AF477381

CROQUET
A Bibliography

CROQUET
A Bibliography

SPECIALIST BOOKS AND PAMPHLETS
COMPLETE TO 1997

compiled by
DAVID H DRAZIN

OAK KNOLL PRESS
ST PAUL'S BIBLIOGRAPHIES
2000

First Edition

Published by **Oak Knoll Press** 310 Delaware Street, New Castle DE 19720
and **St Paul's Bibliographies** West End House, 1 Step Terrace, Winchester, Hampshire SO22 5BW

ISBN: 1-58456-008-8 (USA)
ISBN: 1-873040-57-1 (UK)

Title: Croquet: A Bibliography
Author: David Drazin
Typographer: Rodney Cash
Jacket designer: Dinah Drazin
Publication Director: J Lewis von Hoelle

Copyright: © 1999 David H Drazin

Library of Congress Cataloging-in-Publication Data

Drazin, David H.
    Croquet : a bibliography : specialist books and pamphlets from 1853 to 1997 / David H. Drazin.
        p. cm.
    Includes index.
    ISBN 1-58456-008-8
    1. Croquet--Bibliography. I. Title.

    Z7514.C73 D72 2000
    [GV931]
    016.79635'4—dc21

                                                                99-046911

A CIP catalogue record for this book is available from the British Library

Typeset in Great Britain in Sabon Monotype by Cambridge Photosetting Services, 13 Sturton Street, Cambridge, CB1 2QG

Printed in Great Britain by Alden Press, Osney Mead, Oxford, OX2 0EF

Contents

Preface

My ultimate objective has been, and remains, to compile a 'comprehensive' *catalogue raisonnée* of the literature of the game of croquet. Whereas ideally the product of this exercise might be a single volume, practical considerations have suggested a staged approach. The present work mainly comprises specialist books and pamphlets devoted to the game. A future volume will also include other books and pamphlets, both of fiction and non-fiction, the periodical literature, and literary works in other media. This approach has two merits. The appearance of the present work, it is hoped, will prompt feedback from collectors, librarians, and bookdealers who happen to be aware of relevant publications which have escaped my notice, enabling information from such sources to receive due treatment in future. And an earlier target date than might otherwise have seemed realistic for publishing some account of the core croquet literature is likely to provide the best guarantee that any of this work will see the light of day. Too many epic bibliographies, I am reminded by my publisher, have foundered along the way.

The literature of croquet is arguably an ideal bibliographical subject. It is sufficiently compact to invite comprehensive treatment, much of it is so scarce and ill-documented as to pose a practical need for detailed description and analysis, and no previous attempt has been made to cover the ground in a systematic manner. It is especially satisfying to reflect that this project presented a feasible proposition for an individual compiler because the entire literature, including contributions to serials and references in books and pamphlets not principally devoted to the game, probably comprises no more than a few thousand titles. A similar treatment of any mass sport, which might extend to tens or hundreds of thousands of titles, would necessarily demand far greater resources than could be provided by one life's work.

In the following pages I acknowledge my gratitude to many others for their help in bringing this work into being. I have also to acknowledge that the buck stops with me alone. Though I have taken all the cares I know to avoid error and ambiguity, I would not presume total success in this endeavour. I would invite any reader who should discover such blemish, or be aware of any qualifying work which I have omitted, to let me know, either directly or through the good offices of the co-publishers, so that I may have an opportunity to set the record right.

David Drazin,
Croxley Green, Herts
30 September 1999

Acknowledgements

No man is an island, nor a bibliographer either. I am acutely aware that the compilation of a subject bibliography is essentially a co-operative exercise, and I owe a great debt of gratitude to all who have assisted in bringing this book to birth.

I am especially grateful to Robert Cross, Director of St Paul's Bibliographies, for his early encouragement, for his friendship and hospitality, for instructing me in the art of practical bibliography, and generally for acting as consultant obstetrician throughout a long gestation period; to Alan Oldham, Vice-President and honorary archivist of the Croquet Association, for many kindnesses and, in particular, for bringing to my attention little-known publications issued in the name of the Croquet Association; and to Ashley Heenan, past President of the New Zealand Croquet Council, for his friendship, for his generosity in presenting me with copies of rare publications, and for his constant support and encouragement since I told him of my plans several years ago.

I am also most grateful to Dr Roger Bray, Treasurer of the Croquet Association, a leading authority on the literature of croquet, for much help and advice; to Barry Bloomfield, past Director of Collection Developments at the British Library, for his constructive critique of my original publishing proposal; to Graham Nattrass, Head of German Collections at the British Library, for early encouragement and for initiating me in the mysteries of book 'fingerprinting'; to Dr Simon Goodacre and Edward Wakeling of the Lewis Carroll Society for their help in navigating the Carrollian literary inheritance; to Gail Curry, editor of *The Croquet Gazette*, the official organ of the Croquet Association, for affording me the freedom of its columns to air bibliographical issues; to Brian Bamford for his kindness in promoting this project in the South African *Croquet Chronicle*; to Tremaine Arkley for many kindnesses and for his help in surveying the US croquet literature; to Bob Alman, editor of Croquet World Online, for responding instantly to my frequent email inquiries into literary matters and for affording me limitless space on his sumptuous web site; to Nancy L Rhoades for her friendship and hospitality, for her penetrating comments on my treatment of the Rhodopress of Ashland croquet series, and for giving me the last remainders of these delightful products of her and her late husband's private press; to Steve van Dulken, patent librarian at the British Library, for his patience in fielding my inquiries about industrial property publications and for volunteering a succinct introduction on the subject to this book; to Dr Max Hooper for the benefit of his painstaking investigations into the early history of croquet and for his guidance in researching the Australian literature of the game; to David Tatham, Professor of Fine Art at Syracuse University, for his help in construing Winslow Homer's distinguished contributions to the iconography of croquet; to Sue Kirkham and Margaret McPhee for sharing with me their extensive knowledge of the byways of the Australian croquet literature; to Fred Lake and Jack Ben-Nathan, authorities on the literature of archery and billiards respectively, for bringing to my attention works on those games which also refer to croquet; to Erik Gerdes and Dr Ian Plummer for searching the online systems of overseas libraries on my behalf; to Jonathan Gestetner, Alan Chalmers, and Christopher Saunders for supplying me with copies of scarce books and pamphlets, and to Jonathan Gestetner for suggesting how best to present this work to cater to the antiquarian book trade; to members of my family for many helpful leads and comments; and to the following for their generosity in presenting me copies of works I wanted to see: Cliff Anderson, Judy Anderson, David Appleton, Bill Arliss, David Carpenter, Laverne Carroll,

Winifred Dickinson, Dorothy Miller, Bernard Neal, William Prichard, John Riches, Joyce Ridley, Allen Scheuch, David Shipston, Margaret Woff, Roger Wood.

I was fortunate to find many of the works I wanted to see in the collections of fellow members of the Croquet Association. I am most grateful to all those collectors who entrusted me with their treasured possessions, thus allowing me to examine them at leisure in the comfort of my own home. But I also spent many happy days examining the holdings of institutional collections, and I would especially like to thank the following senior members of staff for their help and hospitality far beyond the call of duty: Becky Hill, Nan Card, and Marlo Keller of the Rutherford B Hayes Presidential Center, Fremont OH; Valerie Warren, past curator of the Wimbledon Lawn Tennis Museum; Michael Bott, archivist of Reading University Library; Bonnie Coles of the Library of Congress, Washington DC; Georgia Barnhill of the American Antiquarian Society, Worcester MA; and Eileen Hart and Richard Pitkin of the Illustrated London News Picture Library, London.

I would also put on record my thanks to the following contemporary authors for illuminating the publishing history of their works: Nigel Aspinall, Don Gaunt, Christopher Hudson, Bill Lamb, John Prince, John Riches, Peter Rudge, John Solomon, Keith Wylie. And I would also thank William Ormerod for insights into the origins of *Croquet* (in the Know the Game series), the best-seller written by his father, Dr GL Ormerod.

Lastly, I would like to thank my wife Anne for her extreme indulgence during so long an excursion from civilised domestic life. I promise her that we shall remind ourselves of the joys of a croquet-free existence before I embark on a sequel to this work.

Introduction

1. Scope. 2. Arrangement. 3. Description and analysis. 4. Usages. 5. Fingerprints. 6. Terminal dates. 7. Patent procedure and terminology. 8. Methods of patent searches. 9. Abbreviations and symbols. 10. Reference bibliography.

1. SCOPE. This first volume of what is planned to be a comprehensive *catalogue raisonnée* of the croquet literature is devoted to what may be described as the core subject material — *ie* books and pamphlets about any aspect of the game, save for periodicals which have appeared more frequently than annually. In order to satisfy, as far as possible, the diverse interests of croquet scholars, book people, and historians, the word 'comprehensive' is used to include all printed books, pamphlets, and leaflets, however originated (in letterpress, typescript, or manuscript), which are principally about any aspect of the game or which include the common noun 'croquet', or its equivalent in another language, on the title page. Also included are some unpublished works of like character which have been issued to restricted user groups (*eg* members of clubs and associations) and one-off works which are accessible to scholars in institutional collections. Hence, this volume includes patents as first published, qualifying works of fiction and literary criticism, musical works, trade catalogues and advertisements, and year books and almanacs, but excludes patent revisions and reissues *etc*, registered trade marks and designs, programmes for croquet events, legal proceedings, letters, recruitment advertisements issued by clubs and associations, and minute books and other archives of clubs and associations.

For present purposes, the word 'croquet' includes modified and related games which share the distinctive characteristics of croquet (*eg* golf croquet, modern croquet, castle croquet, carpet croquet, table croquet), but excludes more distantly related games (*eg* pall mall, lawn billiards, and roque), which have their own unique identities.

The main body of this work (Part A) comprises books and pamphlets which have been seen by the compiler, or which are known to exist or have existed — save for patents of inventions related to the game of croquet, which are listed in Part B. Other books and pamphlets, copies of which had not been seen by the compiler on completion of Part A, but which were then believed on the basis of good evidence to exist or have existed, are listed briefly in Part C; and other patents which may qualify as relevant to the game of croquet, but which had not been seen on completion of Part B, are listed in Part D.

A brief introduction to patent documentation by Stephen van Dulken is given in §7 (*Patent Procedure and Terminology*). Selection of the patents listed in Part B presented three special problems:

Relationship to the game of croquet. The judgement whether or not a given patent is related to the game of croquet is essentially subjective. Here the catchword 'croquet', used in various ways in the indexes prepared at different times by the several patent authorities, was found to be no more than a helpful indicator. Not all patents so indexed have a credible application to the game of croquet. Patent applications tend to be drawn widely to secure maximum protection, much more widely in many instances than can have practical justification.

Specificity of available indexes. The subject indexes available vary in their coverage of patents applicable to the game of croquet and croquet goods. Without actually examining every one of the tens of millions of patents published worldwide, there can be no certainty that all those relating to a particular product or technique will be revealed through official classes or indexed catchwords.

Accessibility of sources. The present searches were undertaken exclusively at the British Library. Though this library is claimed to hold the largest collection of patent documents in the world, the collection is not complete: there are gaps in the subject indexes and in the patent documents themselves.

Since the results of a patent search are necessarily contingent on the sources used, the indexed classes and subclasses selected, and the catchwords accessed, it is fitting to record the methods used in the present instance. These are outlined in §8 (*Methods of Patent Searches*).

It is a matter for speculation how complete the whole compilation here presented is in fact. Suffice to say that it represents over seven years' work, and that the searches on which it is based have benefited from access to the online systems of the leading libraries in most of the developed countries of the world. Taken together, these searches yielded sharply diminishing returns: few new titles came to light during the final year. How many more will surface in future years only time will tell. For want of the requisite language skills, the present work may do less than justice, in particular, to Scandinavia, the countries of the ex-Soviet bloc, and the Orient; and it is hoped that means will be found to make good this weakness in a future edition. It is also possible that some patents of inventions related to the game of croquet, whether registered in territories not covered by the present searches or during periods of time not covered by available sources, have escaped notice. However, any resulting shortfall is unlikely to be appreciable, save possibly within gaps in the French and New Zealand sources. In other countries and colonial territories croquet goods would seem to have been of limited interest to local manufacturers.

2. ARRANGEMENT

Part A (Specialist Books and Pamphlets). These works are numbered serially by first year of publication, or by decade in the case of those which cannot be dated with reasonable confidence, and, within years and decades, alphabetically by title. The serial number given to each entry is prefixed by the letter 'A' or 'AA'. The single-letter prefix 'A' is used to designate every work which was 'published' in the terms of the Copyright Act 1911[1], in which publication is defined as 'the issue of copies . . . to the public'. The double-letter prefix 'AA' is given to designate other ('unpublished') works.

Later editions and variants of the subject works are listed as nearly as possible in chronological order below the first edition. In case of doubt whether an edition recorded as having being the first was preceded by an earlier edition, the description 'First edition' is prefixed by an asterisk. Putative issues which have not been seen are omitted. (There are several known instances in which the said issues of a work do not form a regular numerical sequence, so the existence of a putative intermediate issue which has not been seen cannot be taken for granted.)

In general, the terms used to identify the several issues of a given work are those given by the publisher. Some such descriptions, however, have been modified in the interests of clarity.

Part B (Patents of Inventions Related to the Game of Croquet). Patents are arranged chronologically by nominal date, if any, or otherwise by date of filing, upon which protection was first granted, if only provisionally.

Part C (Checklist of Other Specialist Books and Pamphlets Thought to Exist). The works here listed are arranged alphabetically by name of author and, within authors, alphabetically by title.

Part D (Checklist of Other Putative Patents of Inventions Related to the Game of Croquet). The patents here listed are grouped by national origin and ordered by number.

3. DESCRIPTION AND ANALYSIS

Part A (Specialist Books and Pamphlets). The works recorded in Part A are described and considered in terms of the categories set out below.

Title page: The title page is first reproduced in quasi-facsimile, or as a monochrome illustration at reduced scale, followed where appropriate by the verso of the title page in whole or in part.
Formula: The collational formula, followed by a statement of pagination.
Technical notes: The dimensions of the space given to print, line spacing, leaf dimensions, specification of the paper used for the book block, and details of any inset plates, stickers, and loose inserts.
Contents: The contents of the several parts of the work, including the preliminaries and any supplementary matter.
Binding: Description of the construction of the volume, and the design and content of the outer covers or wrapper. Unless otherwise indicated, case bindings of classical construction are to be construed as having plain white endpapers.
Dust wrapper: Description and design of any loose wrapper.
Copy seen: Details and location of the copy examined by the compiler.
Fingerprint: The short-hand expression or code which identifies the work in accordance with the system formulated by the Institut de Recherche et d'Histoire des Textes[2], as summarised in §5 below.
Notes: Name of printer, price, date of publication if known, ISBN if applicable, details of reviews, and significant information with regard to the work's origins and publishing history.

In the case of works which were reissued at different times or issued in more than one form, any notes with regard to the series as a whole are given in a preliminary '*Foreword*'.

Part B (Patents of Inventions Related to the Game of Croquet). The patent documents recorded in Part B are described more briefly because they conform to national stereotypes. The details given are generally as follows:

Title: Title, name(s) of inventor(s) if cited (or otherwise of proprietor(s) or agent), country, serial number, and nominal date if any
Sub-title: A more detailed description of the invention, if given.
Material dates: Dates of first application, filing of full specification, and acceptance *etc*, as cited.
Contents: Principal contents, including diagrams, and pagination.
Copy seen: Details and location of the copy examined by the compiler.
Notes: Names of publisher and printer, price, and significant information with regard to the patent and patentee.

Part C (Checklist of Other Books and Pamphlets Thought to Exist). The works here listed are given brief citations only, comprising author, title, place of publication, name of publisher, and year of first publication.

Part D (Checklist of Other Putative Patents of Inventions Related to the Game of Croquet). The patents here listed are given brief citations only, comprising country of origin, number, and, save in three instances, title. The titles, derived from secondary sources, some in translation from foreign languages, may not accurately represent the titles of the patent documents themselves.

4. USAGES. The usages in describing the subject works under the foregoing headings generally follow the precepts of Gaskell[3]. The terms used to identify the colours of covers, endpapers, and print conform to the colour 'centroid' definitions of the ISCC-NBS[4].

5. FINGERPRINTS. The system of 'fingerprinting' here adopted is that pioneered by the Institut de Recherche et d'Histoire des Textes. It serves to individuate and identify a printed work in much the same way as true or DNA fingerprinting is used in relation to an individual person. Like those forensic techniques, it is highly, though not absolutely, reliable: the odds against two different books having the same fingerprint are astronomically long but not infinite. The fingerprint of a particular book or pamphlet consists of three parts, followed where appropriate by any notes deemed to be helpful.

Part 1 comprises four groups of characters taken from selected pages. The first group is normally taken from the first recto following the title page, the second group from the fourth recto after the page selected for the first group, the third group from page 13 (or xiii) or, if the second group was taken from p 13 or 15, from p 17 (or xvii), and the fourth group from the verso of the leaf selected for the third group. The group of four characters selected for each recto consists of the last two characters of the last line, followed by the last two characters of the penultimate line; and the group selected for the last (verso) page consists of the first two characters of the last and penultimate lines. Special provisions are made to cover cases in which this formula cannot be applied directly.

Part 2 consists of an alphanumeric code which indicates the page selected for group 3 (in Part 1).

Part 3 consists of the given or inferred year of publication followed by an alphabetical code which indicates whether that year is printed in Arabic (A) or other script, or is not given but inferred (Q).

For example, the fingerprint of this book is 9479 [4].s, y.ed BrBL 7 2000A.

6. TERMINAL DATES. The subject works are confined to those first published up to the end of 1997 and, in cases of later issues, to those published up to the end of 1998.

7. PATENT PROCEDURE AND TERMINOLOGY, BY STEPHEN VAN DULKEN. Patent specifications consist of text and drawings which together describe an invention, plus claims which define the monopoly requested or granted. These specifications were, in most cases, researched by the patent office of the national or international jurisdiction concerned to establish if novelty existed, and published by that office.

A 'patent' is a specification that at some time was granted protection by the patent office concerned. Calling a published document a specification means that it is possible that it was never, or perhaps may not be (if still pending a decision), granted protection. All granted patents are specifications but not all specifications ever get granted. Many of the specifications listed in this book will not have been granted. The United States is one authority which only published granted patents.

The United States has searched applications received for novelty since 1836, but Britain only from 1905. This means that some specifications turn out to be duplicates of earlier specifications.

British patent specifications were numbered within each year from October 1852 to 1915, hence *eg* GB22639/1900 to identify the annual sequence within which it belongs. From 1916 they were numbered in a consecutive series from 100,001.

The patent terminology used in this book is given below. These definitions are generalisations and emphasise British and American practice.

Accepted: the date on which an application to the British Patent Office was accepted for publication and subsequent sealing.

Complete specification: the term used in Britain for the complete description of the invention, often submitted after a provisional specification. From 1962 only the complete specification was ever printed.

Filed: the date on which a specification was handed in to the patent office concerned. Older American patents do not give this date but only the date of grant/publication (it is the same date).

Granted patent: an illustrated description of an invention, accompanied by claims defining the monopoly, which has been published and given protection by a patent office for that jurisdiction.

Provisional specification: the term used in Britain until the 1977 Patents Act for a short, normally unillustrated specification which was meant to be followed within a time limit by a longer, normally illustrated complete specification. Until 1883 only the provisional specification was published even if the complete specification was not submitted within the time-limit. From 1883 to 1962 the provisional specification was published together with the complete specification if both were submitted.

Published application: the term used from the 1977 Patents Act in Britain and from about the same time by some other authorities (but not the United States, which only published a single, granted patent), indicated by an 'A' suffix to the number allocated to the specification. If the invention was granted protection, a 'B' suffix was added to the same number for the granted patent. A suffix 'U' was added to the number of a utility model.

Sealing: the term used by the British Patent Office before the 1977 Patent Act for the act of grant, which was achieved by the applicant paying a fee. Failure to pay the fee meant that the patent was void, *ie* never given protection.

Utility model: the term used for a form of short-term protection granted in some countries. Utility models are less costly than patents.

8. METHODS OF PATENT SEARCHES. The following methods were used, and sources consulted, in tracing candidate patents and identifying those related to the game of croquet, to be entered in Part B. The searches extended to all those countries in which qualifying patents had been published from 1974, when the worldwide *Derwent IPC Index* was introduced, in addition to France, Canada, and New Zealand, where no qualifying patents published during the years 1974–97 could be traced but where the game of croquet is known to have been well established in earlier times. Candidate patents were identified and short-listed by means appropriate to the several sources, but in every case the final judgement whether or not an invention could have practical application to the game was based on consideration of the full patent document.

Worldwide

1974–1996: *Derwent IPC Index* (microfiche). The classes and subclasses searched, given as follows, were selected in the first instance by accessing the word 'croquet' in the IPC catch-word index[6] and then by confirming their status by reference to the IPC manual[7]: Class A63B ('Sports; Games; Amusements'), subclasses 37/00 ('solid balls'), 59/10 ('bats, rackets or the like . . . for croquet'), 63/00 ('targets or goals for ball games'), 71/00 ('games or sports accessories not covered in groups 1/00 to 69/00'). *Derwent IPC Index* lists the full titles of patents selected by class and subclass. All those which it was thought might be relevant to the game of croquet were short-listed.

1997: *Patent Classification Service* (microfiche). The methods used to search this source were the same as those described above in relation to the *Derwent IPC Index*.

Australia

1903–1973: *Australian IPC Index* (microfiche). The class and subclasses searched were the same as those searched worldwide (see above). This source generates brief details of individual patents but not their titles. Relevance to the game of croquet of all those patents generated by the search was considered by referring directly to the full patent documents.

Canada

1873–1919: *The Canadian Patent Office Record* (Ottawa: published by authority). The sole patent listed in the annual alphabetical subject indexes under the word 'croquet' was short-listed.

1920–1973: *Canadian Patent Database*, an online search facility of the Canadian Intellectual Property Office (CIPO). All patents listed by accessing the word 'croquet' in the 'basic' search field were short-listed. (This source evidently uses various indexing criteria. Some of the titles it generated do not include the word 'croquet'.)

France

1791–1876: *Subject-Matter Index of Patents for Inventions (Brevets d'Inventions) Granted in France from 1791 to 1876 Inclusive. Translated, compiled, and published under authority of the Commissioner of Patents* (Washington: Government Printing Office, 1883). All patents listed under the indexed word 'croquet' were short-listed.

1877–1883: *Catalogue des Brevets d'Inventions: Tables* (Paris: Imprimerie et Librairie de Mme V Bouchard-Huzard). Class XX (Articles de Paris et Petites Industries), subclass 1 (Bimbeloterie). All titles in this subclass were searched and those which included the word 'croquet' were short-listed.

1902–1973: *Brevets d'Invention. Tables des Brevets et Certificats d'Addition Imprimés* (Paris: Office Nationale de la Propriété Industrielle). Class XX (Articles de Paris et Petites Industries), subclass 1 (Bimbeloterie). From 1904: Class XX (Articles de Paris et Industries Diverses), subclass 1 (Jeux, jouets, théâtres, courses). All titles in this subclass were searched and those which included the word 'croquet' were short-listed.

New Zealand

1895–1912: *Supplement to The New Zealand Gazette* (Wellington, New Zealand: John Mackay, Government Printer). All patents listed in the quarterly alphabetical subject indexes under the word 'croquet' were short-listed.

1912–49: *New Zealand Patent Office Journal* (Wellington, New Zealand: The Government Printing Office). All patents listed in the annual alphabetical subject indexes under the word 'croquet' were short-listed.

United Kingdom

1855–1908: *Patents for Inventions: Abridgments of Specifications* (London: HMSO). The class and subclasses searched, given as follows, were selected by accessing the word 'croquet' in Part II (Index Headings and Cross References) of *Abridgment Class & Index Key [etc]* (London: HMSO, 1899): Class 132 ('Toys, games, and exercises'), subclasses 'croquet', 'games and sports', 'games and sports, — scoring and marking', 'games and sports, — setting out and marking ground for'. The abridgments of all those patents listed under these subclasses in the annual indexes for Class 132 were examined and those which it was thought might be relevant to the game of croquet were short-listed.

1909–1963: *Patents for Inventions: Abridgments of Specifications* (London: HMSO). From 1909 the abridgments for Class 132 were divided into two classes and Class 132 (ii) ('Games') was reclassified; and from 1931, when the classes themselves were grouped, Class 132 (ii) was placed in Group XV. The following subclasses were selected in place of those referred to above: 'Balls for games, — billiards, bowls, cricket, golf and like games, solid or substantially solid balls for'; 'Bats, clubs, mallets [*etc*], — mallets, croquet and like'; 'Games and sports, scoring and marking apparatus and appliances, and time checks and registers, for, — apparatus of large construction for billiards, tennis, cricket, and like games'; 'Games, outdoor, — Appliances for playing well-known and unspecified games, — — croquet arches, posts, and clips'. The abridgments of all those patents listed under these subclasses in the annual indexes for Class 132 (ii) were examined and those which it was thought might be relevant to the game of croquet were short-listed.

1964–1973: *Patents for Inventions: Abridgments of Specifications* (London: HMSO). A new classification was introduced in 1964. The class and subclasses searched, given as follows, were selected by accessing the word 'croquet' in *Reference Index to the Classification Key Operative from Specification 1,100,001* (London: The Patent Office, 1967): Class A6D ('Games'), subclasses 'Balls for games, — billiards, bowls, cricket, golf, and other games, solid or substantially solid balls for, — — apparatus and processes for, — — — colouring, special' (subclass D1C1), '— — — surfaces, treating' (D1C8), '— — — unclassified making and treating' (D1C5), '— — composition and other balls not composed mainly of indi-arubber, guttapercha, and other readily-yielding materials' (D1A), '— — cores, central, elastic, other than liquid and plastic' (D1C4), '— — cores, central, liquid and plastic' (D1C2), 'Appliances for playing well-known and unspecified games, — croquet arches, posts, and clips' (D11B), 'Mallets for croquet, polo and other games' (D24). The abridgments of all those patents listed under these subclasses in the annual indexes for Class A6D were examined and those which it was thought might be relevant to the game of croquet were short-listed.

USA

1836–1973: *MCFC Classification by Subclass* (Washington DC: United States Department of Commerce, Patent & Trademark Office, Office for Patent and Trademark Information, April 1999), an interactive source on CD-Rom. The class and subclasses searched were selected by accessing the word 'croquet' in *Index to the US Patent Classification System* (Washington DC: US Department of Commerce, December 1997). The class selected is 473 ('Games Using Tangible Projectile'). The selected subclasses are further defined in *Manual of Classification* (Washington DC: US Department of Commerce, Patent and Trademark Office, Search and Information Resources, June 1997) — *viz* 410 ('Croquet; game element or accessory therefor'), 411 ('Arch type of goal or target, *per se* (*ie* croquet wicket)'), 412 ('Player-carried, nonmechanical projector, *per se* (*ie* a mallet *etc*)'). The patent numbers generated by *MCFC Classification by Subclass* on accessing these subclasses were short-listed by reference to the patent abridgments, given in numerical order, in the annual reports of the Commissioner of Patents for the years 1865–1871 and, for the years 1872–1973, in *Official Gazette of the United States Patent Office* (Washington DC: Government Printing Office).

The entries in Part D (*Checklist of Putative Patents of Inventions Related to the Game of Croquet*) are mostly drawn from *esp@cenet*, an online patent information service of the United Kingdom Patents Office. Exceptionally, two patents were listed in sources cited above but are not held by the British Library.

9. ABBREVIATIONS AND SYMBOLS. The following special abbreviations and symbols are used:

Descriptive terms

FC   Front cover
FF   Front flap
FP   Front panel
INID   Internationally Agreed Numbers for the Identification of Data
IPC   International Patent Classification
L   Left, left-hand
nd   No date cited on title page or title page verso
np   No place of publication cited on title page or title page verso
R   Right, right-hand
RC   Rear cover
RF   Rear flap
RP   Rear panel
TBA   To be ascertained
TP   Title page

Institutions

ACA   Australian Croquet Association
ACC   Australian Croquet Council
AECC   All England Croquet Club
AEC<C   All England Croquet & Lawn Tennis Club [originally All England Croquet Club]
AELT&CC   All England Lawn Tennis & Croquet Club [originally All England Croquet Club]
AIC   Associazione Italiana Croquet
CA The Croquet Association [of England *etc*]
CAI   Croquet Association of Ireland
CFA   Croquet Foundation of America
CIPO   Canadian Intellectual Property Office
GNCC   Grand National Croquet Club [United Kingdom]
HMSO   Her [or His] Majesty's Stationery Office
NACA   National American Croquet Association
NCC   National Croquet Club [United Kingdom]
NDCA   Northern District Croquet Association [Australia]
NZCC New Zealand Croquet Council
SCA   Scottish Croquet Association
SFC   Société française du Jeu de Croquet
UAECA The United All England Croquet Association
USCA United States Croquet Association
USFSA   L'Union des Sociétés françaises de Sports athlétiques
VCA   Victorian Croquet Association [Australia]
WACA   West Australian Croquet Association
WCF   World Croquet Federation
WIPO   World Intellectual Property Organization

Collections

AAS   American Antiquarian Society, Worcester MA
BL   British Library, London
BLSRL   British Library Science Reference Library, London (now incorporated within the British Library, Euston Road, London)

BOD   Bodleian Library, Oxford University, Oxford
CA   The Croquet Association, London
CUL   Cambridge University Library, Cambridge, England
HCLHL   Harvard College Library, Houghton Library, Cambridge MA
HCLWL   Harvard College Library, Widener Library, Cambridge MA
HPC   Rutherford B Hayes Presidential Center, Fremont OH
KRWL   Kenneth Ritchie Wimbledon Library, Wimbledon Lawn Tennis Museum, London
LOC   Library of Congress, Washington DC
NLA   National Library of Australia, Canberra
NT   National Trust, London
NYUL   New York University Library, New York NY
PC   Private collection
PUL   Princeton University Library, Princeton NJ
RRCC   Rendell Rhoades Croquet Collection, Rutherford B Hayes Presidential Center, Fremont OH
RSL   Radcliffe Science Library, Bodleian Library, Oxford University, Oxford
RUL   Reading University Library, Reading

National patent authorities

AU   Australia
CA   Canada
CN   China
DE   Germany
FR   France
GB   United Kingdom
JP   Japan
NZ   New Zealand
US   USA

Symbols

§   Section of this Introduction
*   Identification as first edition open to doubt; illegible, of a character selected to form part of the fingerprint of a publication
†   Unreliable owing to uncertainty surrounding the scale of the copying process, of measurements taken from a photocopy supplied by the holder of a document
‡   Letterpress assumed to be wanting due to loss of matter from the copy examined
¶   Seen after completion of Part A (*Specialist Books and Pamphlets*), of a work listed in Part C (*Checklist of Other Specialist Books and Pamphlets Thought to Exist*)

10. REFERENCE BIBLIOGRAPHY

(1) *An Act to amend and consolidate the Law relating to Copyright*, Chapter 47 in *The Public and General Acts of 1911* (London: HMSO, 1911)
(2) *Empreintes I. Guide du releveur* (Paris: Institut de Recherche et d'Histoire des Textes, 1984)
(3) Philip Gaskell, *A New Introduction to Bibliography* (First published by the Oxford University Press in 1972. New Castle DE: Oak Knoll Press, 1995)
(4) Kenneth L Kelly and Deane B Judd, *The ISCC-NBS Method of Designating Colors and a Dictionary of Color Names* (NBS Circular 533. The Inter-Society Color Council, National Bureau of Standards, 1955)
(5) Brenda M Rimmer, *International Guide to Official Industrial Property Publications* (Third edition revised and updated by Stephen van Dulken. London: The British Library, 1992)

(6) *Official Catchword Index to the Sixth Edition (1994) of the International Patent Classification* (Geneva: World International Patent Organization, 1994)
(7) *International Patent Classification* (Sixth Edition. Geneva: World Intellectual Property Organisation, 1994)

Part A:
Specialist Books and Pamphlets

1853

A1 RULES OF THE NEW GAME OF CROQUET.   1853
Isaac Spratt

Not seen. The title was registered by Spratt at the Stationers' Company on 15 November 1856, the date of first publication being given as 2 August 1853. There are three known references to this work in the contemporary press — *viz The Field* (21 August 1858, p 148), *The Queen* (24 September 1864, p 197), *Land and Water* (18 December 1869, p 390) — but no copy is known to have been seen since.

Notes: Spratt — an ivory turner, toymaker, and retailer — is reported to have recorded the rules given to him by a member of the Macnaghten family, but the identity of the informant and the origins of the rules are unclear. See, for example, the accounts of D Prichard (A208, p 5 ff) and Hooper (A256, pp 86–7).

The contents also of Spratt's work are obscure. The last two of the contemporary sources cited above quote specific rules, but the rules they quote are at variance. The significance of these discrepancies is considered by the compiler in *The Croquet Gazette* (January 1996, p 15).

1858

A2 CROQUET. ISM   [1858]

Not seen. There has been no known reported sighting of this work other than that recorded in *"Croquet, I.S.M." Answered* (A4). Its publication in or about 1858 and its character are there attested by the opening lines:

> 'A very great libel has come out in verse,
> Its language poetic, its words choice and terse,
> At least the Composer, he thinks so, no doubt,
> Or else his invectives would not be so stout!
> His book, it is small, as his mind must be too,
> Or else of the game he'd not make such ado;
> And endeavour to prove, in each hoop lay a snare,
> Of which he would have his Compatriots beware,
> As if every stroke that was made at a ball,
> Was intended upon some man's heart to fall ....'

Notes: Tenuous clues as to the authorship of this work are given by the following lines (*op cit*): 'So pray "Sir Professor," tho' great was your wit,' (p 4), 'And thus it is ever with Bachelors old' (p 5), 'Professor I.S.M., before I conclude' (p 6).

A3 RULES AND DIRECTIONS FOR PLAYING CROQUÊT —   1858
A NEW OUTDOOR GAME. John Jaques

Not seen. Though there has been no known sighting of this work, it would nevertheless appear to have been published. Jaques registered the title at the Stationers' Company on 16 July 1858, giving the date of first publication as 14 July 1858. This is consistent with accounts given by Prior (A56, p 43) and Lillie (A98, pp 30–1).

Notes: The authorship of this work may have been shared with Henry Pollock. According to a letter from Pollock to Prior dated 19 January 1870, quoted by Lillie (*op cit*), 'he [Jaques] asked me to give him a code of rules, which I did'.

1859

A4   **"CROQUET, I.S.M." ANSWERED.** [Anon]   1859

"CROQUET, I.S.M.," | ANSWERED. | [double rule] | LONDON: | PRINTED FOR THE AUTHOR, BY | ROBERT HARDWICKE, 192, PICCADILLY. | [rule] 1859. | **Price Threepence.**

Formula: [1⁴]. 4 leaves, pp *1–3 4–8*

Technical notes: 119 × 72 mm (max) (p 6, ragged). 22 lines, 20 = 110 mm. Leaf size 167 × 102 mm; thickness 0.09 mm; wove, unwatermarked, smooth, white

Contents: Title (*1*), blank (*2*), text (verse) (*3–8*)

Binding: Not ascertainable from the copy examined

Copy seen: BL: 11650 a 37 (imperfect, rebound in a library binding)

Fingerprint: e;se l;l, e,e, o;o, C 1859A [all four groups taken from p *3*]

Notes: Printed by Robert Hardwicke, London, price 3d. Year of publication is inferred from a date stamp (4 FE 59), recognisable as that of the BL, on the copy examined. The text offers tenuous clues as to its authorship:

> 'The Author of these little verses to find,
> Allow me to tell you I'm one of the sex
> Whose sweet patient tempers you've tried hard to vex.
> A married one too! or I could not relate
> The cheering effects of the sweet married state;
> But when I was younger, and fairer no doubt,
> I've played Croquet and knew what I was about;
> I aimed at the stick, I struck at my ball,
> I roquet'd my enemy's, tho' my foot's small . . . .'

Croquet, the object of this replication, is here listed as A2.

1861

A5   **ATHLETIC SPORTS AND RECREATIONS FOR BOYS.**   1861
The Rev JG Wood

(a) *First edition (1861)*

ATHLETIC SPORTS | AND | **RECREATIONS FOR BOYS.** | COMPRISING | [in two columns divided by a vertical rule]

CRICKET.	ARCHERY. |
CROQUET.	FENCING. |
LAWN BILLIARDS.	BROADSWORD. |
KNOCK-'EM-DOWN.	RIDING. |
AUNT SALLY.	DRIVING. |
GYMNASTICS.	ROWING. |
SWIMMING.	SAILING. |
SKATING.	ETC. ETC. |

BY | THE REV J.G. WOOD, M.A. | ETC. ETC. | [rule] | [in gothic-revival script] With One Hundred and Twenty-five Illustrations. | [rule] | LONDON: | ROUTLEDGE, WARNE, AND ROUTLEDGE, | FARRINGDON STREET. | NEW YORK: 56, WALKER STREET. | 1861.

Formula: A^2 B–K^8 L^6 [\$1, 3 signed (–A1, L1, 3)]. 80 leaves, pp *i–iii* iv, *1* 2–144, *3* 4–13 *14* [= 160]

Technical notes: 137 × 80 mm (p 4). 50 lines, 20 = 54 mm. Leaf size 165 × 103 mm; thickness 0.12 mm; wove, unwatermarked, smooth, white. Two inset plates (engravings) face pp *i*, 45

Contents: Title (*i*), TP verso (*ii*), contents (*iii*–iv), text (*1*–144), advertisements (*3*–14)

Binding: Dark yellowish Green (137) bead grain cloth over light boards, sewn. The facing pages of the endpapers are coloured pale greenish Yellow (104). FC: gold-blocked title *etc* (ATHLETIC SPORTS | AND | RECREATIONS FOR BOYS | [rule] | REV. J. G. WOOD. M.A.) within a triple-ruled blind-stamped frame with corner ornaments. RC: blind-stamped frame of the same pattern as that on the FC. Spine: gold-blocked title *etc* ([in a convex arc so that the words 'ATHLETIC' and 'RECREATIONS' approximate a circle] ATHLETIC | SPORTS | AND | [in a concave arc] RECREATIONS | FOR BOYS | [rule] | WOOD. | [flourish]) across the head; blind-stamped bands near the head and foot

Copy seen: PC

Fingerprint: 3434 t,t. isr- 4.3. 3 1861A [group 1 taken from the L column of p *iii*]

Notes: Printed by Savill and Edwards, London, price 1/6.

A section entitled 'Croquet' (pp 18–21), largely devoted to the rules of the game, is believed to have been taken from Stonehenge, *Manual of British Rural Sports* (fourth edition, London: George Routledge and Sons, 1859). The entire text, perhaps with minor revisions, is reproduced in *The Boy's Own Treasury of Sports and Pastimes* (London: George Routledge and Sons, [1865]).

The author's code of 40 numbered rules appears to be taken very largely from a letter from HB which appeared in *The Field* (31 July 1858, p 94) and from a letter from Corncrake which appeared in *The Field* (21 August 1858, p 148).

(b) *1871 issue [1871]*

ATHLETIC SPORTS | AND | RECREATIONS FOR BOYS. | COMPRISING | [in two columns divided by a vertical rule]

CRICKET.	ARCHERY. |
CROQUET.	FENCING. |
LAWN BILLIARDS.	BROADSWORD. |
KNOCK-'EM-DOWN.	RIDING. |
AUNT SALLY.	DRIVING. |
GYMNASTICS.	ROWING. |
SWIMMING.	SAILING. |
SKATING.	ETC. ETC. |

BY | THE REV. J. G. WOOD, M.A. | ETC. ETC. | [rule] | [in gothic-revival script] With One Hundred and Twenty-five Illustrations. | [rule] | LONDON: | GEORGE ROUTLEDGE AND SONS, | THE BROADWAY, LUDGATE. | NEW YORK : 416, BROOME STREET.

Formula: A^2 B–K^8 L^4 [\$1 signed (–A1, L1); H4 signed 'P']. 78 leaves, pp *i–iii* iv, *107* 108–250, *1–3* 4 5–8 [= 156]

Technical notes: 135 × 78 mm (p 110). 50 lines, 20 = 54 mm. Leaf size 159 × 104 mm; thickness 0.12 mm; wove, unwatermarked, smooth, white. Two inset plates (engravings) face pp *i*, 241

Contents: Title (*i*), TP verso (*ii*), contents (*iii*–iv), text (*107–250*), advertisements (*1–8*)

Binding: Dark yellowish Green (137) morocco grain cloth over light boards, sewn. The facing pages of the endpapers are coloured pale greenish Yellow (104). FC: an elliptical tinted engraving, depicting three young children and chickens in front of a farmhouse, set centrally within a blocked design, featuring assorted birds, flowers, and foliage. The engraving and surrounding design are set within ruled frames. RC: blocked double-ruled frame, the outer frame in bold. Spine: the title *etc* gold-blocked within a blocked design, featuring foliage ([crosswise within a ruled panel at the head] ATHLETIC | [*do*] SPORTS | [double rule, the lower rule in bold, near the foot] | ROUTLEDGE)

Copy seen: PC

Fingerprint: 4040 t,t. :—in yaTh C 1871Q

Notes: Printed by Savill and Edwards, London. Year of publication is inferred from the date, May 1871, given at the head of p 1 of the advertising supplement.

This issue is remarkable for its irregular pagination and for the incongruity of the cover design with the subject matter. The entire text was evidently extracted from *The Boy's Own Treasury of Sports and Pastimes* (London: George Routledge and Sons, [1865]) together with the pagination, and perhaps other trappings, of that work. The cover design, however, remains a mystery.

The text and the two plates are apparently identical to those of (a). The table of contents is revised to reflect the new pagination, but a page reference given in a foot-note on p 191 remains unaltered. The advertisements are different.

(c) *1884 issue (1884)*

Not seen. The owner of an original copy of this issue describes it as being very similar to (b). In particular, the irregular pagination would appear to be identical. Importantly, however, the supplementary advertisements are different and include an advertisement for the 1884 issue of *Every Boy's Annual* (London: George Routledge and Sons). The FC also is different.

1862

A6   **RULES OF THE GAME OF CROQUET. GVH**   [1862]

(a) *First edition [1862]*

[printed in dark grey artist's rustic script, mostly within an extravagant frame composed of rustic logs entwined with vines in leaf, mallets extending at the four corners and centrally from the uppermost log, male and female figures with mallets raised standing on the top L and R corners respectively and a female figure with parasol raised crouching upon the central structural mallet, a bell suspended from the lower-most log] **RULES** | [*do*] **OF THE GAME** | [*do*] **OF** | [*do*] **CROQUET** | [below the frame, in artist's script] BY | [*do*, a monogram composed of the letters *G, V, H*]

Formula: [1–8¹]. 8 leaves, unnumbered [ff 1–8]

Technical notes: 234 × 185 mm (max) (f 2, ragged). Variable line spacing, some pages divided into three columns. Leaf size 265 × 207 mm; thickness 0.16 mm; wove, unwatermarked, smooth, white, all edges gilt

Contents: Title (*1*), 'THE GAME' (verse) (*2*), 'OUR CROQUET GROUND' (verse) (*3–4*), 'RULES' (*5–6*), 'PLAN OF A CROQUET GROUND' (*7*), cartoon conclusion (*8*)

Binding: Light bluish Grey (190) light laminated boards, apparently stitched through the covers, no endpapers. FC: printed in dark grey ([in artist's script centred within an engraved illustration featuring a large circular chain of 16 ring-shaped croquet hoops and cartoon figures of several players and spectators] **CROQUET** | W H Mc Farlane, Lith^r 19 St James' Sq Edin^h | LONDON : Bosworth & Harrison, 215 Regent S^t | EDINBURGH, John Menzies.   2 Hanover S^t). Inside FC: blank. RC: cartoon in mock-Chinese idiom. Inside RC: blank

Copy seen: BOD: 268 d 2 (disbound)

Fingerprint: s.s, t.il V.g. V.s. C 1862Q [group 1 taken from f 2, groups 2–4 taken from f 6]

Notes: It is unclear whether this work was printed by Bosworth & Harrison or by John Menzies.

Year of publication is inferred from that inscribed in ink on the title page of the copy examined. Special credibility is given to this inscription by the following indications:

(i) An earlier shelf mark ('268 d 6') is erased in what is evidently the same hand.

(ii) The re-marking policy in accordance with which the work received the current shelf mark ceased in the mid-Victorian period.

(iii) The *General Catalogue* of the BL lists a work (shelf mark D-7905 g 13) as destroyed by bombing during the war, which is clearly identifiable as the same work. The year of publication is given as 1862, the author as GVH.

(iv) The fact that Rule 9 is correctly quoted and attributed in a letter by Mallet which appeared in *The Field* (5 September 1863, p 251) clearly indicates that year of first publication could not have been after 1863.

The text includes a code of 15 rules. 'Tight' croquet is mandatory. The word 'roquet' is used throughout to refer to the croquet stroke.

(b) *Rhodopress of Ashland abridged facsimile (1975)*

[TP verso]

The Croquet Series | *One of seventy-five copies* | [swelled rule composed of letters I and inverted letters U, representing a hoop setting] | Only two dim, fragile copies of this | bit of early croquet ephemera are | known. In this new edition, the text | is complete, but the figures have been | reduced in size and numbers. The | original copies are about 19 × 28 cm. | - *Rendell Rhoades*, Editor. | April 5, 1975 | [publisher's device: twin trees in silhouette set at the ends of a line of letterpress in gothic-revival script] Rhodopress of Ashland | [rule] | [in gothic-revival script] Ashland, Ohio. | 1975

Formula: [1¹⁰]. 10 leaves, unnumbered [pp 1–20]

Technical notes: 96 × 57 mm (p 9, ragged). 27 lines, 20 = 71 mm. Leaf size 133 × 107 mm; thickness 0.18 mm; wove, unwatermarked, rough, white. Most illustrative matter is printed in colour — in moderate reddish Orange (37) on pp *1, 10–13, 15, 20,* and in dark yellowish Green (137) on pp *2, 4–9, 14*. Page *3* is illustrated in Orange and Green.

Contents: Title (*1*), TP verso (*2*), sub-title ('THE GAME.') (*3*), text (verse) (*4–9*), text ('OUR CROQUET GROUND.', verse) (*10–14*), text ('RULES') (*15–18*), plan of lawn setting (*19*), cartoon (*20*)

Binding: Pale Yellow (89) laid rough card, stapled, no spine or endpapers. FC: reproduction of the TP, printed in Orange. Inside FC: cartoon in Green. RC: cartoon in Green. Inside RC: cartoon in Orange

Copy seen: PC

Fingerprint: e,e, e.g, e.t, **un C 1975A [groups 1–4 taken from pp *5, 15, 17, 18* respectively]

Notes: Published and printed by Rhodopress of Ashland, Ashland, Ohio. Notwithstanding the editor's claim, this facsimile wants the TP of (a), perhaps because the original from which it was reproduced also wanted the TP of (a).

A7   YE GAME OF CROQUET. Cremer Jr   [1862]

(a) *First edition [1862]*

Formula: [1⁴]. 4 leaves including the rear pastedown, pp *i–ii, 1 2–4 5–6*

Technical notes: 181 × 149 mm (p 4). 48 lines in two columns divided by a vertical rule, 20 = 77 mm. Leaf size 243 × 185 mm; thickness 0.12 mm; wove, unwatermarked, smooth, white

Contents: Title (*i*), blank (*ii*), text (*1–4*), blank (*5*), glued to the RC (*6*)

Binding: Dark bluish Green (165) honeycomb grain cloth, limp, over disjunct front pastedown and 1_4, sewn, no spine or free endpapers. FC: gold-blocked title, centred (CROQUET.). RC: blank

Copy seen: PC

Fingerprint: wops nand heat h,is C 1862Q [all four groups taken from the L column of p *1*]

Notes: Price 6d. Year of publication is conjectural. The stated rules of the game differ from those attributed to the author by a review in *The Queen* (1 October 1864, pp 211–12) and are apparently more primitive. The following issue (b) was probably published late in 1862 or early in 1863. Hence the present issue was probably published early in 1862, or perhaps even earlier.

(b) *Cowell's Anastatic Press issue [1863]*

[The TP as that of (a), extended by the matter which follows]

[at L] ENTERED AT STATIONERS' HALL. [centred] COWELL'S ANASTATIC PRESS, IPSWICH [at R] RIGHT OF TRANSLATION IS RESERVED. | Entertainments provided for Out-door Fetes and Evening Parties by CREMER, Jun., whose only London Establishment is as above. | [at R] Price 6d.

Formula: [1⁶]. 6 leaves including the front and rear pastedowns, unnumbered [pp 1–12]

Technical notes: 180 × 149 mm (p 6). 48 lines in two columns divided by a vertical rule, 20 = 76 mm. Leaf size 242 × 184 mm; thickness 0.12 mm; wove, unwatermarked, smooth, white

Contents: Glued to the FC (*1*), blank (*2*), title (*3*), advertisement (*4*), text (*5–8*), advertisements (*9–10*), blank (*11*), glued to the RC (*12*)

Binding: Dark greyish Green (151) honeycomb grain cloth, sewn, no spine or endpapers. FC: the copy examined has what appears to be an original stick-on paper label, affixed centrally, bearing the title *etc*, printed in black, within an ornamental rectangular frame with rounded corners (THE GAME | OF | [in open display script] **CROQUET**, | By CREMER, JUN., | 210, REGENT STREET, LONDON). RC: blank.

Copy seen: BL: 7920 d 2

Fingerprint: wops nand heat h,is C 1863Q [all four groups taken from the L column of p *1*]

Notes: Printed by Cowell's Anastatic Press, Ipswich, price 6d. The text is apparently a facsimile reprint of (a). Advertising material, including page headings, is added; pagination is omitted.

Approximate year of publication, which differs considerably from that suggested by the *General Catalogue* of the BL (*viz* 1890), is inferred from the following indications:

(i) The rules, featuring a ten-hoop setting and 'tight' croquet, represent a state of the game typical of the early 1860s. Such rules would have been widely seen as obsolescent as early as 1864 or 1865 and would then have been unsuitable for the publisher's purposes, which were presumably the promotion and distribution of the firm's croquet goods.

(ii) Cremer's 'Album of Games' is advertised, apparently as a late addition, at the foot of p *10*. This title would appear to refer to the publisher's *Album of Games and Amusements*, as reviewed in *The Queen* (17 January 1863, p 401).

Hence it is conjectured that this issue was published by Cremer in readiness for the 1863 season. Perhaps the most plausible explanation of his choice of Cowell as printer is that the original plates and type could not be re-used. In such circumstances, the anastatic (facsimile) process for which Cowell was noted could have been seen to offer an attractive solution. Notwithstanding the publisher's stated claim to registration at Stationers' Hall, no record of such registration can be found in the surviving Registry Books of the Stationers' Company.

1863

A8   **CROQUET. Capt Mayne Reid**   1863

(a) *First edition (1863)*

CROQUET. | BY | CAPTAIN MAYNE REID. | [swelled rule] | LONDON: | CHARLES JAMES SKEET, 10, KING WILLIAM STREET, | CHARING CROSS. | 1863. | [*Registered at Stationers' Hall, and Right of Translation reserved.*]

Formula: A⁸ B–C⁸ [$2 signed (–A1, 2)]. 24 leaves, pp *i–iii* iv, 5 6–46 47–48

Technical notes: 155 × 88 mm (pp 6, 46). *ca* 35 lines, 20 = 88 mm. Leaf size 215 × 138 mm; thickness 0.11 mm; wove, unwatermarked, smooth, white. A plate (engraving with letterpress) faces the TP

Contents: Frontispiece (plate), title (*i*), TP verso (*ii*), preface (*iii–*iv), text (5–48)

Binding: Dark reddish Orange (38) bead grain cloth over light boards, sewn. The facing pages of the endpapers are coloured yellowish White (92). FC: gold-blocked title *etc* ([in ornamental letters, swash *R, Q*] CROQUET, | BY | [swash *A, M, A, R*] CAPT : MAYNE REID.) centred within a blind-stamped frame of Greek key pattern design with ruled borders. RC: blind-stamped frame of the same pattern as that on the FC. Spine: blank

Copy seen: PC (imperfect)

Fingerprint: erl, ret. T.em thim 3 1863A

Notes: Printed by Cox and Wyman, London, price 2/6. Published in August 1863. The text includes a code of 126 numbered rules.

Review: *The Queen* (1 October 1864, p 212).

(b) *First American edition (1863)*

CROQUET. | BY | CAPTAIN MAYNE REID. | [rule] | *Boston:* | JAMES REDPATH, PUBLISHER, | 221 WASHINGTON STREET. | 1863.

Formula: 1–4⁶ [$1, 3 signed (–1₁; 1₁–4₁ signed '1*' *etc*)]. 24 leaves, pp *i–ii* iii–iv, 5–48

Technical notes: 129 × 80 mm (p 6). 32 lines, 20 = 81 mm. Leaf size: 172 × 111 mm; thickness 0.12 mm; wove, unwatermarked, smooth, white. A plate (engraving with letterpress) faces the TP

Contents: Title (*i*), TP verso (*ii*), preface (iii–iv), text (5–48)

Bindings: (1) Vivid purplish Blue (194) wavy grain (the waves running vertically) cloth, limp over light Yellow (86) pastedowns, sewn. FC: gold-blocked title ([in ornamental script, swash *R, Q*] CROQUET) in panel with concave rounded corners within a blind-stamped ruled frame. RC: blind-stamped frame of the same pattern as that on the FC. Spine: blank. (2) Moderate reddish Purple (241) bead grain cloth over light boards, otherwise identical to that of (1)

Copies seen: PCs

Fingerprint: m-at hed. T.be ruag 3 1863A

Notes: Printed by Geo C Rand & Avery.

The text apparently differs from that of (a) in accidentals only, notably in the use of American spelling.

(c) *Second English edition (1865)*

CROQUET. | [in gothic-revival script] A Treatise. | BY | CAPTAIN MAYNE REID. | [rule] | LONDON: | HOULSTON AND WRIGHT, | 65, PATERNOSTER ROW. | 1865. | [*Registered at Stationers' Hall, and Right of Translation reserved.*]

Formula: A⁸ B–F⁸ [$2 signed (–A1, 2)]. 48 leaves, *1–5* 6–8 *9* 10–11 *12–13* 14 *15* 16–47 *48* 49–95 *96*

Technical notes: 117 × 71 mm (p 6). 21 lines, 20 = 114 mm. Leaf size 159 × 101 mm; thickness 0.12 mm; wove, unwatermarked, smooth, white

Contents: Blank (*1*), frontispiece (engraving with letterpress) (*2*), title (*3*), TP verso (*4*), preface (*5–8*), preface to the second edition (*9–11*), blank (*12*), contents (*13–14*), text (*15–95*), blank (*96*)

Binding: Dark yellowish Green (137) sand grain cloth over lights boards, sewn. The facing pages of the endpapers are coloured pale Yellow (89). FC: gold-blocked title *etc* in the form of an emblem ([in ornamental script forming a convex arc, swash *R, Q, U, E* with floral strands] CROQUET | [symmetrical design composed of two crossed mallets and winning peg bound together in twine, hoop, and three balls] | [in ornamental script] BY | [swash *A, M, A, Y, N, R*] CAPT. MAYNE REID | [floral feature]) centred within a blind-stamped ruled frame. RC: blind-stamped frame of the same pattern as that on the FC. Spine: blank

Copy seen: PC

Fingerprint: lyhe 6665 h.et IVsu 7 1865A

Notes: Printed by Woodfall and Kinder, London.

The text differs from (a) in a number of substantive, albeit minor, revisions and omissions.

(d) *Third English edition (1866)*

BEETON'S BOOK OF GAMES. | [rule] | **CROQUET.** | [in gothic-revival script] A Treatise. | BY | CAPTAIN MAYNE REID. | [publisher's device, in the form of a medallion surmounted by a beehive] | LONDON: | S. O. BEETON, 248, STRAND, W.C. | (10 DOORS FROM TEMPLE BAR.) | 1866. | [*Registered at Stationers' Hall, and Right of Translation reserved.*]

Formula: a⁶ b⁴ B–G⁶ H⁶ I²) [$1, 3 signed (–a1, b3]. 54 leaves, pp *i–v* vi–ix *x–xi* xii–xiv *xv* xvi *xvii–xx, 1* 2–80 *81–88*

Technical notes: 112 × 62 mm (p 2). 24 lines, 20 = 94 mm. Leaf size 137 × 94 mm; thickness 0.15–0.17 mm; wove, unwatermarked, smooth, white

Contents: Half-title (*i*), blank (*ii*), title (*iii*), TP verso (*iv*), preface, signed 'MAYNE REID', 1863 (*v–ix*), preface to the third edition, signed 'M. R.', 1866 (*xi–xiv*), contents (*xv–xvi*), blank (*xvii*), plan No 1 (*xviii*), plan No 2 (*xix*), blank (*xx*), text (*1–80*), advertisements (*81–88*)

Binding: Deep Red (13) ribbed-morocco grain cloth over light boards, sewn. The facing pages of the endpapers are coloured pale Yellow (89). FC: the title *etc* — identical to that of (c) but extended at the foot to include the price (1/–) — gold-blocked within a triple-ruled blind-stamped frame, the outermost frame in bold, with internal corner ornaments. RC: blind-stamped frame of the same pattern as that on the FC. Spine: blank

Copy seen: PC

Fingerprint: tsf, heno y,ts anqu 3 1866A [group 3 taken from p 13]

Notes: Printed by Virtue and Co, London, price 1/–.

Though reset throughout, the text of this edition is practically identical to that of (c). Plan No 2 is added, an extra footnote is added in recognition of the current prevalence of 'loose' croquet (p 12), and some of the rules dealing with 'misplay' (rules 95–107), together with their footnotes, are altered. The supplementary advertisements are a new feature of this edition.

(e) *Second American edition (1869)*

CROQUET: | [in gothic-revival script] A Treatise, | [swash *W*, *N*, *C*] With Notes and Commentaries. | BY | **CAPTAIN MAYNE REID.** | [swelled rule] | [in gothic-revival script] New-York: | [rule] | [swash *P*, *O*, *N*, *S*] Publishing Office, 119 Nassau Street. | 1869.

Formula: [π1 1–3⁸ χ1]. 26 leaves, pp *i–ii, 1–5 6 7–10 11–28 29 30–45 46 47–48, iii–iv* [= 52]

Technical notes: 178 × 107 mm (p 13). 49 lines, 20 = 73 mm. Leaf size 225 × 145 mm; thickness 0.12 mm; wove, unwatermarked, smooth, white

Contents: Blank *(i–1)*, frontispiece *(2)*, title *(3)*, TP verso *(4)*, preface *(5–6)*, index *(7)*, The Croquet Queen (verse) *(8)*, Plan A *(9)*, Plan B *(10)*, text *(11–48)*, blank *(iii–iv)*

Binding: Moderate olive Green (125) sand grain cloth over stiff boards, sewn. The facing pages of the endpapers are coloured deep yellowish Brown (75). FC: gold-blocked title *etc* in the form of an emblem ([in ornamental script forming a convex arc, swash *R*, *Q*] CROQUET | [symmetrical design composed of hoop, winning peg, two crossed mallets, and two balls] | BY | CAPT.MAYNE REID) centred within a blind-stamped ruled frame. RC: blind-stamped frame of the same pattern as that on the FC. Spine: blank

Copy seen: PC

Fingerprint: ones hely s.ng kepl 7 1869A

Notes: Printed by SW Green, New York.

This edition differs extensively from all earlier editions — notably in expansion of the code of rules (to 184 in number) — and might hence properly be regarded as a new *book*, rewritten to reflect the contemporary state of development of the game and its standing in the US. It is here identified as a variant of its predecessors for ease of reference and because it shares with them a common title.

A9   CROQUÊT: A MACAULAY FLOWER. G   1863

[Apparently the FC, all save the first and last lines within a ruled frame with corner ornaments]

[above the top of the frame] *Entered at Stationers' Hall.* | **CROQUÊT,** | A MACAULAY FLOWER, | (*Which can't be beet.*) | [wavy line] | **CABBAGED** | BY | **G.** | [wavy line] | [wavy line] | LONDON, CANADA WEST, 1863. | [below the frame] [THE RIGHT OF TRANSLATION IS RESERVED]

Formula: Not ascertainable from the photocopy examined. Apparently 16 leaves, unnumbered [pp 1–32]

Technical notes: ca 56 × 73 mm (p *4*, ragged). 9 lines, 20 = *ca* 130 mm. Leaf size *ca* 201 × 151 mm

Contents: Title (*1*), wanting from the photocopy examined (*2*), text (verse: 'The bold Dalzell of Dalzell, …') (*3–32*)

Binding: Not ascertainable from the photocopy examined

Copy seen: PC (incomplete photocopy)

Fingerprint: y!h, l.r, e.e, AnAn C 1863A

Notes: Printed anonymously.

The text consists of a Latin epigram and 30 numbered stanzas of verse, each on a separate page. The poem tells the story of a croquet match, parodying 'Horatius' from Macaulay's *Lays of Ancient Rome*.

AA10   CROQUÊT CASTLES: FOR FIVE PLAYERS.   1863
[Lewis Carroll]

[Heading of p *1*]

CROQUÊT CASTLES. | [swelled rule] | FOR FIVE PLAYERS | [swelled rule]

Formula: [1²]. 2 leaves, pp *1* 2–3 *4*

Technical notes: ca 119 × 77 mm (p *2*). 36 lines, 20 = *ca* 67 mm. Leaf size *ca* 186 × 113 mm

Contents: Title heading (*1*), space, perhaps intended for insertion of a diagram of the hoop setting (*1*), rules, numbered I–VIII, signed 'CH. CH. OXFORD, May 4, 1863' (*1–3*), note (*3*), blank (*4*)

Binding: Apparently none

Copy seen: PUL (photocopy of copy held as part of the Parrish collection)

Fingerprint: D.N. E.K. E.*s.* :—be C 1863A [all four groups taken from p *3*, groups 1–3 from the L column at the foot of the page]

Notes: Printed anonymously, perhaps in London, unpublished.

According to SD Collingwood in *The Life and Letters of Lewis Carroll* (London: T Fisher Unwin, 1898, p 432), this work was probably first printed in London, and reprinted in 1866 in Oxford. However, Carroll later wrote a revised version of the game entitled *Castle Croquet: For Four Players* (AA26), and the reprint mentioned by Collingwood was probably intended to refer to the latter work.

A11   EPITOME OF THE GAME OF BILLIARDS.   1863
Henry Upton Alcock

EPITOME | OF | THE GAME OF BILLIARDS. | BY | HENRY UPTON ALCOCK. | CONTAINING THE MODERN | EUROPEAN AND AMERICAN GAMES, | Copiously illustrated with instructive Diagrams, | TOGETHER WITH AN APPENDIX, COMPRISING | CROQUET OR LAWN BILLIARDS (LADIES' GAME), | BAGATELLE, RIVOLI, ETC.; | [rule] | MELBOURNE: | GEORGE ROBERTSON, 69 ELIZABETH STREET. | Sydney : William Maddock, 383 George Street. | AND ALL BOOKSELLERS | 1863.

Formula: Apparently A⁴ B–J⁸ K–M⁸ N² [$2 signed (–A1, 2, B2, E1, J2, K1, 2, L1, 2, M1, 2, N1, 2)]. 102 leaves, pp *i–viii*, 9 10–11 *12* 13–144 *145* 146–147 *148–149* 150–151 *152–153* 154–155 *156–157* 158–159 *160–161* 162–163 *164–165* 166–167 *168–169* 170–171 *172–173* 174–175 *176–177* 178–179 *180–181* 182–183 *184–185* 186–187 *188–189* 190–191 *192–193* 194–195 *196–197* 198–199 *200–204*

Technical notes: 134 × 80 mm (p *10*). 30 lines, 20 = 91 mm. Leaf size 181 × 120 mm; thickness 0.10 mm; wove, unwatermarked, smooth, white

Contents: Blank (*i*), frontispiece (engraving) (*ii*), title (*iii*), TP verso (*iv*), dedication (*v*), *errata* (*vi*), contents (*vii–viii*), preface, signed 'HENRY UPTON ALCOCK', November 1863 (*9–11*), blank (*12*), text, continued (*13–119*), the game of croquet, or lawn billiards (*120–125*), text, concluded (*126–199*), blank (*200*), advertisements (*201–204*)

Binding: Brilliant purplish Blue (195) bead grain cloth over stiff boards, sewn, advertisements on all pages of the front and rear endpapers. FC: the title *etc* gold-blocked in the form of a medallion, set within a double-ruled blind-stamped frame with internal corner ornaments ([set in a convex arc] ALCOCK | [*do*] ON THE | [set in a concave arc] GAME | [*do*] OF | [*do*] BILLIARDS). RC: blind-stamped frame of the same pattern as that on the FC. Spine: crosswise ([gold-blocked and blind-stamped double band] | ALCOCK | ON THE | GAME | OF | BILLIARDS | [gold-blocked and blind-stamped double band])

Copy seen: PC

Fingerprint: **R.**BY ."to ue.A aboc 7 1863A

Notes: Printed by Clarson, Shallard & Co.

Chapter 4 contains a section on croquet (pp 120–125) which consists principally of an unattributed code of 40 numbered rules. Neither the fourth edition of this work (*Billiards and Other Games of the Table*, 1877) nor the fifth edition (*The Alcock Book of Billiards*, 1901) contains any reference to the game of croquet.

1864

A12   **CROQUÊT: THE LAWS AND REGULATIONS OF THE GAME. John Jaques**   1864

(a) *First edition (1864)*

CROQUÊT: | THE | LAWS AND REGULATIONS OF THE GAME, | THOROUGHLY REVISED, | WITH A DESCRIPTION OF THE IMPLEMENTS, | ETC. ETC. | ILLUSTRATED WITH DIAGRAMS AND ENGRAVINGS. | By JOHN JAQUES. | LONDON: | JAQUES AND SON, 102, HATTON GARDEN. | [rule] | 1864. | [*The Right of Translation is reserved.*]

Formula: A⁸ B⁸ C⁴ [B1 signed]. 20 leaves, pp *1–5* 6–10 *11–12* 13–18 *19–22* 23–24 *25–26* 27–31 *32, 1* 2–8

Technical notes: 169 × 96 mm (p 14). 40 lines, 20 = 85 mm. Leaf size 204 × 132 mm; thickness 0.13–0.15 mm; wove, unwatermarked, smooth, white

Contents: Blank (*1*), frontispiece (engraving, signed '*W THOMAS*') (*2*), title (*3*), TP verso (*4*), text, continued (*5–10*), plate (engraving) (*11*), blank (*12*), text, continued (*13–18*), plate (Plan No 1) (*19*), blank (*20*), plate (Plan No 2) (*21*), blank (*22*), text, continued (*23–24*), plate (engraving) (*25*), blank (*26*), text, concluded (*27–31*), blank (*32*), advertisements (*1–8*)

Binding: Greyish Red (19) diagonal beaded-line grain cloth (the beads running top L to bottom R) over light boards, sewn. FC: gold-blocked illustration (of a woman player dressed in crinoline and bonnet with mallet raised to take 'tight' croquet) and title (CROQUÊT) within a blind-stamped ruled frame, and price (ONE SHILLING) within the base of the frame. RC: blind-stamped frame of the same pattern as that on the FC. Spine: not seen (wanting from the copy examined)

Copy seen: PC (imperfect)

Fingerprint: ewto sser g.he Otal 7 1864A

Notes: Printed by Taylor and Greening, London, price 1/–. It is conjectured that the first issue of this work ran to a few, perhaps several impressions, numbering altogether some 12000 copies — *viz* the number given on the TP of the next known issue (b).

The publishing records of Jaques and Son were lost in a fire which destroyed the company's premises in 1941. However, something of the origins of this work can be pieced together from other sources, notably from the early records of Longmans, who distributed Jaques's croquet publications until about 1874, now held by the RUL. Though the title 'Croquêt' was registered by Jaques at the Stationers' Company on 4 March 1864, the date of first publication being declared as 3 March 1864, Longmans cited a later date — *viz* 18 March 1864 — in their trade publicity material.

Longmans sold this title on commission. Their ledger records that between March 1864 and June 1874 they received a total of 5819 copies, of which 237 were distributed free — 150 to Jaques and 87 described as sundries, probably including review copies. However, these figures may well include some copies of another work distributed by Longmans for Jaques — *viz* Lillie's *The Book of Croquet: Its Tactics, Laws, & Mode of Play* (A54). There is some evidence that Longmans may have confused the two titles, regarding the latter simply as a late edition of the present work.

This issue is assumed to be of the first edition notwithstanding the words 'thoroughly revised' in the title. Those words are thought to have been intended to emphasise that the contents of the present publication were fully up to date, not to imply continuity with an earlier work (*viz* A3).

The text includes a code of 17 numbered laws.

Reviews: *The Queen* (1 October 1864, p 212), *Bristol Mirror* (26 March 1864), *John Bull* (26 March 1864), *Leamington Spa Courier* (April 1864), *Leeds Intelligencer* (26 March 1864), *London Review* (26 March 1864), *Observer* (27 March 1864), *Reading Mercury* (16 April 1864), *Sporting Gazette* (9 April 1864), *Stamford Mercury* (15 April 1864), *Sunday Times* (April 1864), *The Cambridge Independent Press*, *The Chelmsford Chronicle*, *Morning Herald*, *Morning Star*, *The News of the World*, *Shipping Gazette*, *Standard*, *Taunton Courier*, *The Western Times*. The first-mentioned review, though generally consistent with the contents of this work, quotes certain matter *not* contained therein *nor* in any later issue seen. The discrepant matter is expressed in terms different to those used by Jaques — *eg* 'bridge' instead of 'hoop' — and hence it is conjectured that it came from an extraneous source and was attributed to Jaques in error.

(b) *Twelfth thousand issue (1864)*

CROQUÊT: | THE | LAWS AND REGULATIONS OF THE GAME, | THOROUGHLY REVISED, | WITH A DESCRIPTION OF THE IMPLEMENTS, | ETC. ETC. | ILLUSTRATED WITH DIAGRAMS AND ENGRAVINGS. | By JOHN JAQUES. | [rule] | TWELFTH THOUSAND. | [rule] | LONDON: | JAQUES AND SON, 102, HATTON GARDEN. | SOLD ALSO BY | LONGMAN, GREEN, LONGMAN, ROBERTS AND GREEN. | [rule] | 1864. | [*The Right of Translation is reserved.*]

Formula: A⁸ B⁸ C⁴ [B1 signed]. 20 leaves, pp *1–5* 6–10 *11–12* 13–18 *19–22* 23–24 *25–26* 27–31 *32, 1* 2–8

Technical notes: 167 × 97 mm (p 14). 40 lines, 20 = 84 mm. Leaf size 209 × 133 mm; thickness 0.14 mm; wove, unwatermarked, smooth, white

Contents: Blank (*1*), frontispiece (engraving signed '*W THOMAS*') (*2*), title (*3*), TP verso (*4*), text, continued (*5–10*), plate (engraving) (*11*), blank (*12*), text, continued (*13–18*), plate (Plan No 1) (*19*), blank (*20*), plate (Plan No 2) (*21*), blank (*22*), text, continued (*23–24*), plate (engraving) (*25*), blank (*26*), text, concluded (*27–31*), opinions of the press (*32*), advertisements (*1, 2–8*)

Binding: Moderate Purple (223) diagonal beaded-line grain cloth (the beads running top R to bottom L) over light boards, sewn. The facing pages of the endpapers are coloured pale Yellow (89). FC: gold-blocked illustration (of a woman player dressed in crinoline and bonnet with mallet raised to take 'tight' croquet) and title (CROQUÊT) within a blind-stamped ruled frame, and price (ONE SHILLING) within the base of the frame. RC: blind-stamped frame of the same pattern as that on the FC. Spine: blank

Copy seen: BL: 7919 bb 43

Fingerprint: As that of (a)

Notes: Printed by Taylor and Greening, London, price 1/–. It is conjectured that this issue ran to 6000 copies — *viz* the difference between the number given on the TP of the next known issue (c) and 12000 (on the TP as above).

The text would appear to be substantially identical to that of (a) save for the addition of one new law (numbered 11) and the renumbering of all following laws.

Another copy of this issue has been seen in a green paper wrapper without endpapers.

(c) *Eighteenth thousand issue (1864)*

CROQUÊT: | THE | LAWS AND REGULATIONS OF THE GAME, | THOROUGHLY REVISED, | WITH A DESCRIPTION OF THE IMPLEMENTS, | ETC. ETC. | ILLUSTRATED WITH DIAGRAMS AND ENGRAVINGS. | By JOHN JAQUES. | [rule] | EIGHTEENTH THOUSAND. | [rule] | LONDON: | JAQUES AND SON, 102, HATTON GARDEN. | SOLD ALSO BY | LONGMAN, GREEN, LONGMAN, ROBERTS AND GREEN. | [rule] | 1864. | [*The Right of Translation is reserved.*]

Formula: A⁸ B⁸ C⁴ [B1 signed]. 20 leaves, pp *1–5* 6–10 *11–12* 13–18 *19–22* 23–24 *25–26* 27–31 *32, 1* 2–8

Technical notes: 169 × 96 mm (p 14). 40 lines, 20 = 85 mm. Leaf size 205 × 133 mm; thickness 0.14 mm; wove, unwatermarked, smooth, white

Contents: Blank (*1*), frontispiece (engraving signed 'W THOMAS') (*2*), title (*3*), TP verso (*4*), text, continued (*5–10*), plate (engraving) (*11*), blank (*12*), text, continued (*13–18*), plate (Plan No 1) (*19*), blank (*20*), plate (Plan No 2) (*21*), blank (*22*), text, continued (*23–24*), plate (engraving) (*25*), blank (*26*), text, concluded (*27–31*), opinions of the press (*32*), advertisements (*1, 2–8*)

Binding: Moderate reddish Purple (241) diagonal beaded-line grain cloth (the beads running from top R to bottom L) over light boards, sewn. The facing pages of the endpapers are coloured pale Yellow (89). FC: gold-blocked illustration (of a woman player dressed in crinoline and bonnet with mallet raised to take 'tight' croquet) and title (CROQUÊT) within a blind-stamped ruled frame, and price (ONE SHILLING) within the base of the frame. RC: blind-stamped frame of the same pattern as that on the FC. Spine: blank

Copy seen: PC

Fingerprint: As that of (a)

Notes: Printed by Taylor and Greening, London, price 1/–. The text is apparently identical to that of (b).

(d) *A Williams & Co expurgated American edition (1865)*

CROQUÊT: | THE | LAWS AND REGULATIONS OF THE GAME, | **THOROUGHLY REVISED,** | WITH A DESCRIPTION OF THE IMPLEMENTS, | ETC., ETC. | **ILLUSTRATED WITH DIAGRAMS AND ENGRAVINGS.** | By JOHN JAQUES. | [rule] | REPRINTED FROM THE EIGHTEENTH LONDON EDITION. | [rule] | BOSTON: | PUBLISHED BY A. WILLIAMS & CO. | 100 WASHINGTON STREET. | 1865

Formula: $\pi 1$ $1^4 2–3^4 4^4 \chi 1$ [2_1, 3_1 signed]. 18 leaves, pp *i–ii*, 1–5 6–8 9 10 *11–12* 13–18 *19–22* 23–24 25 26–30 *31–34*

Technical notes: 165 × 95 mm (p 6). 35 lines, 20 = 95 mm. Leaf size 233 × 145 mm; thickness 0.14 mm; wove, unwatermarked, smooth, white

Contents: Blank (*i–1*), frontispiece (unsigned engraving) (*2*), title (*3*), TP verso (*4*), text, continued (*5–10*), plate (unsigned engraving) (*11*), blank (*12*), text, continued (*13–18*), plate (Plan No 1) (*19*), blank (*20*), plate (Plan No 2) (*21*), blank (*22*), text, continued (*23–24*), plate (unsigned engraving) (*25*), text, concluded (*26–30*), advertisements (*31–32*), blank (*33–34*)

Binding: Dark yellowish Green (137) sand grain cloth over light boards, sewn. The facing pages of the endpapers are coloured light orange Yellow (70). FC: gold-blocked illustration (of a woman player dressed in crinoline and bonnet with mallet raised to take 'tight' croquet) and title (**CROQUÊT**) within a blind-stamped multiple ruled frame. RC: blind-stamped frame of the same pattern as that on the FC. Spine: blank

Copy seen: PC

Fingerprint: e.ng hes, g.he Otar 7 1865A

Notes: Printed by Stacy and Richardson, Boston. The text and illustrations have been entirely reset but are apparently identical in substance to those of (c), save for the omission of signatures from the illustrations and the name Jaques & Son from the illustration (of a patent clip) on p 17. (The copy examined has been collated with a copy of (a) but not with copies of (b) or (c)). All the illustrations have been copied by hand in the finest detail with meticulous care and are reproduced in sharper outline than those in the original work. The original advertisements for Jaques games and sports equipment have been replaced with advertisements by local manufacturers. The opinions of the press have been omitted.

The omission of original names and signatures, the substitution of new advertising matter, and the fact that none of the original text or illustrations has been reproduced by a facsimile process would strongly suggest that this edition was unauthorised. The description of the present work (on the TP) as 'REPRINTED FROM THE EIGHTEENTH LONDON EDITION' is thought to be an inaccurate reference to the eighteenth thousand London issue (c).

The advertisement by DO Goodrich of Boston on p *34* is of historical interest, implying that this manufacturer had been marketing croquet equipment in America since 1860.

(e) *A Williams & Co expurgated American edition, variant (1865)*

[The TP as that of (d)]

Formula: As that of (d)

Technical notes: 164 × 95 mm (p 6). 35 lines, 20 = 95 mm. Leaf size 232 × 145 mm; thickness 0.16 mm; wove, unwatermarked, smooth, white

Contents: As those of (d)

Binding: As that of (d)

Copy seen: PC

Fingerprint: As that of (d)

Notes: Printed by Stacy and Richardson, Boston.

Close collation of the text with that of (d) has revealed only three minor variations, all in accidentals: (i) '"following stroke;"' replaces '"following stroke,"' in p 7, l 18, (ii) 'croquêtted' replaces 'Croquêtted' in p 8, l 1, and (iii) plain open script replaces the ornamental font used in (d) for the words 'boxwood sets' in p *32*, l 17. The placement of the signatures on the pages also varies, implying that the formes of the earlier impression were dismantled to effect whatever variations were intended in the later. It is conjectured that the present variant derived from (d) rather than *vice versa.*

(f) *Second edition (1865)*

CROQUÊT: | THE | LAWS AND REGULATIONS OF THE GAME, | WITH | A DESCRIPTION OF THE IMPLEMENTS, | ETC. ETC. | ILLUSTRATED WITH DIAGRAMS AND ENGRAVINGS. | BY JOHN JAQUES. | [rule] | NEW EDITION, THOROUGHLY REVISED | [rule] | LONDON: | JAQUES AND SON, 102, HATTON GARDEN. | SOLD ALSO BY | LONGMAN, GREEN, LONGMAN, ROBERTS, AND GREEN. | [rule] | 1865. | [*The Right of Translation is reserved.*]

Formula: A^8 B–C^8 [B1, C1 signed]. 24 leaves, pp *1–7* 8–10 *11* 12 *13–14* 15–26 *27–29* 30–39 *40–48*

Technical notes: 169 × 97 mm (p 16). 40 lines, 20 = 85 mm. Leaf size 204 × 134 mm; thickness 0.11 mm; wove, unwatermarked, smooth, white

Contents: Blank (*1*), frontispiece (engraving, signed 'W *THOMAS*') (*2*), title (*3*), TP verso (*4*), preface to the second edition, signed 'JOHN JAQUES', March 1865 (*5*), blank (*6*), text, continued (*7–12*), plate (engraving) (*13*), blank (*14*), text, continued (*15–26*), plate (engraving) (*27*), blank (*28*), text, concluded (*29–39*), advertisements (*40–48*)

Binding: Dark yellowish Green (137) morocco grain paper over light boards, sewn. The facing pages of the endpapers are coloured pale Yellow (89). FC: heavily gold-blocked illustration, incorporating title ([in rustic script] CROQUÊT | BY | JOHN JAQUES), and other lettering (NEW EDITION. | 1/-), within a decorative ruled blind-stamped frame. The illustration is of a woman player dressed in crinoline and bonnet with mallet raised to take 'tight' croquet, set within a hoop in the form of an arbour entwined with floral shoots. Two mallets lean against the uprights. RC: blind-stamped frame of the same pattern as that on the FC. Spine: blank

Copy seen: HPC: GV931 J3 1865 CROQ

Fingerprint: 5.S. anic ets, apgr 7 1865A [groups 1–4 taken from pp 5, 15, 17, 18 respectively]

Notes: Printed by Taylor and Greening, London, price 1/–.

The code of 25 laws given in the text represents a considerable expansion of that given in (c). Extracts from a poem entitled 'Croquêt', reproduced from *Punch or the London Charivari* (2, 16, 23, 30 July, 13, 20 August 1864) are also added.

(g) *Second edition, twenty-eighth thousand issue (1865)*

CROQUÊT: | THE | LAWS AND REGULATIONS OF THE GAME, | WITH | A DESCRIPTION OF THE IMPLEMENTS, | ETC. ETC. | ILLUSTRATED WITH

DIAGRAMS AND ENGRAVINGS. | By JOHN JAQUES. | [rule] | NEW EDITION, TWENTY-EIGHTH THOUSAND. | [rule] | LONDON: | JAQUES AND SON, 102, HATTON GARDEN. | SOLD ALSO BY | LONGMAN, GREEN, LONGMAN, ROBERTS, AND GREEN. | [rule] | 1865. | [*The Right of Translation is reserved.*]

Formula: A^8 B–C^8 [B1, C1 signed]. 24 leaves, pp *1–7* 8–10 *11* 12 *13–14* 15–26 *27–29* 30–39 *40* [*41–48*]

Technical notes: 169 × 97 mm (p 16). 40 lines, 20 = 85 mm. Leaf size 211 × 136 mm

Contents: Blank (*1*), frontispiece (engraving, signed '*W THOMAS*') (*2*), title (*3*), TP verso (*4*), preface to the second edition, signed 'JOHN JAQUES', March 1865 (*5*), blank (*6*), text, continued (*7–12*), plate (engraving) (*13*), blank (*14*), text, continued (*15–26*), plate (engraving) (*27*), blank (*28*), text, concluded (*29–39*), price list (*40*), apparently wanting from the copy examined ([*41–48*])

Binding: Dark yellowish Green (137) morocco grain cloth over light boards, sewn. The facing pages of the endpapers are coloured pale Yellow (89). FC: heavily gold-blocked illustration, incorporating the title *etc* ([in rustic script] CROQUÊT | BY | JOHN JAQUES), and other lettering (NEW EDITION. | 1/-), within a decorative ruled blind-stamped frame. The illustration is of a woman player dressed in crinoline and bonnet with mallet raised to take 'tight' croquet, set within a hoop in the form of an arbour entwined with floral shoots. Two mallets lean against the uprights. RC: blind-stamped frame of the same pattern as that on the FC. Spine: blank

Copy seen: PC (imperfect, wanting pp [*41–48*])

Fingerprint: As that of (f)

Notes: Printed by Taylor and Greening, London, price 1/–.

The text of this issue is apparently identical to that of (f) save for an addition to footnote (i) on p 33 to the effect that 'pushing' is disallowed in striking the ball. The price list on p 40 appears as p *41* in (f).

It is conjectured that this issue ran to some 4000 copies — *viz* the difference between the number given on the TP of the next known issue (h) and 28000 (on the TP as above).

(h) *Second edition, thirty-second thousand issue (1865)*
CROQUÊT: | THE | LAWS AND REGULATIONS OF THE GAME, | WITH | A DESCRIPTION OF THE IMPLEMENTS, | ETC. ETC. | ILLUSTRATED WITH DIAGRAMS AND ENGRAVINGS. | By JOHN JAQUES. | [rule] | NEW EDITION, THIRTY-SECOND THOUSAND. | [rule] | LONDON: | JAQUES AND SON, 102, HATTON GARDEN. | SOLD ALSO BY | LONGMAN, GREEN, LONGMAN, ROBERTS, AND GREEN. | [rule] | 1865. | [*The Right of Translation is reserved.*]

Formula: A^8 B–C^8 [B1, C1 signed]. 24 leaves, pp *1–7* 8–12 *13–14* 15–16 *17–18* 19–26 *27–29* 30–48

Technical notes: 169 × 97 mm (p 16). 40 lines, 20 = 85 mm. Leaf size 210 × 135 mm; thickness 0.13 mm; wove, unwatermarked, smooth, white

Contents: Blank (*1*), frontispiece (engraving, signed '*W THOMAS*') (*2*), title (*3*), TP verso (*4*), preface to the second edition (*5*), blank (*6*), text, continued (*7–12*), plate (engraving) (*13*), blank (*14*), text, continued (*15–26*), plate (engraving) (*27*), blank (*28*), text, concluded (*29–39*), advertisements (*40–48*)

Binding: As that of (f)

Copy seen: BL: 7920 b 46

Fingerprint: As those of (f) and (g)

Notes: Printed by Taylor and Greening, London, price 1/–. It is conjectured that this issue ran to some 8000 copies — *viz* the difference between the number given on the TP of the next known issue (j) and 32000 (on the TP as above).

The code of 25 laws given in the text is identical to that given in (g).

(j) *Second edition, fortieth thousand issue (1866)*

CROQUET: | THE | LAWS AND REGULATIONS OF THE GAME, | WITH | A DESCRIPTION OF THE IMPLEMENTS, | ETC. ETC. | ILLUSTRATED WITH DIAGRAMS AND ENGRAVINGS. | By JOHN JAQUES. | [rule] | NEW EDITION, FORTIETH THOUSAND. | [rule] | LONDON: | JAQUES AND SON, 102, HATTON GARDEN. | SOLD ALSO BY | LONGMAN, GREEN, LONGMAN, ROBERTS, AND GREEN. | [rule] | 1866. | {*The Right of Translation is reserved.*}

Formula: A^8 B–C^8 [B1, C1 signed]. 24 leaves, pp *1–7* 8–12 *13–15* 16–26 *27–29* 30–48

Technical notes: 169 × 97 mm (p 16). 40 lines, 20 = 85 mm. Leaf size 208 × 133 mm; thickness 0.11 mm; wove, unwatermarked, smooth, white

Contents: Blank *(1)*, frontispiece (engraving, signed '*W THOMAS*') *(2)*, title *(3)*, TP verso *(4)*, preface to the second edition *(5)*, blank *(6)*, text, continued *(7–12)*, plate (engraving) *(13)*, blank *(14)*, text, continued *(15–26)*, plate (engraving) *(27)*, blank *(28)*, text, concluded *(29–39)*, advertisements *(40–48)*

Binding: As that of (h)

Copy seen: HPC: RRCC #417 CROQ

Fingerprint: S.d. uter lyof fean 7 1866A [groups 1–4 taken from pp 5, *15*, 17, 18 respectively]

Notes: Printed by Taylor and Greening, London, price 1/–. It is conjectured that this issue ran to some 5000 copies — *viz* the difference between the number given on the TP of the next known issue (k) and 40000 (on the TP as above).

The code of 25 laws given in the text is identical to that given in (h) but a new footnote (f) is inserted, following footnotes are re-lettered, the circumflex accents over the letter 'e' in the words 'croquet' and 'roquet' are omitted, and some of the pages are recomposed. In the copy examined the markers of Jaques's patent Croquet Indicator, illustrated on p 21, are coloured. It is not known whether the colouring is original.

(k) *Second edition, forty-fifth thousand issue (1866)*

CROQUET: | THE | LAWS AND REGULATIONS OF THE GAME, | WITH | A DESCRIPTION OF THE IMPLEMENTS, | ETC. ETC. | ILLUSTRATED WITH DIAGRAMS AND ENGRAVINGS. | By JOHN JAQUES. | [rule] | NEW EDITION, FORTY-FIFTH THOUSAND. | [rule] | LONDON: | JAQUES AND SON, 102, HATTON GARDEN. | SOLD ALSO BY | LONGMAN, GREEN, LONGMAN, ROBERTS, AND GREEN. | [rule] | 1866. | {*The Right of Translation is reserved.*}

Formula: A–B^8 C^8 [C1 signed]. 24 leaves, pp *1–7* 8–12 *13–15* 16–21 *22* 23–26 *27–29* 30–48

Technical notes: 169 × 96 mm (p 16). 40 lines, 20 = 85 mm. Leaf size 208 × 134 mm; thickness 0.12 mm; wove, unwatermarked, smooth, white

Contents: Blank *(1)*, frontispiece (engraving, signed '*W THOMAS*') *(2)*, title *(3)*, TP verso *(4)*, preface to the second edition *(5)*, blank *(6)*, text, continued *(7–12)*, plate (engraving) *(13)*, blank *(14)*, text, continued *(15–26)*, plate (engraving) *(27)*, blank *(28)*, text, concluded *(29–39)*, advertisements *(40–48)*

Binding: Very light Green (143) paper, sewn. FC: engraving (illustration of a woman player dressed in crinoline and bonnet with mallet raised to take 'tight' croquet) over title (CROQUET. | [rule] By JOHN JAQUES. | [rule] NEW EDITION, PRICE SIXPENCE.) within a ruled frame, and lettering (SAMUEL TAYLOR, PRINTER, GRAYSTOKE PLACE, FETTER LANE, LONDON, E.C.) below the base of the frame, all in black. RC: blank. Spine: not seen (the spine is wanting from the copy examined)

Copy seen: BL: 7919 bb 39 (imperfect, wanting the spine)

Fingerprint: S.d. uter lyof fean 7 1866A [groups 1–4 taken from pp 5, *15*, 17, 18 respectively]

Notes: Printed by Taylor and Greening, London, price 6d. It is conjectured that this issue ran to 9000 copies — *viz* the difference between the number given on the TP of the next known issue (l) and 45000 (on the TP as above).

The text departs from that of (j) at several points. The code of 26 laws includes one new law (numbered 19); all the following laws are renumbered.

(l) *Second edition, fifty-fourth thousand issue (1866)*

CROQUET: | THE | LAWS AND REGULATIONS OF THE GAME, | WITH | A DESCRIPTION OF THE IMPLEMENTS, | ETC. ETC. | ILLUSTRATED WITH DIAGRAMS AND ENGRAVINGS. | By JOHN JAQUES. | [rule] | NEW EDITION, FIFTY-FOURTH THOUSAND. | [rule] | LONDON: | JAQUES AND SON, 102, HATTON GARDEN. | SOLD ALSO BY | LONGMAN, GREEN, LONGMAN, ROBERTS, AND GREEN. | [rule] | 1866. | {*The Right of Translation is reserved.*}

Formula: A–B⁸ C⁸ [C1 signed]. 24 leaves, pp *1–7* 8–12 *13–15* 16–21 *22* 23–26 *27–29* 30–48

Technical notes: 169 × 97 mm (p 16). 40 lines, 20 = 85 mm. Leaf size 215 × 137 mm; thickness 0.12 mm; wove, unwatermarked, smooth, white

Contents: Blank (*1*), frontispiece (engraving, signed 'W *THOMAS*') (*2*), title (*3*), TP verso (*4*), preface to the second edition, signed 'JOHN JAQUES' (*5*), blank (*6*), text, continued (*7–12*), plate (engraving) (*13*), blank (*14*), text, continued (*15–26*), plate (engraving) (*27*), blank (*28*), text, concluded (*29–39*), advertisements (*40–48*)

Binding: Moderate yellowish Green (136) paper glued to the gatherings, sewn, no endpapers. FC: engraving (illustration of a woman player dressed in crinoline and bonnet with mallet raised to take 'tight' croquet) over title *etc* (**CROQUET.** | [wavy line] **By JOHN JAQUES.** | [wavy line] NEW EDITION, PRICE SIXPENCE.) within a double-ruled frame, the outer frame in bold, and lettering (SAMUEL TAYLOR, PRINTER, GRAYSTOKE PLACE, FETTER LANE, LONDON, E.C.) below the base of the frame, all in black. Inside FC: blank. RC: blank. Inside RC: blank. Spine: not seen (wanting from the copy examined)

Copy seen: PC (imperfect, wanting the spine)

Fingerprint: S.d. uter lyof fean 7 1866A [groups 1–4 taken from pp 5, *15*, 17, 18 respectively]

Notes: Printed by Taylor and Greening, London, price 6d. It is conjectured that this issue ran to 11000 copies — *viz* the difference between the number given on the TP of the next known issue (m) and 54000 (on the TP as above).

The text of has not been collated with that of (k) but, judging by the close similarity of the two issues in all other known respects, it is surmised that they are textually identical, or virtually so.

(m) *Second edition, sixty-fifth thousand issue (1867)*

CROQUET: | THE | LAWS AND REGULATIONS OF THE GAME, | WITH | A DESCRIPTION OF THE IMPLEMENTS. | ETC. ETC. | ILLUSTRATED WITH DIAGRAMS AND ENGRAVINGS. | By JOHN JAQUES. | [rule] | *NEW EDITION, SIXTY-FIFTH THOUSAND.* | [rule] | LONDON: | JAQUES AND SON, 102, HATTON GARDEN. | SOLD ALSO BY | LONGMAN, GREEN, READER AND DYER. | [rule] | 1867 | [*The Right of Translation is reserved.*]

Formula: A–B⁸ C⁸ [C1 signed]. 24 leaves, pp *1–7 8–12 13–15 16–26 27–28 29–47 48*

Technical notes: 169 × 96 mm (p 16). 40 lines, 20 = 84 mm. Leaf size 211 × 136 mm; thickness 0.12 mm; wove, unwatermarked, smooth, white

Contents: Blank *(1)*, frontispiece (engraving, signed '*W THOMAS*') *(2)*, title *(3)*, TP verso *(4)*, preface to the second edition *(5)*, blank *(6)*, text, continued *(7–12)*, plate (engraving) *(13)*, blank *(14)*, text, continued *(15–26)*, plate (engraving) *(27)*, blank *(28)*, text, concluded *(29–39)*, price list *(40)*, opinions of the press *(41)*, advertisements *(42–48)*

Binding: Light yellowish Green (135) paper glued to the gatherings, sewn, no endpapers. FC: engraving (illustration of a woman player dressed in crinoline and bonnet with mallet raised to take 'tight' croquet) over title (**CROQUET.** | [rule] **By JOHN JAQUES.** | [rule] NEW EDITION, PRICE SIXPENCE.) within a ruled frame, and lettering (SAMUEL TAYLOR, PRINTER, GRAYSTOKE PLACE, FETTER LANE, LONDON, E.C.) below the base of the frame, all in black. Inside FC: blank. RC: blank. Inside RC: blank. Spine: blank

Copy seen: PC

Fingerprint: S.d. n-i- heor coap 7 1867A

Notes: Printed by Samuel Taylor, London, price 6d.

The text departs from that of (l) at several points. The code of 28 laws includes two new laws (numbered 4 and 10); the laws are renumbered; some of the footnotes are revised; much of the text is rearranged on the page; Jaques's new croquet marking table is described; a new price list is substituted; and there are several variations in the supplementary advertisements. The reviews cited in 'opinions of the press' refer to one source — *viz City Press* — not listed in earlier issues.

(n) *Second edition, sixty-fifth thousand issue, variant [1867]*

The copy examined is apparently identical to (m), save as follows:

Title page: As that of (m) save for the omission of the last but two and penultimate lines ([rule] | 1867.)

Technical notes: Thickness 0.12 mm

Binding: Dark yellowish Green (137) morocco grain paper over light boards, sewn. FC: heavily gold-blocked illustration, incorporating the title *etc* ([in rustic script] CROQUÊT | BY | JOHN JAQUES), and other lettering (NEW EDITION. | 1/-) within a decorative ruled blind-stamped frame. The illustration is of a woman player dressed in crinoline and bonnet with mallet raised to take 'tight' croquet, set within a hoop in the form of an arbour entwined with floral shoots. Two mallets lean against the uprights. RC: blind-stamped frame of the same pattern as that on the FC. Spine: wanting from the copy examined

Copy seen: PC (imperfect, wanting the spine)

Notes: Printed by Samuel Taylor, London, price 1/–. It is not known whether this issue was published before, after, or at the same time as the paperback issue (m).

(o) *Second edition, unnumbered issue [1867]*

CROQUET: | THE | LAWS AND REGULATIONS OF THE GAME, | WITH | A DESCRIPTION OF THE IMPLEMENTS, | ETC. ETC. | ILLUSTRATED WITH DIAGRAMS AND ENGRAVINGS. | By JOHN JAQUES. | [rule] | *NEW EDITION.* | [rule] | LONDON: | JAQUES AND SON, 102, HATTON GARDEN. | SOLD ALSO BY | LONGMAN, GREEN, READER, AND DYER. | [*The Right of Translation is reserved.*]

Formula: [1–3⁸]. 24 leaves, pp *1–7* 8–12 *13–15* 16–26 *27–28* 29–40 *41* 42–47 *48*

Technical notes: 167 × 97 mm (p 16). 40 lines, 20 = 85 mm. Leaf size 210 × 137 mm; thickness 0.12 mm; wove, unwatermarked, smooth, white

Contents: Blank (*1*), frontispiece (engraving, signed 'W *THOMAS*') (*2*), title (*3*), TP verso (*4*), preface to the second edition (*5*), blank (*6*), text, continued (*7–12*), plate (engraving) (*13*), blank (*14*), text, continued (*15–26*), plate (engraving) (*27*), blank (*28*), text, concluded (*29–39*), opinions of the press (*40*), advertisements (*41–48*)

Binding: Apparently as that of (m)

Copy seen: PC (imperfect, wanting the spine)

Fingerprint: S.d. n-i- hang dupa 7 1867Q

Notes: Printed by Samuel Taylor, London. Year of publication is conjectural.

The text is for the most part identical to that of (m). The code of 29 laws includes one new law (number 19); others are renumbered.

On p *41* the header 'ADVERTISEMENTS' is misprinted 'VERTISEMENTS'.

(p) *Second edition, unnumbered issue, variant [1867]*

[The TP as that of (o)]

Formula: [1–3⁸]. 24 leaves, pp *1–7* 8–12 *13–15* 16–26 *27–28* 29–47 *48* (misprinting 42 as '4')

Technical notes: 167 × 97 mm (p 16). 40 lines, 20 = 85 mm. Leaf size 210 × 135 mm; thickness 0.11 mm; wove, unwatermarked, smooth, white

Contents: Apparently as those of (o)

Binding: The copy examined had apparently been rebound.

Copy seen: BL: 7908 e 18 (imperfect)

Fingerprint: As that of (o)

Notes: The text of this variant appears to differ from that of (o) in the following accidentals only: p 41 is now so numbered, the misprinted header on the same page is now corrected, and the page number on p 42 is now misprinted. The paper is also thicker.

(q) *Third edition [1887]*

CROQUET: | THE | LAWS AND REGULATIONS OF THE GAME | WITH | A DESCRIPTION OF THE IMPLEMENTS. | [swelled rule] | *(NEW EDITION.)* | [swelled rule] | LONDON: | J. JAQUES & SON, 102, HATTON GARDEN. | *(The right of Translation is reserved.)*

Formula: [1¹⁶]. 16 leaves, pp *1–5* 6–32

Technical notes: 169 × 97 mm (p 6). 39 lines, 20 = 87 mm. Leaf size 213 × 136 mm

Contents: Title (*1*), blank (*2*), preface (*3*), plate (engraving) (*4*), text (*5–24*), advertisements (*25–32*)

Binding: The copy examined is disbound

Copy seen: HPC: GV931 J3 CROQ (imperfect)

Fingerprint: S.d. y.aa t.so byst C 1887Q [groups 1–4 taken from pp 3, 11, 13, 13 respectively]

Notes: This issue would appear to have been printed anonymously (though the possibility that a library plate may have obscured the printer's name on the original of the photocopy examined cannot be excluded). Year of publication, inferred from an advertisement (p 27) for the publisher's lawn tennis equipment including 'No 26 "1887" Bats', is conjectural. (A reference on p 21 to what might be taken as a recent suggestion by Mr Riky as to how to legislate for playing with the wrong ball or for a wrong point is of no help here. The original source of this suggestion is apparently Riky's letter to the Editor of *The Field* (24 February 1872), some years before the advent of lawn tennis clubs.)

The code of laws is identical to that found in Lillie's *The Book of Croquet* (A54) and hence its authorship by Lillie is inferred. The fact that the price lists and advertisements in this edition and (o) contain several references to WH Peel might suggest that Peel also contributed in some way to the text.

Little of the text of earlier issues remains intact. The code of laws, now 23 in number, is very largely recast. Its brevity, the fact that this edition and (r) are closely similar, and the fact that no price is quoted in (r), would suggest that both editions were designed primarily for distribution with the manufacturer's croquet equipment.

(r) *Fourth edition [1890]*

CROQUET; | THE | LAWS AND REGULATIONS OF THE GAME | WITH | A DESCRIPTION OF THE IMPLEMENTS. | [swelled rule] | *NEW EDITION)* | [swelled rule] | LONDON: | J. JAQUES & SON, 102, HATTON GARDEN. | (*The right of Translation is reserved.*)

Formula: A¹⁶ [A5 signed B]. 16 leaves, pp *i–iv*, 1 2–20 21–28

Technical notes: 172 × 97 mm (p 2). 44 lines, 20 = 79 mm. Leaf size 204 × 138 mm; thickness 0.10 mm; wove, unwatermarked, smooth, white

Contents: Title (*i*), blank (*ii*), preface, signed 'JOHN JAQUES' (*iii*), engraved illustration of croquet ground, signed '*W THOMAS*' (*iv*), text (*1–20*), price list (*21*), advertisements (*22–28*)

Binding: Yellowish Grey (93) paper glued to the fold of the outer sheet, sewn, no spine or endpapers. FC: printed in black within a multiple-ruled frame with an internal decorative pattern and corner ornaments ([engraved illustration of woman and man players, both fashionably dressed, in conversation] | THE | BOOK OF CROQUET | [swelled rule] | NEW EDITION. | [swelled rule] | LONDON: | JAQUES AND SON, 102, HATTON GARDEN. | [*All Rights Reserved.*]). Inside FC: blank. RC: blank. Inside RC: advertisement

Copy seen: PC

Fingerprint: S.d. y.ta adk- thma 3 1890Q

Notes: Printed anonymously.

The text is identical, or virtually so, to that of (q) but for no apparent reason is very largely reset. The price list (p *21*) is extensively revised and the concluding advertisements include new matter. An advertisement for the new game of 'Crobille', invented by WH Peel, may assist in dating this edition more accurately.

The illustration on the FC is identical to that on the FC of Lillie's *The Book of Croquet* (A54b, c).

A13   LAWS OF CROQUET. Walter Miller   [1864]

[Title heading, the title and text set within a double-ruled frame, the inner frame in bold, with corner ornaments]

LAWS OF CROQUET, | BY | WALTER MILLER, | *Corpus Christi College, Oxford.* | [rule] | "Far more free from errors than any published ones which we have seen." — *Field.* | [rule]

Formula: [1¹]. 1 leaf, unnumbered [pp 1–2]

Technical notes: 273 × 184 mm. 43 lines of text. Leaf size 385 × 231 mm

Contents: Title heading, text, and name of printer (*1*)

Binding: None

Copy seen: BL: 1881 c 6 (114 a) (encased between leaves of Japanese paper)

Fingerprint: .]T. O.y. nde. lyd. C 1864Q

Notes: Published and/or printed by Simpkin, Marshall, and Co, London, and Henry Wright, Birmingham.

The text, consisting of a code of 16 numbered laws, is reproduced essentially *verbatim* from a letter by the author which appeared in *The Field* (20 August 1864). Year of publication is inferred from the date of that letter and from the fact that the Editor's review which appeared in the same issue is quoted in the title heading.

Review: *The Field* (20 August 1864, pp 124–5).

A14   **THE LAWS OF CROQUET AS PLAYED BY THE MEDES**   [1864]
           AND PERSIANS. Rab-Mag

THE | LAWS OF CROQUET | AS PLAYED BY THE | MEDES AND PERSIANS | EDITED BY | Rab-Mag | [rule] | "Aballiboozobanganorribo." — *Southey* | [rule] | LONDON | HATCHARD AND CO. 187 PICCADILLY | *Booksellers to H. R. H. the Princess of Wales* | ANNO MUNDI | 5868

Formula: [1⁸]. 8 leaves, pp *i–iii* iv–vi, 7 8–14 *15* [16]

Technical notes: ca 142 × 84 mm (p iv). 35 lines, 20 = *ca* 82 mm. Leaf size *ca* 186 × 123 mm

Contents: Title (*i*), TP verso (*ii*), introduction signed 'RAB-MAG, 'Bou-biar, Ben-Arnan, AM 5868' (*iii*–vi), the laws of croquet, numbered I–XXXIII, misprinting XXXIII as 'XXIII' (*7–14*), blank (*15*), wanting from the photocopy examined ([16])

Binding: Wanting from the photocopy examined

Copy seen: PC (incomplete photocopy of CUL 143 4 39, wanting p [16])

Fingerprint: ."lf t.s— y.he *Fl*mo 3 1864Q

Notes: Printed by James Hedderwick & Son, Glasgow. The introduction, though alluding to the contemporary state of croquet, is pure satire. The code of laws and footnotes are manifestly intended to be read as a serious contribution, though the footnotes are expressed in satirical idiom. Year of publication is inferred from the review cited below.

Review: *The Field* (6 August 1864, pp 106–7).

A15   **ROUTLEDGE'S HANDBOOK OF CROQUET.**   1864
           Edmund Routledge

           (a) *First edition (1864)*

ROUTLEDGE'S | HANDBOOK | OF | CROQUET. | BY | EDMUND

ROUTLEDGE, | EDITOR OF | "EVERY BOY'S MAGAZINE." | WITH ILLUSTRATIONS. | LONDON: | ROUTLEDGE, WARNE, & ROUTLEDGE, | BROADWAY, LUDGATE HILL; | NEW YORK: 129, GRAND STREET. | 1864.

Formula: A–D⁸ [$2 signed (–A1)]. 32 leaves, pp *i–iii* iv *v–vi*, 7 8–61 *62–64*

Technical notes: 104 × 64 mm (p 8). 20 = 68 mm. Leaf size 136 × 89 mm; thickness 0.13 mm; wove, unwatermarked, smooth, white

Contents: Title (*i*), TP verso (*ii*), preface, signed 'Edmund Routledge', March 1864 (*iii*–iv), contents (*v*), blank (*vi*), text (7–61), name of printer (61), advertisements (*62–64*)

Binding: Moderate Yellow (87) paper over light boards, sewn. FC: in black (ROUTLEDGE'S SIXPENNY HANDBOOKS. | [in artist's open letters out of illustration] **CROQUET** | [in artist's solid letters over illustration] **BY** | [*do*] **EDMUND ROUTLEDGE** | [engraved illustration of a woman player in crinoline and bonnet with mallet raised to take 'tight' croquet against the background of a croquet party] | [letterpress] **PRICE SIXPENCE** | [rule] | [letterpress] LONDON : ROUTLEDGE, WARNE,&ROUTLEDGE) apparently within a ruled frame (the R edge of which would appear to have been truncated from the copy examined). RC: advertisement for Routledge's Sixpenny Handbooks (listing 13 titles) and Hoyle's Games Modernized, within a ruled frame, in black. Spine: in black upwards (CROQUET. — SIXPENCE.)

Copy seen: PC

Fingerprint: s.ly e-ur ber, bait 3 1864A

Notes: Printed by Cox and Wyman, London, price 6d. It is conjectured that this issue ran to some 16000 copies — *viz* the number given on the TP of the next known issue (b). The text includes a code of 52 numbered rules.

Review: *The Queen* (1 October 1864, p 212).

(b) *Sixteenth thousand issue (1865)*

ROUTLEDGE'S | **HANDBOOK** | OF | **CROQUET.** | BY | EDMUND ROUTLEDGE. | [in gothic-revival script] Sixteenth Thousand. | LONDON: | ROUTLEDGE, WARNE, & ROUTLEDGE, | BROADWAY, LUDGATE HILL; | NEW YORK: 129, GRAND STREET. | 1865.

Formula: A⁸ B–D⁸ [$2 signed (–A1, 2)]. 32 leaves, pp *1–7* 8–61 *62–64*

Technical notes: 103 × 63 mm (p 8). 31 lines, 20 = 67 mm. Leaf size 135 × 88 mm; thickness 0.13 mm; wove, unwatermarked, smooth, white

Contents: Title (*1*), TP verso (*2*), preface, signed 'Edmund Routledge' (*3–4*), contents (*5*), blank (*6*), text (7–61), name of printer (61), advertisements (*62–64*)

Binding: Moderate Yellow (87) paper over light boards, sewn. FC: in black (ROUTLEDGE'S SIXPENNY HANDBOOKS. | [in artist's open letters out of illustration] **CROQUET** | [in artist's solid letters over illustration] **BY** | [*do*] **EDMUND ROUTLEDGE** | [engraved illustration of a woman player in crinoline and bonnet with mallet raised to take 'tight' croquet against the background of a croquet party] | [letterpress] **PRICE SIXPENCE** | [rule] | [letterpress] LONDON : ROUTLEDGE, WARNE,&ROUTLEDGE) apparently within a ruled frame (the upper and R edges of which would appear to have been truncated from the copy examined). RC: advertisement for Routledge's Sixpenny Handbooks (listing 14 titles) and Hoyle's Games Modernized, apparently within a ruled frame (the lower edge of which would appear to have been truncated from the copy examined), in black. Spine: in black upwards (CROQUET. — SIXPENCE.)

Copy seen: PC

Fingerprint: s.ly e-ur ber, bait 3 1865A

Notes: Printed by Cox and Wyman, London, price 6d. It is conjectured that this issue ran to some 16000 copies — *viz* the difference between the number given on the TP of the next known issue (c) and that given on the TP of this issue.

The text departs little, and mostly in minor detail only, from (a). In particular, it is notable that the author's personal endorsement of Jaques croquet equipment, given on p 51 of the first edition, is omitted.

(c) *Thirty-second thousand issue (1866)*

ROUTLEDGE'S | HANDBOOK | OF | CROQUET. | BY | EDMUND ROUTLEDGE. | [in gothic-revival script] Thirty-second Thousand. | LONDON: | GEORGE ROUTLEDGE AND SONS, | BROADWAY, LUDGATE HILL; | NEW YORK: 416 BROOME STREET. | 1866.

Formula: A^8 $B–D^8$ [\$2 signed (–A1, 2)]. 32 leaves, pp *1–7* 8–61 *62–64*

Technical notes: 103 × 62 mm (p 8). 31 lines, 20 = 67 mm. Leaf size 135 × 92 mm; thickness 0.10 mm; wove, unwatermarked, smooth, white

Contents: Title (*1*), blank (*2*), preface (*3–4*), contents (*5*), blank (*6*), text (*7–61*), advertisements (*62–64*)

Binding: As that of (b)

Copy seen: PC (imperfect)

Fingerprint: s.ly e-ur ber, bait 3 1866A

Notes: Printed by Cox and Wyman, London, price 6d.

The text differs from (b) in minor detail only. The advertisements at the end are all different.

(d) *Thirty-second thousand issue, variant (1866)*

[The TP as that of (c)]

Formula: As that of (c)

Technical notes: 103 × 62 mm (p 8). 31 lines, 20 = 67 mm. Leaf size 136 × 89 mm; thickness 0.10 mm; wove, unwatermarked, smooth, white

Contents: As those of (c)

Binding: Moderate Yellow (87) paper over light boards, sewn. FC: in black and deep reddish Orange (36) ([black] ROUTLEDGE'S SIXPENNY HANDBOOKS. | [in artist's Orange letters with black outlines out of the illustration] CROQUET | [in artist's solid black letters over the illustration] BY | EDMUND ROUTLEDGE | [engraved illustration of a woman player in crinoline and bonnet with mallet raised to take 'tight' croquet against the background of a croquet party, printed in black with some Orange detail] | [letterpress in Orange] PRICE SIXPENCE | [black letterpress within base of frame] LONDON: GEORGE ROUTLEDGE & SONS.), apparently within a ruled frame in Orange (the upper edge of which would appear to have been truncated from the copy examined). RC: advertisement with illustration of woman croquet player on the FC, apparently within a ruled frame (the L edge of which would appear to have been truncated from the copy examined), in black and Orange. Spine: wanting from the copy examined

Copy seen: PC (imperfect, wanting the spine)

Fingerprint: s.ly e-ur ber, bait 3 1866A

Notes: Printed by Cox and Wyman, London, price 6d. This issue is apparently identical to (c) save in respect of the colouring of the covers and the advertising on the RC.

(e) *First American, Beadle's Dime, edition (1866)*

BEADLE'S DIME | HANDBOOK OF CROQUET: | A COMPLETE GUIDE TO THE PRACTICE OF THE GAME. | BY EDMUND ROUTLEDGE; | GIVING ALL THE RULES PROPOSED BY VARIOUS AMERICAN | WRITERS ON THE GAME. | [rule] | NEW YORK: | BEADLE AND COMPANY, PUBLISHERS, | 118 WILLIAM STREET.

Formula: [1¹⁶]. 16 leaves, pp 1–9 10–28 29–32

Technical notes: 133 × 80 (p 13). 40 lines, 20 = 67 mm. Leaf size 160 × 101 mm; thickness 0.11 mm; wove, unwatermarked, smooth, white

Contents: Blank (*1*), frontispiece, engraved illustration of a woman player dressed in crinoline and bonnet with mallet half-raised to take 'tight' croquet, signed 'Norr & Co' (*2*), title (*3*), TP verso (*4*), preface, signed 'The Editor' (*5*), contents (*6*), plan of croquet court (*7*), blank (*8*), text (*9–28*), advertisements (*29–32*)

Binding: Moderate orange Yellow (71) paper, printed in black, glued to the fold of the outer sheet and creased to form a spine, sewn, no endpapers. FC: within a double-ruled frame, the outer frame in bold ([in hatched and shaded open display script, in a convex arc] **BEADLE'S** | [*do*] **DIME** | [within the outer ring of a medallion, superimposed over the line above, in a convex arc] UNITED STATES OF AMERICA | [centred in the foregoing medallion] ONE | [*do*] DIME | [reproduction of frontispiece illustration] **BOOK OF CROQUET.** | [rule] | NEW YORK: | BEADLE COMPANY, 118 WILLIAM ST. | American News Co., 121 Nassau St., N. Y.). Inside FC: advertisement (Beadle's Dime School Series). RC: advertisement (Beadle's Dime Pocket Songster No 4). Inside RC: advertisement (Beadle's Dime Hand-Books for Housewives and Homes). Spine: downwards (Beadle's BOOK OF CROQUET   Dime ‡)

Copy seen: HPC: GV931 R6 1866a CROQ (imperfect)

Fingerprint: R.*e.* ndne rdit suyo 7 1866A

Notes: Apparently printed by American News Co, New York, price 10 cents. This edition appears to be an authorised reprint. The text has not been collated with earlier UK issues, but it is believed to constitute a revised abridgment modelled closely on the original. Like (a), it includes a code of 52 numbered rules. It includes also eleven additional numbered rules 'adopted by some players'.

(f) *First American, Beadle's Dime, edition, variant (1866)*

[The TP as that of (e)]

Formula: [1¹⁶(–1₁₆)]. 15 leaves, pp *1–9* 10 *11–12* 13–30

Technical notes: 133 × 80 (p 13). 40 lines, 20 = 67 mm. Leaf size 160 × 101 mm; thickness 0.12 mm; wove, unwatermarked, smooth, white

Contents: Title (*1*), TP verso (*2*), blank (*3*), frontispiece, as that of (e) (*4*), contents (*5*), blank (*6*), preface (*7*), blank (*8*), text (*9–28*), advertisement (*29*), blank save pagination (*30*)

Binding: Moderate orange Yellow (71) paper, printed in black, glued to the fold of the outer sheet and creased to form a spine, stitched, no endpapers. FC: as that of (e). Inside FC: advertisement (Empire Depot of Games). RC: advertisement

(Martelle, 'The New Summer Game'). Inside RC: advertisement (New York City Base-Ball Emporium and Manufacturing Company). Spine: downwards (Beadle's BOOK OF CROQUET   Dime Bo ‡)

Copy seen: HPC: GV931 R6 1866 CROQ

Fingerprint: 2624 ndne rdit suyo C 1866A [groups 1–4 taken from pp 5, 13, 17, 18 respectively]

Notes: Apparently printed by American News Co, New York, price 10 cents. Some of the early leaves of the copy examined had been printed or collated out of order. It is not clear how this fault arose and hence whether it is likely to be characteristic of the whole issue. Apart from this irregularity, the text is apparently identical to that of (e), the two issues varying only in their advertising matter.

**A16   THE RULES OF CROQUET REVISED AND CORRECTED   [1864]
BY AN OLD HAND. [Capt Mayne Reid]**

(a) *First edition [1864]*

Not seen. Reid refers to this work in the bill of complaint filed by his solicitors in an action against the sixth Earl of Essex in Chancery for breach of copyright of his book *Croquet* (A8).

Notes: This work was apparently published jointly by the Earl of Essex of Cassiobury Park, Watford, and his printer, Miss Emily Faithfull of the City of London and Middlesex, late in 1863 or early in 1864, price 6d. In his decree in the Chancery Court (25 August 1864), Vice Chancellor Kindersley ordered that all stocks held by the publishers be destroyed. It would appear that altogether some hundreds of copies of the first and second editions had by then been sold.

Reid complained that 93 of his 126 rules had been copied *verbatim* or with 'merely colorable alterations of corresponding contents'. Hence the contribution of another hand or other hands is inferred. In a letter to Reid's solicitors, Parke and Pollock, quoted in Reid's bill of complaint, the Earl claimed that his book had been written by 'a friend of mine'.

(b) *Second edition [1864]*

Not seen. According to Reid, this work ran to a 'second edition'. It would appear from Reid's account that this edition, also printed by Emily Faithfull, was issued shortly before he initiated proceedings against the earl for infringement of copyright at the end of July 1864. See also *Notes* to (a).

**A17   THE RULES OF THE GAME OF CROQUET, AS PLAYED   [1864]
AT SHERIFF HUTTON PARK. [Cordeaux & Ernest *et al*]**

(a) **First edition [1864]*

Not seen. The contents of the several known issues of this work evidently reflect the evolution of a tripartite relationship between Cordeaux & Ernest, sports goods manufacturers and publishers, the Sheriff Hutton Park croquet club or fraternity, and Thompson, their patron, owner of Sheriff Hutton Park. The publication of most issues was clearly intended to support the equipment sales of Cordeaux & Ernest, who probably distributed copies with their croquet equipment. Other editions — notably (c) — may have been published independently, or by arrangement with Cordeaux & Ernest, by Thompson or by the group of players who met in his grounds.

Authorship of most parts of the several editions is attributed more or less explicitly to

Cordeaux & Ernest and Thompson. Authorship of the rules themselves, however, is not so attributed and is open to question.

Year of first publication also is uncertain. The game of croquet would appear to have been played at Sheriff Hutton Park according to these rules in 1863 but it may be inferred from a preface to (b) that those rules were not published, at least by Cordeaux & Ernest, until August 1864. Whether or not they had been set in print any earlier is unclear.

(b) *Second edition [1867]*

THE RULES | OF THE | GAME OF CROQUÊT, | AS PLAYED AT | [in gothic-revival script] **Sheriff Hutton Park.** | [rule] | [in open script] PUBLISHED BY PERMISSION. | [rule] | **SECOND EDITION,** | *With Preliminary Remarks and Description of* | *Implements, by the Publishers.* | YORK : | PUBLISHED BY CORDEAUX & ERNEST, | PRINTED BY DEAN & SON, LUDGATE HILL, LONDON.

Formula: Apparently [1^{16}]. 16 leaves, pp *1–9* 10–16 *17* 18–31 *32*

Technical notes: 140 × 86 mm (p 11). 30 lines, 20 = 94 mm. Leaf size 176 × 118 mm; thickness 0.09 mm; wove, unwatermarked, smooth, white

Contents: Blank (*1*), frontispiece (advertisement) (*2*), title (*3*), blank (*4*), preface, signed 'THE PUBLISHERS', 15 March 1867 (*5*), preface to the first edition, signed 'CORDEAUX & ERNEST', 8 August 1864 (*6*), contents (*7*), blank (*8*), preliminary remarks (*9–16*), introduction to the game of croquet by Thompson, including a code of 16 numbered rules (*17–26*), 'TO THE TRADE, &c' (*27*), testimonials, to January 1866 (*28–29*), price lists (*30–31*), advertisement (*32*)

Binding: Not ascertainable from the copy examined

Copy seen: BOD: 250 k 2 (23) (wanting the original wrapper, in a library binding)

Fingerprint: 7.S. d.or asnt scha 7 1867Q

Notes: Printed by Dean & Son, London. Year of publication is inferred from the date appended to the preface on p 5.

It is evident that the publishers acknowledged authorship of the preliminary remarks on pp 9–16 and the matter addressed to the trade on p 27.

(c) *Abridged edition [1869]*

RULES | FOR THE | GAME OF CROQUÊT , | AS PLAYED AT | [in gothic-revival script] **Sheriff Hutton Park,** | IN THE YEAR 1863. | AMENDED 1865, 67, 68, 69.

Formula: Apparently [1^{4} χ1]. 5 leaves, pp *1–3* 4–6 *7–8* 9 [*10*]

Technical notes: ca 132 × 81 mm (p 4). 30 lines, 20 = *ca* 87 mm. Leaf size *ca* 185 × 122 mm

Contents: Title (*1*), rules for the game of croquet and explanations (*2–6*), suggestions for equalising sides or players (*7*), plan for laying out the ground (*8–9*), wanting from the photocopy examined ([*10*])

Binding: Not seen

Copy seen: NT (incomplete photocopy, wanting p 10)

Fingerprint: r.nt ."êt l.s. r-t- C 1869Q [all four groups taken from p *3*]

Notes: Printed anonymously. The code of 18 numbered rules departs from that of (b) in several particulars, including revisions and additions.

(d) *Third edition [1871]*

[Within a ruled frame]

THE RULES | OF THE | GAME OF CROQUÊT, | AS PLAYED AT | *Sheriff Hutton Park.* | [rule] | THE CONFERENCE LAWS ADOPTED IN 1870. | [rule] | REMARKS, CRITICAL AND EXPLANATORY, | OF THE | *Progress of Croquet, with an Introduction to the Game,* | By LEONARD THOMPSON, Esq. | TOGETHER WITH AN | Historical Sketch of the Game, and full description | of the Implements used.   By the Publishers. | [rule] | Illustrated with Diagrams and Engravings. | [rule] | *Entered at Stationers' Hall.* | YORK : | PUBLISHED BY CORDEAUX & ERNEST, | PRINTED BY DEAN & SON, LUDGATE HILL, LONDON.

Formula: Apparently *A*1 B–C^8 D^4 [$1 signed (–A1)]. Apparently 21 leaves, pp *i–ii, 1–3 4 5 6–11 12 13–36 37–40*

Technical notes: ca 143 × 92 mm (p 6). 37 lines, 20 = *ca* 78 mm. Leaf size *ca* 171 × 116 mm

Contents: Title (*i*), blank (*ii*), index (*1*), blank (*2*), preface, signed 'CORDEAUX & ERNEST', 1 March 1871 (*3–4*), text (*5–29*), the laws of croquet as adopted at the Conference of Croquet Players in London, January 1870, copied from *The Times* and other journals (*30–35*), York Croquet Tournament, (abridged) from *Land and Water* (*35–36*), advertisements (*37–38*), testimonials (*39–40*), advertisement (*40*)

Binding: Not seen. From the photocopy examined it would appear that the FC is identical, or virtually so, to that of (f)

Copy seen: PC (imperfect photocopy)

Fingerprint: **38 d.s- s.s. asca 3 1871Q

Notes: Printed by Dean & Son, London. Year of publication is inferred from the date appended to the signature in the preface. The reference to *Land and Water* (pp 35, 36) is unhelpful in dating this edition: the York tournament was reported in that journal on 11 June 1870, several months before the date appended to the preface.

The text includes the rules of the game of croquet as played at Sheriff Hutton Park amended to 1869 (pp 25–28) and the January 1870 'Conference' code of laws (pp 30–33). The rules are identical to those in (c).

Review: *Westminster Papers* (1 July 1871, p 57).

(e) *1873 issue (1873)*

Not seen. A copy of this issue once held by the BL is listed in the *General Catalogue* as having been destroyed by bombing in the war.

(f) *Fourth edition [1873]*

THE RULES | OF THE | GAME OF CROQUÊT, | AS PLAYED AT | *Sheriff Hutton Park,* | [rule] | THE CONFERENCE LAWS ADOPTED IN 1870. | [rule] | REMARKS, CRITICAL AND EXPLANATORY, | OF THE | *Progress of Croquet, with an Introduction to the Game,* | By LEONARD THOMPSON, Esq. | TOGETHER WITH AN | Historical Sketch of the Game, and full description of | the Implements used, by the Publishers. | [rule] | Illustrated with Diagrams and Engravings. | [rule] | *Fourth Edition.   Entered at Stationers' Hall* | YORK: | PUBLISHED BY CORDEAUX AND ERNEST, | PRINTED BY DEAN & SON, LUDGATE HILL, LONDON.

Formula: B^8 C–D^8 [C1, D1 signed]. 24 leaves, pp *1–4 5 6–7 8–13 14 15–42 43–45 46–47 48*

Technical notes: 145 × 92 mm (p 8). 38 lines, 20 = 78 mm. Leaf size 182 × 120 mm; thickness 0.12 mm; wove, unwatermarked, smooth, white

Contents: Title (*1*), blank (*2*), preface, signed 'Cordeaux & Ernest', 1 March 1873 (*3*), preface to the third edition, signed 'Cordeaux & Ernest', 1 March 1871 (*4–5*), index (*6*), text (*7–42*), advertisements (*43–45*), testimonials (*46–47*), advertisement (*48*)

Binding: Vivid purplish Blue (194) moiré-effect embossed cloth, the grain running from top R to bottom L, over light boards, sewn. The facing pages of the endpapers are coloured pale Yellow (89). FC: gold-blocked illustration (of a woman player dressed in crinoline and bonnet with mallet raised to take 'tight' croquet) and title (CROQUET) within a blind-stamped ruled frame. RC: blind-stamped frame of the same pattern as that on the FC. Spine: blank

Copy seen: BL: 7921 dd 21

Fingerprint: 3.T. d.s- d.ed itIn 3 1873Q

Notes: Printed by Dean & Son, London. Year of publication is inferred from the signature appended to the preface (p *3*) and from a pencil annotation, apparently by the BL, on the copy examined.

The text includes the rules of the game of croquet as played at Sheriff Hutton Park amended to 1869 (pp 27–30) and the January 1870 'Conference' code of laws (pp 32–35).

1865

A18   **CROQUET AND ARCHERY. [Anon]**   [1865]

FAMILY HERALD HANDY BOOKS. | CROQUET | AND | ARCHERY. | [rule] | LONDON: | B. BLAKE, FAMILY HERALD OFFICE, | 421, STRAND.

Formula: A^{16} B^{16} [B1, 2 signed]. 32 leaves, pp *1–5 6–25 26–31 32–55 56, 1 2–3 4–8* [= 64]

Technical notes: 110 × 68 mm (p 9). 25 lines, 20 = 88 mm. Leaf size 144 × 89 mm; thickness 0.10 mm; wove, unwatermarked, smooth, white

Contents: Title (*1*), name of printer (*2*), croquet contents (*3*), blank (*4*), text, croquet (*5–25*), blank (*26*), section title ('ARCHERY') (*27*), blank (*28*), archery contents (*29*), blank (*30*), text, archery (*31–55*), blank (*56*), advertisements (*1–8*)

Binding: Light Orange (52) paper, glued to the spine, no endpapers. FC: printed in black, mostly within an elaborate multiple-ruled frame with broad bands at the head and foot ([in Orange out of black] **FAMILY HERALD** | [*do*] HANDY BOOKS | [in black on Orange] Croquet | [*do*] AND | [*do*] Archery. | [*do*, a rule] | [*do*] London : | [*do*] B. Blake, Family Herald Office, | [*do*] 421, Strand. | [in Orange out of black] PRICE THREE PENCE. | [below the frame, L justified, in black on Orange] No. 16.). Inside FC: advertisement. RC: advertisement. Inside RC: advertisement. Spine: blank

Copy seen: BOD: 3843 E 125 (1)

Fingerprint: 2518 ndle g.en tuba 3 1865Q [group 4 taken from p 18]

Notes: Printed by William Stevens, London, price 3d. Year of publication is inferred from that (1865) attributed by Bodley's Librarian and from the advertisement on p *8* for *The Licensed Victuallers' Almanack* for 1864, issued by the same publisher.

The text includes a code of 30 numbered rules.

A19   **CROQUET: AS PLAYED BY THE NEWPORT CROQUET**   1865
        CLUB. [J], 'One of the Members'

(a) *First edition (1865)*

CROQUET. | AS PLAYED BY | THE NEWPORT CROQUET CLUB. | BY | ONE OF THE MEMBERS. | Sic ludus animo debet aliquando dari | Ad cogitandum melior ut redeat tibi. | PHŒD., Lib. iii, Fab. 4. | NEW YORK: | SHELDON & COMPANY, | 498 & 500 BROADWAY. | [rule] | 1865.

[TP verso]

Entered, according to Act of Congress, in the year 1865, by | SHELDON & CO., | In the Clerk's Office of the District Court for the Southern District | of New York. | [one of three lines at the lower L] Stereotyped by | [*do*] SMITH & McDOUGAL, | [*do*] 84 Beekman-st. | [one of three lines at the lower R] Printed by | [*do*] C. S. WESTCOTT & Co., | [*do*] 79 John-st.

Formula: Not ascertainable from the photocopy examined [p 25 signed '3', p 29 signed '3*', p 37 signed '4']. 26 leaves, pp *i–iii* iv–vi *vii–viii*, 9 10–14 *15–17* 18–21 22 *23–50 51 52*

Technical notes: †114 × 64 mm (p iv). 27 lines, 20 = †85 mm. Leaf size †152 mm [17 cm according to the catalogue of the LOC] × 94 mm

Contents: Title (*i*), TP verso (*ii*), preface, signed 'J', 7 July 1865 (*iii*–vi), contents (*vii*), blank (*viii*), text (9–52)

Binding: Not ascertainable from the photocopy examined (the original is in a library binding)

Copy seen: LOC: GV931 N55 (photocopy taken from negative microfilm)

Fingerprint: kers n.he d.on opTu 3 1865A

Notes: Printed by CS Westcott, New York. The close similarity of this edition to (b) suggests that the latter issue was, at least for the most part, an identical reprint, and hence that the format of the present issue, seen only in photocopy, may best be inferred from that of the latter.

The text includes a code of 52 numbered rules together with 9 numbered hints to beginners.

(b) *1867 issue (1867)*

CROQUET. | AS PLAYED BY | THE NEWPORT CROQUET CLUB. | BY | ONE OF THE MEMBERS. | Sic ludus animo debet aliquando dari | Ad cogitandum melior ut redeat tibi. | PHŒD., Lib. iii, Fab. 4. | NEW YORK: | SHELDON & COMPANY, | 498 & 500 BROADWAY. | [rule] | 1867.

Formula: $1^8 \ 2^{10}(-2_{10}) \ 3^6 \ 4^6(-4_1)$ [2_5 signed '3', 2_7 signed '3*', 3_2 signed '4']. 28 leaves, pp *i–iii* iv–vi *vii–viii*, 9 10–14 *15–17* 18–21 22 *23–28 29 30–50 51 52–56*

Technical notes: 122 × 68 mm (p iv). 27 lines, 20 = 91 mm. Leaf size 167 × 107 mm; thickness 0.12 mm; wove, unwatermarked, smooth, white

Contents: Title (*1*), TP verso (*ii*), preface, signed 'J', 7 July 1865 (*iii*–vi), contents (*vii*), blank (*viii*), text (9–52), advertisements (53–56)

Binding: Stitched. Almost all of the wrapper is wanting from the copy examined. Only a small portion of the spine, of brilliant orange Yellow (67) paper, glued to the folds of the gatherings, remains intact. There are no end papers

Copy seen: HPC: GV935 C96 CROQ (imperfect)

Fingerprint: kers n.he d.on opTu 3 1867A

Notes: Printed by CS Westcott & Co, 79 John Street, stereotyped by Smith & McDougal, 84 Beekman Street.

The text of this issue has not been collated with that of (a). It is evident, however, that for the most part they are identical. The present issue is extended to include advertising.

A20 **THE GAME OF CROQUET: ITS APPOINTMENT AND** **1865**
LAWS. R Fellow

(a) *First edition (1865)*

THE GAME OF CROQUET; | ITS | APPOINTMENT AND LAWS; | WITH DESCRIPTIVE ILLUSTRATIONS. | BY R. FELLOW. | NEW YORK: | PUBLISHED BY HURD AND HOUGHTON. | BOSTON: E. P. DUTTON AND COMPANY. | 1865.

Formula: $1^8\ 2^8$ [2_1 signed]. 16 leaves, pp *1–7* 8–15 *16* 17–31 *32*

Technical notes: 132 × 82 mm (p 17). 28 lines, 20 = 94 mm. Leaf size 190 × 121 mm; thickness 0.13 mm; laid, unwatermarked, smooth, white. An inset plate (frontispiece) faces the TP

Contents: Title (*1*), TP verso (*2*), preface (*3*), blank (*4*), contents (*5*), blank (*6*), text (*7–31*), blank (*32*)

Binding: Dark greyish reddish Brown (47) sand grain cloth over light boards, sewn. The facing pages of the endpapers are coloured pale Yellow (89). One additional free endpaper (laid, matching the paper of the book) front and rear. FC: gold-blocked title (CROQUET) and illustration (of a man kneeling, testing the passage of a ball through a hoop with mallet held between his hands) within a blind-stamped frame. RC: blind-stamped, otherwise the same as the FC. Spine: blank

Copy seen: PC

Fingerprint: F.om cex, rmin otpl 3 1865A

Notes: Printed by HO Houghton and Company, Riverside, Cambridge.

The text includes a code of 17 numbered laws, several including numbered sub-clauses. The illustrator has been identified by the American Antiquarian Society as Augustus Hoppin.

(b) *First edition, variant (1865)*

THE GAME OF CROQUET; | ITS | APPOINTMENT AND LAWS; | WITH DESCRIPTIVE ILLUSTRATIONS. | BY R. FELLOW. | NEW YORK: | PUBLISHED BY HURD AND HOUGHTON. | 401 Broadway, cor. Walker Street. | 1865.

Formula: As that of (a)

Technical notes: 132 × 82 mm (p 17). 28 lines, 20 = 94 mm. Leaf size 190 × 125 mm; thickness 0.12 mm; wove, unwatermarked, smooth, white. An inset plate (frontispiece) faces the TP

Contents: As those of (a)

Binding: Strong reddish Brown (40) linen-texture cloth over light boards, sewn. The facing pages of the endpapers are coloured greyish reddish Brown (46). One additional free endpaper (wove, matching the paper of the book) front and rear. FC: gold-blocked title (CROQUET) and illustration (of a man kneeling, testing the passage of a ball through a hoop with mallet held between his hands) within a blind-stamped frame. RC: blind-stamped, otherwise the same as the FC. Spine: blank

Copy seen: HPC: GV931 S43 Copy3 CROQ

Fingerprint: As that of (a)

Notes: Printed by HO Houghton and Company, Riverside, Cambridge. This variant differs from (a) only in not citing an associate publisher on the TP, in the quality of the paper, and in the construction of the binding. In view of the fact that EP Dutton and Company were apparently not involved in the publication of the 1866 issue (c), it is conjectured that this firm was appointed at the outset but disenfranchised soon after the appearance of the first edition.

(c) *1866 issue (1866)*

THE GAME OF CROQUET; | ITS | APPOINTMENT AND LAWS; | WITH DESCRIPTIVE ILLUSTRATIONS. | BY R. FELLOW. | NEW YORK: | PUBLISHED BY HURD AND HOUGHTON. | 1866.

Formula: As that of (a)

Technical notes: 132 × 82 mm (p 17). 28 lines, 20 = 94 mm. Leaf size 186 × 122 mm; thickness 0.13 mm; laid, unwatermarked, smooth, white. An inset plate (frontispiece) faces the TP

Contents: As those of (a)

Binding: Dark greyish reddish Brown (47) sand grain cloth over light boards, sewn. The facing pages of the endpapers are coloured greyish reddish Brown (46). One additional free endpaper (laid, matching the paper of the book) front and rear. FC: gold-blocked title and illustration, the same as (a), within a decorative blind-stamped frame. RC: blind-stamped, otherwise the same as that on the FC. Spine: blank

Copy seen: PC

Fingerprint: F.om cex, rmin otpl 3 1866A

Notes: Printed by HO Houghton and Company, Riverside, Cambridge.

The text is apparently identical to that of (a).

(d) *1867 issue (1867)*

THE GAME OF CROQUET; | ITS | APPOINTMENT AND LAWS; | WITH DESCRIPTIVE ILLUSTRATIONS. | By R. FELLOW. | NEW YORK: | PUBLISHED BY HURD AND HOUGHTON. | 459 Broome Street. | 1867.

Formula: Apparently as that of (a)

Technical notes: ca 131 × 82 mm (p 8). 28 lines, 20 = *ca* 94 mm. Leaf size *ca* 189 × 120 mm. An inset plate (frontispiece) faces the TP

Contents: Title (*1*), TP verso (*2*), preface (*3*), blank (*4*), contents (*5*), blank (*6*), text (*7–31*), not seen ([*32*])

Binding: Apparently bound in a wrapper of pale coloured paper without endpapers. FC: printed within a triple-ruled frame, the centre frame in bold (THE | [in gothic-revival script, decorated *G, C*] ITS | APPOINTMENTS AND LAWS; | *WITH DESCRIPTIVE ILLUSTRATIONS* | By R. FELLOW. | [engraved illustration of a man kneeling, testing the passage of a ball through a hoop with mallet held between his hands] | NEW YORK: | PUBLISHED BY HURD AND HOUGHTON. | 1867.). Inside FC: not seen. RC: advertisement. Inside RC: not seen

Copy seen: HCLWL: SG 1360 3.3 (incomplete photocopy)

Fingerprint: F.om cex, rmin otpl 3 1867A

Notes: Printed by HO Houghton and Company, Riverside, Cambridge.

The text is apparently identical to that of (a).

(e) *New edition, enlarged and corrected (1868)*

THE GAME OF CROQUET; | ITS | APPOINTMENT AND LAWS; | WITH DESCRIPTIVE ILLUSTRATIONS. | By R. FELLOW. | [NEW EDITION, ENLARGED AND CORRECTED.] | NEW YORK: | PUBLISHED BY HURD AND HOUGHTON. | 459 Broome Street. | 1868.

Formula: 1^8 2–3^8 [2_1, 3_1 signed]. 24 leaves, pp *i*–*iii* iv–v *vi*, 7 8–42 43 44–48

Technical notes: 133 × 82 mm (p iv). 25 lines, 20 = 108 mm. Leaf size 185 × 121 mm; thickness 0.14 mm; laid, unwatermarked, smooth, white. An inset plate (frontispiece) faces the TP and one additional free endpaper is appended at the rear.

Contents: Title (*i*), TP verso (*ii*), preface, signed 'R. FELLOW', March 1868 (*iii*–v), contents (*vi*), text (7-48)

Binding: Dark greyish reddish Brown (47) sand grain cloth over light boards, sewn. The facing pages of the endpapers are coloured dark orange Yellow (72). FC: identical or very similar to that of (c). RC: blind-stamped, otherwise the same as that on the FC. Spine: blank

Copy seen: HPC: GV93 S43 1868 CROQ

Fingerprint: skht e-ee etne ReM) 3 1868A

Notes: Printed by HO Houghton and Company.

The text is very largely rewritten and now incorporates the principles of the Field Code, represented by twelve numbered laws (I–XII) with several alphabetical sub-clauses, the principles of arbitration, numbered 1–9, laid down by the writer in *London Society*, and *Castle Croquet: For Four Players* (AA26) by Lewis Carroll, evidently reprinted with great care (deviating only in minor accidentals) from *Aunt Judy's Magazine* (London: Bell and Daldy, August 1867, pp 221–24).

(f) *Abercrombie & Fitch augmented edition (1968)*

THE GAME OF CROQUET | ITS APPOINTMENTT AND LAWS | *by Horace Elisha Scudder* | [swelled rule] | EDITED AND AUGMENTED BY | *Paul Seabury* | WITH A FOREWORD BY | *Rex Stout* | ABERCROMBIE & FITCH | NEW YORK

Formula: [1–4^8]. 32 leaves, pp *1*–*6* 7–19 20–22 23–44 45–46 47–52 53–54 55–63 64

Technical notes: 154 × 89 mm (p 10). 34 lines, 20 = 91 mm. Leaf size 209 × 136 mm; thickness 0.16 mm; wove, unwatermarked, smooth, white

Contents: Half-title (*1*), blank (*ii*), title (*iii*), TP verso (*iv*), contents (*v*), blank (*vi*), foreword, signed 'REX STOUT' (7–8), introduction, signed 'P.S.' (9–19), blank (*20*), sub-title, 'THE GAME OF CROQUET' (*21*), blank (*22*), preface, initialled 'R.F.' (*23*), text (24–44), sub-title, 'CASTLE CROQUET' (*45*), editor's note (*46*), text (47–52), sub-title, 'THE BRITISH GAME OF CROQUET' (*53*), editor's note (*54*), text, a simple synopsis, attributed to John Jaques and Son (54–58), glossary, adapted from *How to Play Croquêt*, 1873 (A22) (59–63), blank (*64*)

Binding: paper, printed in alternate brilliant bluish Green (159) and moderate purplish Red (258) horizontal stripes on a moderate Yellow (87) background, over-lapping a light greyish Olive (109) cloth spine over stiff boards, sewn. FC: blank. RC: blank. Spine: gold-blocked downwards (*Scudder Seabury* THE GAME OF CROQUET *Abercrombie & Fitch*)

Dust wrapper: White paper, printed in moderate olive Green (125), moderate bluish Green (164), and black. FP: bluish Green panel framed in white on an olive Green background ([on olive Green] AN ABERCROMBIE & FITCH BOOK | [in black on bluish Green, L justified] THE GAME OF | [*do*] CROQUET | [*do*] *ITS APPOINT-MENT AND LAWS* | [*do*] *by Horace Elisha Scudder* | [*do*, rule] | [*do*] *Edited and augmented by Paul Seabury* | [*do*] *With a Foreword by REX STOUT*). FF: publisher's blurb, continued, in black on white. RP: editor's note in black on white. RF: publisher's blurb, concluded, in black on white. Spine: in black on olive Green downwards (The Game of Croquet *SCUDDER · SEABURY Abercrombie & Fitch*)

Copy seen: PC

Fingerprint: 5953 tos, r.a- clFu 7 1968A

Notes: Printed anonymously, price $5.00.

Although the editor reproduces the text of the 1868 edition of Scudder's own work (e) without annotation, the introduction is original, and supplementary matter is taken from other sources — Carroll's *Castle Croquet: For Four Players* from AA26a, *Croquet: A Simple Synopsis* from A151b, and the supplemental glossary from one of the several issues of the second edition of *How to Play Croquêt* (A22).

A21   **THE GAME OF CROQUÊT: ITS LAWS AND**   [1865]
       REGULATIONS. [Edmund Routledge]

(a) *First edition [1865]

THE | [in gothic-revival script] **Game of Croquêt,** | ITS | LAWS AND REGULA-TIONS: | WITH A FULL AND | PARTICULAR DESCRIPTION OF THE INSTRUMENTS | USED IN ITS PERFORMANCE, ETC. ETC. | ILLUSTRATED WITH | EXPLANATORY ENGRAVINGS, DIAGRAMS, ETC. | PRINTED FOR THE PROPRIETOR, | AND ENTERED AT STATIONERS' HALL.

Formula: $B^6 C^4 D^{16}$ [B3 signed 'B 3', C1 signed 'C 2', C3 signed 'C 3', D3 signed 'D', D5 signed 'D 3', D9 signed 'E', D11 signed 'F 3']. 26 leaves, pp *1–5* 6–47 *48* 49–52

Technical notes: 126 × 76 mm (p 8). 35 lines, 20 = 72 mm. Leaf size 159 × 100 mm; thickness 0.11 mm; wove, unwatermarked, smooth, white

Contents: Blank (*1*), frontispiece (*2*), title (*3*), blank (*4*), text (*5–43*), advertisements (*44–47*), price lists (*48–52*)

Binding: Dark Green (146) pebble grain cloth limp over pastedowns, sewn. The facing pages of the endpapers are coloured pale greenish Yellow (104). FC: gold-blocked title *etc* centred within a blind-stamped triple-ruled frame, the outermost frame broader than the inner two, with ornaments inside the corners ([illustration of a woman player dressed in crinoline and bonnet with mallet raised to take 'tight croquet'] | CROQUET). RC: blind-stamped frame of the same pattern as that on the FC. Spine: blank

Copy seen: BL: 7921 dd 22

Fingerprint: e,n- r.th t,by isgr 7 1865Q

Notes: Printed anonymously. Year of publication and authorship are inferred from the circumstances in which this work apparently came to be published by the sixth Earl of Essex, manufacturer of the Cassiobury Set of croquet equipment, as a replacement for his earlier rule book, *Rules of the Eglinton Castle and Cassiobury Croquet* (A25). Why the earl should have replaced the one book with another which had much the same contents and was written by the same author is far from clear.

The *General Catalogue* of the BL cites 1865 as conjectural ('?'), and the copy held by the library has an anonymous pencil annotation '? first edition'. The year 1866 may seem more likely: *Rules of the Eglinton Castle and Cassiobury Croquet* (*op cit*), published in 1865, may be supposed to have met the publisher's needs for that year and a replacement may not then have been needed until the following season.

The collation of the copy examined is highly eccentric and the signatures are so chaotic that it is hard to imagine that they could have assisted in controlling the printing process. These oddities could be due to the manner in which *Rules of the Eglinton Castle and Cassiobury Croquet* (*op cit*) was adapted for republication as the present work and/or to the present work having been prepared in haste.

Publication and/or authorship have been attributed, it is thought erroneously, by others to T Turner, probably on account of a citation ('Manufactured by T. Turner, Cassiobury Saw Mills, Watford, Herts.') on the last page of (d) — see also *Notes* to *Rules of the Eglinton Castle and Cassiobury Croquet* (*op cit*).

D Prichard (A208) and others have referred to this work, somewhat cryptically, as 'Eglinton Castle Croquet'. The association would appear to have arisen from its coverage of the Eglinton Castle version of the game and/or from the words 'EGLINTON CASTLE CROQUET' in the frontispiece (an engraved illustration of a croquet party with a castle in the background).

(b) *First edition, paperback [1865]*

[The TP as that of (a)]

Formula: Apparently $X^6 \chi 1\ Y^{22}$ including the front and rear pastedowns [p *3* signed 'B 3', p 13 p signed 'C 2', p 17 signed 'C 3', p 25 signed 'D', p 29 signed 'D 3', p 37 signed 'E', p 41 signed 'F 3']. 29 leaves, pp *i–iv, 1–5* 6–47 *48* 49–52 *53–54*

Technical notes: 126 × 76 mm (p 8). 35 lines, 20 = 72 mm. Leaf size 155 × 100 mm; thickness 0.11 mm; wove, unwatermarked, smooth, white

Contents: Glued to the FC (*i*), blank (*ii–1*), frontispiece (*2*), title (*3*), blank (*4*), text (*5–43*), advertisements (*44–47*), price lists (*48–52*), blank (*53*), glued to the RC (*54*)

Binding: Moderate Yellow (87) paper glued to pp *i, 54* and the spine, sewn. FC: printed in black within a ruled frame ([in gothic-revival script] Game of Croquêt | ITS | **LAWS AND REGULATIONS.** | ([engraved illustration of a woman player dressed in crinoline and bonnet with mallet raised to take 'tight croquet', set within a ruled frame with rounded top corners] | PRINTED FOR THE PROPRIETOR, | AND ENTERED AT STATIONERS'S HALL.). RC: blank. Spine: blank

Copy seen: BOD: Johnson f 2058

Fingerprint: As that of (a)

Notes: Printed anonymously, probably intended for distribution with the manufacturer's croquet equipment.

Year of publication is conjectural. This issue would appear to be a reprint of (a), adapted to take a paper wrapper. The two issues have not been collated systematically but it is believed that their contents are identical or virtually identical.

(c) *First edition, variant [1865]*

[The TP as that of (a)]

Formula: B–F⁶ [B3 signed 'B 3', C2 signed 'C', C4 signed 'C 3', D4 signed 'D 3', E2 signed 'E', E4 signed 'F 3']. 30 leaves, pp *i–ii, 1–3* 4–5 *6* 7 *8–9* 10–47 *48* 49 *50* 51–54 *55 56 57–58*

Technical notes: 127 × 75 mm (p 6). 35 lines, 20 = 72 mm (variable). Leaf size 163 × 101 mm; thickness 0.11 mm; wove, unwatermarked, smooth, white

Contents: Blank (*i*), frontispiece (*ii*), title (*1*), blank (*2*), text (*3–43*), advertisements (*44–49*), price lists (*49–56*), blank (*57–58*)

Binding: Greyish purplish Red (262) pansy grain cloth over light boards, sewn. The facing pages of the endpapers are coloured pale greenish Yellow (104). FC: gold-blocked title *etc* centred within a blind-stamped triple-ruled frame, the outermost frame broader than the inner two, with ornaments inside the corners ([illustration of a woman player dressed in crinoline and bonnet with mallet raised to take 'tight croquet'] | CROQUET). RC: blind-stamped frame of the same pattern as that on the FC. Spine: blank

Copy seen: PC

Fingerprint: e,n- a.e, r.th abpr 3 1865Q

Notes: Printed anonymously.

Year of publication is uncertain. It is conjectured that this issue appeared after (a) because its construction is apparently less irregular and because it contains more advertising matter. If, as is supposed, (a) was rushed out to meet a commercial emergency, then it might have appeared prudent to prepare an improved issue with more advertising as soon as stocks of the first edition were running short.

The text of this issue is apparently identical, or virtually so, to that of (a).

(d) *Second (post-Conference) edition [1870]*

[in gothic-revival script] The Game of Croquêt, | ITS | LAWS AND REGULA-TIONS : | WITH THE | **New Laws of Croquêt,** | AS AGREED TO BY | THE CONFERENCE OF CROQUET PLAYERS, AT THE | CHARING CROSS HOTEL, JANUARY, 1870. | [rule] | ALSO A FULL AND | PARTICULAR DESCRIPTION OF THE INSTRUMENTS USED IN | THE PERFORMANCE OF THE GAME, ETC. | [rule] | ILLUSTRATED WITH | EXPLANATORY ENGRAVINGS, DIAGRAMS, ETC. | [swelled rule] | PRINTED FOR THE PROPRIETOR.

Formula: B–E⁶ [$3 signed (–B1, D1, D3)]. 24 leaves, pp *1–5* 6–31 *32* 33–40 *41* 42–46 *47–48*

Technical notes: 126 × 76 mm (p 8). 35 lines, 20 = 72 mm. Leaf size 161 × 104 mm; thickness 0.11 mm; wove, unwatermarked, smooth, white

Contents: Blank *(1)*, frontispiece *(2)*, title *(3)*, blank *(4)*, text *(5–28)*, advertisements *(29–33)*, price list *(34–40)*, advertisements *(41–46)*, testimonials *(47–48)*, name of manufacturer (T Turner, Cassiobury Saw Mills, Watford, Herts) of most goods referred to in the advertisements *(48)*

Binding: Greyish purplish Red (262) sand grain cloth over light boards, sewn. The facing pages of the endpapers are coloured pale greenish Yellow (104). FC: gold-blocked title *etc* centred within a blind-stamped triple-ruled frame, the outermost frame broader than the inner two, with ornaments inside the corners ([illustration of a woman player dressed in crinoline and bonnet with mallet raised to take 'tight croquet'] | CROQUET). RC: blind-stamped frame of the same pattern as that on the FC. Spine: blank

Copy seen: PC

Fingerprint: e,n- e.to lsn. whfo 7 1870Q

Notes: Printed anonymously. Approximate year of publication is inferred from the fact that the laws given are the 1870 Conference laws (see A52).

The text is extensively revised. Early chapters on the history of the game and how to play it are retained, a chapter on the instruments used in the game is omitted (notwithstanding a reference to such matter on the TP), the rules given in the first edition are replaced by the 1870 Conference laws ('copied from the Times, Daily Telegraph, Sporting Times, and other papers'), and a chapter devoted to Capt Moreton's croquet party is omitted, as also are notes on the new game of Juvenile Carpet Croquet, the Ladies' Game of Parlour Croquet, and the game of L'Étoile. The frontispiece is the same as that in (a). Much of the advertising matter is new.

(e) *Second (post-Conference) edition, variant [1870]*

[The TP as that of (d)]

Formula: B–E⁶ [$1, 3 signed (–B1)]. 24 leaves, pp *1–5* 6–32 *33* 34 *35* 36–41 *42* 43–46 *47* 48

Technical notes: 123 × 75 mm (p 25). 34 lines, 20 = 71 mm. Leaf size 161 × 101 mm; thickness 0.10 mm; wove, unwatermarked, smooth, white

Contents: Blank (*1*), frontispiece (*2*), title (*3*), blank (*4*), text (*5–28*), advertisements (*29–34*), price list (*35–41*), advertisements (*42–46*), testimonials (*47–48*)

Binding: Dark Red (16) moiré-effect embossed cloth over light boards, sewn. The facing pages of the endpapers are coloured vivid greenish Yellow (97). FC: the title (CROQUET), two crossed mallets, two clusters of four balls, and seven hoops form an emblem within a ruled frame, inside the base of which there is a group of three palm stems. The title, set in rustic script within the hoops, and balls are gilt; the crossed mallets and hoops are in black. The frame and palm stems are in black. RC: blind-stamped frame and palm stems, of the same pattern as that on the FC. Spine: blank

Copy seen: PC

Fingerprint: e,n- e.to lsn. whfo 7 1870Q

Notes: Printed anonymously. Approximate year of publication is inferred from close similarities with (d). The text is identical, or virtually identical. Minor variations include the signatures, the pagination, the content and arrangement of some of the advertising, the FC design, and the omission of Turner's name from p 48 of the present variant.

(f) *Second (post-Conference) edition, variant [1870]*

[in gothic-revival script] The Game of Croquêt, | ITS | LAWS AND REGULA-TIONS: | WITH THE | **New Laws of Croquêt,** | AS AGREED TO BY | THE CONFERENCE OF CROQUET PLAYERS, AT THE | CHARING CROSS HOTEL, JANUARY, 1870. | [rule] | ALSO A FULL AND | PARTICULAR DESCRIP-TION OF THE INSTRUMENTS USED IN | THE PERFORMANCE OF THE GAME, ETC. | [rule] | ILLUSTRATED WITH | EXPLANATORY ENGRAVINGS, DIAGRAMS, ETC. | [swelled rule] | PRINTED FOR THE PROPRIETOR.

Formula: Thought to be as that of (b). 24 leaves, pp *1–5* 6–31 *32* 33–40 *41* 42–46 *47* 48

Technical notes: Thought to measure 123 × 75 mm (B3). 34 lines, 20 = 71 mm. Leaf size 161 × 101 mm

Contents: Blank (*1*), frontispiece (*2*), title (*3*), blank (*4*), text (*5–28*), advertisements (*29–33*), price list (*34–40*), advertisements (*41–46*), testimonials (*47–48*)

Binding: Dark red cloth over light boards. FC: title (CROQUET) below a gold-blocked illustration of a woman player dressed in crinoline and bonnet with mallet raised to take 'tight croquet'), within a blind-stamped ruled frame

Copy seen: PC (incompletely examined)

Fingerprint: As that of (e)

Notes: Printed anonymously. It is not known whether this issue preceded or succeeded (e).

The text is apparently identical to that of (e). Some of the advertising matter is different.

(g) *Second (post-Conference) edition, abridged [1870]*

[in gothic-revival script] The Game of Croquêt, | ITS | LAWS AND REGULA-TIONS: | WITH THE | **New Laws of Croquêt,** | AS AGREED TO BY | THE CONFERENCE OF CROQUET PLAYERS, AT THE | CHARING CROSS

HOTEL, JANUARY, 1870. | [rule] | ALSO A FULL AND | PARTICULAR DESCRIP-
TION OF THE INSTRUMENTS USED IN | THE PERFORMANCE OF THE
GAME, ETC. | [rule] | ILLUSTRATED WITH | EXPLANATORY ENGRAVINGS,
DIAGRAMS, ETC. | [swelled rule] | PRINTED FOR THE PROPRIETOR.

Formula: 1^8 2^4 $\chi 1$ 3^6 [p 7 signed 'B3', p 15 signed 'C', p 19 signed 'C3', p 27 signed
'D', p 31 signed 'D3']. 19 leaves, pp *1–5* 6–29 *30* 31–32 *33–34* 35–36 *37 38*

Technical notes: 126 × 76 mm (p 4). 34 lines, 20 = 71 mm. Leaf size 159 ×
100 mm; thickness 0.09 mm; wove, unwatermarked, smooth, white

Contents: Blank (*1*), frontispiece (*2*), title (*3*), blank (*4*), text (*5–28*), advertisements
(*29–36*), testimonials (*37–38*)

Binding: Dark Red (16) sand grain embossed cloth over light boards, sewn. The
facing pages of the endpapers are coloured vivid greenish Yellow (97). FC: the title
(CROQUET), two crossed mallets, two clusters of four balls, and seven hoops form
an emblem within a triple-ruled frame, the central frame in bold, inside the base of
which there is an ornamental feature. The title, set in rustic script within the hoops,
and balls are gilt; the crossed mallets and hoops are in black. The frame and ornamental feature are in black. RC: blank. Spine: blank

Copy seen: PC

Fingerprint: As that of (e)

Notes: Printed anonymously. It is not known whether this issue preceded or
succeeded issues (e) and (f).

The text is apparently identical to that of (e) and (f). Some of the advertising
matter is different.

(h) *Third edition, Thomas Turner issue [1870]*

[Within a double-ruled frame]

THE | [in gothic-revival script] Game of Croquêt, | ITS | LAWS AND REGULA-
TIONS: | WITH THE | **New Laws of Croquêt,** | AS AGREED TO BY | THE
CONFERENCE OF CROQUET PLAYERS, AT THE | CHARING CROSS HOTEL,
JANUARY, 1870. | [rule] | ALSO A FULL AND | PARTICULAR DESCRIPTION OF
THE INSTRUMENTS USED IN | THE PERFORMANCE OF THE GAME, ETC. |
[rule] | ILLUSTRATED WITH | **EXPLANATORY ENGRAVINGS, DIAGRAMS,
ETC.** | [swelled rule] | LONDON:

Formula: B^8 $C–D^8$ [C1, D1 signed]. 24 leaves, pp *1–7* 8–48

Technical notes: 133 × 76 mm (p 6). 40 lines, 20 = 67 mm. Leaf size 201 ×
129 mm; thickness 0.10 mm; wove, unwatermarked, smooth, white

Contents: Blank (*1*), frontispiece (engraved illustration of a croquet party in front
of Windsor Castle with the legend 'The Royal Standard Club Croquet') (*2*), title (*3*),
blank (*4*), text (*5–41*), advertisements (*42–48*)

Binding: Dark Green (146) pebble grain cloth over light boards, sewn. The facing
pages of the endpapers are coloured light Yellow Green (119). FC: the title ([in
rustic script] CROQUET), two crossed mallets, two clusters of four balls, and seven
hoops form an emblem centred within a decorative frame, printed in black with
gold-blocked corner ornaments. The letters of the title (set within the hoops) and
balls are gilt; the mallets and hoops are in black. RC: blind-stamped frame of the
same pattern as that on the FC. Spine: blank

Copy seen: BL: 7921 b 6

Fingerprint: d.es r.us s.e- anan 7 1870Q

Notes: Published and printed anonymously. This edition is thought to have succeeded the putative second edition chiefly because of its larger format and because it introduces 'The Royal Standard Club Croquet'. Year of publication is conjectural.

The TP provides two clues as to the origins of this edition: there is no reference to the 'Proprietor' (*viz* the Earl of Essex) and it concludes *inconclusively* 'LONDON:'. It is hypothesised that the earl had previously disposed of his manufacturing interests in Cassiobury Croquet to Thomas Turner and had licensed him to continue distributing this booklet with this equipment but had reserved the right to licence other manufacturers and retailers to distribute the same booklet with their own croquet equipment. Envisaging that other such licensees might wish to brand their publications, he produced a form of stereotyped TP which could readily be over-printed or otherwise appropriately adapted. If this hypothesis is correct, Thomas Turner, neglecting to add his name or that of the printer, was evidently content to remain anonymous.

The text and illustrations mostly follow the second edition. Significant variations include the introduction of 'The Royal Standard Club Croquet' (possibly an allusion to a new branded range of croquet equipment), abridgment of the treatment given to 'Eglinton Castle Croquet' in earlier editions, and reinstatement of much matter from the first edition which was omitted from the second, notably including the pre-Conference code of 20 rules. The reader is given the interesting choice of playing by the old *rules* or new *laws*.

(j) *Third edition, WH Brown issue [1870]*

[Within a double-ruled frame]

THE | [in gothic-revival script] Game of Croquêt, | ITS | LAWS AND REGULA-TIONS: | WITH THE | **New Laws of Croquêt,** | AS AGREED TO BY | THE CONFERENCE OF CROQUET PLAYERS, AT THE | CHARING CROSS HOTEL, January, 1870. | [rule] | ALSO A FULL AND | PARTICULAR DESCRIPTION OF THE INSTRUMENTS USED IN | THE PERFORMANCE OF THE GAME, ETC. | [rule] | ILLUSTRATED WITH | **EXPLANATORY ENGRAVINGS, DIAGRAMS, ETC.** | [swelled rule] | LONDON:

Formula: B⁸ C–D⁸ [C1, D1 signed]. 24 leaves, pp *1–7* 8–48

Technical notes: 133 × 76 mm (p 6). 40 lines, 20 = 67 mm. Leaf size 201 × 129 mm; thickness 0.10 mm; wove, unwatermarked, smooth, white

Contents: Blank (*1*), frontispiece (engraved illustration of croquet party in front of Windsor Castle with the legend 'The Royal Standard Club Croquet') (*2*), title (*3*), blank (*4*), text (*5–41*), advertisements (*42–48*)

Binding: Yellowish White (2) semi-gloss paper or light card, printed in black, sewn. FC: within a double-ruled frame, the inner frame in bold, with corner ornaments ([in gothic-revival script] The Game of Croquêt, | ITS | LAWS AND REGULA-TIONS: | WITH THE | **New Laws of Croquêt,** | AS AGREED TO BY | THE CONFERENCE OF CROQUET PLAYERS, AT THE | CHARING CROSS HOTEL, January, 1870. | [engraved illustration of a croquet party] | ALSO A FULL AND | PARTICULAR DESCRIPTION OF THE INSTRUMENTS USED IN | THE PERFORMANCE OF THE GAME, ETC. | [rule] | ILLUSTRATED WITH | EXPLANATORY ENGRAVINGS, DIAGRAMS, ETC. | [swelled rule] | LONDON:). RC: within a double-ruled frame, a device featuring two crossed mallets, two balls, and lettering in White out of black ([in a convex arc] TRADE MARK | B). Spine: blank

Copy seen: KRWL: A325

Fingerprint: atd. r.us s.e- anan 7 1870Q

Notes: Published and printed anonymously. Year of publication is conjectural.

It is conjectured that this issue was published by or for WH Brown, whose croquet equipment and sundry other sports goods are presented in the supplementary advertising section. See also *Notes* to (h) above.

(k) *Fourth edition [1896]*

THE | **GAME OF CROQUET:** | ITS | LAWS AND REGULATIONS. | [double rule, the lower longer than the upper] | ALSO A FULL AND | PARTICULAR DESCRIPTION OF THE INSTRUMENTS USED | IN THE PERFORMANCE OF THE GAME, Etc. | [double rule, the upper longer than the lower] | **Illustrated** | *With Explanatory Engravings, Diagrams, &c.*

Formula: [1¹²]. 12 leaves, pp *1–3 4–23 24*

Technical notes: 124 × 76 mm (p *4*). 28 lines, 20 = 89 mm. Leaf size 156 × 105 mm; thickness 0.12 mm; wove, unwatermarked, smooth, white

Contents: Title (*1*), blank (*2*), text (*3–23*), blank (*24*)

Binding: White paper, the outside coloured moderate purplish Pink (250) with a semi-gloss finish, stapled, no spine or endpapers. FC: as the TP, reproduced in black within a ruled frame. Inside FC: blank. RC: blank. Inside RC: blank

Copy seen: PC

*Fingerprint: sh*e, e.o- inke st12 7 1896Q [group 2 taken from p 13]

Notes: Published and printed anonymously. Approximate year of publication is inferred from new matter on p 8 concerning court dimensions, the size and weight of balls *etc.*

The text of earlier issues is streamlined and there are no advertisements. The introductory matter is substantially abridged and the pre-Conference 'rules' are omitted. The laws, though rearranged in minor detail, remain essentially those published in 1870 as the Conference Code and reproduced in earlier issues. The only new matter comprises that referred to above, descriptions and illustrations of the six-, seven-, and eight-hoop settings, and a brief note on a point of etiquette.

It is hypothesised that this late, streamlined edition was offered for sale to any manufacturer or retailer who required such an introductory booklet to distribute with its croquet equipment. It is further conjectured that the publisher, having learnt from experience (with the third edition) that trade customers were generally content to distribute a standard publication in this way, decided to make no special provision for individual branding.

A22   HOW TO PLAY CROQUÊT. [Anon]   [1865]

(a) *First edition [1865]*

HOW TO PLAY CROQUÊT. | A | NEW POCKET MANUAL | OF | [in gothic-revival script] Complete Instructions for American Players. | ILLUSTRATED WITH | ENGRAVINGS AND DIAGRAMS. | TOGETHER WITH | ALL THE RULES OF THE GAME;   HINTS ON PARLOR-CROQUÊT, | AND A GLOSSARY OF TECHNICAL TERMS. | [swelled rule]

[TP verso, p *2*]

Entered according to Act of Congress, in the year 1865, | BY ADAMS & CO. | In the Clerk's office of the District Court of the District | of Massachusetts.

Formula: 1^8 2–3^8 4^6 $\chi1$ [2_1, 3_1 signed]. 31 leaves, pp *1–4* 5–19 *20* 21–45 *46 47* 48–62

Technical notes: 117 × 72 mm (p 6). 27 lines, 20 = 88 mm. Leaf size 160 × 101 mm; thickness 0.09 mm; wove, unwatermarked, smooth, white

Contents: Title (*1*), TP verso (*2*), contents (*3*), advertisement (*4*), text (*5–47*), blank (*48*), catalogue of advertisements (*49–62*)

Binding: Light Yellow (86) paper, stitched. There is a free endpaper, matching the paper of the book, at the front. FC: printed in black within a double-ruled frame, the outer frame in bold (**HOW TO PLAY** | **CROQUÊT.** | [swelled rule] | **FIELD CROQUÊT.** | **Parlor Floor Croquêt.** | **Parlor Table Croquêt.** | BOSTON: | ADAMS & CO., 25 BROMFIELD STREET.). Inside FC: blank. RC: blank. Inside RC: blank. Spine: blank

Copy seen: PC

Fingerprint: 4645 1.g- eses ofde 3 1865Q

Notes: Printed anonymously, price 25 cents. Year of publication is inferred from the statement on the TP verso (p 2). The order in which this issue and (b) appeared is uncertain. The latter issue may have appeared at any time during the period 1865–68.

The text includes a code of 60 rules and regulations. This work has not been collated with A23 but several obvious similarities between the two suggest that, apart from the advertising, they may be identical.

(b) First edition, WF Brown issue [1865]

[The TP as that of (a)]

[TP verso, p 2]

Entered according to Act of Congress, in the year 1865, | BY ADAMS & CO., | In the Clerk's Office of the District Court of the District of Massa- | chusetts. | [rule of interrupted line] | W. F. Brown & Co., Printers, 50 Bromfield Street, Boston.

Formula: Apparently $\pi1$ 1^8 2–3^8 4^6 $\chi1$ [2_1, 3_1 signed]. 26 leaves, pp *i–ii*, *1–4* 5–19 *20* 21–45 *46 47* 48–49 [50]

Technical notes: ca 118 × 72 mm (p 6). 27 lines, 20 = *ca* 88 mm. Leaf size *ca* 156 × 100 mm

Contents: Title (*1*), TP verso (*2*), contents (*3*), advertisement (*4*), text (*5–47*), advertisement (*48*), blank (*49*), wanting from the copy examined ([*50*])

Binding: Not seen. The original, in a library binding, is evidently sewn but may formerly have been stitched

Copy seen: HCLWL: SG 1360 6 (incomplete photocopy of imperfect original in a library binding)

Fingerprint: 4645 1.g- eses ofde 3 1865Q

Notes: Printed by WF Brown & Co, Boston. Year of publication is inferred from the statement on the TP verso (p 2). See also *Notes* to (a). The copy examined bears an inscription signed '1870, June 2.'.

The text is identical, or virtually identical, to that of (a). The two advertisements (pp *4, 48*), for *Sports and Games*, a magazine published by Adams, are identical.

(c) First edition, DB Brooks issue [1868]

[The TP and TP verso as those of (a)]

Formula: 1^8 2–3^8 [2_1, 3_1 signed]. 24 leaves, pp *1–4* 5–19 *20* 21–45 *46 47 48*

Technical notes: 117 × 72 mm (p 6). 27 lines, 20 = 88 mm. Leaf size 157 × 101 mm; thickness 0.10 mm; wove, unwatermarked, smooth, white

Contents: Title (*1*), TP verso (*2*), contents (*3*), blank (*4*), text (*5–47*), blank (*48*)

Binding: Light Yellow (86) paper, stitched, no front endpaper. FC: printed in black within a double-ruled frame, the outer frame in bold (**HOW TO PLAY** | **CROQUÊT.** | [swelled rule] | **FIELD CROQUÊT.** | **Parlor Floor Croquêt.** | **Parlor Table Croquêt.** | BOSTON: | D. B. BROOKS & BRO., 55 WASHINGTON STREET.). Inside FC: blank. RC: wanting from the copy examined. Spine: wanting from the copy examined.

Copy seen: PC (incomplete)

Fingerprint: 4645 1.g- eses ofde 3 1868Q

Notes: Printed anonymously. Year of publication is inferred from an apparently contemporary inscription in pencil on the TP of the copy examined.

This issue would appear to have been prepared for Brooks & Co, a sports and games manufacturer. It would appear to differ from (a) only in the omission of advertising matter and in substitution on the FC of Brooks's name and address for those of Adams.

(d) *First edition, variant [1871]*

[The TP as that of (a)]

[TP verso, p *2*]

Entered according to Act of Congress, in the year 1865, | BY ADAMS & CO. | In the Clerk's Office of the District Court of the District | of Massachusetts.

Formula: 1^8 2–3^8 4^8 [2_1, 3_1 signed]. 32 leaves, pp *1–4* 5–19 *20* 21–45 *46* 47 *48–64*

Technical notes: 118 × 72 mm (p 6). 27 lines, 20 = 87 mm. Leaf size 160 × 101 mm; thickness 0.10 mm; wove, unwatermarked, smooth, white. The fore-edges of 4_7 and 4_8 are uncut in the copy examined

Contents: Title (*1*), TP verso (*2*), contents (*3*), blank (*4*), text (*5–47*), blank (*48*), catalogue of advertisements (*49–64*)

Binding: Light Yellow (86) paper glued to the gatherings, stitched, no endpapers. FC: printed in black within a double-ruled frame, the outer frame in bold (**HOW TO PLAY** | **CROQUÊT.** | [swelled rule] | **FIELD CROQUÊT.** | **Parlor Floor Croquêt.** | **Parlor Table Croquêt.** | BOSTON: | ADAMS & CO., 25 BROMFIELD STREET.). Inside FC: blank. RC: blank. Inside RC: blank. Spine: blank

Copy seen: PC

Fingerprint: 4645 1.g- eses ofde 3 1865Q

Notes: Printed anonymously, price 25 cents. Probable year of publication is inferred from a reference on p *49* to the January 1871 issue of *Sports and Games*, produced by the publisher, but the possibility that it was issued in 1872 cannot be excluded.

The text appears to be identical to that of (a). The only variations would appear to be in the advertisements.

(e) *1871 issue [1871]*

HOW TO PLAY CROQUÊT. | A | NEW POCKET MANUAL | OF | [in gothic-revival script] Complete Instructions for American Players. | ILLUSTRATED WITH | ENGRAVINGS AND DIAGRAMS. | TOGETHER WITH | ALL THE RULES OF THE GAME; HINTS ON PARLOR-CROQUÊT, | AND A GLOSSARY OF TECHNICAL TERMS. | [swelled rule]

[TP verso]

Entered according to Act of Congress, in the year 1865, | BY ADAMS & CO. | In the Clerk's Office of the District Court of the District of Massa- | chusetts.

Formula: 1^8 2–3^8 4^8 [2_1, 3_1 signed]. 32 leaves, pp *1–4 5–7 8 9–10 11 12–19 20 21–45 46 47 48–64*

Technical notes: 118 × 72 mm (p 6). 27 lines, 20 = 88 mm. Leaf size 157 × 100 mm; thickness 0.10 mm; wove, unwatermarked, smooth, white

Contents: Title (*1*), TP verso (*2*), contents (*3*), advertisement (*4*), text (*5–47*), advertisements (*48–64*)

Binding: Light Yellow (86) paper glued to the gatherings, stitched, no endpapers. FC: printed in black within a double-ruled frame, the outer frame in bold (**HOW TO PLAY** | **CROQUÊT.** | [swelled rule] | **FIELD CROQUÊT.** | **Parlor Floor Croquêt.** | **Parlor Table Croquêt.** | BOSTON: | ADAMS & CO., 25 BROMFIELD STREET.). RC: wanting from the copy examined. Spine: blank

Copy seen: PC (wanting the RC and much of the spine)

Fingerprint: 4645 d.ne e.in ofde 3 1871Q

Notes: Printed anonymously, price 25 cents. Year of publication is inferred from an advertisement on p *48* for bound volumes of *Sports and Games for 1870*.

The text departs little from that of (a). The alterations are mostly concerned with developments of equipment, and fashion in dress. The rules of the game remain unaltered. The advertisements are different.

(f) *1871 issue, variant [1871]*

HOW TO PLAY CROQUÊT. | A | NEW POCKET MANUAL | OF | [in gothic-revival script] Complete Instructions for American Players. | ILLUSTRATED WITH | ENGRAVINGS AND DIAGRAMS. | TOGETHER WITH | ALL THE RULES OF THE GAME;   HINTS ON PARLOR-CROQUÊT, | AND A GLOSSARY OF TECHNICAL TERMS. | [swelled rule]

[TP verso, p 2]

Entered according to Act of Congress, in the year 1865, | BY ADAMS & CO. | In the Clerk's Office of the District Court of the District of Massa- | chusetts.

Formula: 1^8 2–3^8 4^8 [2_1, 3_1 signed]. 32 leaves, pp *1–4 5–7 8 9–10 11 12–19 20 21–45 46 47 48–64*

Technical notes: 118 × 72 mm (p 6). 27 lines, 20 = 88 mm. Leaf size 165 × 95 mm; thickness 0.10 mm; wove, unwatermarked, smooth, white

Contents: Title (*1*), TP verso (*2*), contents (*3*), advertisement (*4*), text (*5–47*), advertisements (*48–64*)

Binding: Light Yellow (86) paper glued to the gatherings, stitched, no endpapers. FC: printed in black within a double-ruled frame, the outer frame in bold (**HOW TO PLAY** | **CROQUÊT.** | [swelled rule] | **FIELD CROQUÊT.** | **Parlor Floor Croquêt.** | **Parlor Table Croquêt.** | BOSTON: | ADAMS & CO., 25 BROMFIELD STREET.). RC: wanting from the copy examined. Spine: wanting from the copy examined

Copy seen: PC (wanting the RC and spine)

Fingerprint: 4645 d.ne e.in ofde 3 1871Q

Notes: Printed anonymously, price 25 cents. Probable year of publication is inferred from a reference on p *49* to the January 1871 issue of *Sports and Games*, produced by the publisher, but the possibility that it was issued in 1872 cannot be excluded.

The text appears to be identical to that of (e). The only variation would appear to be in the advertising on p 63. In the present issue, this page is devoted to music for the piano-forte, substituting for the conclusion of advertisements for novelties and for the start of a new section of advertisements for miscellaneous goods, thus destroying the continuity of the advertising matter in the earlier issue. The publisher was evidently more concerned to promote his music sales than to preserve a clear distinction between novelties and sundries.

(g) *Second edition (1873)*

NEW AND REVISED EDITION | OF | **How to Play Croquet.** | A POCKET MANUAL | OF | [some of the letters ornamented] Complete Instructions for all Players. | ILLUSTRATED WITH | ENGRAVINGS AND DIAGRAMS, | TOGETHER WITH | THE RULES OF THE GAME, | *As Adopted by Professional and Amateur Clubs,* | HINTS ON FLOOR AND TABLE CROQUET, | AND DEFINITIONS OF TECHNICAL TERMS. | [swelled rule] | BOSTON: | ADAMS & CO., PUBLISHERS.

[TP verso, p 2]

Entered, according to Act of Congress, in the year 1873, by ADAMS | & Co., in the office of the Librarian of Congress | at Washington.

Formula: [1–2¹²]. 24 leaves, pp *1–5 6–42 43–48*

Technical notes: 127 × 86 mm (p 6). 30 lines, 20 = 85 mm. Leaf size 171 × 113 mm; thickness 0.11 mm; wove, unwatermarked, smooth, white

Contents: Title *(1)*, TP verso *(2)*, contents *(3)*, blank *(4)*, text *(5–42)*, advertisements *(43–48)*

Binding: Light yellowish Brown (76) paper glued to the gatherings, stitched, no endpapers. FC: printed within a triple frame, the central frame ruled, the inner and outer frames in scalloped lines (**NEWLY REVISED EDITION.** | [rule] | **HOW TO PLAY** | **CROQUÊT.** | [swelled rule] | FIELD CROQUET, | PARLOR CROQUET, | [double rule] | **RULES AND REGULATIONS OF** | **AMERICAN PLAYERS.** | [double rule] | BOSTON: | LEONARD, BURDITT & CO. | 55 Washington Street.). Inside FC: advertisement by Leonard, Burditt & Co. RC: advertisement by Leonard, Burditt & Co. Inside RC: advertisement by Leonard, Burditt & Co. Spine: blank

Copy seen: PC

Fingerprint: 3937 ofin e.ot Whbe 3 1873A

Notes: Printed anonymously. Year of publication is inferred from a citation on the TP verso *(qv)*.

This edition is reset, and substantially rewritten and re-illustrated, but much of the original text and many of the original engravings, some rearranged, are retained. The code of rules and regulations is reduced to 58 in number and several are re-arranged in order, but the scope of the code as a whole is apparently unaltered. In general, the intention in revising the work would appear to have been to improve its presentation, not to update or vary its content.

(h) *Second edition, variant (1873)*

NEW AND REVISED EDITION | OF | **How to Play Croquet.** | A POCKET MANUAL | OF | [some of the letters ornamented] Complete Instructions for all Players. | ILLUSTRATED WITH | ENGRAVINGS AND DIAGRAMS, | TOGETHER WITH | THE RULES OF THE GAME, | *As Adopted by Professional and Amateur Clubs,* | HINTS ON FLOOR AND TABLE CROQUET, | AND DEFINITIONS OF TECHNICAL TERMS. | [swelled rule] | BOSTON:

[TP verso, p 2]

Entered, according to Act of Congress, in the year 1873, by ADAMS | & Co., in the office of the Librarian of Congress | at Washington.

Formula: [1–2¹²]. 24 leaves, pp *i–ii, 1–5 6–42 43–46*

Technical notes: 131 × 86 mm (p 6). 30 lines, 20 = 88 mm. Leaf size 168 × 113 mm; thickness 0.12 mm; wove, unwatermarked, smooth, white

Contents: Blank (*i–ii*), title (*1*), TP verso (*2*), contents (*3*), blank (*4*), text (*5–42*), blank (*43–46*)

Binding: Light yellowish Brown (76) paper glued to the gatherings, stitched, no endpapers. FC: printed within a triple frame, the central frame ruled, the inner and outer frames in scalloped lines (**NEWLY REVISED EDITION.** | [swelled rule] | **HOW TO PLAY** | **CROQUET.** | [swelled rule] | FIELD CROQUET. | PARLOR CROQUET. | PARLOR TABLE CROQUET. | [swelled rule] | **RULES AND REGULATIONS** | OF | **AMERICAN PLAYERS.**). Inside FC: blank. RC: blank. Inside RC: blank. Spine: blank

Copy seen: HPC: GV931 H85 1873a CROQ

Fingerprint: 3937 ofin e.ot Whbe 3 1873A

Notes: Published and printed anonymously. Year of publication is inferred from a citation on the TP verso (*qv*). Publication by Adams & Co is inferred from the assertion of copyright on the TP verso and from the close similarity of this issue with all others here recorded.

The text of this issue has not been collated systematically with that of (g), but they are probably identical. The present issue would appear to have been prepared as a prototype in anticipation of branding to the requirements of individual games manufacturers for issue with their own croquet equipment. See, for example, (j). The addition of the reference to parlor table croquet on the FC, in the absence of any reference to this version of the game in the text, may have been thought to be a feature which would appeal to other manufacturers. It will also be noted that this variant marks the passing of the circumflex 'e' in the word 'croquet' on the FC.

(j) *Second edition, DB Brooks issue (1873)*

NEW AND REVISED EDITION | OF | **How to Play Croquet.** | A POCKET MANUAL | OF | [some of the letters ornamented] Complete Instructions for all Players. | ILLUSTRATED WITH | ENGRAVINGS AND DIAGRAMS, | TOGETHER WITH | THE RULES OF THE GAME, | *As Adopted by Professional and Amateur Clubs,* | HINTS ON FLOOR AND TABLE CROQUET, | AND DEFINITIONS OF TECHNICAL TERMS. | [swelled rule] | BOSTON: | ADAMS & CO., PUBLISHERS.

[TP verso, p 2]

Entered, according to Act of Congress, in the year 1873, by ADAMS | & Co., in the office of the Librarian of Congress | at Washington.

Formula: As that of (g)

Technical notes: 126 × 86 mm (p 6). 30 lines, 20 = 85 mm. Leaf size 170 × 111 mm; thickness 0.11 mm; wove, unwatermarked, smooth, white

Contents: As those of (g)

Binding: Light yellowish Brown (76) paper glued to the gatherings, stitched, no endpapers. FC: printed within a triple frame, the central frame ruled, the inner and outer frames in scalloped lines (**NEWLY REVISED EDITION.** | [swelled rule] |

HOW TO PLAY | CROQUET. | [swelled rule] | FIELD CROQUET. | PARLOR CROQUET. | PARLOR TABLE CROQUET. | [swelled rule] | **RULES AND REGULATIONS** | OF | **AMERICAN PLAYERS**.). Inside FC: blank. RC: advertisement by D. B. Brooks & Co. Inside RC: blank. Spine: blank

Copy seen: HPC: GV931 H85 1873 CROQ

Fingerprint: 3937 ofin e.ot Whbe 3 1873A

Notes: Printed anonymously. Year of publication is inferred from a citation on the TP verso (*qv*).

The text of this issue has not been collated systematically with that of (g), but they are probably identical. The present issue would appear to have been prepared for Brooks & Co, a sports and games manufacturer.

(k) *Second edition, Priest, Holmes issue (1873)*

NEW AND REVISED EDITION | OF | **How to Play Croquet.** | A POCKET MANUAL | OF | [some of the letters ornamented] Complete Instructions for all Players. | ILLUSTRATED WITH | ENGRAVINGS AND DIAGRAMS, | TOGETHER WITH | THE RULES OF THE GAME, | *As Adopted by Professional and Amateur Clubs,* | HINTS ON FLOOR AND TABLE CROQUET, | AND DEFINITIONS OF TECHNICAL TERMS.

[TP verso, p 2]

Entered, according to Act of Congress, in the year 1873, by ADAMS | & Co., in the office of the Librarian of Congress | at Washington.

Formula: As that of (g)

Technical notes: 127 × 86 mm (p 6). 30 lines, 20 = 85 mm. Leaf size 166 × 113 mm; thickness 0.11 mm; wove, unwatermarked, smooth, white

Contents: As those of (g)

Binding: Light yellowish Brown (76) paper glued to the gatherings, stitched, no endpapers. FC: printed within a triple frame, the central frame ruled, the inner and outer frames in scalloped lines (**NEWLY REVISED EDITION.** | [swelled rule] | **HOW TO PLAY** | **CROQUET.** | [swelled rule] | FIELD CROQUET. | PARLOR CROQUET. | PARLOR TABLE CROQUET. | [swelled rule] | **PRIEST, HOLMES & CO.,** | **PUBLISHERS,** | KEENE, N. H. | 1875). Inside FC: blank. RC: advertisement by D. B. Brooks & Co. Inside RC: blank. Spine: blank

Copy seen: HPC: GV931 H85 1875 CROQ

Fingerprint: 3937 ofin e.ot Whbe 3 1873A

Notes: Printed anonymously. Year of publication is inferred from a citation on the FC.

This issue would appear to have been produced by and/or for, and to have been published by, a specialist firm of publishers (*viz* Priest, Holmes & Co).

A23   **How to Play Croquêt. [Anon]**   1865

HOW TO PLAY CROQUÊT. | A | NEW POCKET MANUAL | [in gothic-revival script] Complete Instructions for American Players. | ILLUSTRATED WITH | ENGRAVINGS AND DIAGRAMS. | TOGETHER WITH | ALL THE RULES OF THE GAME: HINTS ON PARLOR-CROQUÊT, | AND A GLOSSARY OF TECHNICAL TERMS. | [swelled rule] | BOSTON: | PUBLISHED BY AMSDEN & COMPANY, | 14 BROMFIELD STREET.

Formula: Apparently 1^8 2–3^8 4^8 [2_1, 3_1 signed]. 32 leaves, pp *1–4* 5–19 *20* 21–47 *48–64*

Technical notes: *ca* 116 × 71 mm (p 6). 27 lines, 20 = *ca* 86 mm. Leaf size *ca* 145 × 92 mm

Contents: Title (*1*), TP verso (*2*), contents (*3*), blank (*4*), text (5–47), advertisement (*48*)

Binding: Not included in the photocopy examined, sewn

Copy seen: HPC: GV931 H84 CROQ (photocopy of original from an unknown source)

Fingerprint: 4645 1.g- eses ofde 3 1865A

Notes: Printed anonymously. The text of this work has not been collated systematically with that of A22 but several obvious similarities suggest that, discounting the advertising, they may be identical.

A24   **LAWS AND REGULATIONS OF THE GAME OF**   **[1865]**
             CROQUET. [**Anon**]

[Page *i*, mostly within a ruled frame with corner ornaments]

[above the frame] ENTERED AT STATIONERS' HALL | [in gothic-revival script] Laws and Regulations | OF THE | [in open ornamented display script] **GAME OF CROQUET.** | WITH ILLUSTRATIONS. | **JAMES SOUTTER & SON,** | [in gothic-revival script] **Croquet Implement Manufacturers, etc.,** | 102 PRINCES STREET, EDINBURGH

Formula: Apparently [1^8]. 8 leaves, pp *i–iv*, *1* 2–10 *11–12*

Technical notes: 137 × 85 mm (p 5). 33 lines, 20 = 84 mm. Leaf size 180 × 123 mm; thickness 0.13 mm; wove, unwatermarked, slightly rough, white

Contents: Title (*i*), glued together (*ii–iii*), blank (*iv*), text (2–10), advertisements (*11–12*)

Binding: Apparently sewn, no wrapper

Copy seen: BOD: 250 k 10 (13) (in a library binding)

Fingerprint: f.rs d.ea lle, cehe C 1865Q [groups 2–4 taken from p 9]

Notes: Printed anonymously. According to the Registry Books of the Stationers' Company, date of publication was given by Soutter as 19 May 1865, as entered on 23 May 1865.

The text consists of an unnumbered code of laws.

A25   **RULES OF THE EGLINTON CASTLE AND CASSIOBURY**   **1865**
             CROQUET. [**Edmund Routledge**]

[Within a ruled frame]

RULES | OF THE | EGLINTON CASTLE | AND | CASSIOBURY | **CROQUET.** | [swelled rule] | T. TURNER, | CASSIOBURY SAW MILLS, | WATFORD, HERTS. | 1865.

Formula: A^8 B–D^8 [$2 signed (–A1, A2, B1, B2)]. 32 leaves, pp *1–7* 8–61 *62–64*

Technical notes: 103 × 61 mm (p 8). 31 lines, 20 = 67 mm. Leaf size 160 × 99 mm; thickness 0.12 mm; wove, unwatermarked, smooth, white

Contents: Title (*1*), preface, signed 'Edmund Routledge', March 1864 (2–3), text, directions for playing Eglinton Castle Croquet (5), full page engraved illustration of croquet stand (6), title heading, 'HANDBOOK OF CROQUET' (7), text, concluded (7–61), name of printer (61), price lists (62–64)

Binding: Light olive (106) pebble grain cloth, limp, sewn. The facing pages of the endpapers are coloured pale Yellow (89). FC: gold-blocked illustration (of a woman player dressed in crinoline and bonnet with mallet raised to take 'tight' croquet) and title (CROQUET) within a blind-stamped double-ruled frame with internal corner ornaments. RC: blind-stamped frame of the same pattern as that on the FC. Spine: blank

Copy seen: PC

Fingerprint: 4.E, e-ur ber, bait 3 1865A

Notes: Printed by Cox and Wyman, London.

Though this work is deemed for present purposes to have a separate identity, inasmuch as it has a unique title and ostensibly a unique publisher, it might with equal propriety be classified alternatively as a reprint of *Routledge's Handbook of Croquet* (A15), in that the text, though slightly abridged, is identical to that of the latter work and that both works share common authorship, or as the first edition of *The Game of Croquêt: Its Laws and Regulations* (A21), inasmuch as early issues of the latter work have essentially the same text and share common origins. Notwithstanding its seeming anonymity, it is plain from the preface and from the near identity of the text with that of A15 that Routledge was the author. And, notwithstanding the citation of T Turner as publisher, it is no less certain that its real begetter was the sixth Earl of Essex.

Essex was the manufacturer of the 'Cassiobury Set' of croquet equipment. Until August 1864 this set came with a rule-book (A16) largely plagiarised from M Reid (A8). Reid instituted proceedings in Chancery (Reid v the Earl of Essex and Another) for breach of copyright and, by a decree made by Vice-Chancellor Kindersley on 25 August, the earl was ordered to destroy all stocks of the offending publication. It is conjectured that he tried to procure a replacement as a matter of urgency to protect his equipment sales, and obtained permission to reprint Routledge's recently published handbook which had been well received by the press. This attribution is consistent with the fact that the only departures in the present work from the text of Routledge's book are the prominent treatment given to the Eglinton Castle version of the game (Lord Eglinton was the earl's son-in-law) and the omission of the author's endorsement of Jaques equipment.

Turner would appear to have been employed by the earl at this time as saw mill or factory manager. It is conjectured that his role in the publication of the present work was merely as nominee. For some reason which is far from clear, subsequent 'editions' were given a distinct identity, *The Game of Croquêt: Its Laws and Regulations* (A21), and early issues of the latter work merely bore the cryptic imprint of 'The Proprietor'. Though the earl had been at pains to conceal his identity as manufacturer and publisher, he had been unmasked by an editorial in the *Spectator* of 3 September 1864 in connection with the case brought against him by Reid in Chancery. His reticence as entrepreneur was to persist.

In later years Turner was to become a merchant in his own right. The firm of Thomas Turner & Co Limited, incorporated in or about 1886, was a prominent manufacturer of timber products and continued to produce Cassiobury croquet equipment for many years. The 1900 official edition of the UAECA *The Laws of Croquet* (A100f) contains an advertisement for its wide range of Cassiobury sports goods.

1866

AA26 CASTLE-CROQUÊT: FOR FOUR PLAYERS.   1866
[Lewis Carroll]

(a) *First private printing (1866)*
[Title heading, p *1*]
CASTLE-CROQUÊT. | FOR FOUR PLAYERS. | [rule]
Formula: [1²]. 2 leaves, pp *1* 2–4
Technical notes: ca 143 × 80 mm (p 2). 43 lines, 20 = *ca* 68 mm. Leaf size *ca* 176 ×
113 mm
Contents: Title heading and diagram of hoop setting (*1*), rules, numbered I–VI
(*1–2*), recommended colours for the balls (*3*), advice to the player (*3–4*), date, signed
'*Aug.* 1866.' (*4*), name of printer (*4*)
Binding: Apparently none
Copy seen: PUL (photocopy of copy held by the Parrish collection)
Fingerprint: d.e, t,ur ayit t,r: C 1866A [all four groups taken from p 3]
Notes: Printed by Joseph Vincent, Oxford, unpublished. This work was first
published in the August 1867 issue of *Aunt Judy's Magazine* (vol III, No 16,
pp 221–24), which was later collated with other issues in *Aunt Judy's Christmas
Volume for Young People* (ed Mrs Alfred Gatty, London: Bell and Daldy, 1867).
Carroll developed Castle-Croquêt from an earlier game which he called Croquêt
Castles (see AA10). It has been supposed that he intended to include a revised
version of the game in a proposed new work, *Alice's Puzzle Book*, which was never
in fact published. It has further been supposed that the putative revisions (see (b))
were incorporated by Stuart Collingwood, Carroll's nephew and biographer, in
what has been supposed to be a definitive posthumous reprint of Carroll's work in
his *The Lewis Carroll Picture Book* (London: T Fisher Unwin, 1899, pp 271–74).
The evidence for these hypotheses is considered by the compiler in *The Croquet
Gazette*, March 1999, and found wanting. The true source of Collingwood's
variations, repeated in subsequent editions of the present work — *eg* J Fisher, *The
Magic of Lewis Carroll* (London: Nelson, 1973, pp 42–44) — is unknown. Their
vocabulary suggests an early date, *ca* 1865. This would imply that the present
edition may properly be regarded as the latest version of the game ever contemplated by Carroll.

(b) *Unpublished excerpt (1875)*
[Page headers, no title]
CASTLE-CROQUET.
Formula: [1²]. 2 leaves, pp *1* 2–3 *4*
Technical notes: ca 130 × 88 mm (p 3). 27 lines, 20 = *ca* 97 mm. Leaf size *ca* 189 ×
130 mm
Contents: Inscription in MS, 'Mar 13/75' (*1*), text (*2–3*), blank (*4*)
Binding: None
Copy seen: PUL (photocopy of copy held by the Parrish collection)
Fingerprint: rery tht. beou. isep C 1875A [all four groups taken from p 3]
Notes: Produced, apparently by Macmillan, unpublished. Save for minor acciden-
tals, the text constitutes a verbatim excerpt from (a), extending from line 2 of rule
VI (p 2) to the words 'one or more' in line 3 of the fourth paragraph of advice to
the player (p 3).

Carroll wrote to Macmillan on 9 March 1875, 'I enclose the *Castle Croquet* rules to try the experiment on. Would you get a page of it set up in whatever style you think will look best'. The significance of this cryptic request and the true purpose of the present excerpt are considered by the compiler elsewhere (*op cit*).

A27   **CROQUÊT. The Rev JG Wood (first edition),**   [1866]
F Wood (ed, second edition)

(a) **First edition [1866]*

CROQUÊT. | BY | The Rev. J. G. WOOD, | AUTHOR OF | "THE COMMON SHELLS OF THE SEA-SHORE," | *WITH ILLUSTRATIONS.* | LONDON : | FREDERICK WARNE AND CO. | BEDFORD STREET, COVENT GARDEN.

Formula: Apparently A^8 B–F^8 [\$2 signed (–A1, A2)]. 48 leaves, pp [i] *ii–v* vi–ix *x, 11* 12–94 *95–96*

Technical notes: ca 73 × 51 mm (p 16). 19 lines, 20 = *ca* 78 mm. Leaf size *ca* 94 × 66 mm. Four numbered inset plates face pp 16, 18, 30, 50

Contents: Wanting from the photocopy examined ([i]), frontispiece (engraving) (*ii*), title (*iii*), TP verso (*iv*), contents (*v*–ix), blank (*x*), text (*11*–94), advertisements (*95–96*)

Binding: Illustrated cloth, sewn, all edges gilt (according to the description of Warne's Illustrated Bijou Books in the advertisement on p 95)

Copy seen: PC (imperfect photocopy, wanting p [i])

Fingerprint: 21rs f.me l.ke BuSu 7 1866Q

Notes: Printed by Savill, Edwards and Co, London, price 6d. Year of publication is inferred from a citation in the *General Catalogue* of the BL. This work was reissued, together with companion works on archery and cricket, in *The Bijou Book of Out-door Amusements* (A37).

Comparison with copies seen of *The Bijou Book of Out-door Amusements* (*op cit*) and *Archery*, a component part of that composite volume, suggests that the frontispiece is tinted.

Chapter V includes a code of 21 numbered rules which bears little resemblance to that found in the same author's earlier work, *Athletic Sports and Recreations for Boys* (A5). 'Tight' and 'loose' croquet are now both allowed.

(b) *Second edition [1869]*

WARNE'S BIJOU BOOKS. | [rule] | **CROQUET.** | BY | F. WOOD, | AUTHOR OF "CRICKET," ETC. | [in gothic-revival script] With Illustrations and Coloured Frontispiece. | LONDON : | FREDERICK WARNE AND CO., | BEDFORD STREET, STRAND.

Formula: A^8 B–F^8 [\$2 signed (–A1, A2)]. 48 leaves, pp *i–v* vi–viii, *9* 10–14 *15–17* 18–95 *96*

Technical notes: 73 × 55 mm (p 11). 21 lines, 20 = 70 mm. Leaf size 96 × 67 mm; thickness 0.09 mm; wove, unwatermarked, smooth, white. In the copy examined, four inset plates of diagrams, numbered I–IV, face pp *16*, 18, 30, 51. It may be presumed that the coloured frontispiece mentioned on the TP, wanting from the copy examined, faces the TP

Contents: Half-title (*i*), blank (*ii*), title (*iii*), blank (*iv*), contents (*v*–viii), text (*9*–95), name of printer (*96*)

Binding: Strong Brown (55) cloth over light boards, sewn. The endpapers of the copy examined are coloured light yellowish Brown (76) but may originally have been white. FC: blocked in black and gold ([frieze of abstract design in gold and black] | [in gold] CROQUET | [floral device in black] | [frieze of abstract design incorporating some elements of the upper frieze, in gold and black]). RC: a central floral device, blocked in black. Spine: upwards, centred (CROQUET.).

Copy seen: PC (wanting frontispiece, formerly held by the Warne archive)

Fingerprint: 1817 e.ga g.ts 4.th C 1869Q [groups 1–4 taken from pp *v*, 13, 19, 20 respectively]

Notes: Printed by Savill, Edwards and Co, London. Year of publication is inferred from the stated source of the code of laws set out on pp 20–34 ('the "Field" Code') and the author's comment on this choice: 'Indeed, there is but one other, the "All England" code, which holds any position at all besides it'. The AECC, founded in 1868, played its first championship at the Crystal Palace in 1869 according to the Field Rules as revised by the AECC Committee (A30b). But this code was soon superseded by the Conference Code, of greater authority, which was widely known soon after the Conference held on 19 January 1870 to be in course of preparation. The fact that the present author makes no mention of the latter code suggests that the text was completed before the date of the conference.

A curiosity of this edition is the change of authorship. F Wood, author of Warne's companion Bijou book *Cricket*, is thought to have been retained by the publisher to update this work, presumably on account of JG Wood's unavailability. F Wood is not known to have written or edited any other work on croquet and is hence thought to have played rather an editorial role. This hypothesis receives some support from the fact that a footnote on p *9* is signed 'ED'. It is tempting to suppose that JG Wood was no longer available to Warne after transferring his allegiance to George Routledge and Sons, which he would appear to have done in or about 1865 with the publication of *The Boy's Own Treasury of Sports and Pastimes*. This move may have been linked to a severance in relations between Frederick Warne and the Routledges of Routledge, Warne, and Routledge — see, for example, *Athletic Sports and Recreations for Boys* (A5).

The text is entirely reset and is thought to have little in common with (a).

**A28	CROQUET.** [A Woolnoth]	[1866]

[Title heading, p *1*]

CROQUET. | [swelled rule]

Formula: [1²]. 2 leaves, pp *1* 2–4

Technical notes: 163 × 75 mm (p 2, ragged). 40 lines, 20 = 83 mm. Leaf size 216 × 136 mm; thickness 0.10 mm; wove, unwatermarked, smooth, pale orange Yellow (73)

Contents: Title (*1*), verse (*1*–4), name of printer (4)

Binding: None

Copy seen: PC

Fingerprint: o?!" y,h; o,l. l,u! C 1866Q [all four groups taken from p 3]

Notes: Printed by A Stenhouse, Hillhead, Glasgow. Page 4 is signed 'A. W.'. Year of publication is inferred from the state of the game described in the text, and authorship from an apparently contemporary annotation on the copy examined, the provenance of which is unknown.

A29　CROQUET GALOP. Charles Coote (composer)　　　　[1866]

(a) **First edition [1866]*

Formula: Apparently [1⁴, excluding the cover sheet]. 4 leaves, pp 1–8

Technical notes: 253 × 197 mm, variable (p 2). Leaf size 328 × 243 mm (but see *Copies seen* below); thickness 0.13 mm; wove, unwatermarked, smooth, white

Contents: Music for piano-forte (1–8)

Binding: White paper, printed in black and full colour, apparently sewn, no spine or endpapers. FC: as illustrated. Inside FC: blank. The two copies examined want the RC

Copies seen: (1) PC (imperfect, as illustrated, wanting the RC and substantial material at the foot of all leaves), (2) PC (photocopy, wanting only the RC and the extremities of all leaves)

Fingerprint: Indeterminate

Notes: Published by Hopwood and Crew, London.

The cover illustration is signed in MS '*CONCANEN LEE & SIEBE LITH*'. Year of publication is that suggested by W Longman in a letter which appeared in *The Croquet Association Gazette* (26 October 1922, p 299).

(b) *First American issue [1866]*

[The FC]

[in artist's ornamental open script below a line drawing of two crossed mallets and three balls, in a convex arc, flanked by flourishes] Croquet Galop | [the same coloured illustration as that on (a), but wanting all reference to WH Cremer] | [in artist's ornamental script, flanked by flourishes] **BY** | [*do*] **CHARLES COOTE** | [at the R, outlined by a seven-pointed star] 7½ | [in artist's script] **BOSTON:** | [leaning L, symmetrically with the final italics] Published by [in regular form] **OLIVER DITSON & C⁰** 277 *Washington St.* | W.A. PONDS & CO　J.G. HAYNES & CO JOHN CHURCH JR.　J.E. GOULD　LYON & HEALY. | [the five places set under the names of the five respective publishers] N. YORK.　BOSTON.　CINN.　Phil. CHICAGO

Formula: Not ascertainable from the photocopy examined. 4 leaves, pp *i–ii*, 3–7 [8]

Technical notes: ca 249 × 198 mm (p 4). Leaf size *ca* 348 × 249 mm

Contents: As the contents of (a), except that the initials 'H & C' at the foot of every page are replaced by the publisher's code number 22573 at the foot of pp 3, 5, 6, 7

Binding: Apparently issued as loose leaves

Copy seen: AAS (incomplete black-and-white photocopy, wanting p [8])

Fingerprint: Indeterminate

Notes: It is conjectured that this issue was published at much the same time as (a).

(c) *Ashdown & Parry issue [1866]*

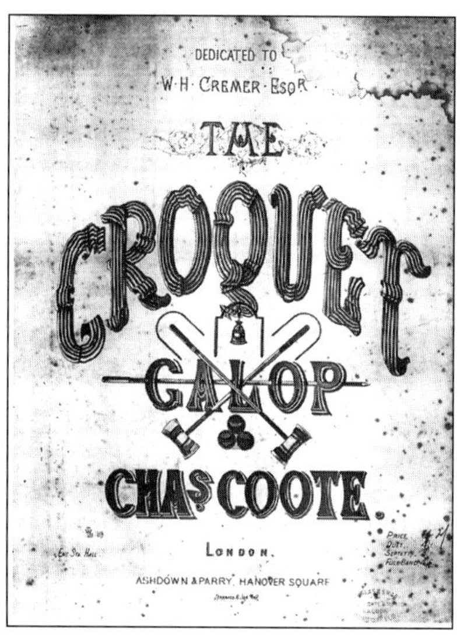

[The FC, seen in the illustration, is printed in black, blue, red, and yellow]

Formula: [1⁶]. 6 leaves including FC, pp *i–ii*, 1–8, *iii–iv*

Technical notes: 263 × 195 mm (p 7). Leaf size 349 × 261 mm; thickness 0.15 mm; wove, unwatermarked, smooth, white

Contents: As those of (a)

Binding: None

Copy seen: PC

Fingerprint: Indeterminate

Notes: Published by Ashdown & Parry, printed by Stannard & Son, price 3/–. Other versions of this work were evidently issued for different ensembles — for piano duet (price 4/–), septet (3/–), and full band (4/6). Year of publication is conjectural.

The musical score is identical to that of (a). The only variation is in substitution of a new inscription, 'C. COOTE, Croquet Galop. (10,703) ASHDOWN & PARRY. LONDON.', at the foot of p 8 and variously abridged on all other pages.

A30   CROQUET: ITS IMPLEMENTS AND LAWS.   **1866**
A Committee of Players Appointed by the Editor of *"The Field"*
(a) *First edition (1866)*

CROQUET: | ITS IMPLEMENTS AND LAWS. | DRAWN UP BY | A COMMITTEE OF PLAYERS | APPOINTED BY | THE EDITOR OF "THE FIELD" | [double rule] | LONDON: | HORACE COX, 346, STRAND, W.C. | [rule] | 1866

Formula: A⁸ [A2 signed]. 8 leaves, pp *1–3* 4–16

Technical notes: 133 × 80 mm (p 4). 36 lines, 20 = 75 mm. Leaf size 183 × 121 mm; thickness 0.11 mm; wove, unwatermarked, smooth, white

Contents: Title (*1*), TP verso (*2*), text (*3–16*)

Binding: Light yellowish Green (135) paper, sewn, no spine or endpapers. FC: the TP is reproduced in black within an outer frame of twine knotted at the corners and an inner ruled frame, with added matter below the base of the frames (Price Sixpence; by post, Seven Stamps.). Inside FC: advertisement. RC: advertisement. Inside RC: advertisement.

Copy seen: BL: 7907 aa 27

Fingerprint: s:ng tod. m.en cehe 3 1866A

Notes: Printed by Horace Cox, London, price 6d.

The text consists of a code of 12 numbered laws with lettered sub-clauses, which came to be called the '*Field* Code'.

(b) *1869 issue (1869)*

CROQUET, | ITS IMPLEMENTS AND LAWS, | DRAWN UP BY | A COMMITTEE OF PLAYERS APPOINTED BY | THE EDITOR OF "THE FIELD," | AND | REVISED IN MAY, 1869, | BY | THE COMMITTEE OF THE A. E. C. C. | LONDON : | HORACE COX, 346, STRAND, W.C. | [rule] | 1869.

Formula: [1⁸ 2⁴ 3²]. 14 leaves, pp *1–3* 4–16 *17* 18–27 *28*

Technical notes: 135 × 80 mm (p 4). 30 lines, 20 = 92 mm. Leaf size 179 × 120 mm; thickness 0.14 mm; wove, unwatermarked, smooth, white

Contents: Title (*1*), TP verso (*2*), text (*3–16*), sub-title ('APPENDIX') (*17*), advertisements (*18–19*), the Eglinton Castle game of croquet (*20–22*), advertisements (*23–27*), name of printer (*28*)

Binding: Dark Green (146) morocco grain cloth, limp over pastedowns, sewn. FC: gold-blocked within a blind-stamped triple-ruled frame, the central rule in bold (THE "FIELD' | CROQUET LAWS, | REVISED BY | THE A.E.C.C. COMMITTEE). RC: blind-stamped frame of the same pattern as that on the FC. Spine: blank

Copy seen: BL: 7907 aa 29

Fingerprint: ofht).om athe ti(*e* 3 1869A

Notes: Printed by Horace Cox, London.

The text, now including a code of 12 numbered laws with lettered sub-clauses, is expanded to cover the Eglinton Castle version of croquet and is entirely reset.

(c) *Copp, Clark edition (1873)*

CROQUET: | ITS IMPLEMENTS & LAWS. | DRAWN UP | BY A COMMITTEE OF PLAYERS APPOINTED BY | THE EDITOR OF "THE FIELD;" | AND | REVISED, MAY, 1869. | BY | THE COMMITTEE OF THE A. E. C. C. | [double rule] | TORONTO: | COPP, CLARK & CO., 17 & 19 KING STREET EAST. | 1870

Formula: Not ascertainable from the photocopy examined, unsigned. 9 leaves, pp *1–3* 4 5 6–18

Technical notes: †163 × †96 mm (p 6). 31 lines, 20 = †106 mm. Leaf size †197 × †144 mm

Contents: Title (*1*), TP verso (*2*), preface, signed 'Q', Toronto, 20 April 1870 (*3–4*), text (*5–18*)

Binding: Apparently pale cover paper or card, sewn. FC: within a double-ruled frame, the inner frame with corner ornaments (CROQUET: | ITS IMPLEMENTS & LAWS. | DRAWN UP | BY A COMMITTEE OF PLAYERS APPOINTED BY | THE EDITOR OF "THE FIELD;" | AND | REVISED, MAY, 1869, | BY | THE COMMITTEE OF THE A. E. C. C. | [rule] | TORONTO: | COPP, CLARK & CO. 67 & COLBORNE STREET. | 1873.). Inside FC: apparently blank. RC: apparently blank. Inside RC: blank

Copy seen: NLA: Mc 756 (photocopy of unknown scale)

Fingerprint: s.of t.nd).ke sior 3 1873A

Notes: Printed by Copp, Clark & Co, Toronto, in 1873. A curiosity of this work is the discrepancy between the years of publication cited on the FC and TP. It is conjectured that Copp, Clark printed the present issue in 1873 and an earlier issue in 1870.

**A31   CROQUET: ITS PRINCIPLES AND RULES [and THE   1866
CROQUET MANUAL]. Prof A Rover**

(a) *First edition (1866)*

[Within a double-ruled frame]

CROQUET; | Its Principles and Rules, | WITH | EXPLANATIONS AND ILLUSTRATIONS, | FOR THE | [in gothic-revival script] LAWN AND PARLOR. | [rule] | PROF. A. ROVER, F. C. R. | [rule] | SPRINGFIELD, MASS.: | MILTON BRADLEY & CO. | 1866.

Formula: 1^6 $2–3^8$ $4^8(4_1+\chi1)$ [$1 signed $(–1_1, 1)$]. 31 leaves, pp *i–iv, 1–3 4 5–7 8–24 25 26 27 28 29 30–42, v–vii, 43–52 53–56* [= 62]

Technical notes: 110 × 65 mm (p 9). 27 lines, 20 = 82 mm. Leaf size 147 × 98 mm; thickness 0.11 mm; wove, unwatermarked, smooth, white

Contents: Advertisements (*i–ii*), blank (*iii*), frontispiece, engraving signed 'A Rover Dec' (*iv*), title (*1*), TP verso (*2*), publisher's notice (*3–4*), contents (*5*), blank (*6*), text (*7–52*), advertisements (*53–56*)

Binding: Light greyish yellowish Brown (79) paper, printed in black, glued to the folds of the gatherings, stitched, no endpapers. FC: within a double-ruled frame ([in outlined display script] **CROQUET:** | [engraved illustration of a croquet game in play] | ITS PRINCIPLES AND RULES. | [rule] | SPRINGFIELD, MASS.: | MILTON BRADLEY & CO. | 1866.). Inside FC: advertisement. RC: advertisement. Inside RC: advertisement. Spine: blank

Copy seen: HPC: GV931 R65 1866 CROQ

Fingerprint: g-ty s.x- taey oftw 3 1866A

Notes: Printed by Samuel Bowles & Company. The text includes a code of 14 rules (numbered I–XIV) with several sub-clauses numbered in Arabic script.

Reviews: *Albany Atlas and Argus, Albany Evening Journal, Ball Players' Chronicle, Boston Post, Boston Transcript, Chicago Republican, Chicago Tribune, Christian Times and Witness, Columbia Republican, Detroit Tribune, Free Press, Godey's Ladies' Book, Hartford Courant, Hartford Evening Press, Holyoke Transcript, Liberal Christian, Lowell Courier, Louisville Democrat, New Orleans Picayune, New Orleans Times, Northampton Courier and Gazette, Our Young Folks,*

Providence Evening Press, *Scientific American*, *Springfield Republican*, *Troy Times*, *Washington Chronicle*.

(b) *Second edition [1866]*

Not seen. This edition is described in specific terms in the publisher's notice to be found in (c), wherein it is stated that the rules given in (a) are revised in detail in the light of comments received from readers.

(c) *Third edition (1867)*

[Within a double-ruled frame]

CROQUET; | ITS PRINCIPLES AND RULES, WITH EX- | PLANATIONS AND ILLUSTRATIONS, | FOR THE LAWN AND | PARLOR. | [rule] | Prof. A. ROVER, F. C. R. | [rule] | SPRINGFIELD, MASS.: | MILTON BRADLEY & CO. | 1867.

Formula: π1 1⁸ 2–4⁸ χ1 5⁴ [$1 signed (–1, 1)]. 38 leaves, pp *i–ii*, *1–3* 4 *5–7* 8–26 *27* 28 *29* 30 *31* 32–48, *iii–iv*, 49–66 *67–72* [= 76]

Technical notes: 110 × 65 mm (p 9). 27 lines, 20 = 82 mm. Leaf size 147 × 98 mm; thickness 0.11 mm; wove, unwatermarked, smooth, white

Contents: Blank (*i*), frontispiece, as that of (a) (*ii*), title (*1*), TP verso (*2*), publisher's notice (*3–4*), contents (*5*), blank (*6*), text, continued (*7–48*), advertisement (*iii*), blank (*iv*), text, concluded (*49–66*), notices of the press (*67*), advertisements (*68–72*)

Binding: Light orange Yellow (70) paper, printed in black, glued to the folds of the gatherings, stitched, no endpapers. FC: within a double-ruled frame ([in outlined display script] **CROQUET,** | [engraved illustration of a boxed croquet set] | **Its Principles and Rules.** | [rule] | THIRD EDITION. | [rule] | SPRINGFIELD, MASS.: | MILTON BRADLEY & CO. | 1867.). Inside FC: advertisement. RC: advertisement. Inside RC: advertisement. Spine: blank

Copy seen: HPC: GV931 R65 1867 CROQ

Fingerprint: ryhe s.en *n*ton inhe 3 1867A

Notes: Printed by Samuel Bowles & Company, Springfield MA.

In the publisher's notice it is stated that this edition incorporates further detailed revisions to the rules and is augmented by a number of croquet problems. The code of rules is recast, now amounting to 14 (I–XIV) with several numbered sub-clauses.

(d) *Fourth edition (1868)*

[Within a double-ruled frame]

CROQUET; | [in gothic-revival script, decorated *I*, *P*, *R*] **Its Principles and Rules,** | WITH | EXPLANATIONS AND ILLUSTRATIONS, | FOR THE | LAWN AND PARLOR. | BY | Prof. A. ROVER, F. C. R. | [rule] | FOURTH EDITION. | [rule] | SPRINGFIELD, MASS.: | MILTON BRADLEY & CO. | 1868.

Formula: π1 1⁸ 2–4⁸ 5⁴ [$1 signed (–π1, 1₁); 5₁ signed '4')]. 37 leaves, pp *1–2*, *i–iii* iv–vi, 7–9 *10–11* 12 13–26 *27* 28 *29* 30 *31–32* 33–45 *46* 47–48 *49–51* 52–59 *60* 61–64 *65* 66–70 *71–72*

Technical notes: 117 × 64 mm (p iv). 25 lines, 20 = 87 mm. Leaf size 146 × 98 mm; thickness 0.10 mm; wove, unwatermarked, smooth, white

Contents: Blank (*1*), frontispiece, as that of (a) (*2*), title (*i*), TP verso (*ii*), preface (*iii–vi*), contents (*7*), blank (*8*), text, continued (*9–49*), blank (*50*), text, concluded (*51–70*), advertisements (*71–72*)

Binding: Moderate orange Yellow (71) paper, printed in black, glued to the folds of the gatherings, stitched, no endpapers. FC: within a double-ruled frame, the outer frame in bold ([in outlined and hatched display script, in a convex arc] **CROQUET,** | [engraved illustration of a boxed croquet set] | [swash *I, P, R*] Its PRINCIPLES AND RULES. | [rule] | FOURTH EDITION. | [rule] | SPRINGFIELD, MASS.: | MILTON BRADLEY & CO. | 1868.). Inside FC: advertisement. RC: advertisement. Inside RC: advertisement. Spine: blank

Copy seen: PC

Fingerprint: inrs e.he thnd plse 3 1868A

Notes: Printed by Samuel Bowles & Company, Springfield MA. The code of rules is now presented as six sections with several numbered sub-clauses.

(e) *Sixth edition (1869)*

[Within a double-ruled frame]

CROQUET: | [in gothic-revival script, swash *I, P, R*] Its Principles and Rules, | WITH | EXPLANATIONS AND ILLUSTRATIONS, | FOR THE | LAWN AND PARLOR. | BY | PROF. A. ROVER, F. C. R. | [rule] | SIXTH EDITION. | [rule] | SPRINGFIELD, MASS.: | MILTON BRADLEY & CO. | 1869.

[Below the frame]

Entered according to Act of Congress, in the year 1866, by MILTON BRADLEY & CO., | In the Clerk's Office of the District Court of Massachusetts.

Formula: 1^8 2–4^8 5^4 [\$1 signed (-1_1; 5_1 signed '4')]. 36 leaves, pp *1–2, i–iii* iv–vi, 9 10–11 *12* 13–26 *27* 28 *29* 30 *31–32* 33–45 *46* 47–48 *49* 50–59 *60* 61–64 *65* 66–70 *71–72* [= 72]

Technical notes: 107 × 64 mm (p iv). 25 lines, 20 = 87 mm. Leaf size 162 × 105 mm; thickness 0.12 mm; wove, unwatermarked, smooth, white

Contents: Blank (*1*), frontispiece (*2*), title (*i*), contents (*ii*), preface (*iii*–vi), text (*9–70*), advertisements (*71–72*)

Binding: Light greenish Blue (172) paper, stitched, no endpapers. FC: printed in black within an elaborately decorated ruled frame ([in shaded display script] CROQUET, | [engraved illustration of a boxed croquet set] | [in gothic-revival script, swash *I, P, R*] Its Principles and Rules. | **BY PROF. A. ROVER.** | [rule] | [swash *S, E*] SIXTH EDITION. | [rule] | SPRINGFIELD, MASS.: | MILTON BRADLEY & CO. | 1869.). Inside FC: advertisement. RC: advertisement. Inside RC: advertisement. Spine: blank.

Copy seen: PC

Fingerprint: inrs thnd ghhe trve C 1869A [groups 1–4 taken from pp *iii*, 13, 21, 22 respectively]

Notes: Printed anonymously.

(f) *Eighth edition (1871)*

[Mostly within a double-ruled frame]

CROQUET: | [in gothic-revival script, decorated *I, P, R*] **Its Principles and Rules,** | WITH | EXPLANATIONS AND ILLUSTRATIONS, | FOR THE | LAWN AND PARLOR. | BY | PROF. A. ROVER, F. C. R. | [rule] | EIGHTH EDITION. | [rule] | SPRINGFIELD, MASS.: | MILTON BRADLEY & CO. | 1871. | [below the frame] Entered according to Act of Congress, in the year 1866, by MILTON BRADLEY & CO., | In the Clerk's Office of the District Court of Massachusetts.

Formula: Complex, not ascertainable from the copy examined. 36 leaves, pp *1–2, i–iii* iv–vi, *9* 10–11 *12* 13–26 *27* 28 *29* 30 *31–32* 33–45 *46* 47–48 *49* 50–59 *60* 61–64 *65* 66–70 *71–72* [= 72]

Technical notes: 108 × 65 mm (p iv). 25 lines, 20 = 87 mm. Leaf size 160 × 103 mm; thickness 0.13 mm; wove, unwatermarked, smooth, white

Contents: Blank (*1*), frontispiece, engraved illustration of a fashionable croquet party (*2*), title (*i*), contents (*ii*), preface (*iii–vi*), text (*9–70*), advertisements (*71–72*)

Binding: Strong Yellow (84) paper, printed in black, glued to the folds of the gatherings, sewn, no endpapers. FC: within a triple-ruled frame, the outermost frame in bold, the innermost frame with corner ornaments ([in shaded and hatched display script] **CROQUET,** | [engraved illustration of a boxed croquet set] | Its Principles and Rules. | *BY PROF. A. ROVER.* | [swelled rule] | [swash *E, E*] EIGHTH EDITION. | [swelled rule] | SPRINGFIELD, MASS.: | MILTON BRADLEY & CO. | 1871.). Inside FC: advertisement. RC: advertisement. Inside RC: advertisement. Spine: blank

Copy seen: HPC: GV931 R65 1871 CROQ

Fingerprint: inrs thnd r-p- onTw C 1871A [group 3 taken from p 19, group 4 taken from p 20]

Notes: Printed anonymously.

This edition has not been collated systematically with (e) but there are several indications that the present edition is essentially a reprint of the latter. The preface is unaltered. Historically, it may be seen as marking a seminal sticking point in the evolution of the American game in so far as it makes no mention of, or concession to, the Conference Code of 1870 (A52), which had established all but universal authority in the UK.

Another copy of this issue has been seen in a light greenish Blue (172) wrapper.

(g) *Eleventh edition (1873)*

[Mostly within a double-ruled frame]

CROQUET: | [in gothic-revival script, decorated *I, P, R*] **Its Principles and Rules,** | WITH | EXPLANATIONS AND ILLUSTRATIONS, | FOR THE | LAWN AND PARLOR. | BY | PROF. A. ROVER, F. C. R. | [rule] | ELEVENTH EDITION. | [rule] | SPRINGFIELD, MASS.: | MILTON BRADLEY & CO. | 1873. | [below the frame] Entered according to Act of Congress, in the year 1866, by MILTON BRADLEY & CO., | In the Clerk's Office of the District Court of Massachusetts.

Formula: Complex, not ascertainable from the copy examined. 36 leaves, pp *1–2*, *i–iii* iv–vi, *9* 10–11 *12* 13–26 *27* 28 *29* 30 *31–32* 33–45 *46* 47–48 *49* 50–59 *60* 61–64 *65* 66–70 *71–72* [= 72]

Technical notes: 108 × 65 mm (p iv). 25 lines, 20 = 87 mm. Leaf size 159 × 105 mm; thickness 0.10 mm; wove, unwatermarked, smooth, white

Contents: Advertisement (*1*), frontispiece, engraved illustration of a fashionable croquet party (*2*), title (*i*), contents (*ii*), preface (*iii*–vi), text (*9–70*), advertisements (*71–72*)

Binding: Moderate greenish Blue (173) paper, printed in black, glued to the folds of the gatherings, stitched, no endpapers. FC: within an elaborate frame incorporating letterpress, the outermost frame ruled in bold, with florid internal corner ornaments ([within the head of the frame between the outermost and the two inner frames] **HAVE YOU SEEN THE NEW GAME,** | [within the base of the frame between the outermost and the two inner frames] **MAGIC HOOPS?** | [within the frame at the L, upwards between the outermost and the two inner frames]

A SPLENDID GAME AND A COMPANION TO CROQUET. | [within the frame at the R, downwards between the outermost and the two inner frames] *FOR THE LAWN, THE GARDEN WALK, OR THE PARLOR.* | [in shaded and hatched display script] **CROQUET,** | [engraved illustration of a boxed croquet set] | –ITS– | [in gothic-revival script with decorated initials, save for the word 'and', which is set aslant] **Principles** AND **Rules,** | BY PROF. A. ROVER, | [swelled rule] | [within a panel composed of rules with decorative end-pieces] **ELEVENTH EDITION.** | [swelled rule] | SPRINGFIELD, MASS.: | MILTON BRADLEY & CO. | 1873.). Inside FC: advertisement. RC: advertisement. Inside RC: advertisement. Spine: blank.

Copy seen: PC

Fingerprint: inrs tho- r-p- onTw C 1873A [group 3 taken from p 19, group 4 taken from p 20]

Notes: Printed anonymously.

This edition has not been collated systematically with (f) but there are several indications that the present edition is essentially a reprint of the latter. The advertisement on the first page is a new feature.

(h) *Twelfth edition (1874)*

[The TP as that of (g)]

Formula: Not ascertainable from the photocopy examined, p 17 signed '2', p 33 signed '3', pp *49* and *65* both signed '4' . 36 leaves, pp [1–2], *i–iii* iv–vi, *9* 10–11 *12* 13–26 *27 28 29* 30 [*31–32*] 33–45 *46* 47–48 *49* 50–59 *60* 61–64 *65* 66–70 *71–72* [= 72]

Technical notes: 108 × 65 mm (p iv). 25 lines, 20 = 87 mm. Leaf size 159 × 105 mm

Contents: Apparently wanting from the copy examined ([1–2]), title (*i*), contents (*ii*), preface (*iii–vi*), text, continued (*9–30*), wanting from the photocopy examined ([*31–32*]), text, concluded (*33–70*), advertisements (*71–72*)

Binding: Apparently printed on pale coloured paper, glued to the folds of the gatherings, stitched, no endpapers. FC: mostly within an elaborate frame incorporating letterpress, the outermost frame ruled in bold, with florid internal corner ornaments ([within the head of the frame between the innermost and two outer frames] **HAVE YOU SEEN THE NEW GAME,** | [within the base of the frame between the innermost and two outer frames] **MAGIC HOOPS?** | [within the frame at the L, upwards between the innermost and two outer frames] A SPLENDID GAME AND A COMPANION TO CROQUET. | [within the frame at the R, downwards between the innermost and two outer frames] FOR THE LAWN, THE GARDEN WALK, OR THE PARLOR. | [in shaded and hatched display script] **CROQUET,** | [engraved illustration of a boxed croquet set] | –ITS– | [in gothic-revival script with decorated initials, save for the word 'and', which is set aslant within a hatched curlicue] **Principles AND Rules,** | BY PROF. A. ROVER, | [swelled rule] | [within a panel composed of rules with decorative end-pieces] **TWELFTH EDITION.** | [swelled rule] | CHICAGO: | W. B. KEEN, COOKE & CO. | 1873. | [below the frame] Clark W. Bryan & Co., Printers, Springfield, Mass.). Inside FC: advertisement. RC: advertisement. Inside RC: advertisement. Spine: blank.

Copy seen: LOC: GV931 R65 1873 (photocopy, apparently wanting the first leaf, the original copy wanting pp [31–32] and rebound in a library binding)

Fingerprint: inrs tho- r-p- onTw C 1874A [group 3 taken from p 19, group 4 taken from p 20]

Notes: Published by WB Keen, Cooke & Co, Chicago, printed by Clark W Bryan & Co, Springfield MA. Curiosities of this edition are the discrepancies between the editions and years of publication cited on the TP and FC. The text is identical, or virtually identical, to that of (g).

(j) *Thirteenth edition (1874)*

[Mostly within a double-ruled frame]

CROQUET: | [in gothic-revival script, decorated *I, P, R*] **Its Principles and Rules,** | WITH | EXPLANATIONS AND ILLUSTRATIONS, | FOR THE | LAWN AND PARLOR. | BY | PROF. A. ROVER, F. C. R. | [rule] | THIRTEENTH EDITION. | [rule] | SPRINGFIELD, MASS.: | MILTON BRADLEY & CO. | 1874. | [below the frame] Entered according to Act of Congress, in the year 1866, by MILTON BRADLEY & CO., | In the Clerk's Office of the District Court of Massachusetts.

Formula: Complex and irregular, not ascertainable from the copy examined. 46 leaves, pp *1–8, i–iii* iv–vi, 9 10–26 *27 28 29 30 31–34 35–47 48 49–50 51 52–61 62 63–66 67 68–72 73–78* [= 92]

Technical notes: 109 × 65 mm (p iv). 25 lines, 20 = 88 mm. Leaf size 167 × 108 mm; thickness 0.08 mm; wove, unwatermarked, smooth, white

Contents: Advertisements (*1–8*), Title (*i*), contents (*ii*), preface (*iii*–vi), text (*9–72*), advertisements (*73–78*)

Binding: Moderate greenish Blue (173) paper, printed in black, glued to the folds of the gatherings, stitched, no endpapers. FC: within an elaborate frame incorporating letterpress, the outermost frame ruled in bold, with florid internal corner ornaments ([within the head of the frame] **HAVE YOU SEEN THE GAME,** | [within the base of the frame] **MAGIC HOOPS?** | [within the frame at the L, upwards in shaded script] *A SPLENDID GAME AND A COMPANION TO CROQUET.* | [within the frame at the R, downwards in shaded script] *FOR THE LAWN, THE GARDEN WALK, OR THE PARLOR.* | [in shaded and hatched display script] **CROQUET,** | [engraved illustration of a boxed croquet set] | –ITS– | [in gothic-revival script with decorated initials, save for the word 'and', which is set aslant in artist's display script] **Principles** and **Rules,** | **BY PROF. A. ROVER,** | [swelled rule] | *THIRTEENTH EDITION.* | [swelled rule] | SPRINGFIELD, MASS.: | MILTON BRADLEY & CO. | 1874.). Inside FC: advertisement. RC: advertisement. Inside RC: advertisement. Spine: blank.

Copy seen: HPC: GV931 R65 1874 CROQ

Fingerprint: inrs tho- r-p- onTw 7 1874A [group 3 taken from p 19, group 4 taken from p 20]

Notes: Printed anonymously.

(k) *Fourteenth edition (1875)*

[Mostly within a double-ruled frame]

CROQUET: | [in gothic-revival script, decorated *I, P, R*] **Its Principles and Rules,** | WITH | EXPLANATIONS AND ILLUSTRATIONS, | FOR THE | LAWN AND PARLOR. | BY | PROF. A. ROVER, F. C. R. | [rule] | FOURTEENTH EDITION. | [rule] | SPRINGFIELD, MASS.: | MILTON BRADLEY & CO. | 1875. | [below the frame] Entered according to Act of Congress, in the year 1866, by MILTON BRADLEY & CO., | In the Clerk's Office of the District Court of Massachusetts.

Formula: Complex and irregular, not ascertainable from the copy examined. 45 leaves, pp *1–6, i–iii* iv–vi, 9 10–11 *12 13–26 27 28 29 30 31–34 35–47 48 49–50 51 52–61 62 63–66 67 68–72 73–78* [= 90]

Technical notes: 108 × 64 mm (p iv). 25 lines, 20 = 88 mm. Leaf size 172 × 111 mm; thickness 0.10 mm; wove, unwatermarked, smooth, white

Contents: Advertisements (*1–5*), frontispiece (*6*), title (*i*), contents (*ii*), preface (*iii*–vi), text (*9–72*), advertisements (*73–78*)

Binding: Dark yellowish Pink (30) paper, printed in black, glued to the folds of the gatherings, stitched, no endpapers. FC: within a triple-ruled frame incorporating letterpress, the outermost frame ruled in bold, with elaborate corner ornaments ([within the head of the frame] PITCH-A-RING. | [within the base of the frame] MAGIC HOOPS. | [upwards within the frame at the L] CORONA IS THE BEST CARD GAME EVER PUBLISHED. | [downwards within the frame at the R] KAKEBA IS THE BEST BOARD GAME EVER INVENTED. | [in shaded and hatched display script] **CROQUET,** | [engraved illustration of a boxed croquet set] | ITS | [in gothic-revival script with decorated initials, save for the word 'and', which is set aslant in artist's display script] **Principles AND Rules,** | **BY PROF. A. ROVER.** | [rule] | **FOURTEENTH EDITION.** | [rule] | MILTON BRADLEY & CO., | SPRINGFIELD, MASS. | AMERICAN NEWS CO., NEW YORK. | 1875.). Inside FC: advertisement. RC: advertisement. Inside RC: advertisement. Spine: blank

Copy seen: HPC: GV931 R65 1875 CROQ

Fingerprint: inrs tho- r-p- onTw 7 1875A [group 3 taken from p 19, group 4 taken from p 20]

Notes: Printed anonymously. This edition has not been collated systematically with (j) but there are several indications that the present edition is essentially a reprint of the latter. The preface is unaltered.

(l) *New abridged edition (1877)*

[Within a double-ruled frame]

CROQUET; | ITS | Principles and Rules, | BY | PROF. A. ROVER. | [rule] | NEW EDITION. | [rule] | 1877. | [rule] Copyright secured, 1877.

Formula: Not ascertainable from the photocopy examined, unsigned. Apparently 14 leaves, pp [i]–*ii*, *1–3* 4–6 *7–9* 10–19 *20* 21–23 *24–25* [26] [= 28]

Technical notes: 112 × 64 mm (p 4). 37 lines, 20 = 59 mm. Leaf size 157 × *ca* 105 mm

Contents: Apparently wanting from the photocopy examined ([i]), blank (*ii*), title (*1*), preface (*2*), text (*3–24*), blank (*25*), apparently wanting from the photocopy examined ([26])

Binding: Deep yellowish Brown (75) paper or card, sewn, no spine or endpapers. FC: printed within a double-ruled frame ([in shaded and hatched display script] **CROQUET,** | [engraved illustration of a boxed croquet set attended by two cherubs arm in arm] | ITS | Principles and Rules. | [rule] 1877). RC: blank

Copy seen: LOC: GV931 R65 1877 (photocopy, the FC and RC in colour, wanting the inside pages of the wrapper and apparently pp [i], [26], the original copy rebound in a library binding)

Fingerprint: d.ce e.ll atl. abqu 3 1877A

Notes: Published and printed anonymously. The preface and text are much abbreviated. The rules alone remain fully intact.

A32 CROQUET TO WHICH IS ADDED TROCO, OR LAWN [1866]
     BILLIARDS. Capt Crawley

CHAMBERS'S USEFUL HAND-BOOKS. | [double rule] | **CROQUET** | TO WHICH IS ADDED | TROCO, OR LAWN BILLIARDS | [in gothic-revival script]

By Captain Crawley | AUTHOR OF 'CHAMBERS'S HAND-BOOK TO CRICKET,' 'THE BILLIARD BOOK,' ETC. | [rule] | [in gothic-revival script] With Illustrations and Diagrams. | [vignette: engraved illustration of two cherubs playing croquet] | W. & R. CHAMBERS, LONDON AND EDINBURGH.

Formula: A⁸ B–D⁸ [$1 signed (–A1)]. 32 leaves, pp *1–9* 10–58 *59* 60–62 *63–64*

Technical notes: 109 × 79 mm (p *10*). 28 lines, 20 = 78 mm. Leaf size 144 × 109 mm; thickness 0.10 mm; wove, unwatermarked, smooth, white

Contents: Title (*1*), TP verso (*2*), dedication (*3*), blank (*4*), preface (*5*), blank (*6*), contents (*7–8*), text: croquet (*9–55*), text: parlour croquet (*56*), text: juvenile carpet croquet (*56–58*), text: troco or lawn billiards (*59–62*), name of printer (*62*), advertisements (*63–64*)

Binding: Moderate Yellow (87) paper over light boards, sewn. There are advertisements on the facing pages of the endpapers. FC: printed in black within a multiple-ruled frame with cross-hatching (CHAMBERS'S USEFUL HAND-BOOKS. | [double rule] | [in display script] **CROQUET** | AND | TROCO | [engraved illustration of a croquet party, within a ruled panel] | W. & R. CHAMBERS, LONDON AND EDINBURGH. | [rule] PRICE SIXPENCE.). RC: advertisement. Spine: blank

Copy seen: BL: 7907 a 64

Fingerprint: R.NT d-s, .'l, ansi 3 1866Q

Notes: Printed by W and R Chambers, Edinburgh, and published, apparently in June 1866, price 6d. Date of publication is deduced from the facts that the laws of the game given in this work are based expressly on those which first appeared in *The Field* on 7 April and were published on 10 April, 'with such deviations as we consider necessary', and that it was reviewed by *The Field* on 30 June.

Review: *The Field* (*op cit*). *The Field* slates the author for his 'deviations': 'With these blunders staring us in the face we cannot do otherwise than caution our readers against trusting to Captain Crawley's "Manual of Croquet"'.

**A33   HALIFAX ARCHERY & CROQUET CLUB [and RULES OF   1866
THE HALIFAX ARCHERY & CROQUET CLUB].**
[Halifax Archery and Croquet Club]

(a) *First edition (1866)*

Not seen. This edition is listed in the *General Catalogue* of the BL as having been published in 1866 by J Bowes & Sons, Halifax, Nova Scotia, but the copy once held by the library has been missing since 1984

(b) *1870 edition (1870)*
[Title heading, p *1*]

HALIFAX | **ARCHERY & CROQUET CLUB** | [swelled rule]

[sub-title, p *1*]

CROQUET REGULATIONS.

Formula: Apparently [1²]. (The copy seen is mounted in a scrapbook and cannot be fully examined.) 2 leaves, unnumbered [pp 1–4]

Technical notes: 283 × 186 mm (p *1*). 68 lines, 20 = 83 mm. Leaf size 337 × 251 mm; thickness 0.11 mm; wove, unwatermarked, smooth, white

Contents: Title heading, sub-title ('croquet regulations'), and text (*1*), blank (*2*), sub-title ('shooting regulations') and text (*3*), apparently blank (*4*)

Binding: None

Copy seen: BL: 1881 c 16 (123)

Fingerprint: n.an gee. hell ors. C 1870Q [all four groups taken from p *3*]

Notes: Published in Halifax, Nova Scotia, and printed anonymously. Approximate year of publication is inferred from the state of development of the game as described in the text and from the fact that the *General Catalogue* of the BL lists this edition as having been issued about 1870, *ie* after (a).

The text includes a code of 15 numbered rules, typical of the period shortly before the passing of 'tight croquet' in club play.

(c) *O'Toole and Kemp edition (1873)*

RULES | OF THE | [in outlined gothic-revival script] **Halifax Archery and Croquet** | [*do*] **Club.** | [rule] | **ESTABLISHED MAY 14, 1866.** | HALIFAX, N. S. | O'TOOLE & KEMP, PRINTERS, 45 GRANVILLE STREET. | 1873.

Formula: Apparently [1⁴(1₁+χ1)]. 10 leaves, apparently pp *1* [2] *i* [*ii*] *3* 4–8

Technical notes: †187 × †135 mm (p *5*). 23 lines, 20 = †164 mm. Leaf size †262 × †189 mm

Contents: Title (*1*), wanting from the copy examined ([2]), *addenda* (*i*), apparently blank, wanting from the copy examined ([ii]), text (*3–8*)

Binding: None apparent in the copy examined, sewn

Copy seen: NLA: Mc 756 (photocopy of unknown scale, wanting p [2])

Fingerprint: ."ir psm- :—he th." C 1873A [all four groups taken from p *i*]

Notes: Printed by O'Toole & Kemp, Halifax, Nova Scotia.

A34   JAQUES'S CROQUET. [Jaques & Son]   1866

[Front page, within a ruled frame]

TWO PRIZE MEDALS AWARDED, 1862. | [engraved illustration, detail from the frontispiece to A12] | **JAQUES'S CROQUET.** | [set between two identical engraved illustrations of a croquet stand and below one of a boxed set of croquet goods] **FOR DESCRIPTIVE PRICE LIST** | [*do*] **SEE OTHER SIDE.** | [*do*, wavy line] | [*do*] **CAUTION. —** To guard | [*do*] against inferior imitations, | [*do*] observe the name "JAQUES | [*do*] AND SON" on the lid of | [*do*] each Box, **WITHOUT WHICH** | [*do*] **NONE IS GENUINE.** | [rule] | **Wholesale, JAQUES & SON, 102, Hatton Garden, E.C.**

Formula: [1¹]. l leaf, unnumbered [pp *1–2*]

Technical notes: 191 × 110 mm (p *2*). 65 lines, 20 = 59 mm. Leaf size 225 × 141 mm; thickness 0.09 mm; wove, unwatermarked, smooth, deep orange Yellow (69)

Contents: Advertisement (*1*), descriptive price list and name of printer (*2*)

Binding: None

Copies seen: PCs (two)

Fingerprint: **C.E. CHof ESS, PRTH** C 1864Q [groups 1–3 taken from p *1*, group 4 taken from p *2*]

Notes: Printed by Taylor and Greening, London. Year of publication is deduced from the following indications:

(i) A substantially identical price list is contained on p 40 of the fortieth thousand issue of Jaques's *Croquet: The Laws and Regulations of the Game* (A12j), published in 1866.

(ii) Up to and including the last known preceding issue of the publisher's popular law book (h), published in 1865, the word 'croquet' is rendered with 'e' circumflex, but in none of the several occurrences of the word in this advertisement or in later issues of the law book is the circumflex accent used.

(iii) The same printers, Taylor and Greening, who had produced all earlier issues of the publisher's law book (*op cit*) were succeeded by Samuel Taylor, who were responsible for the first known issue to appear in 1867 (A12m).

This advertisement was probably distributed in various ways. One of the copies examined has traces of glue along one edge, suggesting that it had originally been tipped in as an insert to a newspaper or magazine.

A35   **THE NICEST KIND OF CROQUET. Christabel**   [1866]
(composer)

[Title heading, p 3]

[in a convex arc] **THE NICEST KIND OF CROQUET.** | [swelled rule] | [R justified] *Music by CHRISTABEL*

Formula: Apparently [1⁴] including the FC and RC. 4 leaves including the FC and apparently the RC, though the latter is wanting from the photocopy examined, pp *1* [2] 3–5 [6–8]

Technical notes: ca 241 × 193 mm (p 4). Leaf size *ca* 330 × 255 mm

Contents: FC (*1*), wanting from the photocopy examined and thought to be blank ([2]), musical score for voice and piano-forte (3–5), wanting from the photocopy examined and thought to be blank ([6–8])

Binding: None, thought to have been issued as loose folded sheets. FC: printed in black-and-white ([in artist's open display script, in a convex arc, within a full-page engraving, signed 'F. N. CARTER. LITH, BOSTON.' and, in MS, 'J. J. Frizzell', depicting a young couple in earnest conversation seated side by side beside a croquet ground] **CROQUET.** | BOSTON, | published by G.D.RUSSELL & COMPANY, 126 tremont, opp. park st. | *ENTERED ACCORDING TO ACT OF CONGRESS IN THE YEAR 1866 BY G. D. RUSSELL & COMPANY IN THE CLERK'S OFFICE OF THE DISTRICT COURT OF MASS.* | [the figure *4* within the outline of a five-pointed star]). Inside FC: wanting from the photocopy examined. RC: wanting from the photocopy examined. Inside RC: wanting from the photocopy examined

Copy seen: AAS (photocopy, wanting pp [2, 6–8])

Fingerprint: Indeterminate

Notes: Printed anonymously. Year of publication is inferred from the stated year of entry in the District Court of MA.

1867

A36   **CROQUET. CH Webb (song writer) and JR Thomas**   [1867]
(composer)

[Front cover, p *1*]

[in shaded gothic-revival script] **To Miss Blanche Carroll** | [in MS-style script] *As a Souvenir of Saratoga these words are respectfully dedicated by the Author* | [in a convex arc, in artist's ornamental display script] **CROQUET** | [black-and-white engraving, signed '*BUFFORD BROS' LITH.*', depicting a young couple fashionably dressed holding hands in earnest conversation seated side by side beside a croquet ground, partly framed by a large arch in the form of a croquet hoop] | [at L, mostly enclosed by a flourish] **WORDS BY** [*do*] **MUSIC BY** | [at the extreme L, the figure 5 within a six-pointed star] [in artist's open display script, the names of the song writer and composer respectively divided by a flourish] **C. H. WEBB. J.R. THOMAS.** | NEW YORK : | Published by **WM. A. POND & CO.** 547 Broadway. | **BOSTON   BUFFALO   CHICAGO   MILWAUKEE** | [the names of the four distributors arranged respectively below the foregoing place names] **OLIVER DITSON & CO.   J. R. BLODGETT.   ROOT & CADY.   H. N. HEMPSTED.** | *ENTERED ACCORDING TO ACT OF CONGRESS IN THE YEAR 1867 BY WM. A. POND & CO. IN THE CLERK'S OFFICE OF THE DISTRICT COURT OF THE SOUTHERN DISTRICT OF NEW YORK.*

Formula: Apparently [1⁴], including the FC. Apparently 4 leaves, including the FC, pp *1* [2] 3 4 *5–6* [7–8]

Technical notes: 209 × 164 mm (p 5). Leaf size 363 × 280 mm

Contents: Title (*1*), apparently blank ([2]), title heading (3), musical score for voice and piano-forte (3–6), apparently blank ([7–8])

Binding: None, thought to have been issued as loose folded sheets

Copy seen: AAS (incomplete photocopy, wanting pp [2, 7–8])

Fingerprint: Indeterminate

Notes: Printed anonymously. Year of publication is inferred from the stated date of entry in the Court of the Southern District of New York.

The heading on p 3 introduces this song 'AS SUNG BY M^RS SOPHIE MOZART'.

1868

A37   **THE BIJOU BOOK OF OUT-DOOR AMUSEMENTS.**   1868
        [JG Wood *et al*]

[The first of three books with separate sub-title pages and pagination, bound jointly with a single TP]

WARNE'S BIJOU LIBRARY. | [rule] | THE | BIJOU BOOK | OF | OUT-DOOR AMUSEMENTS. | [wavy line] | [in gothic-revival script] With Illustrations. | [wavy line] | LONDON: | FREDERICK WARNE AND CO. | BEDFORD STREET, COVENT GARDEN. | 1868

Formula: A⁸ B–E⁸ F⁸(–F5) [$2 signed (–A1, 2)]. 47 leaves, pp *i–v* vi–ix *x, 11* 12–94

Technical notes: 72 × 51 mm (p 12). 19 lines, 20 = 78 mm. Leaf size 95 × 67 mm; thickness 0.10 mm; wove, unwatermarked, smooth, white; five inset plates face pp *i* (engraved illustration of a croquet party), 20, 29, 32, 49

Contents: Title (*i*), blank (*ii*), sub-title ('CROQUET.') (*iii*), blank (*iv*), contents (*v–ix*), blank (*x*), text (*11–94*)

Binding: Very dark Green (147) cloth over boards, sewn. The copy examined has been rebound, displaying the original cloth on the FC, RC, and spine; new boards and endpapers *etc* have evidently been fitted. FC: publisher's device in the form of a monogram (*F, W*) set within a medallion, centred in a double-ruled frame, all gold-blocked. RC: blind-stamped with double-ruled frame. Spine: gold-blocked crosswise ([double rule near the top edge] | [near the top] THE | BIJOU | LIBRARY | [flourish] | [near the centre] OUTDOORGAMES | [near the foot] CROQUET | [rule] | ARCHERY | [rule] | CRICKET | [rule] | [double rule near the lower edge])

Copy seen: BL: 7921 a 28 (imperfect)

Fingerprint: 21rs f.me l.ke Busu 7 1868A

Notes: Printed anonymously. *Croquêt* (A27), and apparently also the other two titles in this composite volume, had been issued separately as Warne's Illustrated Bijou Books at earlier dates. *Croquêt* was published in 1866. The authors of the separate titles were Wood (*Croquêt*), HJB Hancock (*Archery*) and F Wood (*Cricket*).

The text and plates of the book within the present volume which is entitled *Croquet* are apparently identical to those of *Croquêt* (A27). The supplementary advertisements, however, are omitted.

A38   CROQUET TACTICS. Walter Jones Whitmore   1868

CROQUET TACTICS, | WITH | ILLUSTRATIVE COLOURED FIGURES, | AND | DIAGRAMS OF THE VARIOUS CROQUET STROKES. | [double rule] | BY | WALTER JONES WHITMORE. | [double rule] | LONDON: | HORACE COX, 346, STRAND, W.C. | [rule] | 1868.

Formula: π1 A^4 B–C^8 D$^{4\,2}$ [B1, χ2 signed 'B', 'B 2'; C1, 2 signed 'C', 'C 2'; D1 signed 'D']. 27 leaves, pp *i–x, 1* 2–39 *40* 41–44; 13 inset plates face pp 14 (figs 1–8), 19 (fig 9), 20 (fig 10), 23 (2 plates, figs 11 and 12), 25 (fig 13), 27 (2 plates, figs 14 and 15), 28 (fig 16), 30 (fig 17), 31 (figs 18–22), 33 (fig 23), 35 (fig 24); most of the plates are in black, vivid purplish Blue (194), vivid Red (11), and vivid Yellow (82); the plate facing p 14 folds out

Technical notes: 164 $\times$ 101 mm (p 2). 38 lines, 20 = 87 mm. Leaf size 214 $\times$ 137 mm; thickness 0.11 mm; wove, unwatermarked, smooth, white. The plates appear to be hand-coloured

Contents: Advertisements (*i–iv*), title (*v*), TP verso (*vi*), preface, signed 'Walter Jones Whitmore', 18 May 1868 (*vii*), blank (*viii*), contents (*ix*), illustrations (*x*), text (*1–39*), name of printer (*40*), advertisements (*41–44*)

Binding: Dark olive Green (126) sand grain cloth over card, sewn. The facing pages of the endpapers are coloured light Yellow Green (119). FC: gold-blocked title *etc* ([in display script] CROQUET TACTICS | [emblem formed of two crossed mallets and three ringed balls, one either side and one above] | by | [in display script] WALTER JONES WHITMORE | [set in the form of a monogram] 1868) centred within a double blind-stamped ruled frame and a gold-blocked ruled outer frame. RC: blind-stamped inner and outer frames of the same patterns as those on the FC. Spine: blank

Copy seen: BL: 7907 e 22

Fingerprint: 8.<u>E</u>, edis d.ly hoof 3 1868A

Notes: Printed by Horace Cox, London. According to D Prichard (A208, p 22), this work was published in May 1868. In the *Registry Book* of the Stationers' Company, the date of publication is given as June 1868.

The text is an expansion of a series of three articles which the author contributed to *The Field* of 7 December 1867, 4 January 1868, and 28 March 1868. *Cupid and Croquet*, verse by C Scott, is reprinted from *Fun*.

A39   THE NEW HANDBOOK OF CROQUET. Edmund Routledge   1868

(a) **First edition (1868)*

ROUTLEDGE'S | NEW | **HANDBOOK** | OF | **CROQUET.** | BY | EDMUND ROUTLEDGE. | [publisher's device in the form of a medallion] | LONDON: | GEORGE ROUTLEDGE AND SONS | THE BROADWAY, LUDGATE; | NEW YORK: 416, BROOME STREET. | 1868.

Formula: Apparently A^8 B–D^8 [\$2 signed (–A1, A2)]. Apparently 32 leaves, pp *1–3 4–5 6–9 10–32 33 34–38* [*39–42*] *43–61 62–64*

Technical notes: 125 × 79 mm (p 10). 31 lines, 20 = 82 mm. Leaf size 161 × 99 mm; thickness 0.13 mm; wove, unwatermarked, smooth, white

Contents: Title (*1*), blank (*2*), preface, signed 'EDMUND ROUTLEDGE' (*3–5*), blank (*6*), contents (*7*), blank (*8*), text, continued (*9–38*), wanting from the copy examined ([*39–42*]), text, concluded (*43–61*), advertisements (*62–64*), name of printer (*64*)

Binding: Light greenish Blue (172) coated paper over light boards, sewn. There are advertisements on all pages of the front and rear endpapers. FC: in black and moderate Brown (58) over Blue, all the lettering showing as black on Brown (**PRICE SIXPENCE** | [rule] | [in Blue-shaded script] **CROQUET** | **BY** | **EDMUND ROUTLEDGE** | [engraved illustration, in black with Brown detailing in a Blue panel, of a woman player in crinoline and bonnet with mallet half-raised to take 'tight' croquet, with a croquet party in the background] | **LONDON.** | **GEORGE ROUTLEDGE & SONS**) within a ruled frame. RC: advertisement for Gabriel's painless system of dentistry in black on Blue within a double-ruled frame, the outer frame in bold, and below the frame (EDMUND EVANS, ENGRAVER AND PRINTER, RAQUET COURT, FLEET STREET.). Spine: upwards in black on Blue (**ROUTLEDGE'S HANDBOOK OF CROQUET.—Sixpence**)

Copy seen: PC (imperfect, wanting pp [*39–42*])

Fingerprint: se." edto het, bath 3 1868A

Notes: Printed by Wyman and Sons, London, price 6d.

The contents include a code of numbered rules, apparently concluded on pages wanting from the copy examined.

In the preface, the author writes, 'When I wrote my "HANDBOOK OF CROQUET" about six years ago, ...' The implication that his earlier handbook (A15) was written in 1862 could be misleading: there is no other known evidence that that handbook, thought to have been first published in 1864, was written so early.

(b) *First edition, 1869 issue [1869]*

THE NEW | HANDBOOK | OF | **CROQUET.** | BY | EDMUND ROUTLEDGE. | [double rule] | LONDON : | GEORGE ROUTLEDGE AND SONS, | THE BROADWAY, LUDGATE; | NEW YORK : 416, BROOME STREET.

Formula: A^8 B–D^8 [\$2 signed (–A1, A2)]. 32 leaves, pp *1–3 4–5 6–9 10–32 33 34–61 62–64*

Technical notes: 126 × 79 mm (p 10). 31 lines, 20 = 82 mm. Leaf size 161 × 100 mm; thickness 0.13 mm; wove, unwatermarked, smooth, white

Contents: Title (*1*), TP verso (*2*), preface, signed 'EDMUND ROUTLEDGE' (*3–5*), blank (*6*), contents (*7*), blank (*8*), text (*9–61*), advertisements (*62–64*), name of printer (*64*)

Binding: Light greenish Blue (172) coated paper over light boards, sewn. There are advertisements on all pages of the endpapers. FC: in black and moderate Brown (58) over Blue, all the lettering showing as black on Brown (**PRICE SIXPENCE** | [rule] | [in Blue-shaded script] **CROQUET** | **BY** | **EDMUND ROUTLEDGE** | [engraved illustration, in black with Brown detailing in a Blue panel, of a woman player in crinoline and bonnet with mallet half-raised to take 'tight' croquet, with a croquet party in the background] | **LONDON.** | **GEORGE ROUTLEDGE & SONS**) apparently within a ruled frame (the upper edge of which would appear to have been truncated in the production of the copy examined). RC: advertisement for JJ

Thomas's off-court croquet goods in black on Blue within a double-ruled frame. Rear pastedown: advertisement for Routledge's Penny Novels. Spine: wanting from the copy examined

Copy seen: PC (imperfect)

Fingerprint: se." edto het, bath 3 1869Q

Notes: Printed by Wyman and Sons, London, price 6d. Year of publication is conjectural. This issue makes no reference to the 'Conference laws' (A52), so it would seem unlikely that it was published in or after 1870.

The contents include a code of 41 numbered rules.

The text is apparently identical throughout to that of (a). It varies only in the addition of details of the printer on the TP verso and in the advertisements on the endpapers and RC.

(c) *Post-Conference issue [1870]*

THE NEW | HANDBOOK | OF | **CROQUET.** | BY | EDMUND ROUTLEDGE. | [double rule] | LONDON : | GEORGE ROUTLEDGE AND SONS, | THE BROADWAY, LUDGATE; | NEW YORK : 416, BROOME STREET.

Formula: A^8 B–D^8 [$2 signed (–A1, A2)]. 32 leaves, pp *1–3* 4–5 *6–9* 10–32 *33* 34–61 *62* 63–64

Technical notes: 126 × 79 mm (p 10). 31 lines, 20 = 82 mm. Leaf size 162 × 101 mm; thickness 0.13 mm; wove, unwatermarked, smooth, white

Contents: Title (*1*), TP verso (*2*), preface, signed 'Edmund Routledge' (*3–5*), blank (*6*), contents (*7*), blank (*8*), text (*9–61*), the new laws of croquet (*62–64*), name of printer (*64*)

Binding: Identical to that of (b), except for the advertising matter on the rear pastedown. The upper edge of the frame on the FC of the copy examined has been similarly truncated, and the spine is likewise wanting. Rear pastedown: advertisement for Routledge's cheap dictionaries, cheap reckoners, and *Penny Table Book*

Copy seen: PC

Fingerprint: se." edto het, bath 3 1870Q

Notes: Printed by Wyman and Sons, London. Year of publication is inferred from the fact that the text of this issue is extended to include (a preliminary version of) the Conference Code (A52). Apart from this addition, variations in the advertising matter on the endpapers, and correction of the odd typographical fault in (b) — *eg* reprinting 'can' for 'anc' on the last line of p 27 — the two issues are identical.

It is conjectured that this issue was prepared in haste on the basis of early press reports of the 19 January 1870 conference of croquet clubs, and published in readiness for the new season. As reprinted, the code of laws, said to be that drawn up by 'Messrs. Riky and Pryor [*ie* RCA Prior]', departs at several points from the official version which first appeared in April 1870. If more time had allowed, the publisher might have awaited sight of the official version, and the author might have omitted the original 'rules', or at least have suggested when those rules or the new code of laws would be the more appropriate.

(d) *Post-Conference issue, variant [1870]*

THE NEW | HANDBOOK | OF | [the letter Q wanting its lower appendage in the photocopy examined] CROQUET. | BY | EDMUND ROUTLEDGE. | [double rule] | LONDON : | GEORGE ROUTLEDGE AND SONS, | THE BROADWAY, LUDGATE; | NEW YORK : 416, BROOME STREET.

Formula: Apparently as that of (c)

Technical notes: 126 × 79 mm (p 10). 31 lines, 20 = 83 mm.

Contents: Title (*1*), blank (*2*), preface (*3–5*), blank (*6*), contents (*7*), blank (*8*), text (*9–61*), the new laws of croquet (*62–64*), name of printer (*64*)

Binding: Apparently as that of (c), except for the advertising matter on the RC, rear pastedown, and front and rear endpapers. RC: advertisement for Dick Radclyffe and Co's seeds, plants, and horticultural goods within a double-ruled frame, the outer frame in bold. The advertisements on the endpapers include *inter alia* the new titles, *Routledge's Illustrated Dictionary* and *Routledge's Sixpenny Ready Reckoner* (rear pastedown).

Copy seen: PC (imperfect photocopy)

Fingerprint: se." edto het, bath 3 1870Q

Notes: Printed by Wyman and Sons, London. Year of publication is conjectural: this issue has all the outward attributes of a reprint hastily prepared by the publisher to replenish exhausted stock. The text is apparently identical to that of (c).

(e) *Post-Conference issue, variant [1870]*

THE NEW | HANDBOOK | OF | [the letter Q wanting its lower appendage in the copy examined] CROQUET. | BY | EDMUND ROUTLEDGE. | [double rule] | LONDON : | GEORGE ROUTLEDGE AND SONS, | THE BROADWAY, LUDGATE; | NEW YORK : 416, BROOME STREET.

Formula: As that of (c)

Technical notes: As (c), save thickness 0.12 mm

Contents: As those of (d)

Binding: As that of (c), except for the advertising matter on the RC and endpapers. RC: advertisement for Dick Radclyffe and Co's seeds, plants, and horticultural goods within a double-ruled frame, the outer frame in bold. The advertisements on the endpapers are confined to novels published by Routledge. *Routledge's Illustrated Dictionary* and *Routledge's Sixpenny Ready Reckoner* are not included

Copy seen: PC (imperfect, wanting the spine)

Fingerprint: se." edto het, bath 3 1870Q

Notes: Printed by Wyman and Sons, London. Year of publication is conjectural: as (d), this issue has all the outward attributes of a reprint hastily prepared by the publisher to replenish exhausted stock. The text is apparently identical to that of (c).

1869

A40   **CROQUET: DEFINITIONS AND RULES [and CROQUET:**   1869
           TERMS, SUGGESTIONS AND RULES]. [Anon]

(a) *First edition (1869)*

Not seen. The preface to (c) refers to previous editions of this work, and the assertion of copyright on the TP verso of (b) cites 1869 as the year of publication. It is conjectured that that assertion was intended to refer to the year of first publication.

(b) *1871 edition (1871)*

CROQUET. | [rule] | DEFINITIONS & RULES | MADE | **UNIFORM AND CONDENSED** | UNDER THE DIRECTION OF THE | AMERICAN CROQUET COMPANY | OF GENESEO, N. Y. | [rule] | GENESEO: | JAMES W. CLEMENT STEAM JOB PRINTER . | 1871.

[TP verso]

Entered according to an act of Congress, A. D. 1869, by | THE AMERICAN CRO-QUET COMPANY, | In the Clerk's Office of the District Court for the | Northern District of New York.

Formula: [1–2⁸]. 32 leaves, pp *1–7* 8 *9* 10 *11* 12 *13* 14 *15–18* 19–20 *21* 22–26 *27* 28–30 *31* 32

Technical notes: 102 × 67 mm (p 19). 22 lines, 20 = 94 mm. Leaf size 142 × 106 mm; thickness 0.13 mm; wove, unwatermarked, smooth, white

Contents: Blank (*1*), frontispiece (*2*), title (*3*), TP verso (*4*), contents (*5*), blank (*6*), preface (*7–8*), text, continued (*9–14*), blank (*15*), plan of court, game with ten bridges (*16*), plan of court, game with nine bridges (*17*), text, concluded (*18–32*)

Binding: Light bluish Grey (190) semi-gloss paper, laminated over white paper, glued to the gatherings, stitched, no endpapers. FC: printed in black, ornamented with curlicues ([in a convex arc] **AMERICAN CROQUET CO.,** | OF | GENESEO, N. Y. | **HAND-BOOK OF CROQUET.**). Inside FC: blank. RC: blank. Inside RC: blank. Spine: blank

Copy seen: HPC: GV931 A51 1871 CROQ

Fingerprint: 31II orto s.to baot 7 1871A [group 3 taken from the caption to the plan on p 17]

Notes: Printed by James W Clement, Steam Job Printer. A curiosity of this edition is the discrepancy between the year of publication cited on the TP (*viz* 1871) and that cited as the year of copyright on the TP verso (1869). It is conjectured that the latter year was intended to refer to the year of first publication.

The text includes a code of 22 numbered rules.

(c) *Expanded 1871 edition [1871]*

[Within a ruled frame with corner ornaments]

CROQUET. | TERMS, SUGGESTIONS AND RULES, | MADE | UNIFORM AND CONDENSED, | UNDER DIRECTION OF | THE AMERICAN CROQUET COMPANY, | OF GENESEO, N. Y.: | [rule] | [in gothic-revival script] Geneseo, N. Y: | REPUBLICAN STEAM POWER PRESSES. | 1871.

[TP verso, within a ruled frame with corner ornaments]

Entered according to Act of Congress, in the year 1871, by the | AMERICAN CROQUET COMPANY *of GENESEO, N. Y.,* | *In the Office of the Librarian of Congress, at Washington.*

Formula: Not ascertainable, apparently collated in unsigned sections. 22 leaves, pp *1–5* 6–12 *13* 14–15 *16* 17–43 *44*

Technical notes: 100 × 68 mm (p 8). 26 lines, 20 = 76 mm. Leaf size 140 × 106 mm

Contents: Blank (*1*), frontispiece, an engraved illustration of a croquet game (*2*), title (*3*), TP verso (*4*), author's preface (*5–6*), text, continued (*7–12*), blank (*13*), text, continued (*14–15*), blank (*16*), text, concluded (*17–43*), blank (*44*)

Binding: Pale colour card or paper, sewn, no endpapers. FC: ornamented with curlicues ([in a convex arc] **AMERICAN CROQUET CO.,** | OF | GENESEO, N. Y. | **HAND-BOOK OF CROQUET.**). Inside FC: blank. RC: blank. Inside RC: blank. Spine: not seen, perhaps none

Copy seen: LOC: GV931 A51 (photocopy of original copy rebound in library covers)

Fingerprint: aln- d.e- d.it baup C 1871Q [group 2 taken from p 17, group 3 taken from p 19, group 4 taken from p 20]

Notes: Printed by Republican Steam Power Presses, Geneseo NY.

The text of this edition would appear to be have been largely revised. In particular, the code of rules is now considerably extended, amounting to some 50 rules in total, including separately numbered rules relating to misplay (1–4), arches (1–9), roquet (1–9), croquet (1–7), and displaced balls (1–7).

A41   **CROQUET: THE LAWS AND REGULATIONS OF THE**   **1869**
GAME. **The West Essex Croquet Club**

CROQUET: | THE LAWS AND REGULATIONS | OF THE GAME. | BY THE | WEST ESSEX CROQUET CLUB. | [rule] | Ent. Sta. Hall. | [rule] | LONDON: | WALTER BRETTELL, Jun., 336a, OXFORD STREET. W. | [rule] | 1869.

Formula: [1⁸]. 8 leaves, pp *1–5* 6–15 [16]

Technical notes: ca 139 × 85 mm (p 10). 35 lines, 20 = *ca* 79 mm. Leaf size *ca* 186 × 123 mm

Contents: Title (*1*), TP verso (*2*), plan of the ground (*3*), blank (*4*), text (*5–15*), wanting from the photocopy examined ([16]))

Binding: Not apparent from the photocopy examined, sewn

Copy seen: PC (incomplete photocopy of CUL 70 7 230, wanting p [16])

Fingerprint: h.he othe ghed ined C 1869A [group 1 taken from p 5, groups 2–4 taken from p 13]

Notes: Printed by W Brettell, London. According to the applicant's claim to copyright, recorded in the *Registry Book* of the Stationers' Company, this work was published on 30 December 1869.

A42   **THE POCKET GUIDE TO CROQUET.** Cavendish   **1869**

[Front cover, all the letterpress save the last line within a double-ruled outer frame and an inner frame composed of croquet balls and winning pegs]

THE | POCKET GUIDE | TO | [in artist's script composed of stylised croquet mallets, balls, hoops, and winning pegs] CROQUET | BY | CAVENDISH, | AUTHOR OF | "The Laws & Principles of Whist," &c., &c, | LONDON: | THOS. DE LA RUE & CO. | 1869 | [at L] Ent. Sta. Hall. [at R] Price Sixpence. | [under the base of the frame] The right of Translation is reserved.

Formula: [1⁸]. 8 leaves, pp *3* 4–18 [= 16]

Technical notes: 79 × 53 mm (p 4). 32 lines, 20 = 49 mm. Leaf size 94 × 64 mm; thickness 0.12 mm; wove, unwatermarked, smooth, white, all edges gilt

Contents: Title (FC), index (inside FC), text (*3–18*), advertisement (inside RC), publisher's blurb and name of printer (RC)

Binding: Semi-gloss light card or laminate, sewn, no spine or endpapers. The FC and RC are coloured brilliant Green (140), the inner pages white. FC: printed in black as above. Inside FC: index printed in black and strong Red (12). RC: all the letterpress save the last line, and other matter, set within a frame of the same design as that on the FC ([a hoop] THE | POCKET GUIDE | TO | CROQUET | Is intended to supply hints for arranging | and playing the game, together with a | convenient book of reference for deter- | mining questions which may arise in the | course of play. | [device composed of three crossed mallets intersected by eight croquet balls |

[under the base of the frame] THOS. DE LA RUE AND CO. TYP. LONDON.).
Inside RC: advertisement printed in black and Red

Copy seen: BL: 7919 d 34 (imperfect)

Fingerprint: l,wo n.ty enr- ba2. 3 1869A

Notes: Printed by Thos De La Rue, London, price 6d. The text includes a code of
30 laws.

Reviews: The Field (15 May 1869, p 411), *Land and Water* (12 June 1869, p 383).

1860–69

A43   **CROQUET.** [Anon]   *ca* 1866

CASSELL'S SIXPENNY HAND-BOOKS. | [rule] | THE GAME | OF | **CROQUET.** |
[swelled rule] | LONDON: | CASSELL, PETTER, AND GALPIN, | LUDGATE
HILL, E.C.

Formula: A^8 B–D^8 [\$2 signed (–A1, 2)]. 32 leaves, pp *1–7* 8–14 *15* 16–24 *25* 26–60
61–64

Technical notes: 103 × 63 mm (p 8). 28 lines, 20 = 74 mm. Leaf size 134 ×
92 mm; thickness 0.12 mm; wove, unwatermarked, smooth, white

Contents: Half-title (*1*), blank (*2*), title (*3*), blank (*4*), contents (*5*), blank (*6*), text,
continued (*7–14*), engraving (*15*), text, continued (*16–24*), plan of 9-hoop setting
(*25*), plan of 10-hoop setting (*26*), text, concluded (*27–60*), advertisements (*61–64*)

Binding: Greyish Yellow Green (122) semi-gloss paper over light boards, sewn.
There are advertisements printed in black on the facing pages of the endpapers
which are coloured light greenish Yellow (101). FC: printed in black within a ruled
frame in bold (Cassell's Sixpenny Handbooks. | [double rule] | *Croquet.* | [double rule,
the upper rule in bold] | CASSELL, PETTER, AND GALPIN, | LONDON AND
NEW YORK.). RC: advertisement. Spine: apparently blank (part of the spine is
wanting from the copy examined)

Copy seen: BL: 7906 aa 12 (imperfect)

Fingerprint: 6054 erd, y,a- grre 7 1866Q

Notes: Printed anonymously, price 6d. Year of publication is that cited as inferred
in the *General Catalogue* of the BL. This is consistent with the state of development
of the game as presented in the text.

The text includes a synopsis of the laws of croquet, extending to 17 in number. The
'tight' croquet stroke is optional.

A44   **CROQUET: A COMPLETE POCKET MANUAL.** [Anon]   *ca* 1869

[in shaded display script] **CROQUET,** | *A COMPLETE POCKET MANUAL,* | [in
shaded script] **Its Rules and Regulations,** | — WITH — | ILLUSTRATIONS AND
EXPLANATIONS, | — FOR — | LAWN, PARLOR AND TABLE.

Formula: Apparently [1^{12}]. Apparently 12 leaves, pp [*1*] 2–5 6–23 [*24*]

Technical notes: ca 116 × 76 mm (p 6). 33 lines, 20 = *ca* 70 mm. Leaf size *ca* 157 ×
115 mm

Contents: Wanting from the photocopy examined ([*1*]), frontispiece, engraved illustration (*2*), title (*3*), contents (*4*), text (*5–22*), advertisement by C Newman & Sons
(*23*), wanting from the photocopy examined ([*24*])

Binding: Apparently pale coloured paper wrapper, both sewn and stitched, no
endpapers. FC: within a double-ruled frame, the outer frame in bold with corner

and intermediate ornaments ([in shaded display script, in a convex arc] **CROQUET,** | [a monogram composed of the letters *C, N, S,* presumed to be the publisher's device] | [emblem composed of two crossed mallets surmounted by a single ball] | — ITS — | [in shaded gothic-revival script] **Rules** [in regular script, slanted from bottom L to top R] AND [in shaded gothic-revival script] **Principles.**). Inside FC: wanting from the photocopy examined. RC: blank. Inside RC: wanting from the photocopy examined

Copy seen: HPC: RRCC #392 (photocopy)

Fingerprint: nged e.nd e.It bast 7 1869Q

Notes: Apparently published by C Newman & Sons, Richmond IN, assumed to be manufacturers of croquet equipment, and printed anonymously. Approximate year of publication is inferred from the close similarity of the text with A31d and from the similarity of the costume worn by the woman player depicted in the frontispiece with the woman's costume seen in the frontispiece of *Croquet* (A8e), another American treatise on the game.

The text includes a code of rules in the form of six sections with several numbered sub-clauses.

A45   CROQUET AND BILLIARDS. [Anon]   *ca* 1864

CROQUET | AND | BILLIARDS.

Formula: [1¹⁶]. 16 leaves, pp *1–5* 6 7 *8–10 11* 12–28 *29–32*

Technical notes: 115 × 71 mm (p 6, croquet), 119 × 71 mm (p 12, billiards). 27 lines, 20 = 86 mm (p 6); 36 lines, 20 = 66 mm (p 12). Leaf size 156 × 102 mm; thickness 0.09 mm; wove, unwatermarked, smooth, white

Contents: Title (*1*), blank (*2*), contents (*3–4*), text (*5–28*), advertisements (*29–32*)

Binding: Brilliant Yellow (83) paper, sewn, no spine or endpapers. FC: woodcut printed in black and deep reddish Orange (36) ([in black, within a rectangular panel with a saw-tooth inner edge] PRICE TWOPENCE | [in black, within the convex crown of a large hoop, forming a frame] CROQUET | [illustration, in black and Orange, of a man player with mallet raised above his shoulder to take 'tight croquet'] | [in black on Orange within a decorative concave panel] WITH EVERY RULE OF THE GAME. | [in black, within a rectangular panel with a saw-tooth inner edge] LONDON:J. NEAL,61, Sᵀ·JOHN'S SQ.]). RC: advertisement in black.

Copy seen: BL

Fingerprint: .—.— s.nd eee. spye 3 1864Q

Notes: Printed by J Neal, London, price 2d. The copy examined bears the (apparently recent) pencil annotation '1868–71'. In view of the state of the game described in the text, which is typical of 'tight croquet' as widely played in the early 1860s, it is thought that this work was published some years earlier.

The text includes a section entitled 'CROQUET' (pp 5–10) which contains a code of 15 numbered laws.

A46   CROQUÊT: ITS NAME AND ORIGIN. [Anon]   *ca* 1864

(a) *First edition [1864]*

Not seen. The fact that the 'seventh edition' (c) was published two years of the 'fifth' (b) would suggest that this work was effectively an annual serial. Hence it would appear that the first edition was published in or about 1864.

(b) *Fifth edition, enlarged (1867)*

CROQUÊT, | ITS | NAME AND ORIGIN ; | THE ARTICLES USED, | AND | MODE OF PLAYING THE GAME, | FULLY DESCRIBED. | [rule] | FIFTH EDITION. | (ENLARGED.) | [rule] | WITH ILLUSTRATIONS. | [rule] | LONDON: | [rule] | 1867.

Formula: Apparently [π1 1–3⁴]. 13 leaves, pp *1–5* 6–12 *13* 14–25 *26*

Technical notes: 152 × 92 mm (p 6). 29 lines, 20 = 106 mm. Leaf size 210 × 136 mm; thickness 0.11 mm; wove, unwatermarked, smooth, white

Contents: Blank (*1*), frontispiece (*2*), title (*3*), blank (*4*), text (*5–25*), price list (*26*)

Binding: Greyish greenish Yellow (105) light card, printed in black, sewn, no spine or endpapers. FC: within a double-ruled frame, the outer frame in bold (**CROQUÊT :** | A NEW GAME OF SKILL. | [engraved illustration of a croquet party] | LONDON:). Inside FC: blank. RC: blank. Inside RC: blank

Copy seen: HPC: RRCC #32 CROQ

Fingerprint: *v**of s,ey elor inth 7 1867A [group 2 taken from p 15]

Notes: Printed anonymously. The text includes a code of five numbered directions and one supernumerary direction for playing the game.

(c) *Seventh edition, enlarged (1869)*

CROQUÊT: | ITS | **NAME AND ORIGIN;** | THE ARTICLES USED, | AND | MODE OF PLAYING THE GAME | FULLY DESCRIBED. | [rule] | SEVENTH EDITION. | (ENLARGED.) | [rule] | WITH ILLUSTRATIONS. | [rule] | LONDON: | [rule] | 1869.

Formula: [1² 2–4⁴, 1₂ᵦ glued to 2₁ₐ to form a single leaf of double thickness]. 13 leaves, pp *1–5* 6–12 *13* 14–25 *26*

Technical notes: 150 × 92 mm (p 6). 31 lines, 20 = 98 mm. Leaf size 212 × 135 mm; thickness 0.11 mm; wove, unwatermarked, smooth, white

Contents: Blank (*1*), frontispiece (engraving, signed 'WELLS & VICKERS') (*2*), title (*3*), blank (*4*), text (*5–25*), blank (*26*)

Binding: Light Green (144) paper laminate, sewn, no spine or endpapers. FC: title *etc* in black (**CROQUÊT:** | A NEW GAME OF SKILL. | [engraved illustration of a croquet party] | LONDON | 1869.) within a double-ruled frame, the outer frame in bold. RC: blank.

Copy seen: PC

Fingerprint: *v*.of enre lyrn awon 7 1869A [group 2 taken from p 15]

Notes: Printed anonymously. The text includes a code of six numbered directions for playing the game which is identical in substance to that in (b).

This issue has a new frontispiece and price list, incorporates many stylistic revisions, and is entirely reset, but contains no significant new written matter. The price list suggests that it was distributed by a sports goods manufacturer with its croquet equipment.

A47   [JN HEARDER'S GUIDE TO SEA FISHING AND THE   *ca* 1868
RIVERS OF SOUTH DEVON]. **JN Hearder**

(a) **First edition [1868]*

J. N. HEARDER, | 145 UNION STREET, PLYMOUTH, | MANUFACTURER OF | PRIZE | RIVER & SEA FISHING TACKLE, | ARCHERY, CROQUET, |

UMBRELLAS AND PARASOLS. | DEALER IN | [in gothic-revival script] Cricket and fives Bats and Balls, | RACKETS, QUOITS, SKATES, ETC. | MAGIC LANTERNS, | DISSOLVING VIEWS. | Philosophical Apparatus Maker & Electrician. | *Teacher of Chemistry and Experimental Physics in* | *connection with the Science & Art Department,* | *South Kensington.* | FELLOW OF THE CHEMICAL SOCIETY.

Formula: Apparently A^8 B–F^8 [\$1 signed (–A1)]. Apparently 48 leaves, pp *1–5 6–30 31 32–39 40 41–58 59 60–89 90 91–92 93–95* [*96*]

Technical notes: ca 92 × 59 mm (p *6*). 34 lines, 20 = *ca* 54 mm. Leaf size *ca* 113 × 71 mm

Contents: Title (*1*), blank (*2*), advertisement (*3*), blank (*4*), text (*5–92*), advertisement and name of printer (*93*), blank (*94–95*), ([*96*])

Binding: Not ascertainable from the photocopy examined. FC: mostly within a double-ruled frame, the outer frame in bold ([in shaded display script] **J. N. HEARDER'S** | GUIDE TO SEA FISHING | AND THE | [in gothic-revival script] Rivers of South Devon, | AND | DESCRIPTIVE CATALOGUE | OF HIS | PRIZE RIVER AND SEA | FISHING TACKLE, | **CRICKET,** | ARCHERY, CROQUET, | UMBRELLAS, PARASOLS, &c. &c. | [swelled rule] | MANUFACTORY: | 145 UNION STREET, | PLYMOUTH. | [below the frame] ENTERED AT STATIONERS' HALL.)

Copy seen: HCLHL: XF 5205 50.7 (incomplete photocopy)

Fingerprint: h.6. *ee*me /65/ DiDi 3 1868Q

Notes: Printed by JW Skardon, Plymouth.

Year of publication and the serial order of this particular edition are uncertain. However, the following clues strongly suggest that there could have been no more than one previous edition and that the present edition appeared in 1867 or 1868:

(i) The advertisement on p *3* refers to a trade exhibition in 1866. Since trade catalogues for sporting goods and services are typically issued early in the year in preparation for a mid-year season — *eg* (d), which is signed January — it is most unlikely that this edition appeared earlier than 1867. The year 1868 would seem more likely.

(ii) The next known dated edition is that described as the sixth (c), which presumably appeared in 1873, the year appended to the introduction. Since it is considered most unlikely that a major supplier of sports goods would issue more than one complete catalogue in a given year and none in a closely adjacent year, the present edition could not have appeared after 1868.

The text consists of a catalogue of angling and other sports goods, mostly priced (pp *5–39*) and a local guide to angling technique (pp *40–92*). There is a brief section devoted to croquet equipment (p *31*).

(b) *Fifth edition [1872]*

J. N. HEARDER, | 195 UNION STREET, PLYMOUTH, 195, | *Correspondent of the "Field,"* | MANUFACTURER OF | PRIZE | RIVER & SEA FISHING TACKLE, | ARCHERY, CROQUET, | UMBRELLAS AND PARASOLS. | DEALER IN | [in gothic-revival script] Cricket and Fives Bats and Balls, | Rackets, Quoits, Skates, &c. | MAGIC LANTERNS, | DISSOLVING VIEWS, | Philosophical Apparatus Maker and Electrician, | Lecturer on Chemistry and Experimental Physics, | D.Sc., Ph. D., F.C.S.

Technical notes: ca 104 × 68 mm (p 4). 38 lines, 20 = *ca* 55 mm. Leaf size *ca* 131 × 85 mm

Contents: Title (*1*), blank (*2*), introduction (*3–5*), contents (*6–7*), wanting from the photocopy examined ([8 ff]), text ([*9–105*])

Binding: Apparently pale coloured paper wrapper. FC: mostly within a ruled frame with corner ornaments (HEARDER & SON'S | [in open outlined gothic-revival script] **GUIDE TO SEA FISHING** | AND THE | [in gothic-revival script] Rivers of South Devon, | AND | DESCRIPTIVE CATALOGUE | OF HIS | PRIZE RIVER AND SEA | FISHING TACKLE, | CRICKET, | ARCHERY, CROQUET, | UMBRELLAS, PARASOLS, &c. &c. | [swelled rule] | MANUFACTORY: | 195, UNION STREET, 195, | PLYMOUTH.). Inside FC: blank

Copy seen: HCLWL: F 5205 50.5 (photocopy of preliminaries only, the original copy rebound in a library binding)

Notes: Year of publication is inferred from the same premises as those detailed in the *Notes* to (a).

(c) *Sixth edition [1873]*

[L justified] Sixth Edition.] | J. N. HEARDER, | 195, UNION STREET, PLYMOUTH, 195, | *CORRESPONDENT OF "THE FIELD,"* | MANUFACTURER OF | PRIZE | [in gothic-revival script] River & Sea Fishing Tackle, | ARCHERY, CROQUET, | [in open outlined display script] **UMBRELLAS & PARASOLS,** | Cricket & Fives Bats & Balls, | RACKETS, QUOITS, SKATES, &c. | [in display script] MAGIC LANTERNS, | DISSOLVING VIEWS. | PHILOSOPHICAL APPARATUS MAKER AND ELECTRICIAN | Lecturer on Chemistry and Experimental Physics, | D.Sc., Ph. D., F.C.S.

Technical notes: ca 104 × 67 mm (p 4). 31 lines, 20 = *ca* 55 mm. Leaf size *ca* 137 × 87 mm

Contents: Title (*1*), blank (*2*), introduction, signed January 1873 (*3–5*), advertisement (*6*), contents (*7–8*), text, continued (*9*) wanting from the photocopy examined ([*10–125*])

Binding: Apparently pale coloured paper wrapper. FC: mostly within a decorative frame with a ruled inner border and double-ruled outer border (J. N. HEARDER'S | [in open outlined gothic-revival script] **Guide to Sea Fishing** | AND THE | RIVERS OF SOUTH DEVON, | AND | DESCRIPTIVE CATALOGUE | OF HIS | [decorated initials *P, R, S*] Prize River and Sea | **FISHING TACKLE,** | CRICKET, | ARCHERY, CROQUET, | UMBRELLAS, PARASOLS, &c. | [rule] | MANUFACTORY: | 195, UNION STREET, 195, | PLYMOUTH. | SIXTH EDITION, CONSIDERABLY ENLARGED, | AND CONTAINING A MONTHLY TABLE OF | EDIBLE FISH "IN SEASON." | [below the frame] *Entered at Stationers's Hall.*). Inside FC: blank

Copy seen: HCLWL: F 5205 50.6 (photocopy of preliminaries only, the original copy rebound in a library binding)

Notes: Year of publication is taken as that appended to the introduction (p 5).

(d) *Seventh edition [1877]*

[L justified] Seventh Edition.] | THIS SUPERSEDES PREVIOUS EDITIONS. | [rule] | HEARDER & SON, | 195, UNION STREET, PLYMOUTH, 195, | *Correspondent of "The Field" and "Land and Water,"* | MANUFACTURERS OF | Prize River and Sea Fishing Tackle, | ARCHERY, CROQUET, | [in gothic-revival script] Umbrellas and Parasols; | CRICKET AND

FIVE BATS & BALLS, | *RACKETS, QUOITS, SKATES, &c.,* | [in open outlined display script] **MAGIC LANTERNS,** | DISSOLVING VIEWS. | [in gothic-revival script] **Philosophical Apparatus Makers and Electricians,** | [rule] | Plymouth : | R. White Stevens, Printer, 15 Parade.

Technical notes: ca 98 × 70 mm (p 4). 38 lines, 20 = *ca* 52 mm. Leaf size *ca* 115 × 81 mm

Contents: Title (*1*), blank (*2*), introduction, signed January 1877 (*3–5*), advertisement (*6*), contents (*7*), wanting from the photocopy examined ([8 ff]), text ([*9–117*])

Binding: Apparently pale coloured paper wrapper. FC: within a ruled frame with corner ornaments (HEARDER & SON'S | [in open outlined gothic-revival script] **Guide to Sea Fishing** | AND THE | **RIVERS OF SOUTH DEVON,** | AND | DESCRIPTIVE CATALOGUE | OF THEIR | *Prize River and Sea* | FISHING TACKLE, | CRICKET, ARCHERY, CROQUET, | UMBRELLAS, PARASOLS, &c. | [rule] | MANUFACTORY: | [in gothic-revival script] **195, Union Street, Plymouth, 195.** | [rule] | Seventh Edition, considerably enlarged. | *And containing a Monthly Table of* | EDIBLE FISH "IN SEASON." | [below the frame] *Entered at Stationers' Hall.*). Inside FC: blank

Copy seen: HCLWL: XF 5205 50.7 (photocopy of preliminaries only)

Notes: Printed by R White Stevens, Plymouth. Year of publication is inferred from that appended to the introduction (p 5).

(e) *Ninth edition [1885]*

[L justified] Ninth Edition. | THIS SUPERSEDES PREVIOUS EDITIONS. | [rule] | HEARDER & SON, | 195, UNION STREET, PLYMOUTH, 195, | *Correspondent of "The Field," and "Land & Water,"* | MANUFACTURERS OF | [in gothic-revival script with decorative initials *P, R, &, S, F, T*] **Prize River & Sea Fishing Tackle,** | ARCHERY, CROQUET, | UMBRELLAS AND PARASOLS, | DEALERS IN | CRICKET AND FIVES BATS AND BALLS, | *Lawn Tennis, Badminton, Rackets, Quoits,* | *Skates, &c,* | [in shaded display script] **MAGIC LANTERNS,** | DISSOLVING VIEWS. | Philosophical Apparatus Makers and Electricians, | [rule] | Plymouth : | Mansfield & Faull, Printers, Week Street.

Technical notes: ca 104 × 67 mm (p 4). 37 lines, 20 = *ca* 57 mm. Leaf size *ca* 119 × 85 mm

Contents: Title (*1*), heading only, 'MEMORANDUM.' (*2*), introduction, signed January 1885 (*3–5*), heading only, 'MEMORANDUM.' (*6*), contents (*7*), omitted from the photocopy examined ([8 ff]), text ([*9–121*])

Binding: Apparently pale coloured paper wrapper. FC: within a double-ruled frame with corner ornaments ([illustration of a row of prize medals surmounted by the royal warrant] | HEARDER & SON'S | ILLUSTRATED | [in gothic-revival script with decorated initials *G, S, F*] **Guide to Sea Fishing** | AND THE | RIVERS OF SOUTH DEVON, | AND | DESCRIPTIVE CATALOGUE | OF THEIR | PRIZE RIVER AND SEA | [in display script] *FISHING* ❖ *TACKLE,* | *Cricket, Archery, Croquet, Lawn Tennis,* | UMBRELLAS, PARASOLS, &c. | [rule] | MANUFACTORY: | 195, UNION STREET, PLYMOUTH, 195, | ESTABLISHED 1770. | [rule] | *Ninth Edition, considerably reduced prices, and con-* | *taining a Monthly Table of Edible Fish "in Season"* | [below the frame] Entered at Stationers' Hall.). Inside FC: blank

Copy seen: HCLWL: F 5205 50.9 (photocopy of preliminaries only, the original copy rebound in a library binding)

Notes: Printed by Mansfield & Faull, Plymouth. Year of publication is inferred from the signature to the introduction (p 5).

(f) *Twelfth edition [1890]*

[Front cover, mostly within a double-ruled frame, much of which is evidently wanting from the original of the photocopy examined]

[above the frame] ENTERED AT STATIONERS' HALL | [within a transverse panel, at L on one of two lines] ESTAB. | [*do*] 1770. | [centrally within a transverse panel, illustration of a row of prize medals surmounted by the royal warrant] | [within transverse panel, at R on one of two lines] ESTAB. | [*do*] 1770. | [in shaded display script] **HEARDER & SON'S** | ILLUSTRATED | [in display script] **Guide to Sea Fishing** | AND THE | [flourish] RIVERS OF SOUTH DEVON, [flourish] | AND DESCRIPTIVE CATALOGUE OF THEIR | PRIZE RIVER AND SEA FISHING TACKLE | *CRICKET, ARCHERY, CROQUET, LAWN TENNIS AND* | *ATHLETIC REQUISITES.* | [rule] | [‡] **5, UNION STREET, PLYMOUT** [‡] | [engraved illustration of a shore fishing scene] | [below the frame] J. H. KEYS, PRINTER, WHIMPLE STREET, PLYMOUTH

Technical notes: ca 103 × 75 mm (p 1). Variable line spacing. Leaf size *ca* 122 × 85 mm

Contents: Introductory address to customers (1), contents (2), text, continued (3), wanting from the photocopy examined ([4 ff])

Binding: Off-white paper, stitched, no endpapers. FC: printed as above. Inside FC: list of royal and titled customers and patrons. RC: wanting from the photocopy examined. Inside RC: wanting from the photocopy examined

Copy seen: HCLWL: F 5205 50.12 (photocopy of preliminaries only, the original copy rebound in a library binding)

Notes: Printed by JH Keys, Plymouth. This edition is identified as the twelfth in the introductory address (p 1). Approximate year of publication is taken from the HCLWL citation.

A48   MODERN OUT-DOOR AMUSEMENTS. [Anon]   *ca* 1867

MODERN | OUT-DOOR AMUSEMENTS | INCLUDING | SWIMMING— ARCHERY—PEDESTRIANISM—CRICKET—CROQUET | FOOTBALL— GOLF, | ETC. ETC. | [publisher's device in the form of a medallion incorporating a monogram] *F W* | LONDON: | FREDERICK WARNE AND CO., | BEDFORD STREET, COVENT GARDEN. | NEW YORK : SCRIBNER, WELFORD AND CO.

Formula: A⁴ B–M⁸ N⁴ [\$2 signed (–A1, 2)]. 96 leaves, pp *i–v* vi–viii, *1* 2–30 *31* 32–54 *55* 56–92 *93* 94–136 *137* 138–163 *164* 165–175 *176* 177–178 *179* 180–182 *183–184*

Technical notes: 120 × 71 mm (p 3). 44 lines, 20 = 54 mm. Leaf size 152 × 101 mm; thickness 0.12 mm; wove, unwatermarked, smooth, white

Contents: Title (*i*), TP verso (*ii*), preface (*iii*), blank (*iv*), contents (*v–viii*), text (1–178), index (*179–82*), advertisements (*183–184*)

Binding: Light yellowish Brown (76) cloth over stiff boards, sewn. There are advertisements on the facing pages of the front and rear endpapers. FC: in black (PRICE ONE SHILLING | [rule] | [in shaded display script] MODERN | OUT-DOOR | AMUSEMENTS | INCLUDING | SWIMMING—ARCHERY—PEDESTRIANISM— CRICKET | CROQUET—FOOTBALL—GOLF, ETC. ETC. | [publisher's device as on the TP] | LONDON: | FREDERICK WARNE & CO., | BEDFORD STREET,

STRAND.) within a double-ruled frame. RC: advertisement in black within a double-ruled frame. Spine: in black upwards (MODERN OUT-DOOR AMUSE-MENTS.—1s.) within a ruled frame

Copy seen: PC

Fingerprint: s.te ifng d,s. faar 3 1867Q

Notes: Printed by Savill, Edwards & Co, London, price 1/–. Year of publication is inferred from the text, which refers to alterations and revisions of the rules of cricket 'up to the date of February, 1866' (p 94).

The text includes a section entitled 'CROQUÊT' (pp *137–163*) which comprises nine chapters. Chapter V sets out a code of 21 rules, Ch VI comments on some of them. The fact that this code is identical, or virtually so, to that contained in *The Bijou Book of Out-door Amusements* (A37) strongly suggests common authorship. Hence it is thought that the section on croquet in the present work was written by J Wood.

1870

AA49 THE ALL ENGLAND CROQUET CLUB 1870.   1870
[The All England Croquet Club]

[Page *1*, within an ornamental frame]

[an emblem composed of two crossed mallets, a hoop, a ball, and a draped ribbon bearing the club name] | [in display script, swash *T, A, E*] THE ALL ENGLAND | [*do*, swash first C] CROQUET CLUB. | [the figures shaped to fit within a triangular orna-ment] 1870

Collation: A Z-fold leaflet. A single leaf with two folds divided into three panels, unnumbered [pp 1–6]

Technical: Area of letterpress: variable. Variable line spacing. Measurements of each folded panel: *ca* 129 × 72 mm

Contents: Title (*1*, panel 3 of side A), president, vice-president, and committee *etc* (*2*, side B), key plan showing position of the ground (*3–4*, side B), terms and conditions of membership *etc* (*5*, side A), subscription rates (*6*, side A)

Binding: None

Copy seen: PC (photocopy)

Fingerprint: Indeterminate

Notes: Printed anonymously.

A50 BYE LAWS AND REGULATIONS FOR THE MANAGEMENT   1870
OF PRIZE MEETINGS [and REGULATIONS FOR THE
MANAGEMENT OF PRIZE MEETINGS]. [The All England Croquet Club]

(a) **First edition (1870)*

[Page *1*]

ALL ENGLAND CROQUET CLUB. | [wavy line] | BYE LAWS, | AND | REGU-LATIONS | FOR THE | MANAGEMENT OF PRIZE MEETINGS. | [double rule] | LONDON: | HORACE COX, 346, STRAND, W.C. | [rule] | 1870.

Formula: Apparently [1⁸]. 8 leaves, pp *1–3* 4–6 *7* 8–14 *15–16*

Technical notes: 117 × 77 mm (p 11). 19 lines, 20 = 126 mm. Leaf size 154 × 102 mm; thickness 0.11 mm; laid, unwatermarked, smooth, white, all edges gilt

Contents: Title (*1*), name of printer (*2*), bye laws, numbered 1–6 with alphabetical sub-clauses (*3–6*), regulations for the management of prize meetings, numbered 1–20 (*7–14*), name of printer (*14*), blank (*15–16*)

Binding: Apparently none, perhaps sewn

Copy seen: BOD: 250 K 3 (19) (in a library binding)

Fingerprint: e.is ndhe e.nd Lome 3 1870A

Notes: Printed by Horace Cox, London.

(b) *1871 edition (1871)*

[Page *1*]

ALL ENGLAND CROQUET CLUB | **REGULATIONS** | FOR THE | MANAGE-MENT OF PRIZE MEETINGS. | [double rule] | LONDON : | HORACE COX, 346, STRAND, W.C. | [rule] | 1871.

Formula: Apparently [1¹²]. 12 leaves, pp *1–5* 6–12 *13–24*

Technical notes: 118 × 77 mm (p 10). 20 lines, 20 = 117 mm. Leaf size 152 × 92 mm; thickness 0.10 mm; wove, unwatermarked, smooth, white, all edges gilt

Contents: Title (*1*), name of printer (*2*), index (*3*), blank (*4*), text (*5–12*), name of printer (*12*), advertisements (*13–24*)

Binding: Apparently none, perhaps sewn

Copy seen: BOD: 250 K 10 (15) (in a library binding)

Fingerprint: 1110 edp- **n.s.** NOBA 3 1871A

Notes: Printed by Horace Cox, London. The text extends to 21 numbered regulations.

(c) *1873 edition (1873)*

[Page *1*]

ALL ENGLAND CROQUET CLUB | REGULATIONS | FOR THE | MANAGE-MENT OF PRIZE MEETINGS. | [double rule] | LONDON : | HORACE COX, 346, STRAND, W.C. | [rule] | 1873.

Formula: Apparently [1¹²]. 12 leaves, pp *1–5* 6–14 *15–24*

Technical notes: 116 × 77 mm (p 12). 20 lines, 20 = 117 mm. Leaf size 151 × 99 mm; thickness 0.11 mm; wove, unwatermarked, smooth, white, all edges gilt

Contents: Title (*1*), name of printer (*2*), index (*3*), blank (*4*), regulations, numbered 1–28 (*5–14*), name of printer (*14*), advertisements (*15–24*)

Binding: Apparently none, perhaps sewn

Copy seen: BOD: 268 c 498 (15) (in a library binding)

Fingerprint: 1413 s.de chne Lono 3 1873A

Notes: Printed by Horace Cox, London.

(d) *1875 edition (1875)*

[Page *1*]

ALL ENGLAND CROQUET CLUB | REGULATIONS | FOR THE | MANAGE-MENT OF PRIZE MEETINGS. | [double rule] | LONDON : | HORACE COX, 346, STRAND, W.C. | [rule] | 1875.

Formula: As that of (c)

Technical notes: 117 × 79 mm (p 12). 20 lines, 20 = 117 mm. Leaf size 149 × 99 mm; thickness 0.10 mm; wove, unwatermarked, smooth, white, all edges gilt

Contents: As those of (c)

Binding: Apparently none, perhaps sewn

Copy seen: BOD: 268 c 498 (16) (in a library binding)

Fingerprint: 1413 s.de chne Lono 3 1875A

Notes: Printed by Horace Cox, London.

A51   **CROQUET.**   1870

John B Lawreen (song writer) and Vincent Davis (composer)

[The FC]

[in a convex arc, in shaded script] **CROQUET,** | [coloured engraving within a framed panel, arched at top, illustrating a croquet party, 'Young De Bounce of the Blues' in pugilistic pose in the foreground, sundry players in the middle ground, and an imposing stately home in the background, signed 'Alfred Concanen'] | [centred] Young De Bounce of the Blues didnt like it at all, | [centred] For with my Partner he played as a rule, | [centred] So like knights of old we retired to a Wood, | [centred] And with our Mallets there fought a Duel." | [at L, on two lines, the writer's name below] *WRITTEN BY* **JOHN B. LAWREEN,** [device] [at R, on two lines, the composer's name below] *COMPOSED BY* **VINCENT DAVIS,** | *SUNG BY* | [in shaded script] **J. H. MILBURN.** | [at L, in artist's script] *ENT, STA, HALL,* [rule] [at R, in artist's script] *PRICE 3/-* | [the bottoms of the letters and any intended punctuation truncated from the copy examined] LONDON DUFF & STEWART 147 OXFORD STREET

Formula: Not ascertainable from the copy examined. 4 leaves including the cover, pp *i–ii*, 1–5 6

Technical notes: 288 (variable) × 195 mm. Leaf size 348 × 243 mm; thickness 0.13 mm; wove, unwatermarked, smooth, white

Contents: Cover, as above (*i*), blank (*ii*), song for voice and piano, in Tempo Schottische, 'A friend of mine ask'd me, one day if I'd go, To his snug little box out of town …' (1–5), blank (6)

Binding: None

Copy examined: PC (imperfect)

Fingerprint: Indeterminate

Notes: Printed by J & W Pearman, Castle Street East, price 3/–. Year of publication is inferred from an advertisement for this piece of sheet music which appeared in *The Queen* (17 September 1870).

This song was recorded privately in 1997 for reproduction at the Croquet Association Centenary Exhibition at the Wimbledon Lawn Tennis Museum, London.

A52   **THE LAWS OF CROQUET.**   1870

[The Committee of the General Conference of Croquet Clubs]

(a) *First edition (1870)*

THE | LAWS OF CROQUET | ADOPTED AT | THE GENERAL CONFERENCE OF | CROQUET CLUBS, | ON | JANUARY 19, 1870. | LONDON: | THOS. DE LA RUE AND CO. | [rule] | 1870.

Formula: [1⁶]. 6 leaves, pp *1–3* 4–10 *11–12*

Technical notes: 121 × 77 mm (p 4). 28 lines, 20 = 88 mm. Leaf size 155 × 106 mm; thickness 0.13 mm; laid, unwatermarked, smooth, white, all edges gilt

Contents: Title (*1*), TP verso (*2*), text (the laws of croquet) (*3–9*), text (suggestions and recommendations) (10), blank (*11–12*)

Binding: Light Yellow (86) semi-gloss card laminated on white paper, sewn, no spine or endpapers. FC: reproduction of the TP, printed in black within a ruled frame with corner ornaments. Inside FC: blank. RC: blank. Inside RC: blank

Copy seen: BL: 7919 d 35

Fingerprint: bynd n.en keck llt. C 1870A [all four groups taken from p *3*]

Notes: Issued apparently during the week of 17 April 1870, printed by Thomas De La Rue and Co, London, price 6d. According to *The Field* (11 November 1871, p 403), 10000 copies were printed, of which 3000 were cancelled on the publication of the second (1871) edition.

Authorship vested formally in the Committee. The draft was compiled by RCA Prior and J Riky, considered by the Committee clause by clause, and finally edited by McLaughlin and WJ Whitmore. Copyright, assigned initially to the AECC and NCC jointly in equal shares on their undertaking to fund the publication, devolved solely on the AECC when the two clubs merged in 1871.

The text consists principally of a code of 26 numbered laws which became known as the 'Conference Code' or 'Conference Laws'. As subsequently revised from time to time, the code was widely accepted in the UK until the UAECA issued its first official code of laws (A100a) in 1897.

Reviews: *The Field* (22 January 1870, p 71), *ibid* (29 January 1870, pp 91–2), *ibid* (9 July 1870, p 23), *Land and Water* (7 May 1870, p 330), *ibid* (14 May 1870, p 348), *The Queen* (5 February, 1870, p 86), *The Westminster Papers* (2 May 1870, pp 11–12).

(b) *Second edition (1871)*

[Page *1*]

THE | LAWS OF CROQUET | ADOPTED AT | THE GENERAL CONFERENCE OF | CROQUET CLUBS | ON | JANUARY 19, 1870. | REVISED IN 1871. | LONDON: | THOS. DE LA RUE AND CO. | [rule] | 1871.

Formula: [1¹²]. 12 leaves, pp *1–3* 4–6 *7* 8–11 *12–13* 14–24

Technical notes: 121 × 77 mm (p 14). 27 lines, 20 = 89 mm. Leaf size 155 × 106 mm; thickness 0.10 mm; wove, unwatermarked, smooth, white, all edges gilt

Contents: Title (*1*), name of printer (*2*), index (*3–4*), preface (*5–6*), text (recommendations) (*7–11*), text (definitions) (*12*), text (the laws of croquet) (*13–24*)

Binding: Apparently none, perhaps sewn

Copy seen: BOD: 250 k 10 (14) (in a library binding)

Fingerprint: 1616 n.d, y,ut ro10 3 1871A

Notes: Issued apparently during the week commenced 16 April 1871, printed by Thomas De La Rue and Co, London. According to *The Field* (15 July 1871, p 45), the first impression of 5000 copies was 'exhausted in a very few days'.

This edition was revised by a committee consisting of C Lane (chairman), S Maddock, J Walsh, J Hale, C Dalton, R Prior, P Smith, H Wiggin, and H Jones (hon sec). The authority of the committee was called into question at the time, notably by W Whitmore and the GNCC.

The text is revised and extended, now running to 41 numbered laws, reflecting the rapid pace of development of the game. In particular, the laws relating to playing out of turn and with the wrong ball are further developed.

Reviews: *The Field* (*op cit*), *The Queen* (23 December 1871, p 422), *The Westminster Papers* (1 June 1871, pp 33–5), *ibid* (2 October 1871, pp 107–9).

(c) *Second edition*, addenda *(1872)*

Not seen. In an announcement carried by *The Westminster Papers* (1 August 1872, pp 59–60), signed by G Muntz, P Smith, and C Dicking — members of the revising committee — it is stated that 'the revised laws have been printed as "addenda" to the previously existing code of laws ... with the following paragraph prefixed to them:—

 "Addenda et corrigenda, passed in February 1872, by the votes of the Secretaries of the various Croquet Clubs, and accepted by the Commitee of the All England Croquet Club on the 15th February 1872."

'We are informed that about 1800 copies of the book have been sold in this form. . . .'

(d) *Third edition, preliminary issue (1872)*

Not seen. The announcement quoted at (c) above continues, 'We are aware that within the last few weeks a new edition of the Laws of Croquet has been published, in which the revised laws have been properly incorporated in the Code. . . .'

(e) *Judd and Glass edition [1872]*

Not seen. According to D Prichard (A208, p 22), 'Two years later [after publication of the first editon] Walter [Whitmore] wrote a revised version'.

Notes: The bibliography in Prichard's *The History of Croquet* (*op cit*) cites Judd and Glass as the publishers. Year of publication is given as 1870. This is inconsistent with Prichard's own account (above) and unlikely because Whitmore publicly acknowledged the Committee's copyright for the 1870 season (though he rejected its subsequent validity).

(f) *Third edition [1873]*

Not seen. This edition was apparently issued (belatedly) in May 1873. According to *The Queen* (9 May 1874, p 394), 3000 copies were sold in 1873.

The text includes several revisions to the second edition (b), notably concerning pegging-out and playing out of turn, with the wrong ball, or for a wrong point. It is not known whether or not it departs from (d).

(g) *First American edition (1878)*

THE | LAWS OF CROQUET. | ADOPTED AT | The General Conference of Croquet Clubs, | IN ENGLAND. | REVISED BY THE VOTES OF THE CLUB SECRETARIES, AND CON- | TAINING THE CORRIGENDA AUTHORIZED BY THE VOTES | OF THE CLUB SECRETARIES. | [rule] | FIRST AMERICAN EDITION. | [rule] | BOSTON: | NOYES, SNOW AND COMPANY. | 1878.

Formula: [1¹²]. 12 leaves, pp *1–3* 4–23 *24*

Technical notes: 118 × 77 mm (p 16). 29 lines, 20 = 82 mm. Leaf size 165 × 110 mm; thickness 0.14 mm; wove, unwatermarked, smooth, white

Contents: Title (*1*), TP verso (*2*), index (*3–4*), preface to the American edition, dated 1878 (*5*), preface to the English edition (*6*), text (*7–23*)

Binding: Light greyish yellowish Brown (79) light card, glued to the fold of the outer sheet, the covers having a greyish greenish Yellow (105) semi-gloss coating, printed in black, sewn, no spine or endpapers. FC: within a double-ruled frame ([in shaded script, L justified] **THE LAWS** | OF | [in shaded script, the letter C set on a decorative shield] CROQUET. | [vignette, engraved illustration of a boxed croquet set] | ADOPTED AT | The General Conference of Croquet Clubs, in England. | [rule] | FIRST AMERICAN EDITION. | [rule] | BOSTON: | NOYES, SNOW & COMPANY. | 1878.). Inside FC: blank. RC: blank. Inside RC: blank

Copy seen: HPC: GV933 L3 1878 CROQ

Fingerprint: 1818 n.ng p.ot thth 7 1878A

Notes: Printed anonymously. Comments made in the preface to this (American) edition with regard to the inclusion of *addenda* and *corrigenda* suggest that it was reprinted from the third (English) edition (f).

(h) *De La Rue 1894 edition (1894)*

THE | LAWS OF CROQUET | ADOPTED AT | THE GENERAL CONFERENCE OF | CROQUET CLUBS IN 1870 | REVISED AND CORRECTED | BY THE | CLUB SECRETARIES IN 1872 AND 1873 | *NOW RE-PUBLISHED, WITH AN ADDITIONAL* | *SETTING, ETC.* | LONDON: | THOS. DE LA RUE AND CO. | [rule] | 1894

Formula: 1^{12} [1_2 signed 'A2', 1_5 signed 'A*']. 12 leaves, pp *1–3* 4 5 *6–11* *12–13* 14–23 *24*

Technical notes: 122 × 76 mm (p 20). 28 lines, 20 = 89 mm. Leaf size 162 × 104 mm; thickness 0.09 mm; wove, unwatermarked, smooth, white, all edges gilt

Contents: Title (*1*), TP verso (*2*), index (*3–4*), text (recommendations) (*5–11*), text (definitions) (*12*), the laws of croquet, numbered 1–37 (*13–23*), name of printer (*23*), advertisement (*24*)

Binding: Light greenish Blue (172) paper laminated on white paper, sewn, no spine or endpapers. FC: reproduction of the TP, and supplementary matter ([at L:] ENT. STA. HALL.] [at R:] [PRICE SIXPENCE.) printed in black within a double-ruled frame, the outer frame in bold, with flourishes inside the corners. Inside FC: blank. RC: blank. Inside RC: blank

Copy seen: BL: 7919 d 36

Fingerprint: 1717 y.or g;ed plag 3 1894A

Notes: Printed by Thomas De La Rue and Co, London, price 6d.

1871

A53   **HINTS ON CROQUET. 'OMF, Cantab'**   1871

[Within a ruled frame]

HINTS ON CROQUET. | BY | O. M. F., CANTAB. | LONDON: JAQUES AND SON, | 102, HATTON GARDEN.

Formula: Apparently [$1–3^8$], including the front and rear endpapers. 28 leaves including the front and rear endpapers, pp *i–iv*, *1–5* 6–50 *51–52*

Technical notes: *ca* 121 × 77 mm (p 6). 27 lines, 20 = *ca* 91 mm. Leaf size *ca* 166 × 105 mm

Contents: Apparently glued to the FC (*i*), blank (*ii*), advertisement (*iii*), blank (*iv*), title (*1*), TP verso (*2*), preface, signed 'O. M. F.', 1871 (*3*), blank (*4*), text (*5–51*), apparently glued to the RC (*52*)

Binding: Apparently printed on pale coloured sand grain cloth or paper, sewn. The endpapers are apparently printed (see *Contents* above). FC: printed, save the last

line, within a double-ruled frame, the outer frame in bold, with corner ornaments
(HINTS ON CROQUET | BY | O. M. F., CANTAB | [engraved illustrative diagram of
mallet head and balls set for a croquet stroke] | LONDON, JAQUES AND SON, |
102, HATTON GARDEN | [below the frame] ONE SHILLING AND SIXPENCE).
RC: wanting from the photocopy examined. Spine: wanting from the photocopy
examined

Copy seen: PC (imperfect photocopy)

Fingerprint: 1.F. e.ns meof st*W 3 1871A [the third character in group 4 is
printed as an asterisk]

Notes: Printed anonymously, price 1/6.

Reviews: *The Field* (8 July 1871, p 33), *The Westminster Papers* (1 January 1872,
pp 168–9).

1872

A54   **THE BOOK OF CROQUET: ITS TACTICS, LAWS, & MODE**   [1872]
OF PLAY. Arthur Lillie

(a) *First edition [1872]*

[Within a ruled frame]

THE | BOOK OF CROQUET: | *Its Tactics, Laws, & Mode of Play.* | BY | ARTHUR
LILLIE, | WINNER OF THE ALL COMERS' FIRST PRIZE, ALL ENGLAND | CROQUET
CLUB, 1871. | [rule] | "Why hath thy queen | Summoned me hither to this short-
grassed green?" | [at R] *The Tempest.* | [rule] | LONDON: | JAQUES AND SON,
102, HATTON GARDEN. | [rule] | [*ALL RIGHTS RESERVED*]

Formula: A⁸ B–C⁸ [B signed 'B', 'B2'; C signed 'C', 'C2']. 24 leaves, pp *1–5* 6–10
11–12 13–14 *15–16* 17–24 *25* 26–39 *40–41* 42–46 *47–48*

Technical notes: 165 × 97 mm (p 9). 40 lines, 20 = 84 mm. Leaf size 214 × 136 mm;
thickness 0.11 mm; wove, unwatermarked, smooth, white

Contents: Blank (*1*), engraved illustration of a croquet ground, signed 'W *THOMAS*'
(*2*), title (*3*), TP verso (*4*), text, continued (*5–10*), blank (*11*), engraved illustration,
signed 'W *THOMAS*' (*12*), text, continued (*13–14*), engraved illustration, signed
'W *THOMAS*' (*15*), blank (*16*), text, concluded (*17–46*), advertisements (*47–48*)

Binding: Light yellowish Green (135) semi-gloss paper, sewn. There are advertisements on all pages of the endpapers save the front pastedown. FC: printed in black
within a double-ruled frame, the outer frame in bold ([engraved illustration of two
players, a man and a woman, both fashionably dressed, in conversation] | THE |
BOOK OF CROQUET. | [rule] | BY ARTHUR LILLIE. | [rule] | LONDON : |
JAQUES AND SON, 102, HATTON GARDEN. | [*All Rights reserved.*]). RC:
blank. Spine: wanting from the copy examined

Copy seen: BL: 7919 bb 37 (in a library binding)

Fingerprint: nghe t.an i-ry plov 7 1872Q

Notes: Published early in 1872; printed by Edmund Evans, London. The text of this
issue is apparently identical to that of (b); it would appear to differ only in the binding and in the arrangement of blank pages and pages given to advertising. There is
no known evidence as to which preceded the other.

It is conjectured that this work was intended primarily for distribution with the
publisher's croquet equipment, not for separate sale. The text includes a code of
20 laws.

Reviews: *The Field* (13 April 1872, p 335), *The Westminster Papers* (1 June 1872, pp 31–32).

(b) *First edition, variant [1872]*

[The TP as that of (a)]

Formula: Not ascertainable from the copy examined [p 17 signed 'B', p 19 signed 'B2', p 33 signed 'C', p 35 signed 'C2']. 27 leaves including the front and rear paste-downs, pp *1–5* 6–10 *11–12* 13–14 *15–16* 17–24 25 26–39 *40–41* 42–46 *47–54*

Technical notes: 166 × 98 mm (p 9). 40 lines, 20 = 84 mm. Leaf size 214 × 136 mm; thickness 0.11 mm; wove, unwatermarked, smooth, white

Contents: Glued to the FC (*1*), engraved illustration of a croquet ground, signed 'W THOMAS' (*2*), title (*3*), TP verso (*4*), text, continued (*5–10*), blank (*11*), engraved illustration, signed 'W THOMAS' (*12*), text, continued (*13–14*), engraved illustration, signed 'W THOMAS' (*15*), blank (*16*), text, concluded (*17–46*), advertisements (*47–53*), glued to the RC (*54*)

Binding: Light yellowish Green (135) semi-gloss paper, sewn, no separate end-papers. FC: as that of (a). RC: blank. Spine: blank

Copy seen: PC (rebound)

Fingerprint: As that of (a)

Notes: Printed by Edmund Evans, London. This issue apparently differs from (a) only in its construction and in the addition of new advertising matter. See also *Notes* to (a).

(c) *Revised issue [1873]*

[Within a ruled frame]

THE | BOOK OF CROQUET: | *Its Tactics, Laws, & Mode of Play.* | BY | ARTHUR LILLIE, | Champion, Grand National Croquet Club, 1872, and Winner of the All Comers' | First Prize, All England Croquet Club, 1871. | [rule] | "Why hath thy queen | Summoned me hither to this short-grassed green?" | [at R] *The Tempest.* | [rule] | REVISED EDITION. | LONDON: | JAQUES AND SON, 102, HATTON GARDEN. | [rule] | [*ALL RIGHTS RESERVED*]

Formula: A⁸ B–C⁸ D⁴ [B signed 'B1', 'B2'; C signed 'C1', 'C2']. 28 leaves including the front and rear endpapers, pp *1–5* 6–12 *13–14* 15–16 *17–18* 19–25 26 27–40 *41 42 43* 44–48 *49–56*

Technical notes: 165 × 97 mm (p 6). 40 lines, 20 = 84 mm. Leaf size 212 × 136 mm; thickness 0.11 mm; wove, unwatermarked, smooth, white

Contents: Glued to the FC (*1*), engraved illustration of a croquet ground, signed 'W THOMAS' (*2*), title (*3*), TP verso (*4*), text, continued (*5–12*), engraved illustration, signed 'W THOMAS' (*13*), blank (*14*), text, continued (*15–16*), engraved illustration, signed 'W THOMAS' (*17*), blank (*18*), text, concluded (*19–48*), advertisements (*49–54*), blank (*55*), glued to the RC (*56*)

Binding: Very light Purple (221) semi-gloss card, glued to the folds of the sections, sewn, no separate endpapers. FC: printed in black within a double-ruled frame, the outer frame in bold ([engraved illustration of two players, a man and a woman, both fashionably dressed, in conversation] | THE | **BOOK OF CROQUET.** | BY | ARTHUR LILLIE. | [rule] | NEW EDITION. | [rule] | LONDON: | JAQUES AND SON, 102, HATTON GARDEN. | [*All Rights reserved.*]). RC: blank. Spine: blank

Copy seen: PC (imperfect)

Fingerprint: nghe ckle d?re anTh C 1873Q [groups 1–4 taken from pp 5, 15, 19, 20 respectively]

Notes: Printed by Edmund Evans, London. Approximate year of publication is inferred from the contents of the supplementary advertisements.

The text, including a code of 20 laws, and illustrations depart little from those of (a).

(d) *Cloth binding [1874]*

Not seen. In an MS memorandum from Jaques to Longmans dated 8 July 1874, now held by the RUL, the publishers note that they have discontinued a new edition of this work which is bound in cloth. No copy of this issue is known to have survived.

(e) *Second (abridged) edition [1895]*

[The FC]

[engraved illustration of two players, a man and a woman, both fashionably dressed, in conversation] | THE | **BOOK OF CROQUET.** | BY ARTHUR LILLIE. | [rule] | NEW EDITION. | [rule] | LONDON: | JAQUES AND SON, 102, HATTON GARDEN. | [*All Rights reserved.*]

Formula: [1⁶]. 6 leaves including the front and rear pastedowns, pp *i–ii*, 1–9 *10*

Technical notes: ca 165 × 97 mm (p 6). 39 lines, 20 = *ca* 87 mm. Leaf size *ca* 213 × 141 mm

Contents: Glued to the FC (*i*), advertisement (*ii*), text (1–9), advertisement (9), glued to the RC (*10*)

Binding: Apparently pale coloured paper, sewn, no spine or endpapers. FC: printed within a double-ruled frame (as above). RC: blank

Copy seen: PC (photocopy)

Fingerprint: t.so one. s,en nd1. C 1895Q [group 1 taken from p 1, groups 2–4 taken from p 9]

Notes: Printed anonymously. Year of publication is inferred from an advertisement in *The Association Laws of Croquet* (A95, p 9), 'now ready'. That work is known to have been published in 1895.

The text, which is largely rewritten, is confined to a brief introduction devoted to hoop settings (referred to as 'arches'), followed by a code of 23 laws.

AA55   LE CERCLE: THE "QUEEN OF THE SUMMER GAMES".   [1872]
[DB Brooks & Bro]

[Page *1*, within a double-ruled frame, the outer frame in bold]

LE CERCLE, | THE "QUEEN OF THE SUMMER GAMES." | [engraved illustration of Le Cercle in play] | [in open outlined and shaded script] **Brooks' Cue Alleys, Carom Croquet Boards,** | PARLOR & FIELD RING QUOITS, PARLOR BILLIARD TABLES, FIELD | AND PARLOR CROQUET, INDIAN CLUBS—ALL WEIGHTS. | **D. B. BROOKS & BRO.,** | Manufacturers of Field and Parlor Games, | [in solid and outlined script] 55 *Washington Street,* - *Boston, Mass.*

Formula: [1¹]. 1 leaf, unnumbered [pp 1–2]

Technical notes: 117 × 96 mm (p *1*, centred). Variable line spacing. Leaf size 142 × 117 mm; thickness 0.11 mm; wove, unwatermarked, smooth, wite

Contents: Advertisement for Le Cercle *etc* (1), advertisement for Henry F Miller pianos (2)

Binding: None

Copy seen: PC

Fingerprint: s.s, ., S. LDs, ."E, C 1872Q [all four groups taken from p *1*]

Notes: Printed anonymously. Year of publication is inferred from an anonymous annotation on the copy examined.

Though played with mallets, balls, and hoops, Le Cercle bore little resemblance to croquet. The implements used in the game, which was probably introduced in 1870, were the subject of a US patent (19 October 1869, No 95969) by Charles B Barlow of Portsmouth, NH.

**A56   NOTES ON CROQUET: AND SOME ANCIENT BAT AND   1872
       BALL GAMES RELATED TO IT. RCA Prior**

NOTES ON CROQUET: | AND SOME | ANCIENT BAT AND BALL GAMES RELATED | TO IT. | BY | R. C. A. PRIOR, M.D., F.L.S. | AUTHOR OF "POPULAR NAMES OF BRITISH PLANTS," AND TRANSLATOR OF ANCIENT DANISH BALLADS. | [publisher's device, consisting of a medallion incorporating a monogram] | WILLIAMS AND NORGATE, | 14, HENRIETTA STREET, COVENT GARDEN, LONDON; | AND | 20, SOUTH FREDERICK STREET, EDINBURGH. | 1872.

Formula: A–C^8 D^4 χ^2 [$2 signed (–A1, χ1, 2)]. 30 leaves, pp *1–3 4–60*

Technical notes: 158 × 94 mm (p *4*). 34 lines, 20 = 93 mm. Leaf size 216 × 136 mm; thickness 0.14 mm; wove, unwatermarked, smooth, white. Five numbered inset plates consisting of engraved illustrations face pp *1, 19, 21, 29, 36*

Contents: Title (*1*), TP verso (*2*), text (*3–58*), name of printer (*58*), list of illustrations (*59*), blank (*60*)

Binding: Strong reddish Purple (237) sand grain cloth over stiff boards, sewn. The facing pages of the endpapers are coloured light Yellow (86). FC: the title *etc* ([in display script] NOTES ON CROQUET | BY | *R. C. A. Prior*) gold-blocked centrally within inner and outer frames blocked in black, the inner frame double-ruled with rounded corners, the outer frame double-ruled with small rosettes in the corners. RC: blind-stamped inner and outer frames of the same patterns as those on the FC. Spine: blank

Copy seen: PC (imperfect)

Fingerprint: ngom ryd, 0.*of* enpe 3 1872A

Notes: Printed by Gilbert and Rivington, London.

AA57   [NUMERICAL CROQUET]. [Lewis Carroll]   [1872]

Not seen. On 24 October 1872 the author recorded in his diary that he had sent the rules of a game he called 'numerical croquet' (a mental version of the game) to Gwendolen Cecil. The author's original manuscript is not known to have survived.

An MS which describes a revised version of this game, *Arithmetical Croquet*, is here listed as AA89a.

**AA58   THE GRAND NATIONAL CROQUET CLUB: BYE-LAWS   [1872]
        AND REGULATIONS OF PLAY. [Anon]**

[Page *1*, within a florid engraved frame]

THE GRAND | [in display script] NATIONAL | [in gothic-revival script, swash C, C] **Croquet Club.** | [swelled rule] | BYE-LAWS AND REGULATIONS | OF PLAY.

Formula: [1²]. 2 leaves, unnumbered [pp 1–4]

Technical notes: ca 106 × 64 mm (p *2*). 51 lines, 20 = *ca* 42 mm. Leaf size *ca* 133 × 89 mm

Contents: Title (p *1*), text (*2–3*), decorative device (p *4*)

Binding: One sheet with a single fold, apparently unbound

Copy seen: PC (photocopy)

Fingerprint: y.ce eehe asat ise- C 1872Q [all four groups taken from p *3*]

Notes: Printed anonymously. Year of publication is inferred from the text.

1873

A59   **CROQUET: AS PLAYED BY THE PHILADELPHIA CROQUET**   1873
CLUB. [Philadelphia Croquet Club]

[in shaded open script] **CROQUET** | AS PLAYED BY THE | [in gothic-revival script] Philadelphia Croquet Club. | [rule] | PHILADELPHIA: | CLAXTON, REMSEN & HAFFELFINGER. | 1873.)

Formula: Not ascertainable from the copy examined. [P 5 signed '1*', p 13 signed '2', p 17 signed '2*']. 13 leaves, pp *i–ii*, *1–5 6–7 8–9 10–19 20–24*

Technical notes: 101 × 65 mm (p *10*). 17 lines, 20 = 115 mm variable. Leaf size 173 × 104 mm

Contents: Blank (*i*), diagram of court (*ii*), title (*1*), TP verso (*2*), publisher's notice (*3*), blank (*4*), text, continued (*5–7*), blank (*8*), text, concluded (*9–19*), blank (*20*), advertisements (*21–23*), blank (*24*)

Binding: Light greenish Blue (172) paper or card, sewn, no spine or endpapers. FC: printed within a double-ruled frame, the outer frame in bold (CROQUET | AS PLAYED BY THE | [in gothic-revival script] Philadelphia Croquet Club. | [rule] | PHILADELPHIA: | CLAXTON, REMSEN & HAFFELFINGER, | 624, 626, and 628 MARKET STREET. | 1873.). RC: blank

Copy seen: LOC: GV935 P54 (photocopy, wanting the inside pages of the wrapper, the original copy rebound in library covers)

Fingerprint: e.is lsa- onch AbAR 3 1873A

Notes: Printed by Collins. The text includes a code of rules comprising 21 articles, numbered I–XXI.

1874

A60   **THE COMPLETE CROQUET-PLAYER. James Dunbar Heath**   1874

(a) *First edition (1874)*

THE COMPLETE | CROQUET-PLAYER | BY | JAMES DUNBAR HEATH | CHAMPION, 1873 | WITH ILLUSTRATIONS | LONDON | GEORGE ROUTLEDGE AND SONS | THE BROADWAY, LUDGATE | 1874 | [*All rights reserved*]

Formula: B–G⁸ [$2 signed (–B1)]. 48 leaves, pp *i–iii* iv *v* vi, 7 *8–11 12 13–48 49 50–84 85 86–96*

Technical notes: 133 × 77 mm (p *9*). 34 lines, 20 = 79 mm. Leaf size 160 × 99 mm; thickness 0.11 mm; wove, unwatermarked, smooth, white; eight inset plates, apparently in four colours, face pp 60, 64, 67, 69, 70, 72, 73, 74

Contents: Title (*i*), TP verso (*ii*), preface, dated March 1874 (*iii–*iv), contents (*v–*vi), text (*7–96*), name of printer (*96*)

Binding: Pale Yellow (89) paper over light boards, sewn. There are advertisements on all pages of the endpapers. FC: an elaborate design printed in moderate Yellow Green (120) and black, featuring a chequer pattern of flowers, a row of eight balls centred in hoops, and lettering in various scripts within five horizontal oblong panels (**THE COMPLETE** | Croquet | Player | **BY JAMES D. HEATH** | CHAMPION, 1873 | **GEORGE ROUTLEDGE AND SONS.**). RC: advertisement in black. Spine: in black upwards (THE COMPLETE CROQUET PLAYER.)

Copy seen: PC

Fingerprint: ves. n.ur B.ay *Cure* 3 1874A

Notes: Printed by Bradbury, Agnew, & Co, London.

(b) *1875 issue (1875)*

THE COMPLETE | CROQUET-PLAYER | BY | JAMES DUNBAR HEATH | CHAMPION, 1873 AND 1874 | WITH ILLUSTRATIONS | [in gothic-revival script] New and Revised Edition | LONDON | GEORGE ROUTLEDGE AND SONS | THE BROADWAY, LUDGATE | 1875 | [*All rights reserved*]

Formula: B–G[8] [$2 signed (–B1)]. 48 leaves, pp *i–v* vi, 7 8–11 *12* 13–84 85 86–96

Technical notes: 132 × 76 mm (p 8). 34 lines, 20 = 78 mm. Leaf size 163 × 102 mm; thickness 0.10 mm; wove, unwatermarked, smooth, white; eight inset plates, in four colours, face pp 60, 64, 67, 69, 70, 72, 73, 74

Contents: Title (*i*), TP verso (*ii*), preface (*iii*), preface to new edition, dated March 1875 (*iv*), contents (*v–vi*), text (*7–96*), name of printer (*96*)

Binding: Pale Yellow (89) paper over stiff boards, sewn. There are advertisements on all pages of the endpapers. FC: an elaborate design printed in deep Yellow Green (118) and black, featuring a chequer pattern of flowers, a row of eight balls centred in hoops, and lettering in various scripts within five horizontal oblong panels (**THE COMPLETE** | Croquet | Player | **BY JAMES D. HEATH** | CHAMPION, 1873 and 1874. | **GEORGE ROUTLEDGE AND SONS**). RC: advertisement in black. Spine: in black upwards (THE COMPLETE CROQUET PLAYER)

Copy seen: PC (imperfect)

Fingerprint: 4.k. n.ur B.ay *Cure* 3 1875A

Notes: Printed by Bradbury, Agnew, & Co, London.

The plates and almost all of the text are reprinted without alteration. The only departures from (a) appear to be the addition of a new preface, a few minor revisions and excisions, and the addition of the names of champions and prize winners for 1874.

(c) *Third edition (1896)*

THE "OVAL" SERIES | THE COMPLETE | CROQUET-PLAYER | BY | JAMES DUNBAR HEATH | CHAMPION, 1873 AND 1874 | WITH ILLUSTRATIONS | [in gothic-revival script] New and Revised Edition | LONDON | GEORGE ROUTLEDGE AND SONS, Limited | BROADWAY, LUDGATE HILL | MANCHESTER AND NEW YORK | 1896 | [*All rights reserved*]

Formula: B–G[8] [$2 signed (–B1)]. 48 leaves, pp *1–3* 4 5 6 *7* 8–11 *12* 13–84 85 86–96

Technical notes: 132 × 76 mm (p 8). 34 lines, 20 = 78 mm. Leaf size 179 × 121 mm; thickness 0.14 mm; wove, unwatermarked, smooth, white; eight inset plates in four colours face pp 60, 64, 67, 69, 70, 72, 73, 74

Contents: Title (*1*), advertisement (*2*), preface to new edition (*3–4*), contents (*5–6*), text (*7–96*)

Binding: (1) Greyish olive Green (127) cloth over light boards, sewn. FC: printed in black, vivid reddish Orange (34), and light Grey (264) ([black, in artist's script] THE COMPLETE | CROQUET PLAYER | [drawing of a man and woman on court, outlined in black with Orange and Grey infilling] | [black, in artist's script] JAMES DUNBAR HEATH). RC: blank. Spine: in black downwards, in the same script as that on the FC (THE COMPLETE CROQUET PLAYER). (2) As that of (1) save for the background colour of the covers, in light greyish yellowish Brown (79)

Copies seen: PC (2)

Fingerprint: toer n.ur B.ay *Cure* 3 1896A

Notes: Printed by Bradbury, Agnew, & Co, London. The 1896 edition is referred to as the third edition in a preface (p iii) to (d).

The text departs from that of (b) on pp 47, 92 ff. The main variations relate to more recent revisions of the 'Conference Code', other publications, details of croquet clubs, champions, and prize winners.

(d) *Fourth edition (1904)*

THE "OVAL" SERIES | THE COMPLETE | CROQUET-PLAYER | BY | JAMES DUNBAR HEATH | (CHAMPION, 1873 AND 1874) | NEW EDITION REVISED BY | M. A. SAFFERY | *Member of the Croquet Association* | LONDON | GEORGE ROUTLEDGE AND SONS, LIMITED | BROADWAY HOUSE, LUDGATE HILL | NEW YORK : E. P. DUTTON & CO.

Formula: π^4 A–F^8 χ1 G^6 H^{16} [\$1 signed (–π1, χ1, H1)]. 75 leaves, pp *i–ii* iii–viii, *1* 2–110, *1* 2–26 27 28–30 *31* 32 [= 150]

Technical notes: 132 × 84 mm (p 3). 30 lines, 20 = 88 mm. Leaf size 182 × 118 mm. All gatherings other than H^{16}: thickness 0.15 mm, wove, unwatermarked, rough, white. Gathering H^{16}: thickness 0.08 mm, wove, unwatermarked, smooth, white. Eight inset plates in four colours face pp *i*, 63, 66, 68, 70, 72, 73, 74

Contents: Title (*i*), advertisement (*ii*), extracts from the preface to the third edition (1896) (iii–iv), preface to the new edition, signed 'A. S.' (v–vi), contents (vii–viii), text (*1*–110), name of printer (110), advertisements (*1*–32)

Binding: Vivid Red (11) cloth over light boards, sewn. FC: printed in black, greyish Brown (61), and light greyish yellowish Brown (79) ([black, in artist's script] THE COMPLETE | CROQUET PLAYER | [drawing of a man and woman on court, outlined in black with greyish Brown and light greyish yellowish Brown infilling] | [black, in artist's script] JAMES DUNBAR HEATH). RC: blank. Spine: in black downwards, in the same script as that on the FC (THE COMPLETE CROQUET PLAYER)

Copy seen: PC

Fingerprint: y,us asll r.he tuNo 3 1904A

Notes: Printed by Cowan & Co, Perth, price 1/–. Year of publication is taken from the advertisement on p 20 of the advertising section.

Though much of Heath's original text and illustrations (including the plates) remain unaltered, this edition is extensively revised and updated. All the letterpress is reset, some of the plates are relocated in relation to the text, and there are a new preface and two new appendices. Routledge added a substantial advertising section.

(e) *Fourth edition, 1910 issue [1910]*

THE "OVAL" SERIES | THE COMPLETE | CROQUET-PLAYER | BY | JAMES DUNBAR HEATH | (CHAMPION, 1873 AND 1874) | NEW EDITION REVISED BY | H. A. SAFFERY | *Member of the Croquet Association* | LONDON | GEORGE

ROUTLEDGE AND SONS, Limited | BROADWAY HOUSE, LUDGATE HILL | New York : E. P. DUTTON & CO.

Formula: π⁴ A–G⁸ [$1 signed (–π1)]. 60 leaves, pp *i–vi* vii–viii, *1* 2–60 [61–62] 63–111

Technical notes: 131 × 84 mm (p 3). 30 lines, 20 = 87 mm. Leaf size 181 × 119 mm; thickness 0.18 mm, wove, unwatermarked, rough, white. Eight inset plates in four colours face pp *i* ('*To face p 50*'), 36 ('*To face page 66*'), 63, 66, 68, 70, 72, 73, 74

Contents: Blank (*i–ii*), half-title (*iii*), advertisement (*iv*), title (*v*), blank (*vi*), contents (vii–viii), text, continued (*1–60*), wanting from the copy examined ([61–62]), text, concluded (63–111), name of printer (111), blank (*112*)

Binding: Vivid Red (11) cloth over light boards, sewn. FC: printed in black, light greyish Brown (60), and pale yellowish Pink (31) ([black, in artist's script] The Complete | Croquet Player | [drawing of a man and woman on court, outlined in black with Brown and Pink infilling] | [black, in artist's script] James Dunbar Heath). RC: blank. Spine: in black downwards, in the same script as that on the FC (The Complete Croquet Player)

Copy seen: PC (wanting pp [61–62])

Fingerprint: 3837 att. r.he tuNo 3 1910Q

Notes: Printed by The Edinburgh Press, price 1/–. Year of publication is inferred from the lists of championship winners given on pp 109–10.

The text is substantially identical to that of (d) but is updated, notably having regard to the introduction of the B baulk area in 1910 (pp 58–78) and to extend the lists of championship winners. The prefaces and supplementary advertisements in (d) are omitted.

This issue is flawed by irregularities in the numbering and location of the inset plates, as may be seen in the foregoing *technical notes*. The initials of Saffery, the editor, given on the TP are also at variance with (d). Neither MA Saffery nor HA Saffery appear to have been recorded as Associates of the CA.

**A61   THE CROQUET MANUAL OF COMPLETE INSTRUCTIONS   [1874]
FOR ALL PLAYERS. [Prof A Rover]**

(a) **First edition [1874]*

Not seen. Year of first publication is inferred from the citation on the TP of (b).

(b) *Horace Partridge 1876 edition (1876)*

THE | [in gothic-revival script with decorated initials] **Croquet Manual** | OF | COMPLETE INSTRUCTIONS FOR ALL PLAYERS | FULLY ILLUSTRATED WITH DIAGRAMS AND ENGRAVINGS. | SUGGESTIONS ON | PARLOR AND FLOOR CROQUET, | TOGETHER WITH THE | RULES OF THE POPULAR | Game of Lawn Croquet, | BY | PROF. A. ROVER. | Published by permission of Milton, Bradley & Co., Owners of | Copyright | [rule] BOSTON : | Horace Partridge & Co., Publishers. | 1874.

Formula: [1¹⁶ 2⁴]. 20 leaves, pp *1–5* 6–15 *16–17* 18 *19–21* 22–27 *28* 29–33 *34* 35–36 *37* 38–39 *40*

Technical notes: 107 × 73 mm (p 7). 36 lines, 20 = 60 mm. Leaf size 143 × 99 mm; thickness 0.08 mm; wove, unwatermarked, smooth, white

Contents: Engraved illustration of a croquet party, indistinctly signed [?] '*M. BRADLEY*' (*1*), frontispiece, engraved illustration of games of quoits and croquet, unsigned (*2*), title (*3*), preface (*4*), text (5–39), blank (*40*)

Binding: Moderate greenish Blue (173) paper, printed in black, glued to the folds of the gatherings, stitched, no endpapers. FC: within a double-ruled frame (**THE** | Croquet Manual | [vignette, engraved illustration of a boxed croquet set] | **RULES AND REGULATIONS** | FOR THE GAMES OF | [in gothic-revival script] Field Croquet; Parlor Table Croquet; | [*do*] Parlor Floor Croquet. | [swelled rule] | BOSTON, MASS. | **Horace Partridge & Co.** | 1876.). Inside FC: blank. RC and spine: wanting from the copy examined

Copy seen: HPC: GV931 R651 1874 CROQ (imperfect, wanting the RC and spine)

Fingerprint: uton red, x-he thou C 1876A [group 3 taken from p 21, group 4 taken from p 22]

Notes: Printed anonymously. Year of publication is taken from that cited on the FC, not that cited on the TP.

(c) *Anonymous 1878 edition (1878)*

[The FC, within a double-ruled frame, the outer frame in bold]

THE | [in shaded display script] **Croquet Manual** | OF | Complete Instructions for all Players. | FULLY ILLUSTRATED WITH DIAGRAMS AND ENGRAVINGS | SUGGESTIONS ON | [engraved illustration of a boxed croquet set] | PARLOR AND FLOOR CROQUET. | **Together with the Rules of the Popular** | *Game of Lawn Croquet,* | BY PROF. A. ROVER. | Published by permission of Milton Bradley & Co., Owners of the Copyright. | [swelled rule] | BOSTON: | 1878.

Formula: Not ascertainable from the photocopy examined, apparently unsigned. Apparently 20 leaves, pp [1–4] 5 6–15 *16–17* 18 *19–21* 22–27 *28* 29–33 *34* 35–36 *37* 38–39 [40]

Technical notes: ca 105 × 72 mm (p 6). 35 lines, 20 = *ca* 60 mm. Leaf size *ca* 146 × 107 mm

Contents: Wanting from the photocopy examined ([1–4]), text (5–39), wanting from the photocopy examined ([40])

Binding: Light greenish Grey (154) wrapper, apparently stitched. FC: printed in black as above. Inside FC: wanting from the photocopy examined. RC: blank. Inside RC: wanting from the photocopy examined

Copy seen: PC (incomplete photocopy, wanting pp [1–4, 40], the wrapper in colour)

Fingerprint: Not ascertainable from the photocopy examined

Notes: The text of this edition evidently departs little, if at all, from contemporary issues of Prof Rover's own work, *Croquet: Its Principles and Rules* (A31). The fact that the original of the photocopy examined was found in a boxed set of table croquet of the period might suggest that this edition was produced under licence from Milton Bradley — perhaps by Horace Partridge, publishers of (b) — specifically for that purpose. Though most of the text is devoted to the lawn game, a section on 'parlor croquet' and 'the board game' (pp 31–33) would have made it entirely suitable for distribution as an instructional manual with such games.

A62   HAND-BOOK OF CROQUET, WITH RULES FOR PLAYING.   1874
[Anon]

HAND-BOOK | OF | [in outlined script] **CROQUET,** | WITH | RULES FOR PLAYING. | [swelled rule] | ROCHESTER, N. Y. | PUBLISHED BY HOWES & BEEBEE, | MANUFACTURERS OF CROQUET. | 1874.

Formula: [1⁴]. 4 leaves, pp *1–2* 3–8

Technical notes: 112 × 67 mm (p 7). 27 lines, 20 = 85 mm. Leaf size 142 × 96 mm; thickness 0.08 mm; wove, unwatermarked, smooth, white

Contents: Title (*1*), text (*2–8*)

Binding: Light greenish Grey (154) paper, sewn, no spine or endpapers. FC: printed in black within a double-ruled frame, the outer frame in bold, with internal corner ornaments ([in shaded display script, in a convex arc] **HAND-BOOK** | [flourish] OF [flourish] | [in outlined display script] **CROQUET.** | **TRADE** [engraved illustration of two crossed mallets in front of a croquet cage, containing a ball] **MARK.** | [swelled rule] | PUBLISHED BY HOWES & BEEBEE. | 1874.). Inside FC: blank. RC: blank. Inside RC: blank

Copy seen: HPC: GV931 C8H6 1874 CROQ

Fingerprint: n.ny byer T.n. hen, C 1874A

Notes: Printed anonymously. This is one of several beginners' rule books issued in the early 1870s by American manufacturers with their croquet equipment which are in substance identical or virtually identical. There is no known evidence as to their origin.

1875

A63   CROQUET. [A convention of croquet players held in Brooklyn,   1875
5 April 1875]

(a) *First edition (1875)*

[in display script with gothic-revival C within an ornamental panel] **Croquet.** | [1875. | [rule] | Entered according to act of Congress, in the year 1875, by I. BEDWIN, | IN the office of the Librarian of Congress, Washington, D.C. | [rule] | [rule] | WILLIAM T. BORLAND, STATIONER AND PRINTER, 48 BROAD STREET, NEW YORK.

Formula: Apparently [1⁸]. 8 leaves, unnumbered [pp 1–16]

Technical notes: 109 × 75 mm (p 4). 32 lines, 20 = 69, variable. Leaf size 155 × *ca* 90 mm

Contents: Title (*1*), blank (*2*), text (*3–14*), blank (*15–16*)

Binding: Apparently sewn. It is not known whether this work was originally issued in a wrapper

Copy seen: LOC: GV935 C94 (photocopy, the original rebound in library covers)

Fingerprint: s.st y.r– anE. PlCo 3 1875A

Notes: The origins of this work are obscure. It is conjectured that authorship vested in a convention of players which assigned the copyright to I Bedwin, perhaps on his undertaking to publish it. See also *Notes* to (b).

The text consists of a code of 49 rules typical of 'tight croquet' as played in the UK in the early 1860s.

(b) *Rhodopress of Ashland edition (1974)*

[dark reddish Orange (38) display script with gothic-revival C within an ornamental panel] Croquet. | [in Orange] 1875. | [rule] | Entered according to act of Congress, in the year 1875, by I. BEDWIN, in the office of the Librarian of Congress, Washington, D.C. | [rule] | [rule in bold] | WILLIAM T. BORLAND, STATIONER AND PRINTER, 48 BROAD STREET, NEW YORK.

[TP verso]

Originally published by William T. Borland, | June 22, 1875 | Reprinted by

Rhodopress of Ashland, | *March 10, 1974* | [this line and the following line set within a diagram of a croquet lawn, each hoop represented by an inverted letter U and each stake by a letter I] *The Croquet Series.* | *One of fifty copies.* | [publisher's device: twin trees in silhouette set above either end of a long rule] | [in gothic-revival script] Rhodopress of Ashland ◆ Ashland, Ohio. | 1974

Formula: [1⁸]. 8 leaves, unnumbered [pp 1–16]

Technical notes: 114 × 72 mm (p *4*). 34 lines, variable, 20 = 68 mm, variable. Leaf size 132 × 107 mm; thickness 0.17 mm; wove, unwatermarked, rough, white. See also *Notes* below

Contents: Title (*1*), TP verso (*2*), text (*3–14*), advertisement (*14*), blank (*15–16*)

Binding: Pale orange Yellow (73) laid paper, stapled, no spine or endpapers. FC: reproduction of the title matter on the TP within a triple-ruled frame printed in black ([in dark reddish Orange (38) display script with gothic-revival C within an ornamental panel] Croquet. | [in Orange] 1875.). Inside FC: blank. RC: blank. Inside RC: blank

Copy seen: CA

Fingerprint: s.st y.r- anE. PlCo 3 1974A

Notes: Published and printed by Rhodopress of Ashland, Ashland, Ohio.

This edition, described in the TP verso as a 'reprint', was reset and printed on a hand-press.

A64   RULES FOR PLAYING THE GAME OF CROQUET. [Anon]   1875

Foreword: The copies seen of the several publications here described share a common title and, with the possible exception of (d), which has not been seen, other characteristics. Hence there are good grounds for supposing that they may properly be regarded as issues of the same work. Again with the possible exception of (d), all are linked, albeit on the basis of circumstantial evidence only, with the name of FH Ayres, publishers and manufacturers of sports and games. In view of the fact that most of these rule books were published anonymously, it is believed that they were distributed by Ayres with their croquet sets and were not intended for sale separately. It is further conjectured that, on the revival of tournament croquet in the early 1890s, Ayres decided to replace this title with a new work of ostensibly more authority, *The Laws of Croquet and Regulations for the Management of Prize Meetings* (A94), suitable both for sale to experienced players and for distribution with their croquet sets.

(a) *First edition (1875)

RULES | FOR | *PLAYING THE GAME* | OF | CROQUET. | [rule] | WITH DIAGRAM & EXPLANATION OF TERMS. | [rule] | [engraved illustrations of circular and 'upright' eight-piece croquet stands and a mallet in contact with a ringed ball] | [rule] | [in gothic-revival script] **London.** | [rule] | [partially obscured by a stick-on label bearing the name SA Cripps of '*286, Long Dean St. Room*'] 1875. | [*do*, apparently over-printed] LONDON: AN MYERS & Cº BERNERS STREET.W.

Formula: Apparently [1⁸(–1₁)]. 7 leaves, pp *i–ii, 1–3* 4–10 *11–12*

Technical notes: 148 × 102 mm (p *6*). 24 lines, 20 = 125 mm. Leaf size 215 × 136 mm; thickness 0.11 mm; wove, unwatermarked, smooth, white

Contents: Glued to the FC (*i*), advertisement (*ii*), title (*1*), plan of court (*2*), text, continued (*3–7*), the game of Bell Croquet (*8*), diagram of the Eglinton Castle Game of Croquet (*9*), advertisements for Garden Seat Croquet (*10–11*), glued to the RC (*12*)

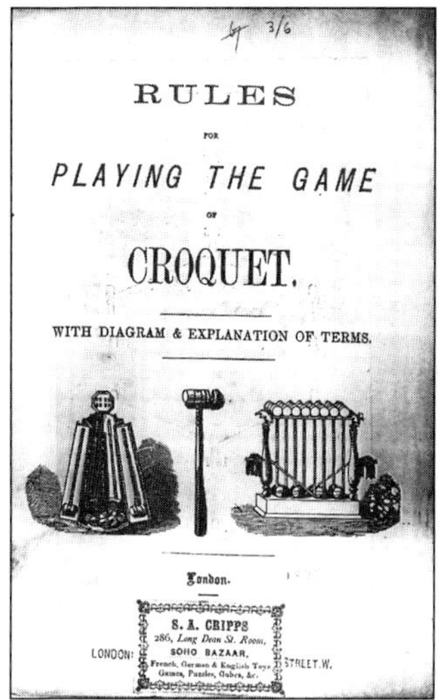

Binding: Strong Blue (178) semi-gloss paper glued to the outer leaves, which serve as pastedowns, no free endpapers or spine, sewn. FC: within a frame composed of a repeated decorative figure, with corner ornaments (**CROQUET.** | [engraved illustration of a woman player, fashionably dressed, with mallet raised to take 'tight' croquet]). RC: blank

Copy seen: PC

Fingerprint: h.es .)T. ofgs isul C 1875A [groups 1, 3, 4 taken from p *3*, group 2 taken from p *11*]

Notes: Published and printed anonymously. Publication by FH Ayres is inferred from the following indications:

(i) The engraved illustration on the TP of the 'upright' croquet stand is identical to one seen in an undated FH Ayres trade catalogue of the same period.

(ii) Goods illustrated in the advertisements on pp *10–11* bear a trademark which incorporates the initials *F, H, A*.

It is conjectured that FH Ayres appointed AN Myers as distributors and supplied them with copies of this work over-printed with their name as merchandising support, and that Myers included them with Ayres croquet goods supplied to SA Cripps and other retailers.

(b) *1876 issue [1876]*

[Within a double-ruled frame, the outer frame in bold, with corner ornaments]

RULES | FOR | PLAYING THE GAME | OF | CROQUET. | [rule] | WITH AUTHORIZED RULES, DIAGRAMS, AND | EXPLANATIONS OF TERMS. | [rule] | LONDON. | [rule] | 1876

Formula: [1¹²]. 12 leaves, pp *1–3 4–6 7 8–24*

Technical notes: 130 × 85 mm (p 4). 30 lines, 20 = 88 mm. Leaf size 180 × 122 mm; thickness 0.11 mm; wove, unwatermarked, smooth, white

Contents: Title (*1*), blank (*2*), text (*3–24*)

Binding: Apparently printed in black on pale-coloured paper, sewn. The copy examined has apparently been rebound in a card cover, displaying a reduced-scale photocopy of the original cover, possibly derived from another copy. It is not known whether the original copy ever had endpapers. FC: printed within a double-ruled frame, the outer frame in bold (RULES | FOR | PLAYING THE GAME | OF | CROQUET. | [rule] | [vignette, engraved illustration of a croquet party in a parkland setting, apparently signed 'A DORRINGTON & CO'] | [swelled rule] | LONDON. | [rule] | 1876.). RC: blank. Spine: none in evidence on the rebound copy examined

Copy seen: BL: 7921 dd 20 (imperfect, in a library binding)

Fingerprint: hend e.by d.ct apho 3 1876A

Notes: Written, published and printed anonymously, unpriced. Publication by FH Ayres is inferred from close similarities of this issue to (c) and from the same indications which suggest that the latter issue was published by Ayres.

The text includes a code of 37 rules of the game, not attributed to any authority.

(c) *1878 issue (1878)*

[Within a double-ruled frame, the outer frame in bold, with corner ornaments]
RULES | FOR | PLAYING THE GAME | OF | CROQUET. | [rule] | WITH AUTHORIZED RULES, DIAGRAMS, AND | EXPLANATIONS OF TERMS. | [rule] | LONDON. | [rule] | 1878

Formula: [1–2⁸]. 16 leaves, pp *1–3* 4–6 7 8–21 *22* 23–24 *25–32*

Technical notes: 130 × 85 mm (p 4). 30 lines, 20 = 88 mm. Leaf size 185 × 121 mm; thickness 0.10 mm; wove, unwatermarked, smooth, white

Contents: Title (*1*), blank (*2*), text (*3–24*), blank (*25*), advertisements (*26–32*)

Binding: Apparently printed in black on pale-coloured paper, sewn. The copy examined has apparently been rebound in a card cover, displaying a reduced-scale photocopy of the original cover, enhanced by some artwork, possibly derived from another copy. It is not known whether the original copy ever had endpapers. FC: printed within a double-ruled frame, the outer frame in bold (RULES | FOR | PLAY-ING THE GAME | OF | CROQUET. | [rule] | [vignette, engraved illustration of a croquet party in a parkland setting, signed 'A DORRINGTON & CO'] | [wavy line] | LONDON. | [rule] | 1877.). RC: blank. Spine: none in evidence on the rebound copy examined

Copy seen: BL: 7921 de 27 (imperfect, in a library binding)

Fingerprint: hend e.by d.ct apho 3 1878A

Notes: Written, published, and printed anonymously. Publication by FH Ayres is inferred from the fact that several of the advertisements contained in this issue — all unpriced, unbranded, and none giving the name or address of a supplier — are also contained in *Guide to the Compendium of Games*, an explicit Ayres publication of the same period.

A curiosity of this issue is the discrepancy between the years of publication cited on the TP and FC. This might suggest that another issue of the same work was published in 1877, remaining stocks of the cover of which were also used for at least some copies of the present issue.

(d) *1889 issue (1889)*

Not seen. A search of the on-line system of the library of Indiana State University has revealed a work with this title dated 1889.

(e) *1892 issue (1892)*

[Within a triple-ruled frame, the inside of the central frame embellished with a wavy border, with corner ornaments]

RULES | FOR | PLAYING THE GAME | OF | CROQUET. | [double rule] | LONDON. | [rule] | 1892.

Formula: [1¹²]. 12 leaves, pp *1–3* 4–6 7 8–24

Technical notes: ca 131 × 83 mm (p 4). 30 lines, 20 = *ca* 88 mm. Leaf size *ca* 185 × 121 mm

Contents: Title (*1*), blank (*2*), text (*3–24*)

Binding: Apparently printed on pale-coloured paper or card, sewn, no spine or endpapers. FC: reproduction of the TP. Inside FC: advertisement. RC: blank. Inside RC: advertisement

Copy seen: PC (photocopy)

Fingerprint: h*nd e.by d.ct apho 3 1892A

Notes: Written, published and printed anonymously. Publication by FH Ayres is inferred from the fact that both advertisements it contains are branded by this supplier of games and sports equipment and from the same indications which suggest that this firm also published issues (b) and (c).

The text would appear to be identical in substance to that of (b) and (c), as is attested by the essential identity of their fingerprints.

(f) *1894 issue (1894)*

[Within a triple-ruled frame, the inside of the central frame embellished with a wavy border, with corner ornaments]

[in shaded display script] **RULES** | FOR | PLAYING THE GAME | OF | [in gothic-revival script] **CROQUET.** | [vignette, engraved illustration of a croquet party in a parkland setting] | [rule] | LONDON. | 1894.

Formula: [1¹⁴]. 14 leaves including the front and rear endpapers, pp *i–ii, 1–3* 4–6 7 8–24, 25–26

Technical notes: 132 × 84 mm (p 4). 30 lines, 20 = 89 mm. Leaf size 183 × 123 mm; thickness 0.09 mm; wove, unwatermarked, smooth, white

Contents: Glued to the FC (*i*), advertisement (*ii*), title (*1*), blank (*2*), text (*3–24*), advertisement (*25*), glued to the RC (*26*)

Binding: Moderate Green (144) semi-gloss paper, sewn, no spine or endpapers. FC: reproduction of the TP. Inside FC: advertisement. RC: advertisement. Inside RC: advertisement

Copy seen: PC

Fingerprint: h*nd e.by d.ct apho 3 1894A

Notes: Publication by FH Ayres is inferred from the fact that all the advertisements in this issue are for Ayres branded goods and from the same indications which suggest that this firm also published issues (b) and (c).

The text would appear to be substantially identical to that of issues (b), (c), and (e), as is attested by the virtual identity of their fingerprints and pagination.

1876

A65   **CROQUET: AS PLAYED BY THE MELROSE CROQUET CLUB.   1876**
[Melrose Croquet Club]

CROQUET: | As played by | THE MELROSE CROQUET CLUB. | [rule] | *Price 10 Cts.* | [rule] | STONEHAM, MASS.: | G. A. KIMBALL AND COMPANY, PUBLISHERS. | 1876.

[TP verso]

Entered according to act of Congress, in the | year 1876, | By FRANK J. STILES, | In the office of the Librarian of Congress, at Wash- | ington.

Formula: Not ascertainable, unsigned. 6 leaves, pp *1–3* 4–12

Technical notes: 87 × 56 mm (p 10). 28 lines, 20 = 62 mm. Leaf size 121 × *ca* 80 mm

Contents: Title (*1*), TP verso (*2*), text (*3–12*)

Binding: Not ascertainable from the photocopy examined

Copy seen: LOC: GV935 C95 (photocopy, no wrapper, the original copy rebound in a library binding)

Fingerprint: t.s, t.er d,ng E.d. C 1876A [groups 2–4 taken from p 11]

Notes: Printed anonymously, price 10 cents. The origins of this work are obscure. It is conjectured that the club assigned the copyright to Stiles, perhaps on his undertaking to publish it.

A66   DIRECTIONS FOR CROQUET, CONTAINING THE RULES   1876 ADOPTED BY THE PRINCIPAL CROQUET CLUBS OF THE UNITED STATES. [Anon]

(a) *First edition (1876)*

[The FC, all the letterpress set within a double-ruled frame, the outer frame in bold]

DIRECTIONS | FOR | **CROQUET,** | CONTAINING THE | RULES | Adopted by the Principal Croquet Clubs | OF THE UNITED STATES. | [rule] | ***PUBLISHED BY*** | SANDUSKY TOOL CO., | MANUFACTURERS OF | **MECHANICS' TOOLS AND FIELD CROQUET,** | ALL DESCRIPTIONS OF WOOD TURNING, | SANDUSKY, O. | [rule] | SANDUSKY: | JOURNAL STEAM PRINTING ESTABLISHMENT. | 1876.

Formula: [1⁸]. 8 leaves, pp *1–2*, 3–11 *12* 13–15 *16*

Technical notes: 116 × 80 mm (p 4). 28 lines, 20 = 83 mm. Leaf size 152 × 100 mm; thickness 0.09 mm; wove, unwatermarked, smooth, white

Contents: Text (*1–15*), blank (*16*)

Binding: Moderate Orange (53) paper glued to the fold of the outer leaf, sewn, no spine or endpapers. FC: printed in black, as above. Inside FC: blank. RC: blank. Inside RC: blank

Copy seen: PC

Fingerprint: n.of .]o- y.ue reyo 3 1876A [group 1 taken from p *1*]

Notes: Printed by Journal Steam Printing Establishment.

The text consists of a brief introduction, a plan of the court, a code of 60 numbered rules which is identical to that found in A22, and a glossary of technical terms.

(b) *Register Steam Printing Company edition (1878)*

[The FC, within a double-ruled frame, the outer frame in bold]

DIRECTIONS | FOR | CROQUET, | CONTAINING THE | RULES | ADOPTED BY THE | PRINCIPAL CROQUET CLUBS | OF THE | **UNITED STATES** | [swelled rule] SANDUSKY : | REGISTER STEAM PRINTING ESTABLISHMENT. | 1878.

Formula: [1⁸]. 8 leaves, pp *1–2* 3–12 *13* 14–16

Technical notes: 114 × 80 mm (p 9). 24 lines, 20 = 96 mm. Leaf size 151 × 105 mm; thickness 0.07 mm; wove, unwatermarked, smooth, white

Contents: Text (*1–15*), blank (*16*)

Binding: Pale Green (149) smooth paper, printed in black, sewn through the wrapper, no spine or endpapers. FC: as above. Inside FC: blank. RC: blank. Inside RC: blank

Copy seen: HPC: GV933 D5 1878 CROQ

Fingerprint: n.of nyly h.as anal 3 1878A [group 1 taken from p 1]

Notes: Printed by Register Steam Printing Establishment, Sandusky OH. As (a), this edition includes a code of 60 numbered rules. The texts of the two editions have not been collated.

A67　　HAND BOOK OF CROQUET. [Anon]　　　　1876

HAND BOOK | OF | [in shaded and hatched open script] **CROQUET** | PUBLISHED BY | TEEL & BADET, | MANUFACTURERS, | SOUTH BEND, IND. | [swelled rule] | SOUTH BEND, IND: | TRIBUNE COMPANY, STEAM PRINTERS, | 1876.

Formula: [1⁸]. 8 leaves, pp *1–3* 4–15 *16*

Technical notes: 104 × 71 mm (p 9). 32 lines, 20 = 60 mm, variable. Leaf size 144 × 93 mm; thickness 0.11 mm; wove, unwatermarked, smooth, white

Contents: Title (*1*), blank (*2*), preface (*3*), plan of croquet court (nine-arch croquet) (*4*), plan of croquet court (ten-arch croquet) (*5*), text (*6–15*), blank (*16*)

Binding: White paper printed in black, sewn through the wrapper, no spine or endpapers. FC: within a ruled frame, in bold, with corner ornaments (TEEL & BADET'S | [in shaded and outlined script] **Hand Book** | OF | [in shaded and outlined script] **CROQUET**.) Inside FC: blank. RC: engraved vignette, illustrating a boxed croquet set. Inside RC: blank

Copy seen: HPC: GV931 H3T4 1876 CROQ

Fingerprint: y.im d.be inry main 3 1876A

Notes: Printed anonymously.

A68　　HAND BOOK [OF] CROQUET. [Anon]　　　　[1876]

(a) **First edition [1876]*

[Within an abstract decorative frame with internal corner ornaments, printed in black] [the letter *H* trailing a floral tailpiece] HAND BOOK | OF | [swash C] CROQUET.

Formula: [1⁸]. 8 leaves, pp *1* 2–3 *4* 5–15 *16*

Technical notes: 113 × 88 mm (p 10). 32 lines, 20 = 71 mm, variable. Leaf size 147 × 110 mm; thickness 0.07 mm; wove, unwatermarked, smooth, white

Contents: Title (*1*), plan of court (nine-arch croquet) (*2*), plan of court (ten-arch croquet) (*3*), preface (*4*), text (*5–15*), engraved illustration of crossed mallet and stake, the latter superimposed over the former, the point uppermost, and a ringed ball (*16*)

Binding: No covers or wrapper, sewn.

Copy seen: HPC: GV931 H3 CROQ C1

Fingerprint: e.k, inry het. wod. C 1876Q [all four groups taken from p 5, group 1 from a L column]

Notes: Printed anonymously. Year of publication is inferred from that cited in A67, a virtually identical work.

This work is one of several handbooks — some issued by named publishers, some anonymous, some thought to be facsimile reprints — with texts which are identical or virtually identical. It is believed that they were supplied to the order of various sports manufacturers to issue with their croquet equipment. There is no known evidence as to their original source or as to which, if any, were properly authorised.

(b) *Variant issue [1876]*

Copy seen: PC (photocopy)

Notes: This variant is apparently identical to (a) in every respect, save for the design of the vignette on p *16*. It shows the point of the stake lowermost and the ball surmounting the crossed mallet and stake, and the designs of both stake and mallet are different. There are no obvious indications as to the order in which they were issued. See also *Notes* to (a).

(c) *Variant issue [1876]*

[The FC, within a decorative frame composed of repeated small sqares with tapered corners, printed in black]

HAND BOOK | CROQUET. | [vignette, a stylised croquet ball]

Formula: [1⁸]. 8 leaves, pp *1* 2–15 *16*

Technical notes: 114 × 86 mm (p 8). 31 lines, 20 = 74 mm, variable. Leaf size 156 × 109 mm; thickness 0.09 mm; wove, unwatermarked, smooth, greyish Yellow (90)

Contents: Title (*1*), plan of court (nine-arch croquet) (2), plan of court (ten-arch croquet) (3), preface (4), text (*5–15*), engraved illustration of mallet, ball, hoop, and stake (*16*)

Binding: No covers or wrapper, sewn

Copy seen: HPC: GV931 H32 CROQ

Fingerprint: e,k, inry het. wod. C 1876Q [all four groups taken from p 5, group 1 from a L column]

Notes: Printed anonymously. This variant and (a) are thought to have been issued by the same publisher by virtue of their close similarity in text and format. There are no obvious indications as to the order in which they were issued. See also *Notes* to (a).

A69   HAND-BOOK OF CROQUET WITH RULES FOR PLAYING.   1876
[Anon]

HAND-BOOK | OF | CROQUET | WITH | RULES FOR PLAYING. | [double rule] | KALAMAZOO, MICH: | PUBLISHED BY THE KALAMAZOO HANDLE MANUFAC- | TURING COMPANY. | 1876.

Formula: [1⁴]. 4 leaves, pp *1–2* 3–8

Technical notes: 106 × 66 mm (p 7). 31 lines, 20 = 69 mm. Leaf size 138 × 100 mm; thickness 0.12 mm; wove, unwatermarked, smooth, white

Contents: Title (*1*), preface (*2*), text (3–8)

Binding: Light yellowish Brown (76) paper, printed in black, sewn through the wrapper, no spine or endpapers. FC: within a frame constructed from a design of figured ribbon ([in outlined and shaded display script] **CROQUET** | PLAYING | [engraved illustration of sundry croquet equipment] | upwards at L in margin between the illustration and the frame, in shaded script] *DEFINITIONS, RULES,* | [downwards at R in margin between the illustration and the frame, in shaded script] *AND SUGGESTIONS.* | MADE EASY. | [swelled rule] KALAMAZOO, MICH: | PUBLISHED BY THE KALAMAZOO HANDLE MANU- | FACTURING COMPANY. | 1876.). Inside FC: blank. RC: advertisement. Inside RC: blank

Copy seen: HPC: GV931 H3K3 1876 CROQ

Fingerprint: n.th l—y- T.n. nyit C 1876A [all four groups taken from p 3]

Notes: Printed anonymously. The text comprises a code of 25 unnumbered rules, together with plans of court settings for 9- and 10-hoop games.

A70   TERMS, SUGGESTIONS AND RULES FOR PLAYING CROQUET. 1876
[Anon]

(a) ***First edition** (1876)*

[Within a ruled frame]

TERMS, SUGGESTIONS & RULES | [in shaded script] *FOR PLAYING* | CROQUET. | [swelled rule] | *Published under the Direction of* | HOWES & BEEBEE, | [in gothic-revival script with decorated initials] **Rochester Croquet Manufactory,** | *ROCHESTER, N. Y.* | 1876.

Formula: 1^8 2^6 [2_1 signed]. 14 leaves, pp *1* 2–27 *28*

Technical notes: 106 × 59 mm (p 5). 25 lines, 20 = 86 mm. Leaf size 146 × 97 mm; thickness 0.10 mm; wove, unwatermarked, smooth, white

Contents: Title (*1*), text (2–27), advertisement (*28*)

Binding: Dark purplish Pink (251) laminated paper, printed in black, glued to the folds of the gatherings, stitched, no endpapers. FC: within a double-ruled frame, the outer frame in bold, with internal ornaments of abstract design ([in a convex arc, in outlined display script] **CROQUET** | BY THE | *ROCHESTER* | [in gothic-revival script with decorated initials] **Croquet Manufactory.** | [engraved illustration, featuring two putti among croquet equipment] | HOWES & BEEBEE. | ROCHESTER, N. Y. | 1876.). Inside FC: blank. RC: blank. Inside RC: blank. Spine: blank

Copy seen: HPC: GV931 C8H6 1876a CROQ

Fingerprint: t.ve r.a- y.oa rusi 7 1876A

Notes: Printed anonymously. The text includes a code of 38 numbered rules. The FC frame closely resembles that of the same publisher's earlier rule book (A62) and hence it is conjectured that this edition preceded (b).

(b) *First edition, variant (1876)*

[The TP as that of (a)]

Formula: As that of (a)

Technical notes: As at (a)

Contents: As those of (a)

Binding: Very pale Green (148) laminated paper, printed in black, glued to the folds of the gatherings, stitched, no endpapers. FC: within a triple-ruled frame, the outermost frame in bold, with internal ornaments of abstract design ([in a convex arc, in outlined display script] **CROQUET** | BY THE | *ROCHESTER* | [in gothic-revival script with decorated initials] **Croquet Manufactory.** | [engraved illustration, featuring two putti among croquet equipment] | HOWES & BEEBEE. | ROCHESTER, N. Y. | 1876.). Inside FC: blank. RC: blank. Inside RC: blank. Spine: blank

Copy seen: HPC: GV931 C8H6 1876 CROQ

Fingerprint: As that of (a)

Notes: This variant is identical to (a), save for the frame design and colour of the FC. See also *Notes* to (a).

1877

A71 CROQUET: RULES OF THE BROOKLYN CROQUET 1877
ASSOCIATION. [Brooklyn Croquet Association]

[in open shaded script] **CROQUET.** | [wavy line] | RULES | OF THE | [in gothic-revival script, oversize *B, C, A*] **Brooklyn Croquet Association.** | [rule] | Entered according to Act of Congresss, in the year 1877, by | C. N. HOAGLAND, in the Office of the Librarian | of Congress, Washington, D. C. | [rule] | PUBLISHED BY | E. L. HORSMAN, | **CROQUET MANUFACTURER,** | 80 & 82 William Street, | AND | 64 & 66 Maiden Lane, | NEW YORK.

Formula: [1⁸]. 16 leaves, pp *1–5 6–16*

Technical notes: 100 × 68 mm (p 12). 25 lines, 20 = 82 mm. Leaf size 134 × 84 mm

Contents: Title (*1*), blank (*2*), preface, dated 5 March 1877 (*3*), diagram of court (*4*), text (*5–16*), name of printer (*16*)

Binding: Paper or card, sewn through the wrapper, no spine or endpapers. FC: printed in black ([in open shaded script] **CROQUET.** | [wavy line] | RULES | OF THE | [in gothic-revival script, oversize *B, C, A*] **Brooklyn Croquet Association.** | [rule] | Entered according to Act of Congresss, in the year 1877, by | C. N. HOAGLAND, in the Office of the Librarian | of Congress, Washington, D. C. | [rule] | PUBLISHED BY | E. L. HORSMAN, | MANUFACTURER OF | **PROFESSIONAL CROQUET,** | 80 & 82 William Street, | AND | 64 & 66 Maiden Lane, | NEW YORK.). Inside FC: blank. RC: blank. Inside RC: blank

Copy seen: LOC: GV935 B87 (photocopy, the covers in colour)

Fingerprint: 7.N. d,S. y.he toth 3 1877A

Notes: Printed by HC Stoothoff, New York. The text consists of a code of rules numbered I–XLII.

1878

A72 CROQUET. Gustav zu Putlitz 1878

[Volume I, in gothic script throughout]

Croquet. | [rule] | Roman | von | **Gustav zu Putlitz.** | [rule] Erster Band. | [publisher's device] | Berlin. | **Verlag von Gebrüder Paetel.** | 1878.

[Volume II, in gothic script throughout]

Croquet. | [rule] | Roman | von | **Gustav zu Putlitz.** | [rule] Zweiter Band. | [publisher's device] | Berlin. | **Verlag von Gebrüder Paetel.** | 1878.

Formula: Volume I: π1 1–16⁸ 17⁴ χ1) [$2 signed (–χ1). 134 leaves, pp *i–ii, 1 2–268*

Volume II: π1 1–16⁸ [$2 signed]. 129 leaves, pp *i–ii, 1 2–256*

Technical notes: 123 × 76 mm (vol I, p 3). 23 lines, 20 = 109 mm. Leaf size 185 × 120 mm; thickness 0.07 mm; wove, unwatermarked, smooth, white

Contents: Volume I: Title (*i*), TP verso (*ii*), text, continued (*1–266*), name of printer (*266*)

Volume II: Title (*i*), TP verso (*ii*), text, concluded (*1–256*), name of printer (*256*)

Binding: The binding of the copy examined, combining both volumes, is apparently a library binding. It provides no indication as to how the separate volumes were originally bound

Copy seen: BL: 12554 cc 1

Fingerprints: Volume I: erte r-k- rdne "Lär 3 1878A

Volume II: enas chn, igde nige 3 1878A

Notes: Printed by Volks-Zeitung, Berlin. A novel in two volumes. The old English game of croquet is first introduced in [chapter] XI (vol I, p 131). The significance of the title in relation to the story is not understood.

A73   **HOW TO PLAY CROQUET: A POCKET MANUAL OF**   [1878]
COMPLETE INSTRUCTIONS FOR ALL PLAYERS. S Kramer

Foreword: The titles of all known issues of this work here recorded incorporate the words 'new and revised edition'. Whether or not an earlier, original (unrevised), edition was ever issued is an open question.

(a) *Selchow & Righter edition [1878]*

NEW AND REVISED EDITION | OF | [swash *H, P, C*] How to Play Croquet | A POCKET MANUAL | OF | [swash *C, P*] Complete Instructions for all Players | ILLUSTRATED WITH | ENGRAVINGS AND DIAGRAMS, | TOGETHER WITH | THE RULES OF THE GAME, | *As Adopted by Professional and Amateur Clubs;* | HINTS ON FLOOR AND TABLE CROQUET, | AND DEFINITIONS OF TECHNICAL TERMS. | [swelled rule] | SELCHOW & RIGHTER. | New York.

[TP verso]

Copyright, | 1878, | By S. Kramer

Formula: [1¹²]. 12 leaves, pp *1–3* 4–24

Technical notes: 131 × 86 mm (p 4). 30 lines, 20 = 88 mm. Leaf size 175 × 115 mm; thickness 0.07 mm; wove, unwatermarked, smooth, pale orange Yellow (73)

Contents: Title (*1*), TP verso (*2*), text (*3–24*)

Binding: Light yellowish Brown (76) paper, stapled, no endpapers or spine. FC: printed in black within a double-ruled frame ([in shaded display script] **CROQUET.** | [swelled rule] **ITS** | **Rules and Regulations** | [engraved illustration of a croquet set featuring eight mallets and the FC of the present work] | **COMPLETE.** | [rule] | *INSTRUCTIONS.* | [rule] | **AMERICAN EDITION.**). Inside FC: advertisements for Selchow & Righter products — Vignette Authors, Anagrams, Corn and Beans. RC: advertisements, all apparently for Selchow & Righter products — Peter Coddle's Trip, Parcheesi, Planchette, Old Maid. Inside RC: advertisements for Selchow & Righter products — Mixed Pickles, Most Laughable Thing on Earth, Komikal Konversation Kards, Snap, Popping the Question

Copy seen: PC

Fingerprint: errs *nerp* t.on Grop 3 1878Q

Notes: Printed anonymously. Year of publication is inferred from the year of copyright, as given above. Selchow & Righter of New York manufactured a wide variety of sports goods and games. It may be safely assumed that this work was distributed with their croquet equipment. It is not known whether it was also marketed independently.

(b) *Selchow & Righter edition, variant [1878]*

[The TP and TP verso as at (a) above]

Formula: As that of (a)

Technical notes: 131 × 86 mm (p 4). 30 lines, 20 = 88 mm. Leaf size 176 × 109 mm; thickness 0.07 mm; wove, unwatermarked, smooth, light yellowish Brown (76)

Contents: As those of (a)

Binding: As that of (a) save for variations in the advertising matter. Inside FC: blank. RC: advertisements for Selchow & Righter products — Parcheesi, Our Donkey Party. Inside RC: blank

Copy seen: PC

Fingerprint: As that of (a)

Notes: Printed anonymously. Year of publication is conjectural.

The text departs from that of (a) on p 6 only — by omission of one brief sentence which attributes a patent date (29 June 1869) to a new design of long-headed mallet and by substitution of an illustration which depicts a mallet with an even longer head. These variations suggest that the present issue succeeded (a), not *vice versa*.

(c) *Anonymous Boston issue [1878]*

NEW AND REVISED EDITION | OF | [swash *H, P, C*] How to Play Croquet. | A POCKET MANUAL | OF | [swash *C, P*] Complete Instructions for all Players. | ILLUSTRATED WITH | ENGRAVINGS AND DIAGRAMS, | TOGETHER WITH | THE RULES OF THE GAME, | *As Adopted by Professional and Amateur Clubs ;* | HINTS ON FLOOR AND TABLE CROQUET, | AND DEFINITIONS OF TECHNICAL TERMS. | [swelled rule] | BOSTON:

[TP verso]

Copyright, | 1878, | By S. Kramer

Formula: [1¹²]. 12 leaves, pp *1–3* 4–24

Technical notes: 131 × 86 mm (p 4). 30 lines, 20 = 88 mm. Leaf size 170 × 113 mm; thickness 0.09 mm; wove, unwatermarked, smooth, white

Contents: Title (*1*), TP verso (*2*), text (*3–24*)

Binding: Greyish Yellow (90) semi-gloss paper, printed in black, glued to the fold of the outer sheet, sewn, no spine or endpaper. FC: within a double-ruled frame, the outer frame in bold ([in shaded display script] **CROQUET.** | [swelled rule] **ITS** | **Rules and Regulations** | [engraved illustration of a croquet set featuring eight mallets and the FC of the present work] | **COMPLETE.** | [rule] | *INSTRUCTIONS.* | [rule] | **AMERICAN EDITION.**). Inside FC: blank. RC: anonymous advertisement for Tournée, 'The New Lawn Cushion Game'. Inside RC: blank

Copy seen: HPC: GV931 H85 1865 CROQ

Fingerprint: As those of (a) and (b)

Notes: Printed anonymously. Year of publication is inferred from the year of copyright, as given above. A curiosity of this issue is the extreme anonymity of the publisher. It is conjectured that it was produced in anticipation of publication under a licence agreement to a sports goods manufacturer but that, for some reason, this plan proved abortive and the publisher made other arrangements to dispose of the issue.

The text has not been collated with those of (a) or (b) but, in view of the fact that the three issues share a common fingerprint, it is safe to assume that it is identical or virtually identical to those two.

(d) *William Bryce edition (1883)*

NEW AND REVISED EDITION | [rule] OF [rule] | HOW TO PLAY CROQUET | [rule] | A POCKET MANUAL | [rule] OF [rule] | *Complete Instructions for all*

Players, illustrated | with Engravings and Diagrams, together with | the Rules of the Game, as adopted by | Professional and Amateur Clubs. | Hints on Floor and Table Croquet, | and Definitions of Technical Terms. | [swelled rule] | [in gothic-revival script] London, Ont.: | Wm. Bryce, Publisher, 123 Dundas St. | [rule] | 1883.

Formula: Not ascertainable from the photocopy examined. 16 leaves, pp *1–3 4–32*

Technical notes: †148 × †107 mm (p 4). 34 lines, 20 = †88mm. Leaf size †210 × †142 mm

Contents: Title (*1*), preface (*2*), text (*3–32*)

Binding: Apparently pale paper or card. FC: (Hand Book & Rules | [rule] OF [rule] | **CROQUET.** | [rule] ALSO [rule] | *RULES FOR TOURNAMENTS.* | [rule] | W. Bryce, London. | [in shaded script] **PRICE,** [two printer's ornaments] **10 CENTS**). Inside FC: wanting from the photocopy examined. RC: wanting from the photocopy examined. Inside RC: blank

Copy seen: NLA: Mc 756 (photocopy of unknown scale, wanting the RC and the inside page of the FC)

Fingerprint: reus etof r-ut Nefo 3 1883A

Notes: Printed anonymously, price 10 cents. The preface is much abridged, but the text is virtually identical to that of earlier issues and extended to include suggestions to beginners (pp 25–26) and rules for tournaments (pp 26–28). All the letterpress is reset, one diagram of a court setting is redrawn and printed in white out of black, and the other is replaced by a table of court dimensions.

1879

A74   **LAWN TENNIS, BADMINTON, CROQUET, TROCO,**   [1879]
        RACQUETS, FIVES [*ETC*]. [Capt Rawdon Crawley]

(a) *First edition [1879]*

Not seen. This work is dated 1879 in the select bibliography of D Prichard's *The History of Croquet* (A208, p 234)

(b) *1883 issue [1883]*

LAWN TENNIS, | BADMINTON, | *CROQUET, TROCO, RACQUETS,* | *FIVES,* | [in gothic-revival script] Nurr and Spell, Bowling, Hurling, | ETC., ETC. | [in gothic-revival script] London: | WARD, LOCK, AND CO., | WARWICK HOUSE, SALISBURY SQUARE, E.C.

Formula: 1^8 2–5^8 $6^8(6_4+\chi^4)$ [\$1 signed (-1_1)]. 52 leaves, pp *1–5 6 7 8–13 14–15 16–29 30 31 32 33–34 35 36–39 40 41–46 47–49 50–62 63 64–67 68 69 70 71–74 75 76–78 79 80–81 82 83–88, 1–2 3–6 7 8 9–16* [= 104]

Technical notes: 101 × 63 mm (p 8). 30 lines, 20 = 67 mm. Leaf size 129 × 94 mm; thickness 0.10 mm; wove, unwatermarked, smooth, white (save χ^4, which is of a thinner paper)

Contents: Half-title ('Tennis') (*1*), advertisement (*2*), title (*3*), blank (*4*), contents (*5–6*), text (lawn tennis) (*7–29*), text (badminton) (*30–39*), text (croquet) (*40–62*), text (troco or lawn billiards) (*63–67*), text (racquets) (*68–74*), text (fives) (*75–78*), text (pallone) (*79–81*), text (nurr and spell) (*82–84*), text (bowling) (*84–86*), text (hurling) (*86–87*), text (balloon ball) (*87–88*), name of printer (*88*), appendix (revised laws of lawn tennis) (*1–8*), advertisements (*9–16*)

Binding: Greyish Green (150) cloth over light boards, sections 1–6 stapled individually, stabbed and glued to 6_8, greenish Grey (155) endpapers. There are advertisements on the facing pages of the endpapers. FC: printed as in oblong panels in black and light Grey (264) ([black rule] | [black on Grey] WARD AND LOCK'S SIXPENNY HANDBOOKS. | [decorative panel in black, Green, and Grey] | [black rule] | [black on Green] **LAWN TENNIS** | [double black rule] | [drawing of a mixed doubles lawn tennis game in black, Green, and Grey] | [black double rule] | [black on Green] **CROQUET, RACQUETS &c** | [in black] **ILLUSTRATED** | [black triple rule, the centre rule in bold] | [black arabesque frieze] | [black on Grey] —— WARD LOCK & Co. SALISBURY SQUARE. —— | [black rule]). RC: blank. Spine: in black (**LAWN TENNIS. *SIXPENCE*.**)

Copy seen: BL: 7908 aa 45

Fingerprint: 3837 r,rs wnen wh3. 7 1883Q

Notes: Printed by Unwin Brothers, Chilworth and London, price 6d. Year of publication is inferred as that cited in the *General Catalogue* of the BL. Authorship is inferred from close similarities with *Croquet and Troco* (A32). The reason why this work was published anonymously is unclear.

The laws of croquet given in the text (pp 53–60) are presented as an (unattributed) revision of the January 1870 'Conference Laws' (A52).

(c) *Second edition [1890]*

LAWN TENNIS, | BADMINTON, | *CROQUET, TROCO, RACQUETS, AND FIVES*. | NEW EDITION. | WARD, LOCK, AND CO., | LONDON, NEW YORK, AND MELBOURNE.

Formula: $1^6(1_3+\chi^2)$ $2–6^8$ [\$1 signed $(–1_1, \chi1)$]. 48 leaves, pp *1–5 6 7 8–14 15–17 18–38 39 40–45 46 47 48 49–50 51 52–56 57 58–63 64–66 67–79 80 81–84 85 86 87 88–91 92 93–95 96*

Technical notes: 103 × 63 mm (p 9). 30 lines, 20 = 68 mm. Leaf size 150 × 93 mm; thickness 0.12 mm; wove, unwatermarked, smooth, white

Contents: Half-title ('Lawn Tennis') (*1*), advertisement (*2*), title (*3*), blank (*4*), contents (*5–6*), text (lawn tennis) (*7–45*), text (badminton) (*46–56*), text (croquet) (*57–79*), text (troco or lawn billiards) (*80–84*), text (racquets) (*85–91*), text (fives) (*92–95*), blank (*96*)

Binding: Greyish Green (150) cloth over light boards, the several sections stapled individually. FC: printed as in oblong panels in black and light Orange (52) on a Green background ([black rule] | [black on Orange] WARD AND LOCK'S SIXPENNY HANDBOOKS. | [decorative panel in black and Orange on Green] | [Orange band] | [black on Green] **LAWN TENNIS** | [Orange band] | [drawing of a mixed doubles lawn tennis game in black, Green, and Grey] | [Orange band] | [black on Green] **CROQUET, RACQUETS&c** | [Orange rule] | [in black] **ILLUSTRATED** | [black triple rule, the centre rule in bold] | [arabesque frieze, in black and Orange] | [black on Orange] WARD LOCK & Co. SALISBURY SQUARE.). RC: blank. Spine: upwards, in black (**LAWN TENNIS. *SIXPENCE*.**)

Copies seen: KRWL; BL: Mic A 8627 (3) (microfilm copy of BOD 38455 f 1)

Fingerprint: 5553 eron .)al feli 7 1890Q

Notes: Printed anonymously. Year of publication is inferred as that cited in the *General Catalogue* of the BL.

The text of this edition is extensively revised. The section on lawn tennis is expanded and integrated with the laws of the game (originally presented as an appendix), and the original sections on pallone, nurr and spell *etc* are omitted, as also are several advertisements. The section on croquet appears to be unchanged.

(d) *Second edition, variant [1890]*

LAWN TENNIS, | BADMINTON, | *CROQUET, TROCO, RACQUETS, AND FIVES.* | NEW EDITION. | WARD, LOCK, AND CO., | LONDON, NEW YORK, AND MELBOURNE.

Formula: As that of (c)

Technical notes: 102 × 63 mm (p 9). 30 lines, 20 = 68 mm. Leaf size 151 × 91 mm; thickness 0.12 mm; wove, unwatermarked, smooth, white

Contents: As those of (c)

Binding: Moderate Olive (107) cloth over light boards, the several sections stapled individually. FC: printed as in oblong panels in black and light greyish yellowish Brown (79) on an Olive background ([black rule] | [black on Brown] WARD AND LOCK'S SIXPENNY HANDBOOKS. | [decorative panel in black and Brown on Olive] | [Brown band] | [black on Olive] **LAWN TENNIS** | [Brown band] | [drawing of a mixed doubles lawn tennis game in black and Brown on Olive] | [Brown band] | [black on Olive] **CROQUET, RACQUETS&c** | [Brown rule] | [in black] **ILLUS-TRATED** | [black triple rule, the centre rule in bold] | [arabesque frieze, in black and Brown] | [black on Brown] WARD LOCK & Co. SALISBURY SQUARE.). RC: blank. Spine: upwards, in black (**LAWN TENNIS. *SIXPENCE.***)

Copy seen: PC

Fingerprint: As that of (c)

Notes: This issue is apparently a minor variant of (c), differing essentially only in colouring of the FC.

1870–79

A75   CROQUET: HAND BOOK AND RULES. [Anon]   *ca* 1870

Foreword: There is no known evidence as to which, if either, of the issues here recorded may properly be regarded as the first edition of this work. A statement in the preface implies the existence of an earlier edition but is not thought to warrant acceptance at face value.

(a) **First edition [ca 1870]*

HAND BOOK | AND | RULES | OF | **CROQUET.** | Revised and Amended. | ALSO | **RULES FOR TOURNAMENTS.**

Formula: [1⁸]. 8 leaves, pp *1–5 6–16*

Technical notes: 104 × 68 mm (p 10). 34 lines, 20 = 61 mm. Leaf size 126 × 93 mm; thickness 0.08 mm; wove, unwatermarked, smooth, white

Contents: Title (*1*), frontispiece, engraved illustration of a croquet party, signed 'Cornell Dean' (*2*), preface (*3*), anonymous advertisement, Index Pins (*4*), text (*5–16*)

Binding: Moderate Yellow (87) semi-gloss paper, printed in black, glued to the fold of the outer sheet, stitched, no spine or endpapers. FC: within a frame composed of a chain link with corner ornaments (HAND+BOOK | AND | RULES | [flourish] OF [flourish] | [within a stylised band slanted from bottom L to top R, in open shaded script, flanked at the extremities by flourishes] **CROQUET** | REVISED AND AMENDED | [flourish] ALSO [flourish] | **RULES FOR TOURNAMENTS.**). Inside FC: blank. RC: blank. Inside RC: blank

Copy seen: HPC: GV933 H3a CROQ

Fingerprint: s.nd isso kega thgr 3 1870Q

Notes: Published and printed anonymously. Approximate year of publication is inferred from the state of development of the game as evidenced by the code of 19 numbered rules included in the text, and by a marked similarity of the frontispiece to that in another rule book (A40), which appears to have been first published in 1869.

(b) *First edition, variant [ca 1870]*

HAND BOOK | AND | RULES | OF | **CROQUET.** | Revised and Amended. | ALSO | **RULES FOR TOURNAMENTS.**

Formula: [1⁸]. 8 leaves, pp *1–5 6–16*

Technical notes: 104 × 68 mm (p 10). 34 lines, 20 = 61 mm. Leaf size 126 × 93 mm; thickness 0.08 mm; wove, unwatermarked, smooth, white

Contents: Title (*1*), frontispiece, engraved illustration of a croquet party, signed 'Cornell Dean' (*2*), preface (*3*), anonymous advertisement, Index Pins (*4*), text (*5–16*)

Binding: Moderate Yellow (87) semi-gloss paper, printed in black, glued to the fold of the outer sheet, stitched, no spine or endpapers. FC: within a frame composed of a chain link with corner ornaments (HAND+BOOK | AND | RULES | [flourish] OF [flourish] | [within a stylised band slanted from bottom L to top R, in open shaded script, flanked either end by flourishes] **CROQUET** | REVISED AND AMENDED | [flourish] ALSO [flourish] | **RULES FOR TOURNAMENTS.**). Inside FC: blank. RC: blank. Inside RC: blank

Copy seen: HPC: GV933 H3a CROQ

Fingerprint: s.nd isso kega thgr 3 1870Q

Notes: Published and printed anonymously. The frontispiece and text of this variant are apparently identical to those of (a).

A76   CROQUET QUADRILLES. Charles Godfrey   *ca* 1870

[The FC, printed in dark reddish Orange (38), moderate yellowish Green (136), moderate Yellow (87), dark Grey (266), and black]

[in ornate Orange, Grey, and black display script over an engraved illustration, signed 'STANNARD & SON, LITH', of two crossed mallets, three hoops, and a collection of ringed balls, standing on rough turf, in Orange, Green, Yellow, and black] CROQUET | [in artist's Orange and black shaded display script] QUADRILLES | [at R, in artist's manuscript, surmounted by a flourish] By | [in ornate Orange, Grey, and black display script, below the engraved illustration described above] CHARLES GODFREY. | [in black] BAND MASTER ROYAL HORSE GUARDS. | [swelled rule in black] | [in black, in artist's script] ENT, STA, HALL.   PRICE 4/– | [in black] LONDON: | [*do*] DUFF & STEWART.147.OXFORD Sᵀ W.

Formula: [1⁶], including the FC and RC. 6 leaves, pp *i–ii*, 1–9 *10*

Technical notes: 279 × 217 mm (p 8). Leaf size 335 × 238 mm; thickness 0.15 mm; wove, unwatermarked, smooth, white. In the copy examined each sheet is constructed of two leaves glued together close to the fold, along which there is a line of regularly spaced faint marks as if to indicate where it might be, or might originally have been, sewn or stitched

Contents: Title (*i*), blank (*ii*), music (1–9), blank (*10*)

Binding: Loose sheets

Copy seen: PC

Fingerprint: Indeterminate

Notes: Printed anonymously, price 4/–. Approximate year of publication is suggested by the design of equipment illustrated on the FC and by the profusion of popular croquet music known to have been published in the late 1860s and early 1870s. See, for example, A29 and A51.

The music consists of a piano score of five quadrilles, entitled 'CROQUET', 'THE PUZZLE — LIFE IS LIKE A GAME OF CROQUET — WISHES', 'A YOUNG LADY'S "NO"', 'TRIPPING THRO' THE MEADOWS — ONLY — THE GOOD-BYE AT THE DOOR', 'WILL JONES AND SUSAN JANE — SPORTS GALOP — ABYSSINIAN GOLD — CROQUET'.

The copy examined includes a single loose leaf which consists of a part transposed for A cornet.

A77   **CROQUET: RULES AND REGULATIONS.** [Anon]   *ca* 1876

[The FC]

CROQUET | [engraved illustration of an upright croquet stand] | **RULES AND REGULATIONS**

Formula: [1⁸]. 8 leaves, pp 1–16

Technical notes: 104 × 75 mm (p 4). 34 lines, 20 = 61 mm. Leaf size 142 × 101 mm; thickness 0.10 mm; wove, unwatermarked, smooth, white

Contents: Title heading (1), text (1–15), name of publisher (16)

Binding: Pale Green (149) paper, printed in very deep Purple (220), sewn through the wrapper, no spine or endpapers. FC: as above. Inside FC: blank. RC: ([within an outlined lozenge, the height of the several letters sized to fit] **McVEAN** | **DRESDEN, CANADA** | Established 1874). Inside RC: blank

Copy seen: HPC: GV933 C8M84 CROQ

Fingerprint: s.of hee. t.by orSp 3 1876Q [group 1 taken from the FC]

Notes: Printed anonymously. Approximate year of publication is suggested by the state of development of the game indicated by the code of 50 numbered rules included in the text and from the close similarity of this work to other American rule books issued about the same time — see, for example, A67.

A78   **HAND BOOK OF CROQUET.** OV Goulette   *ca* 1875

HAND BOOK | OF | [in outlined script] **CROQUET.** | [swelled rule] | O. V. GOULETTE, | GANANOQUE, ONT. | [rule] | REPORTER PRINT.

Formula: Not ascertainable from the photocopy examined. Apparently 6 leaves, pp *1* [2] *3* 4–11 [12]

Technical notes: †180 × †114 mm (p 6). 41 lines, 20 = †89mm. Leaf size †235 × †167 mm

Contents: Title (*1*), wanting from the photocopy examined ([2]), preface (*3*), text (4–11), wanting from the photocopy examined ([12])

Binding: No wrapper apparent in the photocopy examined, apparently sewn, and stapled close to the sheet folds

Copy seen: NLA (photocopy of unknown scale, wanting pp [2], [12])

Fingerprint: y.he e.ts t,i- rees C 1875Q [groups 2–4 taken from p 11]

Notes: Printed by Reporter Print. Approximate year of publication is inferred from the NLA catalogue citation.

The text includes a code of 40 numbered rules, which bears no resemblance to the code of the same number of rules found in A73.

A79   HAND-BOOK OF CROQUET. [Anon]   *ca* 1876

[The FC, p *1*]

[in display script] HAND-BOOK | — OF — | [in display script] CROQUET.

Formula: [1⁸]. 8 leaves, pp *1–3* 4–15 *16*

Technical notes: 104 × 72 mm (p 9). 35 lines, 20 = 60 mm, variable. Leaf size 133 × 87 mm; thickness 0.11 mm; wove, unwatermarked, smooth, white

Contents: Title (*1*), TP verso (*2*), preface (*3*), plan of croquet court (nine-arch croquet) (*4*), plan of croquet court (ten-arch croquet) (*5*), text (*6–15*), blank (*16*)

Binding: None, sewn

Copy seen: HPC: GV901 H31 CROQ

Fingerprint: y.im d.be inry main 3 1876Q

Notes: Printed by Register Printing Company, South Bend, Indiana. Year of publication is inferred from the close similarity of this work with A67. The texts of the two publications are identical or virtually identical.

A80   THE LAWS OF CROQUET. Arthur Lillie   *ca* 1872

[Within a ruled frame with flourishes inside the corners]

THE | LAWS OF CROQUET. | [swelled rule] | BY | ARTHUR LILLIE, | Champion, Grand National Croquet Club, 1872, and Winner of | the All Comers' Prize, 1871. | [swelled rule] | LONDON: | JAQUES & SON   102, HATTON GARDEN.

Formula: [1⁴]. 4 leaves, pp *1–4* 5–7 *8*

Technical notes: 159 × 98 mm (p 5). 34 lines, 20 = 93 mm. Leaf size 201 × 134 mm; thickness 0.12 mm; wove, unwatermarked, smooth, white

Contents: Title (*1*), frontispiece (engraved illustration of a croquet lawn in a parkland setting) (*2*), diagram ('The setting') (*3*), text (*4–7*), advertisement (*8*)

Binding: Very dark Green (147) rib grain cloth (the ribs running top L to bottom R) limp over paper, apparently stapled (the copy examined had been rebound). FC: gold-blocked within a double-ruled blind-stamped frame (Laws of Croquet | BY | ARTHUR LILLIE.). RC: blind-stamped frame of the same pattern as that on the FC. Spine: apparently none.

Copy seen: BL: 7919 bb 38 (imperfect)

Fingerprint: r.ut e.s- s,er e.es C 1872Q [all four groups taken from p 5]

Notes: Printed anonymously. Year of publication is inferred from the putative source of the code of laws presented in this work — *viz* the author's *The Book of Croquet* (A54), first published in April 1872 — and the rejection of that code by the contemporary press. It is conjectured that Jaques & Son planned to reprint the author's laws as a replacement for J Jaques's *Croquet: The Laws and Regulations of the Game* (A12) to distribute with their croquet equipment, but it is thought unlikely that they would have done so long after April 1872 in the knowledge that the croquet establishment had taken such strong exception to the author having published his own set of rules so soon after the 'Conference Laws' had achieved general acceptance. According to *The Field* (see below), 'We should in fairness add that Mr. Lillie, if he gave a code at all, was forced into writing one for himself, as he applied to the publishers for permission to reprint the Conference Laws and was refused'. Lillie won the 1872 GNCC championship in mid-June, by which time Jaques would have had an opportunity to review their publishing plans. It is conjectured that they were then so far committed, perhaps chiefly to support their equipment sales at the height of the season, that they decided to proceed immediately with this reprint as a short-term stop-gap while considering how best to buy into the Conference Code at some future date. But, in the light of subsequent developments, other counsels would seem to have prevailed: Jaques continued to publish Lillie's code of laws at least until 1896 (see A54). The (inferred) year of publication cited in the *General Catalogue* of the BL is 1875.

The text consists of a code of 20 laws.

Reviews: *The Field* (13 April 1872, p 335), *The Queen* (20 April 1872, p 276).

AA81   PRICE LIST OF CROQUET, BADMINTON, AND CRICKET   *ca* 1876
GOODS. FH Ayres

[The FC, within a double-ruled frame, the inner frame in bold, with corner ornaments]

F. H. AYRES, | *Manufacturer of every description of* | [in gothic-revival script] **Indoor & Outdoor Games,** | **111, ALDERSGATE STREET, LONDON E.C.** | [double rule] | [engraved vignette depicting a garden seat] | THE REGISTERED CROQUET GARDEN SEAT. | [wavy line] | [in gothic-revival script] Price List of | [swash *C, B*] CROQUET, BADMINTON, AND | [swash *C, G*] CRICKET GOODS.

Formula: [1⁸] including the front and rear pastedowns. 8 leaves including the front and rear pastedowns, unnumbered, pp *i–ii, 1–12, iii–iv*

Technical notes: 171 × 97 mm (p 3). 61 lines, 20 = 56 mm. Leaf size 218 × 140 mm; thickness 0.08 mm; wove, unwatermarked, smooth, white

Contents: Glued to the FC (*i*), text (*ii, 1–12, iii*), glued to the RC (*iv*)

Binding: Greyish purplish Pink (253) paper glued to the FC, sewn, the front and rear pastedowns included within the text, no spine

Copy seen: PC

Fingerprint: 8000 /6/6 S.S. 6600 C 1876Q [groups 2–4 taken from p 9]

Notes: Printed anonymously. Approximate year of publication is inferred from the facts that this work and other Ayres publications of the same period share common illustrations and that this catalogue includes badminton but not lawn tennis goods.

A82   RULES AND REGULATIONS FOR PLAYING FIELD   *ca* 1875
CROQUET. [Anon]

(a) **First edition [ca 1875]*

[The FC, within a double-ruled frame with corner ornaments]

Rules and | **Regulations** | **For Playing** | **FIELD** | **CROQUET**

Formula: [1⁴]. 4 leaves, unnumbered [pp 1–8]

Technical notes: ca 93 × 64 mm (p 2). 26 lines, 20 = *ca* 72 mm. Leaf size *ca* 120 × 79 mm

Contents: Title (*1*), text (*2–8*)

Binding: None

Copy seen: PC (photocopy)

Fingerprint: k.nd ngt- n-he ERt. C 1875Q

Notes: Published and printed anonymously.

The origins of this work are obscure. Similarities to (b) suggest that it was an earlier edition of the same work. Approximate year of publication is inferred from the state of the game described in the text and from its literary and type style. In view of the fact that (b) and (c) are published by Professional Players, it is relevant to note that the earliest clearly dated reference to professionalism in this bibliography is that to professional clubs on the TP of A22b, published in 1873.

(b) *Single folded sheet [ca 1875]*

[Within a ruled and dotted frame in bold with rounded corners]

RULES | — AND — | **Regulations** | [drawing of a mallet, stake, and ringed ball, within a ruled frame with rounded corners which extends horizontally through, as though overlapping the larger ruled and dotted frame] | FOR PLAYING | **FIELD** | **CROQUET** | [flourish] | PUBLISHED BY | PROFESSIONAL PLAYERS.

Formula: [1⁴]. 4 leaves on a single sheet in a W-fold, pp *1* 2–8 in the order *1, 2, 3, 8, 7, 4, 5, 6* of the external contours of the letter *W* (from L to R)

Technical notes: 116 × 62 mm (p 2). 33 lines, 20 = 70 mm, variable. Leaf size 141 × 76 mm; thickness 0.07 mm; wove, unwatermarked, smooth, pale Green (149)

Contents: Title (*1*), text (*2–8*)

Binding: None

Copy seen: HPC: RRCC #125 CROQ

Fingerprint: k.he san- t-ng llR. C 1875Q [all four groups taken from p 3]

Notes: Printed anonymously. The text, which consists of a code of 18 numbered rules, has not been collated with that of (a).

(c) *Single folded sheet, variant [ca 1875]*

[Mostly within a ruled frame in bold]

RULES | and | **REGULATIONS** | [drawing of a mallet, stake, and ringed ball which extends horizontally through the surrounding frame] | For Playing | **FIELD** | **CROQUET** | Published by | PROFESSIONAL PLAYERS

Formula: [1⁴]. 4 leaves on a single sheet in a W-fold, unnumbered, in the order pp *1, 2, 3, 8, 7, 4, 5, 6* of the external contours of the letter *W* (from L to R)

Technical notes: 109 × 63 mm (p 2). 31 lines, 20 = 71 mm, variable. Leaf size 126 × 77 mm; thickness 0.10 mm; wove, unwatermarked, smooth, pale orange Yellow (73)

Contents: Title (*1*), text, continued (*2–3*), blank (*4*), text, concluded (*5–8*)

Binding: None

Copy seen: PC

Fingerprint: y.ll t.ng eses r.he C 1875Q [all four groups taken from p 6]

Notes: Printed anonymously. The text, though reset throughout, is virtually identical to that of (b), save for the fact that p *4*, replacing a court setting ('ARENA No. 1'), is now blank. This omission is thought to have been inadvertent.

1880

A83   **RULES FOR THE STANDARD GAME OF CROQUET.**   1880
        [**National Croquet League**]

RULES | FOR THE | Standard Game of Croquet. | AS ADOPTED BY | THE NATIONAL CROQUET LEAGUE. | TOGETHER WITH ITS | CONSTITUTION,

BY-LAWS, AND CODE OF GOVERNMENT OF | FRIENDLY CONTESTS. | [rule] | PHILADELPHIA: | J. B. LIPPINCOTT & CO. | 1880.

Formula: Not ascertainable from the copy examined [p 5 signed '1*', p 13 signed '2', p 17 signed '2*', p 25 signed '3']. 17 leaves, pp *1–2* 3 4 *5–29* 30 31–34

Technical notes: 129 × 79 mm (p 6). 32 lines, 20 = 82 mm. Leaf size 166 × 105 mm

Contents: Title (*1*), TP verso (*2*), contents (*3*), blank (*4*), text (*5–29*), blank (*30*), advertisements (*31–34*)

Binding: Very pale Green (148) flecked paper or card, sewn, no spine or endpapers. FC: within a triple frame, the inner and outer frames ruled, the central frame consisting of a continuous chain pattern (RULES | FOR THE STANDARD | **GAME OF CROQUET** | AS ADOPTED BY | THE NATIONAL CROQUET LEAGUE. | [swelled rule] | PHILADELPHIA: | J. B. LIPPINCOTT & CO. | 1880.

Copy seen: LOC: GV935 N3 (photocopy, the wrapper in colour, the original copy rebound in library covers)

Fingerprint: 28EN edld ndhe Noma 3 1880A

Notes: Printed anonymously.

A84   **SPALDING'S OFFICIAL CROQUET MANUAL.**   [1880]
       [National Croquet Convention]

SPALDING'S | OFFICIAL | **CROQUET MANUAL** | CONTAINING A | *SHORT HISTORY OF CROQUET,* | WITH FULL INSTRUCTIONS ON THE PROPER AND SCIENTIFIC USE | OF THE BALL AND MALLET | AS PRACTICED BY SKILLED PLAYERS. | [rule] | IT ALSO CONTAINS THE "AMERICAN RULES OR LOOSE | CROQUET," AS OFFICIALLY | ADOPTED BY THE | *NATIONAL CROQUET CONGRESS,* | Held in Chicago, Sept. 23d and 24th, 1879. | [rule] | THE ONLY BOOK OF RULES ON CROQUET EVER PUBLISHED | UNDER NATIONAL AUTHORITY. | [rule] | *PUBLISHED BY* | A. G. SPALDING & BROS., | 118 RANDOLPH ST., CHICAGO, ILL.

Formula: [1–2¹⁶]. 32 leaves, pp *1–2* 3–64

Technical notes: 118 × 72 mm (p 10). 33 lines, 20 = 73 mm. Leaf size 146 × 100 mm; thickness 0.06 mm; wove, unwatermarked, smooth, white

Contents: Title (*1*), TP verso (*2*), publisher's preface, signed 'A. G. SPALDING & BROS' (*3–4*), preface of the standing committee of the National Croquet Convention, signed 'J. A. KENNICOTT', 'J. A. STODDARD', 'A. FRANK WILLIAMS', 'C. M. HAWLEY', 'W. H. RAND' (*5–7*), contents (*8*), text (*9–57*), advertisements (*58–64*)

Binding: Light yellowish Brown (76) paper, printed in black, glued to the folds of the gatherings, stitched, no endpapers. FC: ([above a ruled frame, enclosing a large upper engraving and a small lower framed panel] **PRICE 15 CENTS.**] | [in shaded open script out of the engraving] SPALDING'S | [*do*, flanked at R by a corner ornament] OFFICIAL | [vignette within the engraving, illustration of a croquet party] | [in shaded open script out of the engraving, describing a serpentine line] CROQUET | [in shaded open script out of the engraving] MANUAL | [within the lower panel] PUBLISHED BY | [*do*] **A. G. SPALDING & BROS.,** | [*do*] 118 RANDOLPH STREET, CHICAGO, ILL.). Inside FC: advertisement and name of printer. RC: advertisement. Inside RC: advertisement. Spine: blank

Copy seen: HPC: GV931 S7 1880 CROQ

Fingerprint: d,he e.nd L.T. beSt 3 1880Q

Notes: Printed by Rand, McNally & Co, Chicago, price 15 cents. Year of publication is inferred from the dates of the 1879 Chicago Croquet Convention, as cited on the TP.

Taking a longer historical view, the authority of the National Croquet Convention was arguably no more universal than that of the National American Croquet Association (of New England) which was to be founded only three years later, in 1882. It is interesting to observe that Spalding was to acquire publishing rights to the latter body's rule book (A85) and was no less effusive in proclaiming its national authority.

1882

A85   **CROQUET: THE RULES GOVERNING THE GAME, AS ADOPTED BY THE NATIONAL AMERICAN CROQUET ASSOCIATION [and CROQUET: THE OFFICIAL RULES GOVERNING THE GAME, AS ADOPTED BY THE NATIONAL AMERICAN CROQUET ASSOCIATION].**   1882
[National American Croquet Association]

(a) *First edition (1882)*

CROQUET: | THE | Rules Governing the Game, | AS ADOPTED BY THE | NATIONAL AMERICAN CROQUET | ASSOCIATION, | OCTOBER 4, 1882.

Formula: [1⁶]. 6 leaves, pp *1–3* 4–11 *12*

Technical notes: 111 × 76 mm (p 4). 32 lines, 20 = 70 mm. Leaf size 152 × 103 mm; thickness 0.07 mm; wove, unwatermarked, smooth, brownish Pink (33)

Contents: Title (*1*), introduction (*2*), text (*3–11*), blank (*12*)

Binding: Light yellowish Brown (76) wove paper, stapled, no spine or endpapers. FC: the lettering on the TP (see above) reprinted in black within a double-ruled frame, the outer frame in bold. Inside FC: blank. RC: blank. Inside RC: blank

Copy seen: PC

Fingerprint: t.at d.e- inn- d,ce C 1882A [groups 2–4 taken from p 11]

Notes: Apparently published by the NACA, printed anonymously. The text of this edition is confined to a brief description of the game and a code of 53 numbered rules.

(b) *First edition, variant (1882)*

CROQUET. | [rule] | THE | Rules Governing the Game, | AS ADOPTED BY THE | NATIONAL AMERICAN CROQUET | ASSOCIATION, | OCTOBER 4, 1882.

Formula: As that of (a)

Technical notes: 111 × 76 mm (p 4). 32 lines, 20 = 70 mm. Leaf size 152 × 103 mm; thickness 0.08 mm; wove, unwatermarked, smooth, pale orange Yellow (73)

Contents: As those of (a)

Binding: Light greyish Olive (109) laid paper, stapled, no spine or endpapers. FC: the lettering on the TP (as above) reprinted in black within a double-ruled frame, the outer frame in bold. Inside FC: blank. RC: blank. Inside RC: blank

Copy seen: PC

Fingerprint: t.e, d.e- inn- edce C 1882A [groups 2–4 taken from p 11]

Notes: Apparently published by the NACA, printed anonymously. The text of this variant appears to be identical in substance to that of (a), though some of the pages are reset. It is not clear which issue preceded the other.

(c) *Authorised edition, 1891 (1891)*

CROQUET, | THE RULES GOVERNING THE GAME, | AS ADOPTED BY THE | NATIONAL AMERICAN CROQUET ASSOCIATION. | AUTHORIZED EDITION. | [rule] | REVISED AND CORRECTED | BY THE | NATIONAL ASSOCIATION. | [rule] | PUBLISHED FOR THE ASSOCIATION | BY | A. G. SPALDING & BROS. | NEW YORK. | 1891.

Formula: [1¹⁶ 2⁸]. 24 leaves, pp *1–4* 5 6 7 8 9 *10* 11 *12* 13 *14* 15–34 *35–48*

Technical notes: 128 × 71 mm (p 7). 46 lines, 20 = 56 mm. Leaf size 169 × 119 mm; thickness 0.08 mm; wove, unwatermarked, smooth, white

Contents: Title (*1*), court layout 1889 (*2*), text (*3–34*), advertisements (*35–48*)

Binding: Brownish Orange (54) paper, printed in black, apparently glued to the gatherings (the FC of the copy examined was detached and the spine wanting), stapled through both gatherings, no endpapers. Inside FC: publisher's notice. RC: advertisement. Inside RC: advertisement

Copy seen: PC (imperfect, the FC detached and wanting matter at all extremities, and subsequently restored)

Fingerprint: y.is t.he s.ll shma 3 1891A [group 4 taken from p 16]

Notes: Printed anonymously, price 10 cents.

The text includes a code of rules, numbered 1–59, and a set of 'tournament rules', numbered 1–11. Several of the former rules depart considerably from those in (a).

(d) *Daniel Gunn edition (1893)*

CROQUET | THE | **Rules Governing the Game,** | AS ADOPTED BY THE | NATIONAL AMERICAN CROQUET | ASSOCIATION, | **OCTOBER 4, 1882.** | [rule] | BOSTON: | DANIEL GUNN & CO., PRINTERS. | 1893.

Formula: [1⁶]. 6 leaves, pp *1–3* 4–11 *12*

Technical notes: 110 × 76 mm (p 5). 32 lines, 20 = 69 mm. Leaf size 147 × 94 mm; thickness 0.08 mm; wove, unwatermarked, smooth, light yellowish Brown (76)

Contents: Title (*1*), introduction (*2*), text (*3–11*), blank (*12*)

Binding: Pale Blue (185) paper, stapled, no spine or endpapers. FC: the letterpress of the TP reprinted in black within a double-ruled frame, the outer frame in bold. Inside FC: blank. RC: blank. Inside RC: blank

Copy seen: PC

Fingerprint: t.he d.s- anin n-d, C 1893A [groups 2–4 taken from p 11]

Notes: Printed and apparently published by Daniel Gunn & Co, Boston.

The text is substantially identical to that of the first edition (a). The fact that the rules of the game had developed considerably during the intervening years — see, for example, (c) — would suggest that this edition was not authorised by the NACA.

(e) *Official edition, 1897–98 (1897)*

CROQUET. | . . The . . | **Rules Governing the Game,** | [double rule] | . . . . . . | AS ADOPTED BY THE | NATIONAL AMERICAN CROQUET | ASSOCIATION. | 1897- '98.

Formula: [1⁶]. 6 leaves, pp *1–3* 4–12

Technical notes: 109 × 76 mm (p 11). 40 lines, 20 = 56 mm. Leaf size 152 × 102 mm; thickness 0.08 mm; wove, unwatermarked, smooth, white

Contents: Title (*1*), blank (*2*), text (*3–12*)

Binding: Light greyish Olive (109) laid paper, printed in black, sewn through the wrapper, no spine or endpapers. FC: the lettering on the TP (as above) reprinted within a double-ruled frame, the outer frame in bold. Inside FC: blank. RC: blank. Inside RC: blank

Copy seen: HPC: GV933 N3 1897 CROQ

Fingerprint: llhe sehe asce iser C 1897A [groups 2–4 taken from p 11]

Notes: Apparently published by the NACA, printed anonymously.

The text of this edition is confined to a code of 59 pre-established rules plus one other adopted by the Association in August 1894.

(f) *1898–1899 edition (1898)*

CROQUET | [rule] | The Official | Rules Governing the Game | [double rule] | [flourish] FOR 1898—1899 [flourish] | AS ADOPTED BY THE | NATIONAL AMERICAN CROQUET | ASSOCIATION

Formula: As that of (e)

Technical notes: 109 × 79 mm (p 4). 40 lines, 20 = 56 mm. Leaf size 146 × 98 mm; thickness 0.06 mm; wove, unwatermarked, smooth, white

Contents: As those of (e)

Binding: Light greyish Olive (109) laid paper, printed in black, sewn through the wrapper, no spine or endpapers. FC: the lettering on the TP (as above) reprinted within a double-ruled frame, the outer frame in bold. Inside FC: blank. RC: blank. Inside RC: blank

Copy seen: PC

Fingerprint: llhe sehe asce iser C 1898A [groups 2–4 taken from p 11]

Notes: Apparently published by the NACA, printed anonymously.

The text of this edition has not been collated with that of (e). It would, however, appear that the two editions are identical or virtually identical.

(g) *Official edition, 1900–1901 (1899)*

CROQUET | [rule] | The Official | Rules Governing the Game | [flourish] FOR 1900—1901 [flourish] | AS ADOPTED BY THE | NATIONAL AMERICAN CROQUET | ASSOCIATION

Formula: [1^6]. 6 leaves, pp *1–3 4–12*

Technical notes: 110 × 75 mm (p 11). 40 lines, 20 = 56 mm. Leaf size 144 × 98 mm; thickness 0.06 mm; wove, unwatermarked, smooth, pale orange Yellow (73)

Contents: Title (*1*), TP verso (*2*), text (*3–12*)

Binding: Light yellowish Brown (76) laid paper, printed in deep Blue (179), sewn through the wrapper, no spine or endpapers. FC: reprinted from the TP (as above) within a double-ruled frame, the outer frame in bold. Inside FC: blank. RC: blank. Inside RC: blank

Copy seen: HPC: GV933 N3 1900–01 CROQ

Fingerprint: llhe sehe asce iser C 1899A [groups 2–4 taken from p 11]

Notes: Printed by Geo H Morse & Co, Boston. Year of publication is inferred from the year of printing cited on the TP verso. The text is identical in substance to that of (e) save for some re-arrangement of the footnotes.

(h) *Official edition, 1900–1901, 1901 reprint (1901)*

[Within a double-ruled frame, the outer frame in bold]

CROQUET | [rule] | The Official | Rules Governing the Game | [flourish] FOR 1900—1901 [flourish] | AS ADOPTED BY THE | NATIONAL AMERICAN CROQUET | ASSOCIATION

Formula: As that of (g)

Technical notes: 110 × 75 mm (p 11). 40 lines, 20 = 56 mm. Leaf size 143 × 96 mm; thickness 0.05 mm; wove, unwatermarked, smooth, white

Contents: As those of (g)

Binding: Greyish reddish Orange (39) paper, printed in black, sewn through the wrapper, no spine or endpapers. FC: reprinted from the TP (as above). Inside FC: blank. RC: blank. Inside RC: blank

Copy seen: HPC: GV933 N3 1900–01a CROQ

Fingerprint: llhe sehe asce iser C 1901A [groups 2–4 taken from p 11]

Notes: Printed by Geo H Morse & Co, Boston. Year of publication is inferred from the year of printing cited on the TP verso. The text is apparently identical to that of (g).

(j) *Official edition, 1902 (1902)*

CROQUET | [rule] | The Official | Rules Governing the Game | [flourish] FOR 1902 [flourish] | AS ADOPTED BY THE | NATIONAL AMERICAN CROQUET | ASSOCIATION

Formula: As that of (g)

Technical notes: 109 × 75 mm (p 11). 40 lines, 20 = 56 mm. Leaf size 146 × 96 mm; thickness 0.07 mm; wove, unwatermarked, smooth, white

Contents: As those of (g)

Binding: Light greyish Olive (109) light card, printed in black, sewn through the wrapper, no spine or endpapers. FC: reprinted from the TP (as above), save for use of a different font for the year ('1902'). Inside FC: blank. RC: blank. Inside RC: blank

Copy seen: HPC: GV933 N3 1902 CROQ

Fingerprint: llhe sehe asce iser C 1892A [groups 2–4 taken from p 11]

Notes: Printed by Geo H Morse & Co, Boston. Year of publication is inferred from the citation on the TP; that cited on the TP verso (1892) is manifestly in error. The text is apparently identical to that of (g).

1885

A86　HOW TO PLAY PROGRESSIVE CROQUET. Mrs AF Devereux　　1885

HOW TO PLAY | [in decorative script] **Progressive Croquet** | BY | MRS. A. F. DEVEREUX | [swelled rule] | CINCINNATI | Robert Clarke & Co | 1865

Formula: [1¹²]. 24 leaves, pp *1–3* 4–24

Technical notes: 95 × 55 mm (p 4), 22 lines, 20 = 89 mm. Leaf size 139 × 82 mm

Contents: Title (*1*), TP verso (*2*), text (*3–24*)

Binding: Greyish Yellow (90) paper, apparently sewn through the wrapper, no spine or endpapers. FC: printed in black ([decorative head border] | HOW TO PLAY | [in gothic-revival script] **Progressive Croquet** | By MRS. DEVEREUX |

[within a ruled panel] CROQUET—AN HISTORIC GAME. | [*do*] ITS CHARMS AND ADVANTAGES | [*do*] HOW TO GIVE A PARTY. | [*do*] INVITATIONS. | [*do*] ALL TAKE PARTNERS. | [*do*] SCORE SHEETS. | [*do*] THE SEND OFF. | [*do*] PRIZES. | [*do*] DEFINITIONS OF TERMS USED. | [*do*] A FEW NECESSARY RULES. | [*do*] HINTS TO THE HOSTESS. | [*do*] POINTERS FOR PLAYERS. | CINCINNATI | ROBERT CLARKE & CO | 1885 | [decorative tail border]). Inside FC: advertisement. RC: advertisement. Inside RC: advertisement

Copy seen: LOC: GV933 D48 (photocopy, the covers in colour, the original copy disbound)

Fingerprint: edme v-l- onn- pawi 3 1885A

Notes: Published and printed by Robert Clarke & Co, Cincinnati OH. The text includes a skeletal code of eleven numbered rules addressed to experienced players.

1887

A87   MANUEL ET REGLEMENT DU JEU DU CROQUET. '**Un Amateur**'   **1887**

MANUEL ET REGLEMENT | DU | JEU DU CROQUET | [wavy line] | Publié à Québec par un Amateur en novembre 1887. | [wavy line] | [publisher's device] | QUÉBEC: | Imprimerie Générale A. COTÉ et Cie | 1887.

Formula: Not ascertainable from the photocopy examined. Apparently 18 leaves, pp *1–5* 6 7 *8–16* 17 [18]

Technical notes: †164 × †106 mm (p 10). 34 lines, 20 = †96 mm. Leaf size †210 × †132 mm

Contents: Title (*1*), blank (*2*), preface, signed 'Et, Legaré' (*3*), blank (*4*), text (*5–16*), tables des matières (*17*), wanting from the photocopy examined ([18])

Binding: Apparently wrapped in pale card or paper, the construction of the original not ascertainable from the photocopy examined. FC: within a triple frame with corner ornaments, the innermost and outermost frames scalloped, the central frame ruled in bold (MANUEL ET REGLEMENT | DU | JEU DU CROQUET | [wavy line] | Publié à Québec par un Amateur en novembre 1887. | [wavy line] | [publisher's device] | QUÉBEC: | J. A. LANGLAIS, LIBRAIRE-EDITEUR | 177, Rue St-Joseph, St-Roch | 1887.). Inside FC: blank. RC: wanting from the photocopy examined

Copy seen: NLA: Mc 756 (photocopy of unknown scale)

Fingerprint: É.l. u.ée art, esn. C 1887A [groups 2–4 taken from p 13]

Notes: Published in November 1887, printed by A Coté et Cie, Quebec.

1888

A88   NOUVELLE ACADÉMIE DES JEUX. Jean Quinola   **1888**

NOUVELLE | ACADÉMIE DES JEUX | CONTENANT | UN DICTIONNAIRE DES JEUX ANCIENS | LE NOUVEAU JEU DE CROQUET | LE BESIGUE CHINOIS | ET UNE ÉTUDE SUR LES JEUX ET PARIS DE COURSES | PAR | **Jean QUINOLA, éditée par Garnier frères** | [swelled rule] | H. ARTHAUD & Cie | 48, FAUBURG SAINT-MARTIN, 48 | PARIS

Formula: Apparently constituted of 26 sections [p *1* signed '1', p *437* signed '25']. Apparently 223 leaves, pp *i–ii*, 1 *2–6* 7 [*8–435*] *436–437* 438–440 *441* [*442–444*]

Technical notes: *ca* 134 × 82 mm (p 2). 28 lines, 20 = *ca* 96 mm. Leaf size *ca* 175 × 104 mm

Contents: Title (*i*), blank (*ii*), avertissement (*1–6*), text (*7–[435]*), blank (*436*), table des matières (*437–440*), table alphabétique (*441–[444]*)

Binding: The original of the photocopy examined is apparently in a half-leatherette binding with boards mostly covered by red paper. The spine has seven raised bands and is gold-blocked (J. QUINOLA | [rule] NOUVELLE | ACADÉMIE | DES JEUX | [floral ornament] | [*do*] | [*do*] | [*do*] | H. ARTHAUD & CIE | PARIS). The raised bands are double-ruled. The facing pages of the front endpaper are marbled

Copy seen: HCLWL: SG 3651 723.15 (incomplete photocopy)

Fingerprint: Not ascertained

Notes: Year of publication is taken as that inferred by the Widener Library. The text is divided into five books. Book II ('Les Jeux d'adresse et de combinaison') contains a section devoted to croquet (pp 167–184).

1889

AA89 ARITHMETICAL CROQUET: FOR TWO PLAYERS.   1889
[Lewis Carroll]

(a) *Unpublished manuscript (1889)*

Copy seen: NYUL (photocopy of original MS held by the library as part of the Berol collection)

Notes: The game of 'arithmetical croquet', evidently intended by the author for his projected *Original Games and Puzzles*, is described in an MS dated 22 April 1889 which was found among his papers after his death. Carroll described an earlier version of the game, which he called 'Numerical Croquet', in a letter to Gwendolen Cecil (A57).

(b) *First separate printing (1965)*

[The FC]

Arithmetical | Croquet | For Two Players | [printer's ornament] | BY | LEWIS CARROLL

[Surrogate TP verso, p 5]

First Separate Printing | *March, 1965, at the Adams & Lowell Press, in the* | *Harvard College Yard, in 14-point Caslon type on wove paper.*

Formula: Apparently [1⁴]. 4 leaves, unnumbered [pp 1–8]

Technical notes: 114 × 76 mm (p 8). 20 lines, 20 = 113 mm. Leaf size 172 × 121 mm; wove

Contents: Apparently wanting from the copy examined ([1–3]), text, continued (4–5), apparently wanting from the copy examined ([6–7]), text, concluded, and surrogate TP verso (8)

Binding: Thick red paper, sewn through the wrapper, no spine or endpapers. FC: printed as above

Copy seen: PUL (photocopy — wanting the RC, the inside page of the RC, and pp [1–3, 6–7] — of a copy held as part of the Berol collection)

Fingerprint: e.he itto er20 0:go C 1965A [all four groups taken from p 5]

Notes: Set by undergraduates under the supervision of WH Bond, Librarian of Harvard University, and printed at the Adams & Lowell Press, Harvard College Yard, Boston, in March 1965.

The construction of the original of the photocopy examined is inferred from the construction of (c).

(c) *First separate printing, variant (1965)*

Arithmetical | Croquet | For Two Players | [printer's ornament] | BY | LEWIS CARROLL

[Surrogate TP verso, p 5]

First Separate Printing | March, 1965, at the Adams & Lowell Press, in the | Harvard College Yard, in 14-point Caslon type on wove paper. | This pamphlet has been printed through the generosity of | Dr Alfred C. Berol, | from a manuscript in his possession.

Formula: Apparently [1²]. 2 leaves, unnumbered [pp 1–4]

Technical notes: 114 × 76 mm (p *4*). 20 lines, 20 = 113 mm. Leaf size 172 × 121 mm; the top edges uncut

Contents: Title (*1*), text (*2–4*), surrogate TP verso (*4*)

Binding: Thick paper, apparently coloured, sewn through the wrapper, no endpapers. Inside FC: blank. Inside RC: blank

Copy seen: LOC: GV1493 D6 1965 (photocopy, wanting the FC and RC)

Fingerprint: e.he itto er20 0:go C 1965A [all four groups taken from p *1*]

Notes: This issue differs from (b) in the extension of the citations on the surrogate TP verso and apparently in its construction. The sewing stitches are more widely spaced (at intervals of *ca* 40 mm). The text is unaltered.

The construction of the original of the photocopy examined is inferred partly from the apparent construction of (c).

A90   OUTDOOR SPORTS AND PASTIMES. [Anon]   [1889]

(a) *First edition [1889]*

Not seen. The earliest issue of this work which has been seen (b) is explicitly presented as the second edition.

(b) *Second edition [1889]*

If those who are the enemies of innocent amusements had the direction of the world, they would | take away the spring and youth, the former from the year and the latter | from the human life.—*Balzac.* | [publisher's device] | [in display script] **Outdoor Sports** and **Pastimes.** | CORRECT RULES | FOR | [in two columns]

LAWN TENNIS,	CROQUET,	
BASE BALL,	CRICKET,	
RACQUETS,	FOOT BALL,	
LACROSSE,	CURLING,	
POLO,	QUOITS.	

SECOND EDITION. | [rule] | COMPLIMENTS PASSENGER DEPARTMENT, | Union Pacific Railway, Omaha, Neb. | [rule] | Copyright October 1889, by E. L. LOMAX, General Passenger Agent.

Formula: Not ascertainable (the copy examined is bound together with other books and pamphlets in a composite library binding), unsigned. 32 leaves, pp *1–4* 5–7 *8* 9–15 *16–17* 18–31 *32* 33–38 *39–40* 41–49 *50* 51–52 *53* 54–57 *58–64*

Technical notes: ca 136 × 88 mm (p *9*). 48 lines, 20 = *ca* 57 mm. Leaf size *ca* 170 × 109 mm

Contents: Title (*1*), list of agents (*2*), text (*3–57*), advertisements (*58–64*)

Binding: Apparently wrapped in covers of pale coloured paper without endpapers. FC: printed over an engraving within a ruled frame ([in artist's display script with outlined and decorated initial capital, to the L of a vignette depicting a baseball scene] **Out-** | [in artist's display script with outlined and decorated initial capital, to the R of a vignette depicting a sailing scene] **Door** | [in artist's display script with outlined and decorated initial capital, to the L of a vignette depicting an angling scene] **Sports** | [in artist's display script with outlined and decorated initial capital *P*] AND **PASTIME·S·** | [in artist's script on two lines, to the R of a vignette depicting a lawn tennis scene] Compliments of | [*do*] Passenger Department | [publisher's device, to the R of a vignette depicting a lawn tennis scene] | [within a decorative panel with ornamental head-piece] **THOS. L. KIMBALL   C. S. MELLEN,** | [*do*, referring respectively to the above names] General Manager.   Traffic Manager. | [*do*] **E. L. LOMAX,** General Passenger Agent. | **OMAHA, NEB.**). Inside FC: advertisement. RC: as the FC save for variation within the lower panel (**E. L. LOMAX,   T.W. LEE,** | [referring respectively to the above names] General Passenger Agent.   Asst. Gen'l Pass. Agent. | **OMAHA, NEB.**). Inside RC: advertisement.

Copy seen: HCLWL: Q 98

Fingerprint: t.o, t.o- only thbe 3 1889Q

Notes: Printed anonymously, issued with compliments of the publisher. Year of publication is inferred from the HCLWL citation.

A section of the text devoted to croquet (pp 8–15) includes a code of 60 numbered rules attributed to 'scientific croquet'.

1880–89

AA91   CROQUETSPIEL. [Anon]   *ca* 1880

[Heading, p *1*]

Croquetspiel.

Formula: [1–2¹]. 2 leaves, unnumbered [pp 1–4]

Technical notes: 249 × 198 mm (pp *1, 2*). 55 lines, 20 = 91 mm. Leaf size 312 × 228 mm; thickness 0.05–0.06 mm; wove, unwatermarked, smooth, pale orange Yellow (73)

Contents: Title (*1*), text (*1–2*), plans (*3*), blank (*4*)

Binding: The copy examined is unbound

Copy seen: PC

Fingerprint: elrf ienn r-d, neuf C 1880Q [all groups taken from p *1*]

Notes: Printed anonymously. The provenance of the copy examined is unknown. The type was set on the page in such a manner as to suggest that the leaves were intended to be bound, perhaps with added pagination, on their own or with other matter.

Approximate year of publication is inferred from the state of development of the game described in the text, the vocabulary, the typography, and the character of the paper.

A92   THE LAWS OF CROQUET. [Anon]   *ca* 1880

[in shaded display script] THE LAWS | OF | CROQUET. | [publisher's device] | PUBLISHED BY | FELTHAM & CO., LTD., | LONDON.

Formula: [1¹²]. 12 leaves, pp *1–5 6–10 11–14 15–24*

Technical notes: 119 × 76 mm (p *14*). 27 lines, 20 = 89 mm. Leaf size 159 × 102 mm; thickness 0.10 mm; wove, unwatermarked, smooth, white

Contents: Title (*1*), index (*2*), laws of croquet (*2–3*), preface (*4*), text (*5–22*), advertisements (*23–24*)

Binding: Folded light white card, stapled. FC: in black within an ornamental frame ([in display script, swash *T, L*] The Laws | of | CROQUET | [swelled rule] | [in shaded script] PUBLISHED BY | [in display script, swash *F, C, L*] FELTHAM & CO., LTD. | [in shaded script] Manufactory: | Victoria Steam Works, | Gillingham Street, Victoria Station, | London, S.W. | [in shaded script] City Show Rooms: | 54 & 55, Aldersgate Street, E.C.). Inside FC: advertisement. RC: advertisement for Feltham's tennis bats. Inside RC: advertisement for Feltham's croquet. Spine: none

Copy seen: PC

Fingerprint: 2222 s.nd heve ro10 3 1880Q

Notes: Approximate year of publication is inferred from a reference in the preface to croquet having 'been first played about thirty years ago, when it was brought over from Ireland as a new game', from the state of the laws given in the text, and from the models of tennis bats presented in the publishers' advertisements for their own products.

1892

A93   **STRATÉGIE RAISONNÉE DU CROQUET FRANÇAIS.**   [1892]
Armand Després

STRATÉGIE RAISONNÉE | DU | [in a convex arc] CROQUET FRANÇAIS | 90 Figures | PAR A. DESPRÉS | [engraved illustration of a circular stand holding eight mallets and striped balls] | [the following lines with italics set to the R of the illustration] *Optarem ut aliquis ludos* | *mathematice tractaret, et* | *tam regularum seu legum* | *rationem redderet, quam* | *artificia primaria trade* | *ret.* (LEIBNITZ.) | [to the L of the illustration] PRIX | 1 fr. 50 | [PARIS | DELARUE, LIBRAIRE-ÉDITEUR | 5 RUE DES GRANDS-AUGUSTINS, 5

Formula: 1^8 $2–5^8$ 6^4 [\$1 signed ($–1_1$)]. 44 leaves, pp *1–5* 6–7 *8–10* 11–20 *21* 22–28 *29* 30–61 *62* 63–72 *73* 74–83 *84 85 86* 87–88

Technical notes: 156 × 90 mm (p 11). 35 lines, 20 = 95 mm. Leaf size 230 × 141 mm; thickness 0.15 mm; wove, unwatermarked, smooth, white

Contents: Half-title (*1*), table des matières, errata des figures (*2*), title (*3*), dedication (*4*), introduction (*5–7*), blank (*8*), text (*9–88*)

Binding: Pale orange Yellow (73) paper, sewn. The leaves of the copy examined are uncut. FC: printed in black as the TP but printed in a shaded ruled frame and omitting the price. Inside FC: blank. RC: intricately drawn device within a simple ruled frame, all in black. Spine: in black upwards (STRATÉGIE RAISONNÉE DU CROQUET FRANÇAIS)

Copy seen: PC

Fingerprint: dee. 8.ne .)r. 1.le 7 1892Q

Notes: Printed by D Dumoulin et Cie, Paris, price 1 fr 50. Year of publication is inferred from a footnote to the introduction (p 7).

1893

A94   **THE LAWS OF CROQUET [AND REGULATIONS FOR THE**   1893
MANAGEMENT OF PRIZE MEETINGS]. BC Evelegh (ed)
(a) *First edition (1893)*
THE | **LAWS OF CROQUET.** | [rule] | *REVISED AND EDITED BY* | B. C.

EVELEGH | (**The "Field"**), | CHAMPION IN 1877 AND 1879. | [rule] | Published by | F. H. AYRES, | 111, ALDERSGATE STREET, LONDON, E.C. | [rule] | 1893.

Formula: 1^{16} [1_1 signed '[1]']. 16 leaves, pp *i–iv*, *1–3* 4–7 8–9 10–16 *17–19* 20–24 *25–28*

Contents: Advertisements (*i–iv*), title (*1*), TP verso (*2*), recommendations (*3–7*), definitions (*8*), the laws of croquet, numbered 1–36 (*9–16*), sub-title: regulations for the management of prize meetings (*17*), blank (*18*), regulations, numbered 1–20 (*19–24*), advertisements (*25–28*)

Binding: Apparently printed on card or paper, stapled. FC: apparently identical to that of (b). Inside FC (apparently): advertisement. RC: advertisement. Inside FC (apparently): advertisement.

Copy seen: BL: Mic A 8892 (5), microfilm copy of BOD 38464 f 2

Fingerprint: in.A s.th erd, peth 3 1893A

Notes: Printed by Horace Cox, London, price 6d. According to an entry in the *Registry Book* of the Stationers' Company, this work was published on 9 September 1893.

Though the work lacked the authority of a duly constituted governing body, which had effectively been abrogated by the AELTC (formerly the AECC) in 1882, it gained widespread acceptance in the UK as the most authoritative contemporary statement of the laws of croquet from the rebirth of the game in 1894 to the emergence of the UAECA in 1897. Taking the latest official revisions of the 1870 'Conference Laws' and the AECC *Bye-laws and Regulations for the Management of Prize Meetings* (A50) as its starting points, it was reissued from time to time (on some occasions, it is supposed, with revisions made on the initiative of the editor). It is believed that until 1892 Ayres had distributed *Rules for Playing the Game of Croquet* (A64) with their croquet sets but then decided to introduce a new title with ostensibly more authority, both for sale to experienced players and to support their equipment sales.

The work is presented as two separate books in a single volume (albeit with through pagination). It is believed that this format was adopted so as to demonstrate that the laws and regulations derived from distinct sources, not to combine books which had previously been issued separately by the same publisher.

(b) *1894 issue (1894)*

THE | **LAWS OF CROQUET.** | [rule] | *REVISED AND EDITED BY* | B. C. EVELEGH | (**The "Field"**), | CHAMPION IN 1877 AND 1879, | [rule] | Published by | F. H. AYRES, | 111, ALDERSGATE STREET, LONDON, E.C. | [rule] | 1894.

Formula: 1^{16} [1_1 signed '[1]']. 16 leaves, pp *i–iv*, *1–3* 4–7 8–9 10–16 *17–19* 20–24 *25–28*

Technical notes: 122 × 77 mm (p 13). 33 lines, 20 = 74 mm. Leaf size 158 × 100 mm; thickness 0.10 mm; wove, unwatermarked, smooth, white

Contents: Advertisements (*i–iv*), title (*1*), TP verso (*2*), recommendations (*3–7*), definitions (*8*), the laws of croquet, numbered 1–36 (*9–16*), sub-title: regulations for the management of prize meetings (*17*), blank (*18*), regulations, numbered 1–20 (*19–24*), advertisements (*25–28*)

Binding: White semi-gloss card, apparently stapled, no spine or endpapers. FC: printed in black within a double-ruled frame, the outer frame in bold, with corner ornaments (THE | **LAWS OF CROQUET** | AND | REGULATIONS | FOR THE | **MANAGEMENT OF PRIZE** | **MEETINGS.** | Revised and Edited by | B. C. EVELEGH | (**The "Field"**, | CHAMPION IN 1877 AND 1879. | Published by |

F. H. AYRES, | 111, ALDERSGATE STREET, LONDON, E.C. | [at L] **Entered at Stationer's Hall.}** [at R] **{Price, SIXPENCE.).** Inside FC: advertisement. RC: advertisement. Inside RC: advertisement

Copy seen: BL: 7920 aa 8 (in a library binding)

Fingerprint: in.A s.th erd, peth 3 1894A

Notes: Printed by Horace Cox, London, price 6d.

The text is identical, or almost identical, to that of (a)

(c) '*Sixth edition*' *(1896)*

THE | LAWS OF CROQUET. | *REVISED AND EDITED BY* | B. C. EVELEGH | (**The "Field"**), | CHAMPION IN 1877 AND 1879. | [rule] | SIXTH EDITION. | [rule] | PUBLISHED BY | F. H. AYRES, | 111, ALDERSGATE STREET, LONDON, E.C. | [rule] | 1896.

Formula: [1¹⁶]. 16 leaves, pp *i–iv*, *1–3* 4–7 *8–9* 10–16 *17–19* 20–24 *25–28*

Technical notes: 121 × 76 mm (p 10). 33 lines = 74 mm. Leaf size 163 × 100 mm; thickness 0.14 mm; wove, unwatermarked, smooth, white

Contents: Advertisements (*i–iv*), title (*1*), advertisement and name of printer (*2*), text (laws of croquet) (*3–16*), companion title ('Regulations for the Management of Prize Meetings') (*17*), blank (*18*), text (management of prize meetings) (*19–24*), advertisements (*25–28*)

Binding: Light greenish Grey (154) paper laminate, sewn, no spine or endpapers. FC: printed in black, all save the first line ([above the frame] SIXTH EDITION.) within a double-ruled frame, the outer frame in bold, with corner ornaments (THE | LAWS OF CROQUET | AND | REGULATIONS | FOR THE | **MANAGEMENT OF PRIZE** | **MEETINGS.** | REVISED AND EDITED BY | B. C. EVELEGH | (**The "Field"**), | CHAMPION IN 1877 AND 1879. | PUBLISHED BY | F. H. AYRES, | [‡] ALDERSGATE STREET, LONDON, E.C. | [‡] **Stationers' Hall.}** [at R] **{Price SIXPENCE.).** Inside FC: advertisement. RC: advertisement. Inside RC: advertisement

Copy seen: PC (imperfect)

Fingerprint: in.A s.th erd, peth 3 1896A

Notes: Printed by Horace Cox, London, price 6d.

1895

A95   **THE ASSOCIATION LAWS OF CROQUET. WH Peel**   1895

(a) *First edition (1895)*

Not seen. In the select bibliography of D Prichard's *The History of Croquet* (A208, p234), 1895 is given as the year of publication.

(b) *Second edition (1896)*

THE ASSOCIATION | LAWS OF CROQUET | TOGETHER WITH | SUGGESTIONS AND ADVICE | FOR THE MANAGEMENT OF | CROQUET TOURNAMENTS AND | PRIZE MEETINGS. | As Approved by many of the Leading Croquet | Players and Authorities. | [swelled rule] | *Edited and Revised by* | W. H. PEEL, | *Champion Croquet Player*, 1870, 1871. | [swelled rule] | PUBLISHED BY | J. JAQUES & SON, 102, HATTON GARDEN, LONDON, E.C.

Formula: [1²⁰]. 40 leaves including the front and rear pastedowns, pp *i–iv*, *1* 2–3 *4–6* 7 8 *9–11* *12* 13 *14* 15–21 *22* 23–32 *33–36*

Technical notes: 132 × 85 mm (p 17). 39 lines, 20 = 69 mm. Leaf size 184 × 121 mm; thickness 0.12 mm; wove, unwatermarked, smooth, white

Contents: Glued to the FC (*i*), blank (*ii*), advertisements (*iii–iv*), title (*1*), list of players who allowed their names to be appended as signifying their adoption (*2–3*), preface signed 'WALTER H. PEEL', May 1896 (*4*), recommendations and suggested alterations for improving the attack (*5–11*), definitions of terms (*12–13*), the laws of croquet, numbered 1–37 (*14--21*), suggestions for the management of prize meetings (*22–32*), advertisements (*33–34*), blank (*35*), glued to the RC (*36*)

Binding: Vivid Yellow (82) semi-gloss paper, sewn, no spine or free endpapers. FC: printed in black, above (PRICE SIXPENCE.) and within a double-ruled and cross-hatched frame with corner ornaments ([at R] **2nd EDITION.** | THE | "ASSOCIATION" | **LAWS OF CROQUET** | TOGETHER WITH | **SUGGESTIONS AND ADVICE** | FOR THE MANAGEMENT OF | CROQUET TOURNAMENTS AND | PRIZE MEETINGS. | As Approved by many of the Leading Croquet Players and Authorities. | [swelled rule] | *Edited by* | W. H. PEEL, | *Champion Croquet Player*, 1870, 1871. | [swelled rule] | PUBLISHED BY | J. JAQUES & SON, 102, HATTON GARDEN, LONDON, E.C. | [at L] **Ent. Stat. Hall.**]). RC: advertisement

Copy seen: PC

Fingerprint: ."ly t.or r.he thro 3 1896A

Notes: Printed anonymously, price 6d. Notwithstanding the publisher's claim, there is no record of this work in the *Registry Book* of the Stationers' Company.

On the revival of croquet in the early 1890s, the revisions of the Conference Code edited by Evelegh and issued by Ayres (A94) would appear to have been widely adopted for tournament play. The code of laws in the present work, adopted by members of the inchoate UAECA in anticipation of the formal foundation of that official governing body, challenged the current formulation of the Conference Code. It is perhaps significant that Evelegh's name is not to be found among the listed testifiers (pp 2–3).

A96   **CROQUET GUIDE AND OFFICIAL RULES GOVERNING**   1895
    THE GAME [and CROQUET AND ITS RULES].
    [National Croquet Association of America and Charles Jacobus]

(a) **First edition (1895)*

Croquet Guide | AND | *OFFICIAL RULES GOVERNING* | *THE GAME,* | 1895. | AS ADOPTED BY THE | National American Croquet Association. | [AUTHORIZED EDITION. | [rule] | REVISED AND CORRECTED | BY THE | NATIONAL ASSOCIATION. | [rule] | PUBLISHED FOR THE ASSOCIATION | BY THE | AMERICAN SPORTS PUBLISHING CO. | [rule] | Copyrighted, 1895, by American Sports Publishing Co

Formula: [1¹⁶ 2⁸]. 24 leaves, unnumbered [pp 1–48]

Technical notes: 128 × 80 mm (p 6). 46 lines, 20 = 55 mm. Leaf size 171 × 127 mm; thickness 0.09 mm; wove, unwatermarked, smooth, white

Contents: Title (*1*), plan of croquet court (*2*), text (*3–33*), advertisements (*34--48*)

Binding: Light greyish yellowish Brown (79) light card, printed in black, glued to the folds of the gatherings, stapled through the gatherings, no spine or endpapers. FC: mostly below a page-width double rule ([L column above a double rule] Vol. 4, No. 38A. | [*do*] Issued Monthly. | [centred above double rule] JUNE, 1895. | [R column above double rule] £1.20 per Year | [*do*] Price, 10 Cents | [double rule] | [in a calligraphic script, the letters arranged in serpentine form, swash *S*, *g*] **Spalding's** |

[swash *A*] *ATHLETIC* | *LIBRARY* | [in a calligraphic script] **Croquet Guide** | [*do*] AND OFFICIAL RULES FOR | [at L, with an ornamental tail-piece, in a calligraphic script] **1895** | [to the R of an engraved sketch of a man player in play, in a calligraphic script] AS ADOPTED BY THE | [*do*] **NATIONAL AMERICAN** | [*do*] **CR^OQUET ASS'N.** | *PUBLISHED BY THE* | *AMERICAN SPORTS PUBLISHING* CO | 241 BROADWAY, NEW YORK | *Entered at the New York Post Office, N. Y., as Second Class Matter.*). Inside FC: advertisement. RC: advertisement. Inside RC: advertisement

Copy seen: PC

Fingerprint: e.nd e.te 7.s. focl C 1895A [groups 1–4 taken from pp *3, 15, 17, 18* respectively]

Notes: Published in June 1895, printed anonymously, price 10 cents. Price is inferred from the citation on the FC of (c).

The text includes a code of 59 numbered rules.

(b) *1899 edition (1899)*

CROQUET GUIDE | AND | OFFICIAL RULES GOVERNING THE GAME | AS ADOPTED BY THE | NATIONAL | CROQUET ASSOCIATION | OF AMERICA | [flourish] | AUTHORIZED EDITION | [flourish] | *Revised and Corrected by the National Association* | *up to 1899* | [flourish] | PUBLISHED FOR THE ASSOCIA-TION BY THE | AMERICAN SPORTS PUBLISHING COMPANY | 16 AND 18 PARK PLACE, NEW YORK | Copyright, 1899, by the American Sports Publishing Company

Formula: [1^16 2^8]. 24 leaves, unnumbered [pp *1–48*]

Technical notes: 128 × 79 mm (p *6*). 46 lines, 20 = 56 mm. Leaf size 171 × 129 mm; thickness 0.07 mm; wove, unwatermarked, smooth, white

Contents: Title (*1*), plan of croquet court (*2*), text (*3–39*), advertisements (*40–48*)

Binding: Light greyish yellowish Brown (79) paper, printed in black, glued to the folds of the gatherings, stapled through the gatherings, no endpapers. FC: mostly within an *art nouveau* frame ([L column above the frame] Vol. IX., No. 101. | [*do*] Issued Monthly. | [centred above the frame] JUNE, 1899. | [R column above the frame] Price, [‡] | [*do*] $1. [‡] | [in a calligraphic script, the letters arranged in serpentine form, swash *S, g*] **Spalding's** | [swash *A*] *ATHLETIC* | *LIBRARY* | [double rule] | [in a calligraphic script, followed by three flourishes] **Croquet Guide** | [in a calligraphic script] and Official Rules | [at L, with ornamental head- and tail-pieces, in a calligraphic script] **1899** | [in a calligraphic script] as adopted by the | [*do*] **National Croquet** | [*do*] **Association of America** | [double rule] *PUBLISHED BY THE* | *AMERICAN SPORTS PUBLISHING* CO | 16 and 18 Park Place, New York | *Entered at the New York Post Office, N. Y., as Second Class Matter.*). Inside FC: advertisement. RC: advertisement. Inside RC: advertisement. Spine: blank

Copy seen: HPC: GV933 C8 1899 CROQ (imperfect)

Fingerprint: e*nd e.te 7.s. PrW. C 1899A [group 1 taken from p *3*, group 2 taken from p *15*, group 4 taken from the caption to the portrait on p *18*]

Notes: Published in June 1899, printed anonymously, price 10 cents. Price is inferred from the citations on the FCs of (a) and (c).

This edition has not been collated with other issues.

(c) *1901 edition (1901)*

[Above a ruled frame]

Spalding's Athletic Library | Croquet Guide | AND | Official Rules Governing the

Game | [floral ornament] | [double rule between two lines of dots] | *Published by the* AMERICAN SPORTS PUBLISHING | COMPANY, 16 AND 18 PARK PLACE, NEW YORK CITY

Formula: [1^{16} 2^8]. 24 leaves, pp 1–3 *4 5 6 7 8 9 10* 11 *12* 13 *14* 15–34 *35–48*

Technical notes: 129 × 80 mm (p 5). 31 lines, 20 = 84 mm. Leaf size 171 × 127 mm; thickness 0.07 mm; wove, unwatermarked, smooth, white

Contents: Title (1), TP verso (2), text (3–34), advertisements (*35–48*)

Binding: Light greyish yellowish Brown (79) paper, printed in black, glued to the folds of the gatherings, stapled through the gatherings, no endpapers. FC: mostly within a frame composed of a repeated clover-leaf figure ([L column above the frame] Vl. XII. No. 138. | [*do*] Issued Monthly. | [centred above the frame] SEPTEMBER, 1901. | [R column above the frame] Price, 10 cents. | [*do*] $1.20 Per Year. | [in a calligraphic script, the letters arranged in serpentine form, swash *S, g*] **Spalding's** | [swash *A*] *ATHLETIC* | *LIBRARY* | [double line composed of a repeated ornamental figure] | CROQUET GUIDE | AND | OFFICIAL RULES GOVERNING THE GAME | | [double line composed of a repeated ornamental figure] | *PUBLISHED BY THE* | *AMERICAN SP*O*RTS PUBLISHING* Co | 16 and 18 Park Place, New York | *Entered at the New York Post Office, N. Y., as Second Class Matter.*). Inside FC: advertisement. RC: advertisement. Inside RC: advertisement. Spine: blank

Copy seen: HPC: GV933 C8 1901 CROQ

Fingerprint: d.is s.ey e.rm lesh 3 1901A [group 4 taken from p 16]

Notes: Published in September 1901, printed anonymously, price 10 cents.

The text of this edition has not been collated with that of (b). Though it incorporates the same code of 59 rules, it would appear that the rest of the text of the present edition is considerably abridged.

(d) *1901 edition (1901)*

[Above a frame of *art nouveau* design composed of two continuous lines] SPALDING'S ATHLETIC LIBRARY | CROQUET GUIDE | AND | OFFICIAL RULES | GOVERNING THE GAME | [floral ornament in *art nouveau* style] | PUBLISHED BY THE | AMERICAN SPORTS PUBLISHING CO. | 21 WARREN STREET, NEW YORK

Formula: [1–2^{16}]. 32 leaves, pp 1–3 *4 5 6 7 8 9 10* 11 *12* 13 *14* 15–32 *33–64*

Technical notes: 130 × 88 mm (p 7). 31 lines, 20 = 85 mm. Leaf size 172 × 127 mm; thickness 0.06 mm; wove, unwatermarked, smooth, white

Contents: Title (1), TP verso (2), text (3–34), advertisements (*35–48*)

Binding: White paper, printed in dark Blue (183), glued to the folds of the gatherings, stapled through the gatherings, no endpapers. FC: set mostly as white out of Blue (Vol. XII.No.   Price 10 cents | [in Blue on white within a figured panel] SPALDING'S ATHLETIC LIBRARY | [in artist's script with dropped and decorated *S, S*] SPALDING'S | [*Official* | CROQUET | GUIDE | [drawing in Blue on white, mostly within a rectangular panel with inward-cut corner arcs, and partly out of the Blue background above the panel, of man and woman players in play] | [in white out of Blue] AMERICAN SPORTS PUBLISHING CO. | [*do*] 16 & 18 Park Place, New York | [tail-piece to the panel above]). Inside FC: advertisement. RC: advertisement. Inside RC: advertisement. Spine: blank

Copy seen: HPC: GV933 C8 1901a CROQ

Fingerprint: asng s.ew e.rm lesh 3 1901A [group 4 taken from p 16]

Notes: Printed anonymously, price 10 cents.

Though the text of this edition has not been collated systematically with that of (c), it is believed that the texts of these two issues are identical, or virtually identical.

(e) *1907 edition (1907)*

[Within a double-ruled frame with corner ornaments]

SPALDING'S ATHLETIC LIBRARY | GROUP XI., No. 138 | **CROQUET** | AND ITS RULES | [ornament] | THOROUGHLY REVISED. WITH | ILLUSTRATIONS AND | EXPLANATIONS | CHARLES JACOBUS | EDITOR | PUBLISHED BY THE | AMERICAN SPORTS PUBLISHING COMPANY | 21 WARREN STREET, NEW YORK

Formula: [1⁸ 2–3¹⁶]. 40 leaves, pp *i–xviii*, *1–4 5–6 7–8 9–10 11–12 13–30 31–32 33–34 35 36–43 44–62*

Technical notes: 129 × 89 mm (p 6). 31 lines, 20 = 71 mm. Leaf size 169 × 126 mm; thickness 0.07 mm; wove, unwatermarked, smooth, white

Contents: Advertisement (*i–xvii*), frontispiece, half-tone photograph of editor (*xviii*), title (*1*), TP verso (*2*), publisher's notice (*3*), plan of croquet court (*4*), text (*5–43*), advertisements (*44–62*)

Binding: White paper, printed in dark Blue (183), glued to the folds of the gatherings, stapled through the gatherings, no endpapers. FC: set mostly as white out of Blue (Group XI.No.138   Price 10 cents | | [in artist's script with dropped and decorated *S, S*] SPALDING'S | [in Blue within a white panel with ornaments at the extremities] | ***Official*** | *CROQUET* | *GUIDE* | [drawing in Blue on white, mostly within a rectangular panel with corner ornaments, and partly out of the Blue background above the panel, of man and woman players in play] | [in white out of Blue] *AMERICAN SPORTS PUBLISHING CO.* | [*do*] 21 Warren Street New York | [tail-piece to the panel above]). Inside FC: advertisement, printed in Blue. RC: advertisement. Inside RC: advertisement, printed in Blue. Spine: printed in Blue, centred downwards (No. 138—SPALDING'S ATHLETIC LIBRARY.   OFFICIAL CROQUET GUIDE.)

Copies seen: HPC: GV933 C8 1907 CROQ; LOC: GV931 J2 (photocopy of original copy in library cover, the wrapper in colour)

Fingerprint: n.wo).CH chs. coco 3 1907A [group 2 taken from the caption to the diagram on p *11*]

Notes: Printed anonymously, price 10 cents. Year of publication is inferred from the year of copyright cited on the TP verso, supported by the date (4 June 1908) added to the accession mark of the LOC.

Though the text of this edition includes the same code of rules as that found in earlier editions, it is here extended to 62 in number, the rest of the text is revised, and the whole is reset.

1896

A97   **THE NEW GAME OF CROQUET-GOLF: A GAME FOR GARDEN PARTIES. [Anon]**   1896

[The FC, all save the lowermost line within a double-ruled frame with corner ornaments]

[in gothic-revival script] **The New Game** | [rule] OF [rule] | **CROQUET-GOLF.** | [swelled rule] | [at L, in ornate script] A GAME FOR | [in ornate script] GARDEN PARTIES. | [rule] | F. H. AYRES, LONDON. | 1896. | [below the base of the frame] *Entered at Stationers' Hall.*

Collation: Apparently 4 leaves including the wrapper, unnumbered [pp 1–8]

Technical notes: ca 149 × 87 mm (p *4*). 43 lines, 20 = *ca* 69 mm. Leaf size *ca* 206 × 130 mm

Contents: Title (*1*), diagram of the court (*2*), blank (*3*), introduction (*4*), rules, numbered 1–10 (*5–6*), handicapping and notes (*6*), apparently wanting from the original of the photocopy examined ([*7–8*])

Binding: Apparently sewn, unbound, no spine or endpapers

Copy seen: CUL (incomplete photocopy)

Fingerprint: f.of e.nd ishe opr. C 1896A [all four groups taken from p 5]

Notes: Printed anonymously. In the *Registry Book* of the Stationers' Company the date of publication is given as 23 September 1896.

1897

A98 CROQUET: ITS HISTORY, RULES, AND SECRETS. Arthur Lillie 1897

CROQUET | ITS HISTORY, RULES, AND SECRETS | BY | ARTHUR LILLIE | (CHAMPION, GRAND NATIONAL CROQUET CLUB, 1872; WINNER OF THE | "ALL-COMERS' CHAMPIONSHIP," MAIDSTONE, 1896) | "Lequel bergier haussa un croquet qu'il tenoit en sa main dont il rechassoit | ses brebis."— *MS., 14th Century* | *WITH ILLUSTRATIONS AND DIAGRAMS BY LUCIEN DAVIS* | *AND OTHERS* | LONGMANS, GREEN, AND CO. | 39 PATERNOSTER ROW, LONDON | NEW YORK AND BOMBAY | 1897

Formula: π^4 1–16^8 17^4 18^{16} [\$1 signed (–π1, 18$_1$)]. 152 leaves, pp *i–viii, 1 2–241 242 257–264, 1–32*

Technical notes: 139 × 84 mm (p 2). 32 lines, 20 = 87 mm. Leaf size 185 × 122 mm; thickness mostly 0.10–0.12 mm (18$_1$–18$_{16}$ 0.07mm); wove, unwatermarked, smooth, white. Four inset plates (black-and-white photographs) face pp *i* (protective tissue tipped-in), 56, 125, 246

Contents: Half-title (*i*), name of printer (*ii*), title (*iii*), blank (*iv*), dedication (*v*), blank (*vi*), contents (*vii*), blank (*viii*), text (*1–264*), publisher's classified catalogue of works in general literature (*1–32*)

Binding: Pale orange Yellow (73) cloth over stiff boards, sewn. The facing pages of the endpapers are coloured black. FC: in black and greyish purplish Pink (253), the lettering in black *art nouveau* script (CROQUET | by | Arthur | Lillie | [black with Pink infilling, drawing of two women players on court]). RC: blank. Spine: mostly gold-blocked, crosswise ([double rule] | Croquet | ITS HISTORY | RULES | AND SECRETS | Arthur | Lillie | [in black, a sketch of two crossed mallets bound by a bow with a ball on either side | LONGMANS & C° | [double rule])

Copies seen: KRWL; PC

Fingerprint: R.TO e-ly iror noan 3 1897A

Notes: Published on 7 July 1897, printed by Aberdeen University Press, price 6/–. According to the publisher's records now held by RUL, 1500 copies were printed, but fewer than 1000 had been sold by December 1903, when the trade price was reduced to 1/6 per dozen (13 for 12). Only 271 of the remaining copies were sold, so about 300 copies in quires were wasted. A ledger of miscellaneous expenses records that 40 blocks were engraved by Naumann, seven negatives provided by Churchill, four half-tone blocks engraved by Swan, and two pages of drawings executed by L Davis.

Reviews: Badminton Magazine of Sports and Pastimes (October 1897, p 429), *The*

Field (4 September 1897, p 415), *The Globe, Illustrated Sporting and Dramatic News, Lady's Own Magazine, Pall Mall Gazette, The Speaker, The Times, Westminster Gazette, The World.*

A99   **KINGBALL: A GAME FOR GARDEN PARTIES.** Arthur Lillie   **1897**

[Within a ruled frame with internal ornaments]

1897. | [in display script] **"KINGBALL."** | A | GAME FOR GARDEN PARTIES. | [double rule] | By ARTHUR LILLIE. | (*Champion, late Grand National Croquet Club.*) | [rule] | F. H. AYRES | [rule] LONDON | *Entered at Stationers' Hall.*

Formula: [1⁶]. 6 leaves, pp *1–4* 5–8 *9* 10–11 *12*

Technical notes: ca 116 × 68 mm (p 6). 26 lines, 20 = *ca* 91 mm. Leaf size *ca* 163 × 101 mm

Contents: Title (*1*), blank (*2*), text (*3–11*), advertisement (*12*)

Binding: Apparently none, sewn

Copy seen: CUL: 97 6 230 (photocopy)

Fingerprint: s.ck t.ck ndst d.nt C 1897A [group 1 taken from p *3*, groups 2–4 taken from p *11*]

Notes: Printed anonymously. Notwithstanding the publisher's claim, there is no record of this work in the *Registry Book* of the Stationers' Company.

A100   **THE LAWS OF CROQUET.** [The United All-England Croquet   **1897**
Association (afterwards The Croquet Association)]

(a) *First edition, Horace Cox issue (1897)*

THE | **LAWS OF CROQUET.** | [rule] | REVISED AND CORRECTED | BY A | SPECIAL COMMITTEE | DULY ELECTED FOR THAT PURPOSE BY THE | GENERAL COMMITTEE OF THE | **UNITED ALL-ENGLAND CROQUET ASSOCIATION.** | [rule] | LONDON : | PUBLISHED BY | HORACE COX, | WINDSOR HOUSE, BREAM'S BUILDINGS, E.C.

Formula: [1¹²]. 12 leaves, pp *i–iii* iv, 5 *6–9* 10–11 *12* 13–15 *16–24*

Technical notes: 122 × 77 mm (p 16). 33 lines, 20 = 74 mm. Leaf size 164 × 104 mm; thickness 0.13 mm; wove, unwatermarked, smooth, white

Contents: Title (*i*), advertisement (*ii*), contents (*iii–iv*), recommendations (5–9), advertisement (*10*), definitions, numbered 1–13 (*11–12*), advertisements (*13–14*), the laws of croquet, numbered 1–36 (*15–24*)

Binding: Light purplish Pink (249) semi-gloss laminated board, sewn through the inner lamina(ae), no spine or endpapers. FC: printed in black, mostly within a double-ruled frame, the outer frame in bold, with corner ornaments ([above the frame] OFFICIAL EDITION. | THE | **LAWS OF CROQUET.** | [rule] | REVISED AND CORRECTED | BY A | SPECIAL COMMITTEE | DULY ELECTED FOR THAT PURPOSE BY THE | GENERAL COMMITTEE OF THE | **UNITED ALL-ENGLAND CROQUET ASSOCIATION.** | [rule] | LONDON: | PUBLISHED BY | HORACE COX, | WINDSOR HOUSE, BREAM'S BUILDINGS, E.C. | [below the frame] *Price Sixpence.*). Inside FC: advertisement. RC: advertisement. Inside RC: advertisement

Copy seen: BOD: Per 38464 f 9

Fingerprint: 1716 n.r- **C.E. FuJ.** 3 1897A

Notes: Printed anonymously, presumably by Horace Cox, the publisher. According to an editorial announcement in *Lawn Tennis and Croquet* (13 May 1897, p 31), which in January 1902 was appointed the official organ of the CA, the Association's own first code of laws had [recently] been published by *The Field*, a Horace Cox publication. There being no mention of this event in the columns of *The Field* at the time, it may be supposed that the code was in fact first issued as a separate publication — *ie* the present work — probably earlier the same month.

(b) *First edition, FH Ayres issue [1897]*

THE | **LAWS OF CROQUET.** | [rule] | REVISED AND CORRECTED | BY A | SPECIAL COMMITTEE | DULY ELECTED FOR THAT PURPOSE BY THE | GENERAL COMMITTEE OF THE | **UNITED ALL-ENGLAND CROQUET ASSOCIATION.** | [rule] | Issued by | F. H. AYRES, | BY PERMISSION OF THE LAWN TENNIS ASSOCIATION, AND THE AUTHORISED PUBLISHER, | HORACE COX.

Formula: 1^{16} [1_1 signed '[1]']. 16 leaves, pp *1–4, i–iii* v, 5 6–9 *10–11* 12 *13* 14–23 *24–28* [= 32]

Technical notes: 122 × 77 mm (p 14). 33 lines, 20 = 74 mm. Leaf size 166 × 104 mm; thickness 0.14 mm; wove, unwatermarked, smooth, white

Contents: Advertisements (*1–4*), title (*i*), TP verso (*ii*), contents (*iii*, v), recommendations (*5–9*), blank (*10*), definitions, numbered 1–13 (*11–12*), the laws of croquet, numbered 1–36 (*13–23*), advertisements (*24–28*)

Binding: Light greenish Blue (172) semi-gloss laminated board, sewn, no spine or endpapers. FC: printed in black, mostly within a double-ruled frame, the outer frame in bold, with corner ornaments ([above the frame] OFFICIAL EDITION. | THE | **LAWS OF CROQUET.** | [rule] | REVISED AND CORRECTED | BY A | SPECIAL COMMITTEE | DULY ELECTED FOR THAT PURPOSE BY THE | GENERAL COMMITTEE OF THE | **UNITED ALL-ENGLAND CROQUET ASSOCIATION.** | [rule] | ISSUED BY | F. H. AYRES, | BY PERMISSION OF THE LAWN TENNIS ASSOCIATION, | AND THE AUTHORISED PUBLISHER, | HORACE COX.). Inside FC: advertisement. RC: advertisement. Inside RC: advertisement

Copy seen: BL: 7924 a 5

Fingerprint: 1716 n.r- erut mama 3 1897Q

Notes: Printed by Horace Cox, London.

A curiosity of this issue, perhaps a typographical oversight, is its reference on the TP and FC to the Lawn Tennis Association, where a reference to the UAECA might seem to have been more appropriate. This apparent fault, omission of the year of publication, and other minor irregularities — notably in the pagination — might suggest that the present issue was rushed out in haste.

(c) *First edition, FH Ayres issue, variant [1897]*

THE | **LAWS OF CROQUET.** | [rule] | REVISED AND CORRECTED | BY A | SPECIAL COMMITTEE | DULY ELECTED FOR THAT PURPOSE BY THE | GENERAL COMMITTEE OF THE | **UNITED ALL-ENGLAND CROQUET ASSOCIATION.** | [rule] | ISSUED BY | F. H. AYRES, | BY PERMISSION OF THE UNITED ALL-ENGLAND CROQUET ASSOCIATION, AND THE AUTHORISED PUBLISHER, | HORACE COX.

Formula: 1^{16} [1_1 signed '[1']. 16 leaves, pp *1–4, i–iii* iv, 5 6 7 8–9 *10–11* 12 *13* 14–23 *24–28*

Technical notes: 122 × 77 mm (p 14). 33 lines, 20 = 74 mm. Leaf size 163 × 103 mm; thickness 0.14 mm; wove, unwatermarked, smooth, white

Contents: Advertisements (*1–4*), title (*i*), TP verso (*ii*), contents (*iii–*iv), recommendations (*5–9*), blank (*10*), definitions, numbered 1–13 (*11–12*), the laws of croquet, numbered 1–36 (*13–23*), advertisements (*24–28*)

Binding: Very light bluish Green (162) semi-gloss laminated board, sewn, no spine or endpapers. FC: a different setting of the letterpress on the TP printed in black within a double-ruled frame, the outer frame in bold, with corner ornaments. Inside FC: advertisement. RC: advertisement. Inside RC: advertisement

Copy seen: BL: 7907 df

Fingerprint: 1716 n.r- erut mama 3 1897Q

Notes: Printed by Horace Cox, London. This issue has all the hall-marks of a second impression of a first edition, incorporating minor corrections. The text would appear to be identical in substance to that of (b).

(d) *Official edition, 1898, Horace Cox issue (1898)*

OFFICIAL EDITION. | THE | **LAWS OF CROQUET.** | TO WHICH ARE ADDED | REGULATIONS FOR PRIZE MEETINGS. | [rule] | REVISED AND CORRECTED | BY A | SPECIAL COMMITTEE | DULY ELECTED FOR THAT PURPOSE BY THE | **UNITED ALL-ENGLAND CROQUET ASSOCIATION.** | [rule] | Lᴏɴᴅᴏɴ : | Pᴜʙʟɪsʜᴇᴅ ʙʏ | HORACE COX, | WINDSOR HOUSE, BREAM'S BUILDINGS, E.C. | 1898. | *Price Sixpence.*

Formula: [1¹⁶]. 16 leaves, pp *i–iii* iv, 5 6–9 *10–11* 12 *13–15* 16–25 26 27–32

Technical notes: 122 × 77 mm (p 16). 33 lines, 20 = 74 mm. Leaf size 165 × 105 mm; thickness 0.14 mm; wove, unwatermarked, smooth, white

Contents: Title (*i*), blank (*ii*), index (*iii–*iv), recommendations (*5–9*), advertisement (*10*), definitions, numbered 1–13 (*11–12*), advertisements (*13–14*), the laws of croquet, numbered 1–36 (*15–25*), regulations for prize meetings, numbered 1–22, approved and adopted March 1898 (*26–32*)

Binding: Moderate purplish Pink (250) semi-gloss laminated board, sewn through the inner lamina(ae), no spine or endpapers. FC: printed in black, mostly within a double-ruled frame, the outer frame in bold, with corner ornaments ([above the frame] OFFICIAL EDITION. | THE | **LAWS OF CROQUET.** | TO WHICH ARE ADDED | REGULATIONS FOR PRIZE MEETINGS. | [rule] | REVISED AND CORRECTED | [rule] | BY A | SPECIAL COMMITTEE | DULY ELECTED FOR THAT PURPOSE BY THE | GENERAL COMMITTEE OF THE | **UNITED ALL-ENGLAND CROQUET ASSOCIATION.** | [rule] | Lᴏɴᴅᴏɴ | Pᴜʙʟɪsʜᴇᴅ ʙʏ | HORACE COX, | WINDSOR HOUSE, BREAM'S BUILDINGS, E.C. | [below the frame] *Price Sixpence.*). Inside FC: advertisement. RC: advertisement. Inside RC: advertisement

Copy seen: BOD: Per 38464 f 9

Fingerprint: 1716 n.r- **C.E. Fu**J. 1898A

Notes: Printed anonymously, presumably by Horace Cox, London.

(e) *Official edition, 1899, Horace Cox issue (1899)*

OFFICIAL EDITION. | THE | **LAWS OF CROQUET.** | TO WHICH ARE ADDED | REGULATIONS FOR PRIZE MEETINGS. | [rule] | REVISED | BY THE | COMMITTEE OF THE | **UNITED ALL-ENGLAND CROQUET ASSOCIA-**

TION. | [rule] | LONDON : | PUBLISHED BY | HORACE COX, | WINDSOR HOUSE, BREAM'S BUILDINGS, E. C. | 1899. | *Price Sixpence.*

Formula: 1^{16} [p *3* signed 'c', p *5* signed 'c']. 16 leaves, pp *i–ii, 1 2, iii–iv, 3 4–12, v–vi, 13 14, vii–viii, 15 16–21 22–24* [= 32]

Technical notes: 122 × 77 mm (p 6). 33 lines, 20 = 73 mm. Leaf size 166 × 103 mm; thickness 0.13 mm; wove, unwatermarked, smooth, white

Contents: Title (*i*), the CA (*ii*), index (*1–2*), the laws of croquet, numbered 1–37, approved and adopted 21 December 1898 (*3–12*), advertisements (*v–vi*), definitions, lettered A–K (*13–14*), advertisements (*vii–viii*), regulations for prize meetings, numbered 1–20, approved and adopted 21 December 1898 (*15–21*), blank (*22*), advertisements (*23–24*)

Binding: Light purplish Pink (249) semi-gloss laminated board, sewn through the inner lamina(ae), no spine or endpapers. FC: printed in black, mostly within a double-ruled frame, the outer frame in bold, with corner ornaments ([above the frame] OFFICIAL EDITION, 1899. | THE | **LAWS OF CROQUET.** | TO WHICH ARE ADDED | REGULATIONS FOR PRIZE MEETINGS. | [rule] | REVISED | BY THE COMMITTEE OF THE | **UNITED ALL-ENGLAND CROQUET ASSOCIATION.** | [rule] | LONDON | PUBLISHED BY | HORACE COX, | WINDSOR HOUSE, BREAM'S BUILDINGS, E.C. | [below the frame] *Price Sixpence.*). Inside FC: advertisement. RC: advertisement. Inside RC: advertisement

Copy seen: BOD: Per 38464 f 9

Fingerprint: ...8...8 isbe s.r, (BAp 3 1899A [group 3 taken from p *13*]

Notes: Printed anonymously, presumably by Horace Cox, London. Letters by officials of the UAECA to the editor of *Lawn Tennis and Croquet* which appeared in the columns of that journal in May 1899 refer to this edition. Hence, it was probably published in April or May.

The signatures, which would appear to be redundant, suggest that much of this issue was also intended to be reprinted elsewhere.

(f) *Official edition, 1900, Horace Cox issue (1900)*

OFFICIAL EDITION 1900. | THE | **LAWS OF CROQUET.** | TO WHICH ARE ADDED | REGULATIONS FOR PRIZE MEETINGS. | [rule] | REVISED | BY THE COMMITTEE OF THE | **UNITED ALL-ENGLAND CROQUET ASSOCIATION.** | [rule] | LONDON : | PUBLISHED BY | HORACE COX, | WINDSOR HOUSE, BREAM'S BUILDINGS, E.C. | 1900. | *Price Sixpence.*

Formula: 1^{18} [1_3 signed 'B2', 1_6 signed 'C', 1_7 signed 'C2']. 18 leaves including the front and rear pastedowns, pp *i–viii, 3 4–12, ix–x, 13 14, xi–xii, 15 16–21 22–26* [= 36]

Technical notes: 121 × 76 mm (p 7). 33 lines, 20 = 74 mm. Leaf size 162 × 104 mm; thickness 0.13 mm; wove, unwatermarked, smooth, white

Contents: Glued to the FC (*i*), advertisement (*ii*), title (*iii*), the UAECA (*iv*), index (*v–vi*), advertisements (*vii–viii*), the laws of croquet, numbered 1–37, approved and adopted 21 December 1898 (*3–12*), advertisements (*ix–x*), definitions, lettered A–K (*13–14*), advertisements (*xi–xii*), regulations for prize meetings, numbered 1–20, approved and adopted 21 December 1898 (*15–21*), advertisements (*22–25*), glued to the RC (*26*)

Binding: Moderate purplish Pink (250) semi-gloss laminated board, apparently, no spine or endpapers. FC: printed in black, mostly within a double-ruled frame with corner ornaments, the outer frame in bold ([above the frame] OFFICIAL

EDITION, 1900. | THE | **LAWS OF CROQUET.** | TO WHICH ARE ADDED | **REGULATIONS FOR PRIZE MEETINGS** | [rule] | REVISED | BY THE COM- MITTEE OF THE | **UNITED ALL-ENGLAND CROQUET ASSOCIATION** | [rule] | LONDON : | PUBLISHED BY | HORACE COX, | WINDSOR HOUSE, BREAM'S BUILDINGS, E.C. | [below the frame] *Price Sixpence.*). RC: advertisement

Copy seen: BL: X449 2917 (in a library binding)

Fingerprint: ...8...8 isbe s.r, (BAp 3 1900A [group 3 taken from p *13*]

Notes: Printed anonymously, presumably by Horace Cox, London, price 6d. The signatures, which would appear to be redundant, suggest that much of this issue was also intended to be reprinted elsewhere.

(g) *1900 edition, FH Ayres issue (1900)*

THE | **LAWS** | OF | **CROQUET.** | [double rule] | Published by F. H. AYRES. | [rule in bold] | [rule] LONDON, 1900. [rule]

Formula: [1^{16}]. 16 leaves including the front and rear pastedowns, pp *i–iv*, *1–3* 4–12 *13* 14 *15* 16–23 *24–28*

Technical notes: 128 × 85 mm (p 4). 29 lines, 20 = 89 mm. Leaf size 181 × 122 mm; thickness 0.10 mm; wove, unwatermarked, smooth, white

Contents: Glued to the FC (*i*), index (*ii*), advertisements (*iii–iv*), title (*1*), advertise- ment (*2*), the laws of croquet, numbered 1–37 (*3–12*), definitions, numbered 1–13 (*13–14*), recommendations for match play (*15–23*), advertisements (*24–27*), glued to the RC (*28*)

Binding: Light yellowish Green (135) paper, apparently stapled, no spine. FC: printed in black within a multiple-ruled frame, the outer frame having a wavy border, with corner ornaments ([swelled rule] | THE | LAWS | OF | CROQUET. | [double rule, the upper rule in bold, with an ornamental tail-piece] | **Revised and Corrected.** | — 1900. — | *Published by* F. H. AYRES, London.). RC: advertisement

Copy seen: BL: 7921 dd 18 (in a library binding)

Fingerprint: t.er s.of Y.et boon 3 1900A

Notes: Printed anonymously.

(h) *Official edition, 1901, Horace Cox issue (1901)*

OFFICIAL EDITION, 1901. | THE | **LAWS OF CROQUET.** | TO WHICH ARE ADDED | REGULATIONS FOR PRIZE MEETINGS. | [rule] | REVISED | BY THE COMMITTEE OF | **THE CROQUET ASSOCIATION.** | [rule] | LONDON : | PUBLISHED BY | HORACE COX, | WINDSOR HOUSE, BREAM'S BUILDINGS, E.C. | 1901. | *Price Sixpence.*

Formula: 1^{22} [p *i* signed '[1]', p *vii* signed 'c', p *1* signed 'c 2', p 7 signed 'd', p 9 signed 'd 2']. 22 leaves, pp *i–viii*, *1* 2–12, *ix–x*, *13* 14, *xi–xii*, *15* 16–25 *26–32* [= 44]

Technical notes: 121 × 76 mm (p 5). 33 lines, 20 = 74 mm. Leaf size 165 × 105 mm; thickness 0.13 mm; wove, unwatermarked, smooth, white

Contents: Advertisements (*i–ii*), title (*iii*), the CA (*iv*), index (*v–vi*), advertisements (*vii–viii*), the laws of croquet, numbered 1–38, approved and adopted 31 December 1901 (*1–12*), advertisements (*ix–x*), definitions, lettered A–K (*13–14*), advertise- ments (*xi–xii*), regulations for prize meetings, numbered 1–14, approved and adopted 18 April 1901 (*15–25*), advertisements (*26–32*)

Binding: Moderate purplish Pink (250) semi-gloss laminated board, sewn through the inner lamina(ae), no spine or endpapers. FC: printed in black, mostly within a double-ruled frame with corner ornaments, the outer frame in bold ([above the frame] OFFICIAL EDITION, 1901. | THE | **LAWS OF CROQUET.** | TO WHICH ARE ADDED | REGULATIONS FOR PRIZE MEETINGS. | [rule] | REVISED | BY THE COMMITTEE OF | THE CROQUET ASSOCIATION. | [rule] | London | Published by | HORACE COX, | WINDSOR HOUSE, BREAM'S BUILDINGS, E.C. | [below the frame] *Price Sixpence.*). Inside FC: advertisement. RC: advertisement. Inside RC: advertisement

Copy seen: BOD: Per 38464 f 9

Fingerprint: ...7...6 t.ot n.in *Ho*(B 3 1901A

Notes: Printed anonymously, price 6d. The signatures, which would appear to be redundant, suggest that much of this issue was also intended to be reprinted elsewhere.

(j) *Official edition, 1902, Horace Cox issue (1902)*

OFFICIAL EDITION, 1902. | THE | **LAWS OF CROQUET.** | TO WHICH ARE ADDED | REGULATIONS FOR PRIZE MEETINGS. | [rule] | REVISED | BY | **THE CROQUET ASSOCIATION.** | [rule] | London : | Published by | HORACE COX, | WINDSOR HOUSE, BREAM'S BUILDINGS, E. C.

Formula: Not ascertainable from the copy examined [p *i* signed 'a', p *iii* signed 'b', p *v* signed 'b 2', p 5 signed 'c', p 7 signed 'c 2']. 18 leaves, pp *i–vi*, *1–5* 6–17 *18* 19 20 *21–28* 29–30

Technical notes: 121 × 76 mm (p 6). 33 lines, 20 = 73 mm. Leaf size 166 × 104 mm; thickness 0.12 mm; wove, unwatermarked, smooth, white

Contents: Advertisements (*i–vi*), title (*1*), the CA (*2*) index (*3–4*), the laws of croquet, numbered 1–41, approved and adopted 31 December 1901 (*5–17*), definitions, lettered A–I and K (*18–19*), regulations for prize meetings, numbered 1–14, approved and adopted 14 January 1902 (*20–28*), advertisements (*29–30*)

Binding: Strong purplish Pink (247) semi-gloss laminated board, no spine or endpapers. FC: printed in black, mostly within a double-ruled frame with corner ornaments, the outer frame in bold ([above the frame] OFFICIAL EDITION, 1902. | THE | **LAWS OF CROQUET.** | TO WHICH ARE ADDED | REGULATIONS FOR PRIZE MEETINGS. | [rule] | REVISED | BY | THE CROQUET ASSOCIATION. | [rule] | London | Published by | HORACE COX, | WINDSOR HOUSE, BREAM'S BUILDINGS, E.C. | 1902. | [below the frame] *Price Sixpence.*). Inside FC: advertisement. RC: advertisement. Inside RC: advertisement

Copy seen: BOD: Per 38464 f 9 (in a library binding)

Fingerprint: 1111 d.ry :—re towi 3 1902A

Notes: Printed anonymously, price 6d. The signatures, which would appear to be redundant, suggest that much of this work was also intended to be incorporated in another work.

(k) *Official edition, 1902, J Jaques & Son issue (1902)*

[The FC, mostly within a double-ruled frame, the outer frame in bold, with corner ornaments]

[above the frame] OFFICIAL EDITION, 1902. | THE | **LAWS OF CROQUET.** | TO WHICH ARE ADDED | REGULATIONS FOR PRIZE MEETINGS. | [rule] | REVISED | BY | THE CROQUET ASSOCIATION. | [rule] | ISSUED BY | **J. JAQUES & SON Ltd.,** | 102, HATTON GARDEN, LONDON, E.C. | BY PERMISSION OF THE CROQUET ASSOCIATION AND THE | AUTHORISED PUBLISHER, HORACE COX.

Formula: π1 *1*[18] [*1*$_2$ signed 'C', *1*$_3$ signed 'C2', *1*$_6$ signed 'D', *1*$_7$ signed 'D2']. 19 leaves, pp *i–ii*, *1–5 6–17*, *iii–iv*, *18 19*, *v–vi*, *20 21–28 29–32* [= 38]

Technical notes: 121 × 76 mm (p 6). 33 lines, 20 = 74 mm. Leaf size 162 × 102 mm; thickness 0.12 mm; wove, unwatermarked, smooth, white

Contents: Title (*i*), index (*1–2*), advertisements (*3–4*), the laws of croquet, numbered 1–41, approved and adopted 31 December 1901 (*5–17*), advertisements (*iii–iv*), definitions, lettered A–I and K (*18–19*), advertisements (*v–vi*), regulations for prize meetings, numbered 1–14, approved and adopted 14 January 1902 (*20–28*), advertisements (*29–32*)

Binding: Vivid Yellow (82) semi-gloss laminated board, stapled, no spine or endpapers. FC: printed in black, mostly within a double-ruled frame with corner ornaments, the outer frame in bold ([above the frame] OFFICIAL EDITION, 1902. | THE | **LAWS OF CROQUET.** | TO WHICH ARE ADDED | REGULATIONS FOR PRIZE MEETINGS. | [rule] | REVISED | BY | THE CROQUET ASSOCIATION. | [rule] | ISSUED BY | **J. JAQUES & SON LTD.,** | 102, HATTON GARDEN, LONDON, E.C. | BY PERMISSION OF THE CROQUET ASSOCIATION AND THE | AUTHORISED PUBLISHER, HORACE COX.). Inside FC: advertisement. RC: advertisement. Inside RC: advertisement

Copy seen: PC (imperfect)

Fingerprint: 1111 t.ot :—re towi 3 1902A [group 1 taken from p *1*]

Notes: Printed anonymously. The signatures, which would appear to be redundant, suggest that much of this work was also intended to be incorporated in another work.

(l) *Official edition, 1903, Horace Cox issue (1903)*

OFFICIAL EDITION, 1903. | THE | **LAWS OF CROQUET.** | TO WHICH ARE ADDED | REGULATIONS FOR PRIZE MEETINGS. | [rule] | REVISED | BY | **THE CROQUET ASSOCIATION.** | [rule] | LONDON : | PUBLISHED BY | HORACE COX, | WINDSOR HOUSE, BREAM'S BUILDINGS, E.C.

Formula: *1*[18] [*1*$_2$ signed 'B', *1*$_3$ signed 'B2', *1*$_6$ signed 'C', *1*$_7$ signed 'C2']. 18 leaves, pp *i–vi*, *1–4 5–17 18 19 20 21–28 29–30*

Technical notes: 121 × 76 mm (p 6). 33 lines, 20 = 74 mm. Leaf size 165 × 105 mm; thickness 0.11 mm; wove, unwatermarked, smooth, white

Contents: Advertisements (*i–vi*), title (*1*), the CA (*2*), index (*3–4*), the laws of croquet, numbered 1–41 (*5–17*), definitions, lettered A–I and K, approved and adopted 31 December 1902 (*18–19*), regulations for prize meetings, numbered 1–14, approved and adopted 28 January 1903 (*20–28*), advertisements (*29–30*)

Binding: Strong purplish Pink (247) semi-gloss laminated board, stapled, no spine or endpapers. FC: printed in black mostly within a double-ruled frame, the outer frame in bold, with corner ornaments ([above the frame] OFFICIAL EDITION, 1903. | THE | **LAWS OF CROQUET.** | TO WHICH ARE ADDED | **REGULATIONS FOR PRIZE MEETINGS.** | [rule] | REVISED | BY | THE CROQUET ASSOCIATION. | [rule] | LONDON : | PUBLISHED BY | HORACE COX, | WINDSOR HOUSE, BREAM'S BUILDINGS, E.C. | 1903. | [below the frame] *Price Sixpence.*). Inside FC: advertisement. RC: wanting from the copy examined

Copy seen: PC (imperfect)

Fingerprint: 1111 edry :—re towi 3 1903A

Notes: Printed anonymously, price 6d. The signatures, which would appear to be redundant, suggest that much of this issue was also intended to be incorporated in another work. The accounts of the CA show that royalties in respect of this work in 1903 amounted to £47 7s 9d (at 1d per copy). Hence it may be inferred that 11193 copies were sold that year. According to a letter from Horace Cox to the CA Committee, about £40 came from sales to distributors who included copies with their croquet sets.

(m) *Official edition, 1903, The Army & Navy Co-operative Society issue (1903)*

OFFICIAL EDITION, 1903. | THE | **LAWS OF CROQUET.** | TO WHICH ARE ADDED | REGULATIONS FOR PRIZE MEETINGS. | [rule] | REVISED | BY | **THE CROQUET ASSOCIATION.** | [rule] | Issued by | THE ARMY & NAVY CO-OPERATIVE SOCIETY LTD., | LONDON, BOMBAY, & CALCUTTA.

Formula: [1^{18}]. 18 leaves, pp *i–iv*, *1–5* 6–17 *18* 19 *20* 21–28 *29–32*

Technical notes: 121 × 77 mm (p 6). 35 lines, 20 = 70 mm. Leaf size 165 × 103 mm; thickness 0.11 mm; wove, unwatermarked, smooth, white

Contents: Advertisements (*i–iv*), title (*1*), the CA (*2*), contents (*3–4*), the laws of croquet, numbered 1–41 (*5–17*), definitions, lettered A–I and K, approved and adopted 31 December 1902 (*18–19*), regulations for prize meetings, numbered 1–14, approved and adopted 28 January 1903 (*20–28*), advertisements (*29–32*)

Binding: Strong purplish Pink (247) semi-gloss paper, stapled, no spine or end-papers. FC: printed in black mostly within a double-ruled frame, the outer frame in bold, with corner ornaments ([above the frame] OFFICIAL EDITION, 1903. | THE | **LAWS OF CROQUET.** | TO WHICH ARE ADDED | **REGULATIONS FOR PRIZE MEETINGS.** | [rule] | REVISED | BY | THE CROQUET ASSOCIATION. | [rule] | Issued by | **THE ARMY & NAVY CO-OPERATIVE SOCIETY LTD.,** | LONDON, BOMBAY, & CALCUTTA. | By permission of the Croquet Association, and the authorised | Publisher, Horace Cox. | [below the frame] *Price Sixpence*). Inside FC: advertisement. RC: advertisement. Inside RC: advertisement

Copy seen: PC

Fingerprint: 1111 edry :—re towi 3 1903A

Notes: Printed anonymously, price 6d. See also *Notes* to (l).

(n) *Official edition, 1904, Horace Cox issue (1904)*

OFFICIAL EDITION, 1904. | THE | **LAWS OF CROQUET.** | TO WHICH ARE ADDED | REGULATIONS FOR PRIZE MEETINGS. | [rule] | REVISED | BY | **THE CROQUET ASSOCIATION.** | [rule] | London : | Published by | HORACE COX, | WINDSOR HOUSE, BREAM'S BUILDINGS, E.C.

Formula: Not ascertainable from the copy examined [p *i* signed '*a*', p *3* signed 'B', p *5* signed 'C 2']. 20 leaves, pp *i–x*, *1–5* 6–17 *18* 19 *20* 21–28 *29–30*

Technical notes: 121 × 76 mm (p 6). 33 lines, 20 = 73 mm. Leaf size 164 × 102 mm; thickness 0.12 mm; wove, unwatermarked, smooth, white

Contents: Advertisements (*i–vi*), title (*vii*), the CA (*viii*), advertisements (*ix–x*), index (*1–2*), advertisements (*3–4*), the laws of croquet, numbered 1–41 (*5–17*), definitions, lettered A–I and K, approved and adopted 31 December 1902 (*18–19*), regulations for prize meetings, numbered 1–15, approved and adopted 4 February 1904 (*20–28*), advertisements (*29–30*)

Binding: Strong purplish Pink (247) semi-gloss laminated board, no spine or end-papers. FC: printed in black mostly within a ruled frame with corner ornaments ([above the frame] OFFICIAL EDITION, 1904. | THE | **LAWS OF CROQUET.** | TO WHICH ARE ADDED | **REGULATIONS FOR PRIZE MEETINGS.** | [rule] |

REVISED | BY | THE CROQUET ASSOCIATION. | [rule] | London : | Published by | Horace Cox, | WINDSOR HOUSE, BREAM'S BUILDINGS, E.C. | 1904. | [below the frame] *Price Sixpence.*). Inside FC: advertisement. RC: advertisement. Inside RC: advertisement

Copy seen: BOD: Per 38464 f 9

Fingerprint: **G.s.** a.ng e.ld orG. 7 1904A [group 2 taken from the caption to the diagram on p 7]

Notes: Printed anonymously, price 6d. The signatures, which would appear to be redundant, suggest that much of this work was also intended to be incorporated in another work.

(o) *Official edition, 1905, Horace Cox issue (1905)*

OFFICIAL EDITION, 1905. | THE | **LAWS OF CROQUET** | AND | Regulations for Prize Meetings. | [rule] | MADE AND AUTHORIZED BY | THE CROQUET ASSOCIATION. | [rule] | London : | Published for the Croquet Association by | **HORACE COX,** | Windsor House, Bream's Buildings, E.C. | 1905.

Formula: [1^{24}]. 24 leaves, pp *i–x, 1–5 6–22, xi–xii, 23–32 33–36* [= 48]

Technical notes: 119 × 76 mm (p 6). 35 lines, 20 = 69 mm. Leaf size 161 × 102 mm; thickness 0.12 mm; wove, unwatermarked, smooth, white

Contents: Advertisements (*i–vi*), title (*vii*), the CA (*viii*), advertisements (*ix–x*), index (*1–2*), advertisements (*3–4*), the laws of croquet, numbered 1–40, approved 9 February 1905 (*5–22*), advertisements (*xi–xii*), regulations for prize meetings, numbered 1–15, approved 2 February 1905 (*23–32*), advertisements (*33–36*)

Binding: Strong Pink (2) semi-gloss laminated board, stapled, no spine or endpapers. FC: printed in black, mostly within a ruled frame ([above the frame] OFFICIAL EDITION, 1905. | THE | **LAWS OF CROQUET** | AND | Regulations for Prize Meetings | MADE AND AUTHORIZED BY | THE CROQUET ASSOCIATION. | [rule] | London : | Published for the Croquet Association by | **HORACE COX,** | Windsor House, Bream's Buildings, E.C. | 1905. | [below the frame] PRICE SIXPENCE.). Inside FC: advertisement. RC: advertisement and name of printer. Inside RC: advertisement

Copy seen: PC

Fingerprint: **G.s.** rne; d.ve noDA C 1905A [groups 1–4 taken from pp *ix*, 9, 13, 14 respectively]

Notes: Printed by the Holmesdale Press, Redhill Junction and London, price 6d.

(p) *Official edition, 1906, Horace Cox issue (1906)*

OFFICIAL EDITION, 1906. | THE | **LAWS OF CROQUET** | AND | Regulations for Prize Meetings. | [rule] | ISSUED BY | THE CROQUET ASSOCIATION. | [rule] | London : | Published for the Croquet Association by | **HORACE COX** | Windsor House, Bream's Buildings, E.C. | 1906.

Formula: [1^{26}]. 26 leaves, pp *i–x, 1–5 6–25, xi–xii, 26–33 34 35 36–40* [= 52]

Technical notes: 118 × 75 mm (p 11). 35 lines, 20 = 67 mm. Leaf size 162 × 99 mm; thickness 0.13 mm; wove, unwatermarked, smooth, white

Contents: Advertisements (*i–vi*), title (*vii*), the CA (*viii*), advertisements (*ix–x*), index (*1–2*), advertisements (*3–4*), the laws of croquet, numbered 1–41, approved February 1906 (*5–25*), advertisements (*xi–xii*), regulations for prize meetings, numbered 1–15, approved February 1906 (*26–35*), advertisements (*36–40*)

Binding: Strong Pink (2) semi-gloss laminated board, stapled, no spine or endpapers. FC: printed in black, mostly within a ruled frame ([above the frame] OFFICIAL EDITION, 1906. | THE | **LAWS OF CROQUET** | AND | REGULATIONS FOR PRIZE MEETINGS | ISSUED BY | THE CROQUET ASSOCIATION. | [rule] | London : | Published for the Croquet Association by | **HORACE COX,** | Windsor House, Bream's Buildings, E.C. | 1906. | [below the frame] PRICE SIXPENCE.). Inside FC: advertisement. RC: advertisement and name of printer. Inside RC: advertisement

Copy seen: BL: 7907 df

Fingerprint: **G.**s. orot byb- crul 3 1906A [groups 1–4 taken from pp *ix*, 11, 13, 14 respectively]

Notes: Printed by the Holmesdale Press, Redhill Junction and London, price 6d.

(q) *Official edition, 1906, J Jaques & Son issue (1906)*

OFFICIAL EDITION, 1906. | THE | **LAWS OF CROQUET** | AND | Regulations for Prize Meetings. | [rule] | MADE AND AUTHORIZED BY | THE CROQUET ASSOCIATION. | [rule] | ISSUED BY | **J. JAQUES & SON,** Lᴛᴅ., | 102, HATTON GARDEN, LONDON, E.C. | *BY PERMISSION OF THE CROQUET ASSOCIA-TION.*

Formula: [1²²]. 22 leaves, pp *i–iv*, *1–5 6–33 34 35 36–40*

Technical notes: 118 × 76 mm (p 11). 35 lines, 20 = 68 mm. Leaf size 160 × 100 mm; thickness 0.13 mm; wove, unwatermarked, smooth, white

Contents: Advertisements (*i–iv*), title (*1*), the CA (*2*), index (*3–4*), the laws of croquet, numbered 1–41, confirmed February 1906 (*5–25*), regulations for prize meetings, numbered 1–15, approved and adopted February 1906 (*26–35*), advertisements (*36–40*)

Binding: Vivid Yellow (82) semi-gloss laminated board, stapled, no spine or endpapers. FC: printed in black, mostly within a ruled frame ([above the frame] OFFICIAL EDITION, 1906. | THE | **LAWS OF CROQUET** | AND | REGULATIONS FOR PRIZE MEETINGS | ISSUED BY | THE CROQUET ASSOCIATION. | [rule] | ISSUED BY | **J. JAQUES & SON LTD.,** | 102, HATTON GARDEN, LONDON, E.C. | *BY PERMISSION OF THE CROQUET ASSOCIATION.*). Inside FC: advertisement. RC: advertisement and name of printer. Inside RC: advertisement

Copy seen: PC

Fingerprint: 1615 orot byb- crut 3 1906A

Notes: Printed by the Holmesdale Press, Redhill Junction and London.

(r) *Official edition, 1907, Horace Cox issue (1907)*

OFFICIAL EDITION, 1907. | THE | **LAWS OF CROQUET** | AND | Regulations for Prize Meetings. | [rule] | ISSUED BY | THE CROQUET ASSOCIATION. | [rule] | London : | Published for the Croquet Association by | **HORACE COX,** | Windsor House, Bream's Buildings, E.C. | 1907.

Formula: [1³⁰] including the front and rear pastedowns. 30 leaves, pp *1–2*, *i–x*, *1–5 6–25*, *xi–xiv*, *26–37 38–44* [= 60]

Technical notes: 118 × 76 mm (p 6). 35 lines, 20 = 68 mm. Leaf size 160 × 105 mm; thickness 0.12 mm; wove, unwatermarked, smooth, white

Contents: Glued to the FC (*1*), advertisements (*2–vi*), title (*vii*), the CA (*viii*), advertisements (*ix–x*), contents (*1–2*), advertisements (*3–4*), the laws of croquet, numbered 1–43, confirmed 7 February 1907 (*5–25*), advertisements (*xi–xiv*), regulations for prize meetings, numbered 1–16, approved and adopted February 1907 (*26–37*), advertisements (*38–43*), glued to the RC (*44*)

Binding: Strong Pink (2) semi-gloss laminated board, no spine or endpapers. FC: printed in black, mostly within a ruled frame ([above the frame] OFFICIAL EDITION, 1907. | THE | **LAWS OF CROQUET** | AND | REGULATIONS FOR PRIZE MEETINGS | ISSUED BY | THE CROQUET ASSOCIATION. | [rule] | London : | Published for the Croquet Association by | **HORACE COX,** | Windsor House, Bream's Buildings, E.C. | 1907. | [below the frame] PRICE SIXPENCE.). Inside FC: advertisement (p *2*). RC: advertisement and name of printer. Inside RC: advertisement (p *44*)

Copy seen: BOD: 38463 f 9 (in a library binding)

Fingerprint: **G.**s. heed e.th sa(b 3 1907A [groups 1–4 taken from pp *ix*, 11, 13, 14 respectively]

Notes: Printed by the Holmesdale Press, Redhill Junction and London, price 6d.

(s) *Benetfink edition, 1907 (1907)*

THE | **LAWS OF CROQUET** | AND | Regulations for Prize Meetings. | [rule] | AS ADOPTED BY | THE CROQUET ASSOCIATION.

Formula: [1¹²]. 12 leaves, pp *1–3* 4–24

Technical notes: 134 × 76 mm (p 9). 45 lines, 20 = 60 mm. Leaf size 165 × 106 mm; thickness 0.08 mm; wove, unwatermarked, smooth, white

Contents: Title (*1*), blank (*2*), the laws of croquet, numbered 1–43, confirmed 7 February 1907 (*3–19*), regulations for prize meetings, numbered 1–16, approved and adopted February 1907 (*19–24*), name of printer (*24*)

Binding: Pale Green (149) paper, apparently, no spine or endpapers. FC: printed in black within a double-ruled frame, the outer frame in bold (1907. | THE | [at L in shaded display script] Laws of | [at R in shaded display script] Croquet | WITH | DEFINITION OF TERMS, PLAN OF THE HOOPS, | RECOMMENDATIONS FOR THE MANAGEMENT | OF PRIZE MEETINGS, &c | [rule] | *REVISED TO DATE.* | [rule] | PUBLISHED BY | Benetfink & co., Ltd., | *The Great City Depot for all Sports and Games,* | *107 & 108,* | *CHEAPSIDE, LONDON, E.C.*). Inside FC: advertisement. RC: advertisement. Inside RC: advertisement

Copy seen: BL: 7921 dd 19 (in a library binding)

Fingerprint: s.de isis toly boli 3 1907A

Notes: Printed by the "Cricket Press", London.

(t) *Official edition, 1907, J Jaques & Son issue (1907)*

OFFICIAL EDITION, 1907. | THE | **LAWS OF CROQUET** | AND | Regulations for Prize Meetings. | [rule] | MADE AND AUTHORIZED BY | THE CROQUET ASSOCIATION. | [rule] | ISSUED BY | **J. JAQUES & SON, Ltd.,** | 102, HATTON GARDEN, LONDON, E.C. | *BY PERMISSION OF THE CROQUET ASSOCIATION.*

Formula: [1²²]. 22 leaves, pp *i–iv, 1–5* 6–33 *34 35 36–40*

Technical notes: 117 × 75 mm (p 14). 35 lines, 20 = 68 mm. Leaf size 162 × 102 mm; thickness 0.13 mm; wove, unwatermarked, smooth, white

Contents: Advertisements (*i–iv*), title (*1*), the CA (*2*), contents (*3–4*), the laws of croquet, numbered 1–43, confirmed 7 February 1907 (*5–25*), regulations for prize meetings, numbered 1–16, approved and adopted February 1907 (*26–37*), advertisements (*38–40*)

Binding: Vivid Yellow (82) semi-gloss laminated board, stapled, no spine or endpapers. FC: printed in black, mostly within a ruled frame ([above frame] OFFICIAL EDITION, 1907. | THE | **LAWS OF CROQUET** | AND | REGULATIONS FOR PRIZE MEETINGS | MADE AND AUTHORIZED BY | THE CROQUET ASSOCIATION. | [rule] | ISSUED BY | **J. JAQUES & SON, LTD.,** | 102, HATTON GARDEN, LONDON, E.C. | *BY PERMISSION OF THE CROQUET ASSOCIA-TION.*). Inside FC: advertisement. RC: advertisement and name of printer. Inside RC: advertisement

Copy seen: PC

Fingerprint: 1515 heed e.th sa(b 3 1907A

Notes: Printed by the Holmesdale Press, Redhill Junction and London.

(**u**) *Official edition, 1908, Horace Cox issue (1908)*

OFFICIAL EDITION, 1908. | THE | **LAWS OF CROQUET** | AND | Regulations for Prize Meetings. | [rule] | ISSUED BY | THE CROQUET ASSOCIATION. | [rule] | London : | Published for the Croquet Association by | **HORACE COX,** | Windsor House, Bream's Buildings, E.C. | 1908.

Formula: [1²⁸]. 28 leaves, pp *i–x, 1–5 6–25, xi–xiv, 26–34 35 36–38 39–42* [= 56]

Technical notes: 117 × 75 mm (p 6). 35 lines, 20 = 67 mm. Leaf size 162 × 100 mm; thickness 0.12 mm; wove, unwatermarked, smooth, white

Contents: Advertisements (*i–vi*), title (*vii*), the CA (*viii*), advertisements (*ix–x*), index (*1–2*), advertisements (*3–4*), the laws of croquet, numbered 1–43, confirmed 7 February 1907 (*5–25*), advertisements (*xi–xiv*), regulations for prize meetings, numbered 1–18, approved and adopted February 1908 (*26–38*), advertisements (*39–42*)

Binding: Strong Pink (2) semi-gloss laminated board, no spine or endpapers. FC: printed in black, mostly within a ruled frame ([above the frame] OFFICIAL EDITION, 1908. | THE | **LAWS OF CROQUET** | AND | REGULATIONS FOR PRIZE MEETINGS | ISSUED BY | THE CROQUET ASSOCIATION. | [rule] | London : | Published for the Croquet Association by | **HORACE COX,** | Windsor House, Bream's Buildings, E.C. | 1908. | [below the frame] PRICE SIX-PENCE.). Inside FC: advertisement. RC: advertisement and name of printer. Inside RC: advertisement

Copy seen: BOD: Per 38364 f 9 (in a library binding)

Fingerprint: **G.**s. s.he ctr, thhe 3 1908A [groups 1–4 taken from pp *ix*, 11, 13, 14 respectively]

Notes: Printed by the Holmesdale Press, Redhill Junction and London, price 6d.

(**v**) *Slazenger & Sons issue [1908]*

THE | **LAWS OF CROQUET** | AND | **Regulations for Prize Meetings.** | [rule] | AS ADOPTED BY | **THE CROQUET ASSOCIATION.**

Formula: [1¹²]. 12 leaves, pp *1–3 4–22 23 24*

Technical notes: 133 × 76 mm (p 4). 45 lines, 20 = 60 mm. Leaf size 165 × 105 mm; thickness 0.11 mm; wove, unwatermarked, smooth, white

Contents: Title (*1*), blank (*2*), the laws of croquet, numbered 1–43, confirmed 7 February 1907 (*3–18*), regulations for prize meetings, numbered 1–18, approved and adopted February 1908 (*18–24*), name of printer (*24*)

Binding: Yellowish White (92) laid, rough paper, stapled, no spine or endpapers. FC: printed in black ([in display script] **CROQUET.** | [rule] | THE | [in shaded display script at L] **Laws of** | [in shaded display script at R] **Croquet.** | AS AUTHORISED BY THE | **CROQUET ASSOCIATION.** | [rule] | ISSUED BY | **Slazenger & Sons,** | **LONDON.**). Inside FC: advertisement. RC: advertisement. Inside RC: advertisement

Copy seen: PC

Fingerprint: 7.eg toan l.an ofof C 1908Q [groups 1–4 taken from pp 9, 17, 17, 17 respectively]

Notes: Printed by the "Cricket Press", London. Year of publication is inferred from the stated date of approval by the Committee of the regulations for prize meetings. The laws of the game, stated to have been approved early the previous year, are identical to those given in the *Official Edition, 1907, J Jaques & Son issue* (t).

(w) *Official edition, 1909, Horace Cox issue (1909)*

OFFICIAL EDITION, 1909. | THE | **LAWS OF CROQUET** | AND | Regulations for Prize Meetings. | [rule] | ISSUED BY | THE CROQUET ASSOCIATION. | [rule] | LONDON : | PUBLISHED FOR THE CROQUET ASSOCIATION BY | **HORACE COX,** | Windsor House, Bream's Buildings, E.C. | 1909.

Formula: [1²⁸ χ1]. 29 leaves, pp *i–x, 1–5 6–27, xi–xiv, 28–37 38 39–40 41–44* [= 58]

Technical notes: 118 × 77 mm (p 13). 35 lines, 20 = 69 mm. Leaf size 164 × 101 mm; thickness 0.11 mm; wove, unwatermarked, smooth, white

Contents: Advertisements (*i–vi*), title (*vii*), the CA (*viii*), advertisements (*ix–x*), contents (*1–2*), advertisements (*3–4*), the laws of croquet, numbered 1–43, signed 'JARVIS KENRICK, Hon. Sec.' (*5–22*), advertisements (*xi–xiv*), regulations for prize meetings, numbered 1–20, approved and adopted 4 February 1909 (*28–40*), advertisements (*41–44*)

Binding: Strong Pink (2) semi-gloss laminated board, no spine or endpapers. FC: printed in black, mostly within a ruled frame ([above the frame] OFFICIAL EDITION, 1909. | THE | **LAWS OF CROQUET** | AND | REGULATIONS FOR PRIZE MEETINGS | ISSUED BY | THE CROQUET ASSOCIATION. | [rule] | LONDON : | PUBLISHED FOR THE CROQUET ASSOCIATION BY | **HORACE COX,** | Windsor House, Bream's Buildings, E.C. | 1909. | [below the frame] PRICE SIX-PENCE.). Inside FC: advertisement. RC: advertisement and name of printer. Inside RC: advertisement

Copy seen: BOD: Per 38364 f 9 (in a library binding)

Fingerprint: **G.s.** s.he ctr, thhe 3 1909A [group 2 taken from p 11]

Notes: Printed by the Holmesdale Press, Redhill Junction and London, price 6d.

(x) *Official edition, 1910, Horace Cox issue (1910)*

OFFICIAL EDITION, 1910. | THE | **LAWS OF CROQUET** | AND | Regulations for Prize Meetings. | [rule] | ISSUED BY | THE CROQUET ASSOCIATION. | [rule] | LONDON : | PUBLISHED FOR THE CROQUET ASSOCIATION BY | **HORACE COX,** | Windsor House, Bream's Buildings, E.C. | 1910.

Formula: [1²⁸]. 28 leaves, pp *i–x, 1–5 6–22, xi–xiv, 23–37 38 39–40 41–42* [= 56]

Technical notes: 118 × 76 mm (p 12). 35 lines, 20 = 69 mm. Leaf size 163 × 103 mm; thickness 0.14 mm; wove, unwatermarked, smooth, white

Contents: Advertisements (*i–vi*), title (*vii*), the CA (*viii*), advertisements (*ix–x*), contents (*1–2*), advertisements (*3–4*), the laws of croquet, numbered 1–45, signed 'CHARLES CRAWLEY, Secretary, C.A.' (*5–27*), advertisements (*xi–xiv*), regulations for prize meetings, numbered 1–23, approved and adopted 6 January 1910 (28–40), advertisements (*41–42*)

Binding: Strong Pink (2) semi-gloss laminated board, no spine or endpapers. FC: printed in black, mostly within a ruled frame ([above the frame] OFFICIAL EDITION, 1910. | THE | **LAWS OF CROQUET** | AND | REGULATIONS FOR PRIZE MEETINGS | ISSUED BY | THE CROQUET ASSOCIATION. | [rule] | London : | Published for the Croquet Association by | **HORACE COX,** | Windsor House, Bream's Buildings, E.C. | 1910. | [below the frame] PRICE SIX-PENCE.). Inside FC: advertisement. RC: advertisement and name of printer. Inside RC: advertisement

Copy seen: BOD: Per 38364 f 9 (in a library binding)

Fingerprint: **G.s.** s.he rnch ba(1 3 1910A [group 2 taken from p 11]

Notes: Printed by the Holmesdale Press, Redhill Junction and London, price 6d.

(y) *Official edition, 1910, Slazenger & Sons issue (1910)*

OFFICIAL EDITION, 1910. | THE | **LAWS OF CROQUET** | AND | Regulations for Prize Meetings. | [rule] | MADE AND AUTHORIZED BY | THE CROQUET ASSOCIATION. | [rule] | ISSUED BY | **SLAZENGER & SONS,** | LAURENCE POUNTNEY HILL, | Cannon Street, LONDON, E.C. | *BY PERMISSION OF THE CROQUET ASSOCIATION.*

Formula: [1²⁴]. 24 leaves, pp *i–iv, 1–5* 6–37 *38* 39–40 *41–44* (misprinting 26 as '6')

Technical notes: 118 × 75 mm (p 12). 35 lines, 20 = 68 mm. Leaf size 162 × 104 mm; thickness 0.13 mm; wove, unwatermarked, smooth, white

Contents: Advertisements (*i–iv*), title (*1*), the CA (*2*), contents (*3–4*), the laws of croquet, numbered 1–45 (*5–27*), regulations for prize meetings, numbered 1–23, approved and adopted 6 January 1910 (28–40), advertisements (*38–40*)

Binding: Very light greenish Yellow (134) semi-gloss laminated board, stapled, no spine or endpapers. FC: printed in black, mostly within a ruled frame ([above frame] OFFICIAL EDITION, 1910. | THE | **LAWS OF CROQUET** | AND | REGULATIONS FOR PRIZE MEETINGS | MADE AND AUTHORIZED BY | THE CROQUET ASSOCIATION. | [rule] | [‡] | [‡] | [‡] | [‡] | *BY PERMISSION OF THE CROQUET ASSOCIATION.*). Inside FC: advertisement. RC: advertisement and name of printer. Inside RC: advertisement

Copy seen: PC (imperfect)

Fingerprint: 1818 s.he rnch ba(1 3 1910A

Notes: Printed by the Holmesdale Press, Redhill Junction and London.

(z) *Official edition, 1911, Horace Cox issue (1911)*

OFFICIAL EDITION, 1911. | THE | **LAWS OF CROQUET** | AND | Regulations for Prize Meetings. | [rule] | ISSUED BY | THE CROQUET ASSOCIATION. | [rule] | London : | Published for the Croquet Association by | **HORACE COX,** | Windsor House, Bream's Buildings, E.C. | 1911.

Formula: [1²⁶]. 26 leaves, pp *i–x, 1–5* 6–22, *xi–xiv, 23* 24–36 *37–38* [= 52]

Technical notes: 118 × 68 mm (p 6). 35 lines, 20 = 68 mm. Leaf size 163 × 104 mm; thickness 0.12 mm; wove, unwatermarked, smooth, white

Contents: Advertisements (*i–vi*), title (*vii*), the CA (*viii*), advertisements (*ix–x*), contents (*1–2*), advertisements (*3–4*), the laws of croquet, numbered 1–37, confirmed and adopted 13 January 1911 (*5–22*), advertisements (*xi–xiv*), regulations for prize meetings, numbered 1–26, approved and adopted 2 February 1911 (*23–36*), advertisements (*37–38*)

Binding: Strong Pink (2) semi-gloss stiff laminated board, no spine or endpapers. FC: printed in black, mostly within a ruled frame ([above the frame] OFFICIAL EDITION, 1911. | THE | **LAWS OF CROQUET** | AND | REGULATIONS FOR PRIZE MEETINGS | MADE AND AUTHORIZED BY | THE CROQUET ASSOCIATION. | [rule] | LONDON : | PUBLISHED FOR THE CROQUET ASSOCIATION BY | **HORACE COX,** | Windsor House, Bream's Buildings, E.C. | 1911. | [below the frame] PRICE SIXPENCE.). Inside FC: advertisement. RC: advertisement and name of printer. Inside RC: advertisement

Copy seen: BOD: Per 38364 f 9 (in a library binding)

Fingerprint: **G.**s. 5.'s lfff anre 3 1911A [group 2 taken from p 9]

Notes: Printed by the Holmesdale Press, Redhill Junction and London, price 6d.

(aa) *Official edition, 1911, J Jaques & Son issue (1911)*

OFFICIAL EDITION, 1911. | THE | **LAWS OF CROQUET** | AND | Regulations for Prize Meetings. | [rule] | MADE AND AUTHORISED BY | THE CROQUET ASSOCIATION. | [rule] | ISSUED BY | **J. JAQUES & SON,** LTD., | HATTON GARDEN, LONDON, E.C. | *BY PERMISSION OF THE CROQUET ASSOCIATION.*

Formula: [1^{22}]. 22 leaves, pp *i–iv, 1–5* 6–22 *23* 24–36 *37–40*

Technical notes: ca 118 × 77 mm (p 11). 34 lines, 20 = *ca* 70 mm. Leaf size *ca* 164 × 102 mm

Contents: Advertisements (*i–iv*), title (*1*), the CA (*2*), contents (*3–4*), the laws of croquet, numbered 1–37, confirmed and adopted 3 January 1911 (*5–22*), regulations for prize meetings, numbered 1–26, approved and adopted 2 February 1911 (*23–36*), advertisements (*37–40*)

Binding: Apparently printed on pale coloured board or paper, stapled. FC: mostly within a ruled frame ([above the frame] OFFICIAL EDITION, 1911. | THE | **LAWS OF CROQUET** | AND | REGULATIONS FOR PRIZE MEETINGS | MADE AND AUTHORIZED BY | THE CROQUET ASSOCIATION. | [rule] | ISSUED BY | **J. JAQUES & SON,** LTD., | HATTON GARDEN, LONDON, E.C. | *BY PERMIS-SION OF THE CROQUET ASSOCIATION.*). Inside FC: advertisement. RC: advertisement. Inside RC: advertisement

Copy seen: PC (photocopy)

Fingerprint: 1515 utr, ifff anre 3 1911A

Notes: Printed anonymously.

(bb) *Official edition, 1912, Horace Cox issue (1912)*

OFFICIAL EDITION, 1912. | THE | **LAWS OF CROQUET** | AND | Regulations for Prize Meetings. | [rule] | ISSUED BY | THE CROQUET ASSOCIATION. | [rule] | LONDON : | PUBLISHED FOR THE CROQUET ASSOCIATION BY | **HORACE COX,** | Windsor House, Bream's Buildings, E.C. | 1912.

Formula: [1^{24} χ1]. 25 leaves, pp *i–x, 1–5* 6–22, *xi–xii, 23* 24–36 *37–38* [= 50]

Technical notes: 129 × 76 mm (p 9). 37 lines, 20 = 70 mm. Leaf size 163 × 105 mm; thickness 0.12 mm; wove, unwatermarked, smooth, white

Contents: Advertisements (*i–vi*), title (*vii*), the CA (*viii*), advertisements (*ix–x*), contents (*1–2*), advertisements (*3–4*), the laws of croquet, numbered 1–37, confirmed and adopted 1 February 1912 (*5–22*), advertisements (*xi–xii*), regulations for prize meetings, numbered 1–25, approved and adopted 7 December 1911 (23–36), etiquette (37), advertisement (38)

Binding: Strong Pink (2) semi-gloss stiff laminated board, no spine or endpapers. FC: printed in black, mostly within a ruled frame ([above the frame] OFFICIAL EDITION, 1912. | THE | **LAWS OF CROQUET** | AND | REGULATIONS FOR PRIZE MEETINGS | MADE AND AUTHORIZED BY | THE CROQUET ASSOCIATION. | [rule] | London : | Published for the Croquet Association by | **HORACE COX,** | Windsor House, Bream's Buildings, E.C. | 1912. | [below the frame] PRICE SIXPENCE.). Inside FC: advertisement. RC: advertisement and name of printer. Inside RC: advertisement

Copy seen: BOD: Per 38364 f 9 (in a library binding)

Fingerprint: **G.**s. eall d.be eatu 3 1912A [group 2 taken from p 9]

Notes: Printed by the Holmesdale Press, Redhill Junction and London, price 6d.

(cc) *Official edition, 1913, Horace Cox issue (1913)*

OFFICIAL EDITION, 1913. | THE | **LAWS OF CROQUET** | AND | Regulations for Prize Meetings. | [rule] | ISSUED BY | THE CROQUET ASSOCIATION. | [rule] | London : | Published for the Croquet Association by | **HORACE COX,** | Windsor House, Bream's Buildings, E.C. | 1913.

Formula: [1²⁸]. 28 leaves, pp *i–x, 1–5 6–25, xi–xiv, 26 27–39 40 41 42* [= 56]

Technical notes: 128 × 76 mm (p 9). 37 lines, 20 = 71 mm. Leaf size 165 × 103 mm; thickness 0.12 mm; wove, unwatermarked, smooth, white

Contents: Advertisements (*i–vi*), title (*vii*), the CA (*viii*), advertisements (*ix–x*), contents (*1–2*), advertisements (*3–4*), the laws of croquet, numbered 1–37, Alternative Laws A and B, and copy regulation, confirmed and adopted 2 January 1913 (*5–25*), advertisements (*xi–xiv*), regulations for prize meetings, numbered 1–25, approved and adopted 2 January 1913 (*26–39*), etiquette (*40–41*), advertisement (*42*)

Binding: Strong Pink (2) semi-gloss stiff laminated board, no spine or endpapers. FC: printed in black, mostly within a ruled frame ([above the frame] OFFICIAL EDITION, 1913. | THE | **LAWS OF CROQUET** | AND | REGULATIONS FOR PRIZE MEETINGS | MADE AND AUTHORIZED BY | THE CROQUET ASSOCIATION. | [rule] | London : | Published for the Croquet Association by | **HORACE COX,** | Windsor House, Bream's Buildings, E.C. | 1913. | [below the frame] PRICE SIXPENCE.). Inside FC: advertisement. RC: advertisement and name of printer. Inside RC: advertisement

Copy seen: BOD: Per 38364 f 9 (in a library binding)

Fingerprint: **G.**s. eall d.aw thwh 3 1913A [group 2 taken from p 9]

Notes: Printed by the Holmesdale Press, Redhill Junction and London, price 6d.

(dd) *Official edition, 1913, FH Ayres issue (1913)*

OFFICIAL EDITION, 1913. | THE | **LAWS OF CROQUET** | AND | Regulations for Prize Meetings. | [rule] | MADE AND AUTHORISED BY | THE CROQUET ASSOCIATION. | [rule] | ISSUED BY | **F. H. AYRES, LTD.,** | 111 ALDERSGATE ST., LONDON, E.C. | *BY PERMISSION OF THE CROQUET ASSOCIATION.*

Formula: [1²⁴]. 24 leaves, pp *i–iv, 1–5 6–25 26 27–39 40 41 42–44*

Technical notes: 130 × 76 mm (p 9). 37 lines, 20 = 70 mm

Contents: Advertisements (*i–iv*), title (*1*), the CA (*2*), contents (*3–4*), the laws of croquet, numbered 1–37, alternative laws A and B, and copy regulation, confirmed and adopted 2 January 1913 (*5–25*), regulations for prize meetings, numbered *1–25*, approved and adopted 2 January 1913 (*26–39*), etiquette (*40–41*), advertisements (*42–44*)

Binding: Apparently stapled, no spine or endpapers. FC: mostly within a ruled frame ([above the frame] OFFICIAL EDITION, 1913. | THE | **LAWS OF CROQUET** | AND | REGULATIONS FOR PRIZE MEETINGS | MADE AND AUTHORIZED BY | THE CROQUET ASSOCIATION. | [rule] | ISSUED BY | **F. H. Ayres, Ltd.,** | 111 ALDERSGATE ST., LONDON, E.C. | *BY PERMISSION OF THE CROQUET ASSOCIATION.*). Inside FC: advertisement. RC: advertisement. Inside RC: advertisement

Copy seen: PC (photocopy)

Fingerprint: 1615 t.th d.aw thwh 3 1913A

Notes: Printed by the Holmesdale Press, Redhill Junction and London.

(ee) *Official edition, 1913, The Army & Navy Co-operative Society issue (1913)*

OFFICIAL EDITION, 1913. | THE | **LAWS OF CROQUET** | AND | Regulations for Prize Meetings. | [rule] | MADE AND AUTHORISED BY | THE CROQUET ASSOCIATION. | [rule] | ISSUED BY | **THE ARMY & NAVY CO-OPERATIVE SOCIETY LTD.,** | LONDON, BOMBAY, & CALCUTTA. | *BY PERMISSION OF THE CROQUET ASSOCIATION*

Formula: [1²²]. 22 leaves, pp *i–ii*, *1–5* 6–25 26 27–39 *40* 41 *42*

Technical notes: 130 × 76 mm (p 9). 37 lines, 20 = 70 mm. Leaf size 165 × 102 mm; thickness 0.11 mm; wove, unwatermarked, smooth, white

Contents: Advertisements (*i–ii*), title (*1*), the CA (*2*), contents (*3–4*), the laws of croquet, numbered 1–37, alternative laws A and B, and copy regulation, confirmed and adopted 2 January 1913 (*5–25*), regulations for prize meetings, numbered *1–25*, approved and adopted 2 January 1913 (*26–39*), etiquette (*40–41*), advertisement (*42*)

Binding: Dark Red (16) board, stapled, no spine or endpapers. FC: mostly within a ruled frame ([above the frame] OFFICIAL EDITION, 1913. | THE | **LAWS OF CROQUET** | AND | REGULATIONS FOR PRIZE MEETINGS | MADE AND AUTHORISED BY | THE CROQUET ASSOCIATION. | [rule] | ISSUED BY | **THE ARMY & NAVY CO-OPERATIVE SOCIETY LTD.,** | LONDON, BOMBAY, & CALCUTTA. | *BY PERMISSION OF THE CROQUET ASSOCIATION.*). Inside FC: advertisement. RC: advertisement. Inside RC: advertisement

Copy seen: PC

Fingerprint: As that of (dd)

Notes: Printed by the Holmesdale Press, Redhill Junction and London.

(ff) *Official edition, 1914, Horace Cox issue (1914)*

OFFICIAL EDITION, 1914. | THE | **LAWS OF CROQUET** | AND | Regulations for Prize Meetings. | [rule] | ISSUED BY | THE CROQUET ASSOCIATION. | [rule] | LONDON : | PUBLISHED FOR THE CROQUET ASSOCIATION BY | **HORACE COX,** | Windsor House, Bream's Buildings, E.C. | 1914.

Formula: [1²⁶]. 26 leaves, pp *i–x*, *1–5* 6–25, *xi–xii*, 26 27–39 *40* [= 52]

Technical notes: 128 × 76 mm (p 9). 38 lines, 20 = 68 mm. Leaf size 164 × 103 mm; thickness 0.11 mm; wove, unwatermarked, smooth, white

Contents: Advertisements (*i–vi*), title (*vii*), the CA (*viii*), advertisements (*ix–x*), contents (*1–2*), advertisements (*3–4*), the laws of croquet, numbered 1–37, Alternative

Laws A and B, and copy regulation, confirmed and adopted 4 December 1913 (*5–25*), advertisements (*xi–xii*), regulations for prize meetings, numbered 1–25, approved and adopted 4 December 1913 (*26–39*), etiquette (*40*)

Binding: Strong Pink (2) semi-gloss laminated board, no spine or endpapers. FC: printed in black, mostly within a ruled frame ([above the frame] OFFICIAL EDITION, 1914. | THE | **LAWS OF CROQUET** | AND | REGULATIONS FOR PRIZE MEETINGS | MADE AND AUTHORIZED BY | THE CROQUET ASSOCIATION. | [rule] | LONDON : | PUBLISHED FOR THE CROQUET ASSOCIATION BY | **HORACE COX,** | Windsor House, Bream's Buildings, E.C. | 1914. | [below the frame] PRICE SIXPENCE.). Inside FC: advertisement. RC: advertisement and name of printer. Inside RC: advertisement

Copy seen: BOD: Per 38364 f 9 (in a library binding)

Fingerprint: **G.**s. eall d.aw math 3 1914A [group 2 taken from p 9]

Notes: Printed by the Holmesdale Press, Redhill Junction and London, price 6d.

(gg) *Official edition, 1915, Horace Cox issue (1915)*

OFFICIAL EDITION, 1915. | THE | **LAWS OF CROQUET** | AND | Regulations for Prize Meetings. | [rule] | ISSUED BY | THE CROQUET ASSOCIATION. | [rule] | LONDON : | PUBLISHED FOR THE CROQUET ASSOCIATION BY | **HORACE COX,** | Windsor House, Bream's Buildings, E.C. | 1915.

Formula: [1²⁴ χ1]. 25 leaves, pp *i–viii, 1–5 6–25, ix–x, 26 27–39 40* [= 50]

Technical notes: 129 × 76 mm (p 6). 37 lines, 20 = 70 mm. Leaf size 164 × 103 mm; thickness 0.11 mm; wove, unwatermarked, smooth, white

Contents: Advertisements (*i–vi*), title (*vii*), the CA (*viii*), contents (*1–2*), advertisements (*3–4*), the laws of croquet, numbered 1–37, Alternative Laws A and B, and copy regulation, confirmed and adopted 4 December 1913 (*5–25*), advertisements (*ix–x*), regulations for prize meetings, numbered 1–25, approved and adopted 4 December 1913 (*26–39*), etiquette (*40*)

Binding: Strong Pink (2) semi-gloss stiff laminated board, no spine or endpapers. FC: printed in black, mostly within a ruled frame ([above the frame] OFFICIAL EDITION, 1915. | THE | **LAWS OF CROQUET** | AND | REGULATIONS FOR PRIZE MEETINGS | MADE AND AUTHORISED BY | THE CROQUET ASSOCIATION. | [rule] | LONDON : | PUBLISHED FOR THE CROQUET ASSOCIATION BY | **HORACE COX,** | Windsor House, Bream's Buildings, E.C. | 1915. | [below the frame] PRICE SIXPENCE.). Inside FC: advertisement. RC: advertisement and name of printer. Inside RC: advertisement

Copy seen: BOD: Per 38364 f 9 (in a library binding)

Fingerprint: 1615 eall d.aw math 3 1915A [group 2 taken from p 9]

Notes: Printed by the Holmesdale Press, Redhill Junction and London, price 6d.

(hh) *Official edition, 1916, Horace Cox issue (1916)*

OFFICIAL EDITION, 1916. | THE | **LAWS OF CROQUET** | AND | Regulations for Prize Meetings. | [rule] | ISSUED BY | THE CROQUET ASSOCIATION. | [rule] | LONDON : | PUBLISHED FOR THE CROQUET ASSOCIATION BY | **HORACE COX,** | Windsor House, Bream's Buildings, E.C. | 1916.

Formula: Not ascertainable from the copy examined. 23 leaves, pp *i–iv, 1–5 6–25 26 27–39 40 41 42*

Technical notes: 129 × 76 mm (p 9). 37 lines, 20 = 70 mm. Leaf size 163 × 101 mm; thickness 0.12–0.15 mm; wove, unwatermarked, smooth, white

Contents: Advertisements (*i–ii*), title (*iii*), the CA (*iv*), contents (*1–2*), advertisements (*3–4*), the laws of croquet, numbered 1–37, Alternative Laws A and B, and copy regulation, confirmed and adopted 4 December 1913 (*5–25*), regulations for prize meetings, numbered 1–25, approved and adopted 4 December 1913 (*26–39*), etiquette (*40–41*), blank (*42*)

Binding: Strong Pink (2) stiff board, no spine or endpapers. FC: printed in black, mostly within a ruled frame ([above the frame] OFFICIAL EDITION, 1916. | THE | **LAWS OF CROQUET** | AND | REGULATIONS FOR PRIZE MEETINGS | MADE AND AUTHORISED BY | THE CROQUET ASSOCIATION. | [rule] | LONDON : | PUBLISHED FOR THE CROQUET ASSOCIATION BY | **HORACE COX,** | Windsor House, Bream's Buildings, E.C. | 1916. | [below the frame] PRICE SIXPENCE.). Inside FC: advertisement. RC: advertisement and name of printer. Inside RC: advertisement

Copy seen: BOD: Per 38364 f 9 (in a library binding)

Fingerprint: 1615 eall d.aw math   3 1916A

Notes: Printed by the Holmesdale Press, Redhill Junction and London, price 6d.

(jj) *Official edition, 1916, J Jaques & Son issue (1916)*

OFFICIAL EDITION, 1916. | THE | **LAWS OF CROQUET** | AND | Regulations for Prize Meetings. | [rule] | MADE AND AUTHORISED BY | THE CROQUET ASSOCIATION. | [rule] | ISSUED BY | **J. JAQUES & SON** LTD., | 15 to 21 KIRBY ST., HATTON GARDEN, LONDON, E.C. | *BY PERMISSION OF THE CROQUET ASSOCIATION.*

Formula: [1²⁴]. 24 leaves, pp *i–iv*, *1–5* 6–25 *26* 27–39 *40–44*

Technical notes: 130 × 74 mm (p 9). 38 lines, 20 = 69 mm. Leaf size 165 × 101 mm; thickness 0.11 mm; wove, unwatermarked, smooth, white

Contents: Advertisements (*i–iv*), title (*1*), the CA (*2*), contents (*3–4*), the laws of croquet, numbered 1–37, and alternative laws A and B, confirmed and adopted 4 December 1913 (*5–25*), regulations for prize meetings, numbered 1–25, approved and adopted 4 December 1913 (*26–39*), etiquette (*40*), advertisements (*41–44*)

Binding: Strong Yellow (84) semi-gloss laminated board, stapled, no spine or endpapers. FC: printed in black, mostly within a ruled frame ([above the frame] OFFICIAL EDITION, 1916. | THE | **LAWS OF CROQUET** | AND | REGULATIONS FOR PRIZE MEETINGS | MADE AND AUTHORISED BY | THE CROQUET ASSOCIATION. | [rule] | ISSUED BY | **J. JAQUES & SON** LTD., | 15 to 21 KIRBY ST., HATTON GARDEN, LONDON, E.C. | *BY PERMISSION OF THE CROQUET ASSOCIATION.*). Inside FC: advertisement. RC: advertisement and name of printer. Inside RC: advertisement

Copy seen: PC

Fingerprint: 1615 t.th d.aw math   3 1916A

Notes: Printed by the Holmesdale Press, Redhill Junction and London.

(kk) *Official edition, 1916, Slazenger issue (1916)*

OFFICIAL EDITION.   1916 | THE | **LAWS OF CROQUET** | AND | Regulations for Prize Meetings. | [rule] | MADE AND AUTHORISED BY | THE CROQUET ASSOCIATION. | [rule] | ISSUED BY | **SLAZENGERS LTD.,** | LAURENCE POUNTNEY HILL, | Cannon Street, LONDON, E.C. | *BY PERMISSION OF THE CROQUET ASSOCIATION.*

Formula: Apparently [1²⁴]. Apparently 24 leaves, pp *i–iv*, *1–5* 6–25 *26* 27–39 *40 41 42–44*

Technical notes: 128 × 75 mm (p 9). 37 lines, 20 = 69 mm. Leaf size 166 × 103 mm; thickness 0.10 mm; wove, unwatermarked, smooth, white

Contents: Advertisements (*i–iv*), title (*1*), the CA (*2*), contents (*3–4*), the laws of croquet, numbered 1–37, and alternative laws A and B, confirmed and adopted 4 December 1913 (*5–27*), regulations for prize meetings, numbered 1–25, approved and adopted 4 December 1913 (*26–30*), etiquette (*40–41*), advertisements (*42–44*)

Binding: Stapled. Vestiges of what appear to have been a laminate wrapper, trapped below the crowns of the two staples, are a yellowish green colour

Copy seen: PC (imperfect, wanting almost all of the wrapper)

Fingerprint: 1615 t.th d.aw math 3 1916A

Notes: The copy examined contains no details of the printer or price.

(ll) *Official edition, 1917, Horace Cox issue (1917)*

OFFICIAL EDITION, 1917. | THE | **LAWS OF CROQUET** | AND | Regulations for Prize Meetings. | [rule] | ISSUED BY | THE CROQUET ASSOCIATION. | [rule] | London : | Published for the Croquet Association by | **HORACE COX,** | Windsor House, Bream's Buildings, E.C. | 1917.

Formula: Not ascertainable from the copy examined. 23 leaves, pp *i–iv*, 1–5 6–39 40 41 *42*

Technical notes: 129 × 76 mm (p 6). 37 lines, 20 = 70 mm. Leaf size 164 × 103 mm; thickness 0.11 mm; wove, unwatermarked, smooth, white

Contents: Advertisements (*i–iv*), title (*1*), the CA (*2*), contents (*3–4*), the laws of croquet, numbered 1–37, Alternative Laws A and B, and copy regulation, confirmed and adopted 4 December 1913 (*5–25*), regulations for prize meetings, numbered 1–25, approved and adopted 4 December 1913 (*26–39*), etiquette (*40–41*), blank (*42*)

Binding: Strong Pink (2) stiff board, no spine or endpapers. FC: printed in black, mostly within a ruled frame ([above the frame] OFFICIAL EDITION, 1917. | THE | **LAWS OF CROQUET** | AND | REGULATIONS FOR PRIZE MEETINGS | MADE AND AUTHORISED BY | THE CROQUET ASSOCIATION. | [rule] | London : | Published for the Croquet Association by | **HORACE COX,** | Windsor House, Bream's Buildings, E.C. | 1917. | [below the frame] PRICE SIX-PENCE.). Inside FC: advertisement. RC: advertisement. Inside RC: advertisement by the Holmesdale Press

Copy seen: BOD: Per 38364 f 9 (in a library binding)

Fingerprint: 1615 t.th d.aw math 3 1917A

Notes: Printed anonymously, presumably by the Holmesdale Press, Redhill, Surrey, price 6d.

(mm) *Official edition, 1918, Horace Cox issue (1918)*

OFFICIAL EDITION, 1918. | THE | **LAWS OF CROQUET** | AND | Regulations for Prize Meetings. | [rule] | ISSUED BY | THE CROQUET ASSOCIATION. | [rule] | London : | Published for the Croquet Association by | **HORACE COX,** | Windsor House, Bream's Buildings, E.C. | 1918.

Formula: [1¹⁸]. 18 leaves, pp *i–iv*, 1–5 6–19 20 21–31 *32*

Technical notes: 129 × 76 mm (p 10). 51 lines, 20 = 51 mm. Leaf size 163 × 104 mm; thickness 0.10 mm; wove, unwatermarked, smooth, white

Contents: Advertisements (*i–iv*), title (*1*), the CA (*2*), contents (*3–4*), the laws of croquet, numbered 1–37, Alternative Laws A and B, and copy regulation, confirmed and adopted 4 December 1913 (*5–19*), regulations for prize meetings, numbered 1–25, approved and adopted 4 December 1913 (*20–31*), etiquette (*32*)

Binding: Moderate yellowish Brown (177) speckled card, no spine or endpapers. FC: printed in black, mostly within a ruled frame ([above the frame] OFFICIAL EDITION, 1918. | THE | **LAWS OF CROQUET** | AND | REGULATIONS FOR PRIZE MEETINGS | MADE AND AUTHORISED BY | THE CROQUET ASSOCIATION. | [rule] | London : | Published for the Croquet Association by | **HORACE COX,** | Windsor House, Bream's Buildings, E.C. | 1918. | [below the frame] PRICE SIXPENCE.). Inside FC: advertisement. RC: advertisement. Inside RC: advertisement and name of printer

Copy seen: BOD: Per 38464 f 9 (in a library binding)

Fingerprint: 1313 d.be itte frst 3 1918A

Notes: Printed by the Holmesdale Press, Redhill, Surrey, price 6d.

(nn) *Official edition, 1918, FH Ayres issue (1918)*

OFFICIAL EDITION, 1918. | THE | **LAWS OF CROQUET** | AND | **Regulations for Prize Meetings.** | [rule] | MADE AND AUTHORISED BY | **THE CROQUET ASSOCIATION.** | [rule] | ISSUED BY | **F. H. AYRES, LTD.,** | **111 ALDERSGATE ST., LONDON, E.C.** | *BY PERMISSION OF THE CROQUET ASSOCIATION.*

Formula: [1¹⁶]. 16 leaves, pp *1–5 6–19 20 21–31 32*

Technical notes: 127 × 75 mm (p 6). 51 lines, 20 = 51 mm. Leaf size 163 × 103 mm; thickness 0.09 mm; wove, unwatermarked, smooth, white

Contents: Title (*1*), the CA (*2*), contents (*3–4*), the laws of croquet, numbered 1–37, alternative laws A and B, and copy regulation, confirmed and adopted 4 December 1913 (*5–19*), regulations for prize meetings, numbered 1–25, approved and adopted 4 December 1913 (*20–31*), etiquette (*32*)

Binding: Greenish Grey (155) light card, stapled, no spine or endpapers. FC: printed in black, mostly within a ruled frame ([above the frame] OFFICIAL LAWS, 1918. | THE | **LAWS OF CROQUET** | AND | REGULATIONS FOR PRIZE MEETINGS | MADE AND AUTHORISED BY | THE CROQUET ASSOCIATION. | [rule] | ISSUED BY | **F. H. Ayres, Ltd.,** | 111, ALDERSGATE ST., LONDON, E.C. | *BY PERMISSION OF THE CROQUET ASSOCIATION.*). Inside FC: advertisement. RC: advertisement. Inside RC: advertisement

Copy seen: HPC: 933 L3 1918 CROQ

Fingerprint: 1313 d.be itte frst 3 1918A

Notes: Printed anonymously.

(oo) *Official edition, 1919, Horace Cox issue (1919)*

OFFICIAL EDITION, 1919. | THE | **LAWS OF CROQUET** | AND | Regulations for Prize Meetings. | [rule] | ISSUED BY | THE CROQUET ASSOCIATION. | [rule] | London : | Published for the Croquet Association by | **HORACE COX,** | Windsor House, Bream's Buildings, E.C. | 1919.

Formula: Not ascertainable from the copy examined. 19 leaves, pp *i–iv, 1–5 6–19 20 21–31 32–34*

Technical notes: 128 × 76 mm (p 10). 51 lines, 20 = 51 mm. Leaf size 164 × 105 mm; thickness 0.10 mm; wove, unwatermarked, smooth, white

Contents: Advertisements (*i–iv*), title (*1*), the CA (*2*), contents (*3–4*), the laws of croquet, numbered 1–37, Alternative Laws A and B, and copy regulation, confirmed and adopted 4 December 1913 (*5–19*), regulations for prize meetings, numbered 1–25, approved and adopted 4 December 1913 (*20–31*), etiquette (*32*), advertisements (*33–34*)

Binding: Moderate Pink (5) paper, no spine or endpapers. FC: printed in black, mostly within a ruled frame ([above the frame] OFFICIAL EDITION, 1919. | THE | **LAWS OF CROQUET** | AND | REGULATIONS FOR PRIZE MEETINGS | MADE AND AUTHORISED BY | THE CROQUET ASSOCIATION. | [rule] | London : | Published for the Croquet Association by | **HORACE COX.** | Windsor House, Bream's Buildings, E.C. | 1919. | [below the frame] PRICE ONE SHILLING.). Inside FC: advertisement. RC: advertisement. Inside RC: advertisement and name of printer

Copy seen: BOD: Per 38464 f 9 (in a library binding)

Fingerprint: 1313 d.be itte frst   3 1919A

Notes: Printed by the Holmesdale Press, Redhill Junction and London, price 1/–.

(pp) *Official edition, 1920, The Field Press issue (1920)*

OFFICIAL EDITION, 1920. | THE | **LAWS OF CROQUET** | AND | Regulations for Prize Meetings. | [rule] | ISSUED BY | THE CROQUET ASSOCIATION. | [rule] | London : | Published for the Croquet Association by | **THE FIELD PRESS LTD.,** | Windsor House, Bream's Buildings, E.C. | 1920.

Formula: Not ascertainable from the copy examined. 19 leaves, pp *i–vi, 1–5 6–19 20 21–31 32–34*

Technical notes: 129 × 76 mm (p 6). 54 lines, 20 = 48 mm. Leaf size 164 × 103 mm; thickness 0.10 mm; wove, unwatermarked, smooth, white

Contents: Advertisements (*i–iv*), title (*1*), the CA (*2*), contents (*3–4*), the laws of croquet, numbered 1–37, Alternative Doubles law, and copy regulation, confirmed and adopted 12 February 1920 (*5–19*), regulations for prize meetings, numbered 1–26, approved and adopted 15 January 1920 (*20–31*), etiquette (*32*), advertisements (*33–34*)

Binding: Moderate Pink (5) paper, no spine or endpapers. FC: printed in black mostly within a ruled frame ([above the frame] OFFICIAL EDITION, 1920. | THE | **LAWS OF CROQUET** | AND | REGULATIONS FOR PRIZE MEETINGS | MADE AND AUTHORISED BY | THE CROQUET ASSOCIATION | [rule] | London : | Published for the Croquet Association by | **THE FIELD PRESS LTD.,** | Windsor House, Bream's Buildings, E.C. | 1920. | [below the frame] PRICE ONE SHILLING). Inside FC: advertisement. RC: advertisement. Inside RC: advertisement

Copy seen: BOD: 38464 f 9 (in a library binding)

Fingerprint: 1313 oten rt2) tash 3 1920A

Notes: Printed anonymously, presumably by the Holmesdale Press which advertises on p *33*, price 1/–.

(qq) *Official edition, 1920, FH Ayres issue (1920)*

OFFICIAL EDITION, 1920 | THE | **LAWS OF CROQUET** | AND | Regulations for Prize Meetings | [rule] | MADE AND AUTHORISED BY | **THE CROQUET ASSOCIATION.** | [rule] | ISSUED BY | **F. H. AYRES, LTD.,** | 111 ALDERSGATE ST., LONDON, E.C.1. | *BY PERMISSION OF THE CROQUET ASSOCIATION.*

Formula: [1¹⁸]. 18 leaves, pp *i–ii, 1–5 6–19 20 21–31 32–34*

Technical notes: 128 × 76 mm (p 6). 52 lines, 20 = 50 mm. Leaf size 163 × 105 mm; thickness 0.10 mm; wove, unwatermarked, smooth, white

Contents: Advertisements (*i–ii*), title (*1*), the CA (*2*), contents (*3–4*), the laws of croquet, numbered 1–37, and unnumbered laws of Alternative Doubles, confirmed and adopted 12 February 1920 (*5–19*), regulations for prize meetings, numbered 1–26, approved and adopted 15 January 1920 (*20–31*), etiquette (*32*), advertisements (*33–34*)

Binding: Moderate greenish Blue (173) rough paper, stapled, no spine or endpapers. FC: printed in black, mostly within a ruled frame ([above the frame] OFFICIAL LAWS, 1920. | THE | **LAWS OF CROQUET** | AND | **REGULATIONS FOR PRIZE MEETINGS** | MADE AND AUTHORISED BY | **THE CROQUET ASSOCIATION.** | [rule] | ISSUED BY | **F. H. A**YRES**, L**TD**.,** | **111, ALDERSGATE ST., LONDON, E.C. 4.** | *BY PERMISSION OF THE CROQUET ASSOCIATION.*). Inside FC: advertisement. RC: advertisement. Inside RC: advertisement

Copy seen: BL: 7920 aa 50

Fingerprint: 1313 oten rt2) tash 3 1920A

Notes: Printed anonymously.

(rr) *Official edition, 1921, The Field Press issue (1921)*

OFFICIAL EDITION, 1921. | THE | **LAWS OF CROQUET** | AND | **Regulations for Prize Meetings.** | [rule] | MADE AND AUTHORISED BY | THE CROQUET ASSOCIATION. | [rule] | L**ONDON** : | P**UBLISHED FOR THE** C**ROQUET** A**SSOCIATION** **BY** | **THE FIELD PRESS, LTD.** | **Windsor House, Bream's Buildings, E.C.** | 1921.

Formula: Not ascertainable from the copy examined. 17 leaves, pp *i–ii*, *1–5* 6–18 *19* 20–29 *30* 31 *32*

Technical notes: 126 × 84 mm (p 6). 45 lines, 20 = 56 mm. Leaf size 160 × 101 mm; thickness 0.09 mm; wove, unwatermarked, smooth, white

Contents: Advertisements (*i–ii*), title (*1*), the CA (*2*), contents (*3–4*), the laws of croquet, numbered 1–37, Alternative Doubles law, and extract from Regulation 1, confirmed and adopted 16 January 1921 (*5–18*), regulations for prize meetings, numbered 1–26, approved and adopted 13 November 1920 (*19–29*), etiquette (*30–31*), name of printer (*32*)

Binding: Pale orange Yellow (73) paper, no spine or endpapers. FC: printed in black mostly within a ruled frame ([above the frame] OFFICIAL EDITION 1921. | THE | **LAWS OF CROQUET** | AND | REGULATIONS FOR PRIZE MEETINGS | MADE AND AUTHORISED BY | THE CROQUET ASSOCIATION | [rule] | L**ONDON** : | P**UBLISHED FOR THE** C**ROQUET** A**SSOCIATION BY** | **THE FIELD PRESS LTD.,** | **Windsor House, Bream's Buildings, E.C.** | 1921. | [below the frame] *PRICE ONE SHILLING*). Inside FC: advertisement. RC: advertisement. Inside RC: advertisement

Copy seen: BOD: Per 38464 f 9 (in a library binding)

Fingerprint: 1313 d.). pter orST 3 1921A

Notes: Printed by Roffey and Clark, Croydon, price 1/–.

(ss) *Official edition, 1922, The Field Press issue (1922)*

OFFICIAL EDITION, 1922. | THE | **LAWS OF CROQUET** | AND | **Regulations for Prize Meetings.** | [rule] | ISSUED BY | THE CROQUET ASSOCIATION. | [rule] | L**ONDON** : | P**UBLISHED FOR THE** C**ROQUET** A**SSOCIATION BY** | **THE FIELD PRESS LTD.,** | Windsor House, Bream's Buildings, E.C. | **1922.**

Formula: Not ascertainable from the copy examined. 18 leaves, pp *i–ii*, *1–6* 7–19 *20* 21–32 *33* 34

Technical notes: 125 × 84 mm (p 7). 45 lines, 20 = 56 mm. Leaf size 163 × 102 mm; thickness 0.10 mm; wove, unwatermarked, smooth, white

Contents: Advertisements (*i–ii*), title (*1*), the CA (*2*), advantages of membership (*3*), contents (*4–5*), the laws of croquet, numbered 1–37, Alternative Doubles law, and extract from Regulation 1, confirmed and adopted 5 January 1922 (*6–19*), regulations for prize meetings, numbered 1–28, approved and adopted 5 January 1922 (*20–32*), etiquette (*33–34*)

Binding: Pale Pink (7) paper, no spine or endpapers. FC: printed in black mostly within a ruled frame ([above the frame] **OFFICIAL EDITION, 1922.** | THE | **LAWS OF CROQUET** | AND | **REGULATIONS FOR PRIZE MEETINGS** | MADE AND AUTHORISED BY | THE CROQUET ASSOCIATION | [rule] | LONDON : | PUBLISHED FOR THE CROQUET ASSOCIATION BY | **THE FIELD PRESS LTD.,** | **Windsor House, Bream's Buildings, E.C.** | **1922.** | [below the frame] *PRICE ONE SHILLING.*). Inside FC: advertisement. RC: advertisement and name of printer. Inside RC: advertisement

Copy seen: BOD: 38464 f 9 (in a library binding)

Fingerprint: l.w, tsor J.rn sqco 3 1922A

Notes: Printed by Roffey and Clark, Croydon, Surrey, price 1/–.

(tt) *Official edition, 1923, The Field Press issue (1923)*

OFFICIAL EDITION, 1923. | THE | **LAWS OF CROQUET** | AND | **Regulations for Prize Meetings.** | [rule] | MADE AND AUTHORISED BY | THE CROQUET ASSOCIATION | [rule] | LONDON : | PUBLISHED FOR THE CROQUET ASSOCIATION BY | **THE FIELD PRESS, LTD.** | **Windsor House, Bream's Buildings, E.C.** | **1923.**

Formula: Not ascertainable from the copy examined. 19 leaves, pp *i–ii*, *1–6* 7–19 *20* 21–32, *iii–iv*, *33* 34 [= 38]

Technical notes: 126 × 84 mm (p 7). 45 lines, 20 = 56 mm. Leaf size 163 × 102 mm; thickness 0.09 mm; wove, unwatermarked, smooth, white

Contents: Advertisements (*i–ii*), title (*1*), the CA (*2*), advantages of membership (*3*), contents (*4–5*), the laws of croquet, numbered 1–37, Alternative Double law, and extract from Regulation 1, confirmed and adopted 14 December 1922 (*6–19*), regulations for prize meetings, numbered 1–28, approved and adopted 14 December 1922 (*20–32*), advertisements (*iii–iv*), etiquette (*33–34*)

Binding: Moderate Pink (5) paper, apparently stapled, no spine or endpapers. FC: printed in black mostly within a ruled frame ([above the frame] **OFFICIAL EDITION, 1923.** | THE | **LAWS OF CROQUET** | AND | **REGULATIONS FOR PRIZE MEETINGS** | MADE AND AUTHORISED BY | THE CROQUET ASSOCIATION | [rule] | LONDON : | PUBLISHED FOR THE CROQUET ASSOCIATION BY | **THE FIELD PRESS, LTD.** | **Windsor House, Bream's Buildings, E.C.** | **1923.** | [below the frame] *PRICE ONE SHILLING.*). Inside FC: advertisement. RC: advertisement and name of printer. Inside RC: advertisement

Copy seen: BOD: Per 38464 f 9 (in a library binding)

Fingerprint: .1w, tsor).rn sepl 3 1923A

Notes: Printed by Roffey and Clark, Croydon, price 1/–.

(uu) *Official edition, 1923, J Jaques & Son issue (1923)*

OFFICIAL EDITION, 1923 | THE | **LAWS OF CROQUET** | AND | **Regulations for Prize Meetings.** | [rule] | MADE AND AUTHORISED BY | THE CROQUET ASSOCIATION | [rule] | ISSUED BY | **J. JAQUES & SON, LTD.,** | 15 to 21, KIRBY ST, | HATTON GARDEN, LONDON, E.C.1. | *By permission of the Croquet Association.*

Formula: [1¹⁶ χ1)]. 17 leaves, pp *1–6* 7–19 *20* 21–32 *33 34*

Technical notes: 125 × 84 mm (p 7). 45 lines, 20 = 56 mm. Leaf size 162 × 101 mm; thickness 0.10 mm; laid, unwatermarked, smooth, white

Contents: Title (*1*), the CA (*2*), advantages of membership (*3*), contents (*4–5*), the laws of croquet, numbered 1–37, details concerning Alternative Doubles, and extract from Regulation 1, confirmed and adopted 14 December 1922 (*6–19*), regulations for prize meetings, numbered 1–22, approved and adopted 14 December 1922 (*20–32*), etiquette (*33–34*)

Binding: Yellowish White (92) semi-gloss paper, stapled, no spine or endpapers. FC: printed in black, mostly within a ruled frame ([above the frame] OFFICIAL EDITION, 1923. | THE | **LAWS OF CROQUET** | AND | REGULATIONS FOR PRIZE MEETINGS | MADE AND AUTHORISED BY | THE CROQUET ASSOCIATION | [rule] | ISSUED BY | **J. JAQUES & SON LTD.** | 15 to 21, KIRBY STREET, | HATTON GARDEN, LONDON, E.C.1. | *BY PERMISSION OF THE CROQUET ASSOCIATION.*). Inside FC: advertisement. RC: advertisement and name of printer. Inside RC: advertisement

Copy seen: PC

Fingerprint: .1w, tsor).rn sepl 3 1923A

Notes: Printed by Roffey & Clark, Croydon.

(vv) *Official edition, 1924, The Field Press issue (1924)*

OFFICIAL EDITION, 1924. | THE | **LAWS OF CROQUET** | AND | Regulations for Prize Meetings. | [rule] | MADE AND AUTHORISED BY | **THE CROQUET ASSOCIATION.** | [rule] | LONDON : | PUBLISHED FOR THE CROQUET ASSOCIATION BY | **THE FIELD PRESS, LTD.** | **Windsor House, Bream's Buildings, E.C.** | **1924.**

Formula: Not ascertainable from the copy examined. 19 leaves, pp *i–ii*, *1–6* 7–18, *iii–iv*, 19 20–31 *32 33 34* [= 38]

Technical notes: 126 × 84 mm (p 7). 45 lines, 20 = 56 mm. Leaf size 160 × 99 mm; thickness 0.10 mm; laid, unwatermarked, smooth, white

Contents: Advertisements (*i–ii*), title (*1*), the CA (*2*), advantages of membership (*3*), contents (*4–5*), the laws of croquet, numbered 1–37, confirmed and adopted 13 December 1923 (*6–18*), advertisements (*iii–iv*), regulations for official tournaments, numbered 1–28, approved and adopted 22 November 1923 (*19–31*), etiquette (*32–33*), blank (*34*)

Binding: Moderate Pink (5) paper, apparently stapled, no spine or endpapers. FC: printed in black mostly within a ruled frame ([above the frame] **OFFICIAL EDITION, 1924.** | THE | **LAWS OF CROQUET** | AND | **REGULATIONS FOR PRIZE MEETINGS** | MADE AND AUTHORISED BY | THE CROQUET ASSOCIATION | [rule] | LONDON : | PUBLISHED FOR THE CROQUET ASSOCIATION BY | **THE FIELD PRESS, LTD.** | **Windsor House, Bream's Buildings, E.C.** | 1924. | [below the frame] *PRICE ONE SHILLING.*). Inside FC: advertisement. RC: advertisement and name of printer. Inside RC: advertisement

Copy seen: BOD: Per 38464 f 9 (in a library binding)

Fingerprint: .1w, tsor d.es peln 3 1924A

Notes: Printed by Roffey and Clark, Croydon, price 1/–.

(ww) *Official edition, 1924, FH Ayres issue (1924)*

OFFICIAL EDITION, 1924. | THE | **LAWS OF CROQUET** | AND | Regulations for Prize Meetings. | [rule] | MADE AND AUTHORISED BY | **THE CROQUET**

ASSOCIATION. | [rule] | ISSUED BY | **F. H. AYRES, LTD.,** | **111, ALDERSGATE ST., LONDON, E.C. 1.** | *By permission of the Croquet Association.*

Formula: [1¹⁸(1₁₇+χ1)]. 19 leaves, pp *i–ii, 1–6 7–18 19 20–31 32 33 34–36*

Technical notes: 125 × 84 mm (p 7). 56 lines, 20 = 50 mm. Leaf size 161 × 102 mm; thickness 0.09 mm; laid, unwatermarked, smooth, white

Contents: Advertisements (*i–ii*), title (*1*), the CA (*2*), advantages of membership (*3*), contents (*4–5*), the laws of croquet, numbered 1–37, confirmed and adopted 13 December 1923 (*6–18*), regulations for prize meetings, numbered 1–28, approved and adopted 22 November 1923 (*19–31*), etiquette (*32–33*), device, a knotted bow of ribbon (*34*), advertisements (*35–36*)

Binding: White paper, stapled, no spine or endpapers. FC: printed in black, mostly within a ruled frame ([above the frame] OFFICIAL EDITION, 1924. | THE | **LAWS OF CROQUET** | AND | **REGULATIONS FOR PRIZE MEETINGS** | MADE AND AUTHORISED BY | THE CROQUET ASSOCIATION | [rule] | ISSUED BY | **F. H. Ayres, ltd.,** | **111, ALDERSGATE ST., LONDON, E.C. 1** | *By permission of the Croquet Association.*). Inside FC: advertisement. RC: advertisement and name of printer. Inside RC: advertisement

Copy seen: BL: 7921 dd 12

Fingerprint: .1w, tsor d.es peIn 3 1924A

Notes: Printed by Roffey & Clark, Croydon.

(xx) *Official edition, 1925, The Field Press issue (1925)*

OFFICIAL EDITION, 1925. | THE | **LAWS OF CROQUET** | AND | Regulations for Official Tournaments. | [rule] | MADE AND AUTHORISED BY | **THE CROQUET ASSOCIATION.** | [rule] | London : | Published for the Croquet Association by | **THE FIELD PRESS, LTD.** | Windsor House, Bream's Buildings, E.C. | 1925.

Formula: [1¹⁸]. 18 leaves, pp *i–ii, 1–6 7–20, iii–iv, 21 22–31 32* [= 36]

Technical notes: 125 × 84 mm (p 7). 45 lines, 20 = 56 mm. Leaf size 164 × 102 mm; thickness 0.10 mm; laid, unwatermarked, smooth, white

Contents: Advertisements (*i–ii*), title (*1*), the CA (*2*), advantages of membership (*3*), contents (*4–5*), the laws of croquet, numbered 1–37, and variations A–D, confirmed and adopted 18 December 1924 (*6–20*), advertisements (*iii–iv*), regulations for official tournaments, numbered 1–22, approved and adopted 18 December 1924 (*21–31*), etiquette (*32*)

Binding: White paper, apparently stapled, no spine or endpapers. FC: printed in black mostly within a ruled frame ([above the frame] OFFICIAL EDITION, 1925. | THE | **LAWS OF CROQUET** | AND | Regulations for Official Tournaments | MADE AND AUTHORISED BY | THE CROQUET ASSOCIATION | [rule] | London : | Published for the Croquet Association by | **THE FIELD PRESS, LTD.** | **Windsor House, Bream's Buildings, E.C.** | 1925. | [below the frame] *PRICE ONE SHILLING.*). Inside FC: advertisement. RC: advertisement. Inside RC: advertisement

Copy seen: BL: 7921 dd 13 (in a library binding)

Fingerprint: .1w, n.of m.he peIn 3 1925A

Notes: Printed anonymously, price 1/–.

(yy) *Official edition, 1925, J Jaques & Son issue (1925)*

OFFICIAL EDITION, 1925. | THE | **LAWS OF CROQUET** | AND | Regulations for Official Tournaments. | [rule] | MADE AND AUTHORISED BY | THE CROQUET ASSOCIATION. | [rule] | ISSUED BY | **J. JAQUES & SON, LTD.,** | 15 to 21, KIRBY ST., | HATTON GARDEN, LONDON, E.C.1. | *By permission of the Croquet Association.*

Formula: [1^{16}]. 16 leaves, pp *1–6 7–20 21 22–31 32*

Technical notes: 125 × 84 mm (p 7). 45 lines, 20 = 56 mm. Leaf size 164 × 102 mm; thickness 0.10 mm; laid, unwatermarked, smooth, white

Contents: Title (*1*), the CA (*2*), advantages of membership (*3*), contents (*4–5*), the laws of croquet, numbered 1–37, and variations A–D, confirmed and adopted 18 December 1924 (*5–20*), regulations for official tournaments, numbered 1–22, approved and adopted 18 December 1924 (*21–31*), etiquette (*32*)

Binding: Not seen

Copy seen: PC (disbound)

Fingerprint: .1w, n.of m.he peln 3 1925A

Notes: Printed anonymously, presumably by Roffey and Clark, Croydon, who advertise on p *i*.

(zz) *Official edition, 1926, The Field Press issue (1926)*

OFFICIAL EDITION, 1926. | THE | **LAWS OF CROQUET** | AND | **Regulations for Official Tournaments.** | [rule] | MADE AND AUTHORISED BY | **THE CROQUET ASSOCIATION.** | [rule] | LONDON : | PUBLISHED FOR THE CROQUET ASSOCIATION BY | **THE FIELD PRESS, LTD.** | **Windsor House, Bream's Buildings, E.C.** | 1926.

Formula: [1^{20}]. 20 leaves, pp *i–ii, 1–6 7–21 22, iii–iv, 23–31 32–33 34 35–36* [= 40]

Technical notes: 125 × 84 mm (p 7). 45 lines, 20 = 56 mm. Leaf size 166 × 104 mm; thickness 0.10 mm; laid, unwatermarked, smooth, white

Contents: Advertisements (*i–ii*), title (*1*), the CA (*2*), advantages of membership (*3*), contents (*4–5*), the laws of croquet, numbered 1–37, and variations A–D, confirmed and adopted 17 December 1925 (*6–21*), advertisements (*iii–iv*), regulations for official tournaments, numbered 1–22, approved and adopted 17 December 1925 (*22–31*), etiquette (*32*), instructions and suggestions to referees and umpires (*33–34*), advertisements (*35–36*)

Binding: White paper, apparently stapled, no spine or endpapers. FC: printed in black mostly within a ruled frame ([above the frame] OFFICIAL EDITION, 1926. | THE | **LAWS OF CROQUET** | AND | **Regulations for Official Tournaments** | MADE AND AUTHORISED BY | THE CROQUET ASSOCIATION | [rule] | LONDON : | PUBLISHED FOR THE CROQUET ASSOCIATION BY | **THE FIELD PRESS, LTD.** | **Windsor House, Bream's Buildings, E.C.** | 1926. | [below the frame] *PRICE ONE SHILLING.*). Inside FC: advertisement. RC: advertisement. Inside RC: advertisement and name of printer

Copy seen: BL: 7921 dd 13 (in a library binding)

Fingerprint: .1w, e.be ."da holy 3 1926A

Notes: Printed by Roffey & Clark, Croydon, price 1/–.

(aaa) *Official edition, 1927, The Field Press issue (1927)*

OFFICIAL EDITION, 1927. | THE | **LAWS OF CROQUET** | AND | **Regulations for Official Tournaments.** | [rule] | MADE AND AUTHORISED BY | **THE CROQUET ASSOCIATION.** | [rule] | LONDON : | PUBLISHED FOR THE CROQUET

Association by | **THE FIELD PRESS, LTD.** | Windsor House, Bream's Buildings, E.C. | 1927

Formula: [1¹⁸]. 18 leaves, pp *i–ii, 1–6 7–20 21 22–31 32–33 34*

Technical notes: 125 × 84 mm (p 7). 45 lines, 20 = 56 mm. Leaf size 166 × 104 mm; thickness 0.10 mm; laid, unwatermarked, smooth, white

Contents: Advertisements (*i–ii*), title (*1*), the CA (*2*), advantages of membership (*3*), contents (*4–5*), the laws of croquet, numbered 1–46, and variations A–D, confirmed and adopted 6 January 1927 (*6–20*), regulations for official tournaments, numbered 1–23, confirmed and adopted 6 January 1927 (*22–31*), etiquette (*32*), instructions and suggestions to referees and umpires (*33–34*)

Binding: White paper, apparently stapled, no spine or endpapers. FC: printed in black mostly within a ruled frame ([above the frame] OFFICIAL EDITION, 1927. | THE | **LAWS OF CROQUET** | AND | **Regulations for Official Tournaments** | MADE AND AUTHORISED BY | THE CROQUET ASSOCIATION | [rule] | London : | Published for the Croquet Association by | **THE FIELD PRESS, LTD.,** | Windsor House, Bream's Buildings, E.C. | 1927.). Inside FC: advertisement. RC: advertisement. Inside RC: advertisement and name of printer

Copy seen: BL: 7921 dd 13 (in a library binding)

Fingerprint: .1w, heer d.to ofto 3 1927A

Notes: Printed by Roffey & Clark, Croydon.

(bbb) *Official edition, 1928, The Field Press issue (1928)*

OFFICIAL EDITION, 1928. | THE | **LAWS OF CROQUET** | AND | Regulations for Official Tournaments. | [rule] | MADE AND AUTHORISED BY | **THE CROQUET ASSOCIATION.** | [rule] | London : | Published for the Croquet Association by | **THE FIELD PRESS, LTD.** | Windsor House, Bream's Buildings, E.C. | 1928.

Formula: [1¹⁸]. 18 leaves, pp *1–6 7–19 20, i–ii, 21 22–32 33 34*

Technical notes: 123 × 84 mm (p 9). 44 lines, 20 = 56 mm. Leaf size 161 × 101 mm; thickness 0.10 mm; laid, unwatermarked, smooth, white

Contents: Title (*1*), the CA (*2*), advantages of membership (*3*), contents (*4–5*), the laws of croquet, numbered 1–49, confirmed and adopted 5 January 1928 (*6–19*), etiquette (*20*), advertisements (*i–ii*), regulations for official tournaments, numbered 1–23, confirmed and adopted 5 January 1928 (*21–32*), instructions and suggestions to referees and umpires, numbered 1–14 (*33–34*)

Binding: White paper, apparently stapled, no spine or endpapers. FC: printed in black mostly within a ruled frame ([above the frame] OFFICIAL EDITION, 1928. | THE | **LAWS OF CROQUET** | AND | **Regulations for Official Tournaments** | MADE AND AUTHORISED BY | THE CROQUET ASSOCIATION | [rule] | London : | Published for the Croquet Association by | **THE FIELD PRESS, LTD.,** | Windsor House, Bream's Buildings, E.C. | 1928.). Inside FC: advertisement. RC: advertisement. Inside RC: advertisement and name of printer

Copy seen: BL: 7921 dd 13 (in a library binding)

Fingerprint: .1w, s.r- erll tosh 3 1928A

Notes: Printed by Roffey & Clark, Croydon.

(ccc) *Official edition, 1928, J Jaques & Son issue (1928)*

OFFICIAL EDITION, 1928. | THE | **LAWS OF CROQUET** | AND | **Regulations for Official Tournaments.** | [rule] | MADE AND AUTHORISED BY | THE

CROQUET ASSOCIATION. | [rule] | ISSUED BY | **J. JAQUES & SON, LTD.** | 15 to 21, KIRBY ST, | HATTON GARDEN, LONDON, E.C.1. | **By permission of the Croquet Association.**

Formula: [1^{16} χ1)]. 17 leaves, pp *1–6* 7–19 *20–21* 22–32 *33* 34

Technical notes: 123 × 84 mm (p 12). 44 lines, 20 = 56 mm. Leaf size 161 × 102 mm; thickness 0.10 mm; laid, unwatermarked, smooth, white

Contents: Title (*1*), the CA (*2*), advantages of membership (*3*), contents (*4–5*), the laws of croquet, numbered 1–49, confirmed and adopted 5 January 1928 (*5–19*), etiquette (*20*), regulations for official tournaments, numbered 1–23, confirmed and adopted 5 January 1928 (*21–32*), referees and umpires (*33–34*)

Binding: White semi-gloss paper, stapled, no spine or endpapers. FC: printed in black mostly within a ruled frame ([above the frame] OFFICIAL EDITION, 1928. | THE | **LAWS OF CROQUET** | AND | **Regulations for Official Tournaments** | MADE AND AUTHORISED BY | THE CROQUET ASSOCIATION | ISSUED BY | **J. JAQUES & SON, LTD.** | 15 to 21, KIRBY STREET, | HATTON GARDEN, LONDON, E.C.1. | **By permission of the Croquet Association.**). Inside FC: advertisement. RC: advertisement. Inside RC: advertisement

Copy seen: PC

Fingerprint: .1w, s.r- erll tosh 3 1928A

Notes: Printed anonymously.

(ddd) *Official edition, 1929, The Field Press issue (1929)*

OFFICIAL EDITION, 1929. | THE | **LAWS OF CROQUET** | AND | **Regulations for Official Tournaments.** | [rule] | MADE AND AUTHORISED BY | **THE CROQUET ASSOCIATION.** | [rule] | London : | Published for the Croquet Association by | **THE FIELD PRESS, LTD.** | **Windsor House, Bream's Buildings,** **E.C.** | 1929.

Formula: [1^{18}]. 18 leaves, pp *1–6* 7–19 *20, i–ii, 21* 22–32 *33* 34

Technical notes: 135 × 84 mm (p 9). 49 lines, 20 = 56 mm. Leaf size 162 × 101 mm; thickness 0.10 mm; laid, unwatermarked, smooth, white

Contents: Title (*1*), the CA (*2*), advantages of membership (*3*), contents (*4–5*), the laws of croquet, numbered 1–49, confirmed and adopted 3 January 1929 (*6–19*), etiquette (*20*), advertisements (*i–ii*), regulations for official tournaments, numbered 1–23, confirmed and adopted 3 January 1929 (*21–32*), instructions and suggestions to referees and umpires, numbered 1–15 (*33–34*)

Binding: White paper, apparently stapled, no spine or endpapers. FC: printed in black mostly within a ruled frame ([above the frame] OFFICIAL EDITION, 1929. | THE | **LAWS OF CROQUET** | AND | **Regulations for Official Tournaments** | MADE AND AUTHORISED BY | THE CROQUET ASSOCIATION | [rule] | London : | Published for the Croquet Association by | **THE FIELD PRESS,** **LTD.,** | **Windsor House, Bream's Buildings, E.C.** | 1929. | [below the frame] PRICE ONE SHILLING.). Inside FC: advertisement. RC: advertisement. Inside RC: advertisement and name of printer

Copy seen: BL: 7921 dd 13 (in a library binding)

Fingerprint: .1w, t.en n.ry ma(d 3 1929A

Notes: Printed by Roffey & Clark, Croydon, price 1/–.

(eee) *Official edition, 1930, The Field Press issue (1930)*

OFFICIAL EDITION, 1930. | THE | **LAWS OF CROQUET** | AND | **Regulations** for Official Tournaments. | [rule] | MADE AND AUTHORISED BY | **THE CROQUET ASSOCIATION.** | [rule] | London : | Published for the Croquet Association by | **THE FIELD PRESS, LTD.** | **Windsor House, Bream's Buildings, E.C.** | 1930.

Formula: [1^18]. 18 leaves, pp *1–2* 3–5 6 7–19 *20, i–ii,* 21 22 23–34 *35 36*

Technical notes: 126 × 84 mm (p 8). 45 lines, 20 = 56 mm. Leaf size 164 × 103 mm; thickness 0.10 mm; laid, unwatermarked, smooth, white

Contents: Title *(1),* the CA *(2),* advantages of membership (3), contents (4–5), the laws of croquet, numbered 1–48, confirmed and adopted 2 January 1930 (6–19), etiquette *(20),* advertisements *(i–ii),* regulations for official tournaments, numbered 1–25, confirmed and adopted 2 January 1930 (22–34), instructions and suggestions to referees and umpires, numbered 1–16 *(35–36)*

Binding: White paper, apparently stapled, no spine or endpapers. FC: printed in black mostly within a ruled frame ([above the frame] OFFICIAL EDITION, 1930. | THE | **LAWS OF CROQUET** | AND | **Regulations for Official Tournaments** | MADE AND AUTHORISED BY | THE CROQUET ASSOCIATION | [rule] | London : | Published for the Croquet Association by | **THE FIELD PRESS, LTD.,** | **Windsor House, Bream's Buildings, E.C.** | 1930. | [below the frame] PRICE ONE SHILLING.). Inside FC: advertisement. RC: advertisement. Inside RC: advertisement and name of printer

Copy seen: BL: 7921 dd 13 (in a library binding)

Fingerprint: .1w, s.r- d.to pabe 3 1930A

Notes: Printed by Roffey & Clark, Croydon, price 1/–.

(fff) *Official edition, 1931, The Field Press issue (1931)*

OFFICIAL EDITION, 1931. | THE | **LAWS OF CROQUET** | AND | **Regulations for Official Tournaments.** | [rule] | MADE AND AUTHORISED BY | **THE CROQUET ASSOCIATION.** | [rule] | London : | Published for the Croquet Association by | **THE FIELD PRESS, LTD.** | **Windsor House, Bream's Buildings, E.C.** | 1931.

Formula: [1^18 χ_{1, 2})]. 20 leaves, pp *1–2* 3–5 6 7–23, *i–ii,* 24–37 *38* [= 40]

Technical notes: 125 × 84 mm (p 7). 45 lines, 20 = 56 mm. Leaf size 165 × 104 mm; thickness 0.10 mm; laid, unwatermarked, smooth, white

Contents: Title *(1),* the CA *(2),* advantages of membership (3), contents (4–5), the laws of croquet, numbered 1–48, confirmed and adopted 4 December 1930 (6–20), etiquette *(21–23),* advertisements *(i–ii),* regulations for official tournaments, numbered 1–25, confirmed and adopted 4 December 1930 (24–35), instructions and suggestions to referees and umpires, numbered 1–17 (36–37), name of printer *(38)*

Binding: White paper, apparently stapled, no spine or endpapers. FC: printed in black mostly within a ruled frame ([above the frame] OFFICIAL EDITION, 1931. | THE | **LAWS OF CROQUET** | AND | **Regulations for Official Tournaments** | MADE AND AUTHORISED BY | THE CROQUET ASSOCIATION | [rule] | London : | Published for the Croquet Association by | **THE FIELD PRESS, LTD.,** | **Windsor House, Bream's Buildings, E.C.** | 1931. | [below the frame] PRICE ONE SHILLING.). Inside FC: advertisement. RC: advertisement. Inside RC: advertisement and name of printer

Copy seen: BL: 7921 dd 13 (in a library binding)

Fingerprint: .1ow).ue t.de be(*d* 3 1931A

Notes: Printed by Roffey & Clark, Croydon, price 1/–.

(ggg) *Official edition, 1932, The Field Press issue (1932)*

OFFICIAL EDITION, 1932. | THE | **LAWS OF CROQUET** | AND | **Regulations for Official Tournaments.** | [rule] | MADE AND AUTHORISED BY | **THE CROQUET ASSOCIATION.** | [rule] | LONDON : | LONDON : | PUBLISHED FOR THE CROQUET ASSOCIATION BY | **THE FIELD PRESS, LTD.** | **Windsor House, Bream's Buildings, E.C.** | **1932.**

Formula: Not ascertainable from the copy examined. 21 leaves, pp *1–2* 3–24, *i–ii*, 25–39 *40* [= 42]

Technical notes: 125 × 84 mm (p 7). 45 lines, 20 = 56 mm. Leaf size 162 × 104 mm; thickness 0.11 mm; laid, unwatermarked, smooth, white

Contents: Title (*1*), the CA (*2*), advantages of membership (*3*), contents (*4–5*), the laws of croquet, numbered 1–48, confirmed and adopted 10 December 1931 (*6–22*), etiquette (*23–24*), advertisements (*i–ii*), regulations for official tournaments, numbered 1–25, confirmed and adopted 10 December 1931 (*25–37*), instructions and suggestions to referees and umpires, numbered 1–17 (*38–39*), name of printer (*40*)

Binding: White paper, apparently stapled, no spine or endpapers. FC: printed in black mostly within a ruled frame ([above the frame] **OFFICIAL EDITION, 1932.** | THE | **LAWS OF CROQUET** | AND | **Regulations for Official Tournaments** | MADE AND AUTHORISED BY | THE CROQUET ASSOCIATION | [rule] | LONDON : | PUBLISHED FOR THE CROQUET ASSOCIATION BY | **THE FIELD PRESS, LTD.** | **Windsor House, Bream's Buildings, E.C.** | 1932. | [below the frame] **PRICE ONE SHILLING.**). Inside FC: advertisement. RC: advertisement. Inside RC: advertisement and name of printer

Copy seen: BOD: Per 38464 f 9 (in a library binding)

Fingerprint: .1w, e.th d.or sain 3 1932A

Notes: Printed by Roffey & Clark, Croydon, price 1/–.

(hhh) *Official edition, 1933, The Field Press issue (1933)*

OFFICIAL EDITION, 1933. | THE | **LAWS OF CROQUET** | AND | **Regulations for Official Tournaments.** | [rule] | MADE AND AUTHORISED BY | **THE CROQUET ASSOCIATION.** | [rule] | LONDON : | PUBLISHED FOR THE CROQUET ASSOCIATION BY | **THE FIELD PRESS, LTD.** | **Windsor House, Bream's Buildings, E.C.** | **1933.**

Formula: Not ascertainable from the copy examined. 21 leaves, pp *1–2* 3–24, *i–ii*, 25–39 *40* [= 42]

Technical notes: 125 × 84 mm (p 7). 45 lines, 20 = 56 mm. Leaf size 165 × 104 mm; thickness 0.10 mm; laid, unwatermarked, smooth, white

Contents: Title (*1*), the CA (*2*), advantages of membership (*3*), contents (*4–5*), the laws of croquet, numbered 1–48, confirmed and adopted 15 December 1932 (*6–22*), etiquette (*23–24*), advertisements (*i–ii*), regulations for official tournaments, numbered 1–25, confirmed and adopted 15 December 1932 (*24–35*), instructions and suggestions to referees and umpires, numbered 1–17 (*38–39*), name of printer (*40*)

Binding: Moderate Pink (5) paper, no spine or endpapers. FC: printed in black mostly within a ruled frame ([above the frame] **OFFICIAL EDITION, 1933.** | THE | **LAWS OF CROQUET** | AND | **Regulations for Official Tournaments** | MADE AND AUTHORISED BY | THE CROQUET ASSOCIATION | [rule] | LONDON : | PUBLISHED FOR THE CROQUET ASSOCIATION BY | **THE FIELD PRESS, LTD.** | **Windsor House, Bream's Buildings, E.C.** | **1933.** | [below the frame] **PRICE ONE**

SHILLING.). Inside FC: advertisement. RC: advertisement. Inside RC: advertisement and name of printer

Copy seen: BOD: Per 38464 f 9 (in a library binding)

Fingerprint: .1w, e.th :—he maof 3 1933A

Notes: Printed by Roffey & Clark, Croydon, price 1/–.

(jjj) *Official edition, 1934, The Field Press issue (1934)*

OFFICIAL EDITION, 1934. | THE | **LAWS OF CROQUET** | AND | **Regulations for Official Tournaments.** | ALSO | **The Laws of Golf-Croquet** | [rule] | MADE AND AUTHORISED BY | **THE CROQUET ASSOCIATION.** | [rule] | London : | Published for the Croquet Association by | **THE FIELD PRESS, LTD.** | **Windsor House, Bream's Buildings, E.C.** | **1934.**

Formula: Not ascertainable from the copy examined. 25 leaves, pp *1–2 3–24, i–ii, 25–42 43 44–48* [= 50]

Technical notes: 127 × 85 mm (p 34). 46 lines, 20 = 56 mm. Leaf size 163 × 104 mm; thickness 0.10 mm; laid, unwatermarked, smooth, white

Contents: Title (*1*), the CA (*2*), advantages of membership (*3*), contents (*4–5*), the laws of croquet, numbered 1–48, confirmed and adopted 14 December 1933 (*6–23*), etiquette, continued (*24*), advertisements (*i–ii*), etiquette, concluded (*25*), regulations for official tournaments, numbered 1–25, confirmed and adopted 15 December 1932 (*26–38*), referees and umpires (*39–40*), decisions on points in the laws (*41–43*), space for notes, headed 'DECISIONS' (*44–45*), space for notes, headed 'NOTES' (*46*), laws of golf-croquet, numbered 1–10 (*47–48*), name of printer (*48*)

Binding: Moderate Pink (5) paper, stapled, no spine or endpapers. FC: printed in black mostly within a ruled frame ([above the frame] **OFFICIAL EDITION, 1934.** | THE | **LAWS OF CROQUET** | AND | **Regulations for Official Tournaments** | ALSO | **The Laws of Golf-Croquet** | MADE AND AUTHORISED BY | THE CROQUET ASSOCIATION | [rule] | London : | Published for the Croquet Association by | **THE FIELD PRESS, LTD.** | **Windsor House, Bream's Buildings, E.C.** | **1934.** | [below the frame] **PRICE ONE SHILLING.**). Inside FC: advertisement. RC: advertisement. Inside RC: advertisement and name of printer

Copy seen: BOD: Per 38464 f 9 (in a library binding)

Fingerprint: .1w, e.ay :—he maof 3 1934A

Notes: Printed by Roffey & Clark, Croydon, price 1/–.

(kkk) *Official edition, 1935, The Field Press issue (1935)*

OFFICIAL EDITION, 1935. | THE | **LAWS OF CROQUET** | AND | **Regulations for Official Tournaments.** | ALSO | **The Laws of Golf-Croquet** | [rule] | MADE AND AUTHORISED BY | **THE CROQUET ASSOCIATION.** | [rule] | London : | Published for the Croquet Association by | **THE FIELD PRESS, LTD.** | **Windsor House, Bream's Buildings, E.C.** | **1935.**

Formula: [1²⁴(1₁₂+χ1)]. 25 leaves, pp *1–2 3–24, i–ii, 25–48* [= 50]

Technical notes: 127 × 84 mm (p 34). 46 lines, 20 = 56 mm. Leaf size 165 × 104 mm; thickness 0.10 mm; laid, unwatermarked, smooth, white

Contents: Title (*1*), the CA (*2*), advantages of membership (*3*), contents (*4–5*), the laws of croquet, numbered 1–48, confirmed and adopted 13 December 1934 (*6–23*), etiquette, continued (*24*), advertisements (*i–ii*), etiquette, concluded (*25*), regulations for official tournaments, numbered 1–25, confirmed and adopted 13 December 1934 (*26–38*), referees and umpires (*39–40*), decisions on points in the laws (*41–43*), space for notes, headed 'DECISIONS' (44–45), space for notes, headed 'NOTES' (46), laws of golf-croquet, numbered 1–10 (47–48), name of printer (48)

Binding: Pale purplish Pink (252) paper, stapled, no spine or endpapers. FC: printed in black mostly within a ruled frame ([above the frame] OFFICIAL EDITION, 1935. | THE | **LAWS OF CROQUET** | AND | **Regulations for Official Tournaments** | ALSO | **The Laws of Golf-Croquet** | MADE AND AUTHORISED BY | THE CROQUET ASSOCIATION | [rule] | LONDON : | PUBLISHED FOR THE CROQUET ASSOCIATION BY | **THE FIELD PRESS, LTD.,** | **Windsor House, Bream's Buildings,** **E.C.** | **1935.** | [below the frame] **PRICE ONE SHILLING.**). Inside FC: advertisement. RC: advertisement. Inside RC: advertisement and name of printer

Copy seen: PC

Fingerprint: .1w, e.nd l.be maof 3 1935A

Notes: Printed by Roffey & Clark, Croydon, price 1/–.

(lll) *Official edition, 1936, The Field Press (1930) issue (1936)*

OFFICIAL EDITION, 1936. | THE | **LAWS OF CROQUET** | AND | **Regulations for Official Tournaments.** | ALSO | **The Laws of Golf-Croquet** | [rule] | MADE AND AUTHORISED BY | **THE CROQUET ASSOCIATION.** | [rule] | LONDON : | PUBLISHED FOR THE CROQUET ASSOCIATION BY | **THE FIELD PRESS (1930), LTD.,** | **Field House, Bream's Buildings, E.C.** | **1936.**

Formula: Not ascertainable from the copy examined. 25 leaves, pp *1–2* 3–24, *i–ii*, 25–48 [= 50]

Technical notes: 126 × 84 mm (p 34). 46 lines, 20 = 56 mm. Leaf size 163 × 104 mm; thickness 0.10 mm; laid, unwatermarked, smooth, white

Contents: Title (*1*), the CA (*2*), advantages of membership (*3*), contents (*4–5*), the laws of croquet, numbered 1–48, confirmed and adopted 12 December 1935 (*6–23*), etiquette, continued (*24*), advertisements (*i–ii*), etiquette, concluded (*25*), regulations for official tournaments, numbered 1–25, confirmed and adopted 12 December 1935 (*26–38*), referees and umpires (*39–40*), decisions on points in the laws (*41–43*), space for notes, headed 'DECISIONS' (*44–45*), space for notes, headed 'NOTES' (*46*), laws of golf-croquet, numbered 1–11 (*47–48*), name of printer (*48*)

Binding: Moderate Pink (5) paper, no endpapers. FC: printed in black mostly within a ruled frame ([above the frame] **OFFICIAL EDITION, 1936.** | THE | **LAWS OF CROQUET** | AND | **Regulations for Official Tournaments** | ALSO | **The Laws of Golf-Croquet** | MADE AND AUTHORISED BY | THE CROQUET ASSOCIATION | [rule] | LONDON : | PUBLISHED FOR THE CROQUET ASSOCIATION BY | **THE FIELD PRESS (1930), LTD.,** | **Windsor House, Bream's Buildings, E.C.** | **1936.** | [below the frame] **PRICE ONE SHILLING.**). Inside FC: advertisement. RC: advertisement. Inside RC: advertisement and name of printer

Copy seen: BOD: Per 38463 f 9 (in a library binding)

Fingerprint: .1w,).ll hem- bybe 3 1936A

Notes: Printed by Roffey & Clark, Croydon, price 1/–.

(mmm) *Official edition, 1937, The Field Press (1930) issue (1937)*

OFFICIAL EDITION, 1937. | THE | **LAWS OF CROQUET** | AND | **Regulations for Official Tournaments.** | ALSO | **The Laws of Golf-Croquet** | [rule] | MADE AND AUTHORISED BY | **THE CROQUET ASSOCIATION.** | [rule] | LONDON : | PUBLISHED FOR THE CROQUET ASSOCIATION BY | **THE FIELD PRESS 1930), LTD.** | **Field House, Bream's Buildings, E.C.** | **1937.**

Formula: Not ascertainable from the copy examined. 25 leaves, pp *1–2* 3–40, *i–ii*, 41–48 [= 50]

Technical notes: 127 × 84 mm (p 34). 46 lines, 20 = 56 mm. Leaf size 163 × 103 mm; thickness 0.10 mm; laid, unwatermarked, smooth, white

Contents: Title (*1*), the CA (*2*), advantages of membership (*3*), contents (*4–5*), the laws of croquet, numbered 1–49, confirmed and adopted 10 December 1936 (*6–24*), etiquette (*25–26*), regulations for official tournaments, numbered 1–25, confirmed and adopted 10 December 1936 (*27–39*), referees and umpires, continued (*40*), advertisements (*i–ii*), referees and umpires, concluded (*41–42*), decisions on points in the laws (*43–45*), space for notes, headed 'DECISIONS' (*46*), laws of golf-croquet, numbered 1–11 (*47–48*), name of printer (*48*)

Binding: White paper, stapled, no spine or endpapers. FC: printed in black mostly within a ruled frame ([above the frame] **OFFICIAL EDITION, 1937.** | THE | **LAWS OF CROQUET** | AND | **Regulations for Official Tournaments** | ALSO | **The Laws of Golf-Croquet** | MADE AND AUTHORISED BY | THE CROQUET ASSOCIA-TION | [rule] | London : | Published for the Croquet Association by | **THE FIELD PRESS (1930), LTD.,** | **Field House, Bream's Buildings, E.C.** | **1937.** | [below the frame] **PRICE ONE SHILLING.**). Inside FC: advertisement. RC: advertisement. Inside RC: advertisement and name of printer

Copy seen: BOD: Per 38464 f 9 (in a library binding)

Fingerprint: .1w,).ll hem- bybe 3 1937A

Notes: Printed by Roffey & Clark, Croydon, price 1/–.

(nnn) *Official edition, 1938, The Field Press (1930) issue (1938)*

OFFICIAL EDITION, 1938. | THE | **LAWS OF CROQUET** | AND | **GOLF-CROQUET** | WITH | **Regulations for Official Tournaments.** | [rule] | MADE AND AUTHORISED BY | **THE CROQUET ASSOCIATION.** | [rule] | London : | Published for the Croquet Association by | **THE FIELD PRESS (1930), LTD.** | **Field House, Bream's Buildings, E.C.** | **1938.** | **PRICE ONE SHILLING**

Formula: Not ascertainable from the copy examined. 29 leaves, pp *1–2* 3–24, *i–ii*, 25–56 [= 58]

Technical notes: 127 × 84 mm (p 34). 46 lines, 20 = 56 mm. Leaf size 163 × 104 mm; thickness 0.09 mm; laid, unwatermarked, smooth, white

Contents: Title (*1*), the CA (*2*), advantages of membership (*3*), contents (*4–5*), the laws of croquet, numbered 1–49, confirmed and adopted 19 December 1937 (*6–24*), advertisements (*i–ii*), etiquette (*25–26*), regulations for official tournaments, numbered 1–25, confirmed and adopted 9 December 1937 (*27–39*), referees and umpires (*40–42*), decisions on points in the laws (*43–45*), space for notes, headed 'DECISIONS' (*46–47*), space for notes, headed 'NOTES' (*48–49*), laws of golf-croquet, numbered 1–10 (*50–56*), name of printer (*56*)

Binding: Moderate Pink (5) paper, no spine or endpapers. FC: printed in black mostly within a ruled frame ([above the frame] **OFFICIAL EDITION, 1938.** | THE | **LAWS OF CROQUET** | AND | **GOLF-CROQUET** | WITH | **Regulations for Official Tournaments** | MADE AND AUTHORISED BY | THE CROQUET ASSOCIATION | [rule] | London : | Published for the Croquet Association by | **THE FIELD PRESS (1930), LTD.,** | **Field House, Bream's Buildings, E.C.** | **1938.** | [below the frame] **PRICE ONE SHILLING.**). Inside FC: advertisement. RC: adver-tisement. Inside RC: advertisement and name of printer

Copy seen: BOD: Per 38464 f 9 (in a library binding)

Fingerprint: .1w,).ll hem- bybe 3 1938A

Notes: Printed by Roffey & Clark, Croydon, price 1/–.

(ooo) *Official edition, 1939, The Field Press (1930) issue (1939)*

OFFICIAL EDITION, 1939 | THE | **LAWS OF CROQUET** | AND | **GOLF-CROQUET** | WITH | **Regulations for Official Tournaments.** | [rule] | MADE AND AUTHORISED BY | **THE CROQUET ASSOCIATION.** | [rule] | LONDON : | PUBLISHED FOR THE CROQUET ASSOCIATION BY | **THE FIELD PRESS (1930), LTD.** | **Field House, Bream's Buildings, E.C.** | **1939** | PRICE ONE SHILLING

Formula: [1²⁸]. 28 leaves, pp *1–2* 3–56

Technical notes: 126 × 84 mm (p 15). 45 lines, 20 = 56 mm. Leaf size 164 × 103 mm; thickness 0.09 mm; laid, unwatermarked, smooth, white

Contents: Title (*1*), the CA (*2*), advantages of membership (*3*), contents (*4–5*), the laws of croquet, numbered 1–49, confirmed and adopted 15 December 1938 (*6–19*), five diagrams of court settings (*20–24*), etiquette (*25–26*), regulations for official tournaments, numbered 1–25, confirmed and adopted 15 December 1938 (*27–39*), instructions and suggestions to referees and umpires, numbered 1–19 (*40–42*), decisions on points in the laws of croquet (*43–45*), blank pages headed 'Decisions' (*46–48*), laws of golf-croquet, numbered 1–11, and laws of croquet which apply to golf-croquet (*49–56*)

Binding: Yellowish White (92) paper, stapled, no spine or endpapers. FC: printed in black mostly within a ruled frame ([above the frame] **OFFICIAL EDITION, 1939.** | THE | **LAWS OF CROQUET** | AND | **GOLF-CROQUET** | WITH | **Regulations for Official Tournaments** | MADE AND AUTHORISED BY | THE CROQUET ASSOCIATION | [rule] | LONDON : | PUBLISHED FOR THE CROQUET ASSOCIATION BY | **THE FIELD PRESS (1930), LTD.,** | **Field House, Bream's Buildings, E.C.** | **1939.** | [below the frame] **PRICE ONE SHILLING.**). Inside FC: blank. RC: blank. Inside RC: blank

Copy seen: PC

Fingerprint: .1w,).ll d.'s sait 3 1939A

Notes: Printed anonymously, price 1/–.

(ppp) *Official edition, 1939, FH Ayres issue (1939)*

OFFICIAL EDITION, 1939 | THE | **LAWS OF CROQUET** | AND | **GOLF-CROQUET** | WITH | **Regulations for Official Tournaments.** | [rule] | MADE AND AUTHORISED BY | THE CROQUET ASSOCIATION. | [rule] | ISSUED BY | **F. H. AYRES, LTD.,** | **111 ALDERSGATE ST., LONDON, E.C. 1** | *By permission of the Croquet Association.*

Formula: [1³⁰]. 30 leaves, pp *i–ii, 1–2* 3–56 57–58

Technical notes: 126 × 84 mm (p 32). 46 lines, 20 = 56 mm. Leaf size 163 × 102 mm; thickness 0.11 mm; laid, unwatermarked, smooth, white

Contents: Advertisements (*i–ii*), title (*1*), the CA (*2*), advantages of membership (*3*), contents (*4–5*), the laws of croquet, numbered 1–49, confirmed and adopted 15 December 1938 (*6–24*), etiquette (*25–26*), regulations for official tournaments, numbered 1–25, approved and adopted 15 December 1938 (*27–39*), referees and umpires (*40–42*), decisions on points in the laws of croquet (*43–45*), blank pages for notes (*46–48*), laws of golf-croquet (*49–56*), name of printer (*56*), advertisements (*57–58*)

Binding: White paper, stapled, no spine or endpapers. FC: printed in black, mostly within a ruled frame ([above the frame] OFFICIAL EDITION, 1939. | THE | **LAWS OF CROQUET** | AND | **GOLF-CROQUET** | WITH | **Regulations for Official Tournaments** | MADE AND AUTHORISED BY | THE CROQUET ASSOCIATION | [rule] | ISSUED BY | F. H. Ayres, Ltd., | 111, ALDERSGATE ST., LONDON, E.C.1. | By permission of the Croquet Association.). Inside FC: advertisement. RC: advertisement. Inside RC: advertisement

Copy seen: PC

Fingerprint: .1w,).ll d.'s sait 3 1939A

Notes: Printed by Roffey & Clark, Croydon.

(qqq) *Official edition, 1940, The Field Press (1930) issue (1940)*

OFFICIAL EDITION, 1940 | THE | **LAWS OF CROQUET** | AND | **GOLF-CROQUET** | WITH | **Regulations for Official Tournaments.** | [rule] | MADE AND AUTHORISED BY | **THE CROQUET ASSOCIATION.** | [rule] | London : | Published for the Croquet Association by | **THE FIELD PRESS (1930), LTD.** | **Field House, Bream's Buildings, E.C.** | 1940 | PRICE ONE SHILLING

Formula: [1²⁸]. 28 leaves, pp *1–2* 3–56

Technical notes: 126 × 84 mm (p 15). 45 lines, 20 = 56 mm. Leaf size 164 × 103 mm; thickness 0.09 mm; wove, unwatermarked, smooth, white

Contents: Title (*1*), the CA (*2*), advantages of membership (*3*), contents (*4–5*), the laws of croquet, numbered 1–49, confirmed and adopted 15 December 1938 (*6–19*), five diagrams of court settings (*20–24*), etiquette (*25–26*), regulations for official tournaments, numbered 1–25, confirmed and adopted 15 December 1938 (*27–39*), instructions and suggestions to referees and umpires, numbered 1–19 (*40–42*), decisions on points in the laws of croquet (*43–45*), blank pages headed 'Decisions' (*46–48*), laws of golf-croquet, numbered 1–11, and laws of croquet which apply to golf-croquet (*49–56*)

Binding: Yellowish White (92) paper, stapled, no spine or endpapers. FC: printed in black mostly within a ruled frame ([above the frame] **OFFICIAL EDITION, 1940.** | THE | **LAWS OF CROQUET** | AND | **GOLF-CROQUET** | WITH | **Regulations for Official Tournaments** | MADE AND AUTHORISED BY | THE CROQUET ASSOCIATION | [rule] | London : | Published for the Croquet Association by | **THE FIELD PRESS (1930), LTD.,** | **Field House, Bream's Buildings, E.C.** | 1940. | [below the frame] **PRICE ONE SHILLING.**). Inside FC: blank. RC: blank. Inside RC: blank

Copy seen: BOD: Per 38464 f 9

Fingerprint: .1w,).ll d.'s sait 3 1940A

Notes: Printed anonymously, price 1/–.

(rrr) *Official edition, 1941, The Field Press (1930) issue (1941)*

OFFICIAL EDITION, 1941. | THE | **LAWS OF CROQUET** | AND | **GOLF-CROQUET** | WITH | **Regulations for Official Tournaments.** | [rule] | MADE AND AUTHORISED BY | **THE CROQUET ASSOCIATION.** | [rule] | London : | Published for the Croquet Association by | **THE FIELD PRESS (1930), LTD.** | **Field House, Bream's Buildings, E.C.** | 1941. | PRICE ONE SHILLING

Formula: [1²⁸]. 28 leaves, pp *1–2* 3–56

Technical notes: 126 × 84 mm (p 15). 45 lines, 20 = 56 mm. Leaf size 164 × 103 mm; thickness 0.09 mm; laid, unwatermarked, smooth, white

Contents: As those of (qqq)

Binding: Pale purplish Pink (252) paper, stapled, no spine or endpapers. FC: printed in black mostly within a ruled frame ([above the frame] **OFFICIAL EDITION, 1939.** | The | **LAWS OF CROQUET** | AND | **GOLF-CROQUET** | WITH | **Regulations for Official Tournaments** | MADE AND AUTHORISED BY | THE CROQUET ASSOCIATION | [rule] | London : | Published for the Croquet Association by | **THE FIELD PRESS (1930), LTD.,** | Field House, Bream's Buildings, E.C. | 1941. | [below the frame] **PRICE ONE SHILLING.**). Inside FC: blank. RC: blank. Inside RC: blank

Copy seen: BOD: Per 38464 f 9

Fingerprint: .1w,).ll d.'s sait 3 1941A

Notes: Printed anonymously, price 1/–.

(sss) *Official edition, 1947 (1947)*

OFFICIAL EDITION, 1947, | THE | **LAWS OF CROQUET** | AND | **GOLF-CROQUET** | WITH | **Regulations for Official Tournaments.** | [rule] | MADE AND AUTHORISED BY | THE CROQUET ASSOCIATION. | [rule] | London : | Published for the Croquet Association by | **THE FIELD PRESS (1930), LTD.** | Field House, Bream's Buildings, E.C.

Formula: [1²⁸]. 28 leaves, pp *1–3* 4–56

Technical notes: 125 × 84 mm (p 11). 45 lines, 20 = 56 mm. Leaf size 166 × 105 mm; thickness 0.08 mm; wove, unwatermarked, smooth, white

Contents: Title (*1*), the CA (*2*), advantages of membership (*3*), contents (*4–5*), the laws of croquet, numbered 1–50, and Variations 'A' and 'B', confirmed and adopted 19 December 1946 (*6–21*), etiquette (*22–23*), regulations for official tournaments, numbered 1–25, confirmed and adopted 19 December 1946 (*24–37*), instructions and suggestions to referees and umpires, numbered 1–19 (*38–40*), decisions on points in the laws of croquet (*41–43*), blank pages headed 'Decisions' (*44–45*), blank page headed 'Notes' (*46*), laws of golf-croquet, numbered 1–11, and laws of croquet which apply to golf-croquet (*47–54*), blank pages headed 'Notes' (*55–56*)

Binding: Pale orange Yellow (73) paper, stapled, no spine or endpapers *etc.* FC: printed in black mostly within a ruled frame ([above frame] OFFICIAL EDITION, 1947. | THE | **LAWS OF CROQUET** | AND | **GOLF-CROQUET** | WITH | **Regulations for Official Tournaments** | MADE AND AUTHORISED BY | THE CROQUET ASSOCIATION | [rule] | **JOHN JAQUES,** | WHITE HEATHER WORKS, | 361, Whitehorse Road, | THORNTON HEATH, SURREY | *By permission of the Croquet Association.*). Inside FC: advertisement. RC: blank. Inside RC: advertisement

Copy seen: BL: 7907 df

Fingerprint: .1w, ryor d.). no37 3 1947A

Notes: Printed anonymously. A curiosity of this issue is the discrepancy between the attributions of publisher on the TP (*viz* The Field Press (1930)) and the FC (*viz* John Jaques). It is conjectured it was issued by Jaques under licence to The Field Press and/or the CA.

(ttt) *Official edition, 1948, The Field Press (1930) issue (1948)*

OFFICIAL EDITION, 1948. | THE | **LAWS OF CROQUET** | AND | **GOLF-CROQUET** | WITH | **Regulations for Official Tournaments.** | [rule] | MADE AND AUTHORISED BY | **THE CROQUET ASSOCIATION.** | [rule] | London : | Published for the Croquet Association by | **THE FIELD PRESS (1930), LTD.,** | Field House, Bream's Buildings, E.C.

Formula: [1²⁶]. 26 leaves, pp i–vi, 1–46

Technical notes: 125 × 84 mm (p 14). 45 lines, 20 = 56 mm. Leaf size 162 × 102 mm; thickness 0.09 mm; wove, unwatermarked, smooth, white

Contents: Title (i), blank save pagination (ii), the CA (iii), official list of referees (iv), space for referees appointed in 1948 (v), advantages of membership (vi), contents (1–2), the laws of croquet, numbered 1–49, and Variation 'A' (The Clip Game), confirmed and adopted 8 January 1948 (3–18), etiquette (19), regulations for official tournaments, numbered 1–25, confirmed and adopted 8 January 1948 (20–34), instructions and suggestions to referees, numbered 1–14 (35–36), decisions on points in the laws of croquet (37–38), laws of golf-croquet, numbered 1–11, and laws of croquet which apply to golf-croquet (39–46)

Binding: Pale Yellow (89) paper, stapled, no spine or endpapers. FC: printed in black mostly within a ruled frame ([above the frame] **OFFICIAL EDITION, 1948.** | THE | **LAWS OF CROQUET** | AND | **GOLF-CROQUET** | WITH | **Regulations for Official Tournaments** | MADE AND AUTHORISED BY | THE CROQUET ASSOCIATION | [rule] | LONDON : | PUBLISHED FOR THE CROQUET ASSOCIATION BY | **THE FIELD PRESS (1930), LTD.,** | **Field House, Bream's Buildings, E.C.**). Inside FC: blank. RC: advertisement. Inside RC: blank

Copy seen: BOD: 38464 f 9

Fingerprint: 27.1 e.ed d.lf onba 1948A

Notes: Printed anonymously.

(uuu) *Official edition, 1949 (1949)*

THE OFFICIAL | **HANDBOOK** | **OF THE LAWS** | OF | ASSOCIATION CROQUET | AND GOLF CROQUET AND | THE REGULATIONS FOR | OFFICIAL TOURNAMENTS | ETC. | [rule] | CONFIRMED AND ADOPTED | BY THE COUNCIL OF | **THE CROQUET** | **ASSOCIATION** | FOR THE YEAR | **1949** | [rule] | LONDON ; | THE CROQUET ASSOCIATION | 4, SOUTHAMPTON ROW, W. C. 1 | [rule] | *Printed by Roffey & Clark, Ltd., 12, High Street, Croydon.*

Formula: [1²⁶ χ1]. 27 leaves, pp *i* ii–vi, 1–48

Technical notes: 125 × 83 mm (p 6). 45 lines, 20 = 56 mm. Leaf size 164 × 102 mm; thickness 0.08 mm; laid, unwatermarked, smooth, white

Contents: Title (*i*), blank save pagination (ii), the CA (iii), official list of referees (iv), heading only: referees appointed in 1949 (v), advantages of membership (vi), contents (1–2), laws of Association Croquet, numbered 1–49, and Variations 'A', 'B', confirmed and adopted 6 January 1949 (3–19), etiquette (20), regulations for official tournaments, numbered 1–25, confirmed and adopted 6 January 1949 (21–35), instructions to referees, numbered 1–15 (36–37), decisions on points in the laws of Association Croquet (38–39), laws of golf croquet, numbered 1–11, and laws of Association Croquet adapted to golf croquet (40–47), blank save pagination (48)

Binding: Brilliant orange Yellow (67) paper, stapled, no spine or endpapers. FC: printed in black within a ruled frame (THE LAWS OF ASSOCIATION | **CROQUET** | AND | **GOLF CROQUET** | AND THE | **REGULATIONS** | FOR OFFICIAL | **TOURNAMENTS** | [rule] | OFFICIAL EDITION | PUBLISHED BY | **THE CROQUET** | **ASSOCIATION** | **1949**). Inside FC: blank. RC: advertisement. Inside RC: blank

Copy seen: BL: 7907 df

Fingerprint: 27.1 e.ed ayet deta 3 1949A

Notes: Printed by Roffey & Clark, Croydon. A note in the Sports Trader edition of the laws for the same year (vvv) suggests that this issue was offered for sale to the general public at 1/–.

(vvv) *The Sports Trader 1949 edition [1950]*

[The FC]

[set between the profiles of two sportsmen in silhouette] *The* | [*do*] "SPORTS TRADER" | [*do*] SERIES | [set within a broken panel in the form of a curtain pelmet framed by twin lines] **CROQUET LAWS** | [*do*] By authority of the Croquet Association | [line drawing of lawn tennis racket, two crossed cricket bats, a golf iron, a croquet mallet, and sundry balls against a background of the rising sun with radiating rays] | [set within a broken rectangular panel framed by twin rules] **W. B. TATTERSALL, LTD.** | [*do*] The "Sports Press," | [*do*] 43/44 Shoe Lane, London, E.C.4

Formula: [1^{18}]. 18 leaves, pp *1–3* 4–36

Technical notes: 83 × 55 mm (p 4). 32 lines, 20 = 52 mm. Leaf size 96 × 68 mm; thickness 0.07 mm; wove, unwatermarked, smooth, white

Contents: The CA (*1*), blank (*2*), the laws of croquet, numbered 1–49, confirmed and adopted 6 January 1949 (*3–33*), Appendix A (standard court setting) (*34*), Appendix B (Variations 'A' and 'B') (*35–36*), name of printer (*36*)

Binding: White semi-gloss paper, stapled, no spine or endpapers. FC: as above, framed by a broad ruled border, printed in strong purplish Blue (196). Inside FC: blank. RC: advertisement, printed in Blue. Inside RC: blank

Copy seen: PC

Fingerprint: y.he orhe esor otco 3 1949Q [group 1 taken from p *1*]

Notes: Printed anonymously, published (or printed) on 1 January 1950. Date of publication (or printing) is taken from what is presumed to be a date code ('500101') on p 36.

(www) *Official edition, 1950, John Jaques issue (1950)*

THE OFFICIAL | **HANDBOOK** | **OF THE LAWS** | OF | ASSOCIATION CROQUET | AND GOLF CROQUET AND | THE REGULATIONS FOR | OFFICIAL TOURNAMENTS | ETC. | [rule] | CONFIRMED AND ADOPTED | BY THE COUNCIL OF | **THE CROQUET** | **ASSOCIATION** | FOR THE YEAR | 1950 | [rule] | LONDON ; | THE CROQUET ASSOCIATION | 4, SOUTHAMPTON ROW, W. C. 1 | [rule] | *Printed by Roffey & Clark, Ltd., 12, High Street, Croydon.*

Formula: [1^{26} χ1]. 27 leaves, pp *i* ii–vi, 1–48

Technical notes: 125 × 84 mm (p 6). 45 lines, 20 = 57 mm. Leaf size 163 × 103 mm; thickness 0.08 mm; wove, unwatermarked, smooth, white

Contents: Title (*i*), blank save pagination (ii), the CA (iii), official list of referees (iv), heading only: referees appointed in 1950 (v), advantages of membership (vi), contents (1–2), laws of Association Croquet, numbered 1–49, and Variations 'A', 'B', confirmed and adopted 6 January 1949 (3–19), etiquette (20), regulations for official tournaments, numbered 1–25, confirmed and adopted 6 January 1949 (21–35), instructions to referees, numbered 1–15 (36–37), decisions on points in the laws of Association Croquet (38–39), laws of golf croquet, numbered 1–11, and laws of Association Croquet adapted to golf croquet (40–47), blank save pagination (48)

Binding: Light greenish Blue (172) paper, stapled, no spine or endpapers. FC: printed in black within a ruled frame (THE LAWS OF ASSOCIATION | **CROQUET** | AND | **GOLF CROQUET** | AND THE | **REGULATIONS** | FOR

OFFICIAL | **TOURNAMENTS** | MADE AND AUTHORISED BY | THE CROQUET ASSOCIATION | [rule] | **JOHN JAQUES & SON LTD.** | WHITE HEATHER WORKS, | 361, Whitehorse Road, | THORNTON HEATH, SURREY | By permission of the Croquet Association.). Inside FC: advertisement. RC: blank. Inside RC: advertisement

Copy seen: BL: 7907 df

Fingerprint: 27.1 e.ed ayet deta 3 1950A

Notes: Printed by Roffey & Clark, Croydon.

(xxx) *Official edition, 1951 (1951)*

THE OFFICIAL | **HANDBOOK** | **OF THE LAWS** | OF | ASSOCIATION CROQUET | AND GOLF CROQUET AND | THE REGULATIONS FOR | OFFICIAL TOURNAMENTS | ETC. | [rule] | CONFIRMED AND ADOPTED | BY THE COUNCIL OF | **THE CROQUET** | **ASSOCIATION** | FOR THE YEAR | **1951** | [rule] | LONDON ; | THE CROQUET ASSOCIATION | 4, SOUTHAMPTON ROW, W. C. 1 | [rule] | *Printed by Roffey & Clark, Ltd., 12, High Street, Croydon.*

Formula: [1²⁶ χ1]. 27 leaves, pp *i* ii–vi, 1–48

Technical notes: 124 × 84 mm (p 6). 44 lines, 20 = 57 mm. Leaf size 164 × 104 mm; thickness 0.10 mm; wove, unwatermarked, smooth, white

Contents: Title (*i*), blank save pagination (ii), the CA (iii), official list of referees (iv), heading only: referees appointed in 1949 (v), advantages of membership (vi), index (1–2), laws of Association Croquet, numbered 1–49, and Variations 'A', 'B', confirmed and adopted 4 January 1951 (3–19), etiquette (20), regulations for official tournaments, numbered 1–26, confirmed and adopted 4 January 1951 (21–35), instructions to referees, numbered 1–15 (36–37), decisions on points in the laws of Association Croquet (38–39), laws of golf croquet, numbered 1–11, and laws of Association Croquet adapted to golf croquet (40–47), blank save pagination (48)

Binding: Brilliant orange Yellow (67) paper, stapled, no spine or endpapers. FC: printed in black within a ruled frame (THE LAWS OF ASSOCIATION | **CROQUET** | AND | **GOLF CROQUET** | AND THE | **REGULATIONS** | FOR OFFICIAL | **TOURNAMENTS** | [rule] | OFFICIAL EDITION | PUBLISHED BY | **THE CROQUET** | **ASSOCIATION** | 1951). Inside FC: blank. RC: advertisement. Inside RC: blank

Copy seen: BL: 7907 df

Fingerprint: 27.1 e.ed ayet deta 3 1951A

Notes: Printed by Roffey & Clark, Croydon.

(yyy) *Official edition, 1951, John Jaques & Son issue (1951)*

THE OFFICIAL | **HANDBOOK** | **OF THE LAWS** | OF | ASSOCIATION CROQUET | AND GOLF CROQUET AND | THE REGULATIONS FOR | OFFICIAL TOURNAMENTS | ETC. | [rule] | CONFIRMED AND ADOPTED | BY THE COUNCIL OF | **THE CROQUET** | **ASSOCIATION** | FOR THE YEAR | **1951** | [rule] | LONDON ; | THE CROQUET ASSOCIATION | 4, SOUTHAMPTON ROW, W. C. 1 | [rule] | *Printed by Roffey & Clark, Ltd., 12, High Street, Croydon.*

Formula: [1²⁶ χ1]. 27 leaves, pp *i* ii–vi, 1–48

Technical notes: 124 × 84 mm (p 6). 44 lines, 20 = 57 mm. Leaf size 163 × 104 mm; thickness 0.08 mm; wove, unwatermarked, smooth, white

Contents: Title (*i*), blank save pagination (ii), the CA (iii), official list of referees (iv), heading only: referees appointed in 1949 (v), advantages of membership (vi), index

(1–2), laws of Association Croquet, numbered 1–49, and Variations 'A', 'B', confirmed and adopted 4 January 1951 (3–19), etiquette (20), regulations for official tournaments, numbered 1–26, confirmed and adopted 4 January 1951 (21–35), instructions to referees, numbered 1–15 (36–37), decisions on points in the laws of Association Croquet (38–39), laws of golf croquet, numbered 1–11, and laws of Association Croquet adapted to golf croquet (40–47), blank save pagination (48)

Binding: Light greenish Grey (154) paper, stapled, no spine or endpapers *etc.* FC: printed in black mostly within a ruled frame ([above the frame] OFFICIAL EDITION, 1951. | THE LAWS OF ASSOCIATION | **CROQUET** | AND | **GOLF CROQUET** | AND THE | **REGULATIONS** | FOR OFFICIAL | **TOURNAMENTS** | MADE AND AUTHORISED BY | THE CROQUET ASSOCIATION | [rule] | **JOHN JAQUES & SON LTD.** | WHITE HEATHER WORKS, | 361, Whitehorse Road, | THORNTON HEATH, SURREY | By permission of the Croquet Association.). Inside FC: advertisement. RC: blank. Inside RC: advertisement

Copy seen: BL: 7907 df

Fingerprint: 27.1 e.ed ayet deta 3 1951A

Notes: Printed by Roffey & Clark, Croydon.

(zzz) *Official edition, 1953 (1953)*

THE OFFICIAL | **HANDBOOK** | **OF THE LAWS** | OF | ASSOCIATION CROQUET | AND GOLF CROQUET AND | THE REGULATIONS FOR | OFFICIAL TOURNAMENTS | ETC. | [rule] | CONFIRMED AND ADOPTED | BY THE COUNCIL OF | **THE CROQUET** | **ASSOCIATION** | **1953** | [rule] | LONDON : | THE CROQUET ASSOCIATION | 4, SOUTHAMPTON ROW, W.C.1 | [rule] | *Printed by Roffey & Clark, Ltd., 12, High Street, Croydon.*

Formula: [1²⁶]. 26 leaves, pp *i* ii–iv, *1* 2–21 22 23–48

Technical notes: 124 × 83 mm (p 8). 45 lines, 20 = 56 mm. Leaf size 163 × 94 mm; thickness 0.08 mm; wove, watermarked ([a crown] | PREMIER PRINCE | 297), smooth, white

Contents: Title (*i*), blank (ii), the CA (iii), official list of referees (iv), advantages of membership (1), index (2–3), plan of court (4), laws of Association Croquet, numbered 1–49, confirmed and adopted 1 January 1953 (5–19), appendix (Variations 'A' and 'B') (20), etiquette (21), regulations for official tournaments, numbered 1–26, confirmed and adopted 1 January 1953 (22–36), instructions to referees, numbered 1–15 (37–38), decisions on points in the laws of Association Croquet (39–40), laws of golf croquet, numbered 1–11 (41–44), laws of Association Croquet adapted to golf croquet (45–48)

Binding: White paper, stapled, no spine or endpapers. FC: printed in black within a ruled frame (THE LAWS OF ASSOCIATION | **CROQUET** | AND | **GOLF CROQUET** | AND THE | **REGULATIONS** | FOR OFFICIAL | **TOURNAMENTS** | [rule] | OFFICIAL EDITION | PUBLISHED BY | **THE CROQUET** | **ASSOCIA-TION** | **1953**). Inside FC: advertisement. RC: blank. Inside RC: advertisement

Copy seen: PC

Fingerprint: 27C1 e.ed tsde scis 3 1953A

Notes: Printed by Roffey & Clark, Croydon.

(aaaa) *Official edition, 1953, John Jaques & Son issue (1953)*

THE OFFICIAL | **HANDBOOK** | **OF THE LAWS** | OF | ASSOCIATION CROQUET | AND GOLF CROQUET AND | THE REGULATIONS FOR |

OFFICIAL TOURNAMENTS | ETC. | [rule] | CONFIRMED AND ADOPTED | BY THE COUNCIL OF | **THE CROQUET** | **ASSOCIATION** | 1953 | [rule] | LONDON ; | THE CROQUET ASSOCIATION | 4, SOUTHAMPTON ROW, W. C. 1 | [rule] | *Printed by Roffey & Clark, Ltd., 12, High Street, Croydon.*

Formula: [1²⁶]. 26 leaves, pp *i–ii* iii–iv, 1–48

Technical notes: 124 × 84 mm (p 8). 44 lines, 20 = 57 mm. Leaf size 165 × 105 mm; thickness 0.08 mm; wove, watermarked ([a crown] | Premier Prince | 297), smooth, white

Contents: Title (*i*), blank (*ii*), the CA (iii), official list of referees (iv), advantages of membership (1), index (2–3), laws of Association Croquet, numbered 1–49, and Variations 'A', 'B', confirmed and adopted 1 January 1953 (4–20), etiquette (21), regulations for official tournaments, numbered 1–26, confirmed and adopted 1 January 1953 (22–36), instructions to referees, numbered 1–15 (37–38), decisions on points in the laws of Association Croquet (39–40), laws of golf croquet, numbered 1–11, and laws of Association Croquet adapted to golf croquet (41–48)

Binding: Brilliant orange Yellow (67) paper, stapled, no spine or endpapers. FC: printed in black mostly within a ruled frame ([above the frame] OFFICIAL EDITION, 1953. THE LAWS OF ASSOCIATION | **CROQUET** | AND | **GOLF CROQUET** | AND THE | **REGULATIONS** | FOR OFFICIAL | **TOURNAMENTS** | MADE AND AUTHORISED BY | THE CROQUET ASSOCIATION | [rule] | **JOHN JAQUES & SON LTD.** | WHITE HEATHER WORKS, | 361, Whitehorse Road, | THORNTON HEATH, SURREY | By permission of the Croquet Association). Inside FC: advertisement. RC: blank. Inside RC: advertisement

Copy seen: BL: 7907 df

Fingerprint: 27C1 e.ed tsde scis 3 1953A

Notes: Printed by Roffey & Clark, Croydon. There were no changes to the laws for 1954 and throughout that year the 1953 edition was used and offered for sale.

(bbbb) *Official edition, 1955 (1955)*

THE OFFICIAL | **HANDBOOK** | **OF THE LAWS** | OF | ASSOCIATION CROQUET | AND GOLF CROQUET AND | THE REGULATIONS FOR | OFFICIAL TOURNAMENTS | ETC. | [rule] | CONFIRMED AND ADOPTED | BY THE COUNCIL OF | **THE CROQUET** | **ASSOCIATION** | 1955 | [rule] | LONDON : | THE CROQUET ASSOCIATION | 4, SOUTHAMPTON ROW, W.C.1

Formula: [1²⁶]. 26 leaves, pp *i–ii* iii–iv, 1–19 *20* 21–29 *30* 31–48

Technical notes: 124 × 84 mm (p 8). 45 lines, 20 = 56 mm. Leaf size 157 × 101 mm; thickness 0.09 mm; wove, watermarked ([a crown] | Premier Prince | 297), smooth, white

Contents: Title (*i*), blank (*ii*), the CA (iii), official list of referees (iv), advantages of membership (1), index (2–3), plan of court (4), laws of Association Croquet, numbered 1–49, and Variations 'A' and 'B', confirmed and adopted 1 January 1955 (5–20), etiquette (21), regulations for official tournaments, numbered 1–26, confirmed and adopted 1 January 1955 (22–36), instructions to referees, numbered 1–15 (37–38), decisions on points in the laws of Association Croquet (39–40), laws of golf croquet, numbered 1–11, and laws of Association Croquet adapted to golf croquet (41–48)

Binding: Very pale Green (148) paper, stapled, no spine or endpaper. FC: printed in black within a ruled frame (THE LAWS OF ASSOCIATION | **CROQUET** | AND

| GOLF CROQUET | AND THE | **REGULATIONS** | FOR OFFICIAL | **TOURNA-MENTS** | [rule] | OFFICIAL EDITION | PUBLISHED BY | **THE CROQUET** | **ASSOCIATION** | 1955). Inside FC: advertisement. RC: name of printer. Inside RC: advertisement

Copy seen: BOD: Per 38464 f 9

Fingerprint: 27C1 e.ed tsde scis 3 1955A

Notes: Printed by Roffey & Clark, Croydon. The Council of the CA confirmed and adopted these laws and regulations at a meeting held on 6 January 1955, notwithstanding the contrary date cited in the text. See also *Notes* to (aaaa)

(cccc) *Official edition, 1956 (1956)*

THE OFFICIAL | **HANDBOOK** | **OF THE LAWS** | OF | ASSOCIATION CROQUET | AND GOLF CROQUET AND | THE REGULATIONS FOR | OFFICIAL TOURNAMENTS | ETC. | [rule] | CONFIRMED AND ADOPTED | BY THE COUNCIL OF | **THE CROQUET** | **ASSOCIATION** | 1955 | [rule] | LONDON : | THE CROQUET ASSOCIATION | 4, SOUTHAMPTON ROW, W. C. 1

Formula: [1²⁶]. 26 leaves, pp *i–ii* iii–iv, 1–19 *20* 21–29 *30* 31–48

Technical notes: 124 × 84 mm (p 8). 45 lines, 20 = 56 mm. Leaf size 157 × 101 mm; thickness 0.09 mm; wove, watermarked ([a crown] | Premier Prince | 297), smooth, white

Contents: Title (*i*), blank (*ii*), the CA (iii), official list of referees (iv), advantages of membership (1), index (2–3), plan of court (4), laws of Association Croquet, numbered 1–49, confirmed and adopted 1 January 1955 (5–19), blank (*20*), etiquette (21), regulations for official tournaments, numbered 1–26, confirmed and adopted 1 January 1955 (22–36), instructions to referees, numbered 1–15 (37–38), decisions on points in the laws of Association Croquet (39–40), laws of golf croquet, numbered 1–11, and laws of Association Croquet adapted to golf croquet (41–48)

Binding: White paper, stapled, no spine or endpapers. FC: printed in black within a ruled frame (THE LAWS OF ASSOCIATION | **CROQUET** | AND | **GOLF CROQUET** | AND THE | **REGULATIONS** | FOR OFFICIAL | **TOURNAMENTS** | [rule] | OFFICIAL EDITION | PUBLISHED BY | **THE CROQUET** | **ASSOCIATION** | **1956**). Inside FC: advertisement. RC: name of printer. Inside RC: advertisement

Copy seen: PC

Fingerprint: 27C1 e.ed tsde scis 3 1956A

Notes: Printed by Roffey & Clark, Croydon. The Council of the CA confirmed and adopted these laws and regulations at a meeting held on 5 January 1956, notwithstanding the contrary date cited in the text.

(dddd) *Official edition, 1957 (1957)*

THE OFFICIAL | **HANDBOOK** | **OF THE LAWS** | OF | ASSOCIATION CROQUET | AND GOLF CROQUET AND | THE REGULATIONS FOR | OFFICIAL TOURNAMENTS | ETC. | [rule] | CONFIRMED AND ADOPTED | BY THE COUNCIL OF | **THE CROQUET** | **ASSOCIATION** | 1957 | [rule] | LONDON ; | THE CROQUET ASSOCIATION | 4, SOUTHAMPTON ROW, W. C. 1

Formula: [1²⁶]. 26 leaves, pp *i–iv*, 1–19 *20* 21–48

Technical notes: 124 × 84 mm (p 8). 44 lines, 20 = 57 mm. Leaf size 164 × 105 mm; thickness 0.08 mm; wove, watermarked ([a crown] | Premier Prince | 297) smooth, white

Contents: Title (*i*), the CA (*ii*), official list of referees (*iii*), the CA (*iv*), index (1–3), laws of Association Croquet, numbered 1–49, confirmed and adopted 1 January 1957 (4–19), blank (*20*), etiquette (21), regulations for official tournaments, numbered 1–26, confirmed and adopted 1 January 1957 (22–36), instructions to referees, numbered 1–14 (37–39), decisions on points in the laws of Association Croquet (39–40), laws of golf croquet, numbered 1–11, and laws of Association Croquet adapted to golf croquet (41–48)

Binding: Yellowish White (92) paper, stapled, no spine or endpapers. FC: printed in black within a ruled frame (THE LAWS OF ASSOCIATION | **CROQUET** | AND | **GOLF CROQUET** | AND THE | **REGULATIONS** | FOR OFFICIAL | **TOURNA-MENTS** | [rule] | OFFICIAL EDITION | PUBLISHED BY | **THE CROQUET** | **ASSOCIATION** | 1957). Inside FC: advertisement. RC: name of printer. Inside RC: advertisement

Copy seen: BL: 7907 df

Fingerprint: wsod e.ed tsde scis 3 1957A

Notes: Printed by Roffey & Clark, Croydon. The Council of the CA confirmed and adopted these laws and regulations at a meeting held on 3 January 1957, notwith-standing the contrary date cited in the text.

(eeee) *The Sports Trader 1959 edition (1959)*

[The FC]

[set between the profiles of two sportsmen in silhouette] *The* | [*do*] "SPORTS TRADER" | [*do*] SERIES | [set within a broken panel in the form of a curtain pelmet framed by twin lines] **CROQUET LAWS** | [*do*] By authority of the Croquet Assn. | [line drawing of a lawn tennis racket, two crossed cricket bats, a golf iron, a croquet mallet, and sundry balls against a background of the rising sun with radiating rays] | [set within a broken rectangular panel framed by twin rules] **W. B. TATTERSALL, LTD.** | [*do*] The "Sports Press," | [*do*] 36-37 Furnival St., London, E.C.4

Formula: [1¹⁸]. 18 leaves, pp *1–3* 4–35 *36*

Technical notes: 83 × 55 mm (p 4). 30 lines, 20 = 56 mm. Leaf size 99 × 68 mm; thickness 0.07 mm; wove, unwatermarked, smooth, white

Contents: The Croquet Association (*1*), blank (*2*), the laws of croquet, confirmed and adopted 11 December 1958 (*3–35*), name of printer (*36*)

Binding: White semi-gloss paper, stapled, no spine or endpapers *etc*. FC: as above, framed by a broad ruled border, printed in deep Red (13). Inside FC: blank. RC: advertisement, printed in Red. Inside RC: blank

Copy seen: PC

Fingerprint: y.he orhe e;ng orot 3 1959A [group 1 taken from p *1*]

Notes: Printed anonymously, published (or printed) on 14 January 1959. Date of publication (or printing) is taken from what is presumed to be a date code ('590114') on p *36*. (Consistent date codes are to be found in other Sports Trader titles.)

(ffff) *New series, first edition (1961)*

THE LAWS OF | [in shaded display script] Association Croquet | [*do*] AND GOLF CROQUET | AND THE REGULATIONS FOR | OFFICIAL TOURNAMENTS | FIRST EDITION | *Published by* | THE CROQUET ASSOCIATION | The Hurlingham Club, London, S.W.6 | 1961

Formula: [1³⁰]. 30 leaves, pp *i–ii* iii–viii, 1–5 6 7–31 *32* 33–52

Technical notes: 126 × 85 mm (p 14). 45 lines, 20 = 56 mm. Leaf size 162 × 104 mm; thickness 0.09 mm; wove, unwatermarked, smooth, white

Contents: Title (*i*), TP verso (*ii*), the Queen's message (iii), message from Sir Compton Mackenzie (iv), forewords by Mrs ML Rawlinson and Mrs MC McClelland (v), Councils (*viz* the CA Council, the ACC, the NZCC) (vi), contents (vii), foreword by Ian C Baillieu (viii), index (1–5), the laws of Association Croquet, numbered 1–57 (6–33), regulations for official tournaments, numbered 1–26 (34–49), laws of golf croquet, numbered 1–7 (50–51), blank save pagination (52)

Binding: Light yellowish Green (135) parchment-effect card, printed in dark yellowish Green (137), stapled, no spine or endpapers. FC: within a triple-ruled frame (THE LAWS OF | ASSOCIATION | [in shaded script] CROQUET | AND | [in shaded script] GOLF CROQUET | AND THE | REGULATIONS | FOR OFFICIAL | TOURNAMENTS). Inside FC: advertisement. RC: blank. Inside RC: advertisement

Copy seen: BL: 7907 df

Fingerprint: 1.R. 2726 p;he baon 3 1961A

Notes: Published in May 1961, printed by RH Johns, Newport, Monmouth. This was the first radical revision of the CA laws of croquet since World War I. The draft was prepared by Ian C Baillieu QC, barrister.

According to the minutes of meetings of the CA Council, 15000 copies were printed in 1961 at a cost of £385, of which 5000 were taken by the ACA, 1000 by John Jaques and Son, and 250 by the NZCC. The CA sold 500 copies during 1961, leaving a balance of 8250 in stock at the end of the year. These were sold piecemeal in subsequent years.

Several amendment sheets printed on gummed paper were issued by the CA in the following years to assist users in updating their copies.

(gggg) *New series, second edition (1968)*

THE LAWS OF | [in shaded display script] **Association Croquet** | [*do*] **AND GOLF CROQUET** | AND THE REGULATIONS FOR | OFFICIAL TOURNAMENTS | SECOND EDITION | *Published by* | THE CROQUET ASSOCIATION | THE HURLINGHAM CLUB, LONDON, S.W.6 | 1968

Formula: [1³⁰]. 30 leaves, pp *i–ii* iii–viii, 1–5 6 7–31 *32* 33–51 52

Technical notes: 126 × 85 mm (p 14). 45 lines, 20 = 56 mm. Leaf size 162 × 102 mm; thickness 0.09 mm; wove, unwatermarked, smooth, white

Contents: Title (*i*), TP verso (*ii*), the Queen's message (iii), message from Sir Compton Mackenzie and foreword by Mrs ML Rawlinson (iv), foreword by Mrs NC McClelland and explanatory note, signed VC Gasson (v), Councils (*viz* the CA Council, the ACC, the NZCC) (vi), contents (vii), foreword by Ian C Baillieu (viii), index (1–5), the laws of Association Croquet, numbered 1–58 (6–33), regulations for official tournaments, numbered 1–26 (34–49), laws of golf croquet, numbered 1–7 (50–51), blank (52)

Binding: Very pale Green (1) rough card, printed in deep Green (142), stapled, no spine or endpapers. FC: within a double-ruled frame, the outer frame in bold (THE LAWS OF | ASSOCIATION | | [in shaded script] **CROQUET** | AND | [in shaded script] **GOLF CROQUET** | AND THE | REGULATIONS | FOR OFFICIAL | TOURNAMENTS). Inside FC: advertisement. RC: blank. Inside RC: advertisement

Copy seen: HPC: GV933 L31 1968 CROQ

Fingerprint: 1.R. 2727 p;he isho 3 1968A

Notes: Published in March 1968, printed by RH Johns, Newport, Monmouth.

(hhhh) *New series, third edition (1972)*

THE LAWS OF | [in shaded display script] Association Croquet | [*do*] AND GOLF CROQUET | AND THE REGULATIONS FOR | TOURNAMENTS | THIRD EDITION | *Published by* | THE CROQUET ASSOCIATION | The Hurlingham Club, London, S.W.6 | 1972

Formula: [1^{34}]. 34 leaves, pp *i–ii* iii–v *vi* vii–viii, 1–57 *58–60*

Technical notes: 126 × 84 mm (p 8). 45 lines, 20 = 56 mm. Leaf size 163 × 104 mm; thickness 0.09 mm; wove, unwatermarked, smooth, white

Contents: Title (*i*), TP verso (*ii*), the Queen's message (iii), foreword by Ian C Baillieu (iv), explanatory note to the third edition, signed 'D.M.C. Prichard' (v), blank (*vi*), councils (vii), contents (viii), index (1–5), the laws of Association Croquet, numbered 1–58 (6–37), regulations for tournaments, numbered 1–24 (38–55), laws of golf croquet, numbered 1–7 (56–57), blank (*58–59*), guide to limits of claims (*60*)

Binding: Deep Red (13) card, stapled, no spine or endpapers. FC: within a double-ruled frame, the outer frame in bold (THE LAWS OF | ASSOCIATION | [in shaded script] **CROQUET** | AND | [in shaded script] **GOLF CROQUET** | AND THE | REGULATIONS | FOR | TOURNAMENTS). Inside FC: advertisement. RC: blank. Inside RC: advertisement

Copy seen: PC

Fingerprint: 1.R. 3030 t.". unco 3 1972A

Notes: Published in March 1972, printed by RH Johns, Newport, Monmouth.

(jjjj) *New series, fourth edition (1984)*

THE LAWS OF | **Association Croquet** | AND GOLF CROQUET | AND THE REGULATIONS FOR | TOURNAMENTS | FOURTH EDITION | *Published by* | THE CROQUET ASSOCIATION | The Hurlingham Club | Ranelagh Gardens | London SW6 3PR | 1984

Formula: [1^{36}]. 36 leaves, pp *i* ii–iv *v* vi–ix, 1–62 *63*

Technical notes: 120 × 78 mm (p 6). 43 lines, 20 = 56 mm. Leaf size 148 × 104 mm; thickness 0.09 mm; wove, unwatermarked, smooth, white

Contents: Title (*i*), TP verso (ii), the Queen's message (iii), preface, signed 'B.G. Neal' (iv), contents (*v*–ix), the laws of Association Croquet, numbered 1–56 (1–35), appendices 1–4 (36–40), laws of golf croquet (41–43), regulations for tournaments, numbered 1–22 (44–59), schedule of bisques in modified games (60), guide to limits of claims (61–62), blank (*63*)

Binding: Light greenish Blue (172) card, stapled, no spine or endpapers. FC: within a double-ruled frame, the outer frame in bold (THE LAWS OF | **ASSOCIATION** | **CROQUET** | AND | GOLF CROQUET | AND THE | REGULATIONS | FOR | TOURNAMENTS). Inside FC: advertisement. RC: advertisement. Inside RC: advertisement

Copy seen: PC

Fingerprint: 4.R. rmNT e.op imst C 1984A [groups 1–4 taken from pp iii, 2, 14, 15 respectively]

Notes: Published in April 1984, printed by Stoate & Bishop (Printers). The pagination of pp 1–63 is irregular in that the rectos and versos are respectively even- and odd-numbered.

(kkkk) *New series, fourth edition, revised (1986)*

THE LAWS OF | **Association Croquet** | AND GOLF CROQUET | AND THE REGULATIONS FOR | TOURNAMENTS | FOURTH EDITION | *Published by* | THE CROQUET ASSOCIATION | The Hurlingham Club | Ranelagh Gardens | London SW6 3PR | 1986

Formula: [1³⁶]. 36 leaves, pp *i* ii–ix, 1–62 63

Technical notes: 120 × 78 mm (p 6). 43 lines, 20 = 56 mm. Leaf size 148 × 104 mm; thickness 0.09 mm; wove, unwatermarked, smooth, white

Contents: Title (*i*), TP verso (ii), the Queen's message (iii), preface, signed 'B.G. Neal' (iv), contents (v–ix), the laws of Association Croquet, numbered 1–56 (1–33), appendices 1–5 (34–40), laws of golf croquet (41–43), regulations for tournaments, numbered 1–22 (44–59), schedule of bisques in modified games (60), guide to limits of claims (61–62), advertisement (*63*)

Binding: Light yellowish Green (135) card, stapled, no spine or endpapers. FC: within a double-ruled frame, the outer frame in bold (THE LAWS OF | **ASSOCIA- TION** | **CROQUET** | AND | GOLF CROQUET | AND THE | REGULATIONS | FOR | TOURNAMENTS). Inside FC: advertisement. RC: advertisement. Inside RC: advertisement

Copy seen: PC

Fingerprint: 4.R. ndrm).et an(*b* C 1986A [groups 1–4 taken from pp iii, 2, 14, 15 respectively]

Notes: Published in 1986, printed by Stoate & Bishop (Printers), Cheltenham. The pagination of pp 1–63 is irregular in that the rectos and versos are respectively even- and odd-numbered.

(llll) *New series, fifth edition (1989)*

THE LAWS OF | **Association Croquet** | AND GOLF CROQUET | AND THE REGULATIONS FOR | TOURNAMENTS | FIFTH EDITION | *Published by* | THE CROQUET ASSOCIATION | THE HURLINGHAM CLUB | RANELAGH GARDENS | LONDON, SW6 3PR | 1989

Formula: [1³⁸]. 38 leaves, pp *1–2, i* ii–ix, 1–62 63–65 [= 76]

Technical notes: 121 × 84 mm (p 10). 44 lines, 20 = 56 mm. Leaf size 148 × 102 mm; thickness 0.10 mm; wove, unwatermarked, smooth, white

Contents: Advertisements (*1–2*), title (*i*), TP verso (ii), the Queen's message (iii), preface, signed 'S.N. MULLINER' (iv), contents (v–viii), diagram of court (ix), the laws of Association Croquet, numbered 1–56 (1–32), appendices 1–5 (33–39), laws of golf croquet (40–42), regulations for tournaments, numbered 1–22 (43–59), schedule of bisques in modified games (60), guide to limits of claims (61–62), advertisements (*63–65*)

Binding: Moderate Red (15) card, stapled, no spine or endpapers. FC: within a double-ruled frame, the outer frame in bold (THE LAWS OF | **ASSOCIATION** | **CROQUET** | AND | GOLF CROQUET | AND THE | REGULATIONS | FOR | TOURNAMENTS). Inside FC: advertisement. RC: advertisement. Inside RC: advertisement

Copy seen: PC

Fingerprint: 9.R. n.it h.er enLa C 1989A [group 3 taken from p 12, group 4 taken from p 13]

Notes: Published in April 1989, printed by DDS Colour Printers, Weston-Super-Mare. The pagination of pp 1–62 is irregular in that the rectos and versos are respectively even- and odd-numbered.

(mmmm) *New series, fifth edition, revised (1992)*

THE LAWS OF | **Association Croquet** | AND GOLF CROQUET | AND THE REGULATIONS FOR | TOURNAMENTS | FIFTH EDITION | *Published by* | THE CROQUET ASSOCIATION | THE HURLINGHAM CLUB | RANELAGH GARDENS | LONDON, SW6 3PR | 1989

Formula: As that of (llll)

Technical notes: 117 × 84 mm (p 11). 42 lines, 20 = 56 mm. Leaf size 147 × 99 mm; thickness 0.10 mm; wove, unwatermarked, smooth, white

Contents: As those of (llll)

Binding: Moderate Red (15) card, stapled, no spine or endpapers. FC: within a double-ruled frame, the outer frame in bold (THE LAWS OF | **ASSOCIATION** | **CROQUET** | AND | GOLF CROQUET | AND THE | REGULATIONS | FOR | TOURNAMENTS). Inside FC: advertisement. RC: advertisement. Inside RC: advertisement

Copy seen: PC

Fingerprint: 9.R. s.ot h.er enLa C 1992A [group 3 taken from p 12, group 4 taken from p 13]

Notes: Published in 1992, printed by Print Seventy, Crewe, Cheshire. The pagination of pp 1–62 is irregular in that the rectos and versos are respectively even- and odd-numbered.

AA101 RULES OF THE WAVENEY BORDERERS' ARCHERY, LAWN   1897
TENNIS & CROQUET CLUB, 1897. [Waveney Borderers' Archery,
Lawn Tennis & Croquet Club]

[Within a double frame with corner ornaments, the inner frame scalloped and the outer frame ruled]

RULES | OF THE | WAVENEY BORDERERS' | **ARCHERY,** | LAWN TENNIS & CROQUET CLUB, | 1897. | [swelled rule] | DISS: | E. CUPISS, PRINTER AND PUBLISHER.

Formula: [1⁸]. 8 leaves, pp *1–4* 5 6 *7–9* 10 11–12 *13* 14 *15–16*

Technical notes: 73 × 51 mm (p 6). 30 lines, 20 = 50 mm. Leaf size 98 × 78 mm; thickness 0.10 mm; wove, unwatermarked, semi-gloss, white

Contents: Title (*1*), officers of the club (*2–3*), text (*4–16*)

Binding: White paper, identical to that of the book block, sewn, no spine or endpapers. FC: printed in black, as the TP. Inside FC: blank. RC: blank. Inside RC: blank

Copy seen: PC

Fingerprint: S.E. zewo s.C. yeth 3 1897A

Notes: Published and printed by E. Cupiss, Diss, Suffolk.

1898

A102   HOW TO PLAY CROQUET. WH Peel   [1898]

(a) *First edition [1898]*

HOW TO PLAY | CROQUET. | *With Hints and Suggestions for the* | *Management of* | CROQUET MEETINGS | AND | PUBLIC TOURNAMENTS. | BY | W. H. PEEL, | *Croquet Champion, 1870-71, and late Hon. Sec. All England* | *Croquet Association.* | PUBLISHED BY | JOHN JAQUES & SON, 102, HATTON GARDEN, LONDON, E.C.

Formula: A⁴ B–F⁸ G⁴ [$2 signed (–A1, A2)]. 48 leaves, pp *1–9* 10–72 *73* 74–92 *93–96*

Technical notes: 133 × 85 mm (p 19). 39 lines, 20 = 68 mm. Leaf size 183 × 120 mm; thickness 0.10 mm; wove, unwatermarked, smooth, white

Contents: Title (*1*), acknowledgement (*2*), contents (*3*), frontispiece (black-and-white photograph) (*4*), preface by A Law (*5–6*), plan of six-hoop setting (*7*), plan of seven-hoop setting (*8*), text (*9–92*), advertisements (*93–96*)

Binding: White paper, printed in moderate Yellow Green (120), black, strong Yellow (84), light Grey (264), and dark Pink (6), over stiff boards, sewn. FC: title *etc* within a Yellow Green panel ([in MS-style script, white out of Yellow Green] *How to Play* | *Croquet.* | WITH | [black on Yellow Green] <u>Hints and Suggestions for the</u> | <u>Management of Croquet Meetings</u> | <u>and Public Tournaments.</u> | [white out of Yellow Green] By W. H. PEEL, | [black on Yellow Green] (Champion 1870 and 1871), | Late Hon. Sec. United All England Croquet Association.), framed by solid coloured discs of the four last-named colours on white, repeated 14 times in clockwise order. RC: advertisement in Pink and Grey on white. Spine: in Pink on white upwards (HOW TO PLAY CROQUET), and across the foot (1/-)

Copy seen: PC

Fingerprint: 8986 r.of *e*.ur maTh 3 1898Q

Notes: Printed by The Ely Press, London, price 1/–. Year of publication is inferred from a date (19 February 1898) cited in the preface.

Review: Lawn Tennis and Croquet (4 May 1898, p 31).

(b) *Second edition [1900]*

HOW TO PLAY | **CROQUET.** | *With Hints and Suggestions for the* | *Management of* | CROQUET MEETINGS | AND | PUBLIC TOURNAMENTS | **SECOND EDITION,** | RE-EDITED BY | COL. THE HON. H. C. NEEDHAM | BY | **W. H. PEEL,** | *Croquet Champion, 1870-71, and late Hon. Sec. All England* | *Croquet Association.* | PUBLISHED BY | JOHN JAQUES AND SON, LIMITED | 102, Hatton Garden, London, E.C.

Formula: A⁴ B–F⁸ G⁴ [$1 signed (–A1, G1)]. 52 leaves, pp *1–6* 7–66 *67* 68 *69* 70–81 *82* 83–92 *93* 94–97 *98–104*

Technical notes: 133 × 84 mm (p 8). 38 lines, 20 = 68 mm. Leaf size 183 × 123 mm; thickness 0.10 mm; wove, unwatermarked, smooth, white

Contents: Title (*1*), blank (*2*), contents (*3*), photograph (*4*), preface by Henry C Needham (*5*), plan of six-hoop setting (*6*), text (*7–97*), advertisements (*98–104*)

Binding: White paper, printed in deep reddish Orange (36) and moderate olive Green (125), over stiff boards, sewn. There are advertisements on the facing pages of the front endpaper, and on all pages of the rear endpaper. FC: title *etc* within a Green panel ([in MS-style script, white out of Green] ***How to Play*** | ***Croquet.*** | [black] WITH | <u>Hints and Suggestions for the</u> | <u>Management of Croquet Meetings</u> |

and Public Tournaments. | *(Second Edition).* | [white out of Green] by **W. H. PEEL,** | [black] (Champion 1870 and 1871). | Late Hon. Sec. United All England Croquet Association. | **LONDON : JOHN JAQUES & SON, Ltd.**) within an Orange ruled frame. RC: advertisement in Orange and Green on white. Spine: in Orange on white upwards (**HOW TO PLAY CROQUET.**)

Copy seen: PC

Fingerprint: 9382 r.er r.be Mywo 3 1900Q

Notes: Printed by The Ely Press, London; noted by *Lawn Tennis and Croquet* (8 August 1900, p 288).

The text of this edition incorporates a number of revisions by its new editor 'to expunge any matter which the progress of a few years has rendered unnecessary, and to add a few words of my own here and there, and footnotes illustrating changes up to date' (preface). There is also a new chapter about the CA.

(c) *Third edition [1903]*

HOW TO PLAY | **CROQUET.** | *With Hints and Suggestions for the* | *Management of* | CROQUET MEETINGS | AND | PUBLIC TOURNAMENTS | BY | **W. H. PEEL,** | *Croquet Champion, 1870-71, and late Hon. Sec. All England* | *Croquet Association.* | **THIRD EDITION,** | RE-EDITED BY | COL. THE HON. H. C. NEEDHAM | PUBLISHED BY | JOHN JAQUES AND SON, LIMITED, | 102, Hatton Garden, London, E.C.

Formula: A^4 B–G^8 H^4 [\$1 signed (–A1, H1)], including front and rear endpapers. 56 leaves, pp *i–ii, 1–6 7–23 24 25–29 30 31–75 76 77–98 99–110*

Technical notes: 133 × 84 mm (p 8). 38 lines, 20 = 68 mm. Leaf size 183 × 123 mm; thickness 0.10 mm; wove, unwatermarked, smooth, white

Contents: Glued to the FC (*i*), advertisement (*ii*), advertisement (*1*), frontispiece, black-and-white photograph of the author (*2*), title (*3*), contents (*4*), list of illustrations (*5*), preface by Henry C Needham (*6*), text (*7–98*), date of revision (February 1903) (*98*), advertisements (*99–109*), glued to the RC (*110*)

Binding: White paper, printed in deep reddish Orange (36) and moderate olive Green (125), over stiff boards, sewn. FC: title *etc* within a Green panel ([in MS-style script, white out of Green] ***How to Play*** | ***Croquet.*** | [black] WITH | Hints and Suggestions for the | Management of Croquet Meetings | and Public Tournaments. | *(Third Edition),* | [white out of Green] by **W. H. PEEL,** | [black] (Champion 1870 and 1871). | Late Hon. Sec. United All England Croquet Association. | **LONDON: JOHN JAQUES & SON, Ltd.**) within an Orange ruled frame. RC: advertisement in Orange and Green on white. Spine: wanting from the copy examined

Copy seen: HPC: GV931 P4 1903 CROQ (imperfect)

Fingerprint: 9597 r.be epp. jule 7 1903Q

Notes: Printed anonymously. Year of publication is inferred from a citation on p 98. The text has not been collated systematically with that of any other edition. However, the close similarity of its fingerprint with that of (d) would suggest that the texts of the two issues are, at least for the most part, identical.

(d) *Fourth edition [1904]*

How to Play Croquet | *With Hints and Suggestions for the* | *Management of* | Croquet Meetings | AND | Public Tournaments | BY | W. H. PEEL | *Croquet Champion, 1870-71, and late Hon. Sec. All England* | *Croquet Association.* | Fourth Edition | REVISED BY | Col. the Hon. H. C. Needham | *Hon. Sec. The Croquet*

Association. | PUBLISHED BY | John Jaques and Son, Limited, | 102, Hatton Garden, London, E.C.

Formula: A^4 B–G^8 H^4 [\$1 signed (–A1, H1)]. 56 leaves including the endpapers, pp *i–ii, 1–6 7–23 24 25–29 30 31–100 101–110*

Technical notes: 132 × 85 mm (p 17). 39 lines, 20 = 68 mm. Leaf size 183 × 121 mm; thickness 0.09 mm; wove, unwatermarked, smooth, white

Contents: Glued to the FC (*i*), advertisements (*ii, 1*), frontispiece (photograph) (*2*), title (*3*), contents (*4*), list of illustrations (*5*), preface, signed 'HENRY C. NEEDHAM', February 1904 (*6*), text (*7–100*), advertisements (*101–109*), glued to the RC (*110*)

Binding: White paper, printed in deep reddish Orange (36) and dark Green (146), over stiff boards, sewn. The end pages of the gatherings serve as the paste-downs. FC: title *etc* within a Green panel ([in MS-style script, white out of Green] ***How to Play*** | [*do*] ***Croquet.*** | [black] WITH | <u>Hints and Suggestions for the</u> | <u>Management of Croquet Meetings</u> | <u>and Public Tournaments.</u> | *(Fourth Edition).* | [white out of Green] by **W. H. PEEL,** | [black] (Champion 1870 and 1871.) | Late Hon. Sec. United All-England Croquet Association | **LONDON : JOHN JAQUES & SON, Ltd.**) within an Orange ruled frame. RC: advertisement in Orange and Green on white. Spine: in Orange on white upwards (**HOW TO PLAY CROQUET**)

Copy seen: BL: 7921 de 33

Fingerprint: 9877 r.be epp. jule 7 1904Q

Notes: Printed anonymously. Year of publication is inferred from the date appended to the author's signature in the preface and from the list of Gold Medallists given on p 99.

The text departs from that of (b) in several places. The main changes are an extension of the section on croquet at garden parties (now Ch IX) and the addition of portraits of newly risen stars. Other matter is rearranged.

The table of contents refers to a list of tournaments for 1904 as on p 102, but this list is not included in the text.

(e) *Fifth edition [1905]*

How to Play Croquet | *With Hints and Suggestions for the* | *Management of* | Croquet Meetings | AND | Public Tournaments | BY | W. H. PEEL | *Croquet Champion, 1870-71, and late Hon. Sec. All England* | *Croquet Association.* | Fifth Edition | PUBLISHED BY | John Jaques and Son, Limited, | 102, Hatton Garden, London, E.C.

Formula: A^4 B–G^8 H^4 [\$2 signed (–A1, 2, H1, 2)]. 56 leaves including the endpapers, pp *i–ii, 1–6 7–29 30 31–63 64 65–69 70 71–78 79 80–99 100–110*

Technical notes: 133 × 85 mm (p 17). 38 lines, 20 = 68 mm. Leaf size 184 × 120 mm; thickness 0.10 mm; wove, unwatermarked, smooth, white

Contents: Glued to the FC (*i*), advertisements (*ii, 1–3*), frontispiece (photograph) (*4*), title (*5*), contents (*6*), text (*7–99*), advertisements (*100–109*), glued to the RC (*110*)

Binding: White paper, printed in deep reddish Orange (36) and moderate olive Green (125), over stiff boards, sewn. The end pages of the gatherings serve as the pastedowns. FC: title *etc* within a Green panel ([in MS-style script, white out of Green] ***How to Play*** | ***Croquet.*** | [black] WITH | <u>Hints and Suggestions for the</u> | <u>Management of Croquet Meetings</u> | <u>and Public Tournaments.</u> | *(Fifth Edition).* |

[white out of Green] by **W. H PEEL,** | [black] (Champion 1870 and 1871), | Late Hon. Sec. United All-England Croquet Association. | **LONDON: JOHN JAQUES & SON, Ltd.**) within an Orange ruled frame with rounded corners. RC: advertisement in Orange and Green on white. Spine: in Orange on white upwards (**HOW TO PLAY CROQUET**)

Copy seen: PC

Fingerprint: s.of d.ys ep**p.** jule 7 1905Q

Notes: Edited and printed anonymously. Year of publication is inferred from the list of winners of the CA's Gold Medal given on p 99.

The text departs from that of (d) in several places. The main omissions are of matter added by earlier editors, notably the preface and an appendix entitled 'The United All England Croquet Association' (afterwards 'The Croquet Association'); and the main addition is a short chapter (Ch VII) on the Willis setting. A portrait of H Needham, a former editor of this work, is replaced by one of V Rowley, Gold Medallist, 1904. Other matter is rearranged and retitled.

(f) *Sixth edition [1906]*

How to Play Croquet | *With Hints and Suggestions for the* | *Management of* | Croquet Meetings | AND | Public Tournaments | BY | W. H. PEEL | *Croquet Champion*, 1870-71, *and late Hon. Sec. All England* | *Croquet Association.* | Sixth Edition. | PUBLISHED BY | JOHN JAQUES & SON, LIMITED, | 102, Hatton Garden, London, E.C.

Formula: A^4 B–G^8 H^4 [\$1 signed (–A1)]. 56 leaves including the endpapers, pp *i–ii*, *1–6* 7–11 *12* 13–23 *24–25* 26 *27* 28–29 *30–31* 32–58 *59* 60–63 *64–66* 67–69 *70–71* *72–79* 80 *81–82* 83 *84–100* *101–110*

Technical notes: 142 × 84 mm (p 10). 39 lines, 20 = 71 mm. Leaf size 181 × 121 mm; thickness 0.09 mm; wove, unwatermarked, smooth, white

Contents: Glued to the FC (*i*), advertisements (*ii, 1–3*), frontispiece (photograph) (*4*), title (*5*), contents (*6*), text (*7–100*), advertisements (*101–109*), glued to the RC (*110*)

Binding: White paper, printed in deep reddish Orange (36) and moderate olive Green (125), over stiff boards, sewn. The end pages of the gatherings serve as the pastedowns. FC: title *etc* within a Green panel ([in MS-style script, white out of Green] *How to Play* | *Croquet.* | [black] WITH | <u>Hints and Suggestions for the</u> | <u>Management of Croquet Meetings</u> | <u>and Public Tournaments.</u> | *(Fifth Edition).* | [white out of Green] by **W. H. PEEL,** | [black] (Champion 1870 and 1871), | Late Hon. Sec. United All-England Croquet Association. | **LONDON: JOHN JAQUES & SON, Ltd.**) within an Orange ruled frame with rounded corners. RC: advertisement in Orange and Green on white. Spine: in Orange on white upwards (**HOW TO PLAY CROQUET**)

Copy seen: PC

Fingerprint: heme d.he rt**p.** poan 7 1906Q

Notes: Edited and printed anonymously. Year of publication is inferred from the list of winners of the CA's Gold Medal given on p *101*.

The letterpress, including that on the cover, is entirely reset, but the text and illustrations are for the most part identical, or virtually so, to those of (e). The only substantive departures from (e) appear to be updates — *viz* the addition of AB Akroyd to the photographs and list of CA Gold Medal winners.

A curiosity of the FC is the retention of the citation '*Fifth Edition*'.

1899

A103 CROQUET. 'Straw Hat' [1899]

DEAN'S CHAMPION HANDBOOKS. | CROQUET. | By "STRAW HAT," | *Author of "Rowing," "Rugby and Association Football," | "Lawn Tennis," &c.* | [publisher's device at L] | [at L] *London:* | [*do*] DEAN & SON, LIMITED, | [*do*] 160a, *Fleet Street, E.C.*

Formula: [1–4⁸]. 32 leaves, pp *1–3* 4–9 *10* 11 *12* 13–21 *22* 23–25 *26–28* 29–32 *33* 34 35 *36–40* 41–42 43–46 *47* 48–58 *59* 60–63 *64*

Technical notes: 119 × 89 mm (p 5). 27 lines, 20 = 89 mm. Leaf size 173 × 116 mm; thickness 0.16 mm; wove, unwatermarked, smooth, white

Contents: Title (*1*), blank (*2*), introduction (*3*), text (*3–64*)

Binding: Dark olive Green (126) cloth, sewn. The copy examined has been fitted with new boards, apparently displaying the original cloth. There are advertisements in black on the facing pages of the front endpaper, and in black and greyish Blue (186) on the facing pages of the rear endpaper. FC: printed in black, brilliant greenish Yellow (98), deep yellowish Pink (27), and pinkish White (9), the lettering in black arranged over and about a sketch of two crossed mallets surmounting two hoops and two balls set in long grass, the mallets coloured White merging at their ends to Yellow, the hoops in White merging downwards to Yellow, the balls and grass in Yellow ([at the top in black, in artist's script] DEAN'S CHAMPION HAND BOOKS. | [at R, in black merging downwards to Yellow] 1/- | [in Pink, swash C] CROQUET | [at L, in Pink merging downwards to white] By | [in White] "Straw [mallet handles] [in Pink merging downwards to White] Hat"). RC: advertisement printed in black. Spine: printed in black upwards (CROQUET.)

Copy seen: BL: 7912 bbb (imperfect)

Fingerprint: s.he t.he dein wowa 3 1899Q

Notes: Printed anonymously, price 1/–. Year of publication is inferred from the citation in the *General Catalogue* of the BL.

The text includes a code of 26 laws which is not attributed to any authority.

A104 CROQUET. Leonard B Williams 1899

The Isthmian Library | Edited by B. Fletcher Robinson | [rule in bold] | **No. XII.** | CROQUET | BY | LEONARD B. WILLIAMS | *ILLUSTRATED.* | LONDON | A. D. INNES & COMPANY | LIMITED | 1899

Formula: π⁴ AA² B–U⁸ V² [$1 signed (–π1, V1)]. 160 leaves, pp *i–xii*, 1–119 *120* 121–300, *1–8*

Technical notes: 131 × 84 mm (p 2). 26 lines, 20 = 101 mm. Leaf size 193 × 130 mm; thickness 0.17 mm; wove, unwatermarked, rough, white. Three inset plates (drawings) face pp *iii* (frontispiece, signed Chas E Dawson, with tipped-in tissue protection), 68, 70; 14 inset plates (photographs) face pp 14, 18, 20, 22, 198, 200, 204, 206, 208, 210, 212, 214, 216, 292

Contents: Half-title (*i*), blank (*ii*), title (*iii*), blank (*iv*), dedication (*v*), blank (*vi*), author's preface (*vii–viii*), contents (*ix*), blank (*x*), list of illustrations (*xi*), blank (*xii*), text (1–274), rules (275–294), index (295–300), advertisements (*1–8*)

Binding: Deep Green (142) sand grain cloth over stiff boards, sewn. FC: gold-blocked (CROQUET | [publisher's device, a statuesque representation of two nude male wrestlers on a pedestal, in the form of a panel containing the words] THE ISTHMIAN LIBRARY). RC: blind-stamped publisher's device in the form of a monogram. Spine: gold-blocked crosswise ([top] CROQUET | [slightly above centre] LEONARD B. | WILLIAMS | [at the foot] THE | ISTHMIAN | LIBRARY)

Copy seen: PC

Fingerprint: K.D, onma ofre saIn 3 1899A

Notes: Printed anonymously, price 5/–. In *Lawn Tennis and Croquet* (2 August 1899, p 242) it is reported that this work 'has now made its appearance'.

The frontispiece, which features a woman player *en déshabillé,* christened 'Roquetetta' by Capt Greenham of Ipswich, has been reproduced elsewhere, notably in S Potter, *The Theory and Practice of Gamesmanship* (London: Rupert Hart-Davis, 1947) and on the FCs of the Spring, Summer, Autumn, and Winter 1970 issues of *The Croquet Gazette.*

Reviews: *Lawn Tennis and Croquet* (31 May 1899, pp 94–5), *The Field* (26 August 1899, p 370), *Athenæum, Daily Chronicle, Daily News, Daily Telegraph, Manchester Guardian, Outlook, Referee, World.*

A105   A POCKET GUIDE TO CROQUET. GH Powell   [1899]

A POCKET GUIDE | TO | CROQUET, | BEING A MANUAL OF THE MODERN "SCIENTIFIC" GAME. | BY | G. H. POWELL, | *Of the Inner Temple,* | AUTHOR OF "EXCURSIONS IN LIBRARIA," "ANIMAL EPISODES," ETC. | TO WHICH IS ADDED THE | *LAWS OF CROQUET:* | *REGULATIONS FOR PRIZE MEETINGS* | (REVISED EDITION, 1899) | OF THE | United All England Croquet Association. | [rule] | LONDON | PUBLISHED BY "LAWN TENNIS AND CROQUET," | LAURENCE POUNTNEY HILL.

Formula: 1^8 2–7^8 8^4 [\$1 signed (–1_1)]. 60 leaves, pp *1–3* 4–10 *11* 12–14 *15* 16–18 *19* 20–40 *41* 42–49 *50* 51–68 *69* 70–76 *77* 78–89 *90 93* 94 95 96–102 *103–104* 105–110 *111–120*

Technical notes: 133 × 84 mm (p 4). 26 lines, 20 = 104 mm. Leaf size 182 × 118 mm; thickness 0.09 mm; wove, unwatermarked, smooth, white

Contents: Title (*1*), TP verso (*2*), introduction (*3–10*), contents (*11–14*), text (*15–89*), blank (*90*), the laws of croquet (*91–110*), advertisements (*111–120*)

Binding: Paperback in light white card, stapled. FC: collage of a large hoop in the form of a three-quarter frame printed in black, over diagonal stripes printed in greyish Green (150), moderate reddish Orange (37), black, and dark greyish Yellow (91), over a sketch of a lawn set out for croquet printed in black, greyish Yellow Green (122), and the aforementioned colours ([black on white background in display script] Price 1/- | [black over the design] THE POCKET | [*do*] GUIDE | [white out of the design] NEW | [white outlined in black in display script over the design] CROQUET | [black over the design] by | [*do*] G.H.Powell.). Inside FC: advertisement. RC: advertisement. Inside RC: advertisement. Spine: blank

Copy seen: PC

Fingerprint: 8.to 6767 s.he ser*u* 7 1899Q

Notes: Printed by George Berridge & Co, London, price 1/–. Year of publication is inferred from the date of the UAECA laws reproduced in the text and from the date of the review cited below.

Review: *Lawn Tennis and Croquet* (16 August 1899, p 284).

1900

A106   **CROQUET. Lt-Col the Hon Henry C Needham**   [1900]

(a) *First edition [1900]*

Not seen. Year of first publication is inferred from the reviews cited below.

Reviews: *Lawn Tennis and Croquet* (20 June 1900, p 152), *The Field* (23 June 1900, p 885).

(b) *1901 issue (1901)*

CROQUET. | BY | Lieut.-Col. the Hon. HENRY C. NEEDHAM, | HON. SEC. C.A. | *WITH ILLUSTRATIONS BY THE AUTHOR.* | WITH THE REVISED LAWS OF 1901. | LONDON: | GEORGE BELL & SONS, YORK ST., COVENT GARDEN, | AND NEW YORK. | 1901.

Formula: $\pi^4(-\pi1)$ A^4 B–F^8 G^4 H^6 [\$1 signed (–A1, H1)]. 57 leaves including the front and rear pastedowns, pp *1–6, i–v* vi *vii–viii, 1* 2–66 *67–69* 70 71 *72–88 89–100*

Technical notes: 127 × 81 mm (p 3). 32 lines, 20 = 80 mm. Leaf size 165 × 110 mm; thickness 0.11 mm; wove, unwatermarked, smooth, white. Four inset plates (black-and-white photographs) face pp 6, 16, 26, 36; one inset leaf of *corrigenda* faces p 76

Contents: Glued to the FC (*1*), advertisements (*2–6*), half-title (*i*), blank (*ii*), title (*iii*), *corrigenda* (*iv*), preface, signed 'Henry C. Needham' (*v–vi*), note to the issue of 1901, signed 'H. C. N.', April 1901 (vi), contents (*vii*), blank (*viii*), text (*1–66*), the laws of croquet *etc* (*67–88*), name of printer (*88*), advertisements (*89–99*), glued to the RC (*100*)

Binding: Greyish olive Green (127) cloth over light boards, sewn, no endpapers. FC: printed in black ([swash *T, A, S*] The All-England Series | [rule] | [swash *Q*] Croquet | [swash *B*] BY | [slanting upwards from L to R] Lt.Col.Hon.H.Needham. | [line drawing of a man instructing a young woman in the croquet stroke] | [in a panel at L] WITH REVISED | [*do*] LAWS, 1901. | [rule] | *Price One Shilling*). RC: printed in black (G. BELL [publisher's device] & SONS). Spine: printed in black upwards ([swash *C, Q*] Croquet – Lt. Col. Hon. H. Needham.)

Copy seen: PC

Fingerprint: e.et tsy. g,re thwh 3 1901A

Notes: Printed by William Clowes and Sons, London, price 1/–.

(c) *1902 issue (1902)*

CROQUET. | BY | Lieut.-Col. the Hon. HENRY C. NEEDHAM, | HON. SEC. C.A. | *WITH ILLUSTRATIONS BY THE AUTHOR.* | WITH THE REVISED LAWS OF 1902. | LONDON: | GEORGE BELL & SONS, YORK ST., COVENT GARDEN, | AND NEW YORK. | 1902.

Formula: π^4 A^4 B–F^8 G^4 H^6 [\$1 signed (–A1, H1)]. 58 leaves including the front and rear pastedowns, pp *1–8, i–viii, 1* 2–66 *67–69* 70 71 *72–81* 82 *83–88 89–100*

Technical notes: 127 × 81 mm (p 3). 32 lines, 20 = 80 mm. Leaf size 166 × 109 mm; thickness 0.10 mm; wove, unwatermarked, smooth, white. Four inset plates (black-and-white photographs) face pp 6, 16, 26, 36; a *corrigenda* slip is tipped over p *1*

Contents: Glued to the FC (*1*), blank (*2–3*), advertisements (*4–8*), half-title (*i*), blank (*ii*), title (*iii*), *corrigenda* (*iv*), preface, signed 'Henry C. Needham', 1900 (*v*), note to the issue of 1902, signed 'H. C. N.', March 1902 (*vi*), contents (*vii*), blank (*viii*), text (*1–66*), the laws of croquet *etc* (67–88), name of printer (88), advertisements (89–99), glued to the RC (*100*)

Binding: As that of (b), except that a solid black rectangle is over-printed, partially obscuring the year of publication on the FC.

Copy seen: PC

Fingerprint: O.L. tsy. g,re thwh 3 1902A

Notes: Printed by William Clowes and Sons, London and Beccles, price 1/–.

The text of this issue is apparently identical to that of (b), only the laws *etc* are updated. In particular, it is notable that the *corrigenda* remain unaltered and some are repeated in the present *corrigenda* slip tipped over p *1*.

A107   CROQUET UP TO DATE. Arthur Lillie   1900

CROQUET UP TO DATE | CONTAINING THE IDEAS AND TEACHINGS | OF THE LEADING PLAYERS AND CHAMPIONS | EDITED BY | ARTHUR LILLIE | HON. SECRETARY FOR CROQUET, ALL ENGLAND LAWN-TENNIS | AND CROQUET CLUB, WIMBLEDON | *WITH ILLUSTRATIONS* | LONGMANS, GREEN, AND CO. | 39 PATERNOSTER ROW, LONDON | NEW YORK AND BOMBAY | 1900 | *All rights reserved*

Formula: a^8 b^2 A–T^8 U^6 [$1 signed (–*a*1)]. 168 leaves, pp *1–2*, *i–iv* v–vii *viii* ix–xviii, *1* 2–179 *180* 181–313 *314–316* [= 336]

Technical notes: 147 × 89 mm (p xii). 29 lines, 20 = 102 mm. Leaf size 223 × 140 mm; thickness 0.17 mm; wove, unwatermarked, rough, white. Fifteen inset plates (photographs) face pp *iii* (tissue protection tipped-in), xiv, 18, 28, 86, 122, 129, 141, 174, 183, 184, 216, 233, 245; two plates face p 141

Contents: Blank (*1–2*), half-title (*i*), blank (*ii*), title (*iii*), blank (*iv*), contents (v–vii), blank (*viii*), list of illustrations (ix–x), introduction (xi–xviii), text (1–297), the laws of croquet 1899 (298–313), blank (*314*), advertisement (*315*), blank (*316*)

Binding: Moderate bluish Green (164) cloth over stiff boards, sewn, the pages uncut. FC: gold-blocked title at the head (CROQUET | UP TO | DATE); illustration, in black at lower L, of a woman player preparing to play a hoop stroke. RC: blank. Spine: gold-blocked crosswise ([double rule at the upper edge] | [at the top] CROQUET | UP TO | DATE | [slightly above centre] ARTHUR LILLIE | [at the foot] LONGMANS & C° | [double rule at the lower edge])

Copy seen: PC

Fingerprint: CE31 s.re ton. pean 7 1900A

Notes: Published on 19 June 1900, printed anonymously, price 10/6. The text includes contributions by H Needham (Ch II), C Locock (Ch III), C Heneage (Ch IV), W Bruce (Ch VI), F Croft (Ch XI), K Waldron (Ch XII), G Powell (Ch XIII), H Wilberforce (Ch XVI).

According to the publisher's records now held by RUL, 1500 copies were printed, of which 197 were remaindered to the trade at 1/9 per dozen (13 for 12) in January 1910.

The KRWL holds what appears to be a contemporary reprint of this work with the author's annotations, which suggests that the publisher contemplated issuing an early revised issue, incorporating the addition of an index and some extension of the photographic plates. No such later issue is thought to have been published. (At the material time the author was a prominent member of the AELT&CC.)

Reviews: *The Queen* (21 July 1900, p 98), *Lawn Tennis and Croquet* (15 August 1900, pp 302–3).

1901

A108   **THE CROQUET ANNUAL 1901–2. 'Diana' of the *Ladies' Field***   1901

The Ladies' Field Handbooks | [bold rule] | THE CROQUET ANNUAL | 1901–2 | COMPILED AND EDITED BY | "DIANA" | OF THE "LADIES' FIELD" | [in gothic-revival script] | GEORGE NEWNES, LIMITED | 8-12, SOUTHAMPTON STREET, STRAND, W.C. | 1901

Formula: 1^4 2–10^8 11^{16} [\$1 signed (-1_1, 11_1)]. 92 leaves, pp *i–iv* v *vi* vii–viii, 1–142 *143–144, 1* 2–32 [= 184]

Technical notes: 135 × 84 mm (p 2). 33 lines, 20 = 82 mm. Leaf size 180 × 120 mm; thickness 0.09 mm; wove, unwatermarked, smooth, white

Contents: Half-title (*i*), blank (*ii*), title (*iii*), advertisement (*iv*), preface (v), advertisement (*vi*), contents (vii–viii), text (1–142), advertisements (*143–144*), publications of George Newnes Limited (*1–32*)

Binding: Dark Pink (6) cloth over light boards, sewn. There are advertisements on the facing pages of the front endpaper and on all pages of the rear endpaper. FC: in black (THE LADIES' FIELD HANDBOOKS | CROQUET ANNUAL | [flourishes above end-points] .1901-1902. | [illustration of a female figure in statuesque pose within an *art nouveau* frame] | 1/6). RC: blank. Spine: blank

Copy seen: PC

Fingerprint: e?re urhe s.of ofwe 3 1901A

Notes: Printed by Unwin Brothers, The Gresham Press, Woking and London, price 1/6.

AA109 **OFFICIAL HANDICAP BOOK. [The Croquet Association]**   1901

(a) **First edition (1901)*

Not seen. Year of first publication is deduced from the fact that this work was first mentioned in the 1901 edition of the association's Regulations for Prize Meetings (Regulation 15 in A100h) in the following terms: 'In handicap events players shall meet at the handicap allotted in the Official Handicap Book, subject to the revision of the Handicapper at the meeting, who shall also handicap entries not entered in the book. A copy of the Official Handicap Book shall be sent to every meeting duly advertised in the Croquet Association Calendar. A player whose form is uncertified shall be entered, if a gentleman, at three bisques from scratch, if a lady at five bisques.' For some years previously, however, handicaps were regulated and listed by a handicapping committee, and may have been set in print for restricted distribution.

(b) *1919 edition (1919)*

[in display script] **The Croquet Association.** | [double rule, the upper longer than the lower] | [swelled rule] | OFFICIAL HANDICAP BOOK, | 1919. | ☐ ☐ ☐ | **Association Handicapper :** | C. D. LOCOCK.

Formula: [1–10^8]. 80 leaves, pp *1–3* 4–158 *159–160*. The copy examined was specially bound for official use with extra interleaved pages for notes. The extra leaves are here discounted

Technical notes: 167 × 109 mm (p 10). *ca* 49 lines, 20 = *ca* 68 mm (the text con-

than the lower] | [swelled rule] | **OFFICIAL HANDICAP BOOK.** | □ □ □ |
Association Handicapper, | Brig.-Gen. J. H. TWISS, C.B., C.B.E.

Formula: [1–8⁸ 4⁶(4₃+χ₁,₂]. 32 leaves including the endpapers, pp *i–iv*, *1–3 4–37 38 39–47 48 49–57 58–60*. The copy examined was specially bound for official use with extra interleaved pages for notes. The extra leaves are here discounted

Technical notes: 172 × 109 mm (p 9). 56 lines, 20 = 64 mm. Leaf size 213 × 134 mm; thickness 0.15 mm; laid, watermarked ([in a convex arc] CONQUEROR | LONDON | [heraldic device]), smooth, white

Contents: Glued to the FC (*i*), blank (*ii–iv*), title (*1*), blank (*2*), contents (*3*), official list of managers (*4*), official list of referees and umpires (*4–5*), official list of handicappers (*5*), managers, referees, and handicappers (*6*), list of Associates with their handicaps (*7–37*), blank (*38*), list of non-Associates with their handicaps (*39–47*), blank (*48*), register of assumed names (*49*), county croquet unions (*49*), registered croquet clubs (*49–54*), Bagnall-Wild system (*55–57*), blank (*58–60*)

Binding: Dark greyish Red (20) morocco grain cloth over and bordering the spine, overlapped by greenish Grey (155) rough paper over stiff boards, sewn. FC: printed in black ([in gothic-revival script] The | [*do*] Croquet Association | [rule] | OFFICIAL HANDICAP BOOK | 1937). RC: blank. Spine: blank

Copy seen: CA (imperfect)

Fingerprint: 5754 chon 7).1 Ke6_ 3 1937A

Notes: Printed anonymously, probably by Roffey & Clark (see also *Notes* to (c)).

1902

A110   **THE CROQUET ASSOCIATION [continued as YEAR BOOK OF   1902
        THE CROQUET ASSOCIATION, HAND BOOK OF THE
        CROQUET ASSOCIATION, ABRIDGED HAND BOOK OF THE
        CROQUET ASSOCIATION, DIRECTORY OF THE CROQUET
        ASSOCIATION, THE CROQUET ASSOCIATION DIRECTORY,
        DIRECTORY OF ASSOCIATES].** [The Croquet Association]

Foreword: This serial has been the principal official work of reference issued to Associates (*ie* members). It has had a chequered history, reflecting the development of the CA and its services, budgetary constraints and other vicissitudes, and the concurrent availability of complementary publications issued by or by arrangement with the CA from time to time — notably those devoted to the laws of the game, regulations for the management of official events, notices of forthcoming events, the names and addresses of members, their current handicaps.

For many years (interrupted only by the first and second world wars), it was issued annually early in the year, in readiness for the new season. More recently, it appeared at irregular intervals, and in some years was supplemented by occasional issues of amendment sheets.

From its inception it was referred to officially as the 'Croquet Association Year Book' but was not actually so entitled until 1949. From 1955 it underwent several name changes, reflecting the current official view as to its key role and having regard to its contents and the contents of other CA publications. In 1954 it was decided, for reasons of economy, to publish it every two or three years, and hence to call it a handbook rather than a year book.

Where standard copies were available for examination, they were selected for the purpose of compiling the entries which follow. It will be seen, however, that for most years the copies examined were specially bound for official purposes and were of anomalous construction. Comparison of the various copies examined over the years suggests that all issues produced for ordinary distribution were constructed in much the same format as the copies here described — *ie* printed on wove paper of about 0.11 thickness and bound in a wrapper of paper or light card.

(a) *First edition (1902)*

1902. | [rule] | [in display script] **The** | [*do*] **Croquet Association.** | [swelled rule] | RULES | AND | LIST OF MEMBERS WITH ADDRESSES AND HANDICAPS. | LIST OF ASSOCIATES WHO ARE MEMBERS | OF SHEEN HOUSE CLUB. | CALENDAR OF FIXTURES, | WITH | NAMES AND ADDRESSES OF LOCAL SECRETARIES. | PARTICULARS AS TO MEMBERSHIP OF THE | C.A., AND S.H.C. | RECORD OF PRINCIPAL WINNERS | AND | C.A. MEDALLISTS. | [swelled rule] | ISSUED ANNUALLY TO ASSOCIATES.

Formula: A^8 B–D^8 [\$1 signed (–A1)]. 32 leaves, pp *1–5* 6–61 *62–63, 64*

Technical notes: 162 × 98 mm (p 7). 36 lines, 20 = 90 mm. Leaf size 203 × 136 mm; thickness 0.12 mm; wove, unwatermarked, smooth, white

Contents: Title (*1*), TP verso (*2*), the CA Committee and Handicapping Committee (*3*), blank (*4*), rules (*5–11*), calendar of fixtures (*12–14*), advantages of membership (*15*), list of Associates who are Members of the Sheen House Club (*16–20*), list of members (*21–54*), list of Irish members (*55–57*), winners of principal events (*58–61*), advertisements (*62–63*), glued to the rear endpaper (*64*)

Binding: Dark yellowish Green (137) calico grain cloth over and bordering the spine, overlapped by greyish Yellow Green (122) paper over stiff boards, sewn. There are advertisements on the facing pages of the endpapers. FC: printed in dark yellowish Green (137) (THE | CROQUET ASSOCIATION, | 1902.). RC: blank. Spine: blank

Copy seen: CA

Fingerprint: M.q. *c*.M, e.re adwi 3 1902A

Notes: Printed by Lowe Bros, London, issued free to Associates. It was announced in *Lawn Tennis and Croquet* (5 March 1902, p 537) that this work would 'shortly be issued'.

(b) *1903 edition (1903)*

1903. | [rule] | [in display script] **The** | [*do*] **Croquet Association.** | [in gothic-revival script] **Contents.** | COMMITTEE. | HANDICAPPING COMMITTEE. | RULES OF C.A. | LIST OF MEMBERS WITH ADDRESSES AND HANDICAPS. | LIST OF ASSOCIATES WHO ARE MEMBERS | OF THE ROEHAMPTON CLUB. | CALENDAR OF FIXTURES, | WITH | NAMES AND ADDRESSES OF LOCAL SECRETARIES. | PARTICULARS AS TO MEMBERSHIP OF THE | C.A., AND R.C. | RECORD OF PRINCIPAL WINNERS | AND | C.A. MEDALLISTS. | [rule] | ISSUED ANNUALLY TO ASSOCIATES.

Formula: A^8 B–E^8 F^4 [\$1 signed (–A1, F1)]. 44 leaves, pp *1–5* 6–82 *83–88*. The copy examined was specially bound for official use with extra interleaved pages for notes. The extra leaves are here discounted

Technical notes: 163 × 98 mm (p 7). 37 lines, 20 = 90 mm. Leaf size 209 × 137 mm; thickness 0.12 mm; wove, unwatermarked, smooth, white

Contents: Title (*1*), TP verso (*2*), Committee *etc* (*3*), sub-committees (*4*), rules (*5–11*), calendar of fixtures (*12–15*), advantages of membership (*16*), list of Associates who are Members of the Roehampton Club (*17–21*), list of members

(22–60), classified list of handicaps (61–76), winners of the principal events (77–82), advertisements (*83–85*), blank (*86–88*)

Binding: Very dark yellowish Green (138) pebble grain cloth over and bordering the spine, overlapped by greyish Yellow Green (122) paper over stiff boards, sewn. There are advertisements on the facing pages of the endpapers. FC: printed in dark yellowish Green (137) (THE | CROQUET ASSOCIATION, | 1903.). RC: blank. Spine: blank

Copy seen: CA (imperfect)

Fingerprint: T.). *c.*M, y.e, Seln 3 1903A

Notes: Printed by Lowe Bros, London, issued free to Associates. Official notices of *addenda* and *corrigenda* appeared in *Lawn Tennis and Croquet* in its issues of 6 May 1903 (p 45), 13 May 1903 (pp 59–60), 20 May 1903 (p 76), 10 June 1903 (p 134), and 17 June 1903 (p 158).

(c) *1904 edition (1904)*

1904. | [rule] | [in display script] **The** | [*do*] **Croquet Association.** | [double rule] | [in gothic-revival script] **Contents.** | COMMITTEE. | SUB-COMMITTEES. | RULES OF C.A. | LIST OF MEMBERS WITH ADDRESSES AND HANDICAPS. | LIST OF ASSOCIATES WHO ARE MEMBERS | OF THE ROEHAMPTON CLUB. | CALENDAR OF FIXTURES, | WITH | NAMES AND ADDRESSES OF LOCAL SECRETARIES. | PARTICULARS AS TO MEMBERSHIP OF | THE C.A., AND R.C. | CLASSSIFIED HANDICAP LIST | RECORD OF PRINCIPAL WINNERS | AND | C.A. MEDALLISTS. | [rule] | ISSUED ANNUALLY TO ASSOCIATES.

Formula: A^8 B–F^8 [$1 signed (–A1)]. 48 leaves, pp *1–5* 6–92 *93–96*. The copy examined was specially bound for official use with extra interleaved pages for notes. The extra leaves are here discounted

Technical notes: 162 × 98 mm (p 7). 37 lines, 20 = 89 mm. Leaf size 203 × 140 mm; thickness 0.11 mm; wove, unwatermarked, smooth, white

Contents: Title (*1*), TP verso (*2*), Committee *etc* (*3*), sub-committees (*4*), rules (5–10), calendar of fixtures (11–14), advantages of membership (14–15), list of Associates who are Members of the Roehampton Club (16–20), list of Members (21–64), classified list of handicaps (65–84), winners of the principal events (85–92), advertisements (*93–96*)

Binding: Very dark yellowish Green (138) pebble grain cloth over and bordering the spine, overlapped by greyish Yellow Green (122) paper over stiff boards, sewn. There are advertisements on the facing pages of the endpapers. FC: printed in moderate deep yellowish Green (132) (THE | CROQUET ASSOCIATION, | 1904.). RC: blank. Spine: blank

Copy seen: CA (imperfect)

Fingerprint: C.s. t.ry r.al Meth 3 1904A [the third and fourth characters of group 1 are in gothic-revival script]

Notes: Printed by Lowe Bros, London, issued free to Associates.

(d) *1905 edition (1905)*

1905. | [rule] | [in display script] **The** | [*do*] **Croquet Association.** | [double rule] | [in gothic-revival script] **Contents.** | COMMITTEE. | SUB-COMMITTEES. | OFFICIAL HANDICAPPERS. | RULES OF THE CROQUET ASSOCIATION. | THE LAWS OF CROQUET, AND REGULATIONS FOR | PRIZE MEETINGS. | DECISIONS ON DISPUTED POINTS ON THE LAWS. | ETIQUETTE. |

PRINCIPAL WINNERS AND SILVER MEDALLISTS. | ADVANTAGES OF MEMBERSHIP. | LIST OF MEMBERS WITH ADDRESSES AND HANDICAPS, | SHOWING ‡MEMBERS [*sic*] OF ROEHAMPTON CLUB, | †LIFE MEMBERS [*sic*], *SPECIALLY [*sic*] HANDICAPPED UNDER | REGULATION 10. | CLASSI-FIED HANDICAP LIST. | AGREEMENT TO QUALIFY FOR CALENDAR FIXTURE. | OFFICIAL CALENDAR OF FIXTURES, WITH NAMES AND | ADDRESSES OF LOCAL HON. SECRETARIES. | [rule] | ISSUED ANNUALLY TO ASSOCIATES ONLY.

Note: The copy examined had apparently been specially bound for official use with extra lined leaves for notes between all pages. The extra leaves were discounted in compiling the notes which follow.

Formula: [1–8⁸ 9⁴]. 68 leaves, pp *1–6* 7–11 *12* 13–23 *24* 25–36 *37* 38–45 *46* 47–98 *99* 100–127 *128–129* 130–131 *132–136*. The copy examined was specially bound for official use with extra interleaved pages for notes. The extra leaves are here dis-counted

Technical notes: 166 × 98 mm (p 7). 37 lines, 20 = 90 mm. Leaf size 208 × 138 mm; thickness 0.12 mm; wove, unwatermarked, smooth, white

Contents: Title (*1*), advertisement (*2*), Committee *etc* (*3*), sub-committees (*4*), official handicappers (*5*), rules of the CA (*6–11*), the laws of croquet (*12–23*), regulations for prize meetings (*24–35*), etiquette (*36*), winners of principal events (*37–43*), advantages of membership (*44–45*), list of Members (*46–98*), classified list of handicaps (*99–125*), agreement to qualify for CA calendar fixture (*126–127*), blank (*128*), calendar of fixtures (*129–131*), blank (*132*), advertisements (*133–136*)

Binding: Very dark yellowish Green (138) pebble grain cloth over and bordering the spine, overlapped by greyish Yellow Green (122) paper over stiff boards, sewn. There are advertisements on all pages of the endpapers. FC: printed in moderate olive Green (125) (THE | CROQUET ASSOCIATION, | 1905.). RC: printed in moderate olive Green (125) (Printed by | THE HOLMESDALE PRESS LIMITED. | Redhill Junction and London.). Spine: blank

Copy seen: CA (imperfect)

Fingerprint: C.s. c.K, s.g; inba 3 1905A [the third and fourth characters of group 1 are in gothic-revival script]

Notes: Printed by The Holmesdale Press, Redhill Junction and London, issued free to Associates.

(e) *1906 edition (1906)*

[Heading, p *1*]

1906. | [rule] | [in display script] **The** | [*do*] **Croquet Association.** | [double rule]

Formula: [1–10⁸]. 80 leaves including the front pastedown, pp *i–iv*, *1–6* 7–11 *12* 13–26 *27* 28–53 *54* 55–116 *117* 118–152 *153–156*. The copy examined was specially bound for official use with extra interleaved pages for notes. The extra leaves are here discounted

Technical notes: 166 × 98 mm (p 8). 37 lines, 20 = 90 mm. Leaf size 210 × 138 mm; thickness 0.09 mm; wove, unwatermarked, smooth, white

Contents: Glued to the FC (*i*), advertisements (*ii–iv*), title heading and contents (*1*), advertisement (*2*), Committee *etc* (*3*), sub-committees (*4*), official handicappers (*5*), rules of the CA (*6–11*), the laws of croquet (*12–26*), regulations for prize meetings (*27–34*), standing orders of the Committee (*35–40*), decisions on disputed points in the laws of croquet (*41–42*), etiquette (*43*), winners of the principal events (*44–51*), advantages of membership (52–53), list of Members (54–116), classified list of handicaps (*117–146*), agreement to qualify for CA calendar fixture (147–149), calendar of fixtures (150–152), blank (*153*), advertisements (*154–156*)

Binding: Very dark yellowish Green (138) pebble grain cloth over and bordering the spine, overlapped by light greenish Grey (154) paper over stiff boards, sewn. No front endpaper. There are advertisements on all pages of the rear endpaper. FC: printed in moderate olive Green (125) (THE | CROQUET ASSOCIATION, | 1906.). RC: publisher's device printed in deep Yellow Green (118) at lower R. Spine: blank

Copy seen: CA (imperfect)

Fingerprint: C.s. c.K, y.om coco 3 1906A [group 1 taken from p *3*, the third and fourth characters of group 1 in gothic-revival script]

Notes: Printed by The Holmesdale Press, Redhill Junction and London, issued free to Associates.

(f) *1907 edition (1907)*

[Heading, p *1*]

1907. | [rule] | [in display script] **The** | [*do*] **Croquet Association.** | [double rule]

Formula: [1–9⁸ 10⁸ χ1 11⁴]. 85 leaves, pp *i–ii, 1–6 7–11 12 13–26 27 28–54 55 56–127 128 129–164 165–168*. The copy examined was specially bound for official use with extra interleaved pages for notes. The extra leaves are here discounted

Technical notes: 166 × 98 mm (p *7*). 37 lines, 20 = 90 mm. Leaf size 210 × 135 mm; thickness 0.11 mm; wove, unwatermarked, smooth, white

Contents: Advertisements (*i–ii*), title heading and contents (*1*), advertisement (*2*), Committee *etc* (*3*), sub-committees (*4*), the Official Handicapper, official referees and handicappers (*5*), rules of the CA (6–11), the laws of croquet (*12–26*), regulations for prize meetings (*27–34*), standing orders of the Committee (35–40), decisions on disputed points in the laws of croquet (41–43), etiquette (44), winners of the principal events (45–52), advantages of membership (53–54), list of Members (55–127), classified list of handicaps (*128–158*), agreement to qualify for CA calendar fixture (159–161), calendar of fixtures (162–164), advertisements (*165–168*)

Binding: Very dark yellowish Green (138) pebble grain cloth over and bordering the spine, overlapped by light greenish Grey (154) paper over stiff boards, sewn. There are advertisements on all pages of the endpapers. FC: printed in deep Yellow Green (118) (THE | CROQUET ASSOCIATION, | 1907.). RC: publisher's device printed in moderate olive Green (125) at lower R. Spine: blank

Copy seen: CA (imperfect)

Fingerprint: C.s. c.K, s.om 7yHo 3 1907A [group 1 taken from p *3*, the third and fourth characters of group 3 in gothic-revival script]

Notes: Printed by The Holmesdale Press, Redhill Junction and London, issued free to Associates.

(g) *1909 edition (1909)*

[Heading, p *1*]

1909. | [rule] | [in display script] **The** | [*do*] **Croquet Association.** | [double rule]

Formula: [1–12⁸ 13⁸(13₁+χ1)]. 105 leaves, pp *i–ii, 1–2 3–14 15 16–204 205–208*. The copy examined was specially bound for official use with extra interleaved pages for notes. The extra leaves are here discounted

Technical notes: 167 × 96 mm (p *10*). 38 lines, 20 = 89 mm. Leaf size 207 × 137 mm;

thickness 0.14 mm; laid, watermarked (OCEANA FINE | LEDGER | [heraldic device]), smooth, white

Contents: Advertisements (*i–ii*), title heading and contents (*1*), advertisement (*2*), Committee *etc* (*3*), sub-committees (*4*), the Official Handicapper, official referees and handicappers (*5*), official managers (*6*), rules of the CA (*7–14*), the laws of croquet (*15–30*), regulations for prize meetings (*31–40*), standing orders of the Committee (*41–46*), decisions on disputed points in the laws of croquet (*47–51*), etiquette (*52*), winners of the principal events (*53–63*), advantages of membership (*64–65*), list of Members (*66–154*), classified list of handicaps (*155–188*), agreement to qualify for CA calendar fixture (*189–191*), registered clubs (*192–200*), calendar of fixtures (*201–204*), advertisements (*205–208*)

Binding: Very dark yellowish Green (138) pebble grain cloth over and bordering the spine, overlapped by light greenish Grey (154) paper over stiff boards, sewn. There are advertisements on all pages of the endpapers. FC: printed in moderate olive Green (125) (THE | CROQUET ASSOCIATION, | 1909.). RC: publisher's device printed in dark Green (146) at lower R. Spine: blank

Copy seen: CA (imperfect)

Fingerprint: C.s. ofe, lyrs HoJA 3 1909A [group 1 taken from p *3*, the third and fourth characters of group 1 in gothic-revival script]

Notes: Printed by The Holmesdale Press, Redhill Junction and London, issued free to Associates.

(h) *1910 edition (1910)*

[Heading, p *1*]

1910. | [rule] | [in display script] **The** | [*do*] **Croquet Association.** | [double rule]

Formula: [1–13⁸ 14⁶]. 110 leaves, pp *i–ii, 1–2 3–20 21 22–205 206 207–214 215–218.* The copy examined was specially bound for official use with extra interleaved pages for notes. The extra leaves are here discounted

Technical notes: 166 × 97 mm (p 10). 38 lines, 20 = 88 mm. Leaf size 207 × 138 mm; thickness 0.12 mm; laid, watermarked (OCEANA FINE | LEDGER | [heraldic device]), smooth, white

Contents: Advertisements (*i–ii*), title heading and contents (*1*), advertisement (*2*), Committee *etc* (*3*), sub-committees (*4*), the Official Handicapper (*5*), official referees and handicappers (*5-6*), official managers (*6*), rules of the CA (*7–14*), standing orders of the Committee (*15–20*), the laws of croquet (*21–37*), regulations for prize meetings (*38–47*), decisions on disputed points in the laws of croquet (*48–53*), etiquette (*54*), winners of the principal events (*55–66*), advantages of membership (*67–68*), list of Members (*69–161*), classified list of handicaps (*162–195*), list of affiliated foreign and colonial associations *etc* (*196*), registered clubs (*197–205*), blank (*206*), agreement to qualify for CA calendar fixture (*207–209*), calendar of fixtures (*210–214*), advertisements (*215–218*)

Binding: Very dark yellowish Green (138) pebble grain cloth over and bordering the spine, overlapped by light greenish Grey (154) paper over stiff boards, sewn. There are advertisements on all pages of the endpapers. FC: printed in moderate olive Green (125) (THE | CROQUET ASSOCIATION, | 1910.). RC: publisher's device printed in dark Green (146) at lower R. Spine: blank

Copy seen: CA (imperfect)

Fingerprint: C.s. y.nd s.de SeCH 3 1910A [group 1 taken from p *3*, the third and fourth characters of group 1 in gothic-revival script]

Notes: Printed by The Holmesdale Press, Redhill Junction, issued free to Associates.

(j) *1912 edition (1912)*

[Heading, p *1*]

1912. | [rule] | [in display script] **The Croquet Association.** | [double rule]

Note: The copy examined had apparently been specially bound for official use with extra lined leaves for notes between all pages. The extra leaves were discounted in compiling the notes which follow.

Formula: [1–13⁸ 14⁶(14₅+χ1)]. 111 leaves, pp *i–ii, 1–2 3–22 23 24–216 217–220*

Technical notes: 166 × 97 mm (p 11). 37 lines, 20 = 89 mm. Leaf size 206 × 137 mm; thickness 0.17 mm; laid, watermarked (Oceana Fine | Ledger | [heraldic device]), rough, white

Contents: Advertisements (*i–ii*), title heading and contents (*1*), advertisement (*2*), Committee *etc* (3), sub-committees (4), the Association Handicapper (5), official referees (5–6), official handicappers (6–7), official managers (7), official referees, handicappers and managers (8), rules of the CA (9–16), standing orders of the Committee (17–22), the laws of croquet (*23–35*), regulations for prize meetings (36–46), decisions on disputed points in the laws of croquet (47), etiquette (48), challenge prizes (49), winners of the principal events (50–62), advantages of membership (63–64), list of Members (65–159), register of assumed names (160), classified list of handicaps (161–195), list of affiliated foreign and colonial associations *etc* (196), registered clubs (197–208), agreement to qualify for CA calendar fixture (209–210), calendar of fixtures (211–216), advertisements (*217–220*)

Binding: Very dark yellowish Green (138) pebble grain cloth over and bordering the spine, overlapped by light greenish Grey (154) paper over stiff boards, sewn. There are advertisements on all pages of the endpapers. FC: printed in moderate olive Green (125) (THE | CROQUET ASSOCIATION, | 1912.). RC: publisher's device printed in dark Green (146) at lower R. Spine: blank

Copy seen: CA (imperfect)

Fingerprint: C.s. s,r- m.om Reof 3 1912A [group 1 taken from p 3, the third and fourth characters of group 1 in gothic-revival script]

Notes: Printed by The Holmesdale Press, Redhill Junction, issued free to Associates.

(k) *1913 edition (1913)*

[Heading, p *1*]

1913. | [rule] | [in display script] **The Croquet Association.** | [double rule]

Formula: [1–13⁸ 14⁸(14₇+χ1) 15⁴]. 117 leaves, pp *i–ii, 1–3 4–22 23 24–230 231–232.* The copy examined was specially bound for official use with extra interleaved pages for notes. The extra leaves are here discounted

Technical notes: 167 × 101 mm (p 11). 37 lines, 20 = 90 mm. Leaf size 205 × 138 mm; thickness 0.17 mm; laid, watermarked (Oceana Fine | Ledger | [heraldic device]), rough, white

Contents: Advertisements (*i–ii*), title heading and contents (*1*), advertisement (*2*), Council *etc* (3), committees (4), the Association Handicapper (5), official referees (5–6), official handicappers (6–7), official managers (7), official referees, handicappers and managers (8), rules of the CA (9–16), standing orders of the Council (17–22), the laws of croquet (*23–37*), regulations for prize meetings (38–48), decisions on disputed points in the laws of croquet (49), etiquette (50), challenge prizes (51), winners of the principal events (52–65), advantages of membership

(66–67), list of Associates (68–169), register of assumed names (170), classified list of handicaps (171–206), list of affiliated foreign and colonial associations *etc* (207), registered clubs (208–220), agreement to qualify for CA calendar fixture (221–223), calendar of fixtures (224–230), advertisements (*231–232*)

Binding: Very dark yellowish Green (138) pebble grain cloth over and bordering the spine, overlapped by light greenish Grey (154) paper over stiff boards, sewn. There are advertisements on all pages of the endpapers. FC: printed in moderate olive Green (125) (THE | CROQUET ASSOCIATION, | 1913.). RC: publisher's device printed in dark Green (146) at lower R. Spine: blank

Copy seen: CA (imperfect)

Fingerprint: C.s. ofy- d.as (stw 3 1913A [group 1 taken from p *3*, the third and fourth characters of group 1 in gothic-revival script]

Notes: Printed by The Holmesdale Press, Redhill Junction and London, issued free to Associates.

(l) *1914 edition (1914)*

[Heading, p *1*]

1914. | [rule] | [in display script] **The Croquet Association.** | [double rule]

Formula: [1–14⁸ 15⁶]. 118 leaves, pp *i–ii*, *1–3* 4–22 *23* 24–232 *233–234*. The copy examined was specially bound for official use with extra interleaved pages for notes. The extra leaves are here discounted

Technical notes: 166 × 97 mm (p 21). 38 lines, 20 = 89 mm. Leaf size 206 × 138 mm; thickness 0.14 mm; laid, watermarked ([the letters OX, LE are not clearly legible] OXFORD | LEDGER | [heraldic device]), smooth, white

Contents: Advertisements (*i–ii*), title heading and contents (*1*), advertisement (2), Council *etc* (3), committees (4), the Association Handicapper (5), official referees (5–6), official handicappers (6–7), official managers (7–8), official referees, handicappers and managers (8), rules of the CA (9–16), standing orders of the Council (17–22), the laws of croquet (*23–38*), regulations for prize meetings (39–49), decisions on points in the laws of croquet (heading only) (50), etiquette (51), challenge prizes (52), winners of the principal events (53–68), official handicap list: Associates (69–172), register of assumed names (173), classified list of handicaps (174–209), list of affiliated foreign and colonial associations *etc* (210), registered clubs (211–223), agreement to qualify for CA calendar fixture (224–225), calendar of fixtures (226–232), advertisements (*233–234*)

Binding: Very dark yellowish Green (138) pebble grain cloth over and bordering the spine, overlapped by light greenish Grey (154) paper over stiff boards, sewn. There are advertisements on all pages of the endpapers. FC: printed in moderate olive Green (125) (THE | CROQUET ASSOCIATION, | 1914.). RC: publisher's device printed in dark Green (146) at lower R. Spine: gold-blocked across the head (C.A. | [rule] | 1914)

Copy seen: CA (imperfect)

Fingerprint: C.s. n.he m.as GaMa 3 1914A [group 1 taken from p *3*, the third and fourth characters of group 1 in gothic-revival script]

Notes: Printed by The Holmesdale Press, Redhill Junction and London, issued free to Associates.

(m) *1915 edition (1915)*

[Heading, p *1*]

1915. | [rule] | [in display script] **The Croquet Association.** | [double rule]

Formula: [1–14⁸ 15⁴]. 116 leaves including the front and rear pastedowns, pp *i–iv*, *1–3 4–22 23 24–223 224–228*. The copy examined was specially bound for official use with extra interleaved pages for notes. The extra leaves are here discounted

Technical notes: 166 × 97 mm (p 21). 38 lines, 20 = 89 mm. Leaf size 206 × 136 mm; thickness 0.17 mm; laid, watermarked (Oceana Fine | Ledger | [heraldic device]), smooth, white

Contents: Glued to the FC (*i*), advertisements (*ii–iv*), title heading and contents (*1*), advertisement (*2*), Council *etc* (*3*), committees (4), the Association Handicapper (5), official referees (5–6), official handicappers (6–7), official managers (7–8), official referees, handicappers and managers (8), rules of the CA (9–16), standing orders of the Council (17–22), the laws of croquet (*23–38*), regulations for prize meetings (*39–49*), decisions on points in the laws of croquet (50), etiquette (51), challenge prizes (52), winners of the principal events (53–71), advantages of membership (72), official handicap list: Associates (73–172), classified list of handicaps (173–207), list of affiliated foreign and colonial associations *etc* (208), registered clubs (209–221), agreement to qualify for CA calendar fixture (222–223), advertisements (*224–227*), name of printer (*227*), glued to the RC (*228*)

Binding: Dark greyish olive Green (128) ribbed-morocco grain cloth over and bordering the spine, overlapped by light olive Grey (112) paper over stiff boards, sewn, no endpapers. FC: printed in dark olive Green (126) (THE | CROQUET ASSOCIATION, | 1915.). RC: blank. Spine: gold-blocked across the head (C.A. | [rule] | 1915)

Copy seen: CA (imperfect)

Fingerprint: /.s. n.he m.as GaMa 3 1915A [group 1 taken from p *3*, the third and fourth characters of group 1 in gothic-revival script]

Notes: Printed by The Holmesdale Press, Redhill and London, issued free to Associates.

(n) *1920 edition (1920)*

[Heading, p *1*]

1920. | [rule] | [in display script] **The Croquet Association.** | [double rule]

Formula: [1–10⁸]. 80 leaves including the rear pastedown, pp *1–3 4–19 20 21–156 157–160*. The copy examined was specially bound for official use with extra interleaved pages for notes. The extra leaves are here discounted

Technical notes: 165 × 101 mm (p 11). 48 lines, 20 = 70 mm. Leaf size 207 × 139 mm; thickness 0.17 mm; laid, watermarked (Oceana Fine | Ledger | [heraldic device]), rough, white

Contents: Title heading and contents (*1*), advertisement (2), Council *etc* (3), committees (4), the Association Handicapper (5), official referees (5–6), official handicappers (6–7), official managers (7), official referees, handicappers, and managers (8), rules of the CA (9–14), standing orders of the Council (15–19), the laws of croquet (*20–32*), regulations for prize meetings (33–42), decisions on points in the laws of croquet (heading only) (43), etiquette (44), challenge prizes (45), winners of the principal events (46–63), advantages of membership (64), official handicap list: Associates (65–136), register of assumed names (137), list of affiliated foreign and colonial associations *etc* (138), registered clubs (139–150), agreement to qualify for CA calendar fixture (151–152), calendar fixtures (153–156), advertisements (*157–159*), glued to the RC (*160*)

Binding: Dark greyish olive Green (128) pebble grain cloth over and bordering the spine, overlapped by light olive Grey (112) embossed linen grain paper over stiff boards, sewn. There are advertisements on all pages of the front endpaper. No rear endpaper. FC: printed in dark olive Green (126) (THE | CROQUET ASSOCIATION, | 1920.). RC: blank. Spine: gold-blocked upwards (C. A. YEAR BOOK 1920.)

Copy seen: CA (imperfect)

Fingerprint: 1.s. s;e- y.es SeCH 3 1920A [group 1 taken from p 3, the third and fourth characters of group 1 in gothic-revival script]

Notes: Printed anonymously, apparently by the Holmesdale Press, issued free to Associates.

(o) *1921 edition (1921)*

[Heading, p 5]

[in gothic-revival script] **The Croquet Association.** | [double rule]

Formula: [1–6⁸]. 48 leaves, pp *1–6 7–94 95–96.* The copy examined was specially bound for official use with extra interleaved pages for notes. The extra leaves are here discounted

Technical notes: 172 × 109 mm (p 13). 61 lines, 20 = 56 mm. Leaf size 211 × 136 mm; thickness 0.15 mm; laid, watermarked (Three Crowns | Ledger | [heraldic device with crowns]), smooth, white

Contents: Blank (*1*), advertisements (*2–4*), title heading and contents (*5*), advertisement (*6*), Council *etc* (*7*), committees (*8*), the Association Handicapper and official referees (*9*), official handicappers (*10*), official managers (*10–11*), official referees, handicappers, and managers (*11*), rules of the CA (*12–15*), standing orders of the Council (*16–18*), the laws of croquet (*19–32*), regulations for prize meetings (*33–43*), etiquette (*44–45*), advantages of membership (*46*), agreement to qualify for CA calendar fixture (*47–48*), challenge prizes (*49*), winners of the principal events (*50–61*), list of Associates with their handicaps (*62–88*), registered clubs (*89–93*), list of affiliated foreign and colonial associations *etc* (*94*), notes (heading only) (*95*), advertisements and name of printer (*96*)

Binding: Dark Red (16) ribbed-morocco grain cloth over and bordering the spine, overlapped by light olive Grey (112) embossed linen grain paper over stiff boards, sewn. FC: printed in dark olive Green (126) ([in gothic-revival script] The | [*do*] Croquet Association, | [*do*] 1921.). RC: blank. Spine: apparently blank (part of the spine of the copy examined is obscured by a stick-on label)

Copy seen: CA (imperfect)

Fingerprint: 1.s. y.Y, r.oa atli 7 1921A [groups 1–4 taken from pp 7, 15, 17, 18 respectively]

Notes: Printed by Roffey & Clark, Croydon, issued free to Associates.

(p) *1922 edition (1922)*

[Heading, p 5]

[in gothic-revival script] **The Croquet Association.** | [double rule]

Formula: [1–6⁸ 7²]. 50 leaves, pp *1–7 8–15 16 17–29 30 31–42 43 44–97 98–100.* The copy examined was specially bound for official use with extra interleaved pages for notes. The extra leaves are here discounted

Technical notes: 169 × 109 mm (p 13). 61 lines, 20 = 56 mm. Leaf size 211 × 138 mm; thickness 0.16 mm; laid, watermarked (James Spicer & Sons | London | [heraldic device]), rough, white

Contents: Blank (*1*), advertisements (*2–4*), title heading and contents (*5*), advertisement (*6*), Council *etc* (*7*), committees (*8*), the Association Handicapper and official referees (*9*), official handicappers (*10*), official managers (*10–11*), official referees, handicappers, and managers (*11*), rules of the CA (*12–15*), the laws of croquet (*16–29*), regulations for prize meetings (*30–42*), etiquette (*43–44*), advantages of membership (*45*), agreement to qualify for CA calendar fixture (*46–47*), challenge prizes (*48*), winners of the principal events (*49–62*), list of Associates with their handicaps (*63–91*), registered clubs (*92–96*), list of affiliated foreign and colonial associations *etc* (*97*), advertisement and name of printer (*98*), advertisement (*99*), blank (*100*)

Binding: Dark Red (16) morocco grain cloth over and bordering the spine, overlapped by light olive Grey (112) embossed linen grain paper over stiff boards, sewn. FC: printed in dark olive Green (126) ([in gothic-revival script] The | [*do*] Croquet Association, | [*do*] 1922.). RC: blank. Spine: apparently blank (part of the spine of the copy examined is obscured by a stick-on label)

Copy seen: CA (imperfect)

Fingerprint: 1.*s*: *y*.Y, meom aynd C 1922A [groups 1–4 taken from pp 7, 15, 17, 17 respectively]

Notes: Printed by Roffey & Clark, Croydon, issued free to Associates.

(q) *1923 edition (1923)*

[Heading, p 5]

[in gothic-revival script] **The Croquet Association.** | [double rule]

Formula: [1–6⁸ 7²(7₁+χ1)]. 51 leaves, pp *1–7* 8–15 *16* 17–29 *30* 31–42 *43* 44–99 *100–102*. The copy examined was specially bound for official use with extra interleaved pages for notes. The extra leaves are here discounted

Technical notes: 169 × 110 mm (p 13). 61 lines, 20 = 56 mm Leaf size 206 × 132 mm; thickness 0.17 mm; laid, watermarked (JAMES SPICER & SONS | LONDON | [heraldic device]), rough, white

Contents: Blank (*1*), advertisements (*2–4*), title heading and contents (*5*), advertisement (*6*), Council *etc* (*7*), committees (*8*), the Association Handicapper and official referees (*9*), official handicappers (*10*), official managers (*10–11*), official referees, handicappers, and managers (*11*), rules of the CA (*12–15*), the laws of croquet (*16–29*), regulations for prize meetings (*30–42*), etiquette (*43–44*), advantages of membership (*45*), agreement to qualify for CA calendar fixture (*46–47*), challenge prizes (*48*), winners of the principal events (*49–62*), list of Associates with their handicaps (*63–93*), registered clubs (*94–98*), list of affiliated foreign and colonial associations *etc* (*99*), advertisement and name of printer (*100*), advertisement (*101*), blank (*102*)

Binding: Dark Red (16) morocco grain cloth over and bordering the spine, overlapped by light greenish Grey (154) embossed linen grain paper over stiff boards, sewn. FC: printed in dark olive Green (126) ([in gothic-revival script] The | [*do*] Croquet Association | [*do*] 1923.). RC: blank. Spine: apparently blank (part of the spine of the copy examined is obscured by a stick-on label)

Copy seen: CA (imperfect)

Fingerprint: 1.*s*: *y*.Y, meom aynd C 1923A [groups 1–4 taken from pp 7, 15, 17, 17 respectively]

Notes: Printed by Roffey & Clark, Croydon, issued free to Associates.

(r) *1924 edition (1924)*

[Heading, p 5]

[in gothic-revival script] **The Croquet Association.** | [double rule]

Formula: [1–6⁸ 7⁴]. 52 leaves, pp *1–10* 11–17 *18* 19–30 *31* 32–43 *44* 45–101 *102–104*. The copy examined was specially bound for official use with extra interleaved pages for notes. The extra leaves are here discounted

Technical notes: 172 × 109 mm (p 15). 62 lines, 20 = 56 mm. Leaf size 206 × 131 mm; thickness 0.14 mm; laid, watermarked (THREE CROWNS | LEDGER | [heraldic device with crowns]), rough, white

Contents: Blank (*1*), advertisements (*2–4*), title heading and contents (*5*), advertisement (*6*), former President, Vice-Presidents, Chairmen, and Vice-Chairmen of Council (*7*), advertisement (*8*), Council *etc* (*9*), committees (*10*), the Association Handicapper and official referees (11), official handicappers (12), official managers (12–13), official referees, handicappers, and managers (13), rules of the CA (14–17), the laws of croquet (*18–30*), regulations for prize meetings (*31–43*), etiquette (*44–45*), advantages of membership (46), agreement to qualify for CA calendar fixture (47–48), challenge prizes (49), winners of the principal events (50–63), list of Associates with their handicaps (64–95), registered clubs (96–100), list of affiliated foreign and colonial associations *etc* (101), advertisement and name of printer (*102*), advertisement (*103*), blank (*104*)

Binding: Dark Red (16) morocco grain cloth over and bordering the spine, over-lapped by light olive Grey (112) embossed linen grain paper over stiff boards, sewn. FC: printed in dark olive Green (126) ([in gothic-revival script] The | [*do*] Croquet Association | [*do*] 1924.). RC: blank. Spine: apparently blank (part of the spine of the copy examined is obscured by a stick-on label)

Copy seen: CA (imperfect)

Fingerprint: 2220 g.ed *y*.Y, grwh 7 1924A [group 1 taken from p 7]

Notes: Printed by Roffey & Clark, Croydon, issued free to Associates.

(s) *1925 edition (1925)*

[Heading, p 5]

[in gothic-revival script] **The Croquet Association.** | [double rule]

Formula: [1–6⁸ 7⁴ 8²]. 54 leaves including the front pastedown, pp *1–10* 11–17 *18* 19–32 *33* 34–46 *47* 48–106 *107–108*. The copy examined was specially bound for official use with extra interleaved pages for notes. The extra leaves are here discounted

Technical notes: 170 × 110 mm (p 15). 61 lines, 20 = 56 mm. Leaf size 206 × 129 mm; thickness 0.15 mm; laid, watermarked ([in a convex arc] CONQUEROR | LONDON | [heraldic device]), smooth, white

Contents: Glued to the FC (*1*), advertisements (*2–4*), title heading and contents (*5*), advertisement (*6*), former President, Vice-Presidents, Chairmen, and Vice-Chairmen of Council (*7*), advertisement (*8*), Council *etc* (*9*), committees (*10*), official list of managers (11), official list of referees (11–12), official list of handicappers (12), managers, referees, and handicappers (13), rules of the CA (14–17), the laws of croquet (*18–32*), regulations for official tournaments (*33–46*), etiquette (*47*), advantages of membership (48), agreement to qualify for official tournament (49), challenge trophies, medals, and other prizes (50–52), winners of CA events (53–67), list of Associates with their handicaps (68–100), registered clubs (101–105), list of affiliated foreign and colonial associations *etc* (106), advertisement (*107*), name of printer (*108*)

Binding: Dark Red (16) ribbed-morocco grain cloth over and bordering the spine, overlapped by light olive Grey (112) embossed linen grain paper over stiff boards, sewn. FC: printed in dark olive Green (126) ([in gothic-revival script] The | [*do*] Croquet Association, | [*do*] 1925.). RC: blank. Spine: apparently blank (part of the spine of the copy examined is obscured by a stick-on label)

Copy seen: CA (imperfect)

Fingerprint: 2422 g.ed *y*.Y, grwh 7 1925A [group 1 taken from p 7]

Notes: Printed by Roffey & Clark, Croydon, issued free to Associates.

(t) *1926 edition (1926)*

[Heading, p 5]

[in gothic-revival script] **The Croquet Association.** | [double rule]

Formula: [1–7^8 8^2]. 58 leaves, pp *1–11* 12–20 *21* 22–37 *38* 39–50 *51–52* 53–73 *74* 75–114 *115–116* (misprinting 26 as '6'). The copy examined was specially bound for official use with extra interleaved pages for notes. The extra leaves are here discounted

Technical notes: 168 × 110 mm (p 17). 60 lines, 20 = 56 mm. Leaf size 204 × 134 mm; thickness 0.16 mm; laid, watermarked ([in a convex arc] Conqueror | London | [heraldic device]), smooth, white

Contents: Blank (*1*), advertisements (*2–4*), publishing details (*4*), title heading and contents (*5*), advertisement (*6*), former President, Vice-Presidents, Chairmen, and Vice-Chairmen of Council (*7*), advertisement (*8*), Council *etc* (*9*), committees (*10*), official list of managers (*11*), official list of referees (*11–12*), official list of handicappers (*12*), managers, referees, and handicappers (*13*), rules of the CA (*14–18*), standing orders of the Council (*19–20*), the laws of croquet (*21–37*), regulations for official tournaments (*38–50*), etiquette (*51*), referees and umpires (*52–53*), advantages of membership (*54*), agreement to qualify for official tournament (*55*), challenge trophies, medals, and other prizes (*56–58*), winners of CA events (*59–74*), list of Associates with their handicaps (*75–108*), registered clubs (*109–113*), list of affiliated foreign and colonial associations *etc* (*114*), advertisement (*115*), blank (*116*)

Binding: Dark Red (16) morocco grain cloth over and bordering the spine, overlapped by light olive Grey (112) embossed linen grain paper over stiff boards, sewn. FC: printed in dark olive Green (126) ([in gothic-revival script] The | [*do*] Croquet Association | [*do*] 1926.). RC: blank. Spine: apparently blank (part of the spine of the copy examined is obscured by a stick-on label)

Copy seen: CA (imperfect)

Fingerprint: 2422 r.an n.b- *Se*CH 7 1926A [group 1 taken from p 7]

Notes: Printed by Roffey & Clark, Croydon, issued free to Associates.

(u) *1928 edition (1928)*

[Heading, p 5]

[in gothic-revival script] **The Croquet Association.** | [double rule]

Formula: [1–7^8 8^2]. 58 leaves including the front pastedown, pp *1–10* 11–21 *22* 23–35 *36–37* 38–51 *52* 53–55 *56* 57–58 *59* 60–116. The copy examined was specially bound for official use with extra interleaved pages for notes. The extra leaves are here discounted

Technical notes: 170 × 111 mm (p 17). 61 lines, 20 = 56 mm. Leaf size 212 × 132 mm;

thickness 0.15 mm; laid, watermarked (PENTLAND | LEDGER | [heraldic device]), smooth, white

Contents: Glued to the FC (*1*), advertisements (*2–4*), publishing details (*4*), title heading and contents (5), advertisement (6), former President, Vice-Presidents, Chairmen, and Vice-Chairmen of Council (7), advertisement (8), Council *etc* (9), committees (*10*), official list of managers (11), official list of referees (11–12), official list of handicappers (12), managers, referees, and handicappers (13), rules of the CA (14–18), standing orders of the Council (19–21), the laws of croquet (*22–35*), etiquette (*36*), regulations for official tournaments (*37–53*), advantages of membership (*54*), agreement to qualify for official tournament (*55*), challenge trophies, medals, and other prizes (*56–58*), winners of CA events (*59–76*), list of Associates with their handicaps (*77–110*), county croquet unions (*111*), registered clubs (*111–115*), list of affiliated overseas associations *etc* (*116*)

Binding: Dark Red (16) morocco grain cloth over and bordering the spine, overlapped by light olive Grey (112) embossed linen grain paper over stiff boards, sewn. No front endpaper. In the copy examined there is an advertisement on a disjunct leaf glued over the rear pastedown. FC: printed in dark olive Green (126) ([in gothic-revival script] The | [*do*] Croquet Association | [*do*] 1928.). RC: blank. Spine: apparently blank (part of the spine of the copy examined is obscured by a stick-on label)

Copy seen: CA (imperfect)

Fingerprint: 2624 r.an n.b- *Se*CH 7 1928A [group 1 taken from p 7]

Notes: Printed by Roffey & Clark, Croydon, issued free to Associates.

(v) *1929 edition (1929)*

[Heading, p 5]

[in gothic-revival script] **The Croquet Association.** | [double rule]

Formula: [1–7⁸ χ1 9²]. 59 leaves including the front and rear pastedowns, pp *1–11* 12–21 22 23–35 *36–37* 38–51 52 53–116 *117–118*. The copy examined was specially bound for official use with extra interleaved pages for notes. The extra leaves are here discounted

Technical notes: 171 × 110 mm (p 21). 61 lines, 20 = 56 mm. Leaf size 208 × 136 mm; thickness 0.15 mm; laid, watermarked (CROXLEY | LION LEDGER | [heraldic device]), smooth, white

Contents: Glued to the FC (*1*), advertisements (*2–4*), publishing details (*4*), title heading and contents (5), advertisement (6), former President, Vice-Presidents, Chairmen, and Vice-Chairmen of Council (7), advertisement (8), Council *etc* (9), committees (*10*), official list of managers (*11*), official list of referees (11–12), official list of handicappers (12), managers, referees, and handicappers (13), rules of the CA (14–18), standing orders of the Council (19–21), the laws of croquet (*22–35*), etiquette (*36*), regulations for official tournaments (*37–53*), advantages of membership (*54*), agreement to qualify for official tournament (*55*), challenge trophies, medals, and other prizes (*56–58*), winners of CA events (*59–77*), list of Associates with their handicaps (*78–111*), county croquet unions (*112*), registered clubs (*112–115*), list of affiliated overseas associations *etc* (*116*), advertisement (*117*), glued to the RC (*118*)

Binding: Dark Red (16) morocco grain cloth over and bordering the spine, over-lapped by light olive Grey (112) embossed linen grain paper over stiff boards, sewn, no endpapers. FC: printed in dark olive Green (126) ([in gothic-revival script] The | [*do*] Croquet Association | [*do*] 1929.). RC: blank. Spine: apparently blank (part of the spine of the copy examined is obscured by a stick-on label)

Copy seen: CA (imperfect)

Fingerprint: 2826 l.ng r.he *Se*CH 7 1929A [group 1 taken from p 7]

Notes: Printed by Roffey & Clark, Croydon, issued free to Associates.

(w) *1930 edition (1930)*

[Heading, p 5]

[in gothic-revival script] **The Croquet Association.** | [double rule]

Formula: [1–8⁸]. 64 leaves including the front and rear pastedowns, pp *1–10* 11–123 *124–128*. The copy examined was specially bound for official use with extra inter-leaved pages for notes. The extra leaves are here discounted

Technical notes: 167 × 109 mm (p 15). 60 lines, 20 = 56 mm. Leaf size 206 × 135 mm; thickness 0.18 mm; laid, watermarked (CROXLEY | LION LEDGER | [heraldic device]), rough, white

Contents: Glued to the FC (*1*), advertisements (*2–4*), publishing details (*4*), title heading and contents (*5*), advertisement (*6*), former President, Vice-Presidents, Chairmen, and Vice-Chairmen of Council (*7*), advertisement (*8*), Council *etc* (*9*), committees (*10*), official list of managers (*11*), official list of referees (*11–12*), official list of handicappers (*12*), managers, referees, and handicappers (*13*), rules of the CA (*14–19*), standing orders of the Council (*20–22*), the laws of croquet (*23–36*), etiquette (*37–38*), regulations for official tournaments (*39–56*), advantages of membership (*57*), agreement to qualify for official tournament (*58*), challenge trophies, medals, and other prizes (*59–61*), winners of CA events (*62–81*), list of Associates with their handicaps (*82–116*), county croquet unions (*117*), registered clubs (*117–122*), list of affiliated overseas associations *etc* (*123*), advertisement (*124*), blank (*125–127*), glued to the RC (*128*)

Binding: Dark Red (16) morocco grain cloth over and bordering the spine, over-lapped by light olive Grey (112) embossed linen grain paper over stiff boards, sewn, no endpapers. FC: printed in dark olive Green (126) ([in gothic-revival script] The | [*do*] Croquet Association | [*do*] 1930.). RC: blank. Spine: apparently blank (part of the spine of the copy examined was obscured by a stick-on label)

Copy seen: CA (imperfect)

Fingerprint: 2826 l.ng y.ly ceAn 7 1930A [group 1 taken from p 7]

Notes: Printed by Roffey & Clark, Croydon, issued free to Associates.

(x) *1931 edition (1931)*

[Heading, p 5]

[in gothic-revival script] **The Croquet Association.** | [double rule]

Formula: [1–7⁸ 8⁴ 9⁴(–9₁)]. 63 leaves including the front and rear pastedowns, pp *1–10* 11–124 *125–126*. The copy examined was specially bound for official use with extra interleaved pages for notes. The extra leaves are here discounted

Technical notes: 168 × 109 mm (p 15). 60 lines, 20 = 56 mm. Leaf size 207 × 134 mm; thickness 0.15 mm; laid, watermarked (CROXLEY | LION LEDGER | [heraldic device]), rough, white

Contents: Glued to the FC (*1*), advertisements (*2–4*), publishing details (*4*), title heading and contents (*5*), advertisement (*6*), former President, Vice-Presidents, Chairmen, and Vice-Chairmen of Council (*7*), advertisement (*8*), Council *etc* (*9*), committees (*10*), official list of managers (*11*), official list of referees (*11–12*), official list of handicappers (*12*), managers, referees, and handicappers (*13*), rules of the CA (*14–19*), standing orders of the Council (*20–22*), croquet — a simple synopsis (*23*), the laws of croquet (24–38), etiquette (39–40), regulations for official tournaments (41–58), advantages of membership (59), agreement to qualify for official tournament (60), challenge trophies, medals, and other prizes (61–63), winners of CA events (64–83), list of Associates with their handicaps (84–117), county croquet unions (118), registered clubs (118–123), list of affiliated overseas associations *etc* (124), advertisement (*125*), glued to the RC (*126*)

Binding: Dark Red (16) morocco grain cloth over and bordering the spine, overlapped by light olive Grey (112) embossed linen grain paper over stiff boards, sewn, no endpapers. FC: printed in olive Green (126) ([in gothic-revival script] The | [*do*] Croquet Association | [*do*] 1931.). RC: blank. Spine: apparently blank (part of the spine of the copy examined is obscured by a stick-on label)

Copy seen: CA (imperfect)

Fingerprint: 3028 l.ng y.ly ceAn 7 1931A [group 1 taken from p 7]

Notes: Printed by Roffey & Clark, Croydon, issued free to Associates.

(y) *1932 edition (1932)*

[Heading, p 5]

[in gothic-revival script] **The Croquet Association.** | [double rule]

Formula: [1–8⁸]. 64 leaves including the front pastedown, pp *1–10* 11–127 *128*. The copy examined was specially bound for official use with extra interleaved pages for notes. The extra leaves are here discounted

Technical notes: 171 × 109 mm (p 15). 61 lines, 20 = 56 mm. Leaf size 210 × 137 mm; thickness 0.13 mm; laid, watermarked (Lerryn | Extra Strong | [heraldic device]), smooth, white.

Contents: Glued to the FC (*1*), advertisements (*2–4*), publishing details (*4*), title heading and contents (*5*), advertisement (*6*), former President, Vice-Presidents, Chairmen, and Vice-Chairmen of Council (*7*), advertisement (*8*), Council *etc* (*9*), committees (*10*), official list of managers (11), official list of referees (11–12), official list of handicappers (12), managers, referees, and handicappers (13), rules of the CA (14–19), standing orders of the Council (20–22), croquet — a simple synopsis (23), the laws of croquet (24–40), etiquette (41–42), regulations for official tournaments (43–60), advantages of membership (61), agreement to qualify for official tournament (62), challenge trophies, medals, and other prizes (63–65), winners of CA events (66–87), list of Associates with their handicaps (88–120), county croquet unions (121), registered clubs (121–126), list of affiliated overseas associations *etc* (127), blank (*128*)

Binding: Dark Red (16) morocco grain cloth over and bordering the spine, overlapped by light olive Grey (112) embossed linen grain paper over stiff boards, sewn. No endpapers. In the copy examined there is an advertisement on a disjunct pastedown glued to the RC. FC: printed in dark olive Green (126) ([in gothic-revival script] The | [*do*] Croquet Association | [*do*] 1932.). RC: blank. Spine: apparently blank (part of the spine of the copy examined is obscured by a stick-on label)

Copy seen: CA (imperfect)

Fingerprint: 3028 l.ng y.ly ceAn 7 1932A [group 1 taken from p 7]

Notes: Printed by Roffey & Clark, Croydon, issued free to Associates.

(z) *1933 edition (1933)*

[Heading, p 5]

[in gothic-revival script] **The Croquet Association.** | [double rule]

Formula: [1–8⁸ χ1]. 65 leaves, pp *1–10* 11–127 *128–130*. The copy examined was specially bound for official use with extra interleaved pages for notes. The extra leaves are here discounted

Technical notes: 172 × 109 mm (p 15). 62 lines, 20 = 56 mm. Leaf size 213 × 135 mm; thickness 0.15 mm; laid, watermarked ([in a convex arc] Conqueror | London | [heraldic device]), rough, white

Contents: Blank (*1*), advertisements (*2–4*), publishing details (*4*), title heading and contents (*5*), advertisement (*6*), former President, Vice-Presidents, Chairmen, and Vice-Chairmen of Council (*7*), advertisement (*8*), Council *etc* (*9*), committees (*10*), official list of managers (11), official list of referees (11–12), official list of handi-cappers (12), managers, referees, and handicappers (13), rules of the CA (14–19), standing orders of the Council (20–22), croquet — a simple synopsis (23), the laws of croquet (24–40), etiquette (41–42), regulations for official tournaments (43–60), advantages of membership (61), agreement to qualify for official tournament (62), challenge trophies, medals, and other prizes (63–65), winners of CA events (66–87), list of Associates with their handicaps (88–120), county croquet unions (121), registered clubs (121–126), list of affiliated overseas associations *etc* (127), blank (*128*), advertisement (*129*), blank (*130*)

Binding: Dark Red (16) morocco grain cloth over and bordering the spine, over-lapped by light olive Grey (112) embossed linen grain paper over stiff boards, sewn. FC: printed in dark olive Green (126) ([in gothic-revival script] The | [*do*] Croquet Association | [*do*] 1933.). RC: blank. Spine: blank

Copy seen: CA (imperfect)

Fingerprint: 3230 n.of y.he of31 7 1933A [group 1 taken from p 7]

Notes: Printed by Roffey & Clark, Croydon, issued free to Associates.

(aa) *1934 edition (1934)*

[Heading, p 5]

[in gothic-revival script] **The Croquet Association.** | [double rule]

Note: The copy examined had apparently been specially bound for official use with extra lined leaves for notes. The extra leaves were discounted in compiling the notes which follow.

Formula: [1–8⁸ 9⁴]. 68 leaves, pp *1–10* 11–133 *134–136*

Technical notes: 172 × 110 mm (p 15). 62 lines, 20 = 56 mm. Leaf size 201 × 135 mm; thickness 0.15 mm; laid, watermarked ([in a convex arc] Conqueror | London | [heraldic device]), rough, white

Contents: Blank (*1*), advertisements (*2–4*), publishing details (*4*), title heading and contents (*5*), advertisement (*6*), former Presidents, Vice-Presidents, Chairmen, and Vice-Chairmen of Council (*7*), advertisement (*8*), Council *etc* (*9*), committees (*10*), official list of managers (11), official list of referees (11–12), official list of handi-cappers (12), managers, referees, and handicappers (13), rules of the CA (14–19), standing orders of the Council (20–22), croquet — a simple synopsis (23), the laws of croquet (24–41), etiquette (42–43), regulations for official tournaments (44–61), decisions on points in the laws of croquet (62–64), laws of golf-croquet (65–66), advantages of membership (67), agreement to qualify for official tournament (68), challenge trophies, medals, and other prizes (69–71), winners of CA events (72–95), list of Associates with their handicaps (96–126), county croquet unions (127), reg-istered clubs (127–132), list of affiliated overseas associations *etc* (133), blank (*134*), advertisement (*135*), blank (*136*)

Binding: Dark Red (16) morocco grain cloth over and bordering the spine, over-lapped by light olive Grey (112) embossed linen grain paper over stiff boards, sewn. FC: printed in dark olive Green (126) ([in gothic-revival script] The | [*do*] Croquet Association | [*do*] 1934.). RC: blank. Spine: blank

Copy seen: CA (imperfect)

Fingerprint: 3332 n.ll y.he of31 7 1934A [group 1 taken from p 7]

Notes: Printed by Roffey & Clark, Croydon, issued free to Associates.

(bb) *1935 edition (1935)*

[Heading, p 5]

[in gothic-revival script] **The Croquet Association.** | [double rule]

Note: The copy examined had apparently been specially bound for official use with extra lined leaves for notes. The extra leaves were discounted in compiling the notes which follow.

Formula: [1–8⁸ 9⁴]. 68 leaves including the front and rear pastedowns, pp *1–10* 11–133 *134–136*

Technical notes: 172 × 110 mm (p 15). 62 lines, 20 = 56 mm. Leaf size 212 × 135 mm; thickness 0.17 mm; laid, watermarked ([in convex arc] CONQUEROR | LONDON | [heraldic device]), rough, white

Contents: Glued to the FC (*1*), advertisements (*2–4*), publishing details (*4*), title heading and contents (*5*), advertisement (*6*), former Presidents, Vice-Presidents, Chairmen, and Vice-Chairmen of Council (*7*), advertisement (*8*), Council *etc* (*9*), committees (*10*), official list of managers (*11*), official list of referees (*11–12*), official list of handicappers (*12*), managers, referees, and handicappers (*13*), rules of the CA (*14–19*), standing orders of the Council (*20–22*), croquet — a simple synopsis (*23*), the laws of croquet (*24–41*), etiquette (*42–43*), regulations for official tournaments (*44–61*), decisions on points in the laws of croquet (*62–64*), laws of golf-croquet (*65–66*), advantages of membership (*67*), agreement to qualify for official tournament (*68*), challenge trophies, medals, and other prizes (*69–71*), winners of CA events (*72–95*), list of Associates with their handicaps (*96–126*), county croquet unions (*127*), registered clubs (*127–132*), list of affiliated overseas associations *etc* (*133*), blank (*134*), advertisement (*135*), glued to the RC (*136*)

Binding: Dark Red (16) morocco grain cloth over and bordering the spine, over-lapped by light olive Grey (112) embossed linen grain paper over stiff boards, sewn. FC: printed in dark olive Green (126) ([in gothic-revival script] The | [*do*] Croquet Association | [*do*] 1935.). RC: blank. Spine: apparently blank (part of the spine of the copy examined is obscured by a stick-on label)

Copy seen: CA (imperfect)

Fingerprint: 3332 n.ll y.he stTh 7 1935A [group 1 taken from p 7]

Notes: Printed by Roffey & Clark, Croydon, issued free to Associates.

(cc) *1936 edition (1936)*

[Heading, p 5]

[in gothic-revival script] **The Croquet Association.** | [double rule]

Formula: [1⁸(–1₁) 2–8⁸ 9⁸(–9₇,₈)]. 69 leaves, pp *3–8* 9–95 *96* 97–127 *128, i–ii,* 129–137 *138* [=138]. The copy examined was specially bound for official use with extra interleaved pages for notes. The extra leaves are here discounted

Technical notes: 173 × 110 mm (p 15). 62 lines, 20 = 56 mm. Leaf size 201 × 130 mm;

thickness 0.15 mm; laid, watermarked ([in a convex arc] CONQUEROR | LONDON | [heraldic device]), rough, white

Contents: Advertisements *(3–4)*, publishing details *(4)*, title heading and contents (5), advertisement (6), former Presidents, Vice-Presidents, Chairmen, and Vice-Chairmen of Council (7), advertisement (8), Council *etc* (9), committees (10), official list of managers (11), official list of referees (11–12), official list of handicappers (12), managers, referees, and handicappers (13), rules of the CA (14–19), standing orders of the Council (20–22), croquet — a simple synopsis (23), the laws of croquet (24–41), etiquette (42–43), regulations for official tournaments (44–61), decisions on points in the laws of croquet (62–64), laws of golf-croquet (65–66), advantages of membership (67), agreement to qualify for official tournament (68), challenge trophies, medals, and other prizes (69–71), winners of CA events (72–95), blank *(96)*, list of Associates with their handicaps (97–127), blank *(128)*, advertisement *(i)*, blank *(ii)*, county croquet unions (129), registered clubs (129–134), list of affiliated overseas associations *etc* (135), the CA chess circle and contract bridge tournament (136), the CA golf meetings (137), blank *(138)*

Binding: Dark Red (16) morocco grain cloth over and bordering the spine, overlapped by light olive Grey (112) embossed linen grain paper over stiff boards, sewn. FC: printed in dark olive Green (126) ([in gothic-revival script] The | *[do]* Croquet Association | *[do]* 1936.). RC: blank. Spine: apparently blank (part of the spine of the copy examined is obscured by a stick-on label)

Copy seen: CA (imperfect)

Fingerprint: 3533 n.ll y.he stTh C 1936A [groups 1–4 taken from pp '7', '15', '17', '18' respectively]

Notes: Printed by Roffey & Clark, Croydon, issued free to Associates.

(dd) *1937 edition (1937)*

[Heading, p 5]

[in gothic-revival script] **The Croquet Association.** | [double rule]

Formula: [1–8⁸ 9⁸(–9₇,₈)]. 71 leaves including the front and rear pastedowns, pp *1–7* 8–129 *130* 131–139 *140–142*. The copy examined was specially bound for official use with extra interleaved pages for notes. The extra leaves are here discounted

Technical notes: 173 × 109 mm (p 15). 62 lines, 20 = 56 mm. Leaf size 202 × 135 mm; thickness 0.16 mm; laid, watermarked ([in open shaded script, in a convex arc as in perspective] DURAFORT), smooth, white, all edges speckled in dark Red (16)

Contents: Glued to the FC *(1)*, advertisements *(2–4)*, publishing details *(4)*, title heading and contents (5), advertisements (6–7), former Presidents, Vice-Presidents, Chairmen, and Vice-Chairmen of Council (8), Council *etc* (9), committees (10), official list of managers (11), official list of referees and umpires (11–12), official list of handicappers (12), managers, referees, and handicappers (13), rules of the CA (14–19), standing orders of the Council (20–21), croquet — a simple synopsis (22), the laws of croquet (23–42), etiquette (43–44), regulations for official tournaments (45–63), decisions on points in the laws of croquet (64–66), laws of golf-croquet (67–68), advantages of membership (69), agreement to qualify for official tournament (70), challenge trophies, medals, and other prizes (71–73), winners of CA events (74–98), list of Associates with their handicaps (99–129), blank *(130)*, county croquet unions (131), registered clubs (131–136), list of affiliated overseas associations *etc* (137), the CA chess circle and contract bridge tournament (138), the CA golf meetings (139), blank *(140)*, advertisement *(141)*, glued to the RC *(142)*

Binding: Dark Red (16) morocco grain cloth over and bordering the spine, over-lapped by light olive Grey (112) embossed linen grain paper over stiff boards, sewn. FC: printed in dark olive Green (126) ([in gothic-revival script] The | [*do*] Croquet Association | [*do*] 1937.). RC: blank. Spine: apparently blank (part of the spine of the copy examined is obscured by a stick-on label)

Copy seen: CA (imperfect)

Fingerprint: s..0 n.ll y.he stTh 7 1937A [groups 1–4 taken from pp 7, 15, 17, 18 respectively; the letterpress in a panel on p 7 is discounted]

Notes: Printed by Roffey & Clark, Croydon, issued free to Associates.

(ee) *1938 edition (1938)*

[Heading, p 7]

The Croquet Association | [double rule]

Formula: [1–9⁸ 10⁴]. 76 leaves including the pastedowns, pp *1–7* 8–23 *24–25* 26–42 [43–44] 45–150 *151–152*. The copy examined was specially bound for official use with extra interleaved pages for notes. The extra leaves are here discounted

Technical notes: 175 × 109 mm (p 15). 63 lines, 20 = 56 mm. Leaf size 207 × 139 mm; thickness 0.16 mm; laid, watermarked (GB | TUB SIZED | LEDGER), smooth, white, all edges speckled in dark Red (16)

Contents: Glued to the FC (*1*), advertisements (*2–4*), publishing details (*4*), advertisements (*5–6*), title heading and contents (*7*), former Presidents, Vice-Presidents, Chairmen, and Vice-Chairmen of Council (8), Council *etc* (9), committees (10), official list of managers (11), official list of referees (11–12), official list of handi-cappers (12), managers, referees, and handicappers (13), rules of the CA (14–19), standing orders of the Council (20–22), croquet — a simple synopsis (23), blank (*24*), the laws of croquet, continued (*25–42*), wanting from the copy examined ([43–44]), the laws of croquet, concluded (45–46), etiquette (47–48), regulations for official tournaments (49–67), decisions on points in the laws of croquet (68–70), laws of golf-croquet (71–77), advantages of membership (78), agreement to qualify for official tournament (79), challenge trophies, medals, and other prizes (80–82), winners of CA events (83–109), ranking lists (110), list of Associates with their handicaps (111–141), county croquet unions (142), registered clubs (142–147), list of affiliated overseas associations *etc* (148), the CA chess circle and contract bridge tournament (149), the CA golf meetings (150), advertisement (*151*), glued to the RC (*152*)

Binding: Dark Red (16) morocco grain cloth over and bordering the spine, over-lapped by light olive Grey (112) embossed linen grain paper over stiff boards, sewn. FC: printed in dark olive Green (126) (The | Croquet Association | 1938). RC: blank. Spine: apparently blank (part of the spine of the copy examined is obscured by a stick-on label)

Copy seen: CA (imperfect, wanting pp [43–44])

Fingerprint: 1.*s:* y.he 38T, BaBa C 1938A [groups 1–4 taken from pp 9, 17, 25, 26 respectively]

Notes: Printed by Roffey & Clark, Croydon, issued free to Associates.

(ff) *1939 edition (1939)*

[Heading, p 7]

THE CROQUET ASSOCIATION | [double rule]

Formula: [1–9⁸ 10⁶]. 78 leaves including the front pastedown, pp *1–7* 8–23 *24–25*

26–42 [43–44] 45–151 *152–156*. The copy examined was specially bound for official use with extra interleaved pages for notes. Except where otherwise indicated, the extra leaves are here discounted

Technical notes: 174 × 110 mm (p 15). 62 lines, 20 = 56 mm. Leaf size 203 × 137 mm; thickness 0.15 mm; laid, watermarked (GB | TUB SIZED | LEDGER), smooth, white, all edges speckled in very dark Red (17)

Contents: Glued to the FC (*1*), advertisements (*2–4*), publishing details (*4*), advertisements (*5–6*), title heading and contents (*7*), former Presidents, Vice-Presidents, Chairmen, and Vice-Chairmen of Council (*8*), Council *etc* (*9*), committees (*10*), official list of managers (*11*), official list of referees and umpires (*11–12*), official list of handicappers (*12*), managers, referees, and handicappers (*13*), rules of the CA (*14–19*), standing orders of the Council (*20–22*), croquet — a simple synopsis (*23*), advertisement (*24*), the laws of croquet, continued (*25–42*), wanting from the copy examined ([*43–44*]), the laws of croquet, concluded (*45–46*), etiquette (*47–48*), regulations for official tournaments (*49–67*), decisions on points in the laws of croquet (*68–70*), laws of golf-croquet (*71–78*), advantages of membership (*79*), agreement to qualify for official tournament (*80*), challenge trophies, medals, and other prizes (*81–83*), winners of CA events (*84–110*), ranking lists (*111*), list of Associates with their handicaps (*112–142*), county croquet unions (*143*), registered clubs (*143–148*), list of affiliated overseas associations *etc* (*149*), the CA chess circle and contract bridge tournament (*150*), the CA golf meetings (*151*), blank (*152*), advertisement (*153*), blank (*154–156*)

Binding: Dark Red (16) morocco grain cloth over and bordering the spine, overlapped by light olive Grey (112) embossed linen grain paper over heavy boards, sewn. In the copy examined the last extra leaf serves as the rear pastedown. FC: printed in dark olive Green (126) (The | Croquet Association | 1939). RC: blank. Spine: blank

Copy seen: CA (imperfect, wanting pp [43–44])

Fingerprint: 1.s: y.he 39T, BaBa C 1939A [groups 1–4 taken from pp 9, 17, 25, 26 respectively]

Notes: Printed by Roffey & Clark, Croydon, issued free to Associates.

(gg) *1948 edition (1948)*

[Heading, p *i*]

THE CROQUET ASSOCIATION | [double rule]

Formula: [1–4⁸ 5⁸(–5₂₋₆) 6⁸ 7⁶]. 49 leaves, pp *i* ii–xvi, 1–50, 61–91 92 [= 98]. The copy examined was specially bound for official use with extra interleaved pages for notes. The extra leaves are here discounted

Technical notes: 169 × 109 mm (p x). 61 lines, 20 = 56 mm. Leaf size 210 × 133 mm; thickness 0.17 mm; laid, watermarked ([in a convex arc] CONQUEROR | LONDON | [heraldic device]), smooth, white, all edges speckled in very dark Red (17)

Contents: Title and contents (*i*), former Presidents, Vice-Presidents, Chairmen, and Vice-Chairmen of Council (ii), Council *etc* (iii), committees (iv), official lists of managers and referees (v), official list of handicappers (vi), managers, referees, and handicappers (vi), rules of the CA (vii–xii), standing orders of the Council (xiii–xv), advertisement (xvi), the laws of croquet (1–18), etiquette (19), regulations for official tournaments (20–34), instructions to referees (35–36), decisions on points in the laws of croquet (37–38), laws of golf croquet (39–46), table of byes (47–48), advantages of membership (49), agreement to qualify for official tournament (50), winners of CA events (61–67), winners of international events and CA medallists

(68–71), rankings (71), list of Associates with their handicaps (72–87), county croquet unions (88), registered clubs (88–91), list of affiliated overseas associations *etc* (92), name of printer (92)

Binding: Very dark Red (17) morocco grain cloth over and bordering the spine, overlapped by light Grey (264) paper over stiff boards, sewn. FC: printed in dark greyish olive Green (128) (The | Croquet Association | 1948). RC: blank. Spine: blank

Copy seen: CA (imperfect)

Fingerprint: 1.s: d.n- g.ce shfo 3 1948A [group 1 taken from p iii]

Notes: Printed by Roffey & Clark, Croydon, price 2/6 to Associates.

(hh) *1949 edition (1949)*

YEAR BOOK | OF THE | CROQUET ASSOCIATION | 1949. | THE CROQUET ASSOCIATION, | 4, SOUTHAMPTON ROW, | W.C.1

Formula: [1–7⁸ χ1)]. 57 leaves, pp *i–ii* iii–xviii, 1–50 *51* 52–94 *95*–96. The copy examined was specially bound for official use with extra interleaved pages for notes. The extra leaves are here discounted

Technical notes: 171 × 110 mm (p xii). 61 lines, 20 = 56 mm. Leaf size 210 × 138 mm; thickness 0.13 mm; wove, unwatermarked, smooth, white

Contents: Title (*i*), blank (*ii*), contents (iii), former Presidents, Vice-Presidents, Chairmen, and Vice-Chairmen of Council (iv), Council *etc* (v), committees (vi), official lists of managers and referees (vii), official list of handicappers (viii), managers, referees, and handicappers (viii), rules of the CA (ix–xiv), standing orders of the Council (xv–xviii), the laws of association croquet (1–19), etiquette (20), regulations for official tournaments (21–35), instructions to referees (36–37), decisions on points in the laws of Association Croquet (38–39), laws of golf croquet (40–47), table of byes (48–49), advertisement (50), advantages of membership (*51*), agreement to qualify for official tournament (52), challenge trophies, medals, and other prizes (53–55), winners of CA events (56–70), winners of international events and CA medallists (71–74), rankings (74), list of Associates with their handicaps (75–90), county croquet unions (91), registered clubs (91–94), list of affiliated overseas associations *etc* (95), name of printer (95), blank (96)

Binding: Very dark Red (17) morocco grain cloth over and bordering the spine, overlapped by light Grey (264) paper over stiff boards, sewn. FC: printed in dark olive Green (126) (The | Croquet Association | 1949). RC: blank. Spine: blank

Copy seen: CA (imperfect)

Fingerprint: 95et l.n, o.or *Se*LO 3 1949A

Notes: Printed by Roffey & Clark, Croydon, price 2/6 to Associates.

(jj) *1950 edition (1950)*

YEAR BOOK | OF THE | CROQUET ASSOCIATION | 1950. | THE CROQUET ASSOCIATION, | 4, SOUTHAMPTON ROW, | W.C.1

Formula: [1–7⁸ χ1)]. 57 leaves, pp *i–ii* iii–xviii, 1–95 96. The copy examined was specially bound for official use with extra interleaved pages for notes. The extra leaves are here discounted

Technical notes: 170 × 110 mm (p xii). 61 lines, 20 = 56 mm. Leaf size 206 × 137 mm; thickness 0.13 mm; laid, watermark composed of lettering set in a design of folded ribbon (DARTMILL | BW | RIBBON), smooth, white, all edges speckled in dark Red (16)

Contents: Title (*i*), blank (*ii*), contents (iii), former Presidents, Vice-Presidents, Chairmen, and Vice-Chairmen of Council (iv), Council *etc* (v), committees (vi), official lists of managers and referees (vii), official list of handicappers (viii), managers, referees, and handicappers (viii), rules of the CA (ix–xiv), standing orders of the Council (xv–xviii), the laws of association croquet (1–19), etiquette (20), regulations for official tournaments (21–35), instructions to referees (36–37), decisions on points in the laws of Association Croquet (38–39), laws of golf croquet (40–47), table of byes (48–49), advertisement (50), advantages of membership (51), agreement to qualify for official tournament (52), challenge trophies, medals, and other prizes (53–55), winners of CA events (56–71), winners of international events and CA medallists (72–75), list of Associates with their handicaps (76–91), registered clubs (92–95), list of affiliated overseas associations *etc* (96), name of printer (96)

Binding: Dark Red (16) morocco grain cloth over and bordering the spine, over-lapped by light olive Grey (112) paper over stiff boards, sewn. FC: printed in dark olive Green (126) (The | Croquet Association | 1950). RC: blank. Spine: blank

Copy seen: CA (imperfect)

Fingerprint: 96et l.n, o.or *Se*LO 3 1950A

Notes: Printed by Roffey & Clark, Croydon, price 3/6 to Associates.

(kk) *1951 edition (1951)*

YEAR BOOK | OF THE | CROQUET ASSOCIATION | 1951. | THE CROQUET ASSOCIATION, | 4, SOUTHAMPTON ROW, | W.C.1

Formula: [1–6⁸ 7¹⁰]. 58 leaves, pp *i–ii* iii–xviii, 1–2 3 4–97 98. The copy examined was specially bound for official use with extra interleaved pages for notes. The extra leaves are here discounted

Technical notes: 173 × 110 mm (p x). 62 lines, 20 = 56 mm. Leaf size 207 × 137 mm; thickness 0.16 mm; laid, watermarked (IMPERATOR | LEDGER | [heraldic device]), smooth, white

Contents: Title (*i*), blank (*ii*), contents (iii), former Presidents, Vice-Presidents, Chairmen, and Vice-Chairmen of Council (iv), Council *etc* (v), committees (vi), official lists of managers and referees (vii), official list of handicappers (viii), managers, referees, and handicappers (viii), rules of the CA (ix–xiv), standing orders of the Council (xv–xviii), the laws of association croquet (1–19), etiquette (20), regulations for official tournaments (21–35), instructions to referees (36–37), decisions on points in the laws of Association Croquet (38–39), laws of golf croquet (40–47), table of byes (48–49), advertisement (50), advantages of membership (51), agreement to qualify for official tournament (52), challenge trophies, medals, and other prizes (53–55), winners of CA events (56–71), winners of international events and CA medallists (72–75), list of Associates with their handicaps (76–92), registered clubs (93–97), list of affiliated overseas associations *etc* (98), name of printer (98)

Binding: Dark Red (16) morocco grain cloth over and bordering the spine, over-lapped by light Grey (264) paper over stiff boards, sewn. FC: printed in dark olive Green (126) (The | Croquet Association | 1951). RC: blank. Spine: blank

Copy seen: CA (imperfect)

Fingerprint: 98et s.a- o.or *Se*LO 3 1951A

Notes: Printed by Roffey & Clark, Croydon, price 3/6 to Associates.

(ll) *1953 edition (1953)*

YEAR BOOK | OF THE | CROQUET ASSOCIATION | 1953. | THE CROQUET ASSOCIATION, | 4, SOUTHAMPTON ROW, | W.C.1

Formula: [1–4⁸ χ1]. 33 leaves, pp *1–2* 3–65 *66*. The copy examined was specially bound for official use with extra interleaved pages for notes. The extra leaves are here discounted

Technical notes: 173 × 110 mm (p 10). 62 lines, 20 = 56 mm. Leaf size 210 × 139 mm; thickness 0.14 mm; laid, watermarked ([in open shaded script, in a convex arc as in perspective] DURAFORT), smooth, white, all edges speckled in dark Red (16)

Contents: Title (*1*), blank (*2*), contents (*3*), former Presidents, Vice-Presidents, Chairmen, and Vice-Chairmen of Council (*4*), Council *etc* (*5*), committees (*6*), official lists of managers and referees (*7*), official list of handicappers (*8*), managers, referees, and handicappers (*8*), rules of the CA (*9–14*), standing orders of the Council (*15–18*), advantages of membership (*19*), agreement to qualify for official tournament (*20*), challenge trophies, medals, and other prizes (*21–23*), winners of CA events (*24–40*), winners of international events and CA medallists (*41–44*), list of Associates with their handicaps (*45–59*), registered clubs (*60–64*), list of affiliated overseas associations *etc* (*65*), name of printer (*65*), blank (*66*)

Binding: Dark Red (16) morocco grain cloth over and bordering the spine, overlapped by light olive Grey (112) paper over stiff boards, sewn. FC: printed in dark olive Green (126) (The | Croquet Association | 1953). RC: blank. Spine: blank

Copy seen: CA (imperfect)

Fingerprint: 65et s.a- o.or *SeLO* 3 1953A

Notes: Printed by Roffey & Clark, Croydon, price 3/6 to Associates.

(mm) *1954 edition (1954)*

YEAR BOOK | OF THE | CROQUET ASSOCIATION | 1954. | THE CROQUET ASSOCIATION, | 4, SOUTHAMPTON ROW, | W.C.1.

Formula: [1–4⁸ χ1]. 33 leaves, pp *1–2* 3–65 *66*. The copy examined was specially bound for official use with extra interleaved pages for notes. The extra leaves are here discounted

Technical notes: 173 × 109 mm (p 10). 62 lines, 20 = 56 mm. Leaf size 207 × 134 mm; thickness 0.14 mm; laid, watermarked (BOYD BROOK | MILLS), smooth, white, all edges speckled in dark Red (16)

Contents: Title (*1*), blank (*2*), contents (*3*), former Presidents, Vice-Presidents, Chairmen, and Vice-Chairmen of Council (*4*), Council *etc* (*5*), committees (*6*), official lists of managers and referees (*7*), official list of handicappers (*8*), managers, referees, and handicappers (*8*), rules of the CA (*9–14*), standing orders of the Council (*15–18*), advantages of membership (*19*), agreement to qualify for official tournament (*20*), challenge trophies, medals, and other prizes (*21–23*), winners of CA events (*24–41*), winners of international events and CA medallists (*42–45*), list of Associates with their handicaps (*46–60*), registered clubs (*61–65*), list of affiliated overseas associations *etc* (*66*), name of printer (*66*)

Binding: Dark Red (16) morocco grain cloth over and bordering the spine, overlapped by light olive Grey (112) paper over stiff boards, sewn. FC: printed in dark olive Green (126) (The | Croquet Association | 1954). RC: blank. Spine: blank

Copy seen: CA (imperfect)

Fingerprint: 66et s.a- o.or *SeLO* 3 1954A

Notes: Printed by Roffey & Clark, Croydon, price 3/6 to Associates.

(nn) *1956–57 edition [1956]*

HAND BOOK | OF THE | CROQUET ASSOCIATION | 1956-7 | THE CROQUET ASSOCIATION, | 4, SOUTHAMPTON ROW, | W.C.1

Formula: [1–3⁸ 4¹⁰]. 34 leaves, pp *1–2* 3–66 *67–68*

Technical notes: 168 × 109 mm (p 10). 60 lines, 20 = 56 mm. Leaf size 212 × 139 mm; thickness 0.10 mm; wove, unwatermarked, smooth, white

Contents: Title (*1*), blank (*2*), contents (*3*), former Presidents, Vice-Presidents, Chairmen, and Vice-Chairmen of Council (*4*), Council *etc* (*5*), committees (*6*), official lists of managers and referees (*7*), official list of handicappers (*8*), managers, referees, and handicappers (*8*), rules of the CA (*9–14*), standing orders of the Council (*15–18*), advantages of membership (*19*), agreement to qualify for official tournament (*20*), challenge trophies, medals, and other prizes (*21–23*), winners of CA events (*24–42*), winners of international events and CA medallists (*43–46*), list of Associates with their handicaps (*47–60*), registered clubs (*61–65*), list of affiliated overseas associations *etc* (*66*), name of printer (*67*), blank (*68*)

Binding: Greyish Green (150) paper glued to the spine, sewn, no endpapers. FC: printed in dark yellowish Green (137) (The | Croquet Association | 1956-7). Inside FC: blank. RC: blank. Inside RC: blank. Spine: blank

Copy seen: CA

Fingerprint: 66et s.a- r.on *SeLO* 3 1956Q

Notes: Printed by Roffey & Clark, Croydon, advertised in the December 1954 issue of *Croquet* (formerly *The Croquet Association Gazette*) at a price of 4/–. Year of publication is further attested by the archives of the CA.

(oo) *1958–59 edition [1958]*

HAND BOOK | OF THE | CROQUET ASSOCIATION | 1958-9 | THE CROQUET ASSOCIATION, | 4, SOUTHAMPTON ROW, | W.C.1

Formula: [1–3⁸ 4¹⁰]. 34 leaves, pp *1–2* 3–66 *67–68*

Technical notes: 172 × 109 mm (p 10). 62 lines, 20 = 56 mm. Leaf size 217 × 138 mm; thickness 0.10 mm; wove, unwatermarked, smooth, white

Contents: Title (*1*), blank (*2*), contents (*3*), former Presidents, Vice-Presidents, Chairmen, and Vice-Chairmen of Council (*4*), Council *etc* (*5*), committees (*6*), official lists of managers and referees (*7*), official list of handicappers (*8*), managers, referees, and handicappers (*8*), rules of the CA (*9–14*), standing orders of the Council (*15–18*), advantages of membership (*19*), agreement to qualify for official tournament (*20*), challenge trophies, medals, and other prizes (*21–23*), winners of CA events (*24–43*), winners of international events and medallists (*44–48*), list of Associates with their handicaps (*49–61*), registered clubs (*62–66*), list of affiliated overseas associations *etc* (*67*), name of printer (*68*)

Binding: Greyish Green (150) paper glued to the spine, sewn, no endpapers. FC: printed in dark yellowish Green (137) (The | Croquet Association | 1958-9). Inside FC: blank. RC: blank. Inside RC: blank. Spine: blank

Copy seen: CA

Fingerprint: 66et s.a- r.on *SeLO* 3 1958Q

Notes: Printed by Roffey & Clark, Croydon, price 4/– to Associates. Year of publication is attested by the archives of the CA.

(pp) *1960–61 edition [1960]*

HAND BOOK | OF THE | CROQUET ASSOCIATION | 1960-1 | THE CROQUET ASSOCIATION, | HURLINGHAM CLUB, | S.W.6

Formula: [1–3⁸ 4¹⁰]. 34 leaves, pp *1–2* 3–65 *66–68*

Technical notes: 172 × 109 mm (p 10). 62 lines, 20 = 56 mm. Leaf size 215 × 136 mm; thickness 0.11 mm; wove, unwatermarked, smooth, white

Contents: Title (*1*), blank (*2*), contents (*3*), former Presidents, Vice-Presidents, Chairmen, and Vice-Chairmen of Council (*4*), Council *etc* (*5*), committees (*6*), official lists of managers and referees (*7*), official list of handicappers (*8*), managers, referees, and handicappers (*8*), rules of the CA (*9–14*), standing orders of the Council (*15–18*), advantages of membership (*19*), agreement to qualify for official tournament (*20*), challenge trophies, medals, and other prizes (*21–23*), winners of CA events (*24–44*), winners of international events and CA medallists (*45–46*), list of Associates with their handicaps (*47–59*), registered clubs (*60–64*), list of affiliated overseas associations *etc* (*65*), blank (*66*), name of printer (*67*), blank (*68*)

Binding: Greyish Green (150) paper glued to the spine, sewn, no endpapers. FC: printed in dark yellowish Green (137) (The | Croquet Association | 1960-1). Inside FC: blank. RC: blank. Inside RC: blank. Spine: blank

Copy seen: CA

Fingerprint: 66et s.ly r.on *SeV.* 3 1960Q

Notes: Printed by Roffey & Clark, Croydon. According to advertisements in *Croquet* (formerly *The Croquet Association Gazette*), this issue was available from May 1961 at a price of 4/6. Year of publication is further attested by the archives of the CA.

(qq) *1962–63 edition [1962]*

ABRIDGED | HAND BOOK | OF THE | CROQUET ASSOCIATION | 1962–3 | THE CROQUET ASSOCIATION | HURLINGHAM CLUB | S.W.6

Formula: [1¹²]. 12 leaves, pp *1–2* 3–24

Technical notes: 174 × 110 mm (p 8, ragged). 61 lines, 20 = 57 mm. Leaf size 215 × 139 mm; thickness 0.09 mm; wove, unwatermarked, smooth, white

Contents: Title (*1*), blank (*2*), Council *etc* (*3*), official lists of managers, referees, and handicappers (*4–5*), blank (*6*), list of Associates with their handicaps (*7–21*), registered clubs (*22–23*), list of affiliated overseas associations *etc* (*24*)

Binding: Strong Yellow Green (117) card, stapled, no spine or endpapers. FC: printed in black, as the TP above. Inside FC: blank. RC: name of printer. Inside RC: blank

Copy seen: PC

Fingerprint: 6.s: 0)re .121 Me7M 3 1962Q

Notes: Printed by RH Johns, Newport, Monmouthshire. Published early in 1962, price 2/6 to Associates, 3/6 to non-Associates.

(rr) *1964 edition (1964)*

HAND BOOK | OF THE | Croquet Association | 1964 | THE CROQUET ASSOCIATION, | HURLINGHAM CLUB, | S.W.6

Formula: [1–4⁸ 5⁴]. 36 leaves, pp *1–2* 3–21, *i*, 22–48, *ii*, 49–69 *70* [= 72]

Technical notes: 171 × 109 mm (p 8). 61 lines, 20 = 56 mm. Leaf size 214 × 139 mm; thickness 0.10 mm; wove, unwatermarked, smooth, white

Contents: Title (*1*), blank (*2*), contents (*3*), former Presidents, Vice-Presidents, Chairmen, and Vice-Chairmen of Council (*4*), Council *etc* (*5*), official lists of managers, referees, and handicappers (*6*), rules of the CA (*7–12*), standing orders of the Council (*13–16*), advantages of membership (*17*), qualifications for an official tournament (*18*), challenge trophies, medals, and other prizes (*19–21*), blank (*i*), winners of CA events (*22–46*), winners of international events and CA medallists (*47–48*), blank (*ii*), list of Associates with their handicaps (*49–66*), registered clubs (*67–69*), list of affiliated overseas associations *etc* (*70*), name of printer (*70*)

Binding: Greyish Yellow Green (122) paper glued to the spine, sewn, no endpapers. FC: printed in dark yellowish Green (137) (The | Croquet Association | 1964). Inside FC: blank. RC: blank. Inside RC: blank. Spine: blank

Copy seen: CA

Fingerprint: .6B, r.is e.al ofsp 3 1964A

Notes: Printed by Roffey & Clark, Croydon. Published in April 1964, price 7/6.

(ss) *1968–70 edition [1968]*

abridged | **HANDBOOK** | *of the* | **CROQUET ASSOCIATION** | *1968-70* | Croquet Association, Hurlingham Club, S.W.6 | TELEPHONE : Renown 3148

Formula: [1¹⁴]. 14 leaves, unnumbered [pp 1–28]

Technical notes: 177 × 119 mm (p 6, ragged). 51 lines, 20 = 70 mm. Leaf size 201 × 155 mm; thickness 0.12 mm; wove, unwatermarked, smooth, white

Contents: Title (*1*), blank (*2*), the CA: patron and secretary (*3*), official lists of managers, referees, handicappers, umpires (*4*), list of Associates with their handicaps (*5–23*), list of registered clubs (*24–27*), list of affiliated overseas associations *etc* (*28*)

Binding: Pale Green (149) card, stapled, no spine or endpapers. FC: printed in black, the title set within a frame composed of repeated calligraphic figures (*abridged* | **HANDBOOK** | *of the* | **CROQUET ASSOCIATION** | *1968-70*). Inside FC: blank. RC: printed in black close to the foot (Creative Offset Limited, Park Works, Borough Road, Kingston upon Thames. 01-549 0111). Inside RC: blank

Copy seen: CA

Fingerprint: 48.6 e.6) d.h, NoMa V 1968Q [groups 1–4 taken from pp *3, 11, 13, 14* respectively]

Notes: Printed by Creative Offset. Year of publication is attested by the archives of the CA.

(tt) *1970 edition (1970)*

HAND BOOK OF | THE CROQUET ASSOCIATION | 1970 | [double rule] | Patron: | HER MAJESTY THE QUEEN | CONTENTS | [details of contents listed under *Contents* below] | All Communications should be addressed to the Secretary: | **THE CROQUET ASSOCIATION** | **HURLINGHAM   CLUB** | **S.W.6.** | TELEPHONE 736-3148

Formula: [1²⁰]. 20 leaves, pp *1* 2–40

Technical notes: 171 × 102 mm (pp 3 and 17, ragged). Variable number of lines per page, 20 = 62–69 mm. Leaf size 214 × 141 mm; thickness 0.10 mm; wove, unwatermarked, smooth, white

Contents: Title and contents (*1*), Presidents, Vice-Presidents, and Chairmen of Council (*2*), rules of the CA (*3–8*), important dates in the history of croquet (*9*), challenge trophies, medals, and other prizes (*10–13*), winners of CA events (*14–34*), results of international events (34), medals presented to overseas associations (35–36), CA silver medallists (36), list of registered clubs (37–39), list of affiliated overseas associations *etc* (40), notice (40)

Binding: Very pale Green (148) card, stapled, no spine or endpapers. FC: printed in black (The | Croquet Association | 1970 | THE CROQUET ASSOCIATION, | HURLINGHAM CLUB, | S.W.6.). Inside FC: blank. RC: blank. Inside RC: blank

Copy seen: PC

Fingerprint: n.ne y.l. d.e- 1919 3 1970A

Notes: Printed anonymously by FH Brown, Burnley, Lancs, at a cost to the CA of £129.

(uu) *1970–72 edition [1970]*

abridged | HANDBOOK | *of the* | CROQUET ASSOCIATION | *1970–1972* | Croquet Association, Hurlingham Club, S.W.6. | Telephone: 01 736 3148

Formula: [1¹⁴]. 14 leaves, unnumbered [pp 1–28]

Technical notes: 171 × 130 mm (p 6, ragged). 49 lines, 20 = 70 mm. Leaf size 202 × 153 mm; thickness 0.10 mm; wove, unwatermarked, smooth, white

Contents: Title (*1*), blank (*2*), the CA (*3*), managers, referees, handicappers, examining referees, umpires (*4*), list of Associates with their handicaps (*5–22*), list of registered clubs (*23–27*), list of affiliated overseas associations *etc* (*27–28*)

Binding: Light bluish Green (163) card, stapled, no spine or endpapers. FC: printed in black within a decorative frame (*abridged* | HANDBOOK | *of the* | CROQUET ASSOCIATION | *1970–1972*). Inside FC: blank. RC: blank. Inside RC: blank

Copy seen: PC

Fingerprint: 486. s.2) h.7. Le1M C 1970Q

Notes: Printed anonymously. The copy examined encloses a loose leaf of amendments up to 10 June 1970.

(vv) *1972–74 edition [1972]*

DIRECTORY | *of the* | CROQUET ASSOCIATION | *1972-1974* | Croquet Association, Hurlingham Club, S.W.6. | Telephone: 01 736 3148

Formula: [1³²]. 32 leaves, pp *1–4* 5–30 *31–32*. The copy examined is interleaved with blank sheets for notes (see *Notes*). The extra leaves are here discounted

Technical notes: 177 × 136 mm (p 9, ragged). 51 lines, 20 = 70 mm. Leaf size 202 × 153 mm; thickness 0.10 mm; wove, unwatermarked, smooth, white

Contents: Title (*1*), blank (*2*), the CA: patron and secretary (*3*), blank (*4*), official lists of managers, examining referees, referees, handicappers (*5*), list of Associates with their handicaps (*6–23*), list of registered clubs (*24–28*), list of affiliated overseas associations *etc* (*29–30*), blank (*31–32*)

Binding: Pale Yellow (89) light card, stapled, no spine or endpapers. FC: printed in black, the title set within a frame composed of repeated calligraphic figures (**DIRECTORY** | *of the* | **CROQUET ASSOCIATION** | *1972-1974*). Inside FC: blank. RC: blank. Inside RC: blank

Copy seen: CA (wanting amendment sheets)

Fingerprint: 486. t.a. 6)x. 3L–½ C 1972Q [groups 1–4 taken from pp *3*, 11, 13, 14 respectively]

Notes: Printed anonymously by Browns Typewriting Services at a cost to the CA of

£89.90. Seven amendment sheets were issued at sporadic intervals after this edition was first published. Year of publication is attested by the archives of the CA. It is believed that all copies of this edition were interleaved with blank sheets for notes.

(ww) *1974–76 edition [1974]*

DIRECTORY | *of the* | CROQUET ASSOCIATION | *1974-1976* | Croquet Association, Hurlingham Club, S.W.6. | Telephone: 01 736 3148

Formula: [1⁴⁰]. 40 leaves, pp *1–3 4–37 38–40*. The copy examined is interleaved with blank sheets for notes (see *Notes* to (vv)). The extra leaves are here discounted

Technical notes: 176 × 128 mm (p 9, ragged). 50 lines, 20 = 70 mm. Leaf size 203 × 151 mm; thickness 0.11 mm; wove, watermarked crosswise ([in a convex arc] CROXLEY | [in a concave arc] SCRIPT), smooth, white

Contents: Title (*1*), blank (*2*), the CA: patron and secretary (*3*), blank save pagination (*4*), list of authorised tournament officials (*5–6*), list of Associates with their handicaps (*7–27*), members of New York Croquet Club enrolled as Associates (*29–30*), members of Palm Beach Croquet Club enrolled as Associates (*30*), list of registered clubs (*31–35*), list of affiliated overseas associations *etc* (*36–37*), notice (*37*), blank (*38–40*)

Binding: Very light greenish Blue (171) light card, stapled, no spine or endpapers. FC: printed in black, the title set within a frame composed of repeated calligraphic figures (**DIRECTORY** | *of the* | CROQUET ASSOCIATION | *1974-1976*). Inside FC: blank. RC: blank. Inside RC: blank

Copy seen: CA (wanting amendment sheets)

Fingerprint: 486. s.d. c.o. 5H4_ C 1974Q [groups 1–4 taken from pp *3*, 11, 13, 14 respectively]

Notes: Printed anonymously by FH Brown, Burnley, Lancs, at a cost to the CA of £148.10 (for 400 copies). 'Extra' copies were offered to Associates at a price of 50p. Associates were invited to subscribe to amendment sheets, to be issued from time to time, at a composite price of 50p. Year of publication is attested by the archives of the CA.

(xx) *1976–78 edition [1976]*

DIRECTORY | *of the* | CROQUET ASSOCIATION | *1976-1978* | Croquet Association, Hurlingham Club, S.W.6. | Telephone: 01 736 3148

Formula: [1⁴⁸]. 48 leaves, pp *1–4 5–41 42–48*. The copy examined is interleaved with blank sheets for notes (see *Notes* to (vv)). The extra leaves are here discounted

Technical notes: 176 × 125 mm (p 9, ragged). 50 lines, 20 = 70 mm. Leaf size 204 × 154 mm; thickness 0.10 mm; wove, unwatermarked, smooth, white

Contents: Title (*1*), blank (*2*), the CA: patron and secretary (*3*), blank (*4*), list of authorised tournament officials (*5–6*), list of Associates with their handicaps (*7–30*), members of New York Croquet Club enrolled as Associates (*31–32*), members of Palm Beach Croquet Club enrolled as Associates (*32*), list of croquet clubs in England, Wales, and Ireland (*33–38*), clubs which are members of the SCA (*39*), federations of clubs (*39*), list of affiliated overseas associations *etc* (*39–40*), notice (*41*), blank (*42–48*)

Binding: Very light greenish Blue (171) light card, stapled, no spine or endpapers. FC: printed in black, the title set within a frame composed of repeated calligraphic figures (**DIRECTORY** | *of the* | CROQUET ASSOCIATION | *1976-1978*). Inside FC: blank. RC: printed in black, near the foot (Printed by F. H. Brown Ltd , Litho Division, Helena Street Burnley, Lancs.). Inside RC: blank

Copy seen: CA (wanting amendment sheets)

Fingerprint: 486. 0.th 0.., GL5_ C 1976Q [groups 1–4 taken from pp *3*, 11, 13, 14 respectively]

Notes: Printed by FH Brown, price £1.00 to Associates, who were invited to subscribe to amendment sheets, to be issued from time to time, at a composite price of £1.00. Eight such amendments sheets were subsequently issued. Year of publication is attested by the archives of the CA.

(yy) *1978–79 edition [1978]*

DIRECTORY | *of the* | **CROQUET ASSOCIATION** | *1978-1979* | Croquet Association, Hurlingham Club, S.W.6. | Telephone: 01 736 3148

Formula: [1⁴⁸]. 48 leaves, pp *1–2* 3–46 *47–48*. The copy examined is interleaved with blank sheets for notes (see *Notes* to (vv)). The extra leaves are here discounted

Technical notes: 172 × 126 mm (p 9, ragged). 49 lines, 20 = 70 mm. Leaf size 203 × 153 mm; thickness 0.11 mm; wove, watermarked crosswise ([in a convex arc] CROXLEY | [in a concave arc] SCRIPT), smooth, white

Contents: Title (*1*), blank (*2*), the CA: patron and secretary (3), blank save pagination (4), list of authorised tournament officials (5–6), list of Associates with their handicaps (7–35), list of croquet clubs in England, Wales, and Ireland (36–43), clubs which are members of the SCA (44), federations of clubs (44), list of affiliated overseas associations *etc* (44–45), notice (46), blank (*47–48*)

Binding: Brilliant Yellow (89) light card, stapled, no spine or endpapers. FC: printed in black, the title set within a frame composed of repeated calligraphic figures (**DIRECTORY** | *of the* | **CROQUET ASSOCIATION** | *1978-1979*). Inside FC: blank. RC: printed in black, near the foot (Printed by F.H.Brown Ltd., Litho Division, Helena Street, Burnley, Lancs.). Inside RC: blank

Copy seen: CA (wanting amendment sheets)

Fingerprint: 48R. 6.G. e.8. RD4S C 1978Q [groups 1–4 taken from pp 3, 11, 13, 14 respectively]

Notes: Printed by FH Brown, price £1.25 to Associates, who were invited to subscribe to amendment sheets, to be issued from time to time, at the composite price of £1.25. Year of publication is attested by the archives of the CA.

(zz) *1980–81 edition [1980]*

DIRECTORY | *of the* | **CROQUET ASSOCIATION** | *1980-1981* | The Croquet Association, Hurlingham Club, Ranelagh Gardens, London SW6 3PR | Telephone: 01-736 3148

Formula: [1⁴⁸]. 48 leaves, pp *1* 2–48. The copy examined is interleaved with blank sheets for notes (see *Notes* to (vv)). The extra leaves are here discounted

Technical notes: 171 × 127 mm (p 9, ragged). 49 lines, 20 = 70 mm. Leaf size 202 × 147 mm; thickness 0.11 mm; wove, unwatermarked, smooth, white

Contents: Title (*1*), notice (2), the CA: patron, vice-presidents, and secretary (3), blank save pagination (4), list of authorised tournament officials (5–6), list of Associates with their handicaps (7–37), list of croquet clubs in England, Wales, and Ireland (38–45), SCA and affiliated clubs (46), federations of clubs (46), list of affiliated overseas associations *etc* (46–48)

Binding: Pale Green (149) light card, stapled, no spine or endpapers. FC: printed in black, the title set within a frame composed of repeated calligraphic figures (**DIRECTORY** | *of the* | **CROQUET ASSOCIATION** | *1980-1981*). Inside FC:

blank. RC: printed in black, near the foot (Printed by F.H.Brown Ltd., Litho Division, Helena Street Burnley, Lancs.). Inside RC: blank

Copy seen: CA (wanting amendment sheets)

Fingerprint: 48PR 93y, 55r, 8SDe C 1980Q [groups 1–4 taken from pp 3, 11, 13, 14 respectively]

Notes: Printed by FH Brown, price £1.50 to Associates and non-registered clubs, issued free to registered clubs and associations. Associates were invited to subscribe to amendment sheets, to be issued from time to time, at the composite price of £1.50. Year of publication is attested by the archives of the CA.

(aaa) *1985 edition (1986)*

[The FC]

<u>THE CROQUET ASSOCIATION</u> | <u>DIRECTORY</u> | of Associates and Clubs | <u>1985</u> | [R justified] January 1985

Formula: [1–53¹]. 53 leaves, ff 1–53

Technical notes: 238 × 174 mm (p 4, ragged). 56 lines, 20 = 85 mm. Leaf size 297 × 210 mm; thickness 0.10 mm; wove, unwatermarked, smooth, white

Contents: Index and notes (1), officials (2), list of UK Associates with their handicaps (3–33), registered clubs (34–42), schools and universities (43–44), federations (44), SCA and affiliated clubs (45), list of affiliated overseas associations *etc* (46–48), list of authorised tournament officials (49–52), members of Council (53)

Binding: The covers of very light greenish Blue (171) card, slotted, in a black plastic comb, no endpapers. FC: printed in black as above. Inside FC: blank. RC: none

Copy seen: PC

Fingerprint: n.he 11me 71l: 3014 C 1985A [group 1 taken from f 1, groups 3 and 4 taken from f 13]

Notes: Printed anonymously.

(bbb) *1986 edition (1986)*

[The FC]

THE CROQUET ASSOCIATION | DIRECTORY | of Associates and Clubs. | 1986 | [R justified] June 1986.

Formula: [1–60¹]. 60 leaves, ff 1–60

Technical notes: 235 × 183 mm (p 4, ragged). 56 lines, 20 = 85 mm. Leaf size 296 × 210 mm; thickness 0.10 mm; wove, unwatermarked, smooth, white

Contents: Index and notes (1), officials (2), list of UK Associates with their handicaps (3–34), list of overseas Associates (35–38), registered clubs (39–49), schools and universities (50–51), affiliated organisations, and federations (52), SCA and affiliated clubs (53), list of affiliated overseas associations *etc* (54–56), list of authorised tournament officials (57–60)

Binding: The FC of white card, slotted, in a black plastic comb, no endpapers. FC: printed in black as above. Inside FC: blank. RC: none

Copy seen: PC

Fingerprint: h.ES 55l: 51me 74me 3 1986A [group 1 taken from f 1, groups 3 and 4 taken from f 13]

Notes: Printed anonymously.

(ccc) *1987 edition (1987)*

[The FC]

THE | **CROQUET ASSOCIATION** | DIRECTORY | of Associates and Clubs | 1987

Formula: [1–36¹]. 36 leaves, pp 1–65 66 67–72

Technical notes: 250 × 177 mm (p 8, ragged). 58 lines, 20 = 86 mm. Leaf size 299 × 208 mm; thickness 0.09 mm; wove, unwatermarked, smooth, white

Contents: Index and notes (1), officials (2), list of UK Associates and their handicaps (3–39), list of overseas Associates (40–43), registered clubs (44–55), schools and universities (56–58), affiliated organisations (59), federations (60), SCA and affiliated clubs (61–62), list of affiliated overseas associations *etc* (63–65), non-affiliated clubs (66), list of authorised tournament officials (67–71), members of Council (72)

Binding: Light greenish Yellow (101) card, slotted, in a black plastic comb, no endpapers. FC: printed in black as above. Inside FC: blank. RC: none

Copy seen: PC

Fingerprint: n.om T.15 94l: o7SF 3 1987A [group 1 taken from p 1]

Notes: Printed anonymously by The Ludo Press.

(ddd) *1988 edition (1988)*

[The FC]

[in a convex arc, forming the crown of the association's device] · THE CROQUET ASSOCIATION · | [within the association's device] 1988 | [*do*] DIRECTORY | ASSOCIATES and CLUBS

Formula: [1–42¹]. 42 leaves, pp *i–ii*, 1–72 73 74–81 82

Technical notes: 169 × 129 mm (p 3, ragged). 60 lines, 20 = 56 mm. Leaf size 210 × 147 mm; thickness 0.12 mm; wove, unwatermarked, smooth, white

Contents: Index and notes (*i*), list of officials (*ii*), list of UK Associates and their handicaps (1–42), list of overseas Associates (43–47), registered clubs (48–60), schools and universities (61–64), affiliated organisations (65–66), federations (67), SCA and affiliated clubs (68–69), list of affiliated overseas associations *etc* (70–73), non-affiliated clubs (74–75), list of authorised tournament officials (76–81), blank (*82*)

Binding: Front cover of light greenish Grey (154) card, slotted, in a black plastic comb, no endpapers. FC: printed in black as above. Inside FC: blank. RC: none

Copy seen: PC

Fingerprint: 8)5. 12W. 89me PE5S 3 1988A [group 1 taken from p i]

Notes: Printed anonymously by Instant Print West One.

(eee) *1989 edition (1989)*

[The FC]

[in a convex arc, forming the crown of the association's device] · THE CROQUET ASSOCIATION · | [within the association's device] 1989 | [*do*] DIRECTORY | ASSOCIATES and CLUBS

Formula: [1–54¹]. 54 leaves, pp *a, i*, 1–103 *104–106* [= 108]

Technical notes: 151 × 119 mm (p 2, ragged), some of the text divided into two columns. 58 lines, 20 = 52 mm. Leaf size 206 × 143 mm; thickness 0.12 mm; wove, unwatermarked, smooth, white

Contents: Contents (*a*), officers and officials (*i*), list of UK and Irish Associates (1–66), list of overseas Associates (67–73), registered clubs (74–84), schools and universities (85–87), federations (88), overseas affiliated clubs (89–90), affiliated governing bodies (91–92), other affiliated entities (93–94), non-affiliated clubs in England (95), SCA affiliated clubs (96), CA referees (97–98), CA managers (99), CA coaches (100–101), CA handicappers (102–103), blank (*104–106*)

Binding: Very light greenish Blue (171) card glued to the edges of the leaves, scored hinges front and rear, no endpapers. FC: printed in black as above. Inside FC: blank. RC: blank. Inside RC: blank. Spine: blank

Copy seen: PC

Fingerprint: 0302 H)L. H1H1 TeNC 3 1989 [group 1 taken from p *a*]

Notes: Printed anonymously.

(fff) *1990 edition (1990)*

[The FC]

[in a convex arc, forming the crown of the association's device] · THE CROQUET ASSOCIATION · | [within the association's device] 1990 | [*do*] DIRECTORY | ASSOCIATES and CLUBS

Formula: [1–72¹]. 72 leaves, pp *i–ii, 1,* 2–139 *140–142*

Technical notes: 157 × 111 mm (p 2, ragged), some of the text divided into two columns. 53 lines, 20 = 60 mm. Leaf size 205 × 144 mm; thickness 0.10 mm; wove, unwatermarked, smooth, white

Contents: Contents (*i*), officers and officials (*ii*), list of UK and Irish Associates (*1–93*), list of overseas Associates (94–103), registered clubs (104–118), schools and universities (119–123), overseas affiliated clubs (124–126), affiliated governing bodies (127–130), SCA affiliated clubs (131), CA referees (132–133), CA managers (134), CA coaches (135–136), CA handicappers (137–138), official club handicappers (139), blank (140–142)

Binding: Moderate Pink (5) card glued to the edges of the leaves, scored hinges front and rear, no endpapers. FC: printed in black as above. Inside FC: blank. RC: blank. Inside RC: blank. Spine: blank

Copy seen: PC

Fingerprint: 3937 H)h, J,l, DoVC 3 1990A [group 1 taken from p *i*]

Notes: Printed anonymously.

(ggg) *1993 edition (1993)*

[The FC]

[in a convex arc, forming the crown of the association's device] THE CROQUET ASSOCIATION | DIRECTORY | 1993

Formula: [1³⁴]. 34 leaves, pp *i–ii, 1* 2–66

Technical notes: 172 × 102 mm (p 2, ragged), mostly divided into two columns. Variable number of lines per page, irregularly spaced; thickness 0.10 mm; wove, unwatermarked, smooth, white

Contents: Contents and key to symbols (*i*), officers and officials (*ii*), list of UK and Irish Associates and their handicaps (*1–46*), list of overseas Associates (46–48), registered clubs (48–55), federations (55), schools and universities (55–57), UK associated organisations (58), overseas associated organisations (58–59), SCA affiliated clubs (59), CA referees (60–62), CA managers (62), CA coaches (63–64), CA handicappers (65–66)

Binding: Brilliant greenish Yellow (98) paper, stapled, no spine or endpapers. FC: printed in black as above. Inside FC: blank. RC: advertisement. Inside FC: blank

Copy seen: PC

Fingerprint: s)ry *5ex *82- SuTF 3 1993A [group 1 taken from p *i*]

Notes: Printed anonymously from the association's database, designed by W Gillott.

(hhh) *1995 edition (1995)*

[The FC]

[within a border composed of asterisks, with cut-outs in the upper corners] **1995** | [*do*] **DIRECTORY OF** | [*do*] **ASSOCIATES** | [association's device] | Published by: The Croquet Association | The Hurlingham Club | Ranelagh Gardens | London SW6 3PR

Formula: [1–28¹]. 28 leaves, unnumbered [pp 1–56]

Technical notes: 235 × 179 mm (p *2*). 56 lines, 20 = 85 mm. Leaf size 297 × 210 mm; thickness 0.10 mm; wove, unwatermarked, smooth, white

Contents: Contents (*1*), blank (*2*), list of home Associates (*3–28*), list of overseas Associates (*29–30*), UK affiliated clubs (*31–44*), federations and their secretaries (*45*), blank (*46*), coaches (*47–50*), handicappers (*51–52*), referees (*53–56*)

Binding: Light Green (144) card, stapled, no spine or endpapers. FC: printed in black as above. Inside FC: blank. RC: blank. Inside RC: blank

Copy seen: PC

Fingerprint: 5959 6398 1794 MrMr C 1995A [group 1 taken from p *1*]

Notes: Printed anonymously.

(jjj) *1996 edition (1996)*

[The FC]

[within a border composed of asterisks, with cut-outs in the upper corners] **1996** | [*do*] **DIRECTORY OF** | [*do*] **ASSOCIATES** | [association's device] | Published by: The Croquet Association | The Hurlingham Club | Ranelagh Gardens | London SW6 3PR | Tel/Fax: 0171-736 3148

Formula: [1–27¹]. 27 leaves, unnumbered [pp 1–54]

Technical notes: 235 × 170 mm (p *4*). 56 lines, 20 = 85 mm. Leaf size 297 × 210 mm; thickness 0.11 mm; wove, unwatermarked, smooth, white

Contents: Contents (*1*), blank (*2*), list of home Associates (*3–28*), list of overseas Associates (*29–30*), registered clubs (*31–44*), federations and their secretaries (*45*), blank (*46*), coaches (*47–48*), handicappers (*49*), blank (*50*), tournament managers (*51*), blank (*52*), referees (*53–54*)

Binding: Very light greenish Blue (171) card, stapled, no spine or endpapers. FC: printed in black as above. Inside FC: blank. RC: blank. Inside RC: advertisement

Copy seen: PC

Fingerprint: esrs 5400 0073 MrMr C 1996A [group 1 taken from p *1*]

Notes: Printed anonymously, probably by Kall Kwik Printing, London. Kall Kwik undertook several printing commissions for the CA at about this time and supplied the sole advertisement in this edition. The copy examined contains a loose *errata* slip which apparently accompanied the booklet when it was issued.

(kkk) *1998 edition (1998)*

[The FC]

[within a border composed of asterisks, with cut-outs in the upper corners] **1998** | [*do*] **DIRECTORY OF** | [*do*] **ASSOCIATES** | [association's device] | Published by: The Croquet Association | The Hurlingham Club | Ranelagh Gardens | London SW6 3PR | Tel/Fax: 0171-736 3148 | E mail:caoffice@croquet.org.uk

Formula: [1–32¹]. 32 leaves, unnumbered [pp 1–64]

Technical notes: 235 × 170 mm (p *4*). 56 lines, 20 = 85 mm. Leaf size 297 × 210 mm; thickness 0.11 mm; wove, unwatermarked, smooth, white

Contents: Contents (*1*), blank (*2*), list of home Associates (*3–30*), list of overseas members (*31–32*), registered clubs (*33–47*), blank (*48*), federation secretaries (*49*), blank (*50*), coaches (*51–54*), handicappers (*55–57*), blank (*58*), tournament managers (*59–60*), referees (*61–64*)

Binding: Pale orange Yellow (73) light card, stapled, no spine or endpapers. FC: printed in black as above. Inside FC: blank. RC: blank. Inside RC: advertisement.

Copy seen: PC

Fingerprint: esrs 7707 8947 MrMr C 1998A [group 1 taken from p *1*]

Notes: Printed anonymously, probably by Kall Kwik Printing, London (see also *Notes* to (jjj)).

**A111   GARDEN LAWNS, TENNIS LAWNS, CROQUET GROUNDS,   [1902]
BOWLING GREENS, PUTTING GREENS, CRICKET
GROUNDS.** [Sutton & Sons]

(a) *First edition [1902]*

Not seen. That later editions appear to have been issued annually suggests that the first edition was published in this year.

(b) *Eleventh edition (1912)*

[From half-title heading *etc*, p *i*]

LAWNS | BY | Sutton & Sons, Reading. | *ELEVENTH EDITION.* | ... | SIMKIN, MARSHALL, HAMILTON, KENT & CO., Limited, LONDON.

[The TP, p *v*]

[L justified] | Garden Lawns | [*do*] Tennis Lawns | [*do*] Croquet Grounds | [*do*] Bowling Greens | [*do*] Putting Greens | [*do*] Cricket Grounds | [at R] By Sutton & Sons | [*do*] Reading | [at L] Eleventh | [*do*] Edition | [at L, outlined by a circle] 1/- | LONDON | SIMPKIN, MARSHALL, HAMILTON, KENT & CO., Ltd. | 1912 | *All rights reserved*

Formula: A⁸(A¹+χ²) B–E⁸ F⁴ [\$2 signed (–A1, 2, F2)]. 46 leaves including the front and rear pastedowns, pp *1–2, i–viii*, 1 2–6 *7* 8–10 *11* 12–14 *15* 16–18 *19* 20–22 *23* 24–26 *27* 28–30 *31* 32–34 *35* 36–38 *39* 40–44 *45* 46–48 *49* 50–54 *55* 56–58 *59* 60–63 *64–65* 66–68 *69–71* 72–75 *76–82* [= 92]

Technical notes: 166 × 197 mm (p *2*). 35 lines, 20 = 96 mm. Leaf size 216 × 138 mm. Pp *i–iv*: thickness 0.10 mm, wove, unwatermarked, smooth, white. Other pp: thickness 0.13 mm, wove, unwatermarked, semi-gloss, white

Contents: Glued to the FC (*1*), blank (*2*), half-title heading, contents, price, reviews, and advertisement (*i*), advertisements (*ii–iv*), title (*v*), blank (*vi*), contents (*vii*), half-tone photograph (*viii*), text (*1–75*), advertisements (*76–80*), name of printer (*80*), blank (*81*), glued to the RC (*82*)

Binding: Dark Green (146) card, glued to the section folds, sewn. FC: silver-blocked ([at top L] LAWNS | [at R, at the foot] SUTTON & SONS | [*do*] READING). RC: blank. Spine: blank

Copy seen: RSL: 19188 e 37

Fingerprint: 7165 ldn- e.he grob 1912A [group 1 taken from p *vii*]

Notes: Printed by Spottiswoode & Co, London, Colchester, and Eton, price 1/–, free of charge to customers. The copy examined bears the library accession mark, dated 14 June 1912.

Reviews quoted on p *i* are attributed to *The Times* and *Ladies' Field*.

1904

A112   HOW TO PLAY CROQUET. WW Bruce   [1904]

(a) *First edition [1904]*

HOW TO PLAY | *CROQUET* | BY | W. W. BRUCE | [rule] | LONDON | BEETON & CO., LTD., | 10 & 11, FETTER LANE, E.C.

Formula: Apparently *1 2–6*[8] [\$1signed (*–1*[1])]. Apparently 48 leaves including the front and rear pastedowns, pp [i–iii] *iv–vi, 1 2–7 8 9–15 16 17–21 22 23–28 29 30–37 38 39–44 45 46–51 52 53–57 58 59–64 65 66–71 72 73–79 80 81–87* [88–90]

Technical notes: 129 × 88 mm (p 4). 27 lines, 20 = 96 mm. Leaf size 186 × 126 mm

Contents: Apparently glued to the FC (*i*), wanting from the photocopy examined ([ii–iii]), plan of croquet ground (*iv*), title (*v*), blank (*vi*), text (*1–87*), name of printer (87), wanting from the photocopy examined ([88–89]), apparently glued to the RC (*90*)

Binding: Not seen

Copy seen: PC (incomplete photocopy of CUL: 1904 7 1061, wanting pp [i–iv, 88–90])

Fingerprint: heB. m.lp isen —tfo 3 1904Q

Notes: Printed by WJ Pack & Co, Norwich. Year of publication is inferred from the CUL accession mark (dated '3 JU 04') on the photocopy examined.

(b) *1906 issue [1906]*

HOW TO PLAY | *CROQUET* | BY | W. W. BRUCE | [rule] | LONDON | BEETON & CO., LTD., | 10 & 11, FETTER LANE, E.C.

Formula: Not ascertainable from the copy examined. 52 leaves, pp *1–4, i ii–viii, 1 2–7 8 9–15 16 17–21 22 23–28 29 30–37 38 39–44 45 46–51 52 53–57 58 59–64 65 66–71 72 73–79 80 81–87 88–92*

Technical notes: 127 × 84 mm (p ii). 31 lines, 20 = 75 mm. Leaf size 182 × 116 mm; thickness 0.10–0.12 mm; wove, unwatermarked, smooth, white

Contents: Blank (*1*), plan of croquet ground (*2*), title (*3*), blank (*4*), preface ('The latest laws of croquet, 1906'), signed 'W. W. Bruce' (*i–viii*), text (*1–87*), name of printer (87), advertisements (*88–92*)

Binding: The copy examined had been restitched and rebound, displaying most of the original FC and a leaf bearing an advertisement which was apparently the original front pastedown. FC: printed on white paper in black, strong Red (12) and greyish Yellow (90) on and out of a deep yellowish Brown (90) background, the lettering arranged within a sketch which features dandelion seeds in white over a lawn set out with a hoop, two mallets, and three balls, and an irregular *art nouveau* style panel in Yellow ([white out of Brown] HOW TO PLAY | [in Red display script outlined in black] Croquet | [within panel, in Red] BY | [*do*] W. W. Bruce | [*do*] ONE | [*do*] SHIL^LING).

Copy seen: BL: 7912 df 44

Fingerprint: ayre heB. isen —tfo 3 1906Q

Notes: Printed by WJ Pack & Co, Norwich, price 1/–. Year of publication is inferred from the edition of the laws of croquet reproduced in the preface, which are described as 'the latest laws of croquet'.

The text and preliminaries have not been collated with those of (a). In view of similarities in their pagination and fingerprints, however, it would appear that the present issue departs little from the first edition — perhaps only in the addition of the 1906 laws of croquet and the supplementary advertising matter.

1905

A113   THE NEW COMBINATION OF PARLOUR GAMES. [Anon]   [1905]

THE NEW | [flourish] *Combination* [flourish] | [flourish] OF [flourish] | [in ornamental script] **Parlour** [flourish] **Games.** | [double rule] | [ornamental tail piece] | **CONTENTS.** | [divided into two columns:]

CROQUET.	TRAILS.	
TON TON.	PUFF and DART.	
BALL SOLITAIRE.	GO BANG.	
EXPERT ANGLER.	GERMAN TACTICS.	
FOX and GEESE.	PARLOUR AUNT SALLY.	
SKITTLES.	STAR RINGOLETTE.	
STEEPLECHASE and RACE GAME.	
The SNAIL or YOU GO BACK.	

[double rule]   [double rule] | [in gothic-revival script] **London.** | [R justified, in minuscule script] Y⁻10⁻05.

Formula: [1⁶]. 6 leaves, pp *1* 2–12

Technical notes: ca 127 × 84 mm (p 6). 29 lines, 20 = *ca* 89 mm. Leaf size *ca* 186 × 120 mm

Contents: Title (*1*), text (*2–12*)

Binding: Blue paper or light card, sewn, no spine or endpapers. FC: printed in black ([within the upper of two inter-connected panels, described by twin rules, surmounted by corner ornaments in bold on either side] THE NEW | [*do*, in ornamental script] **COMBINATION** | [*do*, in ordinary script] OF | [*do*, in ornamental script] *Parlour Games* | [*do*, a wavy line] | [*do*, an ornamental tail-piece] | [between the upper and lower panels] **CONTENTS.** | [wavy line] | [within the lower panel, divided into two columns by a double saw-toothed vertical rule:]

CROQUET.	TRAILS.	
STEEPLECHASE and RACE GAME.	PUFF and DART.	
GERMAN TACTICS.	
TON TON.	BALL SOLITAIRE.	
GO BANG.	FOX and GEESE.	
EXPERT ANGLER.	PARLOUR AUNT SALLY.	
The SNAIL or YOU GO BACK.	STAR RINGOLETTE.	
SKITTLES.	

[within the lower panel, a double rule] | [*do*] **LONDON.**). Inside FC: advertisement by FH Ayres. RC: blank. Inside RC: advertisement by FH Ayres

Copy seen: PC (photocopy)

Fingerprint: hehe s.he e.re n.ch C 1905Q [groups 2–4 taken from p 11]

Notes: Published and printed anonymously. The publisher is thought to be FH Ayres, the sole advertiser. This inference is consistent with the facts that the copy examined was found within a boxed compendium of parlour games and that Ayres are known to have marketed similar boxed compendia of games previously. Year of publication is inferred from the following indications:

(i) reference to the term 'motor car' (in the advertisement inside the FC), the first recorded use of which given by the *Oxford English Dictionary* (Oxford University Press, 1971) is in 1895, and

(ii) the lowermost line of the TP, which is taken to be a date code, signifying July or October 1905.

Page 2 of the text is devoted to the game of croquet. It constitutes six numbered paragraphs of directions, consistent with 'tight' croquet as played widely in the 1860s. (The design of croquet equipment contained in the boxed compendium of games in which the copy examined was found also harks back to this period.)

1906

A114   **CATALOGUE "A": SILVER, HORN, AND WICKER WARE,**   **1906**
LEATHER GOODS, SEAGRASS AND HARDWOOD
FURNITURE, CARRIAGES, CARROMATAS, CALESINS,
CARTS, TRUCKS, WAGONS, BASEBALL OUTFITS,
CROQUET SETS [*ETC*].[Philippines Bureau of Prisons]

CATALOGUE | "A" | [flourish] | SILVER, HORN AND WICKER | WARE, LEATHER GOODS, | SEAGRASS AND HARDWOOD | FURNITURE, CARRIAGES, | CARROMATAS, CALESINS, | CARTS, TRUCKS, WAGONS, | BASEBALL OUTFITS, CRO- | QUET SETS, HAMMOCKS, | AND VARIOUS ARTICLES | [flourish] | SALESROOM AT BILIBID PRISON | BUREAU OF PRISONS | GEORGE N. WOLFE | DIRECTOR OF PRISONS | MANILA | BUREAU OF PRINTING | 1906 | 41310 3

Formula: Apparently [1¹⁸]. 36 leaves, pp 3 [4] 5 [6] 7–37 [38] [= 36]

Technical notes: ca 187 × 109 mm (p 10). 67 lines, 20 = *ca* 56 mm. Leaf size *ca* 232 × 149 mm

Contents: Title (3), wanting from the photocopy examined ([4]), general information (5), wanting from the photocopy examined ([6]), text (7–37), wanting from the photocopy examined ([38])

Binding: Apparently bound in a pale colour paper wrapper, sewn through the folds of the leaves, no endpapers. FC: printed within a ruled frame (CATALOGUE | "A" | [flourish] | SILVER, HORN AND WICKER | WARE, LEATHER GOODS, | SEAGRASS AND HARDWOOD | FURNITURE, CARRIAGES, | CARROMATAS, CALESINS, | CARTS, TRUCKS, WAGONS, | BASEBALL OUTFITS, CRO- | QUET SETS, HAMMOCKS, | AND VARIOUS ARTICLES | [flourish] | SALESROOM AT BILIBID PRISON | BUREAU OF PRISONS | GEORGE N. WOLFE | DIRECTOR OF PRISONS | MANILA | BUREAU OF PRINTING | 1906 | 41310). Inside FC: photograph of Bilibid Prison. RC: wanting from the photocopy examined. Inside RC: wanting from the photocopy examined

Copy seen: HCLWL: Soc 3955.03 (incomplete photocopy)

Fingerprint: e.ll 0021 00l; thAf 7 1906A

Notes: Printed by Manila Bureau of Printing, Manila.

Croquet equipment features in a price list of sporting goods subtitled 'BASEBALL' (p 11).

1907

A115   MODERN CROQUET TACTICS. CD Locock   1907

(a) *First edition (1907)*

MODERN CROQUET | TACTICS | BY | C. D. LOCOCK | *WITH AN INTRO-DUCTION* | BY | JARVIS KENRICK | THE HOLMESDALE PRESS | Redhill, and 47 Fleet Street, E.C. | 1907 | *All rights reserved*

Formula: A^8 B–O^8 P^6 [\$1 signed (–A1)]. 118 leaves, pp *1–9* 10–30 *31* 32–37 *38* 39–41 *42* 43–56 *57* 58–68 *69* 70–74 *75* 76–86 *87* 88–97 *98* 99–112 *113* 114–122 *123* 124–142 *143* 144–157 *158* 159–172 *173* 174–182 *183* 184–190 *191* 192–211 *212* 213–231 *232* 233–234 *235–236*

Technical notes: 129 × 84 mm (p 10). 28 lines, 20 = 93 mm. Leaf size 185 × 126 mm; thickness 0.21 mm; wove, unwatermarked, rough, white. Three inset plates (photographs) face pp *3* (with tissue protection tipped-in), 24, 26; 63 inset diagrams (several printed in four colours) face pp *31, 36, 40, 41, 44, 45, 46, 49, 50, 53, 54, 62, 64, 66, 69, 70, 71, 72, 73, 75, 79, 80, 82, 83, 84, 88, 96, 97, 101, 105, 106, 110, 111, 115, 117, 118, 125, 127, 132, 138, 141, 147, 148, 149, 151, 153, 159, 162, 164, 167, 178, 188, 192, 193, 197, 199, 201, 204, 205, 206, 208*; Diagrams 16, 17 face p 70; Diagrams 33 and 34 back pp 108, 109; Diagram 42 is repeated facing pp 132, 138

Contents: Half-title *(1)*, blank *(2)*, title *(3)*, blank *(4)*, preface *(5)*, blank *(6)*, contents *(7)*, advertisement *(8)*, text *(9–234)*, blank *(235)*, advertisement *(236)*

Binding: Deep Yellow Green (118) cloth over stiff boards, sewn. The fore-edges and lower edges of the copy examined were uncut. There are advertisements on the facing pages of the front endpaper and on all pages of the rear endpaper. FC: in black, white, strong reddish Orange (35), strong Yellow (84), and moderate Blue (182) ([white, in display script] Modern | [*do*] Croquet Tactics | [black, in irregular script] 1907 | [schematic illustration of three balls in Orange, Yellow, and Blue, a mallet in black, and a boundary corner in white]). RC: blank. Spine: gold-blocked across the head, centre, and foot (MODERN | CROQUET | TACTICS. | C. D. LOCOCK. | [publisher's device])

Copy seen: PC

Fingerprint: K.s. s.ng ofre lain 7 1907A

Notes: Published in May 1907, printed anonymously, price 6/–, offered to Associates of the CA at 4/6 before 30 April.

Review: *The Field* (29 June 1907, p 1086).

(b) *Second edition [1910]*

MODERN CROQUET | TACTICS | Together with the Laws (1910) | By | C. D. Locock | With an Introduction by | Jarvis Kenrick | SECOND EDITION | LONDON | E. J. LARBY | 1, PATERNOSTER AVENUE, E.C. | All rights reserved

Formula: a^8 b^8 B–O^8 P^8(–P8) [\$1 signed (–a1)]. 127 leaves including the front and rear endpapers (*a*1, P7), pp *1–4, i–iii* iv–v *vi* vii *viii* ix–xxviii, 1–219 *220–222*

Technical notes: 132 × 84 mm (p x). 29 lines, 20 = 92 mm. Leaf size 182 × 123 mm; thickness 0.15–0.17 mm; wove, unwatermarked, rough, white. Three inset plates (black-and-white photographs) face pp *iii*, xxii, xxiv; 63 inset diagrams (several printed in four colours) face pp 1, 8, 10, 11, 14, 15, 16, 19, 20, 23, 24, 32, 34, 36, 39, 40, 41, 42, 43, 46, 49, 50, 52, 53, 54, 57, 65, 66, 70, 74, 75, 77, 78, 79, 80, 84, 86, 87, 95, 97, 102, 107, 110, 116, 117, 118, 120, 122, 128, 130, 133, 137, 147, 157, 161, 163, 166, 168, 171, 173, 174, 175, 178; Diagrams 16, 17 face p 40; Diagram 42 is repeated facing pp 102, 107

Contents: Glued to the FC (*1*), advertisements (*2–4*), half-title (*i*), blank (*ii*), title (*iii*), preface (iv), preface to the second edition, signed 'C. D. L.', March 1910 (v), advertisement (*vi*), contents (vii), advertisement (*viii*), introduction (ix–xxviii), text (1–201), the laws of croquet (1910) (202–219), name of printer and printer's device (219), advertisements (*220–221*), glued to the RC (*222*)

Binding: Deep Yellow Green (118) cloth over stiff boards, sewn. FC: in white, black, strong reddish Orange (35), strong Yellow (84), and moderate Blue (182) ([white, in display script] Modern | [*do*] Croquet Tactics | [black, at R] TOGETHER WITH THE LAWS | [black, at L] 1910 | [schematic illustration of three balls in Orange, Yellow, and Blue, a mallet in black, and a boundary corner in white]). RC: blank. Spine: gold-blocked across the head, centre, and foot (MODERN | CROQUET | TACTICS. | C. D. LOCOCK. | [publisher's device])

Copy seen: BL: 7921 de 31

Fingerprint: L.n.   alhe   k.i-   Clin   7   1910Q

Notes: Printed by Butler and Tanner, Frome, price 6/–. Year of publication is taken to be that cited on the FC.

In the preface to the second edition, the author observes, 'The book has been revised throughout and several clerical errors … corrected. The chapter on the Pegged-out Game has necessarily been for the most part re-written, and many alterations have been made in the chapters on Wiring and the Openings. The Laws of Croquet for 1910 are included by permission of the Committee of the Croquet Association.'

(c) *Second edition, variant [1910]*

MODERN CROQUET | **TACTICS** | Together with the Laws (1910) | By | C. D. LOCOCK | With an Introduction by | JARVIS KENRICK | SECOND EDITION | LONDON | E. J. LARBY | 1, PATERNOSTER AVENUE, E.C | *All rights reserved*

Formula: a⁸ b⁸ B–O⁸ P⁸ [$1 signed (–a1)]. 127 leaves including the front and rear endpapers (*a*1, P7), pp *1–4*, *i–iii* iv–v *vi* vii *viii* ix–xxviii, 1–219 *220–222*

Technical notes: 132 × 84 mm (p x). 29 lines, 20 = 92 mm. Leaf size 182 × 123 mm; thickness 0.15–0.17 mm; wove, unwatermarked, rough, white. Three inset plates (black-and-white photographs) face pp *iii*, xxii, xxiv; 63 inset diagrams (several printed in four colours) face pp 1, 8, 10, 11, 14, 15, 16, 19, 20, 23, 24, 32, 34, 36, 39, 40, 41, 42, 43, 46, 49, 50, 52, 53, 54, 57, 65, 66, 70, 74, 75, 77, 78, 79, 80, 84, 86, 87, 95, 97, 102, 107, 110, 116, 117, 118, 120, 122, 128, 130, 133, 137, 147, 157, 161, 163, 166, 168, 171, 173, 174, 175, 178; Diagrams 16, 17 face p 40; Diagram 42 is repeated facing pp 102, 107

Contents: Glued to the FC (*1*), advertisements (*2–4*), half-title (*i*), blank (*ii*), title (*iii*), preface (iv), preface to the second edition, signed 'C. D. L.', March 1910 (v), advertisement (*vi*), contents (vii), advertisement (*viii*), introduction (ix–xxviii), text

(1–202), the laws of croquet (1910) (203–219), name of printer and printer's device (219), advertisements (*220–221*), glued to the RC (*222*)

Binding: Deep Yellow Green (118) cloth over stiff boards, sewn. FC: in white, black, strong reddish Orange (35), strong Yellow (84), and moderate Blue (182) ([white, in display script] Modern | [*do*] Croquet Tactics | [black, at R] TOGETHER WITH THE LAWS | [black, at L] 1910 | [schematic illustration of three balls in Orange, Yellow, and Blue, a mallet in black, and a boundary corner in white]). RC: blank. Spine: gold-blocked across the head, centre, and foot (MODERN | CROQUET | TACTICS. | C. D. LOCOCK. | [publisher's device])

Copy seen: PC

Fingerprint: L.n. alhe k.i- Clin 7 1910Q

Notes: Printed by Butler and Tanner, Frome, price 6/–. Year of publication is taken to be that cited on the FC.

The text of this variant would appear to depart very little from that of (b). The title pages of the two issues vary in accidentals only. The order in which they were published is unclear.

(d) *Second edition, 1912 issue (1912)*

MODERN CROQUET | **TACTICS** | Together with the Laws (1912) | By | C. D. LOCOCK | With an Introduction by | JARVIS KENRICK | SECOND EDITION | LONDON | E. J. LARBY | 1, PATERNOSTER AVENUE, E.C | *All rights reserved*

Formula: a^8 b^8 B–N^8 O^8(–O6, 7, 8) P^2(P1+P*8) [\$1 signed (–*a*1)]. 127 leaves including the front and rear endpapers (*a*1, P2), pp *1–4, i–iii* iv–v *vi* vii *viii* ix–xxviii, 1–219 *220–222*

Technical notes: 132 × 84 mm (p x). 29 lines, 20 = 92 mm. Leaf size 184 × 123 mm; thickness 0.15–0.18 mm; wove, unwatermarked, rough, white. Three inset plates (photographs) face pp *iii*, xxii, xxiv; 63 inset diagrams (several printed in four colours) face pp 1, 8, 10, 11, 14, 15, 16, 19, 20, 23, 24, 32, 34, 36, 39, 40, 41, 42, 43, 46, 49, 50, 52, 53, 54, 57, 65, 66, 70, 74, 75, 77, 78, 79, 80, 84, 86, 87, 95, 97, 102, 107, 110, 116, 117, 118, 120, 122, 128, 130, 133, 137, 147, 157, 161, 163, 166, 168, 171, 173, 174, 175, 178; Diagrams 16, 17 face p 40; Diagram 42 is repeated facing pp 102, 107

Contents: Glued to the FC (*1*), advertisements (*2–4*), half-title (*i*), blank (*ii*), title (*iii*), preface (iv), preface to the second edition (v), advertisement (*vi*), contents (vii), advertisement (*viii*), introduction (ix–xxviii), text (1–202), the laws of croquet (pp 203–219), name of printer (219), advertisements (*220–221*), glued to the RC (*222*)

Binding: Deep Yellow Green (118) cloth over stiff boards, sewn. FC: in white, black, strong reddish Orange (35), strong Yellow (84), and moderate Blue (182) ([white, in display script] Modern | [*do*] Croquet Tactics | [black] TOGETHER WITH THE LAWS | [schematic illustration of three balls in Orange, Yellow, and Blue, mallet in black, and corner of boundary in white]). RC: blank. Spine: gold-blocked across the head, centre, and foot (MODERN | CROQUET | TACTICS. | C. D. LOCOCK. | [publisher's device])

Copy seen: PC

Fingerprint: L.et alhe k.i- Clin 7 1912Q

Notes: Printed by Butler and Tanner, Frome and London. Year of publication is inferred from the date of the CA laws of croquet given in pp 203–19. Apart from the laws, the text is apparently identical, or almost identical, to that of (b).

(e) *Third edition [1913]*

MODERN CROQUET | TACTICS | Together with the Laws (1913) | By | C. D. LOCOCK | THIRD EDITION | LONDON | E. J. LARBY | 1, PATERNOSTER AVENUE, E.C | *All rights reserved*

Formula: A^6 B–O^8 P^8(P4+χ1) [\$1 signed (–A1); χ1 signed 'P*']. 119 leaves including the front and rear endpapers, pp *1–2, i–vi* vii *viii* ix *x*, 1–224 *225–226*

Technical notes: 132 × 85 mm (p 6). 29 lines, 20 = 92 mm. Leaf size 182 × 120 mm; thickness 0.16–0.19 mm; wove, unwatermarked, rough, white. 63 inset plates (diagrams, several printed in four colours) face pp 1, 8, 10, 11, 14, 15, 16, 19, 20, 23, 24, 32, 34, 36, 39, 40, 41, 42, 43, 46, 49, 50, 52, 53, 54, 57, 65, 66, 70, 74, 75, 77, 78, 79, 80, 84, 86, 87, 95, 97, 102, 107, 110, 116, 117, 118, 120, 122, 128, 130, 133, 137, 147, 157, 161, 163, 166, 168, 171, 173, 174, 175, 178; Diagrams 17, 18 face p 40; Diagram 42 is repeated facing pp 102, 107

Contents: Glued to the FC (*1*), advertisements (*2–ii*), half-title (*iii*), blank (*iv*), title (*v*), advertisement (*vi*), preface to the third edition (vii), advertisement (*viii*), contents (ix), advertisement (*x*), text (1–206), the laws of croquet (207–224), advertisement (*225*), glued to the RC (*226*)

Binding: As that of (b)

Copy seen: PC

Fingerprint: 3.L. Inls wnme baal 3 1913Q

Notes: Printed by Butler and Tanner, Frome and London. Year of publication is inferred from the (1913) version of the laws of croquet given in the text.

In the preface the author observes, 'This edition has again been revised throughout and brought up to date. It includes a new chapter on the "Alternative Laws" … of 1913. Other alterations in the 1913 code are taken into account in the body of the work. The historical Introduction printed in the former editions is omitted from this, so that Tactics, and the Laws which control them … now form the sole contents. The Appendix has also been removed.'

1909

A116   **IMPROQUET. [Anon]**   [1909]

IMPROQUET | A New Form | of Croquet | London | JARROLD & SONS, 10 & 11, WARWICK LANE, EC. | [*All Rights Reserved*] | PRICE TWO SHILLINGS AND SIXPENCE.

Formula: [1^8]. 8 leaves, pp *1–2* 3–15 *16*

Contents: Title (*1*), blank (*2*), text (3–16), name of printer (*16*)

Copy seen: BL: Mic A 8028 (photocopy of BOD: 38491 e 19 M)

Fingerprint: isny llss hend 14ag 3 1909Q

Notes: Printed by Jarrold and Sons, Norwich. Year of publication is inferred from the BOD accession mark (20 March 1909) on p *2* of the photocopy examined and from the citation in the BL *General Catalogue*.

The text includes a code of 22 numbered rules.

1900–09

A117   **BUSSEY'S TABLE CROQUET. [Geo G Bussey & Co]**   *ca* 1905

[Title heading, p *1*]

BUSSEY'S TABLE CROQUET | (STRONG'S PATENT.)

Formula: [1¹]. 1 leaf, unnumbered [pp 1–2]

Technical notes: ca 312 × 169 mm (p *1*). 92 lines, 20 = *ca* 68 mm. Leaf size *ca* 325 × 217 mm

Contents: Title heading, testimonials, general description of game, and price list (*1*), instructions for setting and rules of play (*2*)

Binding: None

Copy seen: PC (photocopy)

Fingerprint: E.ON /6or /6or /6/6 C 1905Q [all four groups taken from p *1*]

Notes: Issued by Geo G Bussey & Co, London, together with their sets of table croquet. Printed anonymously. Approximate year of publication is inferred from the stated qualifications of the testimonializers quoted on p *1*.

1910

A118 **THE ABC OF CROQUET. Maj Arthur Mainwaring**   [1910]

(a) **First edition [1910]*

THE | ABC | OF | CROQUET | BY | **MAJOR ARTHUR MAINWARING,** | WITH INTRODUCTION | BY | **CYRIL CORBALLY.** | LONDON : | HENRY J. DRANE, | Danegeld House, 82a, Farringdon Street, E.C.

Formula: π² A–G⁸ [\$1 signed (–π1); A1–G1 signed '*Croquet. A.*' *etc* with variable punctuation]. 58 leaves, pp *i–iv, 1* 2–3 *4–7* 8–15 *16* 17–33 *34* 35–42 *43* 44–51 *52* 53–62 *63* 64–69 *70* 71–89 *90* 91–105 *106* 107–110 *111–112*

Technical notes: 93 × 63 mm (p 2). 18 lines, 20 = 106 mm. Leaf size 137 × 96 mm; thickness 0.17 mm; wove, unwatermarked, rough, white

Contents: Title (*i*), blank (*ii*), dedication (*iii*), plan of croquet court (*iv*), preface, signed 'CYRIL CORBALLY' (*1–3*), blank (*4*), contents (*5*), blank (*6*), text (*7–110*), advertisements (*111–112*)

Binding: Vivid Red (11) cloth over light boards, sewn. FC: in white with scattered illustrations of a ball, mallet, and hoop with a semi-circular crown ([in a convex arc] A·B·C | OF | CROQUET | 1/- | A·Mainwaring). RC: blank. Spine: in white upwards (**A.B.C. OF CROQUET**)

Copy seen: PC

Fingerprint: 9.M. ofof hefa Whla 3 1910Q

Notes: Printed anonymously, price 1/–. Year of publication is inferred from references on p *106*–110 to the 1910 alterations to the baulk and wiring laws (which were approved by the Committee of the CA on 6 January 1910).

Reviews (as cited in an advertisement in (c)): *Madam, Scotsman, Cork Times.*

(b) *First edition, variant [1910]*

[The TP as that of (a)]

Formula: As that of (a)

Technical notes: 93 × 63 mm (p 2). 18 lines, 20 = 105 mm. Leaf size 134 × 95 mm. All leaves other than π²: thickness 0.18 mm; wove, unwatermarked, rough, white. π²: thickness 0.06 mm; wove, unwatermarked, smooth, white

Contents: Dedication (*i*), plan of croquet court (*ii*), title (*iii*), blank (*iv*), preface, signed 'CYRIL CORBALLY' (*1–3*), blank (*4*), contents (*5*), blank (*6*), text (*7–110*), advertisement (*111–112*)

Binding: Vivid Red (11) cloth over light boards, sewn. FC: in white with scattered illustrations of a ball, mallet, and a hoop with a semi-circular crown ([in a convex arc] A·B·C | OF | CROQUET | 1/- | A·MAINWARING). RC: blank. Spine: in white upwards (**A.B.C. OF CROQUET**)

Copy seen: PC

Fingerprint: s.ee n-as hefa Whla 3 1910Q

Notes: Printed anonymously, price 1/–. It is presumed that this variant, which would appear to differ only in the transposition of some of the preliminaries, and (a) were published at about the same time. It is unclear which was published first.

(c) *Second edition [1910]*

THE | ABC | OF | CROQUET. | BY | MAJOR ARTHUR MAINWARING, | WITH INTRODUCTION | BY | CYRIL CORBALLY. | LONDON : | DRANE'S | DANEGELD HOUSE | 82A, FARRINGDON STREET, E.C.

Formula: A^8 B–D^8 E^8 [\$1 signed (–A1, E1; misprinting B as 'A')]. 40 leaves, pp *1–6* 7–64 *65–80*

Technical notes: 103 × 84 mm (p 9). 23 lines, 20 = 91 mm. Leaf size 136 × 100 mm; thickness 0.22 mm; wove, unwatermarked, rough, white

Contents: Title *(1)*, dedication *(2)*, preface, signed 'CYRIL CORBALLY' *(3–4)*, contents *(5)*, plan of croquet court *(6)*, text (7–64), advertisements *(65–80)*

Binding: Strong Red (12) cloth over light boards, sewn. FC: blocked in white with scattered illustrations of a ball, mallet, and hoop with a slightly arched crown ([in a convex arc] **A·B·C** | **OF** | **CROQUET** | **1/6** | **A·MAINWARING**). RC: blank. Spine: blind stamped or in white upwards (**A.B.C OF CROQUET**): the lettering on the copy examined is indistinct

Copy seen: PC (imperfect)

Fingerprint: bym. t.ng lyts wism 3 1910Q

Notes: Printed anonymously, price 1/6. Year of publication is conjectural. The letterpress is entirely reset but the text is apparently identical in substance to that of (a). All the supplementary advertisements are new.

A119 CROQUET: A GUIDE TO THE STROKES OF THE GAME. [1910]
GF Handel Elvey

(a) **First edition [1910]*

CROQUET | A Guide to the Strokes | of the Game | By | G. F. HANDEL ELVEY, B.A. (OXON) | LONDON | E. J. LARBY | 1, PATERNOSTER AVENUE, E.C

Formula: A^8 B–C^8 D^6 [\$1 signed (–A1)]. 30 leaves, pp *1–4 5 6* 7–12 *13* 14–26 *27* 28–32 *33* 34–42 *43* 44–46 *47* 48–58 *59–60*

Technical notes: 137 × 84 mm (p 10). 28 lines, 20 = 99 mm. Leaf size 183 × 117 mm; thickness 0.26–0.30 mm; wove, unwatermarked, rough, white

Contents: Half-title *(1)*, blank *(2)*, title *(3)*, TP verso *(4)*, preface, signed 'G. F. HANDEL ELVEY', 8 June 1910 *(5)*, blank *(6)*, contents (7–8), text, continued (9–12), blank *(13)*, text, continued (14–26), blank *(27)*, text, continued (28–32), blank, save signature *(33)*, text, continued (34–42), blank *(43)*, text, concluded (44–58), printer's device *(59)*, blank *(60)*

Binding: Printed in dark yellowish Green (137) on white paper glued flush over stiff boards, sewn. There are advertisements in greyish Yellow Green (122) on the facing pages of the endpapers. FC: in white out of Yellow Green, the title *etc* set within a frame, broken by a smaller elliptical frame as described below, composed of alternate white and coloured squares with corner ornaments ([in display script] **CROQUET** | **The Strokes of** | **the Game** | BY | G.F. HANDEL ELVEY, B.A. (Oxon) | [sketch of a hoop, mallet, and three balls on a lawn, within an elliptical frame which breaches the main frame described above] | **1/- LONDON** [the tops of the letters describing a concave arc parallel to the curvature of the elliptical frame above] **NET** | E.J. LARBY, 1, PATERNOSTER AVENUE). Spine: blank

Copy seen: PC

Fingerprint: 0.Y. 7.6. ptr- tila 7 1910Q

Notes: Printed by Butler & Tanner, Frome and London, price 1/–. Year of publication is inferred from the date appended to the author's signature in the preface. This inference is supported by the author's statement in his later work *Croquet (Association Croquet)* (A165, p 3) that he wrote the present work in 1910.

(b) *First edition, variant [1910]*

[The TP as that of (a)]

Formula: π² A⁸ B–C⁸ D⁶ χ² [B1, C1, D1 signed]. 34 leaves, pp *i–ii* iii–iv, *1–6* 7–12 *13* 14–26 *27* 28–32 *33* 34–42 *43* 44–46 *47* 48–58 *59–64*

Technical notes: 137 × 84 mm (p 10). 28 lines, 20 = 99 mm. Leaf size 185 × 116 mm. Pages *1–60*: thickness 0.20 mm; wove, unwatermarked, rough, white. Pages *i–iv, 61–64*: thickness 0.12 mm; wove, unwatermarked, smooth, white

Contents: Blank *(i)*, advertisements *(i–iii)*, blank *(iv)*, half-title *(1)*, blank *(2)*, title *(3)*, TP verso *(4)*, preface, signed 'G. F. HANDEL ELVEY', 8 June 1910 *(5)*, blank *(6)*, contents *(7–8)*, text, continued *(9–12)*, blank *(13)*, text, continued *(14–26)*, blank *(27)*, text, continued *(28–32)*, blank *(33)*,), text, continued *(34–42)*, blank *(43)*, text, concluded *(44–58)*, printer's device *(59)*, blank *(60–61)*, advertisements *(62–63)*, blank *(64)*

Binding: Printed in dark yellowish Green (137) on white paper, sewn, apparently no endpapers (the copy examined has been rebound). FC: in white out of Green, the title *etc* set within a frame, broken by a smaller elliptical frame as described below, composed of alternate white and coloured squares with corner ornaments ([in display script] **CROQUET** | **The Strokes of** | **the Game** | BY | G.F. HANDEL ELVEY, B.A. (Oxon) | [sketch of a hoop, mallet, and three balls on a lawn, within an elliptical frame which breaches the main frame described above] | **1/- LONDON** [the tops of the letters describing a concave arc parallel to the curvature of the elliptical frame above] **NET** | E.J. LARBY, 1, PATERNOSTER AVENUE). Inside FC: blank. RC: advertisement. Inside RC: blank. Spine: wanting from the copy examined

Copy seen: BL: 07911 de 19 (imperfect, in a library binding)

Fingerprint: As that of (a)

Notes: Printed by Butler & Tanner, Frome and London, price 1/–. It is conjectured that this issue, incorporating appreciably more advertising, was published shortly after (a).

A120 LAWNS AND GREENS: THEIR FORMATION AND   **[1910]**
MANAGEMENT. TW Sanders

LAWNS AND GREENS: | THEIR FORMATION AND | MANAGEMENT. | Garden, Tennis and Croquet Lawns, Bowling and | Golf Greens, Cricket Grounds, Grass Paths, etc. | BY | T. W. SANDERS, F.L.S., F.R.H.S., | *Knight of the First Class of the Royal Order of Wasa, Sweden.* | *Editor of "Amateur Gardening" and "Farm and Garden," also Author* | *of "The Flower Garden," "Encyclopædia of Gardening," "Alphabet* | *of Gardening," "Amateur's Greenhouse," "Bulbs and their Cultivation,"* | *"Vegetables and their Cultivation," etc.* | [rule] | ILLUSTRATED. | [rule] | LONDON : | W. H. & L. COLLINGRIDGE, 148 & 149, Aldersgate Street, E.C.

Formula: B–C⁸ D–K⁸ L² [\$2 signed (–B1, 2)]. 74 leaves, pp *1–5* 6 *7–9* 10 *11* 12–28 *29* 30–32 *33* 34–36 *37* 38–40 *41* 42–44 *45* 46–50 *51* 52–56 *57* 58–78 *79* 80 *81* 82–86 *87* 88–92 *93* 94–98 *99* 100–106 *107* 108–110 *111* 112–113 *114–115* 116–120 *121* 122–134 *135* 136–137 *138*, 1–9 *10*

Technical notes: 139 × 89 mm (p 10). 41 lines, 20 = 68 mm. Leaf size 184 × 123 mm; thickness 0.09 mm; wove, unwatermarked, smooth, white

Contents: Blank (*1*), frontispiece (black-and-white photograph) (*2*), title (*3*), TP verso (*4*), forewords, signed 'TWS' (*5–6*), contents (*7*), blank (*8*), text (*9–138*), advertisements (*1–10*)

Binding: Dark Green (146) cloth over and about the spine, overlapped by moderate Yellow Green (12) paper over stiff boards, sewn. FC: printed in black within four irregularly drawn adjoining rectangular panels in strong reddish Orange (35) ([in the first panel] **LAWNS** | [*do*] **AND GREENS:** | [*do*] THEIR FORMATION AND MANAGEMENT | [in the second panel] By T. W. SANDERS, F.L.S. | [*do*, a rule] | [*do*] *ILLUSTRATED.* | [in the third panel: line drawing of a behatted greensman mowing a domestic garden lawn with a hand-mower] | [in the fourth panel] **The "Amateur Gardening" Office, 148 & 149, Aldersgate St., E.C.** | [below the lowermost panel] ONE SHILLING NET.). RC: advertisement printed in black and Orange. Spine: printed in deep orange Yellow (69) downwards (**LAWNS.**).

Copy seen: BL: 07029 eee 30

Fingerprint: ndof ento idea wipo 7 1910Q

Notes: Printed by WH and L Collingridge, London, price 1/–. Year of publication is inferred from the BL's accession mark (8 FE 10) on the copy examined.

1911

AA121 BROOKLYN CROQUET CLUB: CONSTITUTION, BY-LAWS   **1911**
AND REVISED RULES 1911. [Brooklyn Croquet Club]

BROOKLYN | CROQUET CLUB | [double rule] | CONSTITUTION, BY-LAWS | AND | REVISED RULES | 1911 | PRICE TWENTY-FIVE CENTS

Formula: [1¹⁴]. 14 leaves, pp *1–2* 3–27 *28*

Technical notes: 185 × 75 mm (p 7). 33 lines, 20 = 71 mm. Leaf size 152 × 108 mm; thickness 0.11 mm; wove, unwatermarked, smooth, white

Contents: Title (*1*), Brooklyn Croquet Club (*2*), rules of play (*3–13*), constitution and by-laws (*15–16*), active members, 1910 (*17*), members, 1876–1910 (*18–21*), advertisements (*22–27*), plan of croquet court (*28*)

Binding: Dark greenish Grey (156) rough paper, printed in gold and black, sewn through the wrapper, no spine or endpapers. FC: within a double-ruled and patterned frame in gold ([in gold, within an upper panel ruled in black] **TWENTIETH** | [*do*] **CENTURY** | [*do*] **CROQUET** | [in black, within a central panel ruled in black] THE SCIENCE OF | [in gold, within a central panel ruled in black] | **BALL** | [*do*] **AND** | [*do*] **MALLET** | [in black, within a lower panel ruled in black] BROOKLYN CROQUET CLUB | [*do*] PROSPECT PARK, BROOKLYN, N. Y.).

Inside FC: blank. RC: at the foot ([in black] BROOKLYN EAGLE PRESS). Inside RC: blank

Copy seen: HPC: GV935 B87 1911 CROQ

Fingerprint: r.nd y.ng h.l. behi 3 1911A

Notes: Printed anonymously, price 25 cents. The text includes a code of rules numbered I–XXXI.

AA122 THE CHAMPION CUP 1911. HF Crowther Smith   **1911**

[in artist's script] THE | [in artist's script, in a convex arc, strong Red (12) outlined in black] CHAMPION | [in artist's script, light greenish Yellow (101) outlined in black] CUP | [a cartoon anthropomorphisation in watercolours of the Champion Cup] | [in moderate Blue (182) artist's script, within a tail-piece to the cartoon above] 1911

Formula: [1–11¹]. 11 leaves, unnumbered [pp 1–22]

Technical notes: Leaf size 258 × 180 mm; thickness 0.99–1.10 mm, variable; wove, unwatermarked, very rough, white

Contents: Title (*1*), MS and artwork alternately (*2–21*), blank (*22*)

Binding: Moderate Blue (182) buckram over stiff boards, the leaves tipped between sewn linen stubs. FC: blocked in black centrally within a blind-stamped ruled frame (**THE CROQUET ASSOCIATION.** | [swelled rule] | **"TEN BEST"** | **1911.**). RC: blind-stamped frame of the same pattern as that on the FC. Spine: blank

Copy seen: CA

Fingerprint: Indeterminate

Notes: Unpublished. This work consists of original signed portraits (on the rectos) in line and watercolours of the ten players who contested the Champion Cup (afterwards the President's Cup) in 1911, together with MS notes (on the facing versos) as to the numbers of games they won. All the portraits are dated '1911'.

A123 CROQUET: RULES AND REGULATIONS WITH   **1911**
INSTRUCTIONS. [Anon]

(a) **First edition (1911)*

[The FC, set in a scalloped frame with corner ornaments]

CROQUET | [triple rule] | **RULES AND** | **REGULATIONS** | With Instructions | AMERICAN EDITION | [triple rule] | Manufactured by | ROY BROS., EAST BARNET, VT. | 1911

Formula: [1⁸]. 8 leaves, pp 1–16

Technical notes: 115 × 76 mm (p 2). 33 lines, 20 = 70 mm. Leaf size 142 × 95 mm; thickness 0.07 mm; wove, unwatermarked, smooth, white

Contents: Text (*1–16*), advertisement (*16*)

Binding: Light Grey (264) speckled paper, printed in black, sewn through the outer wrapper, no spine or endpapers. FC: title (as above). Inside FC: blank. RC: plan of croquet court. Inside RC: blank

Copy seen: HPC: GV933 C8R6 1911 CROQ

Fingerprint: nted d,t, e.g. by**Ro** 3 1911A

Notes: Published and printed anonymously. The text, which includes a code of 50 rules, is subtantially identical to that of a similar rule book (A131) issued by

H Rademaker & Sons of Grand Rapids, Michigan, another manufacturer of croquet equipment. Its authorship and original source are unknown.

(b) *Variant edition [1911]*

[The FC, set in a double-ruled frame]

CROQUET | [double rule] | RULES *and* REGULATIONS | WITH INSTRUC-TIONS | [rule] | *AMERICAN EDITION* | [rule] | MANUFACTURED BY | ROY BROTHERS | EAST BARNET, VERMONT

Formula: [1⁸]. 8 leaves, pp 1–16

Technical notes: 111 × 75 mm (p 4). 31 lines, 20 = 73 mm. Leaf size 141 × 103 mm; thickness 0.07 mm; wove, unwatermarked, smooth, light yellowish Pink (28)

Contents: Text (1–16, inside RC), advertisement (inside RC)

Binding: Light greyish yellowish Brown (79) paper, stapled, no spine or endpapers. FC: title (as above). Inside FC: plan of a croquet court. RC: blank. Inside RC: text

Copy seen: PC

Fingerprint: onnd man- h.to inLo 3 1911Q [group 1 taken from p 1]

Notes: Printed anonymously. Year of publication is conjectural.

(c) *Variant edition [1911]*

[The FC, set in a double-ruled frame with corner ornaments]

CROQUET | [triple rule] | RULES & REGULATIONS | *with instructions* | [flourish] | *American Edition* | [flourish] | *Manufactured by* | ROY BROTHERS | EAST BARNET VERMONT

Formula: [1⁸]. 8 leaves, pp 1–16

Technical notes: 117 × 76 mm (p 2). 33 lines, 20 = 72 mm. Leaf size 143 × 100 mm; thickness 0.09 mm; wove, unwatermarked, smooth, white

Contents: Text (1–16), advertisement (16)

Binding: Light Grey (264) paper, stapled, no spine or endpapers. FC: title (as above). Inside FC: plan of a croquet court. RC: blank. Inside RC: blank

Copy seen: PC

Fingerprint: hee; e.l, e.t. anRo 3 1911Q [group 1 taken from p 1]

Notes: Printed anonymously. Year of publication is conjectural.

Collation of the text with that of (b) reveals no substantive variation. These two editions are, however, entirely distinct in that they are set in different fonts. This would suggest that when the first edition appeared Roy Bros did not envisage the work running to a further issue. Perhaps they under-estimated demand for their newly introduced croquet goods.

(d) *Variant issue [1911]*

[The FC as that of (c)]

Formula: As that of (c)

Technical notes: 116 × 76 mm (p 2). 32 lines, 20 = 73 mm. Leaf size 142 × 112 mm; thickness 0.08 mm; wove, unwatermarked, smooth, white

Contents: Text (1–16), advertisement (16)

Binding: Light Grey (264) speckled paper printed in black, sewn through the outer wraper, no spine or endpapers. FC: title (as above). Inside FC: plan of a croquet court. RC: at the foot (FREE PRESS PRINTING CO., BURLINGTON, VT.). Inside RC: blank

Copy seen: HPC: GV933 C8R6 CROQ

Fingerprint: ore- d.he t.ne **PuPe** 3 1911Q [group 1 taken from p 1]

Notes: Printed by Free Press Printing Co, Burlington, VT. Year of publication is conjectural.

The text of this issue has not been collated with that of (c). The fact that the two issues have different fingerprints does not exclude the possibility that they are identical in substance.

A124   **LAWN-TENNIS: GOLF: CROQUET: POLO.**   [1911]
Paul Champ, F de Bellet, A Després, F Caze de Caumont

(a) *First edition [1911]*

Lawn-tennis | **Golf – Croquet** | [flourish] **Polo** [flourish] | [in open script] Par MM. Paul CHAMP, | [*do*] F. DE BELLET, A DESPRÉS, | [*do*] F. CAZE DE CAUMONT. | [publisher's device with large letter *L* and the words] JE SÊME À TOUT VENT | 50 GRAVURES | [publisher's monogram set in outline of a square at L, opposite the two lines which follow] | [in open script at R] Bibliothèque Larousse | [*do*] Paris. – 13-17, rue Montparnasse

[Half-title]

[in open script] LAWN-TENNIS – GOLF | [*do*] [flourish] CROQUET – POLO [flourish]

Formula: Apparently 1^8 2–5^8 χ^6 [\$1 signed (-1_1, 1); 2_1–5_1 signed 'LAWN-TENNIS. 2' etc]. 46 leaves, pp *1*–*5* 6–20 *21* 22–25 [26–27] 28–48 *49* 50–64 *65* 66–71 *72* 73–75 *76*–*77* 78 79 80 *81*–*92*

Technical notes: 141 × 89 mm (p 24). 42 lines, 20 = 67 mm. Leaf size 192 × 129 mm. Twelve leaves of plates are inset: two (the first signed '8*') follow p 8, one (signed '16*') follows p 16, three (the second signed '24**' quired within the first, signed '24*', and third) follow p 24, one (signed '30*') follows p 30, two (the first signed '56*') follow p 56, one (signed '60*') follows p 60, two (the first signed '72*') follow p 72

Contents: Half-title (*1*), blank (*2*), title (*3*), blank (*4*), text, continued (*5–25*), wanting from the photocopy examined ([26–27]), text, concluded (*28–75*), blank (*76*), table des matières (*77–78*), table des gravures (*79–80*), name of printer (*80*), advertisements (*81–92*)

Binding: Apparently identical to that of (b)

Copy seen: LOC: GV861 C6 (photocopy, the covers in colour, wanting pp [26–27])

Fingerprint: esté 9.). 0.e; qupr 7 1911Q

Notes: Printed by Imp[rimerie] Larousse, Paris, price 2 fr. Year of publication is inferred from the catalogue of the LOC and from an inscription on the TP of the photocopy examined which cites the year 1911 as the year of copyright.

Authorship of a section entitled 'Croquet' (pp *49–64*) is attributed to Després.

(b) *Deuxième mille issue [1911]*

Lawn-tennis | **Golf – Croquet** | [flourish] **Polo** [flourish] | [in open script] Par MM. Paul CHAMP, | [*do*] F. DE BELLET, A DESPRÉS, | [*do*] F. CAZE DE CAUMONT. | [publisher's device with large letter *L* and the words] JE SÊME À TOUT VENT |

50 GRAVURES | [publisher's monogram set in outline of a square at L, opposite the two lines which follow] | [in open script at R] Bibliothèque Larousse | [*do*] Paris. – 13-17, rue Montparnasse

[Half-title]

[in open script] LAWN-TENNIS – GOLF | [*do*] [flourish] CROQUET – POLO [flourish] | [at R] <u>DEUXIÈME MILLE</u>

Formula: 1^8 $2–5^8$ χ^6 [\$1 signed (-1_1, $\chi1$); $2_1–5_1$ signed 'LAWN-TENNIS. 2' *etc*]. 46 leaves, pp *1–5 6–20 21 22–48 49 50–64 65 66–71 72 73–75 76–77 78 79 80 81–92*

Technical notes: 141 × 89 mm (p 24). 42 lines, 20 = 67 mm. Leaf size 192 × 129 mm. $1^8–5^8$: thickness 0.13 mm; wove, unwatermarked, rough, white. χ^6: thickness 0.06 mm; wove, unwatermarked, smooth, white. Twelve leaves of photographic plates are inset: two (the first signed '8*') follow p 8, one (signed '16*') follows p 16, three (the second signed '24**' quired within the first, signed '24*', and third) follow p 24, one (signed '30*') follows p 30, two (the first signed '56*') follow p 56, one (signed '60*') follows p 60, two (the first signed '72*') follow p 72

Contents: Half-title (*1*), blank (*2*), title (*3*), blank (*4*), text (*5–75*), blank (*76*), table des matières (*77–78*), table des gravures (*79–80*), name of printer (*80*), advertisements (*81–92*)

Binding: Pale Yellow (89) cloth, limp over the pastedowns, sewn. The outer corners of the cover and the leaves are rounded (radius *ca* 6 mm). FC: printed in dark yellowish Pink (30) ([in a rectangular panel flanked by quatrefoil ornaments] *Bibliothèque Larousse* | **Lawn-tennis** | **Golf** [flourish] **Croquet** | [in upper R corner cut out of illustrative panel below] **Polo** | [a half-tone black-and-white photograph of a woman lawn-tennis player about to serve is glued to the cover cloth in the form of an irregularly shaped panel set within a ruled frame over a decorative tail-piece] | [at the foot, at R] Prix : 2 francs net.). RC: publisher's monogram (*B L*) set as the flower of a dandelion in process of dissemination. Spine: in Pink upwards, set between double rules across the head and foot (**Lawn-tennis. – Golf. – Croquet. – Polo.**)

Copy seen: PC

Fingerprint: esté 9.). 0.e; qupr 7 1911Q

Notes: Printed by Imp[rimerie] Larousse, Paris, price 2 fr. Year of publication is inferred as being the same as (a). Save for the statement of the number of copies printed appended to the half-title of the present issue, the two issues are identical or virtually identical.

(c) *1913 issue (1913)*

Not seen. A copy of an issue dated 1913 is described in the catalogue issued by Christie's South Kensington for a sale held on 20 June 1997 (lot 10, sale BKS-7635).

(d) *Huitième mille issue [1921]*

Lawn-tennis | **Golf – Croquet** | [flourish] **Polo** [flourish] | [in open script] Par MM. Paul CHAMP, | [*do*] F. DE BELLET, A DESPRÉS, | [*do*] F. CAZE DE CAUMONT. | [publisher's device with large letter *L* and the words] JE SÊME À TOUT VENT | 50 GRAVURES | [publisher's monogram set in outline of a square at L, opposite the two lines which follow] | [in open script at R] Bibliothèque Larousse | [*do*] Paris. – 13-17, rue Montparnasse

[Half-title]

[in open script] LAWN-TENNIS – GOLF | [*do*] [flourish] CROQUET – POLO [flourish] | *Édition contenant le règlement* | *officiel de l'U.S.F.S.A.* (1921). | [at R] <u>HUITIÈME MILLE</u>

Formula: 1^8 $2–5^8$ χ^8 [\$1 signed $(–1_1, \chi1)$; $2_1–5_1$ signed 'LAWN-TENNIS. 2' *etc*]. 48 leaves, pp *1–5 6–18 19–21 22–48 49 50–64 65 66–75 76–77 78 79 80 81–96*

Technical notes: 141 × 89 mm (p 24). 42 lines, 20 = 67 mm. Leaf size 193 × 128 mm; wove, unwatermarked, white. Twelve leaves of photographic plates are inset following the same pages as those in (b)

Contents: Half-title (*1*), blank (*2*), title (*3*), blank (*4*), text (*5–75*), blank (*76*), table des matières (*77–78*), table des gravures (*79–80*), name of printer (*80*), advertisements (*81–96*)

Binding: Pale Yellow (89) light card glued to the gatherings, sewn, no endpapers. The outer corners of the cover and pages of the copy examined are rounded (radius *ca* 6 mm). FC: printed in strong Red (12) ([in a rectangular panel flanked by quatrefoil ornaments] *Bibliothèque Larousse* | **Lawn-tennis** | **Golf** [flourish] **Croquet** | [in upper R corner cut out of illustrative panel below] **Polo** | [half-tone black-and-white photograph of a woman lawn-tennis player about to serve, glued to the cover, in the form of an irregularly shaped panel set within a ruled frame over a decorative tail-piece]). RC: publisher's monogram (*B L*) set as the flower of a dandelion plant in process of dissemination, printed in Red. Spine: wanting from the copy examined

Copy seen: BL: 7921 de 28 (in a library binding, the leaves preserved in translucent sleeves)

Fingerprint: esté e:rs sius 5/4/ 7 1921Q

Notes: Printed by Imp[rimerie] Larousse, Paris, price 2 fr. Year of publication is inferred from the citation in the half-title (as above).

The preliminaries and text evidently follow (b) very closely, but the supplementary advertisements differ.

1913

A125　　**A CROQUET ALPHABET.** HF Crowther Smith　　[1913]

A | CROQUET | ALPHABET | RHYMED AND PICTURED | BY | H. F. CROWTHER SMITH | ENGRAVED AND PRINTED BY | HENRY STONE & SON LTD., BANBURY.

Formula: [1^6 $2–4^8$]. 30 leaves, unnumbered [pp 1–60]

Technical notes: 167 × 125 mm (p 6). 34 lines, 20 = 99 mm. Leaf size 245 × 185 mm; thickness 0.15 mm; wove, unwatermarked, semi-gloss, white

Contents: Title (*1*), dedication (*2*), preface, signed 'H. F. Crowther Smith', December 1912) (*3*), blank (*4*), text (*5–60*)

Binding: Dark greyish Yellow (91) paper over stiff boards, sewn. The endpapers are coloured yellowish White (92). FC: printed in artist's scripts ([in dark reddish Orange (38) outlined in black, slanting upwards to R] *A* | [*do*] Croquet | [*do*] Alphabet | [in open letters, at R] RHYMED | [at R] AND | [in Orange outlined in black, at R] PICTURED | BY | [in black, in a flowing hand] H. F. Crowther Smith | [swelled rule, apparently as an appendage to the signature on the above line]). RC: blank. Spine: blank

Copy seen: PC

Fingerprint: 12y. n.TH y.t" alto C 1913Q

Notes: Published privately, printed by Henry Stone & Son, Banbury. Year of publication is inferred from the date appended to the preface and to a citation in the *General Catalogue* of the BL.

The text consists of two alphabets. The first, entitled 'EXPLANATIONS' (pp 5–7) comprises two or three lines of prose for each letter, mostly the initial letters of the surnames or of other words referring to noted contemporary players. The second, untitled (pp 8–59), comprises a couplet of verse on each verso and a colour cartoon on the opposing recto, referring to the same players and situations previously 'explained'.

A126   HOW TO WIN AT GOLF CROQUET. HF Crowther Smith   1913

HOW TO WIN | AT | GOLF CROQUET | [rule] | BY | H. F. CROWTHER SMITH. | [rule] | PRICE 6d. | [rule] | Printed by PHILLIPSON'S PRESS, LTD., St. James' Rd., Kingston. | AND PUBLISHED BY THE AUTHOR, AT LONG DITTON, SURREY.

Formula: [1⁸]. 8 leaves, pp *1–3* 4–16

Technical notes: 136 × 84 mm (p 10). 31 lines, 20 = 89 mm. Leaf size 175 × 117 mm; thickness 0.18 mm; wove, unwatermarked, rough, white

Contents: Title (*1*), plan of croquet court (*2*), preface, signed 'H. F. Crowther Smith', August 1913 (*3*), text (4–16)

Binding: Deep Red (13) paper, no endapers or spine. The copy examined has been rebound; the original binding was apparently stapled. FC: printed in black within a frame composed of leaves connected by wavy lines with rosettes at the corners (How to Win | [rule] AT [rule] | Golf Croquet | BY | H. F. CROWTHER SMITH. | [vignette of wreath] | PRICE SIXPENCE.). Inside FC: blank. RC: blank. Inside RC: blank

Copy seen: BL: 7921 dd 15 (imperfect, in a library binding)

Fingerprint: 3.n, ofot err. hish 3 1913A

Notes: Printed by Phillipson's Press, Kingston, Surrey, price 6d.

1914

A127   CROQUET. Lord Tollemache   1914

CROQUET | BY | LORD TOLLEMACHE | LONDON: | STANLEY PAUL & CO. | 31, ESSEX STREET, STRAND, W.C.

[Page *iv*]

First Published 1914.

Formula: A⁸ B–N⁸ [$1 signed (–A1)]. 104 leaves, pp *i–iv* v–x, *1* 2–195 *196–198*

Technical notes: 160 × 102 mm (p 4). 38 lines, 20 = 84 mm. Leaf size *ca* 221 (variable) × 138 mm; thickness 0.30 mm, variable; wove, unwatermarked, very rough, white; 66 leaves of inset plates printed in black-and-white on one side only, 3 of unnumbered (and unlisted) diagrams and 63 of photographic illustrations (comprising 94 listed figures), follow p 6 (diagram on verso), p 8 (figs 1, 2 on recto; fig 3 on recto; fig 5 on verso; fig 5(a) on recto; fig 5(b) on verso; fig 5(c) on recto; figs 6, 7, 8 on recto; fig 4 on verso; figs 9, 10 on recto; fig 11 on verso; fig 12 on recto; fig 13 on recto; figs 14, 17 on verso; figs 15, 16 on recto; fig 18 on verso; fig 19 on recto; fig 20 on recto), p 10 (figs 21, 22 on verso; figs 23, 24 on recto), p 12 (diagram on verso; fig 25 on verso; fig 26 on recto), p 14 (figs 27, 28 on verso; figs 29, 30 on recto; figs 31, 32 on verso; figs 33, 34 on recto), p 16 (fig 35 on recto), p 18 (figs 36, 37 on verso; figs 38, 39 on recto; fig 40 on verso; figs 41, 42 on recto), p 20 (fig 81 on recto), p 22 (fig 43 on verso; fig 44 on recto; fig 45 on recto; figs 46, 47 on recto; fig 48 on verso; fig 49 on verso; fig 50 on recto), p 26 (fig 83 on verso; fig 84 on recto), p 28 (fig 85 on recto; figs 86, 87 on recto; figs 88, 89 on recto), p 30 (figs 90, 91 on verso; diagram on verso), p 34 (figs 63, 64 on verso; fig 65 on recto; figs 66, 67 on verso; figs 68, 69 on verso; fig 70 on recto), p 36 (figs 51, 52 on verso; fig 53 on recto; figs 54, 55 on verso; fig 56 on recto; figs 57, 58 on recto; fig 59 on recto; figs 60, 61 on verso; fig 62 on recto), p 40 (figs 73, 74 on verso; figs 71, 72 on recto; figs 77, 78 on verso; figs 75, 76 on recto), p 112 (figs 79, 80 on verso), p 132 (fig 82 on recto)

Contents: Half-title (*i*), blank (*ii*), title (*iii*), TP verso (*iv*), preface (*v*–vi), contents (vii–viii), list of illustrations (ix–x), text (*1–195*), blank (*196–198*)

Binding: Greyish Green (150) cloth over stiff boards, sewn. The lower edges of all of the copies examined are cut unevenly. FC: gold-blocked ([near the top] CROQUET | [near the foot at R, slanted upwards from L to R, a crown] | [set aslant *do*, in a flowing hand] Tollemache). RC: blank. Spine: gold-blocked crosswise ([at the top] CROQUET | [just below] LORD TOLLEMACHE | [at the foot] STANLEY PAUL & C°). Inside RC, glued to the pastedown, a pocket with gussets along the fore-edge, upper, and lower edges, open along the inner edge, trimmed with cloth matching the cover, containing the following loose items: (1) an untitled scale plan of a croquet court marked in 1 yd (= 1 inch) squares, printed in black and strong Yellow Green (117), the northings numbered serially and the eastings lettered alphabetically along the yard-line areas, folded first into four crosswise and then into seven lengthwise, (2) six diagrams illustrating tactical situations ('Diagrame's I–VI), printed in deep Yellow Green (118), strong Blue (178), vivid reddish Orange (34), black, and strong orange Yellow (68), quired laterally, (3) two diagrams 'To illustrate Page 39' ('Diagramme's I, II), printed in black and deep Blue (179), quired laterally, and (4) a manilla envelope, measuring 95 × 54 mm, containing twelve 16-mm diameter cardboard counters, three each coloured (on both sides) strong Blue (178), strong reddish Brown (40), black, and light Yellow (86)

Dust wrapper: Greyish yellow Green (122) rough paper, printed in black. FP: within a ruled frame ([at the head] CROQUET | [near the foot at R, slanted upwards from L to R, a crown] | [set aslant *do*, in a flowing hand] Tollemache). FF: blank. RP: blank. RF: blank. Spine: crosswise ([near the head] CROQUET | LORD TOLLEMACHE | [near the foot] STANLEY PAUL & C°)

Copies seen: PCs (3)

Fingerprint: t,an m!ry d.p- loOn 3 1914A

Notes: Printed by Wyman and Sons, London and Reading, price 10/6.

This singular work is characterised by various oddities, notably eccentric orthography and chaotic ordering of the figures. In all of the copies examined, the order of the figures, though irregular, corresponds precisely with the list of illustrations (pp ix–x).

Entries in the catalogues of the BL and BOD, which might be construed as referring to a second (1926) edition of this work, were probably intended to refer to another work by same author, *Croquet: Hints on Practice, Tactics and Stroke Play* (A138). Certainly there is no known evidence that the present work was ever re-issued.

1915

A128 LAWN SPORTS. [Anon]   1915

(a) **First edition (1915)*

[Within a frame of abstract geometrical design]

SPALDING "RED COVER" SERIES OF | ATHLETIC HANDBOOKS | No. 43R | LAWN SPORTS | COMPRISING | [divided into two columns]

Roque	Archery |
Croquet	Tether Ball |
Golf-Croquet	Garden Hockey |
Clock-Golf	Lawn Hockey |

American and British Croquet Rules | IN ADDITION TO WHICH ARE | INCLUDED RULES FOR | CRICKET | AND | [divided into two columns]

Pin Ball	Hand Tennis |
Basket Goal	Hand Polo |
Badminton	Wicket Polo |

Drawing Room Hockey | PUBLISHED BY | AMERICAN SPORTS PUBLISHING | COMPANY | 21 WARREN STREET, NEW YORK

[TP verso]

Copyright, 1915 | BY | American Sports Publishing Company | New York

Formula: Complex, not ascertainable from the copy examined. 104 leaves, pp *i–iv*, 1–2 3–7 8 9–16 *17–20* 21–39 *40* 41–64 65–66 67–84 85–86 87–102 *103* 104–136 *137–138* 139–154 *155–156* 157–163 *164* 165–185 *186–204*

Technical notes: 130 × 89 mm (p 4). 36 lines, 20 = 72 mm. Leaf size 171 × 124 mm. All leaves other than those paginated *i–vi, 17–20, 85–86, 103–104, 137–138, 155–156, 189–204*: thickness 0.13 mm, wove, unwatermarked, smooth, white. Leaves paginated *i–vi, 17–20, 85–86, 103*–104, *137–138, 155–156, 189–204*: thickness 0.09 mm, wove, unwatermarked, semi-gloss, white

Contents: Advertisements (*i–iii*), frontispiece, a black-and-white photograph with archery reference (*iv*), title (*1*), TP verso (*2*), text, the game of roque (*3–39*), 'Croquet and its rules' (*41–84*), text continued, hockey (*85–104*), text continued, 'Golf-Croquet' (*105–109*), text, concluded (*110–185*), advertisements (*186–204*)

Binding: Grey (264) paper, stapled. FC: printed in black, vivid reddish Orange (34), and dark yellowish Green (137), artist's illustrations of archery meeting and croquet game divided vertically by the title set in a broad band slanting upwards from L to R ([in black, at L] Group XII, No. 43R [at R] Price 25 Cents | [in Orange display script, outlined in black, dropped and decorated *S, S*] SPALDING'S | [in Green] **ATHLETIC LIBRARY** | [in Orange, under- and over-lined, out of an oblique black band] *LAWN SPORTS* | [in Green] *AMERICAN SPORTS PUBLISHING CO.* | [in Green] *21 Warren Street, New York*). Inside FC: advertisement, printed in Orange. RC: advertisement, printed in Orange. Inside RC: advertisement, printed in Orange. Spine: in Orange, downwards (**No 43R. SPALDING'S "RED COVER" SERIES. LAWN SPORTS AND VOLLEY BALL. 25 CENTS.**)

Copy seen: HPC: GV701 L3 1915 CROQ

Fingerprint: ndhe e.al heng atst 3 1915A

Notes: Printed anonymously, price 25 cents. Year of publication is inferred from the assertion of copyright on the TP verso. A cipher ('12.16.14') repeated on pp *i–iii* would appear to be a date code, suggesting that this work was produced on 16 December 1914.

The text includes anonymous sections entitled 'CROQUET AND ITS RULES' (pp 40–84) and 'GOLF-CROQUET' (pp 105–109). The former includes a code of 62 rules 'adapted to the playing of *Loose Croquet*' and a code of 37 laws, apparently a précis of the laws of Association Croquet, represented as the 'official laws of the British Croquet Association'. Some other sections are attributed to named sources.

(b) *1916 issue (1916)*

[The TP as that of (a)]

Formula: Complex, not ascertainable from the copy examined. 96 leaves, pp *i–iv*, *1–2 3–7 8 9–16 17–20 21–39 40 41–64 65–66 67–84 85–86 87–102 103 104–136 137–138 139–154 155–156 157–163 164 165–185 186–188*

Technical notes: 130 × 88 mm (p 4). 37 lines, 20 = 71 mm. Leaf size 170 × 124 mm. All leaves other than those paginated *i–vi, 17–20, 85–86, 103–104, 137–138, 155–156*: thickness 0.14 mm, wove, unwatermarked, rough, white. Leaves paginated *i–vi, 17–20, 85–86, 103–104, 137–138, 155–156*: thickness 0.10 mm, wove, unwatermarked, semi-gloss, white

Contents: Advertisements (*i–iii*), frontispiece, a black-and white photograph with archery reference (*iv*), title (*1*), TP verso (*2*), text, the game of roque (*3–39*), 'Croquet and its rules' (*41–84*), text continued, hockey (*85–104*), text continued, 'Golf-Croquet' (*105–109*), text, concluded (*110–185*), advertisements (*186–188*)

Binding: White paper, stapled. FC: as that of (a). Inside FC: advertisement, printed in black. RC: advertisement, printed in Orange. Inside RC: advertisement, printed in black. Spine: in Orange, downwards (**No 43R.** [above] **SPALDING'S** [below] **"RED COVER" SERIES.** [centrally] **Lawn Sports and Volley Ball. 25 Cents.**)

Copy seen: HPC: GV701 L3 1916 CROQ

Fingerprint: ndhe e.al heng atst 3 1916A

Notes: Printed anonymously, price 25 cents. Year of publication is inferred from the assertion of copyright on the TP verso. A cipher ('4.15.16') repeated on pp *i–iii* would appear to be a date code, suggesting that this work was produced on 15 April 1916.

The text would appear to be identical to that of (a). Collation with (a) revealed only one minor editorial revision, namely the insertion of a page reference. The advertising matter, however, is mostly different.

(c) *1921 issue (1921)*

[Within a frame of abstract geometrical design]

Spalding "Red Cover" Series of | Athletic Handbooks | No. 43R | Lawn Sports | comprising | [divided into two columns]

Roque	Archery	
Croquet	Tether Ball	
Golf-Croquet	Garden Hockey	
Clock-Golf	Lawn Hockey	

American and British Croquet Rules | IN ADDITION TO WHICH ARE | INCLUDED RULES FOR | CRICKET | AND | [divided into two columns]

Pin Ball	Hand Tennis	
Basket Goal	Hand Polo	
Badminton	Wicket Polo	

Drawing Room Hockey | PUBLISHED BY | AMERICAN SPORTS PUBLISHING | COMPANY | 21 Warren Street, New York

Formula: [1–6^{16}]. 96 leaves, pp *i–iv, 1–2 3–7 8 9–16 17–20 21–39 40 41–64 65–66 67–80 81 82–84 85–86 87–104 105 106–135 136–145 146–154 155–156 157–163 164 165–185 186–188*

Technical notes: 130 × 88 mm (p 4). 37 lines, 20 = 71 mm. Leaf size 169 × 124 mm; thickness 0.07 mm; wove, unwatermarked, semi-gloss, white

Contents: Advertisements (*i–iii*), frontispiece, a black-and white photograph with archery reference (*iv*), title (*1*), TP verso (2), text, the game of roque (3–39), 'Croquet and its rules' (41–84), text continued, hockey (*85–104*), text continued, 'Golf-Croquet' (105–109), text, concluded (110–185), advertisements (*186–188*)

Binding: White semi-gloss light card glued to the folded edges of the gatherings, stapled, no endpapers. FC: as that of (a). Inside FC: advertisement, printed in black. RC: advertisement, printed in Orange. Inside RC: advertisement, printed in black. Spine: in Orange, downwards (**No. 43R. SPALDING'S "RED COVER" SERIES. LAWN SPORTS and VOLLEY BALL. Price, 25c.**)

Copy seen: HPC: GV701 L3 1921 CROQ

Fingerprint: ndhe e.al heng atst 3 1921A

Notes: Printed anonymously, price 25 cents. Year of publication is inferred from the assertion of copyright on the TP verso. Ciphers ('7-21' and '10-21') on pp *i–iii* would appear to be date codes, suggesting that this work was produced late in the year.

The text is apparently identical to that of (b), except for the substitution of a section devoted to cricket for one previously devoted to volley ball. Curiously, the new section is unpaginated, and reference to the latter game on the spine is in error. The advertising matter is different.

(d) *1925 issue (1925)*

[The TP as that of (c)]

Formula: [1–6¹⁶]. 96 leaves, pp *i–iv*, *1–2* 3–7 *8* 9–16 *17–20* 21–39 *40* 41–64 *65–66* 67–80 *81* 82–84 *85–86* 87–104 *105* 106–133 *134* 135 *136–145* 146–154 *155–156* 157–163 *164* 165–185 *186–188*

Technical notes: 130 × 88 mm (p 4). 37 lines, 20 = 71 mm. Leaf size 170 × 124 mm; thickness 0.06 mm; wove, unwatermarked, very smooth, white

Contents: As the contents of (c)

Binding: As that of (c)

Copy seen: HPC: GV701 L3 1925 CROQ

Fingerprint: ndhe e.al heng atst 3 1925A

Notes: Printed anonymously, price 25 cents. Year of publication is inferred from the assertion of copyright on the TP verso. A cipher ('1-25') repeated on pp *i–iii* would appear to be a date code, suggesting that this issue was produced early in the year.

The text is apparently identical to that of (c). The advertising matter is different. The erroneous reference to volley ball on the spine is perpetuated.

(e) *1926 issue (1926)*

[The TP as that of (c)]

Formula: [1–6¹⁶]. 96 leaves, pp *i–iv*, *1–2* 3–7 *8* 9–16 *17–20* 21–39 *40* 41–43 *44* 45–64 *65–66* 67–80 *81* 82–84 *85–86* 87–104 *105* 106–120 *121* 122–133 *134* 135 *136–145* 146–154 *155–156* 157–163 *164* 165–185 *186–188*

Technical notes: 130 × 88 mm (p 4). 37 lines, 20 = 71 mm. Leaf size 170 × 124 mm; thickness 0.06 mm; wove, unwatermarked, very smooth, white

Contents: As the contents of (c)

Binding: As that of (c)

Copy seen: HPC: GV701 L3 1926 CROQ

Fingerprint: ndhe e.al heng atst 3 1926A

Notes: Printed anonymously, price 25 cents. Year of publication is inferred from the assertion of copyright on the TP verso. Ciphers ('5-26' and '4-26') on pp *i–iii* would appear to be date codes, suggesting that this issue was produced mid-year.

The text is apparently identical to that of (d). The advertising matter is different. The erroneous reference to volley ball on the spine is further perpetuated.

(f) *1927 issue (1927)*

[The TP as that of (c)]

Formula: As that of (e)

Technical notes: 131 × 88 mm (p 4). 37 lines, 20 = 71 mm. Leaf size 170 × 126 mm; thickness 0.07 mm; wove, unwatermarked, smooth, white

Contents: As contents of (c)

Binding: As that of (c)

Copy seen: HPC GV701 L3 1927 CROQ

Fingerprint: ndhe e.al heng atst 3 1927A

Notes: Printed anonymously, price 25 cents. Year of publication is inferred from the assertion of copyright on the TP verso. A cipher ('6-27') repeated on pp *i–iii* would appear to be a date code, suggesting that this issue was produced mid-year.

The text is apparently identical to that of (e). Some of the advertising matter is different. The erroneous reference to volley ball on the spine is further perpetuated.

(g) *1930 issue (1930)*

[Within a frame of abstract geometrical design]

SPALDING "RED COVER" SERIES OF | ATHLETIC HANDBOOKS | No. 43R | LAWN SPORTS | COMPRISING | [divided into two columns]

Roque	Archery |
Croquet	Tether Ball |
Golf-Croquet	Garden Hockey |
Clock-Golf	Lawn Hockey |

American and British Croquet Rules | IN ADDITION TO WHICH ARE | INCLUDED RULES FOR | CRICKET | AND | [divided into two columns]

Pin Ball	Hand Tennis |
Basket Goal	Hand Polo |
Badminton	Wicket Polo |

Drawing Room Hockey | PUBLISHED BY | AMERICAN SPORTS PUBLISHING | COMPANY | 45 ROSE STREET, NEW YORK

Formula: [1–6^{16}]. 96 leaves, pp *i–iv*, *1–2* 3–7 *8* 9–16 *17–20* 21–22 *23* 24–36 *37* 38–39 *40* 41–64 *65–66* 67–70 *71* 72–75 *76* 77–80 *81* 82–84 *85–86* 87–95 *96* 97–104 *105* 106–133 *134* 135–155 *156–157* 158–164 *165* 166–186 *187–188*

Technical notes: 130 × 88 mm (p 4). 37 lines, 20 = 71 mm. Leaf size 170 × 125 mm; thickness 0.08 mm; wove, unwatermarked, smooth, white

Contents: Advertisements (*i–iii*), frontispiece, a black-and-white photograph with archery reference (*iv*), title (*1*), TP verso (*2*), text, the game of roque (*3–39*), 'Croquet and its rules' (*41–84*), text continued, hockey (*85–104*), text continued, 'Golf-Croquet' (*105–109*), text, concluded (*110–186*), advertisements (*187–188*)

Binding: White semi-gloss light card glued to the edges of the gatherings, stapled, no endpapers. FC: as that of (a). Inside FC: advertisement, printed in black. RC: advertisement, printed in Orange. Inside RC: advertisement, printed in black. Spine: in Orange, downwards (**No. 43R. SPALDING'S "RED COVER" SERIES. LAWN SPORTS. Price, 25c.**)

Copy seen: HPC: GV701 L3 1930 CROQ

Fingerprint: ndhe e.al heng atst 3 1930A

Notes: Printed anonymously, price 25 cents. Year of publication is inferred from the assertion of copyright on the TP verso. A cipher ('9-29') repeated on pp *i–iii* would appear to be a date code, suggesting that this issue was produced in September 1929.

The text is apparently identical to that of (f), save for major changes in its treatment of badminton, extending the text to p 186 at the expense of one page of advertisements. Some of the advertising matter is different. The erroneous reference to volley ball on the spine of earlier issues is discontinued.

(h) *1930 re-issue (1930)*

[The TP as that of (g)]

Formula: [1–6¹⁶]. 96 leaves, pp *i–iv, 1–2 3 4 5–7 8 9–16 17–20 21–22 23 24–27 28 29–36 37 38–39 40 41–64 65–66 67–70 71 72–75 76 77–80 81 82 83 84 85–86 87–95 96 97–104 105 106–109 110 111–133 134 135–155 156–157 158–164 165 166–186 187–188*

Technical notes: 132 × 88 mm (p 13). 37 lines, 20 = 72 mm. Leaf size 170 × 125 mm; thickness 0.07 mm; wove, unwatermarked, smooth, white

Contents: Advertisements (*i–iii*), frontispiece (black-and-white photograph) (*iv*), title (*1*), TP verso (*2*), text (*3–186*), advertisements (*187–188*)

Binding: White paper, stapled. FC: as that of (a). Inside FC: advertisement printed in Green. RC: advertisement printed in black and Orange. Inside RC: advertisement printed in Green. Spine: printed downwards in Orange (**No. 43R. SPALDING'S "RED COVER" SERIES. LAWN SPORTS. Price, 25 Cents.**)

Copy seen: PC

Fingerprint: ndhe e.al heng atst 3 1930A

Notes: Printed anonymously, price 25 cents. A cipher repeated on pp *i–iii* would appear to be a date code. Hence it is inferred that this issue was published in or after March 1930.

The text has not been collated with that of (g), but the two issues are thought to be identical or virtually identical.

(j) *1931 issue (1931)*

[Within a double-ruled frame of abstract geometrical design with internal corner ornaments]

Spalding's "Red Cover" Series of | Athletic Handbooks | No. 43R | **Lawn Sports** | Comprising | Roque [twin downwards-pointing chevrons] Croquet [*do*] Modern Croquet | Golf-Croquet [*do*] Clock-Golf [*do*] Archery | Tether Ball [*do*] Garden Hockey [*do*] Lawn Hockey | American and British Croquet Rules | In Addition to which are Included Rules for | **Cricket** | and | Pin Ball [twin downwards-pointing chevrons] Basket Goal | Badminton [*do*] Hand Tennis [*do*] Hand Polo | Wicket Polo [*do*] Drawing Room Hockey | Published by | AMERICAN SPORTS PUBLISHING CO. | 45 Rose Street, New York

Formula: [1–6¹⁶ 7¹²]. 108 leaves, pp *i–iv, 1–2 3 4 5–7 8 9–16 17–20 21–22 23 24–27*

28 *29–36* 37 *38–39* 40 *41–49* 50 *51–60* 61 *62–85* 86–87 88–105 *106* 107 *108* 109–176 *177–178* 179–207 *208–212*

Technical notes: 130 × 88 mm (p 4). 37 lines, 20 = 71 mm. Leaf size 170 × 125 mm; thickness 0.10 mm; wove, unwatermarked, smooth, white

Contents: Advertisements (*i–iii*), frontispiece, a black-and-white photograph with archery reference (*iv*), title (*1*), TP verso (*2*), text, the game of roque (*3–39*), 'Modern Croquet' (*40–61*), 'Croquet and its rules' (*62–105*), text continued, hockey (*106–125*), text continued, 'Golf-Croquet' (*126–130*), text, concluded (*131–207*), advertisements (*208–212*)

Binding: Apparently as that of (h)

Copy seen: HPC: GV701 L3 1931a CROQ

Fingerprint: ndhe e.al heng atst 3 1931A

Notes: Printed anonymously, price 25 cents. Year of publication is inferred from the assertion of copyright on the TP verso. Ciphers ('12-30', '4-31', '11-30') on pp *i–iii* would appear to be date codes, suggesting that this issue was produced in the spring of 1931.

The text departs from that of earlier issues in introducing a new section devoted to 'modern croquet', as distinct from the mainstream American game of 'croquet' and the version of the game attributed to the British Croquet Association. Those sections devoted to the latter game and to golf-croquet remain unaltered.

(k) *1935 issue (1935)*

[Within a double-ruled frame of abstract geometrical design with internal corner ornaments]

Spalding's "Red Cover" Series of | Athletic Handbooks | No. 43R | **Lawn Sports** | Comprising | Roque [twin downwards-pointing chevrons] Croquet [*do*] Modern Croquet | Golf-Croquet [*do*] Clock-Golf [*do*] Archery [*do*] Tether Ball | American and British Croquet Rules | In Addition to which are Included Rules for | **Cricket** | and | Pin Ball [twin downwards-pointing chevrons] Basket Goal | Hand Tennis [*do*] Wicket Polo [*do*] Hand Polo | Published by | AMERICAN SPORTS PUBLISHING CO. | 45 Rose Street, New York

Formula: Thought to be [1–5¹⁶ 6⁴], the collation of the last four leaves unverified. 84 leaves, pp *1–2* 3–7 8 *9–16* 17–18 *19–37* 38 *39–47* 48 *49–58* 59 *60–83* 84–85 86–142 *143–144* 145–163 *164–168*

Technical notes: 130 × 88 mm (p 4). 37 lines, 20 = 71 mm. Leaf size 170 × 125 mm; thickness 0.07 mm; wove, unwatermarked, smooth, white

Contents: Title (*1*), TP verso (*2*), the game of roque (*3–37*), 'Modern Croquet' (*38–58*), 'Croquet and its rules' (*59–103*), text, continued (*104–106*), 'Golf-Croquet' (*107–111*), text, concluded (*112–163*), advertisements (*164–168*)

Binding: White semi-gloss light card glued to the folds of the gatherings, stapled, no endpapers. FC: as that of (a). Inside FC: advertisement, printed in black. RC: advertisement, printed in Orange. Inside RC: advertisement, printed in black. Spine: blank

Copy seen: HPC: GV701 L3 1931 CROQ

Fingerprint: ndhe e.al heng atst 3 1935A

Notes: Printed anonymously, price 25 cents. Year of publication is inferred from the ciphers ('12-30', '4-31', '11-30'), taken to be date codes, which appear in this issue on the supplementary advertising pages *164–166*. In earlier issues such ciphers had been appended to the preliminary advertising matter. The year of copyright asserted on the TP is 1931.

The text omits a number of sports treated in earlier issues. Those sections devoted to modern croquet, croquet, and golf-croquet remain unaltered.

(l) *1936 issue (1936)*

[Within a frame of abstract geometrical design]

Spalding's "Red Cover" Series of | Athletic Handbooks | No. 43R | **Lawn Sports** | Comprising | Roque [twin downwards-pointing chevrons] Croquet [*do*] Modern Croquet | Golf-Croquet [*do*] Clock-Golf [*do*] Archery [*do*] Tether Ball | American and British Croquet Rules | In Addition to which are Included Rules for | Cricket | and | Pin Ball [*do*] Basket Goal | Hand Tennis [do] Wicket Polo [*do*] HAND POLO | PUBLISHED BY | American Sports Publishing Co. | 45 Rose Street, New York

[TP verso]

Copyright. 1931 | By | American Sports Publishing Company | New York

Formula: [1–5^{16} 6^4]. 84 leaves, pp *1–2* 3–7 *8* 9–16 *17–18* 19–37 *38* 39–47 *48* 49–58 *59* 60–83 *84–85* 86–142 *143–144* 145–163 *164–168*

Technical notes: 133 × 78 mm (p 13). 37 lines, 20 = 72 mm. Leaf size 170 × 128 mm; thickness 0.06 mm; wove, unwatermarked, smooth, white

Contents: Title (*1*), TP verso (*2*), text (3–163), advertisements (*164–168*)

Binding: As that of (k)

Copy seen: PC

Fingerprint: ndhe e.al heng atst 3 1936Q

Notes: Printed anonymously, price 25 cents. A cipher repeated on pp 164–6 is thought to be a date code. Hence it is inferred that this issue was published in or after July 1936.

Though this issue has not been collated with (k), it is believed that those sections devoted to all versions of the game of croquet in these two issues are identical or virtually identical.

(m) *1939 issue [1939]*

[Within a double-ruled frame of abstract geometrical design with internal corner ornaments]

SPALDING'S ATHLETIC LIBRARY | No 343 | **Lawn Sports** | Comprising | Roque [twin downwards-pointing chevrons] Croquet [*do*] Modern Croquet | Golf-Croquet [*do*] Clock-Golf [*do*] Archery [*do*] Tether Ball | American and British Croquet Rules | In Addition to which are Included Rules for | **Cricket** | and | Basket Goal [twin downwards-pointing chevrons] Wicket Polo [*do*] Hand Polo | PUBLISHED BY | AMERICAN SPORTS PUBLISHING | COMPANY | NEW YORK

Formula: [1–5^{16}]. 80 leaves, pp *1–2* 3–7 *8* 9–16 *17–18* 19–37 *38* 39–47 *48* 49–58 *59* 60–83 *84–85* 86–138 *139–140* 141–159 *160*

Technical notes: 130 × 89 mm (p 4). 37 lines, 20 = 71 mm. Leaf size 170 × 126 mm; thickness 0.09 mm; wove, unwatermarked, semi-gloss, white

Contents: Title (*1*), TP verso (*2*), text, the game of roque (3–37), 'Modern Croquet' (*38–58*), 'Croquet and its rules' (59–103), text, continued (104–106), text, 'Golf-Croquet' (107–111), text, concluded (112–159), advertisement (*160*)

Binding: White semi-gloss light card glued to the folds of the gatherings, printed in strong Green (141), stapled, no endpapers. FC: in white out of a half-tone photograph of a lawn in a parkland setting, overlaid by an oblique rectangular panel and by a narrow band at the foot ([in Green outlined in white out of half-tone background illustration, dropped and decorated S, S] SPALDING'S [in white out of half-tone background illustration] 50 Cents | [do, partially eclipsed by the line below] ATHLET [‡] ARY | [in white out of half-tone background illustration] **LAWN GAMES** | [in white out of Green panel] **ARCHERY** | [do] **BASKET GOAL** | [do] **CRICKET** | [do] **CLOCK-GOLF** | [do] **CROQUET** | [do] **GOLF-CROQUET** | [do] **HAND POLO** | [do] **ROQUET** | [do] **TETHER BALL** | [do] **WICKET POLO** | [in white out of a Green tail-band] **AMERICAN SPORTS PUBLISHING CO.**). Inside FC: advertisement, in Green. RC: advertisement. Inside RC: advertisement, in Green. Spine: blank

Copy seen: HPC: GV701 L3 1939 CROQ (imperfect)

Fingerprint: ndhe e.al heng atst 3 1939Q

Notes: Printed anonymously, price 50 cents. Year of publication is inferred from the assertion of copyright on the TP verso.

Though this issue and (l) have not been collated, the text of the present issue would appear to be identical or virtually identical to that of (l) save for the omission of a section on hand tennis. The FC design and cover title are new and the space given to advertisements is reduced. The date codes given in earlier issues are discontinued.

A129   **[VICTORIAN CROQUET ASSOCIATION ANNUAL].**   1915
[The Victorian Croquet Association]

(a) *First edition (1915)*

Not seen. J Ridley gives an account of the first publication of this work in A206 (p i).

(b) *1959–60 edition (1959)*

Formula: Apparently [1⁵⁶]. Apparently 56 leaves, pp [1–4] 5–108 [109–112] [= 112]

Technical notes: 151 × 84 mm (p 32). Mostly 53 lines, 20 = 57 mm. Leaf size 176 × 116 mm; thickness 0.10 mm; wove, unwatermarked, smooth, white

Contents: Wanting from the copy examined ([1–4]), official referees (5–6), advertisement (6), officers of associated clubs (7–10), winners of principal events (11–21), association fixtures 1959–60 (22–28), advertisement (29), constitution and rules (30–54), laws of Association Croquet 1957 (55–70), regulations for official tournaments (71–83), instructions to referees (84–86), etiquette (87), affiliated clubs (88), names, addresses, and handicaps of club members (89–108), wanting from the copy examined ([109–112])

Binding: Apparently greyish Green (150) paper, stapled through the wrapper, no endpapers

Copy seen: CA (incomplete, wanting the wrapper and pp [1–4, 109–112])

Fingerprint: Not ascertainable from the photocopy examined.

1916

A130   **CROQUET: RULES OF THE GAME.** [Anon]   1916

(a) **First edition (1916)*

[Within a ruled frame]

SPALDING'S ATHLETIC LIBRARY | **CROQUET** | [rule] | Rules of the Game | AND |

Official Laws | British Croquet Association | Published by | AMERICAN SPORTS PUBLISHING COMPANY | 21 Warren Street, New York

Formula: Not ascertainable from the photocopy examined. 24 leaves, pp *i–iv*, 41–64 65–66 67–84 [= 48]

Technical notes: 129 × 90 mm (p 42). 37 lines, 20 = 72 mm. Leaf size 173 × 125 mm

Contents: Title (*i*), TP verso (*ii*), publisher's notice (*iii*), plan of croquet court (*iv*), text (41–84)

Binding: White semi-gloss light card or paper, printed in dark bluish Grey (192), glued to the folds of the gatherings, the gatherings stapled together close to the folds, no spine or endpapers. FC: in Grey within a white panel with ornaments at the extremities] **ATHLETIC LIBRARY** | [in white out of Grey] Auxiliary Series | [in Grey, on a white panel within a multiple decorative frame] **CROQUET** | [*do*, rule] | [*do*] **Rules of the Game** | [*do*] AND | [*do*] **OFFICIAL LAWS** | [*do*] **British Croquet Association** | [*do*] PRICE 10 CENTS | [below white panel] AMERICAN SPORTS PUBLISHING CO. | [*do*] 21 *Warren Street, New York*). Inside FC: advertisement, in black. RC: advertisement, in white out of Grey, for Spalding's Athletic Library and athletic goods. Inside RC: Spalding's quality guarantees

Copy seen: LOC: GV931 C8 1916 (photocopy of original copy rebound in library covers, the wrapper in colour)

Fingerprint: s.lo .]ee t.da saEv C 1916A

Notes: Printed anonymously, price 10 cents. Year of publication is inferred from the assertion of copyright. A curiosity of this work is the irregular pagination. This is due to the text having been transcribed, largely or in its entirety, complete with original pagination, from the same publisher's larger companion, *Lawn Sports* (A128).

The text includes an (American) code of 62 rules based on a ten-wicket setting, unattributed to any convention or authority, and an undated version of the CA code, extending to 37 laws plus 'Alternative Laws' A and B. The former code appears to be based on that of the National American Croquet Association (see, for example, A85).

(b) *1920 issue (1920)*

[The TP as that of (a)]

Formula: [1²⁴]. 24 leaves, pp *i–iv*, 41–44 45 46–64 65–66 67–84 [= 48]

Technical notes: 129 × 89 mm (p 42). 37 lines, 20 = 71 mm. Leaf size 172 × 142 mm

Contents: As the contents of (a)

Binding: White semi-gloss light card or paper, printed in dark bluish Grey (192), stapled through the folds of the sheets, no spine or endpapers. FC: as that of (a). Inside FC: advertisement, as that of (a). RC: as that of (a). Inside RC: advertisement, in black, for Spalding's sports goods

Copy seen: LOC: GV931 C8 1920 (photocopy of original copy rebound in library covers, the wrapper in colour)

Fingerprint: s.lo e.rs t.da saEv C 1920A

Notes: Printed anonymously, price 10 cents. The text of this issue is identical, or virtually identical, to that of (a).

(c) *1925 abridged issue (1925)*

[Within a ruled frame]

SPALDING'S ATHLETIC LIBRARY | **CROQUET** | [swelled rule] | Rules of the Game |

Published by | AMERICAN SPORTS PUBLISHING CO. | 45 Rose Street, New York

Formula: [1¹⁶]. 16 leaves, pp *i–iv*, 41–43 *44* 45–64 65–68 [= 32]

Technical notes: 129 × 89 mm (p 42). 37 lines, 20 = 71 mm. Leaf size 170 × 125 mm

Contents: Title (*i*), TP verso (*ii*), publisher's notice (*iii*), plan of croquet court (*iv*), text (41–66), advertisements (67–68)

Binding: White semi-gloss light card or paper, printed in black and deep reddish Orange (36), apparently stapled through the wrapper, no spine or endpapers. FC: mostly in white out of Orange ([in Orange on white panels at L and R] **No. 119R PRICE 25 CENTS** | [in artist's script with dropped and decorated *S, S*] SPALDING'S | [in Orange within a white panel with ornaments at the extremities] **ATHLETIC LIBRARY** | [in black, centrally in a double-ruled frame, the outer frame in bold, with corner ornaments, within a white panel] **CROQUET** | [*do*, symmetrical flourish] | [*do*] RULES | [*do*] *of the* | [*do*] GAME | [below white panel] AMERICAN SPORTS PUBLISHING CO. | [*do*] 45 *Rose Street, New York*). Inside FC: advertisement, in black, for Spalding's athletic goods. RC: advertisement, in white out of Orange, for Spalding's Athletic Library and athletic goods. Inside RC: advertisement, in black, 'The Real Meaning of a Trade Mark'

Copy seen: LOC: GV931 C8 1925 (photocopy of original copy rebound in library covers, the wrapper in colour)

Fingerprint: s.lo e.rs t.da saEv C 1925A

Notes: Printed anonymously, price 25 cents. The text of this issue is identical, or virtually identical, to that of earlier issues, save for the omission of the section previously devoted to the British game.

(d) *1926 abridged issue (1926)*

[The TP as that of (c)]

Formula: [1¹⁶]. 16 leaves, pp *i–iv*, 41–64 65–68 [= 32]

Technical notes: 129 × 89 mm (p 42). 37 lines, 20 = 71 mm. Leaf size 170 × 127 mm

Contents: As the contents of (c)

Binding: As that of (c)

Copy seen: LOC: GV931 C8 1926 (photocopy of original copy in library covers, the wrapper in colour)

Fingerprint: s.lo e.rs t.da saEv C 1926A

Notes: Printed anonymously, price 25 cents. The text of this issue is identical, or virtually identical, to that of (c).

(e) *1927 abridged issue (1927)*

[Within a ruled frame]

CROQUET | [swelled rule] | Rules of the Game | Published by | AMERICAN SPORTS PUBLISHING CO. | 45 Rose Street, New York

Formula: [1¹⁶]. 16 leaves, pp *i–iv*, 41–64 65–68 [= 32]

Technical notes: 129 × 89 mm (p 42). 37 lines, 20 = 71 mm. Leaf size 171 × 126 mm; thickness 0.16 mm; wove, unwatermarked, rough, white

Contents: Title (*i*), TP verso (*ii*), publisher's notice (*iii*), plan of croquet court (*iv*), text (41–66), advertisements (67–68)

Binding: White semi-gloss light card, printed in dark Green (146) and deep reddish Orange (36), sewn through the wrapper, no spine or endpapers. FC: mostly in white out of Orange ([in Orange on white panels at L and R] **No. 119R PRICE 25 CENTS** | [in artist's script with dropped and decorated *S, S*] Spalding's | [in Orange within a white panel with ornaments at the extremities] **ATHLETIC LIBRARY** | [in Green, centrally in a double-ruled frame, the outer frame in bold, with corner ornaments, within a white panel] **CROQUET** | [*do*, flourish] | [*do*] RULES | [*do*] *of the* | [*do*] GAME | American Sports Publishing Co. | *45 Rose Street, New York*). Inside FC: advertisement, in Green. RC: advertisement, in white out of Orange, for Spalding's Athletic Library and athletic goods. Inside RC: advertisement, in Green

Copy seen: HPC: GV933 C81 1927 CROQ

Fingerprint: s.l* e.rs t.da saEv C 1927A

Notes: Printed anonymously, price 25 cents. This issue has not been collated with (d) but it would appear that the text is an identical reprint.

(f) *1928 abridged issue (1928)*

[Within a ruled frame]

Spalding's Athletic Library | **CROQUET** | [swelled rule] | Rules of the Game | Published by | American Sports Publishing Co. | 45 Rose Street, New York

Formula: As that of (e)

Technical notes: 128 × 89 mm (p 42). 37 lines, 20 = 71 mm. Leaf size 171 × 128 mm; thickness 0.18 mm; wove, unwatermarked, smooth, white

Contents: As the contents of (e)

Binding: As that of (e), save for the advertising on the RC: advertisement for Spalding Equipment in Green and Orange

Copy seen: HPC: GV933 C81 1928 CROQ

Fingerprint: s.l* e.rs t.da saEv C 1928A

Notes: Printed anonymously, price 25 cents. The text of this issue is apparently identical in substance to that of (e).

(g) *1929 edition (1929)*

[Mostly within a ruled frame]

Spalding'a Athletic Library | CROQUET | [swelled rule] | Rules of the Game | *Also* | Modern Croquet | [swelled rule] | Instructions for Play | Published by | American Sports Publishing Co. | 45 Rose Street, New York | [below the frame] Copyright, 1929, by American Sports Publishing Company

Formula: [1–3⁸]. 24 leaves, pp *i–ii*, 41–63 64–66 67–86 [= 48]

Technical notes: 129 × 89 mm (p 42). 37 lines, 20 = 71 mm. Leaf size 169 × 123 mm; thickness 0.24 mm; wove, unwatermarked, rough, white

Contents: Title (*i*), plan of croquet court (*ii*), text, rules of croquet (41–65), plan of croquet court (66), text, modern croquet (67–85), advertisement (86)

Binding: White semi-gloss light card, printed in dark Green (146) and deep reddish Orange (36), stitched through the wrapper, no endpapers. FC: as that of (a). Inside FC: advertisement, in Green. RC: advertisement, in Green and Orange, for Spalding's sportswear. Inside RC: advertisement, in Green. Spine: in Orange (blank)

Copy seen: HPC: GV933 C81 1929 CROQ

Fingerprint: r-or t.da held ofhi C 1929A

Notes: Printed anonymously, price 25 cents. In this edition, the text is extended to include the game of 'modern croquet'. The advertisements differ from those in (e) and the preliminaries are abridged.

(h) *1931 issue (1931)*

[Mostly within a ruled frame]

Spalding's Athletic Library | CROQUET | [swelled rule] | Rules of the Game | *Also* | Modern Croquet | [swelled rule] | Instructions for Play | Published by | American Sports Publishing Co. | 45 Rose Street, New York | [below the frame] Copyright, 1931, by American Sports Publishing Company.

Formula: Apparently [1–3^8]. 24 leaves, pp *39–40, 41–63 64–66 67–85 86* [= 48]

Technical notes: 129 × 89 mm (p 42). 37 lines, 20 = 71 mm. Leaf height 170 mm, the width not ascertainable from the photocopy examined

Contents: Title *(39)*, plan of croquet court *(40)*, text, rules of croquet *(41–65)*, plan of croquet court *(66)*, text, modern croquet *(67–85)*, advertisement *(86)*

Binding: Printed in deep reddish Orange *(ca 36)* and black on white, apparently stitched through the wrapper, no endpapers. FC: mostly in white out of Orange ([in Orange on white panels at L and R] **No. 119R   PRICE 25 CENTS** | [in artist's script with dropped and decorated *S, S*] Spalding's | [in Orange within a white panel with ornaments at the extremities] **ATHLETIC LIBRARY** | [in black, centrally in a double-ruled frame with corner ornaments, within a white panel] **CROQUET** | [*do*, flourish] | [*do*] RULES | [*do*] *of the* | [*do*] GAME | [in white out of Orange at the foot] American Sports Publishing Co. | [*do*] *45 Rose Street, New York*). Inside FC: advertisement, in black. RC: advertisement, in Orange and black, for Spalding's sportswear. Inside RC: advertisement, in black. Spine: wanting from the photocopy examined

Copy seen: LOC: GV931 C8 1931 (photocopy of original copy rebound in library covers, the wrapper in colour)

Fingerprint: r-or t.da held ofhi   C 1931A

Notes: Printed anonymously, price 25 cents. This issue has not been collated with (g) but the texts of the two issues would appear to vary little if at all.

(j) *1931 issue, variant (1931)*

[Mostly within a ruled frame]

Spalding'a Athletic Library | CROQUET | [swelled rule] | Rules of the Game | *Also* | Modern Croquet | [swelled rule] | Instructions for Play | Published by | American Sports Publishing Co. | New York | [below the frame] Copyright, 1931, by American Sports Publishing Company

Formula: [1–3^8]. 24 leaves, pp *1–2 3–25 26–28 29–47 48*

Technical notes: 129 × 89 mm (p 4). 37 lines, 20 = 71 mm. Leaf size 171 × 126 mm; thickness 0.24 mm; wove, unwatermarked, rough, white

Contents: Title *(1)*, plan of croquet court *(2)*, text, rules of croquet *(3–27)*, plan of croquet court *(28)*, text, modern croquet *(29–47)*, advertisement *(48)*

Binding: White semi-gloss light card, printed in deep reddish Orange *(36)* and black, stitched through the wrapper, no endpapers. FC: mostly in white out of Orange ([in Orange on white panels at L and R] **No. 119R   PRICE 25 CENTS** | [in artist's script with dropped and decorated *S, S*] Spalding's | [in Orange within a white panel with ornaments at the extremities] **ATHLETIC LIBRARY** | [in black, centrally in a double-ruled frame, the outer frame in bold, within a white panel] **CROQUET** |

[*do*, flourish] | [*do*] RULES | [*do*] *of the* | [*do*] GAME | *AMERICAN SPORTS PUBLISHING Co.* | *45 Rose Street, New York*). Inside FC: advertisement, in black. RC: advertisement, in Orange and black, for Spalding's garden services. Inside RC: advertisement, in black. Spine: blank

Copy seen: PC

Fingerprint: r-or t.da held ofhi 3 1931A

Notes: Printed anonymously, price 25 cents. The text of this issue is apparently identical to that of (h). The only significant variation is in the introduction of regular pagination.

<h2 style="text-align:center">1910–19</h2>

A131   CROQUET: RULES AND REGULATIONS. [Anon]   *ca 1911*

(a) **First edition [ca 1911]*

[Title heading, p 1]

CROQUET | RULES AND | REGULATIONS | How to Play Croquet

[Conclusion, p 16]

H. Rademaker & Son, Inc. | Grand Rapids, Mich.

Formula: [1⁸]. 8 leaves, pp 1–3 [4–5] 6–16

Technical notes: ca 113 × 77 mm (p 3). 39 lines, 20 = *ca* 58 mm. Leaf size *ca* 134 × 76 mm

Contents: Text, continued (1–3), wanting from the photocopy examined ([4–5]), text, concluded (6–16), name of distributor (16)

Binding: No wrapper, sewn.

Copy seen: HPC: GV933 C8R3b CROQ (photocopy, wanting pp [4–5])

Fingerprint: t,of onet y.e. thwi 3 1911Q

Notes: Published and printed anonymously, issued by H Rademaker & Son, Grand Rapids, Michigan. Approximate year of publication is inferred from the fact that the text, including a code of 50 numbered rules, is virtually identical to that of a similar manual (A123) issued in 1911 by Roy Bros, East Barnet, VT.

The hoop setting, illustrated on p 2, is of nine hoops.

(b) *Variant edition [ca 1911]*

[The FC, within a double-ruled frame]

CROQUET | [double rule, the upper rule in bold] | **RULES AND | REGULATIONS | WITH INSTRUCTIONS** | [double rule, the upper rule in bold] | **H. RADEMAKER & SONS** | Manufacturers | GRAND RAPIDS, MICH., U. S. A.

Formula: [1⁸]. 8 leaves, pp 1–16

Technical notes: ca 109 × 76 mm (p 2). 31 lines, 20 = *ca* 71 mm. Leaf size *ca* 133 × 94 mm

Contents: Text (1–16), name of distributor (16)

Binding: Apparently pale coloured paper, sewn through the wrapper, no spine or endpapers. FC: printed as above. Inside FC: advertisement for the distributor's croquet sets. RC: engraved illustration of a boxed croquet set in landscape format. Inside RC: diagram of hoop setting

Copy seen: HPC: GV933 C8R3a CROQ (photocopy)

Fingerprint: n.ry d.or y.e. wian 3 1911Q

Notes: Published and printed anonymously, issued by H Rademaker & Sons, Grand Rapids, Michigan. The change of company name from H Rademaker & Son to H Rademaker & Sons would suggest that this edition was published after (a).

Though entirely re-set, the text is substantially identical to that of (a). The hoop setting illustrated inside the RC, however, is of ten hoops.

(c) *Variant edition* [ca 1911]

[The FC, within a double-ruled frame]

CROQUET | [triple rule] | **RULES and** | **REGULATIONS** | WITH INSTRUC-TIONS | [triple rule] | **H. RADEMAKER & SONS** | MANUFACTURERS | GRAND RAPIDS, MICH., U. S. A.

Formula: [1⁸]. 8 leaves, pp 1–15 *16*

Technical notes: ca 112 × 85 mm (p 3). 31 lines, 20 = *ca* 72 mm. Leaf size *ca* 136 × 98 mm

Contents: Text (1–16), name of distributor (*16*)

Binding: Apparently pale coloured paper, sewn through the wrapper, no spine or endpapers. FC: printed as above. Inside FC: advertisement for the distributor's croquet sets. RC: engraved illustration of a boxed croquet set, labelled 'IMPERIAL', in landscape format. Inside RC: diagram of ten-hoop setting

Copy seen: HPC: GV933 C8R3 CROQ (photocopy)

Fingerprint: ndll d,he e.t. eias 3 1911Q [group 1 taken from p 1]

Notes: Published and printed anonymously, issued by H Rademaker & Sons, Grand Rapids. The fact that the Imperial croquet set is altogether more impressive than the unnamed set illustrated in (b) would suggest that this edition was published later.

Though entirely re-set, the text is substantially identical to those of (a) and (b). The hoop setting, illustrated inside the RC, is of ten hoops.

A132 **THE LAWS OF CROQUET.** [Anon]   *ca* 1910

[The FC]

THE | LAWS | OF | CROQUET | [swelled rule]

Formula: [1⁶]. 6 leaves, pp *i–ii, 1* 2–8 *9–10*

Technical notes: 109 × 85 mm (p 2). 52 lines, 20 = 42 mm. Leaf size 137 × 108 mm; thickness 0.12 mm; laid, unwatermarked, rough, white

Contents: Plan (setting No 1) (*i*), plan (setting No 2) (*ii*), title heading ('The laws of croquet') (*1*), text (*1–8*), plan (setting No 3) (*9*), plan (setting No 4) (*10*)

Binding: Dark yellowish Pink (30) smooth wove paper, apparently stapled, no spine or endpapers. FC: cover title (see above) printed in black within a double-ruled frame. Inside FC: blank. RC: blank. Inside RC: blank

Copy seen: BL: 7921 dd 17 (imperfect, in a library binding)

Fingerprint: y.ya d.nd chn, ord. C 1910Q [all four groups taken from p 3]

Notes: Published and printed anonymously. Approximate year of publication is given as the earliest consistent with the state of development of the (official CA) laws presented in the text, which contains 45 in number including No 44 ('striker's opinion to prevail'). The (conjectural) year of publication given in the *General Catalogue* of the BL is 1870, at least 40 years too early.

This work is apparently an unauthorised reprint of the official CA laws, issued perhaps by a sports goods manufacturer or retailer with their croquet equipment.

A133   **MR PUNCH'S BOOK OF SPORTS. JA Hammerton (ed)**   *ca* 1910

MR. PUNCH'S BOOK | OF SPORTS | THE HUMOURS OF CRICKET, FOOT-BALL, | TENNIS, POLO, CROQUET, HOCKEY, | RACING, &c. | [centred to L of cartoon depicting Mr Punch as a rugger player] AS PICTURED BY | [fully justified, to L of cartoon] LINLY SAMBOURNE, PHIL | [*do*] MAY, L. RAVEN-HILL, F. H. | [*do*] TOWNSEND, E. T. REED, | [*do*] GEORGE DU MAURIER | [*do*] CHARLES KEENE, FRANK | [*do*] REYNOLDS, LEWIS BAUMER, | [*do*] GUNNING KING, G.D. | [*do*] ARMOUR, ARTHUR HOPKINS, | [*do*] EVERARD HOPKINS, J. A. | [centred, to L of cartoon] SHEPHERD, AND OTHERS. | *WITH 225 ILLUSTRA-TIONS* | PUBLISHED BY ARRANGEMENT WITH | THE PROPRIETORS OF "PUNCH" | [leaf ornament, repeated three times] | THE EDUCATIONAL BOOK CO. LTD.

Formula: A[8] B–M[8] [$2 signed (–A1, 2)]. 96 leaves, pp *1–4 5–192*

Technical notes: 130 × 90 mm (p 13, variable). Variable line spacing. Leaf size 190 × 127 mm; thickness 0.18–0.21 mm; wove, unwatermarked, smooth, white, top edges gilt

Contents: Half-title (*1*), frontispiece (*2*), title (*3*), The Punch Library of Humour (*4*), preface (*5–6*), text (*7–192*), name of printer (*192*)

Binding: Very deep Red (14) rib grain cloth over stiff boards, sewn. FC: gold-blocked head of Mr Punch at top R with lettering below (BOOK OF | SPORTS). RC: blank. Spine: gold-blocked crosswise ([at the head] PUNCH | [*do*] LIBRARY | [*do*, printer's ornament] |

Copy seen: PC

Fingerprint: thne !"?" ."er be*Th* 3 1910Q

Notes: Printed by Bradbury, Agnew, & Co, London and Tonbridge. Approximate year of publication is that cited in the catalogue online system of the LOC.

The text consists of cartoons and literary contributions which had appeared in *Punch* from its inception in 1841.

A134   **RÈGLE DU JEU DE CROQUET. [La Société française du Jeu de**   *ca* 1900
        Croquet and L'Union des Sociétés françaises de Sports athlétiques]

Règle | DU | **Jeu de Croquet** | ADMISE | [in shaded script] Par la SOCIÉTÉ FRANÇAISE du Jeu de CROQUET | ET | L'UNION DES SOCIÉTÉS FRANÇAISES | DE SPORTS ATHLÉTIQUES | [ornament]

Formula: [1[10]]. 10 leaves, pp *i–ii, 1* 2–4 *5* 6–16 *17–18*

Technical notes: 141 × 90 mm (p 6). 42 lines, 20 = 68 mm. Leaf size 170 × 118 mm; thickness 0.08 mm; wove, unwatermarked, smooth, white

Contents: Title (*i*), blank (*ii*), introduction, signed 'André Després, Président de la Commission de l'USFSA, Président de la SFJC' (*1–2*), plan (tracé No 3) (*3*), plans (tracés Nos I, II, IV, V) (*4*), 'règlements du jeu de croquet', 15 numbered 'articles' (*5–16*), 'considérations matérielles' (*17*), advertisement and name of printer (*18*)

Binding: Greyish Yellow Green (122) light card, sewn, no spine or endpapers. FC: printed in black within a double-ruled frame, the outer frame in bold (**Règle** | DU | **Jeu de Croquet** | ADMISE | PAR LA SOCIÉTÉ FRANÇAISE DU JEU DE CROQUET | ET | L'UNION DES SOCIÉTÉS FRANÇAISES | DE SPORTS

ATHLÉTIQUES | [double rule, the upper rule in bold and longer than the lower, with an ornamental tail-piece] | [equipment manufacturer's device] | Exiger cette Marque sur les Maillets | [swelled rule] | Reproduction interdite). Inside FC: 'table memento', continued inside the RC. RC: advertisement. Inside RC: 'table memento', concluded

Copy seen: BL: 7921 dd 14

Fingerprint: onté c-ui uxp, **g.co** 3 1900Q

Notes: Printed by P Goffi, Paris. Year of publication given is that inferred in the *General Catalogue* of the BL. This is consistent with a textual reference to the *Almanach Hachette* of 1898. An advertisement by Chapitre.com in June 1999 on the Advanced Book Exchange, an internet medium, offering for sale an 1895 edition of this title, suggests that the work may have been first published in the 1890s.

<h2 style="text-align:center">1920</h2>

A135   CROQUET AND ITS VARIETIES. CD Locock   1920

CROQUET | AND ITS VARIETIES | BY | C. D. LOCOCK | AUTHOR OF "MODERN CROQUET TACTICS" | LONDON | PUBLISHED AT THE OFFICES OF "COUNTRY LIFE," 20, | TAVISTOCK STREET, COVENT GARDEN, W.C.2, AND BY | GEORGE NEWNES, LTD., 8-11, SOUTHAMPTON STREET, | STRAND, W.C.2. NEW YORK : CHARLES SCRIBNER'S SONS | 1920

Formula: [1¹⁶]. 16 leaves, pp *1–2* 3–32

Technical notes: 148 × 89 mm (p 6). 42 lines, 20 = 71 mm. Leaf size 186 × 122 mm; thickness 0.18 mm; wove, unwatermarked, rough, white

Contents: Title (*1*), blank (*2*), preface, signed 'C. D. L.' (*3*), contents (*4*), text (*5–25*), the laws of croquet (1920) (*26–32*), name of printer (*32*)

Binding: White semi-gloss card, stapled, no endpapers or spine. FC: printed in black, the first line exceptionally in vivid Red (11) ([in Red] **CROQUET | AND ITS VARIETIES | How to Excel at the Game | By C. D. LOCOCK** | [black-and-white photograph of behatted man at play near a hoop] | ONE OF THE "COUNTRY LIFE" BOOKLETS | *Ninepence Net*). Inside FC: advertisement. RC: advertisement. Inside RC: advertisement

Copy seen: BL: 7911 df 46

Fingerprint: L.*d.* ngh" wsto stby 3 1920A

Notes: Printed by Hazell, Watson & Viney, London and Aylesbury, price 9d.

<h2 style="text-align:center">1921</h2>

A136   CROQUET IN THE SIXTIES. William Longman   1921

Croquet in the Sixties | BY | WILLIAM LONGMAN | LONGMANS, GREEN AND CO. | 39 PATERNOSTER ROW, LONDON, E.C.4. | FOURTH AVENUE AND 30TH STREET, NEW YORK | BOMBAY, CALCUTTA AND MADRAS. | 1921

Formula: [1¹²]. 12 leaves, pp *1–5* 6–23 *24*

Technical notes: 146 × 75 mm (p 16). 42 lines, 20 = 70 mm. Leaf size 183 × 120 mm; thickness 0.08 mm; wove, unwatermarked, smooth, white

Contents: The CA: advantages of membership (*1*), frontispiece (reproduction of frontispiece of A12) (*2*), title (*3*), acknowledgement, signed 'W. LONGMAN', October 1921 (*4*), text (*5–23*), name of printer (*24*)

Binding: Greyish Green (150) paper, apparently stapled, no spine. FC: printed in black within a ruled frame ([in display script] Croquet in the Sixties | [vignette, drawing of period cage-type hoop with hanging bell] | BY | WILLIAM LONGMAN) and below the frame (PRICE ONE SHILLING). RC: blank

Copy seen: BL: 7911 cc 29 (imperfect)

Fingerprint: l.r. e.se iset nolo 7 1921A

Notes: Published in December 1921, printed by The Holmesdale Press, Redhill, Surrey, price 1/–. This work was reprinted from *The Croquet Association Gazette* (20 October 1921, pp 226–32).

1922

A137 CROQUET: A HANDBOOK ON THE STROKES OF THE   1922
GAME AND BREAK-MAKING, ETC. GF Handel Elvey

CROQUET | A Handbook on the Strokes of the Game | and Break-making, etc. | BY | G. F. HANDEL ELVEY, M.A. (Oxon.) | LONDON | E. J. LARBY, LTD. | 30 PATERNOSTER ROW, E.C.4

Formula: A^8 B–D^8 [$1 signed (–A1)]. 32 leaves, pp *1–8* 9–17 *18* 19–21 *22* 23–29 *30* *31–33* *34* 35–39 *40* 41–47 *48* 49–53 *54* 55–63 *64*

Technical notes: 135 × 84 mm (p 11). 32 lines, 20 = 85 mm. Leaf size 184 × 122 mm; thickness 0.18 mm; wove, unwatermarked, rough, white

Contents: Half-title (*1*), advertisement (*2*), title (*3*), blank (*4*), preface, signed 'G. F. HANDEL ELVEY' (*5*), blank (*6*), contents (*7*), seven diagrams (*8*), text, continued (*9–17*), three diagrams (*18*), text, continued (19–21), two diagrams (*22*), text, continued (23–29), five diagrams (*30*), text, continued (*31–33*), diagram (*34*), text, continued (35–39), diagram (*40*), text, continued (41–47), diagram (*48*), text, continued (49–53), diagram (*54*), text, concluded (55–63), name of printer (*64*)

Binding: White linen grain paper, sewn, no endpapers. FC: printed as white out of dark yellowish Green (137), the lettering and illustration falling mostly within a frame, enlarged at the corners, consisting of alternate white and Green squares ([in ornamental script] **CROQUET** | A Handbook on the | Strokes of the Game | and Break-making etc. | BY | G.F. HANDEL ELVEY. M.A.(Oxon.) | [drawing of hoop, mallet, and three balls on a greensward with a line of trees in background, mostly within an elliptical border which extends horizontally outside the main frame] | [the tops of the letters in bold shaped parallel to the elliptical border above] **1/6 LONDON NET** | E.J. LARBY. L^{TD} 30,PATERNOSTER ROW.). Inside FC: advertisement in Green. RC: advertisement in Green. Inside RC: advertisement in Green. Spine: in Green downwards (CROQUET G. F. HANDEL ELVEY)

Copy seen: PC

Fingerprint: Y.m. eris m.or sss. C 1922Q [groups 1–4 taken from pp 5, 13, 17, 17 respectively]

Notes: Printed by Butler & Tanner, Frome & London, price 1/6. Year of publication is inferred from a reference to the Championship croquet ball advertised on the RC: 'ADOPTED AGAIN FOR 1922'.

Notwithstanding their closely similar titles and common publisher, this work is distinguished from the author's earlier work *Croquet: A Guide to the Strokes of the Game* (A119) because it makes no claim to continuity; rather the reverse, the author referring in the preface to his earlier work as its 'predecessor'.

1923

**A138   CROQUET: HINTS ON PRACTICE, TACTICS AND STROKE   [1923]
PLAY. Lord Tollemache**

(a) *First edition [1923]*

[The FC, printed in black, mostly within a double-ruled frame, the outer frame in bold]

[at L] <u>CROQUET</u> [two flourishes in the form of leaves] | Hints on [double rule] | [at R] "PRACTICE" [two flourishes in the form of leaves] | [at R] "TACTICS" [two flourishes in the form of leaves] | and | [at R] "STROKE PLAY" | [at R, engraved image of a crown] | [in a flowing hand] Tollemache | [at L] Also : : | HOW TO PLAY THE BREAK | [at L] with the | [at L] No. 2 HOOP-SETTING | [below the frame] Sold by Messrs. PHILLIPSON & GOLDER, Eastgate Row, Chester.   2/6 Post free.

Formula: [1¹²]. 12 leaves, pp *1* 2–4 5 6–11 *12–13* 14 15 16–24

Technical notes: 203 × 145 mm (p 2). 52 lines, 20 = 77 mm. Leaf size 280 × 220 mm; thickness 0.09 mm; wove, unwatermarked, semi-gloss, white

Contents: Title heading (*1*), text (*1–24*), name of printer (24)

Binding: Light greyish Olive (109) paper, no endpapers or spine. The copy examined had been rebound; the original binding was apparently stapled. FC: printed in black (see TP as above). Inside FC: blank. RC: blank. Inside RC: blank

Copy seen: BL: 7920 d 24 (in a library binding)

Fingerprint: t.NE h.en e.rs Does 7 1923Q [groups 1–4 taken from pp *1*, 9, 17, 18 respectively]

Notes: Printed by Wyman & Sons, London, Reading, and Fakenham, price 2/6. Year of publication is inferred from the citation in the *General Catalogue* of the BL.

Review: *The Croquet Association Gazette* (8 February 1923, p 17).

(b) *Second edition [1926]*

[The FC, mostly within a double-ruled frame, the outer frame in bold]

[at L] <u>CROQUET</u> | [at R, one of two lines] SECOND EDITION | [*do*] Revised with additional Chapter. | Hints on [double rule across the page] | [R justified] "PRACTICE" [twin flourishes in the form of leaves] | [R justified] "TACTICS" [twin flourishes in the form of leaves] | [R justified] "STROKE PLAY" | [author's device, a crown] | [signed in a flowing hand] *Tollemache* | Also : : | HOW TO PLAY THE BREAK | with the | No. 2 HOOP-SETTING | and the | No. 3 HOOP-SET-TING | [below the frame] PHILLIPSON & GOLDER, Ltd., Eastgate Row, Chester. 2/9 Post free.

Formula: [1¹⁴]. 14 leaves, pp *1* 2–4 5 6–11 *12–13* 14 15 16–28

Technical notes: 203 × 145 mm (p 2). 52 lines, 20 = 78 mm. Leaf size 280 × 214 mm; thickness 0.10 mm; wove, unwatermarked, smooth, white

Contents: Title heading and contents (*1*), text, continued (2–4), diagram (*5*), text, continued (6–11), framed half-tone photograph (*12*), plan of court (*13*), text, continued (14), diagram (*15*), text, concluded (16–28), name of printer (28)

Binding: Grey paper, sewn, no spine or endpapers. FC: printed in black as above. Inside FC: blank. RC: blank. Inside RC: blank

Copy seen: BOD 38464 d 3

Fingerprint: t.NE h.en e.rs Dopr 7 1926Q

Notes: Printed by Wyman & Sons, London, Reading, and Fakenham, Price 2/6, 2/9

post free. Year of publication is inferred from the dates of the BOD accession mark (26 August 1926) and the review cited below.

This edition is revised and enlarged with an additional chapter on the new No 3 setting, comprising general remarks, hints on practice for first-class players, and two new maps of the court. The publisher also distributed the two maps unmounted with two sets of Halma men as balls in four colours (price 1/6 post free), the same two maps *etc* mounted on stiff cardboard (price 2/6), and a double set of Halma men only (price 6d).

Review: *The Croquet Association Gazette* (24 April 1926, p 56).

A139 **THE LATEST RULES OF CRICKET, HOCKEY, LAWN TENNIS,** **1923**
BADMINTON, CROQUET. [Fisher & Sons]

(a) **First edition, Joseph Clark & Sons issue (1923)*

The Latest Rules | of | *CRICKET* | [R justified] Page 7 | *HOCKEY* | [R justified] Page 41 | *LAWN TENNIS* | [R justified] Page 68 | *BADMINTON* | [R justified] Page 86 | *CROQUET* | [R justified] Page 99 | [rule] | Issued by | M. C. C. Company, Ltd., | BEDFORD, ENGLAND. | Copies available from the Publishers: | Fisher & Sons, Printers, Bedford.

Formula: [1⁶⁴]. 64 leaves, pp *1–6 7–37 38–40 41–53 54 55–62 63–67 68–84 85–86 87–98 99 100–128*

Technical notes: 72 × 50 mm (p 9). 27 lines, 20 = 54 mm. Leaf size 91 × 50 mm; thickness 0.06 mm; wove, unwatermarked, smooth, white

Contents: Title, incorporating contents (*i*), advertisements (*ii–vi*), laws of cricket (*7–37*), advertisements (*38–40*), rules of hockey, continued (*41–53*), advertisement (*54*), rules of hockey, concluded (*55–62*), advertisements (*63–67*), laws of tennis (*68–84*), advertisement (*85*), laws of badminton (*86–98*), laws of croquet, numbered 1–37, note relating to alternative doubles, and extract from Regulation 1 (*99–128*)

Binding: Rough medium Grey (265) paper, printed in black, stapled, no spine or endpapers. FC: mostly within a double-ruled frame, the outer frame in bold, broken by line drawings of players of the five sports represented in the text ([above the frame] PRICE 3ᴰ | 19 [illustration of cricketer] 23 | LATEST | [in MS] Rules | [*do*] CRICKET | LAWN TENNIS | HOCKEY | CROQUET | BADMINTON | [below the frame] **Joseph Clark & Sons, Ltd.,** | **Y.M.C.A. Buildings,** | **Station Road, Doncaster.**). Inside FC: advertisement. RC: advertisement and name of printer. Inside RC: advertisement

Copy seen: PC

Fingerprint: d.l. w-ty ndr. Whig 3 1923A

Notes: Printed and published by Fisher & Sons, Bedford, in association with Joseph Clark & Sons and MCC Co, manufacturers of sports equipment, price 3d. It may be surmised that Fishers offered this publication to a number of wholesalers and retailers of sports goods, including Joseph Clark and Alltree (see also (b)). It is not known whether this issue and (b) were published simultaneously and, if not, which appeared first.

The laws of croquet given in the text are identical in substance to the official laws for 1923 promulgated by the CA.

(b) **Alltree Bros issue [1923]*

Title page: As that of (a)

Formula: As that of (a)

Technical notes: 72 × 50 mm (p 9). 27 lines, 20 = 54 mm. Leaf size 91 × 59 mm; thickness 0.06 mm; wove, unwatermarked, smooth, white

Contents: As the contents of (a)

Binding: Rough medium Grey (265) paper, printed in black, stapled, no spine or endpapers. FC: mostly within a ruled frame ([above the frame] Price 3d. | [double-underlined, the upper rule extending beyond the lettering, and the lower rule extending beyond the upper] Latest Rules of | CRICKET, | LAWN TENNIS, | HOCKEY, | BADMINTON, | CROQUET. | [rule] | ALLTREE BROS., LTD. | *The A.B. Sports Depot,* | 43 Castle Street, | SHREWSBURY. | [below the frame] *Fisher & Sons. Printers, Bedford.*). Inside FC: advertisement, as that inside the FC of (a). RC: advertisement, different to that on the RC of (a). Inside RC: advertisement, as that inside the RC of (a)

Copy seen: PC

Fingerprint: d.l. w-ty ndr. Whig 3 1923Q

Notes: Printed and published by Fisher & Sons, Bedford, in association with Alltree Bros and MCC Co, manufacturers of sports equipment, price 3d. See also *Notes* to (a).

A140   **THE NEW ZEALAND CROQUET ANNUAL** [and   [1923]
THE NEW ZEALAND CROQUET YEAR BOOK].
[The New Zealand Croquet Council]

(a) *First edition, 1923–24 [1923]*

[The TP, perhaps also the FC]

[in display script] **The New Zealand** | [*do*] **Croquet Annual** | [rule] | [in display script] **1923–24** | [an elaborate ornament] | Printed by CHAS. F. SPOONER & CO. | Rangitikei Street :: Palmerston North | For the :: New Zealand Croquet Council | This book may be procured from | Messrs. G. H. BENNETT & CO., LTD., | Booksellers and Stationers, Palmerston No [‡]

Formula: Not ascertainable from the photocopy examined. Apparently 27 leaves, pp *i–ii, 1–2 3–51* [52]

Technical notes: ca 161 × 103 mm (p 8). Variable line spacing. Leaf size *ca* 203 × 139 mm

Contents: Contents (*i*), blank (*ii*), advertisements (*1–2*), introduction, signed 'R. CAUGHLEY' (*3–4*), officers of the NZCC (*4*), winners of principal events (*5–6*), constitution and rules (*6–11*), laws of croquet (*12–22*), drawing of byes (*23–24*), handicaps of New Zealand players (*25–51*), wanting from the photocopy examined ([*52*])

Binding: Not ascertainable from the photocopy examined

Copy seen: NZCC (incomplete photocopy, wanting the covers or wrapper and p [52])

Fingerprint: 5149 s.e- y.th cano 3 1923Q

Notes: Printed by Chas F Spooner & Co, Palmerston North, published by the NZCC, and sold through representative clubs to members. In the Annual Report of the Executive, presented and confirmed at the Annual Meeting of the Council on 21 January 1924, it is stated that 'Nearly all the representative clubs sold their books and applied for more, but the Association have not been so successful, over 300 having been returned.' It was further reported that the Council was facing a loss of about £12 on this first edition. The total membership of the Council was given as 'approximately 2521'. Hence it may be supposed that about one or two thousand copies were printed.

The principal compilers of this first edition were R Caughley and J Murray, members of the handicapping committee.

(b) *1950–51 edition (1950)*

Formula: [1^4 2^8 $3–6^{16}$]. 152 leaves, pp 1–152

Technical notes: 170 × 101 mm (p 15). Variable line spacing. Leaf size 218 × 139 mm; thickness 0.10 mm; wove, unwatermarked, smooth, white

Contents: Officers of the NZCC (1), winners of principal events (2–7), associations and clubs (8–12), constitution and rules (13–17), laws of Association Croquet, continued (18–19), advertisement (19), laws of Association Croquet, concluded (20–32), advertisement and announcement (32), etiquette (33), explanatory notes on the laws of play (34–36), hints worth remembering (37–38), general handicap regulations (39), handicaps of New Zealand players (40–112), regulations for official tournaments (113–122), general tournament conditions (123), association and club tournaments (124–152)

Binding: Sewn. The copy examined is in a special presentation binding, wanting the original wrapper

Copy seen: PC (special presentation copy)

Fingerprint:).). u.on s.r- MaAU 3 1950A [group 1 taken from p 1]

Notes: Some of the pages of the copy examined are uncut.

(c) *1960–61 edition (1961)*

[The FC]

[interrupting a triple rule, the central rule in bold] THE NEW ZEALAND | [*do*, in gothic-revival script] **Croquet Annual** | [*do*] 1960-61 | [at R, at the foot] *No. 38* | [at L, a rule] | [at L] MAWERA STAR PRINT

Formula: Not ascertainable from the copy examined. 73 leaves, pp 1–143 *144–146*

Technical notes: 170 × 101 mm (p 2). Variable line spacing, mostly 59 lines, 20 = 58 mm. Leaf size 213 × 134 mm; thickness 0.12 mm; wove, unwatermarked, smooth, white

Contents: Officers of the NZCC (1), winners of principal events (2–10), associations and clubs (11–15), constitution and rules (16–20), laws of Association Croquet (21–34), laws of golf croquet (35–36), referees (37–38), explanatory notes on the laws of play (39–40), etiquette (41), hints worth remembering (42–43), editorial notice (43), general handicap regulations (44), handicaps of New Zealand players (45–99), regulations for official tournaments (100–107), general tournament conditions (108), association and club tournaments (109–141), Silver Badge Competition (142), country inter-club competitions (143), statement of receipts and payments on General Account for the year ended (*144*), balance sheet as at 31 July 1959 (*145*), sundry financial information (*146*)

Binding: Pale orange Yellow (73) leather-effect light paper glued to the folds of the gatherings, stapled through the gatherings, no endpapers. FC: printed in black as above. Inside FC: blank. RC: blank. Inside RC: blank. Spine: blank

Copy seen: CA

Fingerprint: q.q. tuon n.n. EKGR 3 1960A [group 1 taken from the L column of p 1]

Notes: Printed by Mawera Star.

(d) *1962–63 edition (1962)*

[The FC]

[interrupting a triple rule, the central rule in bold] THE NEW ZEALAND | [*do*, in gothic-revival script] **Croquet Annual** | [*do*] 1962-63 | [at R, at the foot] *No. 40* | [at L, a rule] | [at L] MAWERA STAR PRINT.

Formula: Not ascertainable from the copy examined. 76 leaves, pp 1–149 *150–152*

Technical notes: 170 × 101 mm (p 18). Variable line spacing, mostly 59 lines, 20 = 58 mm. Leaf size 214 × 139 mm; thickness 0.10 mm; wove, unwatermarked, smooth, white

Contents: Officers of the NZCC (1), winners of principal events (2–11), associations and clubs 12–16), constitution and rules (17–21), laws of Association Croquet, continued (22–25), advertisement (25), laws of Association Croquet, concluded (26–46), laws of golf croquet (47), explanatory notes on the laws of play (48–49), general handicap regulations (49), handicaps of New Zealand players (50–99), regulations for official tournaments (100–110), general tournament conditions (111), instructions to managers (112), association and club tournaments (113–147), Silver Badge Competition (148), country inter-club competitions (149), statement of receipts and payments on General Account for the year ended (*150*), balance sheet as at 31 July 1961 (*151*), sundry financial information (*152*)

Binding: Moderate Yellow Green (120) leather-effect light card stapled through the gatherings, no endpapers. FC: printed in black as above. Inside FC: blank. RC: blank. Inside RC: blank. Spine: blank

Copy seen: PC

Fingerprint: q.q. rynd d.a. TAWA 3 1962A [group 1 taken from the L column of p 1]

Notes: Printed by Mawera Star.

(e) *1972–73 edition (1972)*

[The FC]

[interrupting a triple rule, the central rule in bold] THE NEW ZEALAND | [*do*] **Croquet Annual** | [*do*] 1972-73 | [at R, at the foot] *No. 50*

Formula: Apparently [1–10^8]. 80 leaves, pp 1–160

Technical notes: 178 × 100 mm (p 17). Variable line spacing, mostly 59 lines, 20 = 58 mm. Leaf size 215 × 136 mm; thickness 0.10 mm; wove, unwatermarked, smooth, white

Contents: Contents (inside the FC), officers of the NZCC (1–2), winners of principal events (2–15), associations and clubs 12–16), constitution and rules (16–22), associations and clubs (23–28), laws of Association Croquet (29–53), explanatory notes on the laws of play (54), etiquette (54–55), regulations governing NZCC events (55), Silver Badge Competition (56), country inter-club competitions (57), regulations for official tournaments (58–69), general tournament conditions (70), instructions to managers (71), general handicap regulations (72), handicaps of New Zealand players (73–117), association and club tournaments (118–160, inside the RC), laws of golf croquet (RC)

Binding: Light orange Yellow (70) paper, stapled through the gatherings, no endpapers. FC: printed in black as above. Inside FC: printed in black as above. RC: printed in black as above. Inside RC: printed in black as above. Spine: blank

Copy seen: CA

Fingerprint:).d. nsns stui 1919 3 1972A [group 1 taken from p 1]

Notes: Printed anonymously.

(f) *1986–87 edition (1986)*

[The FC]

The New Zealand | Croquet Council | in association with | **N.Z.I. FINANCE** | [rule] | **YEAR BOOK** | 1986–1987 | [rule] | [publisher's device] | [at R, at the foot] No. 64

Formula: Apparently [1–11⁸]. 88 leaves, pp 1–176

Technical notes: 182 × 101 mm (p 21). Variable line spacing, mostly 64 lines, 20 = 57 mm. Leaf size 213 × 138 mm; thickness 0.09 mm; wove, unwatermarked, smooth, white

Contents: Contents (inside the FC), officers of the NZCC (1–2), winners of principal events (2–19), constitution and rules (20–26), laws of Association Croquet (27–53), explanatory notes on the laws of play (54), regulations for official tournaments (54–66), etiquette (66), regulations governing NZCC events (66), general tournament conditions (67), laws of golf croquet (68–69), Silver Badge Competition (70), The NZI Finance Handicap Singles (71), country inter-club competitions (72), instructions to managers (73), general handicap regulations (74), associations, clubs, and members (75–117), association and club tournaments (118–172), sundry accounts for the year ended 31 July 1985 (173–174), advertisements (175), index of advertised tournaments (176). The imprint of NZI Finance is repeated at the foot of several pages

Binding: Very light Green (143) paper, stapled through the gatherings, the spine wrapped in strong Green (141) PVC textured linen tape, no endpapers. FC: printed in black as above. Inside FC: printed in black as above. RC: advertisement of NZI Finance, printed in black. Inside RC: blank. Spine: blank

Copy seen: CA

Fingerprint: thq. sess ngck 1919 3 1986A [groups 1–3 taken from the L columns of pp 1, 19, 13 respectively]

Notes: Printed anonymously.

(g) *1995–96 edition (1995)*

[device of the NZCC] | **The New Zealand Croquet Council** | **YEAR BOOK** | **1995 - 1996** | Published by | The New Zealand Croquet Council (Inc) | P O Box 11-259 | Sports House, Level 4, Central Library | 65 Victoria Street, Wellington | Ph. (04) 473 7947 Fax. (04) 471 2152   **No. 73**

Formula: [1–124¹]. 124 leaves, pp *1–4* 5–224 *225* 226–247 *248*

Technical notes: 175 × 118 mm (p 36). Variable line spacing, mostly 50 lines, 20 = 70 mm. Leaf size 210 × 148 mm; thickness 0.10 mm; wove, unwatermarked, smooth, white

Contents: Title (*1*), blank (*2*), contents (*3*), surrogate TP verso and notice of AGM (*4*), officers of the NZCC (*5*), associations and clubs (*6–18*), laws of Association Croquet (*19–51*), explanatory notes on the laws of play (*52*), official rulings and interpretations (*53–56*), laws of golf croquet (*57–58*), regulations for tournaments (*59–75*), constitution and rules (*76–87*), handicap regulations (*88*), handicaps of association members (*89–129*), presidents and life members (*130*), winners of principal events (*131–158*), general tournament conditions (*159*), instructions to managers (*160*), Arthur Ross Memorial Event (*161*), country inter-club competitions (*162*), Silver Badge Competition (*163–164*), etiquette (*165–166*), tournament calendar (167–168), NZCC fixtures (169–186), association and club tournaments (187–242), advertisements (243–244), fixtures application form (*245–248*)

Binding: White semi-gloss card printed in strong yellowish Green (131) and black, glued to the edges of the leaves, scored hinges front and rear, no endpapers. FC: equally divided longitudinally, the upper half printed in black on white ([device of the NZCC] | The New Zealand Croquet Council), the lower half in white out of Green (**YEAR BOOK** | **1995/1996** | [at R, at the foot] No 74). Inside FC: blank. RC: divided laterally into white and Green portions, continuously with the FC and spine. Inside RC: blank. Spine: downwards ([in black on white, device of the NZCC] [*do*] The New Zealand [in white out of Green] Croquet Year Book 1995/96) and crosswise at the foot on two lines (No | 73)

Copy seen: PC

Fingerprint: **4544** 51ei 34ra Phwe 3 1965A

Notes: Designed and produced by Alltex Design, Wellington, NZ.

(h) *1996–97 edition (1996)*

[device of the NZCC] | **The New Zealand Croquet Council** | **YEAR BOOK** | **1996 - 1997** | Published by | The New Zealand Croquet Council (Inc) | P O Box 11-259 | Sports House, Level 4, Central Library | 65 Victoria Street, Wellington | Ph. (04) 473 7947 Fax. (04) 471 2152   **No. 74**

Formula: [1–124¹]. 124 leaves, pp *1–4* 5–245 *246–248*

Technical notes: 175 × 118 mm (p 21). Variable line spacing, mostly 50 lines, 20 = 70 mm. Leaf size 209 × 146 mm; thickness 0.12 mm; wove, unwatermarked, smooth, white

Contents: Title (*1*), blank (*2*), contents (*3*), surrogate TP verso and notice of AGM (*4*), officers of the NZCC (5), associations and clubs (6–18), laws of Association Croquet (19–51), explanatory notes on the laws of play (52), official rulings and interpretations (53–56), laws of golf croquet (57–58), regulations for tournaments (59–76), constitution and rules (77–88), general handicap regulations (89–92), umpires, referees, and coaches (93–98), associations, clubs, and members (99–137), presidents and life members (138), winners of principal events (139–163), general tournament conditions (164), instructions to managers (165), Arthur Ross Memorial Event (166), country inter-club competitions (167), Silver Badge Competition (168–169), etiquette (170–171), NZCC fixtures (172–188), association and club tournaments (189–243), advertisements (243–245), fixtures application form (*246–248*)

Binding: White semi-gloss card printed in black and vivid purplish Blue (194), glued to the edges of the leaves, scored hinges front and rear, no endpapers. FC: equally divided laterally, the upper half printed in black and Blue on white ([device of the NZCC] | [in black] The New Zealand Croquet Council) , the lower half in white out of Blue (**YEAR BOOK** | **1996/1997** | [at R, at the foot] No 74). Inside FC: blank. RC: advertisement in Blue on white. Inside RC: advertisement. Spine: downwards ([in black on white, device of the NZCC] [*do*] The New Zealand [in white out of Blue] Croquet Year Book 1996/97) and crosswise at the foot on two lines (No | 74)

Copy seen: PC

Fingerprint: thq. sess ngck 1919 3 1996A [groups 1–3 taken from the L columns of pp 1, 9, 13 respectively]

Notes: Designed and produced by Alltex Design, Wellington, NZ, price NZ$7.00.

(j) *1998–99 edition (1998)*

[R justified]

[NZCC device, incorporating the image of a fernleaf] | **1998–99** | **YEAR BOOK** | No. 76 | Published by | The New Zealand Croquet Council (Inc), | P O Box 11-259, Level 4, Sports House | Central Library, 65 Victoria Street, Wellington | Phone: (04) 473 7947 Fax: (04) 473 7941

Formula: Not ascertainable from the copy examined. 90 leaves, pp *1–4* 5–177 *178–180*

Technical notes: 174 × 120 mm (p 21). 52 lines, 20 = 67 mm. Leaf size 210 × 148 mm; thickness 0.10 mm; wove, unwatermarked, smooth, white

Contents: Title (*1*), blank (*2*), contents (*3*), surrogate TP verso and notice of AGM (*4*), officers of the NZCC (*5*), associations and clubs (*6–18*), regulations for tournaments (*19–35*), accredited coaches (*36–38*), general handicap regulations (*39–42*), associations, clubs, and members (*43–80*), general tournament conditions and miscellaneous information (*81–82*), instructions to managers (*83*), Arthur Ross Memorial Event (*84*), country inter-club competitions (*85*), Silver Badge Competition (*86–87*), etiquette (*88–89*), tournament calendar (*90–91*), NZCC fixtures (*92–111*), association tournaments (*112–147*), club tournaments (*148–166*), club weekend tournaments (*167–169*), major Australian tournaments (*170*), advertisements (*171–173*), fixtures application form (*174–175*), accommodation form (*176–177*), blank (*178–180*)

Binding: White semi-gloss card, apparently glued to the edges of the leaves, no endpapers. FC: the title *etc* printed over and out of a full-length double portrait of Trixey and Aaron Westerby in a landscape setting, printed in full colour ([NZCC device, incorporating the image of a fernleaf, in Blue and Green, outlined by a bright fringe] | [in Grey] **1998–99** | [*do*, outlined by a bluish fringe] **YEAR BOOK**). Inside FC: advertisement by Guardian Trust. RC: advertisement in Blue by Guardian Trust. Inside RC: at the foot (Cover Photo: Courtesy of Waikato Times | Aaron and Trixey Westerby). Spine: extension of the colour photograph on the FC

Copy seen: CA

Fingerprint: **7674** 64.,).59 **CoPu** 3 1998Q

Notes: Printed by Alltex Design, Wellington, price NZ$7.00.

1924

A141   **LE TENNIS, LE BASKET-BALL ET LE CROQUET.** [Anon]   1924

BIBLIOTHÈQUE PRATIQUE GARNIER | [wavy line] | JACK DE TRÉVIÈRES | [rule] | LE TENNIS | LE BASKET-BALL | ET LE CROQUET | [rule] *RÈGLES - TACTIQUE et CONSEILS* | [publisher's device] | PARIS | LIBRAIRIE GARNIER FRÈRES | 6, RUE DES SAINTS.PÈRES, 6 | 1924

Formula: 1^8 2–6^8 [\$1 signed (–1_1)]. 48 leaves, pp *1–5* 6–7 *8–9* 10–18 *19* 20–34 *35* 36–50 *51* 52–66 *67* 68–72 *73 74 75 76*–82 *83* 84–87 *88* 89–96

Technical notes: 125 × 79 mm (p 10). 28 lines, 20 = 90 mm. Leaf size 153 × 108 mm; thickness 0.17 mm; wove, unwatermarked, rough, pale orange Yellow (73)

Contents: Half-title (*1*), name of printer (*2*), title (*3*), blank (*4*), text (5–96)

Binding: White paper, sewn, no endpapers. FC: printed over and out of a vivid Yellow (82) background ([in an outlined rectangular panel with rounded corners, moderate greenish Blue (173) on white out of a Yellow background] BIBLIO-THÈQUE PRATIQUE GARNIER | [Blue over Yellow background] JACK DE

Trévières | [*do*, swelled rule] | [in Blue script with outlines separated by white, out of Yellow background] Le TENNIS . . . . | [*do*] Le BASKET-BALL | [*do*] .. & Le CROQUET | [Blue over Yellow background, set to R of a vignette described below] RÈGLES. | [*do*] TACTIQUE. | [*do*] CONSEILS. | [vignette, signed 'A DESPINASSE', of a woman player with tennis racket raised overhead to serve, in Blue and deep reddish Orange (36) on wh•te, mostly out of an Orange disc outlined in Blue but with racket-head over, and feet out of Yellow background] | [in an outlined rectangular panel with rounded corners, Blue on white out of Yellow background] LIBRAIRIE GARNIER FRÈRES · PARIS). Inside FC: blank. RC: in Blue, advertisement within decorative frame and, below the frame (Paris — Eymenié — 9 24). Inside RC: blank. Spine: in Blue upwards, the vertical rules rendered in letterpress (| PRIX: 3 FR. | **LE TENNIS, LE BASKET-BALL & LE CROQUET** | [on two lines, 'JACK' above] JACK DE TRÉVIÈRES)

Copy seen: PC

Fingerprint: sas.).ne ntp; chse 7 1924A

Notes: The book was printed by Paul Dupont, Paris, the cover by Eymenié, Paris, price 3 fr. De Trévières is taken to be the executive editor of Bibliothèque Pratique Garnier, not the author or editor of this particular work.

The text has two sections on croquet (pp 83–96), including a code of eight 'articles' which is not attributed to any authority.

1925

**AA142 THE CROQUET ASSOCIATION: THE "BEST TEN" 1925.   1925
HF Crowther-Smith**

(a) *Original unpublished artwork (1925)*

The | CROQUET ASSOCIATION | THE "BEST TEN" | 1925 | [rule] | CARICATURED | BY | H. F. CROWTHER-SMITH

Formula: Apparently a trade book of *ca* 12 gatherings, each of 8 blank leaves, almost all cut close to the gutter so as to provide padding, the leaves bearing letterpress, manuscript, and artwork tipped in to some of the remaining page stubs. 18 leaves, unnumbered, f 4 formed of two of the original trade book leaves glued together

Technical notes: Leaves *1–3, 5, 16–18:* size 254 × 185 mm, corners rounded (radius = *ca* 7 mm), thickness 0.15 mm, wove, unwatermarked, smooth, yellowish White (92). Leaf *4:* size 254 × 185 mm, corners rounded (radius = *ca* 7 mm), thickness 0.30 mm, wove, unwatermarked, smooth, White. Leaves *6–15:* size 254 × 173 mm, corners rounded (radius = *ca* 7 mm), thickness 2.00 ± 0.05 mm, cardboard laminate, rough, White

Contents: Blank (*1–6*), title (*7*), blank (*8–9*), captions in red and black MS on the versos, the corresponding caricatures in full colour on the facing rectos (*10–29*), blank (*30–36*)

Binding: Dark yellowish Green (137) cloth over heavy boards with rounded corners (radius *ca* 10 mm), the original trade book leaves sewn. The facing pages of the endpapers are marbled in white, gold, dark greenish Blue (174), and greenish blue gradations. FC: gold-blocked (THE | CROQUET ASSOCIATION | THE "BEST TEN" | 1925). RC: blank. Spine: blank

Copy seen: CA

Fingerprint: Indeterminate

Notes: Unpublished. This work consists of original signed caricatures in line and watercolour of the ten players who contested the Champion Cup (afterwards the President's Cup) in 1925 — *viz* W Longman, P Duff Mathews, GL Reckitt, DLG Joseph, DD Steel, JC Windsor, CR Elwes, KH Coxe, Ben C Apps, H Wright — together with MS notes on facing pages as to their rankings and the numbers of games they won. Since four of the players came from beyond the home counties (JC Windsor from Australia), the artist probably completed the work during the tournament in August 1925. The book was bequeathed to the CA by Mrs Kay Longman in February 1992.

The verso of the front free endpaper is inscribed in pencil with a monogram composed of the letters *L, W*. W Longman, the winner, is the obvious candidate.

An irregular feature of this work is the transposition of the seventh and eighth ranked players, together with their caricatures.

(b) *Limited facsimile edition (1997)*

[Mostly in black]

[in vivid reddish Orange (34)] THE "BEST TEN" | [*do*] 1925 | [swelled rule] | CARICATURED BY | *H.F. Crowther Smith* | A facsimile edition | published in association with | [in Orange] The Croquet Association, London | 1997

Formula: [1–8²]. 16 leaves, unnumbered [pp 1–32]

Technical notes: 138 × 112 mm, variable (p *13*, unframed caricature in full colour). Leaf size 243 × 181 mm; thickness 0.16 mm; wove, unwatermarked, semi-gloss, yellowish White (92); all edges gilt

Contents: Half-title (*1*), blank (*2*), title (*3*), TP verso (*4*), editor's foreword, signed 'David Drazin' (*5*), blank (*6*), copy number (*7*), blank (*8*), facsimile of original TP (*9*), blank (*10–11*), captions in red and black MS on the versos, the corresponding caricatures in full colour on the facing rectos (*12–31*), blank (*32*)

Binding: Dark yellowish Green (137) buckram over stiff boards, sewn, marbled endpapers (in several gradations of red, brown, yellow, and blue). The front and rear free endpapers are laminated with laid white paper. FC: gold-blocked centrally (THE | CROQUET ASSOCIATION | THE "BEST TEN" | 1925). RC: blank. Spine: gold-blocked downwards (THE "BEST TEN" 1925   H.F. CROWTHER SMITH)

Copy seen: PC

Fingerprint: Indeterminate

Notes: Published privately in association with the CA on 1 September 1997; printed by PJ Reproductions, London; bound by Sarratt Bookbinders, Watford, Herts; price £113 to advance subscribers, £150 to others.

This edition was limited to 50 numbered copies. Nine additional copies out of series are rubber-stamped in deep Blue (179) 'SURPLUS TO LIMITED EDITION'.

1928

A143   **ODDS AND ENDS. E Trevor Hardman**   [1928]

ODDS AND ENDS | E. TREVOR HARDMAN. | Price 2/6 post free.

Formula: [1¹²]. 12 leaves, pp *1–2* 3–23 *24*. The copy examined has a loose printed insert, a form consisting of a single folded sheet (*i–iv*) for the reader's solutions to puzzle limericks which constitute part of the text (see *Notes* below)

Technical notes: Pp *1–24*: 151 × 93 mm (p *5*), variable line spacing, leaf size 204 × 126 mm, thickness 0.17 mm, wove, unwatermarked, smooth, white. Pp *i–iv*: 168 ×

92 mm (p *iii*), 23 lines, 20 = 147, leaf size 203 × 125 mm, thickness 0.08 mm, wove, unwatermarked, smooth, white

Contents: Title (*1*), blank (*2*), text (*3–23*), blank (*24*), blank (*i*), dotted lines for reader's limerick solutions (*ii–iii*), blank (*iv*)

Binding: Pale Yellow (89) card, sewn through the wrapper, no spine or endpapers. FC: printed in black (**ODDS** AND **ENDS** | A Medley of Original Compositions, | Croquet Limericks, Acrostics, | and Prize Translations. | E. TREVOR HARDMAN.). Inside FC: blank. RC: blank. Inside RC: blank

Copy seen: PC

Fingerprint: e.d— y.e! m.am FoSh 3 1928Q

Notes: Published privately, printed anonymously, price 2/6. Year of publication is inferred from the announcement which concludes the text: 'Solutions, on printed form, should be sent to Mr. E. Trevor Hardman, 31, Adelaide Crescent, Hove, before the end of September, 1928.'

1929

A144   A CROQUET NONSENSE BOOK. Horace Francis Crowther Smith   [1929]

Formula: [1–7⁴]. 28 leaves, pp *1–7* 8–55 *56*

Technical notes: 204 × 126 mm (p 8). 28 lines, 20 = 148 mm. Leaf size 280 × 202 mm; thickness 0.19 mm; wove, unwatermarked, semi-gloss, white; printed in black, deep yellowish Pink (27), very light yellowish Green (134), and moderate reddish Brown (43)

Contents: Half-title (*1*), blank (*2*), title (*3*), list of original subscribers (*4*), preface (*5*), blank (*6*), text (*7–55*), name of printer (*56*)

Binding: Strong Yellow Green (117) cloth over stiff boards, sewn. FC: gold-blocked, all lettering in artist's script ([at the head] A | CROQUET | [lower parts of the letters E, N, S truncated by the illustration below] NONSENSE | [cartoon depicting a man player on court about to strike a ball] | [at L] BOOK | [at the foot, at L] BY | [at R, in a bold hand, heavily underlined] H·F.Crowther Smith). RC: blank. Spine: blank

Copy seen: PC

Fingerprint: 9.Y. t.ay y-ng atts C 1929Q [groups 2–4 taken from p 13]

Notes: Published privately in July 1929, printed by Welbecson Press, London, price 21/– to original subscribers, 25/– to non-subscribers. In a letter the Editor, which appeared in *The Croquet Association Gazette* (19 January 1929, p 9), the author stated that it would not be economic to print this work until he had received at least 350 advance subscriptions; and publication was delayed for some months until it became apparent that this number might be reached. Hence it is thought that no more than about 500 copies were produced. The list of original subscribers (p *4*) cites the names of 264 individuals, who subscribed in advance to 348 copies.

In *The Croquet Association Gazette* (31 August 1929, p 269), it was reported that 'HM The King has been graciously pleased to accept a copy'.

The full page caricatures of BC Apps (p 39), W Longman (p 47), and DD Steel (p 49) closely resemble those in the artist's earlier work, *The Croquet Association: The "Best Ten" 1925* (A142).

A145   MODERN CROQUET. [Anon]   **1929**

[Within a double-ruled frame with rounded corners]

Modern Croquet | [ornament] | INSTRUCTIONS *for* PLAY | *and* RULES *of* THE GAME | *as used by* | Brooklyn Croquet Club | Union Croquet Club, New York | Prospect Park Croquet Cub | Long Meadow Croquet Club | Manhattan Croquet Club

[TP verso]

COPYRIGHT, 1929 | BY | AMERICAN SPORTS PUBLISHING COMPANY | NEW YORK

Formula: [1¹²]. 12 leaves, pp *1–4* 5–23 *24*

Technical notes: 130 × 88 mm (p 7). 45 lines, 20 = 58 mm. Leaf size 170 × 124 mm

Contents: Title (*1*), TP verso (*2*), contents (*3*), diagram of the court (*4*), text (5–23), blank (*24*)

Binding: White paper or card, printed in vivid reddish Orange (*ca* 34), stapled through the folds of the sheets, no spine or endpapers. FC: in Orange and white out of Orange ([in white display script, dropped and decorated *S, S*] SPALDING'S | [in Orange within a white rectangular panel with decorated extremities] **ATHLETIC LIBRARY** | [in white out of Orange] Auxiliary Series | [in Orange on white within a decorated rectangular frame with concave curved corners and a floral outer frame] MODERN CROQUET | [*do,* symmetrical twin flourishes] | [*do*] *Instructions for Play and Rules* | [*do*] *of the game as used by* | [*do*] **BROOKLYN CROQUET CLUB** | [*do*] **UNION CROQUET CLUB, NEW YORK** | [*do*] **PROSPECT PARK CROQUET CLUB** | [*do*] **LONG MEADOW CROQUET CLUB** | [*do*] **MANHATTAN CROQUET CLUB** | [between the inner and outer frames, in white out of Orange] AMERICAN SPORTS PUBLISHING CO. | [*do*] *45 Rose Street, New York*). Inside FC: blank. RC: blank. Inside RC: blank

Copy seen: LOC: GV931 M6 (photocopy of original copy in a library binding, the wrapper in colour)

Fingerprint: 2323 t.he edbe wiin 3 1929A [group 2 taken from the last two lines of text on p 11]

Notes: Printed anonymously. The text includes a code of 25 numbered rules with alphabetically listed sub-clauses.

A146   **MODERN CROQUET. Edgar Whitaker**   **1929**

WARNE'S "RECREATION" BOOKS | MODERN | CROQUET | BY | *EDGAR WHITAKER* | [publisher's device] | FREDERICK WARNE & CO., LTD. | LONDON & NEW YORK

[TP verso]

COPYRIGHT | FREDERICK WARNE & CO., LTD. | LONDON | 1929 | *Printed in Great Britain.*

Formula: [1–4⁸]. 32 leaves, pp *1–7* 8–64

Technical notes: 130 × 84 mm (p 10). 31 lines, 20 = 85 mm. Leaf size 183 × 124 mm; thickness 0.13 mm; wove, unwatermarked, smooth, white

Contents: Title (*1*), TP verso (*2*), contents (*3*), blank (*4*), foreword (*5*), blank (*6*), text (7–64)

Binding: White paper, sewn. Advertisements on the facing pages of the front and rear endpapers. FC: printed in strong Yellow Green (117), light orange Yellow (70), pale orange Yellow (73), and light yellowish Brown (76) ([in artist's open script against a Yellow Green background, in light orange Yellow, outlined in black] MODERN CROQUET | [at L, in artist's script] BY | [*do*] EDGAR | [*do*] WHITAKER | [artist's illustration of a man player preparing to strike a ball, with details in light orange Yellow, pale orange Yellow, and Brown, against a Yellow Green background] | [at L, in artist's script] 6ᴰNET | [at L, publisher's device outlined in black out of Yellow Green, set within a broad horizontal black band] | **WARNE'S RECREATION BOOKS**). RC: advertisement printed in black and strong Yellow Green (117) on white. Spine: wanting from the copy examined

Copy seen: PC (imperfect)

Fingerprint: 5350 Song lsas boba 3 1929A

Notes: Printed by The Premier Press, London and Bletchley, price 6d.

A147   **TWELVE HINTS TO LONG-BISQUERS [and CROQUET:**   **[1929]**
          TWELVE HINTS TO BEGINNERS]. RLJ

(a) *First edition [1929]*

[The FC]

[at L] <u>PRICE SIXPENCE.</u> | **Twelve Hints** | to | **Long-Bisquers** | BY | R. L. J. | [rule] *Reprinted by permission of* | *"The Croquet Association Gazette."* | [rule] | [at L] THE HOLMESDALE PRESS LTD., | [at R] REDHILL JUNCTION, SURREY.

Formula: [1⁸]. 8 leaves, unnumbered [pp 1–16]

Technical notes: 81 (variable) × 75 mm (p 8). 29 lines, 20 = 56 mm. Leaf size 139 × 107 mm; thickness 0.12 mm; wove, watermarked (CROXLEY DE LU[‡]), smooth, white. The watermark does not appear in full on any sheet of the copy examined

Contents: Contents (*1*), '*Reprinted from the*"The Croquet Association Gazette."' (*2*), introduction, signed 'R. L. J.', July 1929 (*3*), blank (*4*), text (5–16)

Binding: White card folded, stapled, no spine or endpapers. FC: title (as above). Inside FC: blank. RC: blank. Inside RC: blank

Copy seen: BL: 7918 a 68

Fingerprint: T.C. n.is *k!ep* isar C 1929Q

Notes: Printed by the Holmesdale Press, Redhill Junction, price 6d. The first impression of 100 copies had been sold by 24 August 1929. A second impression was available in September.

This work reprints a series of twelve articles by the author which appeared in successive issues of *The Croquet Association Gazette*, under his editorship, during the early months of 1929.

(b) *Second edition [1949]*

[The FC]

[double rule] | [in shaded script] | CROQUET | TWELVE HINTS | TO BEGINNERS | *By* | R. L. J.

Formula: [1⁸]. 8 leaves, pp *1* 2–16

Technical notes: 104 × 75 mm (pp 4, 5). 30 lines, 20 = 70 mm. Leaf size 138 × 107 mm; thickness 0.09 mm; wove, unwatermarked, smooth, white

Contents: Title heading and contents (*1*), '*Reprinted from "The Croquet Association Gazette,"*' (2), introductory note, signed RLJ (3), text (4–16)

Binding: Light greenish Grey (154) leather-effect card, stapled, no spine or end-papers. FC: as above, printed in black. Inside FC: blank. RC: in black at lower R ([rule] *R. H. Johns Ltd., Newport, Mon.*). Inside RC: blank

Copy seen: PC

Fingerprint: T.C. n.nt *k!ep* isar 3 1949Q [group 1 taken from p*1*]

Notes: Printed by RH Johns, Newport, Monmouthshire. This edition was apparently published by the CA. It was reported in *The Croquet Association Gazette* of August 1960 that the Publicity Committee had decided to change the name to 'Twelve Hints to Beginners'.

Review: The Croquet Association Gazette (August 1960).

1930

A148   CROQUET AND HOW TO PLAY IT. Arthur GF Ross   [1930]

(a) *First edition [1930]*

Not seen. Publication of this work by The Richard Wedderspoon Publicity Company of Wanganui, New Zealand, price 3/6, was reported in *The Croquet Association Gazette* (10 May 1930, p 66).

(b) *Second edition (1933)*

[Within a ruled frame]

CROQUET | AND HOW TO | PLAY IT. | [publisher's device] | [swash *B*] *By* | ARTHUR G. F. ROSS | Seven Times New Zealand Champion. | Nine Times Canterbury Champion. | Twice North Island (New Zealand) Champion. | Twice South Island (New Zealand) Champion. | [*st* joined by a ligature in each instance] Winner New Zealand's First Gold Medal Contest | [*st* joined by a ligature] and Test Preliminaries. | [rule] | SECOND EDITION | REVISED & ENLARGED | [rule] | *Published and Produced by* | Richard Wedderspoon & Co., Wanganui, New Zealand. | Printed by | The Hereford Printing Co. Ltd., Wellington, New Zealand. | 1933.

Formula: [1–7⁸] plus 16 leaves of inset plates. 72 leaves, pp *i* ii–xiii, *a*, *1* 2–8, xiv, *b*, 9–14, xv–xxiv, 15–20, xxv–xxvi, 21–22, xxvii, *c*, 23–26, xxviii–xxix, 27–112 [= 144]

Technical notes: 170 × 93 mm (p 4). 43 lines, 20 = 77 mm. Leaf size 211 × 137 mm. Pp *1*–112: thickness 0.15 mm, laid, unwatermarked, rough, white. Pp *i*–xxix, *a*–*c*: thickness 0.09 mm, wove, unwatermarked, semi-gloss, white. Pp ii, iv xiv–xxix are plates of black-and-white photographs, pp xiv–xxix preceding pp 9 (1 leaf, p xiv),

15 (5 leaves, pp xv–xxiv), 21 (1 leaf, pp xxv–xxvi), 23 (1 leaf, p xxvii), 27 (1 leaf, pp xxviii–xxix). Pp *a–c* are blank

Contents: Title (*i*), frontispiece (black-and-white photograph) (ii), The MacRobertson International Croquet Contest, including black-and-white photograph (iii), black-and-white photographs (iv), index to chapters and contents (v–ix), index to illustrations (x), introduction (xi), in appreciation (xii–xiii), blank (*a*), text (*1–112*)

Binding: Pale orange Yellow (73) paper with Yapp-style projecting edges, stapled through the gatherings, no endpapers. FC: printed in black within a multiple-ruled frame, the lettering arranged within a drawing, signed 'HOWELL HADDON.', of the corner of a furnished croquet lawn set in parkland ([at R] SECOND [‡] EDITION | [*do*] REVISED & ENLARGED [‡] | [at R, in artist's overlapping open shaded script, swash *q*] Croquet | [rule, intersecting the descender of *q* above] | [*do*, in artist's script] and how to | [*do*] play it | [*do*, rule] | [at lower L, in artist's script] Arthur. | [*do*] **G.F.ROSS.** | [at L, near the base of the frame, in artist's script] *Published & Produced by* | [*do*] Richard Wedderspoon&Co. | *Wanganui N·Z·* | [set in the side of a mallet head, in artist's script, in a convex arc] The Arthur Ross | [*do*, parallel to the mallet head] PATENT). Inside FC: blank. RC: advertisement. Inside RC: blank. Spine: blank

Copy seen: PC

Fingerprint: y.by *d.h, S.d. heat* 3 1933A [groups 1–4 taken from pp iii, xi, xiii, xiii respectively]

Notes: Printed by The Hereford Printing Co, Wellington, NZ, price UK 5/6.

Review: *The Croquet Association Gazette* (10 March 1934, p 11).

(c) *Second edition, unpublished German translation (1936)*

[Surrogate cover, f *i*, in artist's MS in Indian ink, within a ruled frame in pencil]

[in open script] **Croquet** | und wie es gespielt wird | von | [*A, G, F, R* in open script] **Arthur G.F.Ross.**

[The TP, f 1]

C R O Q U E T | und wie es gespielt wird. | von | Arthur C. F. Ross | [L justified] siebenfacher Champion von Neuseeland | [*do*] neunfacher Champion von Canterbury | [*do*] zweifacher Champion von Nordisland (Neuseeland) | [*do*] Sieger im ersten Wettstreit um Neuseeland's | Goldmedaille und in den Vorkämpfen. | Zweite durchgesehene und | erweiterte Auflage | Veröffentlich und hergestellt von | Richard Wedderspoon & Co | Wanganui Neuseeland. | [L justified] Vom Englischen in's Deutsche übertragen | durch H. C. C. Wach Croquetspieler in Murnau Oberbayern und Uebersetzer des | [*do*] Handbuches wom modernen Croquetspiel | [*do*] der Croquet Association in London W 1.

Formula: [loose leaves]. 126 leaves, ff *i*, 1–125

Technical notes: 290 × 182 mm (f 7, ragged typescript carbon copy with MS revisions in ink). 34 lines, 20 = 172 mm. Leaf size 330 × 211 mm; thickness 0.07 mm; wove, unwatermarked, smooth, white. The text includes numerous illustrations drawn in Indian ink with typescript captions and legends in MS

Contents: Surrogate cover (*i*), title (1), description of text and illustrations on pp ii–iii of (b) (2), summary of contents (2), introduction, signed 'A. G. F. Ross' (3), 'Empfehlendes Geleitwort', signed 'F. COLCHESTER-WEMYSS' (4–5), text (6–125), name of printer (125)

Binding: The copy examined consists of loose leaves gathered in a card sleeve, retained in a spring-back trade binder with Grey cardboard covers. FC: printed in black ([interrupted rule] | [space intended for title or *etc* to be inserted] | [interrupted rule] | [manufacturer's device *etc*). Inside FC: blank. RC: blank. Inside RC: blank. Spine: in black upwards (Nr. [interrupted rule] Name [interrupted rule] Wohnort [interrupted rule] Jahrgang [interrupted rule])

Copy seen: CA

Fingerprint: l.er nder .)ht helt C 1936A [groups 1–4 taken from ff 2, 6, 13, 13 respectively]

Notes: Unpublished typescript carbon copy produced during the period 21 February – 21 May 1936 (as stated on f 125). It is believed that other copies were produced at the same time and had limited circulation in Germany.

(d) *Fourth edition (1947)*

[Mostly within a double frame, the outer frame formed of wavy lines with the outlines of squares at the corners, the inner frame ruled]

[C intersecting the frame at L] Croquet | AND HOW TO | PLAY IT . . . | [ornament] | [swash *B*] *By* | ARTHUR G. F. ROSS | REFEREE, NEW ZEALAND CROQUET COUNCIL | COMPILER OF THE OFFICIAL HANDBOOK | "THE POWERS AND DUTIES OF AN UMPIRE" | NEW ZEALAND OPEN CHAMPION EIGHT TIMES | • | *Published by* | R. Wedderspoon and Co. | Hereford Printing Co. Ltd., P.O. Box 160 Te Aro, | Wellington, New Zealand. | 1947

Formula: [1–10⁸]. 80 leaves, pp *i* ii–viii, *1* 2–152

Technical notes: 179 × 92 mm. 48 lines, 20 = 73 mm. Leaf size 216 × 138 mm; thickness 0.13 mm (inset leaves 0.09 mm); wove, unwatermarked, smooth, white; ten leaves of inset plates with numerical pagination, mostly of black-and-white photographs, precede pp *1* (1 leaf, pp ix–x), 9 (2 leaves, pp xi–xiv), 25 (2 leaves, pp xv–xviii), 41 (2 leaves, pp xix–xxii), *57* (3 leaves, pp xxiii–xxviii)

Contents: Title (*i*), introduction (ii), index to chapters and contents (iii–viii), index to illustrations and *erratum* (ix), black-and-white photograph (x), text (*1*–152), *erratum* (p ix) repeated (152)

Binding: Moderate Blue (182) leather-effect card, stapled, no endpapers. FC: printed in deep Blue (179) ([*CROQ* intersecting seven evenly spaced vertical bands, running from top to bottom at L] **CROQUET** | [at R] AND | [at R] **HOW TO PLAY IT** | [at R] *by* | [at R] ARTHUR | [at R] G. F. ROSS | [at R] price **10/6** each | [at lower R] **Fourth Edition   Revised and Enlarged**). Inside FC: blank. RC: blank. Inside RC: blank. Spine: blank

Copy seen: PC

Fingerprint: 2525 r-ys ifd- vaeq 3 1947A [groups 1–4 taken from pp iii, *1*, 13, 14 respectively]

Notes: Printed by Hereford Printing Co, Wellington, NZ, price NZ 10/6.

In the Introduction the author writes, 'Almost no change has been made in the Stroke-making and Break Sections ... but the chapters dealing with tactics have been remodelled completely. I have also made some very slight mention of Croquet from the international point of view ...'.

1931

A149   A HANDBOOK ON MODERN CROQUET.   1931
[Sir Francis Colchester-Wemyss (ed)]

(a) *First edition (1931)*

[at L] *THE CROQUET ASSOCIATION* | A HANDBOOK ON | MODERN CROQUET | *With a Foreword by* | THE VISCOUNT DONERAILE | LONGMANS, GREEN AND CO. | LONDON :: NEW YORK :: TORONTO | 1931

Formula: A⁸ B–E⁸ F⁴ [$1 signed (–A1)]. 44 leaves, pp *i–iv* v–viii *ix* x–xii, 1–3 4 5–75 76

Technical notes: 143 × 88 mm (p vi). 34 lines, 20 = 84 mm. Leaf size 184 × 123 mm; thickness 0.15 mm; wove, unwatermarked, rough, white

Contents: Half-title (*i*), names of publisher's associate companies (*ii*), title (*iii*), TP verso (*iv*), foreword (v–viii), contents (*ix*–x), 'Croquet: A simple synopsis' (xi–xii), text (1–75), advertisement and name of printer (76)

Binding: Light bluish Green (163) parchment-effect paper, sewn. FC: printed in black (**THE CROQUET ASSOCIATION** | [triple rule, the top and bottom rules in bold] | **A** | **HANDBOOK** | **ON** | **MODERN** | [in display script] **CROQUET** | **WITH A FOREWORD BY** | **THE VISCOUNT DONERAILE**). RC: printed in black at the foot near the fore-edge (2/–). Spine: blank

Copy seen: PC

Fingerprint: aply chee e.er haNe 3 1931A

Notes: Published on 30 April 1931, printed by The Burleigh Press, Bristol, price 2/–. Editorship is attributed to F Colchester-Wemyss by *The Croquet Association Gazette* (7 June 1930, p 110).

The text includes contributions by Lord Doneraile (Foreword), M Reckitt (Ch I), R Jones (Ch II), B Apps (Ch III), J Edkins (Ch IV), G Elvey (Ch V).

Review: *The West Australian* (reprinted in *The Croquet Association Gazette* of 5 September 1931).

(b) *German translation [1935]*

Not seen. According to an editorial note in *The Croquet Association Gazette* (21 November 1935, p 345), this work was translated into German by HCC Wach. A typescript of the translation was made available for inspection at the CA offices. It is not known whether it was ever published more widely.

(c) *Second CA issue (1937)*

[at L] *THE CROQUET ASSOCIATION* | A HANDBOOK ON | MODERN CROQUET | *With a Foreword by* | THE VISCOUNT DONERAILE | LONGMANS, GREEN AND CO. | LONDON :: NEW YORK :: TORONTO

[TP verso]

Revised Edition, 1937 | *Made in Great Britain*

Formula: A⁸ B–E⁸ F⁴ [$1 signed (–A1, C1)]. 44 leaves, pp *i–iv* v–viii *ix* x–xii, 1–76. An *erratum* slip is tipped-in over p xi

Technical notes: 143 × 87 mm (p vii). 34 lines, 20 = 84 mm. Leaf size 183 × 121 mm; thickness 0.16 mm; wove, unwatermarked, rough, white

Contents: Half-title (*i*), names of publisher's associate companies (*ii*), title (*iii*), TP verso (*iv*), foreword (v–viii), contents (*ix*–x), 'Croquet: A simple synopsis' (xi–xii), text (1–76), name of printer (p 76)

Binding: Pale Green (149) parchment-effect laminated paper, sewn, apparently glued to the gatherings without endpapers. FC: printed in black (**THE CROQUET ASSOCIATION** | [triple rule, the top and bottom rules in bold] | **A** | **HANDBOOK** | **ON** | **MODERN** | [in display script] **CROQUET** | **WITH A FOREWORD BY** |

THE VISCOUNT DONERAILE). RC: wanting from the copy examined. Spine: wanting from the copy examined

Copy seen: BL: 07908 e 67 (imperfect, in a library binding)

Fingerprint: aply chee e.er bean 3 1937A

Notes: Published on 11 June 1937, printed by The Burleigh Press, Bristol.

The text would appear to vary from (a) chiefly in details given in the appendices, which document the contemporary states of the CA and the game.

1932

A150 THE ART OF CROQUET. HF Crowther-Smith   1932

THE ART OF CROQUET | A PRACTICAL HANDBOOK ON ALL PHASES | OF THE GAME AND ITS RULES | *By* | H. F. CROWTHER-SMITH | WITH | *SKETCHES AND DIAGRAMS* | [in gothic-revival script] | The | [*do*] Sports and Pastimes | [*do*] Library | H. F. & G. WITHERBY | 326 HIGH HOLBORN, LONDON, W.C.

[TP verso]

[publisher's device] | *First Published* 1932 | *Printed for Messrs. H. F. & G. Witherby | at Middle Row Place, London*

Formula: A^8 B–N^8 O^4(O1+χ1) [\$1 signed (–A1)]. 109 leaves, pp *1–8 9–217 218*

Technical notes: 163 × 93 mm (p 10). 29 lines, 20 = 114 mm. Leaf size *ca* 220 (uneven) × 137 mm; thickness 0.22 mm; wove, unwatermarked, rough, white; five inset plates (black-and-white photographs) face pp *3* (with tipped-in protective tissue), 54, 76, 112, 150

Contents: Half-title (*1*), blank (*2*), title (*3*), TP verso (*4*), contents (*5–6*), list of illustrations (*7–8*), text (*9–217*), blank (*218*)

Binding: Dark orange Yellow (72) cloth over stiff boards, sewn. FC: printed ([in black] THE ART OF CROQUET | [*do*] H. F. CROWTHER-SMITH | [in greyish Blue (186), drawing of a man player about to strike a ball, within a double-ruled elliptical frame]). RC: blank. Spine: printed crosswise ([in black] THE | [*do*] ART OF | [*do*] CROQUET | [*do*] H. F. | [*do*] CROWTHER | [*do*] SMITH | [vignette in Blue, as on the FC but in reduced scale] | [in Blue gothic-revival script] The Sports | [*do*] and Pastimes | [*do*] Library | [in black at the foot] WITHERBY)

Copy seen: PC

Fingerprint: s.le r-67 mehe MrCl 7 1932A

Notes: Printed anonymously, London.

1933

A151 CROQUET: A SIMPLE SYNOPSIS. [The Croquet Association] [1933]

(a) **First edition [1933]*

[Heading]

CROQUET—A SIMPLE SYNOPSIS.

Formula: [1^1]. 1 leaf, unnumbered [pp 1–2]

Technical notes: 171 × 99 mm (p *1*). 60 lines, 20 = 57 mm. Leaf size 220 × 136 mm.

Contents: Title heading and text (*1*), not visible on the copy examined ([2])

Binding: None

Copy seen: PC (imperfect)

Fingerprint: e.he heak itnd asd. C 1933Q

Notes: Printed anonymously. This work is identical to a note in the CA Year Book of 1932 (A110y), incorporating minor revisions of phraseology from a similar note in the CA Year Book of 1931 (A110x) which is identical save in accidentals to a preliminary note in *A Handbook on Modern Croquet* (A149, pp xi–xii) of the same year. The fact that most of the text of the last-mentioned work is attributed expressly to other named writers, but exceptionally this note is not so acknowledged, suggests that it was compiled by the editor, F Colchester-Wemyss.

According to *The Croquet Association Gazette* (17 June 1933, p 123), a stereo of this work was prepared by the CA and offered on loan to the Hon Secretaries of tournaments for inclusion in their programmes and for issue to local newspapers. It is thought that the copy examined was printed from one such stereo, perhaps on behalf the CA.

(b) *Second edition [1933]*

[Heading]

CROQUET—A SIMPLE SYNOPSIS.

Formula: [1¹]. 1 leaf, unnumbered [pp 1–2]

Technical notes: 169 × 98 mm (p *1*). 60 lines, 20 = 56 mm. Leaf size 203 × 126 mm; thickness 0.12 mm; wove, unwatermarked, smooth, white

Contents: Title heading and text (*1*), plan of court and name of publisher (2)

Binding: None

Copy seen: PC

Fingerprint: s.ip ison d.of ras. C 1933Q

Notes: Published by the CA, printed anonymously. Year of publication is conjectural. The text, though reset throughout, is identical to that of (a) save for the final paragraph. This edition makes no reference to the provisions of the advanced laws of croquet, the revision presumably being made in the interest of further simplification.

(c) *John Jaques edition [1968]*

[double rule] | **CROQUET** | A Simple Synopsis | [double rule] | Published by : | JOHN JAQUES & SON, LTD. | The Croquet Specialists | [double rule] | JOHN JAQUES & SON, LTD., | 361, WHITEHORSE ROAD, | THORNTON HEATH, SURREY. | [the following lines divided into two columns]

Telephones:	Telegrams :	
THOrnton Heath 4242-3.	CROQUET, THORNTON HEATH.	
STD. 01—684—4242-3.		

[double rule]

Formula: [1²]. 2 leaves, unnumbered [pp 1–4]

Technical notes: 177 × 109 mm (p *3*). 50 lines, 20 = 71 mm. Leaf size 204 × 127 mm; thickness 0.10 mm; wove, unwatermarked, smooth, yellowish White (92)

Contents: Title (*1*), text (*2–4*)

Binding: None

Copy seen: PC

Fingerprint: t.ot aser ont. wnon C 1960Q [all four groups taken from p *3*]

Notes: Printed anonymously. Approximate year of publication is conjectural. The over-stamped statement on the TP of (c) would suggest that this edition was intended for issue with the publisher's croquet sets.

(d) *John Jaques edition, reprint [1970]*

[double rule] | <u>**CROQUET**</u> | A Simple Synopsis | [double rule] | Published by : | JOHN JAQUES & SON, LTD. | The Croquet Specialists | [double rule] | JOHN JAQUES & SON, LTD., | 361, WHITEHORSE ROAD, | THORNTON HEATH, SURREY. | [the following lines divided into two columns]

Telephones: | Telegrams : |
THOrnton Heath 4242-4. | CROQUET, THORNTON HEATH. |
STD. 01—684—4242-4. |
[double rule]

Formula: [1²]. 2 leaves, unnumbered [pp 1–4]

Technical notes: 176 × 109 mm (p 3). 51 lines, 20 = 70 mm. Leaf size 202 × 126 mm; thickness 0.09 mm; wove, unwatermarked, smooth, white

Contents: Title (*1*), text (*2–4*)

Binding: None

Copy seen: PC

Fingerprint: t.ot aser ont. wnon C 1960Q [all four groups taken from p *3*]

Notes: Printed anonymously. Approximate year of publication is conjectural, The copy examined is over-stamped in red above the title 'NO CLIPS ARE PROVIDED WITH THIS SET', suggesting that it was issued with one of the publisher's inexpensive sets of garden croquet equipment. The text is identical to that of (b).

1935

A152　OFFICIAL CROQUET: RULES OF PLAY. [Anon]　　　　1935

(a) *First edition (1935)*

Not seen. This work is referred to explicitly in the foreword to (b), wherein it is stated that the eponymous rules of play were first published on 26 August 1935. Whether or not the title of the first edition was as here given, however, is unclear.

(b) *Revised edition (1939)*

OFFICIAL CROQUET | RULES OF PLAY | Approved and Adopted | by the | **NATIONAL RECREATION** | **ASSOCIATION** | **CROQUET ASSOCIATION** | of **Kentucky** | **DIVISION OF RECREATION** | **City of Louisville** | **DEPT. OF RECRE-ATION** | **Miami, La.** | **PUBLIC RECREATION COMMISSION** | **Cincinnati, Ohio** | **DEPT. OF RECREATION** | **Lincoln, NEB.** | Also endorsed by many other | recreation centres.

Formula: [1⁸]. 8 leaves, pp *1* 2–16

Technical notes: 160 × 70 mm (p 12). 44 lines, 20 = 74 mm. Leaf size 194 × 101 mm; thickness 0.14 mm; wove, unwatermarked, smooth, white

Contents: Title (*1*), foreword, signed 'A. W. Garrett' for Croquet Association of Kentucky (*2*), text (*3–16*)

Binding: White semi-gloss light card, sewn through the wrapper, no spine or endpapers. FC: printed in deep Blue (179) (Official | **RULES** | [double rule] | [emblematic line drawing of a ball and two crossed mallets in front of a hoop flanked by two stakes, incorporating the lettering] **CROQUET** | [double rule] | Revised and

Copyrighted | 1939 | **By Croquet Association of Kentucky** | Division of Recreation | LOUISVILLE,   KENTUCKY | [rule]). Inside FC: blank. RC: blank. Inside RC: blank

Copy seen: HPC: GV933 C8C8 1939 CROQ

Fingerprint: t.st l.as chon AYt. C 1939A [group 1 taken from p 5, groups 2–4 taken from p 13]

Notes: Printed anonymously. The text consists of a code of 38 numbered rules.

1936

A153   **THE ART OF GOLF-CROQUET. HF Crowther-Smith**   1936

[in open display script] The Art | OF | [in open display script] Golf-Croquet | by | H. F. Crowther-Smith | [dotted line] | [swash *P*] *Price One Shilling* | [dotted line] | Printed by Prompt Press, Duke Street, Richmond, Surrey. | Published by The Author, at 13 Mount Ararat Road, | Richmond, Surrey

Formula: [1¹⁰]. 10 leaves, pp *1–4 5–9 10 11–19 20*

Technical notes: 137 × 84 mm (p 12). 34 lines, 20 = 80 mm. Leaf size 181 × 122 mm; thickness 0.15 mm; wove, unwatermarked, smooth, white; an *addendum* slip is tipped-in on p 19

Contents: Title (*1*), blank (*2*), preface (*3*), blank (*4*), text (*5–19*), blank (*20*)

Binding: Greyish olive Green (127) paper, stapled, no endpapers. FC: printed in black (**THE ART** | **OF** | **GOLF-CROQUET** | by | **H. F. Crowther-Smith** | [cartoon vignette depicting a man player dressed in plus-fours with mallet raised in an exaggerated golf-style backswing] | **Price 1s.**). Inside FC: blank. RC: blank. Inside RC: blank

Copy seen: PC

Fingerprint: y.d. a.). ulnd mith 3 1936Q

Notes: Published in April 1936, printed by Prompt Press, Richmond, Surrey, price 1/–.

Review: *The Croquet Association Gazette* (18 April 1936).

A154   **THE CROQUET PLAYER. HG Wells**   1936

(a) *First edition (1936)*

THE | CROQUET PLAYER | A Story | H. G. WELLS | 1936 | CHATTO & WINDUS | LONDON

Formula: A⁸ B–F⁸ [$1 signed (– A1)]. 48 leaves, pp *i–x, 1–81 82–86*

Technical notes: 123 × 81 mm (p 2). 26 lines, 20 = 95 mm. Leaf size 188 × 123 mm; thickness 0.17 mm; laid, unwatermarked, smooth, white

Contents: Blank (*i–iv*), half-title (*v*), blank (*vi*), title (*vii*), TP verso (*viii*), dedication (*ix*), blank (*x*), text (*1–82*), name of printer (*83*), blank (*84–86*)

Binding: Mottled black and Green cloth over stiff boards, sewn. FC: blank. RC: blank. Spine: the title and author are printed in black on a piece of white paper glued to the head ([multiple-ornamented rule] *The* | *Croquet* | *Player* | [small stylised illustration of a ball] | H. G. | WELLS | [multiple ornamented rule])

Dust wrapper: Printed in black and Green on Yellow paper. FP: the title ([near the head in artist's script, L justified] *The* | [in artist's script, in a convex arc] *Croquet Player*) and author ([near the foot in artist's script] *H.G.Wells*) set within a line drawing in black and Green, signed 'Harold Jones', of a man croquet player and a primitive humanoid, the former standing on a croquet ground and the latter knee-deep in marsh. FF: publisher's direction and price. RP: publisher's blurb. RF: blank. Spine: the title ([in black artist's script diagonally from upper L to lower R] The | [do] Croquet | Player), name of author ([in black artist's script diagonally from lower L to upper R] H.G. | [do] Wells), and name of publisher ([in black artist's script diagonally from upper L to lower R] Chatto | [in black artist's script at L] & | [in black artist's script diagonally from lower L to upper R] Windus) set within a line drawing in black and Green, featuring a spade, skull, croquet mallet, and ball

Copy seen: PC

Fingerprint: anch hyal t.im wape 3 1936A [group 1 taken from p 1]

Notes: Printed by R and R Clark, Edinburgh, price 3/6 net. A novel.

Reviews: *The Daily Mail, Isis, Manchester Guardian, Observer, Sunday Times*

(b) *First American edition (1937)*

[Within a mitred, cross-hatched frame]

H. G. WELLS | [a small stylised line drawing of a ball] | *THE* | CROQUET PLAYER | *New York* | *THE VIKING PRESS* | *1937*

Formula: [1–6⁸ 7⁴]. 52 leaves, pp *i–iv*, *1–8 9–16 17–18 19–47 48–50 51–72 73–74 75–98 99–100*

Technical notes: 140 × 80 mm (p 10). 25 lines, 20 = 113 mm. Leaf size 206 × 128 mm; thickness 0.19 mm; wove, unwatermarked, smooth, white

Contents: Blank (*i–ii*), half-title (*iii*), blank (*iv*), title (*1*), TP verso (*2*), contents (*3*), blank (*4*), half-title (*5*), blank (*6*), illustration (*7*), blank (*8*), text, continued (*9–47*), blank (*48*), illustration (*49*), blank (*50*), text, continued (*51–72*), illustration (*73*), blank (*74*), text, concluded (*75–98*), blank (*99–100*)

Binding: Printed in black and silver on Grey cloth over stiff boards, sewn. FC: an arrangement of one black panel and seven smaller ones, the title *etc* ([in silver] H. G. Wells | [illustration a man in Grey out of black] | THE CROQUET | PLAYER) set within the large panel. RC: blank. Spine: downwards in silver on black (H. G. WELLS [stylised line drawing of a ball] THE CROQUET PLAYER [do] THE VIKING PRESS)

Dust wrapper: Printed in colour on white paper. FP: artist's collage in line and colour, featuring the principal characters in the story, continued on the spine, with lettering in white (The Croquet Player | H. G. WELLS). FF: excerpts from English reviews, continued on the RP. RP: publisher's blurb and excerpts from English reviews, concluded. RF: advertisement. Spine: in white out of an extension to the illustration on the FP, downwards (THE CROQUET PLAYER *by* H. G. WELLS) and crosswise at the foot (VIKING)

Copy seen: PC

Fingerprint: 75st onup s.he goou 3 1937A

Notes: Illustrated by Clifton Line, printed by the Haddon Craftsmen, USA.

(c) *French edition, Librairie Arthème Fayard (1937)*

les œuvres libres | **recueil littéraire mensuel ne publiant que de** | [double-underlined, the lower rule in bold] **l'inédit** | CXCV | H. G. Wells | LE JOUEUR DE CROQUET | grande nouvelle inédite. | L. Bourgeois-Borgex | LA FIN D'UN SIÈCLE | chose vues inédites. | Fernande Sestiery | MARI-SOL | roman inédit et complet. | Jean Merilys | UN DICTATEUR COSAQUE | AU XVIIIᵉ SIÈCLE | variété historique inédite. |

Mildred Cram | AMOUR ÉTERNEL | grande nouvelle inédite. | **ABONNEMENTS** | *FRANCE : Un an 86 fr.   Union postale : un an 106 fr.* | [set so as to create the second of two lines divided into four columns] – *Six mois 44 fr.   –   Six mois 58 fr.* | LIBRAIRIE A. FAYARD, 18–20, RUE DU SAINT-GOTHARD, PARIS

Formula: Apparently *1*[16] *2–9*[16] *10*[4] *11*[10] [$1 (*–1*₁, *11*₁)]. 158 leaves, pp *1–5* 6–78 *79* 80–123 *124* 125–228 *229* 230–278 *279* 280–316 *316*, misprinting 257 as '25'

Technical notes: 131 × 81 mm (p 7). 39 lines, 20 = 67 mm. Leaf size 178 × 111 mm; thickness 0.09 mm; wove, unwatermarked, smooth, white

Contents: Half-title (*1*), advertisement (*2*), title (*3*), summary of contents of recent issues of *Les œuvres libres* (*4*), 'Le Joueur de Croquet', editor's introduction (*5–6*), text (*6–78*), other contributions, as listed on the TP (*79–315*), table des matières (*316*)

Binding: Apparently white paper wrapper glued to the folds of the gatherings, sewn, no endpapers. FC: printed mostly in black, the initials letters of the series title and the authors' names in deep Yellow Green (118) (Nᵒ 195. — Septembre 1937.   Huit francs. | **les œuvres libres** | **recueil littéraire mensuel ne publiant que de** | [double-underlined, the lower rule in bold] **l'inédit** | CXCV | H. G. Wells | LE JOUEUR DE CROQUET | grande nouvelle inédite. | L. Bourgeois-Borgex | LA FIN D'UN SIÈCLE | chose vues inédites. | Fernande Sestiery | MARI-SOL | roman inédit et complet. | Jean Merilys | UN DICTATEUR COSAQUE | AU XVIIIᵉ SIÈCLE | variété historique inédite. | Mildred Cram | AMOUR ÉTERNEL | grande nouvelle inédite. | [in Green] *toutes les œuvres sont complètes dans ce livre* | LIBRAIRIE ARTHÈME FAYARD, PARIS). Inside FC: blank. RC: in black, advertisement and production details (*Le Gérant :* A. QUEROL. "Imprimé en France" CORBEIL. — IMP. CRÉTÉ. | [R justified] 141). Inside RC: blank. Spine: wanting from the copy examined

Copy seen: BL: 12208 ee 195 (imperfect, in a library binding)

Fingerprint:).ur ise. u-ès ve—E 7 1937A

Notes: Printed by Crété, price 8 fr.

(d) *Ian Henry Publications reprint (1982)*

THE CROQUET | **PLAYER** | A story by | H. G. Wells | IAN HENRY PUBLICA-TIONS | 1982

Formula: A/B[16] C/D[16] E/F[16] including the endpapers [A/B9 signed 'B', C/D1 signed 'C', C/D9 signed 'D', E/F1 signed 'E', E/F9 signed 'F']. 48 leaves including the end-papers, pp *i–x*, 1–81 *82–86*

Technical notes: 122 × 81 mm (p 2). 26 lines, 20 = 95 mm. Leaf size 198 × 126 mm; thickness 0.14 mm; wove, unwatermarked, smooth, white

Contents: Glued to the FC (*i*), blank (*ii–iv*), half-title (*v*), blank (*vi*), title (*vii*), TP verso (*viii*), dedication (*ix*), blank (*x*), text (1–82), blank (*83–85*), glued to the RC (*86*)

Binding: Moderate Yellow Green (120) linen grain paper over stiff boards, sewn. FC: blank. RC: blank. Spine: gold-blocked downwards ([in half-open display script] [‡] **PLAYER   WELLS**) and crosswise at the foot ([publisher's device, a monogram formed of the letters *I, H*)

Copy seen: BL: Nov 48022 (imperfect)

Fingerprint: anch hyal t.im Wape 3 1982A [group 1 taken from p 1, group 2 taken from p 9]

Notes: ISBN 0 86025 153 5, printed and bound by Biddles, Guildford and King's Lynn.

A155   LAWN TENNIS: CROQUET, CRICKET: BOWLS, POLO. [Anon]   [1936]

[Mostly within a double-ruled frame, the outer frame printed in deep Orange (51), in bold, encapsulating a white repeated saw-tooth pattern out of Orange, with indented corner ornaments at the top and a downward-facing serpentine base]

[in outlined script] **SLAZENGERS** | [*do*] **L I M I T E D** | [Orange rule in bold encapsulating a white repeated saw-tooth pattern out of Orange] | LAWN TENNIS | CROQUET,CRICKET | BOWLS,   POLO | [Orange rule in bold encapsulating a white repeated saw-tooth pattern out of Orange] | BRANCHES:- | PARIS [rule] 82, Rue de Muncie | TORONTO [rule] 53, Young Street | SYDNEY [rule] 496–512, Crown Street | [double rule] | AGENCIES THROUGHOUT | THE WORLD | [rule] | [publisher's device in the form of a medallion] | [forming a column at L of the tail-piece to the frame] TELEGRAMS | [*do*] SLAZENGER | [*do*] CANNON | [*do*] LONDON | [forming a column at R of the tail-piece to the frame] TELEPHONE | [*do*] MANSION HOUSE | [*do*] ⋯ 7755 ⋯ | [*do*] BRANCH EXCHANGE | [in outlined script] LAURENCE POUNTNEY HILL, CANNON ST., LONDON, E.C.4 | [*do*] ALSO AT PARA WORKS. WOOLWICH. S. E. | THE CODE WORDS HEREIN ARE THE COPYRIGHT OF E. L. BENTLEY, 4, FENCHURCH AVENUE, LONDON, E.C.3.

Formula: [1³²]. 32 leaves, pp *1* 2–63 *64*

Technical notes: 184 × 250 mm (p 6, variable). Variable line spacing. Leaf size 250 × 185 mm; thickness 0.10 mm; wove, unwatermarked, semi-gloss, cream

Contents: Title (*1*), introduction (2), index (3), explanation of 'telegraphic code' (4), text (4–63), blank (*64*)

Binding: Moderate Orange (53) light card, stapled, no spine or endpapers. FC: printed in blackish Blue (188) and brownish Orange (54), mostly within a ruled frame in broken line, in bold ([in Blue, outlined in brownish Orange] **SLAZENGERS** | [*do*] **LIMITED** | [line drawing in brownish Orange of man lawn-tennis player about to serve] | [in Blue, outlined in brownish Orange, in MS-style script] *Summer Catalogue* | [below the frame] *Printed in England.*). Inside FC: blank. RC: printed in Blue and brownish Orange ([line drawing in brownish Orange of a man lawn-tennis player about to serve, apparently a reduced-scale reproduction of that on the FC] | [in Blue] SLAZENGERS). Inside RC: blank

Copy seen: PC

Fingerprint: 4162 **h.UD h.d.** haPl 3 1936Q

Notes: Printed anonymously. Year of publication is inferred from a reference in the introduction to the 1935 Wimbledon lawn-tennis championships as having been held 'last year'.

1937

A156   SOME CROQUET VERSES. GDR Tucker and HF Crowther-Smith   1937

SOME | CROQUET | VERSES | By G. D. R. TUCKER | Illustrated by H. F. CROWTHER-SMITH | LONGMANS GREEN AND CO. | LONDON - NEW YORK - TORONTO

Formula: A⁴(A3+χ1) B–C⁴ D⁶ [\$1 signed (+D2; –A1); D1 signed 'E')]. 19 leaves, pp *1–6, i–ii,* 7 8 *9–10* 11 12 *13* 14 *15* 16–23 *24* 25–27 *28* 29–33 *34* 35 *36*

Technical notes: 137 × 74 mm (p 20, ragged). 25 lines, 20 = 112 mm. Leaf size 249 × 173 mm; thickness 0.20 mm; wove, unwatermarked, smooth, white

Contents: Half-title (*1*), blank (*2*), title (*3*), TP verso (*4*), dedication (*5*), acknowledgement (*6*), *erratum* (*i*), blank (*ii*), contents (*7*), blank (*8*), text (*9–36*)

Binding: Strong Orange (50) paper over stiff boards, sewn. FC: printed in black ([cartoon of a man player on court, puzzling over a wired position] | [at L] SOME | CROQUET | [at R] VERSES | [at L] *Illustrated by* | [*do*] H. F. *CROWTHER-SMITH* | [at R, overlapping the line above] *by G. D. R.* | [at R] *TUCKER*). RC: printed in black ([cartoon of a man player with mallet raised to strike a worm]). Spine: blank

Copy seen: PC

Fingerprint: 3635 m.um g.ng WeNo 7 1937A

Notes: Published on 24 May 1937, printed by Western Printing Services, Bristol.

AA157 SUMMER SPORTS 1937. [EJ Riley Ltd]   1937

[The FC]

[across a horizontal band in light orange Yellow (70) with dark orange Yellow (172) borders over a vivid yellow Green (115) panel and moderate reddish Brown (43) background, in Brown script shaded with white] **E·J·RILEY L**^{TD} | [across a horizontal band, the upper of two lines, in black, swash W, M] *Willow Mills* [across the same horizontal band, the lower of two lines, in black] ACCRINGTON | [sketch of sundry sports goods over the panels and Brown background] | [over Yellow Green panel, in black] Manufacturers | [*do*] & Exporters of | [*do*] CRICKET | [*do*] TENNIS | [*do*] GOLF | [*do*] BOWLS | [*do*] CROQUET | [*do*] *ETC.* | [over a nesting set of panels in gradations of Yellow, in black] SUMMER | [*do*] SPORTS | [*do*] 1937

Formula: [1^{60}]. 60 leaves, pp *1* 2–118 *119–120*; and a single-sheet insert, pp *i–ii*

Technical notes: 208 × 110 mm (p 14). variable line spacing. Leaf size 244 × 138 mm; thickness 0.06 mm; wove, unwatermarked, smooth, white. In the copy examined the single-sheet insert, measuring 60 × 95 mm, was found glued to a page of the text

Contents: EJ Riley Limited, terms of trade, and reference to index (*1*), index and sundry notes (2), warranty (3), open letter to readers (4), text (5–118), order form (*119–120*), trade terms (*i*), blank (*ii*)

Binding: White paper, stapled through the wrapper, no spine or endpapers. FC: printed, as above. Inside FC: advertisement. RC: identical to FC. Inside RC: advertisement

Copy seen: PC

Fingerprint: WOe. t.**m.** t.r. oron 3 1937A [the first two characters of group 2 taken from the caption to the illustration on p 9]

Notes: Printed anonymously, probably issued free of charge early in the year in anticipation of the 1937 summer sports season.

Page 99 is devoted to croquet goods. The insert sheet found in the copy examined was probably intended for copies issued to *bona fide* dealers only.

1930–39

AA158 CROQUET. [Roy Brothers]   *ca* 1930

[Within a double-ruled frame]

[double-underlined] **CROQUET** | Manufactured by | **ROY BROTHERS** | **East Barnet, Vt.** | [device, the mirror-image of a swastika] | [extended rule, bisecting the frame] | **FACTORY AND OFFICE OPPOSITE PASSENGER DEPOT | FREIGHT AND EXPRESS OFFICE, INWOOD, VT.**

Formula: [1^{10}]. 10 leaves, pp *ONE*, TWO–TWENTY

Technical notes: 96 × 114 mm (p THREE). 23 lines, 20 = 24 mm. Leaf size 129 × 172 mm; thickness 0.14 mm; wove, unwatermarked, semi-gloss, white

Contents: Title (*ONE*), to the trade (TWO), catalogue of croquet goods, illustrated with black-and-white photographs (THREE–NINETEEN), plan of croquet ground (TWENTY)

Binding: Greyish Yellow (90) calico-effect embossed card, stapled, no spine or endpapers. FC: printed in very dark bluish Green (166), greyish Yellow Green (122), and dark Green (146) ([in artist's display script, in very dark bluish Green shaded with dark Green] **CROQUET** | [triple rule in very dark bluish Green, the space between the uppermost and central rules filled in dark Green] | [elaborate tail-piece in Yellow Green]). Inside FC: blank. RC: at the foot, in black (The Ranlet Press | St. Johnsbury | Vermont). Inside RC: blank

Copy seen: PC

Fingerprint: e$G e$g. e$g. Paru 3 1930Q [the penultimate line of p THREE (group 1) consisting of a single character]

Notes: Printed by The Ranlet Press, St Johnsbury, VT. Approximate year of publication is inferred from the manufacturer's claim to 'twenty years' experience in the manufacture of Croquet' (p TWO), publication of their rule book (A123) in 1911 suggesting that they started making croquet goods about 1910.

Most of the croquet sets illustrated in this trade catalogue are shown to contain copies of the manufacturer's own rule book. Two distinct issues are illustrated, neither of which is here recorded.

AA159 SHEPPARTON CROQUET CLUB: HINTS ON THE GAME.   *ca* 1935
[Anon]

(a) *First edition (ca 1935)*

Not seen. The continued existence of this work from about 1935 is well remembered by senior members of the club.

(b) *1990s reprint (ca 1995)*

[The FC]

SHEPPARTON | CROQUET | CLUB | HINTS ON THE GAME

Formula: [1⁶]. 12 pages, pp 1–12

Technical notes: 179 × 114 mm (p 5). 38 lines, 20 = 94 mm. Leaf size 211 × 148 mm; thickness 0.10 mm; wove, unwatermarked, smooth, white

Contents: Text (1–12)

Binding: Very light yellowish Green (134) paper, stapled through the folds of the leaves, no spine or endpapers. FC: printed in black as above. Inside FC: blank. RC: blank. Inside RC: blank

Copy seen: PC

Fingerprint: w.in r.re ver. tee. C 1995Q [group 1 taken from p 1, groups 2–4 taken from p 9]

Notes: Printed anonymously. Year of publication is conjectural: it is understood that small batches are produced from time to time as stocks held by the club are exhausted.

1944

A160 THE QUEEN'S CROQUET GROUND. Lewis Carroll   [1944]
[page *1*, divided laterally, the upper part consisting of a drawing in several colours,

the lower part consisting of the title in white and vivid reddish Orange (34) out of a black background]

[in MS-style script, mostly in white out of black, the top out of the drawing above] *The* | [in MS-style script, swash *Q*, in Orange] *Queen's Croquet* | [*do*] *Ground*

[From p *24*]

THIS IS A PERRY COLOUR BOOK | [in MS-style script] Devised by Powell Perry | FROM LEWIS CARROL'S [*sic*] 'ALICE IN WONDERLAND' | ILLUSTRATED FROM DRAWINGS BY LESLIE BUTLER

Formula: [1^{12}]. 12 leaves, unnumbered [pp 1–24]

Technical notes: Variable height × 86 mm (p *3*). The text is set in white panels of variable height out of drawings in several colours. Variable number of lines, 20 = 142 mm. Leaf size 180 × 213 mm; thickness 0.13 mm; wove, unwatermarked, smooth, white

Contents: Title, as above (*1*), text (*2–24*), surrogate TP verso (*24*)

Binding: Stapled, no covers, wrapper, endpapers, or spine.

Copy seen: BL: 12807 e 55

Fingerprint: ?"se e.ly !"ay Thwo C 1944Q [group 3 taken from p*17*, group 4 taken from p *18*]

Notes: Printed anonymously. Year of publication is taken as that given in the *General Catalogue* of the BL.

The text is a reprint of Ch VIII (The Queen's Croquet Ground) from Carroll's *Alice's Adventures in Wonderland*.

1946

A161   **HOW TO PLAY CROQUET.** [Anon]   1946

[The FC, printed in deep yellowish Green (132) and black]

[in white out of Green] *Price 25c Postpaid* | [slanted from lower L to upper R in black on an irregularly shaped white panel out of Green, the background also featuring a diagram depicting the passage of a ringed croquet ball through an arched hoop] **HOW** | [*do*] **TO PLAY** | [*do*] **CROQUET** | [in the L column of text, in white out of black, within a band divided into two columns by a vertical dotted line] **SOUTH BEND TOY MFG. CO.** | [*do*] CROQUET MANUFACTURERS SINCE 1874 | [*do*] SOUTH BEND, INDIANA | [in the R column, *H*, *B* separated by an extension to the upper portion of the letter *C* below] *SOUTH BEND* | [*do*, in artist's script, the upper portion of the letter *C* dividing *H*, *B* in the line above] **Croquet**

Formula: [1^{8}]. 8 leaves, unnumbered [pp 1–16]

Technical notes: 152 × 104 mm (pp *5, 7*). 37 lines, 20 = 82 mm. Leaf size 184 × 139 mm; thickness 0.12 mm; wove, unwatermarked, smooth, white

Contents: Title (*1*), assertion of copyright (*2*), text (*2–14*), advertisement (*15*), repeat of TP, save the price (*16*)

Binding: None, sewn

Copy seen: HPC: GV931 S69 1946 CROQ

Fingerprint: ngs, n.me t.at siar C 1946A

Notes: Printed anonymously, price 25 cents postpaid. Year of publication is inferred from the assertion of copyright (p *2*). The text includes a code of 19 numbered rules.

1947

A162   LE CROQUET, LE BADMINTON, LE BILLARD DE PELOUSE.   1947
Jean Perrot

(a) *First edition (1947)*

[The FC, printed in orange and black against a pale green background]

[in black on a white panel out of green] TOUS LES JEUX ET LEUR [‡] | [in artist's open script outlined in black] **LE** | [in artist's open script outlined in black, in a convex arc] **CROQUET** | [in white out of green] **LE BADMINTON** | [*do*] **LE BILLARD DE PELOUSE** | [sketch of a cage-type hoop and two ringed balls] | [at R] PAR | [*do*] JEAN PERROT | [*do*] 16 illustrations de Louis POULAIN

Formula: [1¹⁶]. 16 leaves, pp *1* 2–22 *23* 24–31 *32*

Technical notes: ca 136 × 89 mm (p 3). 36 lines, 20 = *ca* 76 mm. Leaf size *ca* 178 × 113 mm

Contents: Title (*1*), le croquet (*1–22*), extrait du règlement de la Société Française de Croquet, a code of 47 numbered 'articles' (*23–27*), le badminton (*28*), le billard de pelouse (*29–31*), table de matières (*32*), name of printer (*32*)

Binding: White paper, stapled, no spine or endpapers. FC: see TP above. Inside FC: blank. RC: advertisement. Inside RC: blank

Copy seen: PC (photocopy of imperfect original)

Fingerprint: r-n. oner h*s. quré 3 1947A

Notes: Printed by A Steinbach, Enghien, apparently in the autumn of 1947 ('Dépot [*sic*] légal effectué dans le 4ᵉ trimestre 1947'). In the heading to the text on 'le croquet' (p *1*), the author's forename is given as 'Jan'.

(b) *1957 issue (1957)*

[The FC, printed in vivid Orange (48) and black against a brilliant bluish Green (159) background]

[in black on a white panel out of green] TOUS LES JEUX ET LEUR RÈGLES | [in artist's open script, in Orange outlined in black] **LE** | [in artist's open script, in Orange outlined in black, in a convex arc] **CROQUET** | [in white out of green] **LE BAD-MINTON** | [*do*] **LE BILLARD DE PELOUSE** | [sketch of a 'cage' and two ringed balls] | [at R] PAR | [*do*] JEAN PERROT | [*do*] 16 illustrations de Louis POULAIN

Formula: As that of (a)

Technical notes: 136 × 89 mm (p 3). 36 lines, 20 = 76 mm. Leaf size 181 × 113 mm; thickness 0.15 mm; wove, unwatermarked, smooth, white

Contents: As the contents of (a)

Binding: White semi-gloss light card, stapled, no spine or endpapers. FC: as the TP above. Inside FC: blank. RC: advertisement. Inside RC: blank

Copy seen: PC

Fingerprint: r-n. oner hes. quré 3 1957A

Notes: Printed by A Steinbach, Enghien, apparently in the spring of 1957 ('Dépôt légal effectué dans le 1ᵉ trimestre 1957'). This text is identical, or virtually identical, to that of (a).

A163   MODERN CROQUET: TIPS AND PRACTICE. Lord Tollemache   [1947]
MODERN CROQUET | TIPS AND PRACTICE | BY | LORD TOLLEMACHE |

[rule] | *A new book on the Art and* | *Practice of Playing Croquet* | [rule] | PUB-
LISHED BY | STRANGE THE PRINTER LTD. | YORK ROAD, EASTBOURNE | SUSSEX,
ENGLAND | *Price 10/- (postage extra)*

Formula: A⁸ B–E⁸ F⁸(F4+χ²) [\$1 signed (–A1)]. 50 leaves, pp *1–8 9–96, 1–4* (pp *1–2*
and *3–4* folded along the fore-edge)

Technical notes: 167 × 100 mm (p *10*). 32 lines, 20 = 106 mm. Leaf size 203 × 136
mm; thickness 0.13 mm; wove, unwatermarked, smooth, white; one inset plate
backs p *1*

Contents: Half-title (p *1*), blank (*2*), title (*3*), blank (*4*), contents (*5*), blank (*6*),
preface (*7–8*), text (*9–83*), blank (*84*), additional chapter (IX) (*85–96*), folded plan
(*1–4*)

Binding: Strong Yellow Green (117) cloth over stiff boards, sewn. FC: gold-blocked
([at the head] MODERN CROQUET | TIPS & PRACTICE | [near the foot at R,
slanted upwards from L to R: a crown] | [*do*, set aslant, signed in a flowing hand]
Tollemache). RC: blank. Spine: blank

Copy seen: PC

Fingerprint: 68ME s.nd edng *of*be 7 1947Q

Notes: Printed anonymously, price 10/–. It is believed that this work was printed by
Strange the Printer, Eastbourne, and published privately in 1947.

1948

A164   SHOTS AND STROKES IN CROQUET. 'Fanwy Llyn'   1948

SHOTS | AND | STROKES | IN CROQUET | By | "FANWY LLYN" | 1948 |
ROBERTSON & MULLENS LIMITED | MELBOURNE

Formula: [1³²]. 32 leaves, pp *i–ii, 1–4 5–47 48 49–60 61–62*

Technical notes: 136 × 88 mm (p *12*). 38 lines, 20 = 72 mm. Leaf size 178 × 122
mm

Contents: Half-title (*i*), blank (*ii*), title (*1*), TP verso (*2*), 'THE CROQUET CREED'
(verse) (*3*), contents (*4*), text (*5–47*), blank (*48*), the laws of croquet 1939 confirmed
and adopted by the Council 15 December 1938 (*49–60*), blank (*61–62*)

Binding: Moderate reddish Orange (37) rough paper, stapled, no spine or endpapers. FC: printed in black within a moderate Yellow (87) double frame, the inner
frame ruled and the outer frame composed of bead-like figures (**Shots and Strokes**
| IN | **CROQUET** | *By* | **"FANWY LLYN"** | [diagram of the croquet stroke, show-
ing the positions of the mallet and balls] | ROBERTSON & MULLENS LIMITED
| MELBOURNE). Inside FC: blank. RC: advertisement. Inside RC: blank

Copy seen: PC

Fingerprint: l.n" e.ll by). reAs 3 1948A

Notes: Printed by The National Press, Melbourne.

1949

A165   CROQUET (ASSOCIATION CROQUET). The Rev GF Handel Elvey   1949

CROQUET | (ASSOCIATION CROQUET) | [double rule] |A Handbook on the
Strokes and Tactics of | the Game. | Also a Short Description of Golf and Polo | or
Robber Croquet | [double rule] | BY | The Rev. G. F. HANDEL ELVEY, M.A. | [double
rule] Published by | JOHN JAQUES & SON, LIMITED, | 361, WHITEHORSE
ROAD, | THORNTON HEATH, SURREY. | 1949.

Formula: 1^8 2–5^8 [\$1 signed (-1_1); 2_1, 3_1 *etc* signed '(2)', '(3)' *etc*]. 40 leaves, pp *1–2 3 4 5–80*

Technical notes: 142 × 93 mm (p 7). 40 lines, 20 = 72 mm. Leaf size 185 × 122 mm; thickness 0.16 mm; wove, unwatermarked, rough, white. An *errata* slip is tipped-in over the TP

Contents: Title (*1*), blank (*2*), preface, signed 'G. F. Handel Elvey' (*3*), blank (*4*), contents (*5*), text (*6–80*)

Binding: Pale orange Yellow (73) parchment-effect card glued to the folds of the gatherings, sewn, no endpapers. FC: printed in dark yellowish Brown (78), the letter press set in a design composed of four panels variously ornamented ([in uppermost panel] **CROQUET** | [*do*] (ASSOCIATION CROQUET) | [in the second panel, white out of Brown] *A* | [*do*] *Handbook on the Strokes* | [*do*] *and* | [*do,* swash *f*] *Tactics of the Game.* | [in the third panel, set in a convex arc] ALSO | [*do*] A SHORT DESCRIPTION OF | [*do*] GOLF & POLO or ROBBER CROQUET. | [in the fourth panel] *by* | [*do*] <u>The Rev. G. F. HANDEL ELVEY, M. A.</u> | [*do*] *(Chairman of* | [*do*] *The Croquet Association Council* | [*do*] FROM | [*do*] *1939–1948))*. Inside FC: blank. RC: blank. Inside RC: blank. Spine: printed downwards (CROQUET by The Rev. G. F. HANDEL ELVEY , M. A.)

Copy seen: PC

Fingerprint: Y.t. lebs beto mith 1949A

Notes: Printed anonymously, price 7/6.

Review: *The Croquet Association Gazette* (May 1949).

1940–49

A166 CROQUET: RULES & REGULATIONS. [Anon]   *ca* 1942

[within a double-ruled frame]

[double-underlined] **CROQUET** | RULES & REGULATIONS | [line drawing of a croquet set in an open rack] | **Garton Toy Co.** | SHEBOYGAN, WISCONSIN

Formula: [1^3]. 3 leaves on a single sheet in a C-fold, pp *1–6* in the order *1, 6, 5* of the external contours of the letter *C* (from top to bottom) and then *2, 3, 4* of the internal contours

Technical notes: 98 × 66 mm (p 6). 28 lines, 20 = 71 mm, variable. Leaf size 126 × 75 mm; thickness 0.12 mm; wove, unwatermarked, smooth, light yellowish Brown (76)

Contents: Title (*1*), text (*2–6*)

Binding: None

Copy seen: HPC: GV933 C8G3 CROQ

Fingerprint: t.to RNnd uthe ERls C 1942Q [all four groups taken from p *2*]

Notes: Printed anonymously. Year of publication is inferred from a cipher ('Form 17 20M 3-42') at the foot of p 6. This work was presumably issued by the publisher together with its croquet equipment.

The text includes a code of 17 numbered rules.

A167 HISTORY OF THE SUSSEX COUNTY CROQUET AND   *ca* 1947
LAWN TENNIS CLUB, SOUTHWICK. Maj H Jellicorse

[Title heading, p *1*]

History of the Sussex County | Croquet and Lawn Tennis Club, | Southwick | By MAJOR H. JELLICORSE, | *President and one of the Trustees of the Club* | [rule]

Formula: [1⁴]. 4 leaves, unnumbered [pp 1–8]

Contents: Title heading (*1*), text (*1–8*), name of printer (*8*)

Binding: Apparently none, stapled

Copy seen: PC (photocopy of unknown scale)

Fingerprint: asnd p.be edhe one. C 1947Q [all four groups taken from p *3*]

Notes: Printed by Moore & Tillyer, Chichester. Approximate year of publication is inferred from the text.

AA168 JEU DE CROQUET. [Manufrance]   *ca* 1947

[Title heading]

ST ETIENNE −MANUFRANCE− ST ETIENNE | **JEU DE CROQUET** | [swelled rule]

Formula: [1¹]. 1 sheet, unnumbered [pp 1–2]

Technical notes: ca 260 × 173 mm. 50 lines, 20 = *ca* 105 mm. Leaf size *ca* 272 × 198 mm

Contents: Title heading and text (*1*), wanting from the photocopy examined (*2*)

Binding: None

Copy seen: PC (photocopy, wanting the verso)

Fingerprint: E,rt rse. *ete t.il C 1947Q [all four groups taken from p *1*]

Notes: Printed anonymously. Approximate year of publication is inferred from the provenance of the copy examined. It is conjectured that this work was distributed by Manufrance with their croquet equipment.

1954

A169   CROQUET TODAY. Maurice B Reckitt   1954

MAURICE B. RECKITT | [swelled rule] | *Croquet Today* | [swelled rule] | *Instructional Photographs by* | HARRY HARDY, A.I.B.P. | MACDONALD : LONDON

[TP verso]

First published in 1954 by | Macdonald & Co. (Publishers), Ltd. | 16 Maddox Street, W.1 | Made and printed in Great Britain by | Purnell and Sons, Ltd. | Paulton (Somerset) and London

Formula: A⁸ B–Q⁸ [$1 signed (−A1)]. 128 leaves, pp *1–6* 7 8 *9–11* 12–13 14–17 *18* 19–28 *29* 30–256

Technical notes: 156 × 97 mm (p *15*). 37 lines, 20 = 84 mm. Leaf size 197 × 128 mm; thickness 0.11 mm; wove, unwatermarked, smooth, white; a frontispiece and eight other leaves of plates on semi-gloss paper with 16 numbered black-and-white photographic illustrations follow pp 2, 48 (1), 64 (2), 80 (2), 96 (2), 112 (1)

Contents: Half-title (*1*), blank (*2*), title (*3*), TP verso (*4*), dedication (*5*), blank (*6*), acknowledgements (*7*), blank (*8*), contents (*9–10*), list of illustrations (*11*), blank (*12*), introduction, signed 'M. B. R.' (*13–16*), select bibliography (*17*), blank (*18*), text (*19–256*)

Binding: Moderate Green (145) cloth over stiff boards, sewn. FC: blank. RC: blank. Spine: gold-blocked crosswise (*Croquet | Today* | MAURICE B. | RECKITT | [emblem formed of two crossed mallets and a ball] | [at the foot] *MACDONALD*)

Dust wrapper: Printed on white wove paper. FP: in brilliant Yellow Green (116), black, and white on a deep Yellow Green (116) background ([in brilliant Yellow Green calligraphic script] CROQUET | [*do*] TODAY | [in brilliant Yellow Green] MAURICE RECKITT | [sketch of a mallet, hoop, and ball in black, brilliant Yellow Green, and white, signed 'B L'). FF: publisher's blurb (28 lines) and price (12/6 net). RP: contents, in deep Yellow Green on white. RF: blank. Spine: crosswise in brilliant Yellow Green and white on a deep Yellow Green background ([in calligraphic script] CROQUET | [*do*] TODAY | [emblem formed of two crossed mallets in white and a ball in brilliant Yellow Green] | [in brilliant Yellow Green] MAURICE RECKITT | [at the foot, in white] MACDONALD).

Copy seen: PC

Fingerprint: 52us llse 9.le *es*3. C 1954A [groups 1–4 taken from pp 5, 13, 17, 17 respectively]

Notes: Printed by Purnell and Sons, Paulton (Somerset) and London, price 12/6.

1957

A170   CROQUET HANDBOOK. Arthur GF Ross   1957

(a) *First edition (1957)*

CROQUET | **HANDBOOK** | *by* | **ARTHUR G. F. ROSS** | Author of | "CROQUET AND HOW TO PLAY IT" | (4 editions) | British Open Champion, 1954; South of England | Open and Men's Champion 1956; eleven times | New Zealand Champion | • | Published by | **Hereford Printing Co. Ltd., Te Aro** | **Wellington, New Zealand** | 1957

Formula: [1⁴ 2–9⁸ 10²]. 70 leaves, pp *1–8* 9–140

Technical notes: 178 × 100 mm (p 10). 50 lines, 20 = 72 mm. Leaf size 212 × 137 mm; thickness 0.12 mm; wove, unwatermarked, smooth, white

Contents: Title (*1*), foreword, signed 'A. G. F. Ross' (*2*), 'The Alphabet of Croquet' (diagram) (*3*), contents (*4–8*), text (*9–140*)

Binding: Strong Red (12) leather-effect card, glued to the folds of the gatherings, stapled through the gatherings, hinged at the front, no endpapers. FC: printed in black, the title interrupting eight parallel vertical rules at the L ([L justified] **CROQUET** | [*do*] **HANDBOOK** | *by* | **ARTHUR G. F. ROSS** | • | 18/6). Inside FC: blank. RC: blank. Inside RC: blank. Spine: blank

Copy seen: PC

Fingerprint: e.k. r.i- esat evCr 3 1957A [group 1 taken from the L column of the legend of the diagram on p *3*]

Notes: Printed by Hereford Printing Co, Wellington, New Zealand, price 18/6. The copy examined bears a bookseller's label which partially obscures the price mark on the FC.

(b) *First English edition (1959)*

CROQUET HANDBOOK | by | ARTHUR G. F. ROSS | [set between round brackets together with the line below] *British Open Champion, 1954* | [set between round brackets together with the line above] *Eleven times New Zealand Champion* | [publisher's device in the form of a monogram] | IN THE CITY OF LONDON | NICHOLAS KAYE

[TP verso]

First published | in New Zealand | 1957 | in Great Britain | 1959 | [assertion of copyright] | Printed in England by | STRAKER BROTHERS LIMITED | London

Formula: A–D¹⁶ E⁸ [$1 signed]. 72 leaves, pp *1–6* 7–12 *13* 14–19 *20 21 22* 23–27 *28* 29–35 *36* 37–39 *40* 41–48 *49* 50–55 *56* 57–63 *64* 65–67 *68* 69–78 *79* 80–84 *85* 86–87 *88 89–93 94 95–96 97* 98–101 *102* 103–110 *111* 112–115 *116* 117–130 *131* 132–134 *135* 136–144

Technical notes: 176 × 92 mm (p 14). 51 lines, 20 = 70 mm. Leaf size 213 × 134 mm; thickness 0.12 mm; wove, unwatermarked, smooth, white

Contents: Half-title (*1*), by the same author (*2*), title (*3*), TP verso (*4*), foreword, signed 'A. G. F. Ross' (*5*), blank (*6*), contents (*7–11*), plan ('THE ALPHABET OF CROQUET') (*12*), text (*13–144*)

Binding: Moderate Yellow Green (120) linen grain paper over stiff boards, sewn. FC: blank. RC: blank. Spine: gold-blocked downwards (ARTHUR G. F. ROSS **Croquet Hand-book** [publisher's device in the form of a monogram crosswise at the foot])

Dust wrapper: Printed in black on strong reddish Orange (35) matt paper. FP: the lettering arranged within a design composed of geometrical elements and croquet equipment, the background mostly in black ([in black within an Orange irregular rhomboid panel out of black] **CROQUET** | [sketch of a croquet mallet in Orange out of black] | [in black within an Orange irregular rhomboid panel out of black] **HAND-** | [sketch of a croquet mallet in Orange out of black] | [in black within an Orange irregular rhomboid panel out of black] **BOOK** | [in Orange out of black within a panel consisting of a hoop with a semi-circular arched crown in Orange out of black] **ARTHUR** | [*do*] **G. F.** | [*do*] **ROSS** | [publisher's device in the form of a monogram in Orange out of black within a bold ruled frame in Orange, L of hoop panel] | [sketch of ball in black on Orange out of black, R of hoop panel]). FF: publisher's blurb and price in black on Orange. RP: advertisement in black on Orange for the publisher's books on other sporting and recreational subjects. RF: blank. Spine: printed downwards in Orange out of black (ARTHUR. G.F.ROSS **Croquet Hand-book** *NICHOLAS KAYE*)

Copy seen: PC

Fingerprint: Z.gs eds, esat evtr 7 1959A

Notes: Printed by Straker Brothers, London, price 15/– net.

A171   CROQUET: RULES AND STRATEGY FOR HOME PLAY.   1957
Paul Brown

CROQUET | **Rules and Strategy for Home Play** | *by* | **PAUL BROWN** | WITH ILLUSTRATIONS BY THE AUTHOR | [line drawing in strong Red (12) of a man player negotiating a hoop] | D. VAN NOSTRAND COMPANY, INC. | PRINCETON, NEW JERSEY | [at L] TORONTO [at R] LONDON | NEW YORK

[TP verso]

EDITED BY EUGENE V. CONNETT | [rule] | FIRST EDITION | PRINTED IN THE UNITED STATES OF AMERICA | [publisher's device] | COPYRIGHT © 1957 BY | D. VAN NOSTRAND COMPANY, INC. | Published simultaneously in Canada by | D. VAN NOSTRAND COMPANY (Canada), LTD. | [rule] | *All Rights Reserved* | *This book, or any part thereof, may not be* | *reproduced in any form without written* | *per-* | *mission from the author and the publisher.* | [rule] | Library of Congress Catalog Card No. 57-12490 | D. VAN NOSTRAND COMPANY, INC. | 120 Alexander St., Princeton, New Jersey | 257 Fourth Avenue, New York 10, New York | 25 Hollinger Rd., Toronto 16, Canada | *All correspondence should be addressed to the* | *principal office of the company at Princeton, N. J.*

Formula: Apparently [1–3⁸ 4⁴ 5⁸]. 36 leaves, pp *i–x*, 1–60 *61–62*

Technical notes: 185 × 114 mm (p 3). 35 lines, 20 = 106 mm. Leaf size 253 × 178 mm; thickness 0.19–0.22 mm; wove, unwatermarked, rough, white. There are several line drawings; all except the frontispiece are printed in black, strong Red (12), and moderate Blue (182)

Contents: Half-title (*i*), frontispiece, a framed drawing, with legend in MS, of five players in play (*ii*), title (*iii*), TP verso (*iv*), foreword, signed 'Carl Spaatz' in MS (*v*), blank (*vi*), preface (*vii*), blank (*viii*), contents (*ix*), blank (*x*), text (1–61), blank (62)

Binding: Moderate Blue (182) cloth over stiff boards, apparently sewn (the copy examined exhibited no threads or stitch marks). FC: reduced scale facsimile of the illustration on the TP, gold-blocked centrally. RC: blank. Spine: gold-blocked downwards (BROWN   CROQUET—**Rules and Strategy for Home Play**   VAN NOSTRAND)

Dust wrapper: Printed in moderate Pink (5), moderate Blue (182), and black on semi-gloss paper. FP: ([in artist's open script with Pink infill] Croquet | [*do* with Blue infill] **Rules and Strategy** | [*do*] **For Home Play** | [diagram of croquet situations with Pink, Blue, and black infill] | [in artist's open script with Pink infill] **Paul Brown**). FF: publisher's blurb, printed in black, continued on the RF. RP: black-and-white half-tone portrait of the author and biographical notes. RF: publisher's blurb, concluded. Spine: ([in Blue] **CROQUET** • Rules and Strategy For Home Play   [in black] BROWN   van nostrand)

Copy seen: PC

Fingerprint: TZt. d,c- s.i- galw 3 1957A

Notes: Printed anonymously. The colouring of the illustrations corresponds with the irregular colours of the balls with which the author and his associates played — *viz* red, blue, black, white.

1958

A172   NUDE CROQUET. Leslie A Fiedler   [1958]

(a) **First printing in book form [1958]*

[R justified] **NUDE** | [*do*] **CROQUET** | [*do*] **and other stories of** | [*do*] **the joys and terrors of marriage by** | [L justified] **LESLIE A. FIEDLER** | [*do*] **JOHN CHEEVER** | [*do*] **MORRIS PHILIPSON** | [*do*] **EDWARD NEWHOUSE** | [*do*] **W. SOMERSET MAUGHAM** | [*do*] **ALBERTO MORAVIA** | [*do*] **WILLIAM FAULKNER** | [publisher's device] | BERKLEY PUBLISHING CORP. | 145 West 57th Street • New York 19, N. Y.

Formula: Apparently [1–5¹⁶]. 80 leaves, pp *i–ii*, *1–4* 5–155 *156–158*

Technical notes: 135 × 87 mm (p 6). 39 lines, 20 = 69 mm. Leaf size 162 × 103 mm; thickness 0.13 mm; wove, unwatermarked, smooth, white, all edges moderate greenish Yellow (102)

Contents: Publisher's blurb (*i*), blank (*ii*), title (*1*), assertion of copyright, acknowledgements, place of printing (*2*), contents (*3*), blank (*4*), text (5–155), advertisements (*156–158*)

Binding: Semi-gloss white light card glued to the folds of the gatherings, apparently stitched, no endpapers. FC: printed in black and deep reddish Orange (102) over a lurid artist's sketch, signed in illegible MS, in full colour of a man and woman making love — she scantily clad, he in an unclear state of undress — with croquet accessories in evidence ([one of five lines at the top L] 35ᶜ | [*do*] BERKLEY | [*do*, publisher's device] | [*do*] BOOKS | [*do*] G-97 | [one of two lines at the top, centred, in Orange] **NUDE** | [*do*] **CROQUET** | [R justified in Orange] and other stories of |

[*do*] the joys and terrors of marriage by | [R justified in black] LESLIE A. FIEDLER | [*do*] W. SOMERSET MAUGHAM | [*do*] ALBERTO MORAVIA | [*do*] WILLIAM FAULKNER | [*do*] JOHN CHEEVER | [*do*] and others). Inside FC: blank. RC: publisher's blurb in black on dark purplish Pink (251). Inside RC: blank. Spine: in black on Pink, downwards (**NUDE CROQUET** FIEDLER, FAULKNER and others) and crosswise (BERKLEY | [publisher's device] | BOOKS | G-97)

Copy seen: PC

Fingerprint: 34ND ,ang t-es fivi 3 1958Q

Notes: Printed anonymously in the USA, price 35c. Year of publication is inferred from the year of copyright, as cited on p *2*.

A collection of short stories, some extended, reprinted from sundry sources. In the title story (pp *5–39*), which first appeared in the September 1957 issue of *Esquire* magazine (p 134 ff), an impromptu wife-swapping party degenerates into a desultory game of coarse indoor croquet. The text of the story in this reprint is identical, or virtually identical, in substance to that first published in the magazine.

(b) ***Stein and Day anthology (1969)***

Nude | **Croquet** | *the stories of* | **Leslie A. Fiedler** | [publisher's monogram, S, D] | STEIN AND DAY | *Publishers* | New York

Formula: [1–9¹⁶]. 144 leaves, pp *1–7* 8–53 *54–55* 56–67 *68–69* 70–133 *134–135* 136–227 *228–229* 230–249 *250–251* 252–265 *266–267* 268–288

Technical notes: 158 × 101 mm, variable (p 9). 37 lines, 20 = 86 mm. Leaf size 211 × 142 mm; thickness 0.17 mm; wove, unwatermarked, smooth, white; the top edges only are guillotined

Contents: Half-title and publisher's blurb (*1*), by the same author (*2*), title (*3*), TP verso (*4*), contents (*5*), blank (*6*), text, continued (*7–53*), blank (*54*), text, continued (*55–67*), blank (*68*), text, continued (*69–133*), blank (*134*), text, continued (*135–227*), blank (*228*), text, continued (*229–249*), blank (*250*), text, continued (*251–265*), blank (*266*), text, concluded (*267–288*)

Binding: Deep Yellow (85) leather-effect embossed paper over-lapping moderate bluish Green (164) calico spine, over stiff boards, sewn. FC: gold-blocked at the foot in MS, apparently in the author's hand ('Leslie A. Fiedler'). RC: blank. Spine: gold-blocked crosswise (**Nude** | **Croquet** | [wavy line] | **Leslie A.** | **Fiedler** | [near the foot: publisher's monogram, S, D] | STEIN | and | DAY)

Copy seen: BL: X989/15360

Fingerprint: 7567 v-me ."e, gr"I 7 1969Q

Notes: Printed anonymously, SBN 8128–1244–1. Year of publication is inferred from the year of copyright, as cited on the TP verso.

A collection of short stories, some extended, reprinted from sundry sources. The title story is reprinted on pp *7–53*. To quote from the publisher's blurb (p *1*), this story is a 'superb exposé of the bitterness and bitchiness of failed intellectuals'. The text of the story in this volume is substantially revised and extended.

(c) ***First English issue (1970)***

[The TP as that of (b)]

Formula: As that of (b)

Technical notes: 158 × 101 mm, variable (p 9). 37 lines, 20 = 86 mm. Leaf size 215 × 137 mm; thickness 0.13 mm; wove, unwatermarked, smooth, white

Contents: Half-title and publisher's blurb (*1*), by the same author (*2*), title (*3*), TP verso (*4*), contents (*5*), blank (*6*), text, continued (*7–53*), blank (*54*), text, continued (*55–67*), blank (*68*), text, continued (*69–133*), blank (*134*), text, continued (*135–227*), blank (*228*), text, continued (*229–249*), blank (*250*), text, continued (*251–265*), blank (*266*), text, concluded (*267–288*)

Binding: Strong Purple (218) linen grain paper over stiff boards, sewn. FC: blank. RC: blank. Spine: gold-blocked, mostly downwards (NUDE CROQUET   Leslie A. Fiedler), and crosswise at the foot (SECKER & | [*do*] WARBURG)

Dust wrapper: Printed in deep Pink (3), strong purplish Pink (247), and deep purplish Pink (248) on smooth white matt paper. FP: set within a deep purplish Pink panel framed in white against a strong purplish Pink background which is continued on the spine ([in white out of deep purplish Pink] NUDE | [*do*] CROQUET | [in deep Pink out of deep purplish Pink] LESLIE.A.FIEDLER | [line drawing of six figures in deep purplish Pink and deep Pink on white, overlaid by a deep purplish Pink ball with white high-light and framed within a white arched croquet hoop]). FF: publisher's blurb, credit to the designer of the dust wrapper, and price. RP: contents, in strong purplish Pink on white. RF: about the author, in strong purplish Pink on white. Spine: mostly downwards ([in white out of strong purplish Pink] NUDE CROQUET [in deep Pink out of strong purplish Pink] LESLIE.A.FIEDLER]), and crosswise at the foot ([in white out of strong purplish Pink] SECKER & | [*do*] WARBURG).

Copy seen: PC

Fingerprint: 7567 v-me ."e, gr"I 7 1970A

Notes: Published by Martin, Secker & Warburg, London; printed by Redwood Press, Trowbridge and London, price £2.10 net.

The text of this issue is apparently identical to that of (b).

AA173   RULES OF KING-BALL CROQUET. [Anon]   1958

[Page *1*]

[wavy line] | **Rules of** | **KING-BALL CROQUET** | 1958 | [wavy line]

Formula: [1²]. 2 leaves, [pp 1–4]

Technical notes: 127 × 82 mm (p *3*). 35 lines, 20 = 73 mm. Leaf size 152 × 101 mm; thickness 0.08 mm; wove, unwatermarked, smooth, white

Contents: Title (*1*), introduction (*2*), rules, numbered 1–10 with alphabetical sub-clauses (*3–4*)

Binding: None

Copy seen: PC

Fingerprint: t.to erl. ngr. opy, C 1958A [all four groups taken from p *3*]

Notes: Published and printed anonymously.

1950–59

A174   HOW TO LAY OUT A CROQUET SET. [Anon]   *ca* 1950

[Title heading, L justified]

HOW TO LAY OUT | A CROQUET SET

Formula: [1⁴]. 4 leaves, unnumbered [pp 1–8]

Technical notes: 143 × 96 mm (p *5*). 27 lines, 20 = 105 mm. Leaf size 190 × 134 mm;

thickness 0.22 mm; laid, watermarked ([a crown] | [in calligraphic script] *Glastonbury*), rough, white

Contents: Title heading (*1*), text (*1–7*), name of publisher and/or printer (*7*), blank (*8*)

Binding: Self-cover, stapled

Copy seen: PC

Fingerprint: t.'s heke nds. 'snd C 1950Q [all four groups taken from p 5]

Notes: Printed and/or published by CW & Co, printed in England. Approximate year of publication is inferred from the typography and the state of development of the (American) game described in the text. Though apparently of UK origin (the orthography is English), this work was evidently designed for distribution in north America.

The text includes a code of 19 numbered rules.

1960

A175 **TACKLE CROQUET THIS WAY. EPC Cotter**   1960

Tackle Croquet | This Way | E. P. C. COTTER | [publisher's device] | STANLEY PAUL | *London*

[From the TP verso]

STANLEY PAUL & CO. LTD | [set in the publisher's device] AN IMPRINT OF THE HUTCHINSON GROUP | London Melbourne Sydney | Auckland Bombay Toronto | Johannesburg New York | ★ | *First published 1960*

Formula: A⁸ B–H⁸ [$1 signed (–A1)]. 64 leaves including the rear pastedown, *1–10* 11–15 *16* 17–25 *26* 27–33 *34* 35–61 *62* 63–75 *76* 77–91 *92* 93–124 *125–128*

Technical notes: 139 × 88 mm (p 14). 36 lines, 20 = 78 mm. Leaf size 184 × 128 mm; thickness 0.16 mm; wove, unwatermarked, smooth, white

Contents: Half-title (*1*), blank (*2*), title (*3*), TP verso (*4*), dedication (*5*), acknowledgement (*6*), contents (*7*), blank (*8*), list of illustrations (*9*), blank (*10*), text (11–124), blank (*125–127*), glued to the RC (*128*)

Binding: Black simulated-buckram embossed paper over stiff boards, sewn. FC: blank. RC: blank. Spine: blocked in gold and moderate Red (15) crosswise ([in gold] Tackle | [in Red] CROQUET | [in gold] This | [*do*] Way | [*do*] E. P. C. | [*do*] COTTER | [publisher's device in gold near the foot] | [at the foot, in gold] STANLEY | [*do*] PAUL)

Dust wrapper: Printed on white wove paper. FP: black-and-white photograph of the author in play, superimposed by a moderate Red (15) panel at the top L, bearing the lettering ([black] Tackle | [white] CROQUET | [black] This Way | E.P.C.COTTER). FF: publisher's blurb (29 lines) and price (12s 6d net). RP: black-and-white photographs of the wrappers of nine other books in the 'Tackle' series in a three-by-three array separated by two broad horizontal bands in Red. RF: list of other titles in the 'Tackle' series. Spine: printed crosswise on a Red background in black and in white out of Red ([black] Tackle | [white] CROQUET | [black] This | [black] Way | [white] E.P.C. | [white] COTTER | [publisher's device in black near the foot] | [at the foot, in white] STANLEY | [white] PAUL). FF: publisher's blurb (29 lines) and price (12s 6d net)

Copy seen: PC

Fingerprint: l.se t.le t.rs ¹Ten 7 1960A

Notes: Printed by the Anchor Press, Tiptree, Essex, price 12/6.

1961

A176   CROQUET. [GL Ormerod, the fourth edition revised by WE Lamb]   1961

(a) *First edition (1961)*

Not seen. All issues of the first edition of this work which have been seen cite the number of copies previously printed or contain other indications that they were preceded by an earlier issue.

(b) *5000 issue (1961)*

'KNOW THE GAME' SERIES | CROQUET | *in collaboration with* | THE CROQUET ASSOCIATION | **EDUCATIONAL PRODUCTIONS LIMITED**

Formula: [1^{18}]. 18 leaves, pp *1–3 4–36*

Technical notes: 109 × 177 mm (p 6). All pages except pp *1–2* are divided into two columns. 29 lines, 20 = 79 mm. Leaf size 134 × 202 mm; thickness 0.08 mm; wove, unwatermarked, semi-gloss, white. The figures are printed in black and strong Yellow Green (117)

Contents: Title (*1*), foreword, by JW Solomon (*2*), contents and name of printer (*3*), text (*4–36*)

Binding: White high-gloss card laminate, stapled, no spine or endpapers. FC: divided into a narrow panel (at L) and a broad panel (at R). The narrow panel is printed in black and vivid orange Yellow (66) against a pale Yellow (89) background ([in black] *KNOW THE GAME* | [in orange Yellow] **CROQUET** | [in black] **Published in** | [*do*] **collaboration with** | [*do*] **THE CROQUET ASSOCIATION** | [*do*] **U.K. Price 2/6**); the broad panel, printed in black, orange Yellow, and pale Yellow on a moderate Yellow Green (120) background contains a sketch of a man player in play overlapping a diagram which illustrates a hoop approach. Inside FC: advertisement. RC: surrogate TP verso, printed in black between two swelled rules in orange Yellow, the upper rule broken centrally by a device in the form of a monogram (Published by | THE NIBLICK PUBLISHING CO. LTD. | FOR | **EDUCATIONAL PRODUCTIONS LIMITED** | 17 Denbigh Street, London, SW1 | in collaboration with | **THE CROQUET ASSOCIATION** | **c/o The Hurlingham Club, Fulham, London, SW6** | 1st Edition 1961 - Total copies printed 5000 | **WORLD COPYRIGHT RESERVED**). Inside RC: advertisements for the CA and Know the Game books

Copy seen: PC

Fingerprint: x.*es* t.ng s.i- Fije 3 1961A [the last two characters of group 1 taken from the L column of p *3*, all four characters of group 2 taken from the first column of the legend to fig 11 on p 11, all four characters of group 3 taken from the L column of the text on p 13, the first two characters of group 4 taken from the caption to fig 15 on p 14, and the last two characters of group 4 taken from the text on p 14]

Notes: Printed by Fawcett, Greenwood & Co, Halifax, price 2/6.

(c) *10000 issue (1961)*

[The TP as that of (b)]

Formula: As that of (b)

Technical notes: As at (b)

Contents: As the contents of (b)

Binding: White high-gloss card laminate, stapled, no spine or endpapers. FC:

divided into a narrow panel (at L) and a broad panel (at R). The narrow panel is printed in black and vivid orange Yellow (66) against a pale Yellow (89) background ([in black] *KNOW THE GAME* | [in orange Yellow] **CROQUET** | [in black] **Published in** | [*do*] **collaboration with** | [*do*] **THE CROQUET ASSOCIATION** | [*do*] **U.K. Price 2/6**); the broad panel, printed in black, orange Yellow, and pale Yellow on a moderate Yellow Green (120) background contains a sketch of a man player in play overlapping a diagram which illustrates a hoop approach. Inside FC: advertisement. RC: surrogate TP verso, printed in black between two swelled rules in orange Yellow, the upper rule broken centrally by a device in the form of a mono-gram (Published by | THE NIBLICK PUBLISHING CO. LTD. | FOR | **EDUCA-TIONAL PRODUCTIONS LIMITED** | 17 Denbigh Street, London, SW1 | in collaboration with | **THE CROQUET ASSOCIATION** | **c/o The Hurlingham Club, Fulham, London, SW6** | 1st Edition 1961 - Total copies printed 10,000 | **WORLD COPYRIGHT RESERVED**). Inside RC: advertisements for the CA and Know the Game books

Copy seen: PC

Fingerprint: As that of (b)

Notes: Printed by Fawcett, Greenwood & Co, Halifax, price 2/6.

(d) *16000 issue (1961)*

[The TP as that of (b)]

Formula: As that of (b)

Technical notes: As at (b)

Contents: As the contents of (b)

Binding: White high-gloss card laminate, stapled, no spine or endpapers. FC: as that of (b). Inside FC: as that of (b). RC: surrogate TP verso, printed in black between two swelled rules in orange Yellow, the upper rule broken centrally by a device in the form of a monogram (Published by | THE E.P. PUBLISHING CO. LTD. | for | **EDUCATIONAL PRODUCTIONS LIMITED** | 17 Denbigh Street, London, SW1 | in collaboration with | **THE CROQUET ASSOCIATION** | **c/o The Hurlingham Club, Fulham, London, SW6** | 1st Edition 1961 - Total copies printed 16,000 | **WORLD COPYRIGHT RESERVED**). Inside RC: advertisements

Copy seen: PC

Fingerprint: As that of (b)

Notes: Printed by Fawcett, Greenwood & Co, Halifax, price 2/6.

This issue is identical, or virtually identical, to (b), save for the RC and the publisher's advertisement inside the RC.

(e) *23000 issue (1961)*

'KNOW THE GAME' SERIES | **CROQUET** | *in collaboration with* | THE CROQUET ASSOCIATION | **EDUCATIONAL PRODUCTIONS LIMITED**

Formula: As that of (b)

Technical notes: 109 × 84 mm per column (p 6). All pages except pp *1–2* are divided into two columns. 28 lines, 20 = 78 mm. Leaf size 133 × 202 mm; thickness 0.10 mm; wove, unwatermarked, semi-gloss, white. The figures are printed in black and strong Yellow Green (117)

Contents: As the contents of (b)

Binding: White high-gloss card laminate, stapled, no spine or endpapers. FC:

divided into a narrow panel (at L) and a broad panel (at R). The narrow panel is printed in black and vivid orange Yellow (66) against a pale Yellow (89) background ([in black] *KNOW THE GAME* | [in orange Yellow] **CROQUET** | [in black] **Published in** | [*do*] **collaboration with** | [*do*] **THE CROQUET ASSOCIATION** | [*do*] **U.K. Price 3/6**); the broad panel, printed in black, orange Yellow, and pale Yellow on a moderate Yellow Green (120) background contains a sketch of a man player in play overlapping a diagram which illustrates a hoop approach. Inside FC: advertisement. RC: surrogate TP verso, printed in black between two swelled rules in orange Yellow, the upper rule broken centrally by a device in the form of a mono-gram (Published by | THE E.P. PUBLISHING CO. LTD. | for | **EDUCATIONAL PRODUCTIONS LIMITED** | 17 Denbigh Street, London, SW1 | in collaboration with | **THE CROQUET ASSOCIATION** | **c/o The Hurlingham Club, Fulham, London, SW6** | 1st Edition 1961 - Total copies printed 23,000 | **WORLD COPY-RIGHT RESERVED** | B144). Inside RC: advertisements

Copy seen: PC

Fingerprint: As that of (b)

Notes: Printed by Fawcett, Greenwood & Co, Halifax, price 3/6. This issue has not been collated with (b), but it is believed that their texts are identical throughout.

(f) *36000 issue [1968]*

'KNOW THE GAME' SERIES | **CROQUET** | *in collaboration with* | THE CROQUET ASSOCIATION | **EDUCATIONAL PRODUCTIONS LIMITED**

Formula: As that of (b)

Technical notes: 109 × 177 mm (p 6). All pages except pp *1–2* are divided into two columns. 28 lines, 20 = 78 mm. Leaf size 133 × 202 mm; thickness 0.11 mm; wove, unwatermarked, semi-gloss, white. The figures are printed in black and strong Yellow Green (117)

Contents: As the contents of (b)

Binding: White high-gloss card laminate, stapled, no spine or endpapers. FC: divided into a narrow panel (at L) and a broad panel (at R). The narrow panel is printed in black and vivid orange Yellow (66) against a pale Yellow (89) background ([in black] *KNOW THE GAME* | [in orange Yellow] **CROQUET** | [in black] **Published in** | [*do*] **collaboration with** | [*do*] **THE CROQUET ASSOCIATION** | [*do*] **U.K. PRICE 3/6** NET | [*do*] (Limp cover edition)); the broad panel, printed in black, orange Yellow, and pale Yellow on a moderate Yellow Green (120) back-ground contains a sketch of a man player in play overlapping a diagram which illustrates a hoop approach. Inside FC: advertisement. RC: surrogate TP verso, printed in black between two swelled rules in orange Yellow, the upper rule broken centrally by a device in the form of a monogram (Published by | THE E.P. PUBLISHING CO. LTD. | for | **EDUCATIONAL PRODUCTIONS LIMITED.** | 17 Denbigh Street, London, SW1 | in collaboration with | **THE CROQUET ASSOCI-ATION** | **c/o The Hurlingham Club, Fulham, London, SW6** | 1st Edition 1961 - Total copies printed 36,000 | **WORLD COPYRIGHT RESERVED** | © Educational Productions Ltd., 1968 | 7158 0144 9). Inside RC: advertisements for the CA and Know the Game Books

Copy seen: PC

Fingerprint: x.es t.ng s.i- Fije 3 1968Q [the last two characters of group 1 taken from the L column of p 3, all four characters of group 2 taken from the first column of the legend to fig 11 on p 11, all four characters of group 3 taken from the L column of the text on p 13, the first two characters of group 4 taken from the caption to fig 15 on p 14, and the last two characters of group 4 taken from the text on p 14]

Notes: Printed by Fawcett, Greenwood & Co, Halifax, price 3/6. Year of publication is inferred from the year of copyright given on the RC.

The text of this issue is apparently identical to that of earlier issues, save for some minor variations in Law 5 on pp 19–20 and the selection of recommended books given on p 36. Further, the advertisements inside the RC vary and more colour is used in several of the illustrations in the present issue. It has, however, been collated systematically with (b) only.

(g) *44000 issue [1968]*

'KNOW THE GAME' SERIES | CROQUET | *in collaboration with* | THE CROQUET ASSOCIATION | **EDUCATIONAL PRODUCTIONS LIMITED**

Formula: As that of (b)

Technical notes: 109 × 177 mm (p 6). All pages except pp *1–2* are divided into two columns. 28 lines, 20 = 78 mm. Leaf size 133 × 202 mm; thickness 0.10 mm; wove, unwatermarked, semi-gloss, white. The figures are printed in black and strong Yellow Green (117)

Contents: As the contents of (b)

Binding: White high-gloss card laminate, stapled, no spine or endpapers. FC: divided into a narrow panel (at L) and a broad panel (at R). The narrow panel is printed in black and vivid orange Yellow (66) against a pale Yellow (89) background ([in black] *KNOW THE GAME* | [in orange Yellow] **CROQUET** | [in black] **Published in** | [*do*] **collaboration with** | [*do*] **THE CROQUET ASSOCIATION** | [*do*] **U.K. PRICE** | [*do*] **4/- (20p) net** | [*do*] (Limp cover edition)); the broad panel, printed in black, orange Yellow, and pale Yellow on a moderate Yellow Green (120) background contains a sketch of a man player in play overlapping a diagram which illustrates a hoop approach. Inside FC: advertisement. RC: surrogate TP verso, printed in black between two swelled rules in orange Yellow, the upper rule broken centrally by a device in the form of a monogram (Published by | THE E.P. PUBLISHING CO. LTD. | for | **EDUCATIONAL PRODUCTIONS LIMITED.** | 17 Denbigh Street, London, S.W.1 | *Stores Department: Bradford Road, East Ardsley, Wakefield, Yorks.* | in collaboration with | **THE CROQUET ASSOCIATION** | c/o **The Hurlingham Club, Fulham, London, SW6** | 1st Edition 1961 - Total copies printed 44,000 | **WORLD COPYRIGHT RESERVED** | © Educational Productions Ltd., 1968 | 7158 0144 9). Inside RC: advertisements for the CA and Know the Game books

Copy seen: PC

Fingerprint: As that of (f)

Notes: Printed by Fawcett, Greenwood & Co, Halifax, price 4/–. Year of publication is inferred from the year of copyright given on the RC.

The text of this issue is identical, or virtually identical, to that of (f). The only variations are thought to be in the FC, RC, and in the advertisement for the CA inside the RC.

(h) *52000 issue [1971]*

'KNOW THE GAME' SERIES | CROQUET | *in collaboration with* | THE CROQUET ASSOCIATION | **EDUCATIONAL PRODUCTIONS LIMITED**

Formula: As that of (b)

Technical notes: 109 × 177 mm (p 6). All pages except pp *1–2* are divided into two columns. 28 lines, 20 = 78 mm. Leaf size 133 × 203 mm; thickness 0.10 mm; wove, unwatermarked, semi-gloss, white. The figures are printed in black and strong Yellow Green (117)

Contents: Title (*1*), foreword, by JW Solomon (2), contents (3), text (4–36), name of printer (36)

Binding: White high-gloss card laminate, stapled, no spine or endpapers. FC: divided into a narrow panel (at L) and a broad panel (at R). The narrow panel is printed in black and vivid orange Yellow (66) against a pale Yellow (89) background ([in black] **KNOW THE GAME** | [in orange Yellow] **CROQUET** | [in black] **Published in** | [*do*] **collaboration with** | [*do*] **THE CROQUET ASSOCIATION** | [*do*] **U.K. PRICE** | [*do*] **25p net** | [*do*] (Limp cover edition)); the broad panel, printed in black, orange Yellow, and pale Yellow on a moderate Yellow Green (120) background contains a sketch of a man player in play overlapping a diagram which illustrates a hoop approach. Inside FC: advertisement. RC: surrogate TP verso, printed in black between two swelled rules in orange Yellow, the upper rule broken centrally by a device in the form of a monogram (Published by | THE E.P. PUBLISHING CO. LTD. | for | **EDUCATIONAL PRODUCTIONS LIMITED.** | 27-28 Maunsel Street, London, S.W.1 | Sales Department: Bradford Road, East Ardsley, Wakefield, Yorkshire. | in collaboration with | **THE CROQUET ASSOCIATION** | **c/o The Hurlingham Club, Fulham, London, SW6** | 1st Edition 1961 - Total copies printed 52,000 | **WORLD COPYRIGHT RESERVED** | © Educational Productions Ltd., 1971 | I.S.B.N.   O   7158   0144   9). Inside RC: advertisements

Copy seen: PC

Fingerprint: x.*es* t.ng s.i- Fije 3 1971Q [the last two characters of group 1 taken from the L column of p *3*, all four characters of group 2 taken from the first column of the legend to fig 11 on p 11, all four characters of group 3 taken from the L column of the text on p 13, the first two characters of group 4 taken from the caption to fig 15 on p 14, and the last two characters of group 4 taken from the text on p 14]

Notes: Printed by Sunstreet Printing Works (Keighley), price 25p. Year of publication is inferred from the year of copyright given on the RC.

The text of this issue is apparently identical to that of (g) save for the prices of the recommended books given on p 36. The advertisements inside the RC also vary.

(j) *1984 (metric) issue (1984)*

[The L column of the TP]

[monogram, *K, T, G,* in white out of a black ellipse, at L] | [to R] know | [*do*] the | [*do*] game | **CROQUET** | *in collaboration with* | THE CROQUET ASSOCIATION | **Adam & Charles Black - London** | ISBN 0 7136 2554 6 | Printed in Great Britain by | The Stanley Press Ltd., Dewsbury, West Yorkshire.

Formula: As that of (b)

Technical notes: 115 × 178 mm (p 6). All pages save pp *1–2* are divided into two columns. 28 lines, 20 = 78 mm. Leaf size 134 × 204 mm; thickness 0.08 mm; wove, unwatermarked, semi-gloss, white. The figures are printed in black and strong Yellow Green (117)

Contents: Title (*1*), contents (2–3), foreword, by John W Solomon (3), text (4–36)

Binding: White high-gloss card laminate, stapled, no spine or endpapers. FC: printed in black, vivid reddish Orange (34), vivid greenish Yellow (97), strong Blue

(178), and vivid yellowish Green (129) ([monogram, *K*, *T*, *G*, in white out of a black ellipse, at L] | [to R] know | [*do*] the | [*do*] game | [in Orange, at R, at the same level as the foregoing matter] **Croquet** | [illustration of the legs of a player about to perform a corner cannon, in black, Orange, Yellow, Blue, and Green, within a panel outlined in black] | Published in collaboration with The CROQUET ASSOCIATION). Inside FC: advertisement. RC: list of 'KNOW THE GAME' titles at L and surrogate TP verso at R (**CROQUET** | Produced in collaboration with | *The Croquet Association.* | Published by A & C Black (Publishers) Ltd | 35 Bedford Row | London | WC1R 4JH | 1st edition 1961 | **2nd reprint 1984** | Copyright © A & C Black (Publishers) Ltd 1984 | ISBN 0 7136 2554 6 | **ADAM & CHARLES BLACK** | **LONDON**). Inside RC: advertisement

Copy seen: PC

Fingerprint: t.ea t.ng s.i- Fije 3 1984A [group 2 taken from column 1 of the legend to fig 11 on p 11, the first two characters of group 4 taken from the legend to fig 15 on p 14, the last two characters of group 4 taken from the text]

Notes: Printed by The Stanley Press, Dewsbury, West Yorkshire, price 99p.

The text and illustrations depart from those of (h) only in the insertion of metric measurements in parentheses and in a few other minor particulars. The TP and contents are also rearranged.

(k) *Third edition, 1985 issue (1985)*

[The L column of the TP]

[monogram, *K*, *T*, *G*, in white out of a black ellipse, at L] | [to R] know | [*do*] the | [*do*] game | **CROQUET** | Produced in collaboration with | The Croquet Association | Hurlingham Club | Ranelagh Gardens | London SW6 3PR | Telephone 01 736 3148 | Published by A & C Black (Publishers) Ltd | 35 Bedford Row, London WC1R 4JH

Formula: [1^{18}]. 18 leaves, pp *1* 2–36

Technical notes: 109 × 174 mm (p 6), divided into two columns. 29 lines, 20 = 78 mm. Leaf size 134 × 201 mm; thickness 0.11 mm; wove, unwatermarked, semi-gloss, white. The figures are printed in black and white

Contents: Title, acknowledgement, and advertisement (*1*), contents (*1*–2), foreword, by John W Solomon (3), text, continued (4–36) text, concluded (inside the RC)

Binding: White high-gloss card laminate, stapled, no spine or endpapers. FC: printed in black and white over and out of a colour photograph of a man player in play ([monogram, *K*, *T*, *G*, in white out of photograph, at L] | [to R] know | [*do*] the | [*do*] game | [in white out of photograph, at the same level as the foregoing matter] Croquet | [in black] Published in collaboration with The Croquet Association). Inside FC: frontispiece (black-and-white photograph). RC: list of 85 'KNOW THE GAME' titles in three columns divided by broad vertical rules in strong yellowish Green (131) at L, and surrogate TP verso at R (**CROQUET** | Produced in collaboration with | *The Croquet Association.* | [publisher's blurb] | 3rd edition 1985 | © 1984, 1985 A & C Black | (Publishers) Ltd | A & C Black · London | ISBN 0-7136-5620-4 | [bar code] | 9 780713 656206 | **£1.25 net**). Inside RC: text, concluded

Copy seen: PC

Fingerprint: seto heng reee Fibe 3 1985A [the first two characters of group 4 taken from the legend to fig 13 on p 14, the last two characters of group 4 taken from the first column of the text]

Notes: Printed anonymously, price £1.25 net. This edition is identified by the publisher as the third edition, implying the prior publication of a second edition. The basis of this identification is unknown, as also is the first issue recognised by the publisher as the second edition.

The foreword is entirely rewritten, the text is revised in minor detail, the illustrative figures are replaced by black-and-white photographs, and the explanatory diagrams are reproduced in black and white.

(l) *Third edition, 1987 issue (1987)*

[The TP as that of (k)]

Formula: As that of (k)

Technical notes: 110 × 174 mm per column (p 6), divided into two columns. 28 lines, 20 = 77 mm. Leaf size 135 × 201 mm; thickness 0.10 mm; wove, unwatermarked, smooth, white. The figures are printed in black and white

Contents: As the contents of (k) with the addition of the name of the printer (p 36)

Binding: White high-gloss card laminate, stapled, no spine or endpapers. FC: as that of (k). Inside FC: as that of (k). RC: as that of (k) save for variations in the list of (78) 'KNOW THE GAME' titles, the surrogate TP verso (3rd edition 1985, reprinted 1987 | © 1985 A & C Black (Publishers) Ltd), and price (**£1.50 net**). Inside RC: as in (g)

Copy seen: PC

Fingerprint: seto heng reee *Fi*be 3 1987A [the first two characters of group 4 taken from the legend to fig 13 on p 14, the last two characters of group 4 taken from the first column of the text]

Notes: Printed by Hollen Street Press, Slough, Berkshire, price £1.50 net.

The text departs from that of (k) in minor particulars only.

(m) *Fourth edition (1994)*

[Inside the FC, flanked at the R by a full-colour photograph of a man player in play]

[in vivid yellowish Green (129)] **Croquet | Produced in collaboration with | The Croquet Association** | First published 1994 by | A & C Black (Publishers) Ltd | 35 Bedford Row. London WC1R 4JH | © 1994 The Croquet Association | ISBN 0 7136 3671 8 | [publisher's assertion of copyright] | A CIP catalogue record for this book | is available from the British Library | Printed and bound in Hong Kong

Formula: Apparently [1⁴ 2–3⁸ 4⁴]. 24 leaves, pp 1–48

Technical notes: 110 × 170 mm (p 6), divided into three columns. 30 lines, 20 = 74 mm. Leaf size 133 × 202 mm; thickness 0.09 mm; wove, unwatermarked, smooth, white. The headings and sub-headings are printed in vivid yellowish Green (129) and vivid reddish Orange (34) respectively. The figures consist of colour photographs and diagrams in various colours; some extend across two columns of text, others across the full width of the page

Contents: Contents, acknowledgements, and note (1), text, continued (2–48) text, concluded (inside the RC)

Binding: White high-gloss card laminate glued to the folds of the gatherings. FC: colour photograph of a man player in play, with broad borders at the top and L in vivid reddish Orange (34), divided both vertically and horizontally by black rules in bold. In the upper L quadrant in white out of Orange (*KNOW* | *THE* | *GAME*); in the upper R quadrant in white out Orange (**Croquet**); in the lower L quadrant in brilliant Yellow (83) out of Orange (Produced in | collaboration with | The Croquet

| Association). Inside FC: title and colour photograph (as above). RC: four quadrants formed as on the FC, each upper quadrant containing the same matter as that on the FC. In the lower L quadrant in black on Orange near the foot (ISBN 0-7136-3671-8 | [bar code] | 9 780713 636710 >); in the lower R quadrant to the R of an inset colour photograph illustrating a mallet grip ([publisher's blurb] | A & C Black · London | [inset photographs of red, blue, and yellow balls] | **£3.99 net**). Inside RC: diagram (concluding the text), list of 56 *Know The Game* titles, and publisher's note. Spine: downwards ([in white out of Orange] *KNOW THE GAME* [in Yellow out of Orange] CROQUET [in white out of Orange] BLACK)

Copy seen: PC

Fingerprint: 1918 g.ll *ngow An*ru 3 1994A [groups 1 and 2 taken from pp 1 and 11 respectively, the first two characters of group 3 taken from the legend to the photograph on p 13, the last two characters of group 3 taken from the first column of the text, the first two characters of group 4 taken from the legend to the photograph on p 14, the last two characters of group 4 taken from the first column of the text]

Notes: Printed anonymously in Hong Kong, price £3.99 net.

This edition was extensively revised by Bill Lamb with the assistance of J McCullough. It is identified as an edition of a pre-existing work, notwithstanding change of authorship and the publisher's description (*viz* 'First published in 1994'), having regard to its unchanged title and format, and the continued role of this title in the ongoing *Know The Game* series.

The text — though freely rewritten, updated, rearranged, and re-illustrated — is modelled quite closely on earlier editions and incorporates much of their phraseology.

(n) *Fourth edition, First American issue (1997)*

[Inside the FC, flanked at the R by a full-colour photograph of a man player in play]

[in vivid yellowish Green (129)] **Croquet** | Copyright © 1994 The Croquet Association | Published in 1997 by | STACKPOLE BOOKS | 5067 Ritter Road | Mechanicsburg, PA 17055 | [publisher's assertion of copyright] | Produced in collaboration with | A & C Black (Publishers) Ltd., London | Printed in Hong Kong | 10 9 8 7 6 5 4 3 2 1 | First edition | [Library of Congress Cataloging-in-Publication Data]

Formula: Not ascertainable from the copy examined. 24 leaves, pp 1–48

Technical notes: As at (m)

Contents: Contents, acknowledgements, and notes (1), text, continued (2–48), text, concluded (inside the RC)

Binding: White high-gloss card laminate glued to the folds of the gatherings. FC: colour photograph of a man player in play with broad borders at the top and L in vivid reddish Orange (34), divided both vertically and horizontally by black rules in bold. In the upper L quadrant in white out of Orange (*KNOW* | *THE* | *SPORT*); in the upper R quadrant in white out of Orange (**Croquet**). Inside FC: title and colour photograph (as above). RC: four quadrants formed as on the FC, each upper quadrant containing the same matter as that on the FC. In the lower R quadrant to the R of an inset colour photograph illustrating a mallet grip, in black ([publisher's blurb] | ISBN 0-8117-2833-1 | [to the R of bar code] STACKPOLE | [*do*] BOOKS | [*do*] $5.95 U.S. | [*do*] **Printed in Hong Kong**). Inside RC: diagram, concluding the text. Spine: downwards ([in white out of Orange] *KNOW THE GAME* [in Yellow out of Orange] CROQUET [in white out of Orange] STACKPOLE)

Copy seen: PC

Fingerprint: 1918 g.ll *ngow Anru* 3 1997A [groups 1 and 2 taken from pp 1 and 11 respectively, the first two characters of group 3 taken from the legend to the photograph on p 13, the last two characters of group 3 taken from the first column of the text, the first two characters of group 4 taken from the legend to the photograph on p 14, the last two characters of group 4 taken from the first column of the text]

Notes: Printed anonymously in Hong Kong, price US$5.95.

The text is identical to that of (m). The only variations, introduced by the publisher for the American market, are to be found on the covers and in a note on p 1.

(o) *Fifth edition (1998)*

[Inside the FC, flanked at the R by a full-colour photograph of a man player in play]

[in vivid yellowish Green (129)] **Croquet** | Produced in collaboration with | The Croquet Association | Published by A & C Black (Publishers) Ltd | 35 Bedford Row. London WC1R 4JH | Second edition 1998 | Copyright © 1998 by | The Croquet Association | ISBN 0 7136 4994 1 | [publisher's assertion of copyright] | A CIP catalogue record for this book | is available from the British Library. | Printed in Hong Kong

Formula: Not ascertainable from the copy examined. 24 leaves, pp 1–48

Technical notes: 110 × 170 mm (p 20), divided into three columns. 30 lines, 20 = 74 mm. Leaf size 133 × 202 mm; thickness 0.09 mm; wove, unwatermarked, semi-gloss, white. The headings and sub-headings are printed in vivid yellowish Green (129) and vivid reddish Orange (34) respectively. The figures consist of colour photographs and diagrams in various colours; some extend across two columns of text, others across the full width of the page

Contents: Contents, acknowledgements, and note (1), text, continued (2–48) text, concluded (inside the RC)

Binding: White high-gloss card laminate, glued to the folds of the gatherings, no spine or endpapers. FC: divided both vertically and horizontally by black rules in bold. In the upper L quadrant in black on vivid Yellow (82) (*KNOW* | *THE* | *GAME*); in the upper R quadrant in black on Yellow (**Croquet**); in the lower L quadrant in black on Yellow (Produced in | collaboration with | The Croquet | Association | [device of the CA] | Second edition); in the lower R quadrant a colour photograph of a man player in play. Inside FC: title and colour photograph (as above). RC: four quadrants formed as on the FC, each upper quadrant containing the same matter as that on the FC. In the lower L quadrant in black on white out of Yellow near the foot (ISBN 0-7136-4994-1 | [bar code] | 9 780713 649949 >); in the lower R quadrant to the R of a colour photograph of a man player in play ([publisher's blurb] | [inset photographs of red, blue, and yellow balls] | A & C Black · London | **£4.99**). Inside RC: colour photograph, concluding the text, and list of 45 *Know The Game* titles. Spine: downwards ([in black on Yellow] *KNOW THE GAME* CROQUET BLACK)

Copy seen: PC

Fingerprint: 2019 y.ay i-ry *ruma* 3 1998A

Notes: Printed anonymously in Hong Kong, price £4.99. Though presented by the publisher as the 'second edition', it is here identified as the fifth edition by virtue of its following (k) in the Know the Game series (see *Notes* to (m)).

The text, reset throughout, departs from that of (m) in minor particulars only.

Several new photographs are substituted for old, and the text and illustrations are rearranged.

1965

A177   CROQUET: INSTRUCTIONS TO BEGINNERS. JW Solomon   [1965]

(a) **First edition [1965]*

[The FC, within a frame composed of a decorative frieze]

CROQUET | [in shaded half-open script] **Instructions** | [*do*] **to** | [*do*] **Beginners** | [swelled rule] | *compiled by* | *J.W.Solomon* | WITH THE AUTHORITY OF THE CROQUET ASSOCIATION

Formula: [1⁴]. 4 leaves, pp 1–7 8

Technical notes: 144 × 101 mm (p 3, ragged). 34 lines, 20 = 84 mm. Leaf size 179 × 128 mm; thickness 0.12 mm; wove, unwatermarked, smooth, white

Contents: Text (1–8)

Binding: Pale Green (149) card, stapled, no spine or endpapers. FC: printed in black as above. Inside FC: advertisement for Charles Webber and Co croquet goods, citing London address as Phoenix House, 11 Wellesley Road, Croydon. RC: advertisement. Inside RC: advertisement

Copy seen: PC

Fingerprint: !)en n.ll in:- l.er C 1965Q [all four groups taken from p 1]

Notes: Published in October 1965, printed anonymously by Prestoprint, Kingston upon Thames, price 1/–.

(b) *First edition, variant [1965]*

[The FC as that of (a)]

Formula: As that of (a)

Technical notes: 144 × 101 mm (p 3, ragged). 34 lines, 20 = 84 mm. Leaf size 185 × 126 mm; thickness 0.12 mm; wove, watermarked (***Plus*** | ***Fabric***), smooth, white

Contents: As the contents of (a)

Binding: Light Green (144) card, stapled, no spine or endpapers. FC: printed in black as above. Inside FC: advertisement for Charles Webber and Co croquet goods, citing London address as 6 Lisford Street, SE15. RC: advertisement and name of printer. Inside RC: advertisement

Copy seen: PC

Fingerprint: As that of (a)

Notes: Printed by Prestoprint, Kingston upon Thames. The fact that the printer is not named in (a) would suggest that (a) was issued first.

A178   THE LAWS OF CROQUET SIMPLIFIED. E Antony Roper   [1965]

[The FC, within a frame composed of a repeated trefoil figure]

[in shaded open display script] **The Laws of** | **CROQUET** | [in shaded open display script] **Simplified** | [swelled rule] | *compiled by* | *E. Antony Roper* | With the Authority of the Croquet Association

Formula: [1⁶]. 6 leaves, pp 1–12

Technical notes: 141 × 84 mm. 36 lines, 20 = 79 mm. Leaf size 166 × 104 mm; thickness 0.11 mm; wove, watermarked indistinctly in open script ([the only word, apparently one of three, clearly legible in the copy examined] *Plus*), smooth, white

Contents: Text (1–9), lined pages for notes (10–12)

Binding: Pale Green (149) card printed in black, stapled, no spine or endpapers. FC: as above. Inside FC: blank. RC: at the foot ((*Printed by PRESTOPRINT Ltd. Kingston*))

Copy seen: PC

Fingerprint: nyor d̲.es r-he ayhe C 1965Q [group 1 taken from p 1, groups 2–4 taken from p 9]

Notes: Published by the CA, printed by Prestoprint, Kingston upon Thames, price 1/6. Publication by the CA is inferred from the proceedings of its Council, as reported in the April 1965 issue of *Croquet*. Year of publication is as stated in the Chairman's annual report, given in *Croquet* (April 1966, p 4).

1966

A179   CROQUET. JW Solomon   **1966**

(a) *First edition (1966)*

Croquet | J W Solomon | B T Batsford Ltd | London

[TP verso]

First published 1966 | © J W Solomon 1966 | Made and printed in Great Britain | by Jarrold and Sons Ltd   London and Norwich | for the publishers B T BATSFORD LTD | 4 Fitzhardinge Street   London W1

Formula: [$1^8(-1_1)$ 2–7^8 $8^8(-8_8)$]. 62 leaves including the endpapers, pp *i–ii, 1–4* 5–115 *116* 117–118 *119–122*

Technical notes: 169 × 109 mm (p 14). 40 lines, 20 = 84 mm. Leaf size 221 × 149 mm; thickness 0.23–0.26 mm; wove, unwatermarked, smooth, white; four leaves of inset plates (black-and-white photographs) follow pp 28, 44, 60, 76

Contents: Glued to the FC (*i*), blank (*ii*), half-title (*1*), blank (*2*), title (*3*), TP verso (*4*), contents (*5*), acknowledgement (*6*), list of line illustrations (*7*), list of plates (*8*), text (*9–115*), blank (*116*), index (*117–118*), blank (*119–121*), glued to the RC (*122*)

Binding: Dark Blue (183) simulated pig skin over stiff boards, sewn. FC: blank. RC: blank. Spine: gold-blocked downwards (Solomon   CROQUET   Batsford)

Dust wrapper: Printed in black, pale Yellow (89), and vivid yellowish Green (129) on white paper. FP: lettering out of Green monochrome photograph of the author in play ([in Yellow] **CROQUET** | [in white at R] J W Solomon). FF: price and publisher's blurb printed in black. RP: coloured Green all over, no letterpress. RF: list of championship titles won to date (1965) by the author. Spine: downwards ([in Yellow out of Green] Solomon [in Yellow out of Green] **CROQUET** [in black on Green in the form of a monogram] **ep**)

Copy seen: PC

Fingerprint: 1714 s.on *rBto* Bufr 3 1966A

Notes: Published in May or June 1966, printed by Jarrold and Sons, London and Norwich, price 25/– net. Seven thousand copies are believed to have been printed.

Review: MB Reckitt in *Croquet* (September 1966).

(b) *EP Publishing issue (1983)*

Croquet | J W Solomon | E P Publishing Limited

[TP verso]

First published 1966 by B T Batsford Ltd., London. | Republished 1983 by EP Publishing Limited, | Bradford Road, East Ardsley, Wakefield, | West Yorkshire, England WF3 2JN | © J W Solomon 1966, 1983 | ISBN 0 7158 0884 2 | Printed and bound in Great Britain | by The Moxon Press Ltd | Ben Rhydding, Ilkley | West Yorks.

Formula: [1–8⁸]. 64 leaves including the endpapers, pp *i–iv*, 1–4 5–115 *116* 117–118 *119–124*

Technical notes: 169 × 109 mm (p 14). 40 lines, 20 = 84 mm. Leaf size 219 × 149 mm; thickness 0.16 mm; wove, unwatermarked, smooth, white; four leaves of inset plates (black-and-white photographs) follow pp 28, 44, 60, 76

Contents: Glued to the FC (*i*), blank (*ii–iv*), half-title (*1*), blank (*2*), title (*3*), TP verso (*4*), contents (*5*), acknowledgement (*6*), list of line illustrations (*7*), list of plates (*8*), text (*9–115*), blank (*116*), index (*117–118*), blank (*119–123*), glued to the RC (*124*)

Binding: Deep Blue (179) linen grain paper over stiff boards, sewn. FC: blank. RC: blank. Spine: gold-blocked downwards (Solomon   **CROQUET**), and crosswise at the foot ([in the form of a monogram] **ep**)

Dust wrapper: Printed in black and vivid yellowish Green (129) on white paper. FP: lettering in white out of Green monochrome photograph of the author in play (**CROQUET** | [at R] J W Solomon). FF: publisher's blurb and ISBN printed in black. RP: in black on Green at the foot (E P Publishing Limited). RF: list of championship titles won by the author. Spine: in white out of Green downwards (Solomon | **CROQUET**), and crosswise at the foot ([in black on Green, in the form of a monogram] **ep**)

Copy seen: PC

Fingerprint: 1714 s.on *rBto* Bufr 3 1983A

Notes: Printed by the Moxon Press, Ben Rhydding, Ilkley, West Yorks. Two thousand copies are believed to have been printed at the instigation of the CA. The author waived royalties.

The text is apparently identical to that of (a) except for the table on p 115 which is revised to bring the results of the MacRobertson International Shield series up to date as at 1982.

(c) *A & C Black issue (1989)*

[in display script] *Croquet* | *J.W. SOLOMON* | A & C Black · London

[TP verso]

Published in paperback 1989 by | A & C Black (Publishers) Ltd | 35 Bedford Row, London WC1R 4JH | First published 1966 by B. T. Batsford Ltd, London | Republished 1983 by EP Publishing Ltd, Wakefield | © 1966, 1983, 1989 J.W. Solomon | ISBN 0 7136 5636 0 | [assertion of copyright: 6 lines] | A CIP catalogue record for this book is available | from the British Library. | Printed and bound in Great Britain by | Hollen Street Press Ltd of Slough

Formula: [1–4¹⁶]. 64 leaves, pp *1–4* 5–36, *i–ii*, 37–40, *iii–iv*, 41–70, *v–vi*, 71–90, *vii–viii*, 91–120 [= 128]

Technical notes: 168 × 109 mm (p 29). 40 lines, 20 = 84 mm. Leaf size 214 × 137 mm; thickness 0.11 mm; wove, unwatermarked, smooth, white

Contents: Half-title (*1*), frontispiece (black-and-white photograph) (*2*), title (*3*), TP verso (*4*), contents (*5*), acknowledgement and record of the author's achievements

(6), list of line illustrations (7), list of (black-and-white) photographs (8), text (9–118), index (119–120)

Binding: High-gloss heavy white card with hinges front and rear, printed in full colour, glued to the folds of the gatherings; sewn, no endpapers. FC: against a dark Blue (183) background ([in vivid yellowish Green (129), at R] *J.W. SOLOMON* | [Green rule in bold at R] | [in white display script out of Blue] *Croquet* | [Green rule in bold at R] | [panel containing a colour photograph of the author in play, within a ruled frame, the verticals in white, the horizontals bold in white and Green]). Inside FC: blank. RC: against a Blue background ([panel containing publisher's blurb with a ruled frame of similar design to that on the FC] | [ISBN bar code in black on white within a smaller panel at the lower R]). Inside RC: blank. Spine: downwards in white out of Blue (*J.W. Solomon   CROQUET   Black*)

Copy seen: PC

Fingerprint: 1917 s.on nde, baa*f* 7 1989A

Notes: Printed by Hollen Street Press, Slough, price £7.95 net. Ten thousand copies are believed to have been printed, of which a few hundred were remaindered in 1997.

New black-and-white photographs replace those in the original inset plates. The text varies little from that of (a). The main variations are the addition of a new section on recent developments in the game (pp 112–15) and an extension of a table (now on p 118) to bring the results of the MacRobertson International Shield series up to date as at 1986.

A180   **CROQUET AND HOW TO PLAY IT. David Miller and Rupert Thorp   1966**

[in open script] CROQUET AND | [*do*] HOW TO PLAY IT | *by* | DAVID MILLER | *and* | RUPERT THORP | [flourish] | *With a Foreword by* | MAURICE B. RECKITT | *and* | *10 sketches by* | JANE LILLY | FABER AND FABER | 24 Russell Square | London

[TP verso]

First published in mcmlxvi | *by Faber and Faber Limited* | *24 Russell Square London WC1* | *Printed in Great Britain by* | *Latimer Trend & Co Ltd Plymouth* | *All rights reserved* | *© David Miller and Rupert Thorp 1966*

Formula: A^8 B–K^8 L^4(L1+χ^8) [$1 signed (–A1); χ1 signed 'L$_*$']. 90 leaves, pp *1–8 9 10 11 12 13–15 16 17–18 19–20 21–177 178–180*

Technical notes: 167 × 101 mm (p 14). 40 lines, 20 = 84 mm. Leaf size 215 × 136 mm; thickness 0.13 mm; wove, unwatermarked, smooth, white. Three inset plates on semi-gloss paper, each comprising black-and-white photographs, face pp 5, 28, 40

Contents: Blank (*1–2*), half-title (*3*), blank (*4*), title (*5*), TP verso (*6*), dedication (*7*), blank (*8*), contents (*9*), blank (*10*), list of plates (11), blank (*12*), foreword, signed 'Maurice B. Reckitt' (13–15), blank (*16*), preface signed 'D. W. M.' and 'R. F. T.', London, 1965 (17–18), quotation from CM Yonge (19), blank (*20*), text (21–177), blank (*178*), plan of croquet court (*179–180*)

Binding: Moderate bluish Green (164) cloth over stiff boards, sewn. FC: blank. RC: blank. Spine: gold-blocked crosswise (*Croquet* | *and* | *How to* | *Play it* | ★ | *Miller* | *&* | *Thorp* | *Faber*

Dust wrapper: Printed on white semi-gloss paper in black, light greenish Blue (172), vivid reddish Orange (34), and brilliant greenish Yellow (98). FP: ([in blue] **CROQUET** | [*do*] **& HOW TO PLAY IT** | [in black] **DAVID MILLER & RUPERT THORP** | [row of discs in black, Blue, Orange, and Yellow, preceded by R edge of similar Blue disc centred on the spine] | [circular vignette, a black-and-white photograph consisting of a detail from the frontispiece depicting John Bolton in play). FF: publisher's blurb and price (clipped from the copy examined), flanked by R edge of Yellow disc on the FP. RP: list of Faber and Faber sports titles in black with a rule in Orange, flanked at the R by the L edge of a Blue disc centred in the spine. RF: publisher's blurb in relation to other sports titles. Spine: downwards ([in Orange at L] **CROQUET &** | [*do*] **HOW TO PLAY IT** | [Blue disc] | [to R of Blue disc in black] **DAVID MILLER &** | [*do*] **RUPERT THORP**), and crosswise at the foot ([in Yellow] **FABER**)

Copy seen: PC

Fingerprint: etof TTp. d.17 *LoD.* 7 1966R

Notes: Printed by Latimer Trend & Co, Plymouth, price £1 8s.

Review: *Croquet* (August 1966).

1967

AA181 CROQUETTES. Maurice B Reckitt   1967

CROQUETTES | [double rule] | Pen Pictures from the Past | of some great figures in the game | - by - | Maurice B. Reckitt | [rule] 1967. | [rule]

Formula: Loose-leaf typescript with revisions and additions in MS. 55 leaves, pp *i*, 1–2, *ii*, 3–53

Technical notes: 190 × 157 (max) mm (p 4, ragged). 23 lines, 20 = 169 mm. Leaf size 254 × 203 mm; thickness 0.06 mm; wove, watermarked (Melior), smooth, white

Contents: Title (*i*), foreword, signed 'M. B. R.' (1–2), contents (*ii*), text (3–53)

Binding: The copy examined is bound by a paper fastener

Copy seen: CA

Fingerprint: noid ldas stIn elhe 3 1967A [groups 1–4 taken from pp 1, 4, 13, 13 respectively]

Notes: Though unpublished, it is thought that this work was originally intended by the author for publication in 1967, to coincide with the CA's celebrations of the centenary of the Open Championships.

1968

AA182 A HISTORY OF CROQUET AND OF THE CROQUET   1968
ASSOCIATION. Maurice B Reckitt

[File 1 of 7]

A HISTORY OF CROQUET | and of the | CROQUET ASSOCIATION | from the revival of | the game in the Nineties | - by - | Maurice B. Reckitt | 1962–1967 | [double rule]

Formula: [loose-leaf typescript with revisions, additions and some additional leaves in MS, in 7 'files' and 11 loose leaves]. File 1: 153 leaves, pp *1–2*, i–iii, 1–75 75a 76–147; File 2: 95 leaves, pp i–iii, *1*, 148–189 189A 190–211 211A 212–236; File 3: 194 leaves, pp *i*, 237–429; File 4: 205 leaves, pp *i*, 430–633; File 5: 184 leaves, pp *i*, 634–816; File 6: 159 leaves, pp *i*, 836–973, 817–835, 974; File 7: 136 leaves, pp *i*, 975–1109; 11 loose leaves, pp i–xi

Technical notes: Files 1–5: 198 × 159 (max) mm (File 1, p 7, ragged). 24 lines, 20 = 170 mm. Leaf size 253 × 203 mm; thickness 0.08 mm; wove, watermarked

(PLANTAGENET • | BRITISH MAKE •) in heraldic device, smooth, white. Files 6–7 and concluding loose leaves: 198 × 162 (max) mm (File 6, p 837, ragged). 24 lines, 20 = 169 mm. Leaf size 252 × 201 mm; thickness 0.07 mm; wove, watermarked (Melior), smooth, white

Contents: File 1: Title (*1*), contents (*2*), preface, signed 'M. B. R.' (i–iii), introduction (1–9), text, Part I [1894–1908] (10–147); File 2: appendix (Past and Present) (i–iii), contents (*1*), text, Part I [1909–14] (148–236); File 3: contents (*i*), text, Part II [1914–28] (237–429); File 4: contents (*i*), text, Part II [1929–39] (430–633); File 5: contents (*i*), interchapter [1939–45] (634–659), text, Part III [1946–53] (660–816); File 6: contents (*i*), text, Part III [1954–61] (836–973, 817–835, 974); File 6: contents (*i*), text, Part III [1962–67] (975–1109); concluding loose leaves (epilogue, signed 'M. B. R.', New Year's Day 1968) (i–xi)

Binding: When seen in April 1996, all but the epilogue of the copy examined was bound in seven Gayfile quarto binders

Copy seen: CA

Fingerprint: cest J.ee hee, hehe C 1968A [the four groups taken from File 1, pp i, 2, 13, 13]

Notes: Unpublished. This work, largely based on the contents of *The Croquet Association Gazette* (continued as *Croquet*), was compiled during the years 1962–67. Although it is entitled a history, and the author originally intended that it should be a history, 'It soon became evident to me, however, that what I was producing could not claim to be in any true sense the History as which I had imprudently described it on the title page of my typescript, but should more properly be called Annals, prepared as a contribution to our Association's archives' (Epilogue, p i). It would appear that at some stage the author decided to complete it on or soon after getting up to date, in or about his eightieth year. It is perhaps significant that the last chapter but one, which is chiefly concerned with events of 1966 and must have been completed late that year or early in 1967, is entitled 'Penultimate' and that the final chapter is fittingly entitled 'Centenary'. The Epilogue is dated the day after the end of the year (1967) in which the CA celebrated the centenary of the Open Championships.

All or almost all the revisions and additions in the copy examined appear to be in the author's own hand. The original MS is held by the CA, and at least one other copy of the typescript is thought to exist.

<h1 style="text-align:center">1969</h1>

A183   **CROQUET ASSOCIATION FIXTURES** [and **CROQUET**   1969
       ASSOCIATION FIXTURES LIST, FIXTURES LIST].
       [The Croquet Association]

Foreword: This work was conceived by D Caporn, who compiled the first few editions himself. Copies were originally issued free of charge to Associates of the CA on payment of their subscriptions. Subsequently they were issued free of charge to Tournament members only.

(a) *First edition, 1969 (1969)*

[The FC]

[L justified, flanked on the L by triple vertical rules which extend to near the foot] **CROQUET** | [*do*] **ASSOCIATION** | [*do*] **FIXTURES** | [at L, below the triple vertical rule:] **C.A.** [at the R:] **1969** | [triple rule]

Formula: [1¹⁶]. 16 leaves, pp *1* 2–31 *32*

Technical notes: 231 × 173 mm (p 7, ragged). 55 lines, 20 = 85 mm. Leaf size 249 × 201 mm; thickness 0.12 mm; wove, watermarked (**64 Mill** | **HARD-SIZED**), smooth, white

Contents: Calendar of fixtures with page references (*1*), subscriptions, levy, and tribute (2), general conditions and information (3), official tournaments (4–12), club tournaments (13–*32*)

Binding: Pale Yellow (89) paper watermarked ([in a convex arc] Croxley | [in a concave arc] **SCRIPT**), stapled, no spine or endpapers. FC: as above. Inside FC: blank. RC: blank. Inside RC: blank

Copy seen: CA

Fingerprint: ndrk h.he d.by ThTh 3 1969A [group 1 taken from the fore-edge of p *1*, not from the R of the L-hand column]

Notes: Printed anonymously by Browns Typewriting Services, Burnley, Lancs, in March 1969. The accounts of the CA show that 600 copies were produced. The copy examined includes a loose leaf of 'ADDITIONS'.

(b) *1970 edition (1970)*

[The FC]

[L justified, flanked on the L by a vertical rule in bold which extends to near the foot, where it makes a right-angle with an extended horizontal rule in bold] **CROQUET** | [*do*] **ASSOCIATION** | [*do*] **FIXTURES** | [in open script] **1970** | [within a circle described by two lines, the outer line in bold, which represents a face of a mallet which stands on the lower horizontal rule and leans against the extended vertical rule] **C.A.**

Formula: [1^{18}]. 18 leaves, pp *1* 2–36

Technical notes: 216 × 171 mm (p 31, ragged). 51 lines, 20 = 85 mm. Leaf size 245 × 196 mm; thickness 0.14 mm; wove, watermarked (Croxley | duplicator), smooth, white

Contents: Calendar of fixtures with page references (*1*), subscriptions, levy, and tribute (2), general conditions and information (3), official tournaments (4–14), club tournaments (15–35), conditions for invitation events (36)

Binding: Very light greenish Blue (171) paper watermarked ([in a convex arc] Croxley | [in a concave arc] **SCRIPT**), stapled, no spine or endpapers. FC: as above. Inside FC: blank. RC: blank. Inside RC: blank

Copy seen: CA

Fingerprint: 1912 n.l. d.ll 8.po 3 1970A [group 1 taken from p *1*]

Notes: Printed anonymously by Browns Typewriting Services, Burnley, Lancs.

(c) *1971 edition (1971)*

[The FC]

[L justified, flanked on the L by a vertical rule in bold which extends to near the foot, where it makes a right-angle with an extended horizontal rule in bold] **CROQUET** | [*do*] **ASSOCIATION** | [*do*] **FIXTURES** | [in open script] **1971** | [within a circle described by two lines, the outer line in bold, which represents a face of a mallet which stands on the lower horizontal rule and leans against the extended vertical rule] **C.A.**

Formula: [1^{18}]. 18 leaves, pp 1–36

Technical notes: 227 × 167 mm (p 10, ragged). 54 lines, 20 = 85 mm. Leaf size 250 × 204 mm; thickness 0.13 mm; wove, watermarked (**64 Mill | HARD-SIZED**), smooth, white

Contents: Calendar of fixtures with page references (1), subscriptions, levy, and tribute (2), general conditions and information (3), official tournaments (4–14), club tournaments (15–35), conditions for invitation events (36)

Binding: Very light greenish Blue (171) paper watermarked ([in a convex arc] Croxley | [in a concave arc] **SCRIPT**), stapled, no spine or endpapers. FC: as above. Inside FC: blank. RC: blank. Inside RC: blank

Copy seen: CA

Fingerprint: psup y.h. 1.y. 8.fi 3 1971A [group 1 taken from p 1]

Notes: Printed anonymously by Browns Typewriting Services, Burnley, Lancs.

(d) *1972 edition (1972)*

[The FC]

[L justified, flanked on the L by a vertical rule in bold which extends to near the foot, where it makes a right-angle with an extended horizontal rule in bold] **CROQUET** | [*do*] **ASSOCIATION** | [*do*] **FIXTURES** | [in open script] **1972** | [within a circle described by two lines, the outer line in bold, which represents a face of a mallet which stands on the lower horizontal rule and leans against the extended vertical rule] **C.A.**

Formula: [1^{18}]. 18 leaves, pp *1* 2–36

Technical notes: 230 × 167 mm (p 10, ragged). 55 lines, 20 = 85 mm. Leaf size 254 × 203 mm; thickness 0.14 mm; wove, watermarked (**64 Mill | HARD-SIZED**), smooth, white

Contents: Calendar of fixtures with page references (*1*), subscriptions, levy, and tribute (2), general conditions and information (3), official tournaments (4–14), club tournaments (15–35), conditions for invitation events (36)

Binding: Very light greenish Blue (171) paper watermarked ([in a convex arc] Croxley | [in a concave arc] **SCRIPT**), stapled, no spine or endpapers *etc.* FC: as above. Inside FC: blank. RC: blank. Inside RC: blank

Copy seen: CA

Fingerprint: P8P7 Y.41 h.te 7.po 3 1972A [group 1 taken from p 1]

Notes: Printed anonymously by Browns Typewriting Services, Burnley, Lancs.

(e) *1973 edition (1973)*

[The FC]

[L justified, flanked on the L by a vertical rule in bold which extends to near the foot, where it makes a right-angle with an extended horizontal rule in bold] **CROQUET** | [*do*] **ASSOCIATION** | [*do*] **FIXTURES** | [in open script] **1973** | [within a circle described by two lines, the outer line in bold, which represents a face of a mallet which stands on the lower horizontal rule and leans against the extended vertical rule] **C.A.**

Formula: [1^{20}]. 20 leaves, pp *1* 2–39 *40*

Technical notes: 226 × 179 mm (p 5, ragged). 53 lines, 20 = 86 mm. Leaf size 251 × 201 mm; thickness 0.13 mm; wove, watermarked (**64 Mill | HARD-SIZED**), smooth, white

Contents: Calendar of fixtures with page references (*1*), subscriptions, levy, and tribute (2), general conditions and information (3), official tournaments (4–16), club tournaments (16–38), conditions for invitation events (39), blank (*40*)

Binding: Very light greenish Blue (171) paper watermarked ([in a convex arc] CROXLEY | [in a concave arc] **SCRIPT**), stapled, no spine or endpapers. FC: as above. Inside FC: blank. RC: blank. Inside RC: blank

Copy seen: CA

Fingerprint: 8)20 r.he e.on whfr 3 1973A [group 1 taken from p *1*]

Notes: Printed anonymously by Browns Typewriting Services, Burnley, Lancs.

(f) *1974 edition (1974)*

[The FC]

[L justified, flanked on the L by a vertical rule in bold which extends to near the foot, where it makes a right-angle with an extended horizontal rule in bold] **CROQUET** | [*do*] **ASSOCIATION** | [*do*] **FIXTURES** | [in open script] **1974** | [within a circle described by two lines, the outer line in bold, which represents a face of a mallet which stands on the lower horizontal rule and leans against the extended vertical rule] **C.A.**

Formula: [1–20¹]. 20 leaves, pp 1–39 *40*

Technical notes: 231 × 165 mm (p 23, ragged). 54 lines, 20 = 86 mm. Leaf size 249 × 202 mm; thickness 0.13 mm; wove, watermarked (**64 MILL | HARD-SIZED**), smooth, white

Contents: Calendar of fixtures with page references (1–2), subscriptions, levy, and tribute (3), general conditions and information (4), official tournaments (5–17), club tournaments (18–38), conditions for invitation events (39), blank (*40*)

Binding: Brilliant Yellow (83) paper wrapped around the edges of the leaves, stapled, no endpapers. FC: as above. Inside FC: blank. RC: blank. Inside RC: blank. Spine: blank

Copy seen: CA

Fingerprint: k.27 4.s. d.ry <u>COAN</u> 3 1974A [group 1 taken from p *1*]

Notes: Printed anonymously by Browns Typewriting Services, Burnley, Lancs.

(g) *1975 edition (1975)*

[The FC]

[L justified, flanked on the L by a vertical rule in bold which extends to near the foot, where it makes a right-angle with an extended horizontal rule in bold] **CROQUET** | [*do*] **ASSOCIATION** | [*do*] **FIXTURES** | [in open script] **1975** | [within a circle described by two lines, the outer line in bold, which represents a face of a mallet which stands on the lower horizontal rule and leans against the extended vertical rule] **C.A.**

Formula: [1–19¹]. 19 leaves, pp 1–38

Technical notes: 228 × 168 mm (p 36, ragged). 53 lines, 20 = 86 mm. Leaf size 248 × 196 mm; thickness 0.14 mm; wove, watermarked (**64 MILL | HARD-SIZED**), smooth, white

Contents: Calendar of fixtures with page references (1–2), subscriptions, levy, and tribute (3), general conditions and information (4), official tournaments (5–17), club tournaments (17–37), conditions for invitation events (38)

Binding: Light greenish yellow (101) paper wrapped around the edges of the leaves, stapled, no endpapers. FC: as above. Inside FC: blank. RC: blank. Inside RC: blank. Spine: blank

Copy seen: CA

Fingerprint: 2726 t.s. s.be <u>COSE</u> 3 1975A [group 1 taken from p 1]

Notes: Printed anonymously by Browns Typewriting Services, Burnley, Lancs.

(h) *1976 edition (1976)*

[The FC]

[L justified, flanked on the L by a vertical rule in bold which extends to near the foot, where it makes a right-angle with an extended horizontal rule in bold] **CROQUET** | [*do*] **ASSOCIATION** | [*do*] **FIXTURES** | [in open script] **1976** | [within a circle described by two lines, the outer line in bold, which represents a face of a mallet which stands on the lower horizontal rule and leans against the extended vertical rule] **C.A.**

Formula: [1–19¹]. 19 leaves, pp *1* 2–38

Technical notes: 232 × 164 mm (p 33, ragged). 54 lines, 20 = 86 mm. Leaf size 251 × 204 mm; thickness 0.12 mm; wove, watermarked ([in a convex arc] Superfine Papers | [manufacturer's device, combining the letters Y, D] | [in a concave arc] Made in Britain), smooth, white

Contents: Calendar of fixtures with page references (*1–2*), subscriptions, levy, and tribute (3), general conditions and information (4), official tournaments (5–17), club tournaments (17–37), conditions for invitation events (38)

Binding: Very pale Green (148) paper wrapped around the edges of the leaves, stapled, no endpapers. FC: as above. Inside FC: blank. RC: blank. Inside RC: blank. Spine: blank

Copy seen: CA

Fingerprint: 2717).he s.be <u>COS</u>. 3 1976A [group 1 taken from p *1*]

Notes: Printed anonymously by FH Brown, Burnley, Lancs.

(j) *1977 edition (1977)*

[The FC]

[L justified, flanked on the L by a vertical rule in bold which extends to near the foot, where it makes a right-angle with an extended horizontal rule in bold] **CROQUET** | [*do*] **ASSOCIATION** | [*do*] **FIXTURES** | [in open script] **1977** | [within a circle described by two lines, the outer line in bold, which represents a face of a mallet which stands on the lower horizontal rule and leans against the extended vertical rule] **C.A.**

Formula: [1–21¹]. 21 leaves, pp *1* 2–42

Technical notes: 245 × 156 mm (p 8, ragged). 57 lines, 20 = 86 mm. Leaf size 254 × 204 mm; thickness 0.12 mm; wove, watermarked ([in a convex arc] Superfine Papers | [manufacturer's device, combining the letters Y, D] | [in a concave arc] Made in Britain), smooth, white

Contents: Calendar of fixtures with page references (*1–2*), subscriptions, levy, and tribute (3), general conditions and information (4), official tournaments (5–17), club tournaments (18–41), conditions for invitation events (41), schedule of play for Eights Weeks (42)

Binding: Light greenish Yellow (101) paper wrapped around the edges of the leaves, stapled, no endpapers. FC: as above. Inside FC: blank. RC: blank. Inside RC: blank. Spine: blank

Copy seen: CA

Fingerprint: 2926).he s.he <u>COS</u>. 3 1977A [group 1 taken from p *1*]

Notes: Printed anonymously by FH Brown, Burnley, Lancs.

(k) *1978 edition (1978)*

[The FC]

[L justified, flanked on the L by a vertical rule in bold which extends to near the foot, where it makes a right-angle with an extended horizontal rule in bold] **CROQUET** | [*do*] **ASSOCIATION** | [*do*] **FIXTURES** | [in open script] **1978** | [within a circle described by two lines, the outer line in bold, which represents a face of a mallet which stands on the lower horizontal rule and leans against the extended vertical rule] **C.A.**

Formula: [1–21¹]. 21 leaves, pp *1* 2–41 *42*

Technical notes: 242 × 171 mm (p 32, ragged). 57 lines, 20 = 85 mm. Leaf size 249 × 199 mm; thickness 0.13 mm; wove, watermarked (Croxley | duplicator), smooth, white

Contents: Calendar of fixtures with page references (*1–2*), subscriptions, levy, and tribute (3), general conditions and information (4), official tournaments (5–17), club tournaments (18–40), conditions for invitation events (40), schedule of play for Eights Weeks (41), blank (*42*)

Binding: Very light bluish Green (162) paper wrapped around the edges of the leaves, stapled, no endpapers. FC: as above. Inside FC: blank. RC: blank. Inside RC: blank. Spine: blank

Copy seen: CA

Fingerprint: 2925).he s.be <u>COS</u>. 3 1978A [group 1 taken from p *1*]

Notes: Printed anonymously by FH Brown, Burnley, Lancs. The copy examined includes a loose leaf of *errata*.

(l) *1979 edition (1979)*

[The FC]

[L justified, flanked on the L by a vertical rule in bold which extends to near the foot, where it makes a right-angle with an extended horizontal rule in bold] **CROQUET** | [*do*] **ASSOCIATION** | [*do*] **FIXTURES** | [in open script] **1979** | [within a circle described by two lines, the outer line in bold, which represents a face of a mallet which stands on the lower horizontal rule and leans against the extended vertical rule] **C.A.**

Formula: [1–23¹]. 23 leaves, pp *1* 2–45 *46*

Technical notes: 238 × 164 mm (p 5, ragged). 56 lines, 20 = 86 mm. Leaf size 250 × 200 mm; thickness 0.12 mm; wove, watermarked ([in a convex arc] Superfine Papers | [manufacturer's device, combining the letters Y, *D*] | [in a concave arc] Made in Britain), smooth, white

Contents: Calendar of fixtures with page references (*1–2*), subscriptions, levy, and tribute (3), general conditions and information (4), official tournaments (5–17), club tournaments (18–44), conditions for invitation events (44–45), schedule of play for Eights Weeks (45), blank (*46*)

Binding: Light greenish Yellow (101) paper wrapped around the edges of the leaves, stapled, no endpapers. FC: as above. Inside FC: blank. RC: blank. Inside RC: blank. Spine: blank

Copy seen: CA

Fingerprint: g.e- n)s. h.th then 3 1979A [group 1 taken from p *1*]

Notes: Printed anonymously by FH Brown, Burnley, Lancs. The accounts of the CA record that 900 copies were produced.

(m) *1980 edition (1980)*

[The FC]

[L justified, flanked on the L by a vertical rule in bold which extends to near the foot, where it makes a right-angle with an extended horizontal rule in bold] **CROQUET** | [*do*] **ASSOCIATION** | [*do*] **FIXTURES** | [in open script] 1980 | [within a circle described by two lines, the outer line in bold, which represents a face of a mallet which stands on the lower horizontal rule and leans against the extended vertical rule] **C.A.**

Formula: [1–24^1]. 24 leaves, pp *1* 2–47 *48*

Technical notes: 241 × 171 mm (p 10, ragged). 57 lines, 20 = 85 mm. Leaf size 250 × 200 mm; thickness 0.13 mm; wove, watermarked ([in a convex arc] Superfine Papers | [manufacturer's device, combining the letters Y, D] | [in a concave arc] Made in Britain), smooth, white

Contents: Calendar of fixtures with page references (*1–2*), subscriptions, levy, and tribute (3), general conditions and information (4), official tournaments (5–17), club tournaments (18–46), conditions for invitation events (47), schedule of play for Eights Weeks (47), blank (*48*)

Binding: Very light greenish Blue (171) paper watermarked ([in convex arc] CROXLEY | [in concave arc] **SCRIPT**) wrapped around the edges of the leaves, stapled, no endpapers. FC: as above. Inside FC: blank. RC: blank. Inside RC: blank. Spine: blank

Copy seen: CA

Fingerprint: 3430 n)s. s.m. then 3 1980A [group 1 taken from p *1*]

Notes: Printed anonymously by FH Brown, Burnley, Lancs.

(n) *1981 edition (1981)*

[The FC]

[L justified, flanked on the L by a vertical rule in bold which extends to near the foot, where it makes a right-angle with an extended horizontal rule in bold] **CROQUET** | [*do*] **ASSOCIATION** | [*do*] **FIXTURES** | [in open script] 1981 | [within a circle described by two lines, the outer line in bold, which represents a face of a mallet which stands on the lower horizontal rule and leans against the extended vertical rule] **C.A.**

Formula: [1–24^1]. 24 leaves, pp *1* 2–48

Technical notes: 235 × 176 mm (p 8, ragged). 55 lines, 20 = 85 mm. Leaf size 250 × 200 mm; thickness 0.13 mm; wove, watermarked ([in a convex arc] Superfine Papers | [manufacturer's device, combining the letters Y, D] | [in a concave arc] Made in Britain), smooth, white

Contents: Calendar of fixtures with page references (*1–2*), subscriptions, levy, and tribute (3), general conditions and information (4), official tournaments (5–17), club tournaments (18–47), conditions for invitation events (48), schedule of play for Eights Weeks (48)

Binding: Light Yellow (86) paper wrapped around the edges of the leaves, stapled, no endpapers. FC: as above. Inside FC: blank. RC: blank. Inside RC: blank. Spine: blank

Copy seen: CA

Fingerprint: d.21 n)k) s.ll then 3 1981A [group 1 taken from p *1*]

Notes: Printed anonymously by FH Brown, Burnley, Lancs.

(o) *1982 edition (1982)*

[The FC]

[L justified, flanked on the L by a vertical rule in bold which extends to near the foot, where it makes a right-angle with an extended horizontal rule in bold] **CROQUET** | [*do*] **ASSOCIATION** | [*do*] **FIXTURES** | [in open script] **1982** | [within a circle described by two lines, the outer line in bold, which represents a face of a mallet which stands on the lower horizontal rule and leans against the extended vertical rule] **C.A.**

Formula: [1–25¹]. 25 leaves, pp *1* 2–49 *50*

Technical notes: 232 × 176 mm (p 18, ragged). 54 lines, 20 = 86 mm. Leaf size 254 × 202 mm; thickness 0.11 mm; wove, watermarked (***Plus*** | ***Fabric*** | ***Duplicator***), smooth, white

Contents: Calendar of fixtures with page references (*1–2*), subscriptions, levy, and tribute (3), general conditions and information (4), official tournaments (5–17), club tournaments (18–48), conditions for invitation events (49), schedule of play for Eights Weeks (49), blank (*50*)

Binding: Very pale Green (148) paper wrapped around the edges of the leaves, stapled, no endpapers. FC: as above. Inside FC: blank. RC: blank. Inside RC: blank. Spine: blank

Copy seen: CA

Fingerprint: ly21 5.S. ofed Erfi 3 1982A [group 1 taken from p *1*]

Notes: Printed anonymously by FH Brown, Burnley, Lancs. The copy examined includes a loose leaf of *errata*.

(p) *1983 edition (1983)*

[The FC]

[rule] | • CROQUET ASSOCIATION • | [rule] | • FIXTURES 1983 • | [device of sponsor, Mateus Croquet] | **MATEUS CROQUET**

Formula: [1–28¹]. 28 leaves, pp *1* 2, *i–iv*, 3–52

Technical notes: 241 × 171 mm (p 5, ragged). 57 lines, 20 = 86 mm. Leaf size 254 × 204 mm; thickness 0.13 mm; wove, watermarked (***Plus*** | ***Fabric*** | ***Duplicator***), smooth, white

Contents: Calendar of fixtures with page references (*1–2*), croquet lawns, by Ashley Stephenson (*i–iii*), blank (*iv*), subscriptions, levy, and tribute (3), memorandum (3), general conditions and information (4), official tournaments (5–18), club tournaments (19–51), conditions for invitation events (51), schedule of play for Eights Weeks (52)

Binding: Pale Yellow Green (121) semi-gloss paper printed in moderate Green (145) wrapped around the edges of the leaves, stapled, no endpapers. FC: as above. Inside

FC: blank. RC: ([at the foot] • THE CROQUET ASSOCIATION ACKNOWL-
EDGE WITH GRATEFUL THANKS THE SUPPORT OF MATEUS IN THE
PRODUCTION OF THIS COVER). Inside RC: blank. Spine: blank

Copy seen: CA

Fingerprint: ly22 EKe. e.ll then 3 1983A [group 1 taken from p *1*]

Notes: Printed anonymously by Ward Knowles.

(q) *1984 edition (1984)*

[The FC]

[rule] | • CROQUET ASSOCIATION • | [rule] | • FIXTURES • | 1984 | [device
of sponsor, Mateus Croquet] | **MATEUS CROQUET** | • THE CROQUET
ASSOCIATION ACKNOWLEDGE WITH GRATEFUL THANKS THE
SUPPORT OF MATEUS IN THE PRODUCTION OF THIS COVER •

Formula: [1–29^1]. 29 leaves, pp *i, 1–2 3, ii–iii,* 4–53 *54–55* [= 58]

Technical notes: 234 × 175 mm (p 6, ragged). 56 lines, 20 = 84 mm. Leaf size 254
× 204 mm; thickness 0.12 mm; wove, unwatermarked, smooth, white

Contents: advertisement (*i*), blank (*1*), calendar of fixtures with page references
(*2–3*), advertisement (*ii*), blank (*iii*), subscriptions, levy, and tribute (4), general
conditions and information (5), official tournaments (6–19), club tournaments
(20–52), conditions for invitation events (52), schedule of play for Eights Weeks
(53), advertisement (*54*), blank (*55*)

Binding: Pale Yellow Green (121) semi-gloss paper printed in moderate Green (145)
wrapped around the edges of the leaves, stapled, no endpapers. FC: as above. Inside
FC: blank. RC: blank. Inside RC: blank. Spine: blank

Copy seen: CA

Fingerprint: 42d, K.e. n)s. Te74 C 1984A [groups 1–4 taken from pp *i*, 6, 10, 11
respectively]

Notes: Printed anonymously by Ward Knowles.

(r) *1985 edition (1985)*

[The FC]

CROQUET ASSOCIATION | **FIXTURES** | [in open script] 1985 | [device of
sponsor, The Royal Bank of Scotland] | THE CROQUET ASSOCIATION GRATE-
FULLY ACKNOWLEDGES THE SUPPORT | GIVEN BY THE ROYAL BANK OF
SCOTLAND TO THE GAME OF CROQUET

Formula: [1–29^1]. 29 leaves, pp *i–vi,* 1–50 *51–52*

Technical notes: 238 × 171 mm (p 6, ragged). 56 lines, 20 = 85 mm. Leaf size 296
× 208 mm; thickness 0.12 mm; wove, unwatermarked, smooth, white

Contents: advertisement (*i*), blank (*ii*), advertisement (*iii*), blank (*iv*), calendar of
fixtures with page references (*v–vi*), books available from the CA (1), preface, signed
'Barry Keen' (2), subscriptions, levy, and tribute (3), general conditions and information (3–4), official tournaments (4–20), club tournaments (21–50), tournament
entry form (*51–52*)

Binding: Brilliant greenish Blue (168) Astrolux card printed in deep Blue (179)
wrapped around the edges of the leaves, stapled, no endpapers. FC: as above. Inside
FC: blank. RC: blank. Inside RC: blank. Spine: blank

Copy seen: CA

Fingerprint: esre b.re e.y. <u>CH</u>Lu 3 1985A [group 1 taken from p *i*]

Notes: Printed anonymously by Ward Knowles. The accounts of the CA show that 900 copies were produced. The copy examined contains two loose leaves of *addenda*.

(s) *1986 edition (1986)*

[The FC]

CROQUET ASSOCIATION | FIXTURES | [in open script] **1986 |** [device of sponsor, The Royal Bank of Scotland] **| THE CROQUET ASSOCIATION GRATEFULLY ACKNOWLEDGES THE SUPPORT | GIVEN BY THE ROYAL BANK OF SCOTLAND TO THE GAME OF CROQUET**

Formula: [1–36¹]. 36 leaves, pp i–iii *iv*, 1–9 *10* 11–21 *22* 23–39 *40* 41–62 *63–68*

Technical notes: 254 × 159 mm (p 3, ragged). 61 lines, 20 = 84 mm. Leaf size 297 × 210 mm; thickness 0.12 mm; wove, unwatermarked, smooth, white

Contents: Calendar of fixtures with page references (i–ii), contents (iii), advertisement (*iv*), introduction, signed 'Barry Keen' (1), subscriptions, levy, and tribute (2), general conditions and information (3–4), official tournaments, continued (5–9), advertisement (*10*), official tournaments, continued (11–15), advertisement (16), official tournaments, continued (17–21), advertisement (*22*), official tournaments, concluded (23–25), club tournaments, continued (25–39), advertisement (*40*), club tournaments, concluded (41–60), golf croquet (61), short croquet (62), tournament entry forms (*63–68*)

Binding: Brilliant greenish Blue (168) Astrolux card printed in deep Blue (179) wrapped around the edges of the leaves, stapled, no endpapers. FC: as above. Inside FC: blank. RC: blank. Inside RC: blank. Spine: blank

Copy seen: CA

Fingerprint: 2651 1)he ofy. HoEr 3 1986A [group 1 taken from p i]

Notes: Printed anonymously by Instant Print West One. The accounts of the CA show that 1500 copies were produced at a cost of £1250. This edition was edited by Alan Girling.

(t) *1987 edition (1987)*

[The FC]

CROQUET ASSOCIATION | FIXTURES | 1987

Formula: [1–39¹]. 39 leaves, pp *i–v*, 1–17 *18* 19–41 *42* 43–53 *54* 55–68 *69–73*

Technical notes: 270 × 161 mm (p 16, ragged). 64 lines, 20 = 85 mm. Leaf size 297 × 210 mm; thickness 0.12 mm; wove, unwatermarked, smooth, white

Contents: Calendar of fixtures with page references (*i–ii*), calendar by club (*iii–iv*), contents (*v*), introduction, signed 'Barry Keen' (1), subscriptions, levy, tribute, and silver medals (2), general conditions and information (3–4), representative matches (5–6), invitation events (7–9), Loughborough Summer School (10), championships (11–16), advertisements (*17–18*), national events (19–24), week CA tournaments (25), coaching weekends (26), week club tournaments (27–41), advertisement (*42*), open singles weekends (43–53), advertisement (*54*), handicap weekends (55–65), golf croquet (66), short croquet tournaments (66–68), hoop setting, ball specification, and inspection requirements (69), application forms (*70–73*)

Binding: Very pale Green (148) card front and rear, slotted and bound by a black plastic comb, no endpapers. FC: printed in black as above. Inside FC: blank. RC: blank. Inside RC: blank. Spine: blank

Copy seen: CA

Fingerprint: 3147 t.at r.<u>ns</u> ifCo C 1987A [groups 1–4 taken from pp *i*, 4, 8, 9 respectively]

Notes: Printed anonymously by Instant Print West One. The accounts of the CA show that 900 copies were produced.

(u) *1988 edition (1988)*

[The FC]

[device of the CA, incorporating its name in a convex arc (THE CROQUET ASSOCIATION) and the title (**1988** | **FIXTURES**)]

Formula: [1–41^1]. 41 leaves, pp *i–vi*, 1–10 *11* 12–69 *70–76*

Technical notes: 190 × 121 mm (p 31, ragged). 64 lines, 20 = 60 mm. Leaf size 211 × 149 mm; thickness 0.13 mm; wove, unwatermarked, smooth, white

Contents: Calendar of fixtures with page references (*i–iii*), calendar by club (*iv–v*), contents (*vi*), introduction, signed 'Jan MacLeod' (1), subscriptions, levy, tribute, and silver medals (2), general conditions and information (3–4), representative matches (5–7), invitation events (8–10), advertisement (*11*), championships (12–20), national events (21–23), week CA event (24), week club tournaments (25–37), open singles weekends (38–49), grading system (50), coaching courses (51), Loughborough summer school (52), handicap weekends (53–62), golf croquet (63–64), short croquet tournaments (65–69), hoop setting, ball specification, and inspection requirements (*70*), pegging down sheet (*71–72*), application forms (*73–76*)

Binding: Very pale Green (148) card front and rear, slotted and bound by a black plastic comb, no endpapers. FC: printed in black as above. Inside FC: blank. RC: blank. Inside RC: blank. Spine: blank

Copy seen: CA

Fingerprint: er13 tdn. d.t. Ev2. 3 1988A [group 1 taken from p *i*]

Notes: Printed anonymously by Instant Print West One. The accounts of the CA show that 1350 copies were produced.

(v) *1989 edition (1989)*

The Croquet Association | [device of the CA] | Fixtures List 1989 | Published by: The Croquet Association | The Hurlingham Club | Ranelagh Gardens | London SW6 3PR | Revised & Typeset by: Jane Rogers | Edited by: John Walters | AT TOWNSEND CROQUET | Co-ordinated by: Keith Aiton | CA TOURNAMENTS CHAIRMAN

Formula: [1–58^1]. 58 leaves, pp *i–xii*, 1–69 *70* 12–69 *70* 71–98 *99–104*

Technical notes: 175 × 112 mm (p 11, ragged). 60 lines, 20 = 59 mm. Leaf size 205 × 146 mm; thickness 0.12 mm; wove, unwatermarked, smooth, white

Contents: Notice (*i*), blank (*ii*), title (*iii*), calendar of fixtures with page references (*iv–vi*), calendar by club (*vii–ix*), contents (*x–xi*), advertisement (*xi*), blank (*xii*), introduction, signed 'Keith M.H. Aiton' (1–2), subscriptions, levy, and tribute (2–3), silver medals and award scheme (4–5), general conditions and information (6–7), representative matches (8–12), invitation events (12–16), championships (17–29), national events (30–34), week CA events (35–36), week club tournaments (37–53), open singles weekends (54–68), grading system (69), advertisement (*70*), handicap weekends (71–86), golf croquet (87–88), short croquet tournaments (89–94), coaching courses (95), summer schools (96), hoop setting, ball specification, and inspection requirements (97–98), pegging down sheet (99–100), application forms (*101–104*)

Binding: Light greenish Yellow (101) card, scored for hinges front and rear, glued to the edges of the leaves, no endpapers. FC: printed in black ([device of the CA, incorporating its name in a convex arc (THE CROQUET ASSOCIATION) and the title (**1989** | **FIXTURES**). Inside FC: blank. RC: blank. Inside RC: blank. Spine: blank

Copy seen: CA

Fingerprint: 1919   s.A.   r.ns   AsCo   3   1989A   [group 1 taken from the second column of p *v*]

Notes: Printed anonymously.

(w) *1990 edition (1990)*

The Croquet Association | [device of the CA] | Fixtures List 1990 | **Published by: The Croquet Association | The Hurlingham Club | Ranelagh Gardens | London SW6 3PR | Typed and Edited by D.L.Gaunt**

Formula: [1–60¹]. 60 leaves, pp *1–2*, i–viii, 1–99 *100–110*

Technical notes: 164 × 113 mm (p 9, ragged). 55 lines, 20 = 60 mm. Leaf size 209 × 147 mm; thickness 0.10 mm; wove, unwatermarked, smooth, white

Contents: Title (*1*), advertisement (*2*), contents (i–ii), editor's note (ii), calendar of fixtures with page references (iii–viii), subscriptions and levy (1–2), grading system (2), silver medals and award scheme (3–4), general conditions and information (4–6), representative matches (7–10), invitation events (11–16), championships (17–29), national club events (30–36), week CA events (35–36), week tournaments (37–55), open singles weekends (56–71), handicap weekends (72–87), golf croquet (88–89), short croquet tournaments (90–96), coaching courses (97), summer schools (98–99), hoop setting, ball specification, and inspection requirements (99–100), tournament entry forms (*101–110*)

Binding: Very pale Green (148) card, scored for hinges front and rear, glued to the edges of the leaves, no endpapers. FC: printed in black ([device of the CA, incorporating its name in a convex arc (THE CROQUET ASSOCIATION) and the title (**1990** | **FIXTURES**). Inside FC: blank. RC: blank. Inside RC: blank. Spine: blank

Copy seen: CA

Fingerprint: ndld   r.ip   r.ns   CoCo   3   1990A

Notes: Printed anonymously.

(x) *1991 edition (1991)*

The Croquet Association | [device of the CA] | Fixtures List 1991 | **Published by: The Croquet Association | The Hurlingham Club | Ranelagh Gardens | London SW6 3PR | Typed and Edited by D.L.Gaunt**

Formula: [1–55¹]. 55 leaves, pp *1–2*, i–x, 1–83 *84–98*

Technical notes: 165 × 105 mm (p 8, ragged). 55 lines, 20 = 60 mm. Leaf size 209 × 147 mm; thickness 0.10 mm; wove, unwatermarked, smooth, white

Contents: Title (*1*), blank (*2*), contents (i–ii), editor's note (ii), letter to reader, signed 'Nigel Aspinall' (iii), calendar of fixtures with page references (iv–vii), calendar by club (viii–x), subscriptions and levy (1–2), grading system (2), silver medals and award scheme (3–4), general conditions and information (4–6), representative matches (7–9), invitation events (10–13), championships (14–26), national club events (27–33), week CA events (34–36), club events (37–75), golf croquet (76–77), The Garden Croquet Classic (78–79), coaching courses (80), summer schools (81), hoop setting, ball specification, and inspection requirements (82–83), regulations for best-of-five matches (83), blank (*84*), entry form for national club events (*85–86*), notice of availability for invitation events (*87–88*), tournament entry forms (*89–98*)

Binding: Very pale Green (148) card, scored for hinges front and rear, glued to the edges of the leaves, no endpapers. FC: printed in black ([device of the CA, incorporating its name in a convex arc (THE CROQUET ASSOCIATION) and the title (**1991** | **FIXTURES**). Inside FC: blank. RC: blank. Inside RC: blank. Spine: blank

Copy seen: CA

Fingerprint: ntnt epun).he cois 3 1991A [group 2 taken from the column of dates on p ix]

Notes: Printed anonymously.

(y) *1992 edition (1992)*

The Croquet Association | [device of the CA] | Fixtures List 1992 | **Published by: The Croquet Association | The Hurlingham Club | Ranelagh Gardens | London SW6 3PR | Typed and Edited by D.L.Gaunt**

Formula: [1–53¹]. 53 leaves, pp *1–2*, i–xii, 1, xiv xiii, *2–84 85–86* [*87–88*] *89–90* [= 106]

Technical notes: 172 × 107 mm (p 9, ragged). 58 lines, 20 = 60 mm. Leaf size 210 × 148 mm; thickness 0.09 mm; wove, unwatermarked, smooth, white

Contents: Title (*1*), advertisement (*2*), contents (i–ii), editor's notes (ii), sundry information (iii–vii), calendar of fixtures with page references (viii–xi), calendar by club, continued (xii), subscriptions and levy, continued (1), calendar by club, concluded (xiv, xiii), subscriptions and levy, concluded (2), grading system (2), silver medals and award scheme (3–4), general conditions and information (4–6), representative matches (7–10), invitation events (10–13), championships (14–26), national club events (27–33), week CA events (34–36), club events (37–76), golf croquet (77–78), The Garden Croquet Classic (79–80), coaching courses (81), summer schools (82), hoop setting, ball specification, and inspection requirements (82–83), regulations for best-of-five matches (84), tournament entry forms, continued (*85–86*), wanting from the copy examined ([*87–88*]), tournament entry forms, concluded (*89–90*)

Binding: White card, scored for hinges front and rear, glued to the edges of the leaves, no endpapers. FC: printed in black ([device of the CA, incorporating its name in a convex arc (THE CROQUET ASSOCIATION), intersected by device of the sponsor, Angostura aromatic bitters] | 1992 | FIXTURES). Inside FC: blank. RC: advertisement. Inside RC: blank. Spine: blank

Copy seen: CA (imperfect, wanting pp [*87–88*])

Fingerprint: ntrs 6848 r.ip epug C 1992A [group 1 taken from p i, group 2 taken from the extreme R column of p ix, group 3 taken from p 1, group 4 taken from the column of dates on p xiv]

Notes: Printed anonymously. It will be noted that the collation of the copy examined is anomalous.

(z) *1993 edition (1993)*

The Croquet Association | [device of the CA] | Fixtures List 1993 | **Published by: The Croquet Association | The Hurlingham Club | Ranelagh Gardens | London SW6 3PR | Typed and Edited by D.L.Gaunt**

Formula: [1–49¹]. 49 leaves, pp *1*, i–xi, 1–82 *83–86* [= 98]

Technical notes: 166 × 115 mm (p 8, ragged). 56 lines, 20 = 60 mm. Leaf size 216 × 153 mm; thickness 0.11 mm; wove, unwatermarked, smooth, white

Contents: Title (*1*), contents (i–ii), editor's notes (ii), calendar of fixtures with page references (iii–vi), calendar by club (vii–x), introduction, signed 'John Walters' (x–xi), subscriptions and levy (1–2), grading system (2), silver medals and award scheme (3–4), general conditions and information (4–6), representative matches (7–9), invitation events (10–13), championships (14–25), national club events (26–32), advertisement (32), CA week events (33–35), club events (36–74), golf croquet (75–76), The Garden Croquet Classic (77–78), coaching courses (79), summer schools and refereeing courses (80), hoop setting, ball specification, and inspection requirements (81–82), tournament entry forms (*83–86*)

Binding: Yellowish White (92) card glued to the edges of the leaves, no endpapers. FC: printed in black ([device of the CA, incorporating its name in a convex arc (THE CROQUET ASSOCIATION) and the title (1993 | FIXTURES). Inside FC: blank. RC: blank. Inside RC: blank. Spine: blank

Copy seen: CA

Fingerprint: H.d. u.of r.ip B.Wo C 1993A [groups 1–4 taken from pp ii, x, 1, 2 respectively]

Notes: Printed anonymously.

(aa) *1994 edition (1994)*

[set centrally within the outline of a folded ribbon] FIXTURES LIST 1994 | [device of the CA] | Published by: The Croquet Association | The Hurlingham Club | Ranelagh Gardens | London SW6 3PR | [R justified] Typed and edited by D.L.Gaunt

Formula: [1–50¹]. 50 leaves, pp *1*, i–xi, 1–82 *83–86* [87–88] [= 100]

Technical notes: 166 × 114 mm (p 2, ragged). 57 lines, 20 = 58 mm. Leaf size 210 × 147 mm; thickness 0.11 mm; wove, unwatermarked, smooth, white

Contents: Title (*1*), contents (i–ii), editor's notes (ii), calendar of fixtures with page references (iii–vi), calendar by club (vii–x), introduction (xi), subscriptions and levy (1–2), grading system (2), silver medals and award scheme (2–4), general conditions and information (4–6), representative matches (7–10), invitation events (10–13), championships (14–24), national club events (25–31), CA week events (31–33), advertisement (33), club events (34–75), notice to club secretaries (75), golf croquet (76–77), The Garden Croquet Classic (78), coaching courses (79), summer schools and refereeing courses (80), hoop setting, ball specification, and inspection requirements (81–82), tournament entry forms (*83–86*), wanting from the copy examined ([87–88])

Binding: Strong reddish Orange (35) card, scored for hinges front and rear, glued to the edges of the leaves, no endpapers. FC: printed in black ([device of the CA, incorporating its name in a convex arc (THE CROQUET ASSOCIATION) and the title (1994 | FIXTURES). Inside FC: blank. RC: blank. Inside RC: blank. Spine: blank

Copy seen: CA (imperfect, wanting pp [87–88])

Fingerprint: H.d. epug t3t2 then 3 1994A [group 1 taken from p ii, group 2 taken from p x, group 3 taken from the L column of the table on p 13]

Notes: Printed anonymously. The copy examined contains two loose A4 folded leaves of *addenda*, headed 'AMENDMENTS TO THE 1994 FIXTURES LIST' and 'THE 5th WORLD CROQUET CHAMPIONSHIP'.

(bb) *1995 edition (1995)*

[set centrally within a rectangular frame composed of small five-pointed stars]
FIXTURES LIST 1995 | [device of the CA] | Published by: The Croquet Association
| The Hurlingham Club | Ranelagh Gardens | London SW6 3PR | [R justified] Typed
and edited by D.L.Gaunt

Formula: [1–52^1]. 52 leaves, pp *1*, i–xi, 1–85 *86–92* [= 104]

Technical notes: 166 × 114 mm (p 3, ragged). 57 lines, 20 = 58 mm. Leaf size 210
× 149 mm; thickness 0.10 mm; wove, unwatermarked, smooth, white

Contents: Title (*1*), contents (i–ii), editor's notes (ii), calendar of fixtures with page
references (iii–vi), calendar by club (vii–x), advertisement (x), introduction, signed
'D W Shaw' (xi), notice by the chairman of the trophies committee, signed in MS
'A. Oldham', but apparently not in his hand (xi), subscriptions and levy (1–2),
grading system (2), silver medals and award scheme (2–4), general conditions
and information (4–6), representative matches (7–9), invitation events (10–12),
championships (13–23), national club events (24–30), advertisement (30), CA week
events (31–32), club events (33–75), notice to club secretaries (75), advertisement
(75), golf croquet (76–78), The Garden Croquet Classic (79), courses and summer
schools (80–83), hoop setting, ball specification, and inspection requirements
(84–85), advertisement (85), blank (86), tournament entry forms (*87–92*)

Binding: Moderate yellowish Green (136) card, scored for hinges front and rear,
glued to the edges of the leaves, no endpapers. FC: printed in black ([device of the
CA, incorporating its name in a convex arc (THE CROQUET ASSOCIATION)
and the title (**1995** | FIXTURES). Inside FC: blank. RC: blank. Inside RC: blank.
Spine: blank

Copy seen: CA

Fingerprint: 07H. 1.nt s.e. beEx 3 1995A

Notes: Printed anonymously.

(cc) *1996 edition (1996)*

[set centrally within a decorative frame] **FIXTURES LIST 1996** | [device of the CA]
| Published by: The Croquet Association | The Hurlingham Club | Ranelagh
Gardens | London SW6 3PR | Tel: 0171-736-3148 | [R justified] Typed and edited by
D.L.Gaunt

Formula: [1–51^1]. 51 leaves, pp *1*, i–xi, 1–84 *85–90*

Technical notes: 160 × 108 mm (p 5, ragged). 57 lines, 20 = 56 mm. Leaf size 210
× 147 mm; thickness 0.10 mm; wove, unwatermarked, smooth, white

Contents: Title (*1*), contents (i–ii), editor's notes (ii), calendar of fixtures with page
references (iii–vi), calendar by club (vii–x), advertisement (x), introduction, signed
'D W Shaw' (xi), notice by the chairman of the trophies committee, signed
'A.Oldham' (xi), subscriptions and levy (1–2), grading system (2), silver medals and
award scheme (2–4), general conditions and information (4–6), representative
matches (7–9), invitation events (10–12), championships (13–24), international
events (25), advertisement (25), national club events (26–32), CA week events
(33–35), notice and advertisement (35), club events (36–74), advertisement (74), golf
croquet (75–77), The Garden Croquet Classic (78), courses and summer schools
(79–83), hoop setting, ball specification, and inspection requirements (83–84), tournament entry forms (*85–90*)

Binding: Very light greenish Blue (171) card, scored for hinges front and rear, glued
to the edges of the leaves, no endpapers. FC: printed in black ([device of the CA,

incorporating its name in a convex arc (THE CROQUET ASSOCIATION) and the title (1996 | FIXTURES). Inside FC: blank. RC: blank. Inside RC: blank. Spine: blank

Copy seen: CA

Fingerprint: 07H. e.YB ndof acsp 3 1996A

Notes: Printed anonymously.

(dd) *1997 edition (1997)*

FIXTURES LIST 1997 | [1997 centenary device of the CA] | Published by: The Croquet Association | The Hurlingham Club | Ranelagh Gardens | London SW6 3PR | Tel/Fax 0171-736 3148 | [R justified] Typed and edited by DL Gaunt

Formula: [1–54¹]. 54 leaves, pp *i* ii–xii, 1–91 92–96

Technical notes: 166 × 115 mm (p 14, ragged). 56 lines, 20 = 59 mm. Leaf size 210 × 147 mm; thickness 0.10 mm; wove, unwatermarked, smooth, white

Contents: Title (*i*), contents (ii–iii), editor's notes (iii), calendar of fixtures with page references (iv–vii), calendar by club (viii–xi), advertisement (xi), introduction, signed 'Bill Arliss' (xii), notice by the chairman of the trophies committee, signed 'A.Oldham' (xii), subscriptions and levy (1–2), grading system (2), silver medals and award scheme (2–4), general conditions and information (4–6), notice to club secretaries (6), centenary celebration with introduction, signed 'Stephen Badger' (7–10), advertisement (10), representative matches (11–13), invitation events (14–16), championships (17–30), international events, continued (30), advertisement (30), international events, concluded (31), advertisement (31), national club events (32–37), CA week events (38–40), notice and advertisement (40), club events, continued (41–65), advertisement (66), club events, continued (67–70), advertisements (71), club events, concluded (72–82), advertisement (82), golf croquet (83–85), courses and summer schools (86–90), hoop setting, ball specification, and inspection requirements (90–91), tournament entry forms (92–94), blank (95–96)

Binding: High-gloss laminated gold Astrolux card, scored for hinges front and rear, glued to the edges of the leaves, no endpapers. FC: printed in black ([1997 centenary device of the CA] | 1997 FIXTURES). Inside FC: blank. RC: blank. Inside RC: blank. Spine: blank

Copy seen: PC

Fingerprint:).H. e.YB k.es frth 3 1997A

Notes: Printed anonymously.

(ee) *1998 edition (1998)*

[within a panel framed by an ornamental border] FIXTURES LIST 1998 | [device of the CA] | Published by: The Croquet Association | The Hurlingham Club | Ranelagh Gardens | London SW6 3PR | Tel: 0171-736-3148 | Email: caoffice@ croquet.org.uk | [R justified] Typed and edited by D.L. Gaunt

Formula: [1–52¹]. 52 leaves, pp *i* ii–xvii, 1–79 80–87

Technical notes: 170 × 115 mm (p 8, ragged). 57 lines, 20 = 60 mm. Leaf size 210 × 148 mm; thickness 0.10 mm; wove, unwatermarked, smooth, white

Contents: Title (*i*), contents (ii–iii), editor's notes (iii), calendar of fixtures with page references (iv–ix), advertisement (ix), calendar by club (x–xiii), introduction, signed 'Bill Arliss', and notice by the chairman of the trophies committee, signed 'A.Oldham' (xiv), advertisements (*xv–xvii*), subscriptions and levy (1), grading system and silver medals (2), award scheme (3), general conditions and information (3–5), notice to club secretaries (5), representative matches (6–9), invitation events (9–11), championships (12–24), national club events (25–28), other CA events (29–31), notice and advertisement (31), club events (32–67), golf croquet events (68–71), short croquet events (72–73), courses and summer schools (74–78), hoop setting, ball specification, and inspection requirements (78–79), tournament entry and availability forms (*80–87*)

Binding: Pale yellowish Pink (31) card, scored for hinges front and rear, glued to the edges of the leaves, no endpapers. FC: printed in black ([device of the CA] | **Fixture Booklet** | **1998**). Inside FC: blank. RC: blank. Inside RC: blank. Spine: blank

Copy seen: PC

Fingerprint:).H. alEY almp CA5. 3 1998A

Notes: Printed anonymously.

1971

A184   CROQUET ANCIENT AND MODERN. Eng-Lt-Comdr A Clark   1971

C R O Q U E T | ANCIENT   AND   MODERN | BY | Engnr.-Lieut.-Comndr, A. Clark | S.A. Open Champion 1954 | S.A. Open Doubles Champion 1952, 1954, 1961. | Silver & Bronze Medallist.

Formula: [1^{10}]. 10 leaves, pp *i–iv*, 1–14 *15–16*

Technical notes: 181 × 140 mm (p 3, ragged). 43 lines, 20 = 84 mm; thickness 0.09 mm; wove, unwatermarked, smooth, white

Contents: Title (*i*), dedication (*ii*), contents (*iii*), author's preface, signed 'Alexander Clark' (*iv*), text (1–14), blank (*15–16*)

Binding: White card, stapled, no spine or endpapers. FC: line drawing of a croquet trophy bordered by the title ([in artist's script, respectively across and down the head, L, foot, and R] CROQUET | ANCIENT | AND | MODERN) within a double-ruled frame with concave corners. Inside FC: blank. RC: blank. Inside RC: blank

Copy seen: PC

Fingerprint: r.s. nda, eyle ExBe 3 1971Q

Notes: Published and printed anonymously.

**AA185 LAWNPLAY: CROQUET [and LAWNPLAY: CROQUET AND   1971
OTHER OUTDOOR FAMILY GAMES]. [Anon]**

(a) **First edition (1971)*

[Page *1*]

[in black over a photograph of a game of backyard croquet] ninety-seventh anniversary **1971** [in white out of the foregoing photograph, the title but not the sub-title in MS-style script] *Lawnplay*$_®$ [sub-title] **CROQUET** | [in white out of illustration] **BY SOUTH BEND** | [*do*] A MILTON BRADLEY COMPANY | [*do*] For Family Fun in Outdoor Living | [photo-vignettes of two croquet sets in trolley stands, separated by a column of descriptive copy extending to 42 lines] | SOUTH BEND TOY MANUFACTURING COMPANY, INC. | A Milton Bradley Company, South Bend, Indiana 46623 © 1970 South Bend Toy Mfg. Co., Inc. Under Berne Universal Copyright Convention.

Formula: Not ascertainable from the photocopy examined. 6 leaves, unnumbered [ff 1–6] and 4 additional smaller leaves, unnumbered [ff i–iv], which apparently form a species of spine

Technical notes: †272 × †209 mm (p *1*, ragged). 97 lines, 20 = †56 mm. Pp *1–6*: leaf size †275 × †215mm. Pp *i–iv*: leaf size †72 × †275 mm

Contents: Title (*1*), text (*1–4*), price list No 160, 2 September 1970 (*5–6*, loose), half-title (*i*), photograph of the publisher's factory and a summary of its croquet product range (*ii–iii*), addresses and telephone numbers of the company's office sites (*iv*)

Binding: Not ascertainable from the photocopy examined

Copy seen: HPC: RRCC #461 CROQ (photocopy)

Fingerprint: **C. s.r- ors. edne C 1971A [all four groups taken from p *3*]

Notes: Printed anonymously. Some of the croquet sets illustrated in the text include what appear to be copies of an earlier version of this trade catalogue.

(b) *1975 edition (1975)*

[Page *1*, apparently out of a plain background]

[in white] 1975 | [publisher's device and, in black] *Lawnplay* ® | [in white out of plain background] **CROQUET and OTHER OUTDOOR FAMILY GAMES** | [photograph of merchandising unit stocked with the publisher's boxed products] | [two framed photographs of outdoor family games] | [between photographs of two more indoor family games, in white out of plain background] OVER ONE HUNDRED YEARS | [*do*] OF QUALITY AND PROGRESS | [*do*] IN OUTDOOR FAMILY GAMES | [in white out of plain background] SOUTH BEND TOY MFG. CO. INC., A MILTON BRADLEY COMPANY, SOUTH BEND, INDIANA 46628 | [*do*] © 1974 South Bend Toy Mfg. Co. Inc. Under Berne & Universal Copyright Convention

Formula: Not ascertainable from the photocopy examined. 4 pp, unnumbered [pp 1–4]

Technical notes: †251 × †200 mm (p 2). 107 lines, 20 = †47 mm. Leaf size †276 × †209 mm

Contents: Title (*1*), text (*1–4*)

Binding: Not ascertainable from the photocopy examined

Copy seen: HPC: RRCC #461 CROQ (photocopy)

Fingerprint: s.n, edor **G—s. eds. C 1975A [all four groups taken from the L column of p *3*]

Notes: Printed anonymously.

1973

A186   **COMMENTARY ON THE LAWS OF CROQUET. DMC Prichard   1973
[fifth edition revised by Bill Lamb]**

(a) *First edition (1973)*

Not seen. The publication of this work in 1973 is well documented in the archives of the CA.

(b) *Revised edition (1973)*

[The FC]

COMMENTARY | ON THE LAWS | OF | CROQUET | BY | D. M. C. PRICHARD | 1973 | REVISED EDITION

Formula: [1¹⁸]. 18 leaves, pp *1–4 5–36*

Technical notes: 177 × 101 mm (p 8). 42 lines, 20 = 84 mm. Leaf size 216 × 139 mm; thickness 0.10 mm; wove, unwatermarked, smooth, white

Contents: Contents (*1–2*), introduction (*3–4*), text (*5–36*)

Binding: Brilliant Yellow (83) light card, stapled, no spine or endpapers. FC: printed in black (as above). Inside FC: blank. RC: blank. Inside RC: blank

Copy seen: PC

Fingerprint: 2118 :-". d.or thco 3 1973A

Notes: Published and printed anonymously.

(c) *Fourth revised edition (1984)*

[Page *i*]

COMMENTARY | ON THE LAWS | OF | CROQUET | BY | D.M.C. PRICHARD | 1984 | FOURTH REVISED EDITION

Formula: [1–34¹]. 34 leaves, ff *i–ii, 1 2–32*

Technical notes: 271 × 166 mm (p 6, ragged). 65 lines, 20 = 84 mm. Leaf size 297 × 210 mm; thickness 0.11 mm; wove, unwatermarked, smooth, white

Contents: Title (*i*), contents (*ii–1*), preface (*2*), introduction (*3*), text (*4–32*)

Binding: In a black extruded plastic binder, no wrapper or endpapers

Copy seen: CA

Fingerprint: 2121 w.he o.ll heil C 1984A [group 4 taken from f 13]

Notes: Produced in typescript, printed anonymously by a photographic process, probably in-house by the CA.

(d) *Fourth revised edition, re-issue [1984]*

[Page *i*]

COMMENTARY | ON THE LAWS | OF | CROQUET | BY | D.M.C. PRICHARD | 1984 | FOURTH REVISED EDITION

Formula: [1¹⁸]. 18 leaves, pp *i–iii, 1 2–5 6 7–24 25 26–32 33*

Technical notes: 191 × 124 mm (p 6, ragged). 64 lines, 20 = 60 mm. Leaf size 210 × 148 mm; thickness 0.10 mm; wove, unwatermarked, smooth, white

Contents: Title (*i*), contents (*ii–iii*), blank (*1*), preface (*2*), introduction (*3*), text (*4–32*), blank (*33*)

Binding: None

Copy seen: CA

Fingerprint: 3130 w.es).ed maun C 1984Q [group 1 taken from p *iii*, group 2 taken from p 8, group 3 taken from p 14, group 4 taken from p 15]

Notes: Produced in typescript, printed anonymously by a photographic process at reduced scale, probably in-house by the CA. The script is new, and was apparently produced by a photographic process, varying (c) to incorporate minor corrections.

(e) *Fifth edition (1996)*

[The FC]

[publisher's device] | **COMMENTARY** | **ON THE** | **LAWS OF CROQUET** | **by** | **D.M.C. Prichard** | **1996 Fifth Edition (revised by Bill Lamb)**

Formula: [1¹⁸]. 18 leaves, pp *1–2 3–36*

Technical notes: 174 × 126 mm (p 9). 42 lines, 20 = 84 mm. Leaf size 210 × 139 mm; thickness 0.10 mm; wove, unwatermarked, smooth, white

Contents: Title and assertion of copyright (*1*), contents (*1–2*), introduction, signed 'Bill Lamb' (*3*), blank save pagination (*4*), text (*5–36*)

Binding: Deep yellowish Pink (27) card, stapled, no spine or endpapers. FC: as above, printed in black. Inside FC: blank. RC: blank. Inside RC: blank

Copy seen: PC

Fingerprint: 1515 beed uphe plst 3 1996A [group 1 taken from p *1*]

Notes: Published by the CA, printed by Kall Kwik, price £5 to Associates. It is believed that the initial print run was of 500 copies. Copyright is vested in the CA.

A187   CROQUET. [GN Aspinall, BG Neal, JW Solomon, and RW Bray]   1973

[Mostly L justified]

[R justified] **Croquet** | [publisher's device] | **Training Associates** | 41 Paradise Walk, London SW3 4JW | Telephone 01-351 1151 | **A member of the Talking Pictures Group**

[TP verso, L justified]

Published–1973 | © Training Associates 1973 | World Copyright reserved | I.S.B.N. 0 85961 005 5 | [...] | Printed in England by National Westminster Bank, Stationery Office   TA6

Formula: [1⁴⁸]. 48 leaves, pp *i–iv*, *1–90 91–92*

Technical notes: 193 × 131 mm (p 2). Most of the text divided into two columns, the R column consisting of illustrative black-and-white photographs (some with legends), the L column consisting of explanation. 46 lines, 20 = 84 mm. Leaf size 213 × 150 mm; thickness 0.09 mm; wove, unwatermarked, semi-gloss, white

Contents: Title (*i*), TP verso (*ii*), foreword, signed in MS 'Peter Lawson' (*iii*), introduction, signed 'ROGER BRAY' (*iv*), text (*1–90*), blank (*91–92*)

Binding: White semi-gloss card, stapled, no spine or endpapers. FC: the title *etc* ([publisher's device] **National Westminster Bank Sport Coaching Series** | [R justified] **Croquet**) set in black on a broad vivid Green (139) upper panel, above a three-by-three array of square colour photographs representing nine sports, the price (**35p**) set in black above the lower edge of the lower R illustration. Inside FC: advertisement for Coaching Books in the same series. RC: ([publisher's device in black at L] | [a three-by-three array of square colour photographs representing nine sports] | [at R in black] I.S.B.N.   0 85961 005 5). Inside RC: notes on Audio-Visual Sport Coaching Programme

Copy seen: PC

Fingerprint: onry l.he s.is 2.1. 3 1973A

Notes: Printed by National Westminster Bank, Stationery Office, price 35p. This work was also issued by Training Associates in the form of 35 mm single-frame colour filmstrips with synchronised sound on standard compact cassettes.

AA188 CROQUET & CROQUET POOL. [Anon]   1973

[The FC]

[R of publisher's device, printed in vivid purplish Blue (194) and vivid Red (11) on a white ellipse out of a Blue horizontal band] **CROQUET &** | [*do*] **CROQUET POOL** | [in white out of Red] *for leisure-time, outdoor family fun* | [in white out of

Blue] *and other Forster leisure-time products* | [in white out of Red] **FORSTER MFG. CO., INC. WILTON, MAINE 04294 U.S.A.**

Formula: One M-fold leaf. Pages *A* B–F [lettered in order of the contours of the letter *M*, reading from L to R: *A* E D H G C B F]

Technical notes: 367 × 189 mm (p B). 119 lines, 20 = 62 mm. Leaf size 280 × 200 mm; thickness 0.11 mm; wove, unwatermarked, semi-gloss, white

Contents: Title (*A*), text, continued (B–E), text, continued, and surrogate TP verso (F), text, concluded (G–H)

Binding: None

Copy seen: HPC: RRCC #400 CROQ

Fingerprint: s.es H:d. S:e. e,K: C 1973A [all four groups taken from p B]

Notes: Printed anonymously, dated December 1973.

A189   OLD-TIME CROQUET IN HIGHLAND COUNTY, OHIO.   1973
'Harry of Carmel'

Old-time Croquet | *in* | **Highland County, Ohio.** | *by* | "Harry of Carmel" | • • • | [publisher's device: twin trees in silhouette set at the ends of a long rule] | [in gothic-revival script] Rhodopress of Ashland ◆ Ashland, Ohio. | 1973

Formula: [1⁸]. 8 leaves, unnumbered [pp 1–16]

Technical notes: 93 × 76 mm (p *4*). 22 lines, 20 = 84 mm. Leaf size 132 × 108 mm; thickness 0.17 mm; wove, unwatermarked, rough, white

Contents: Title (*1*), TP verso (*2*), introduction, signed 'Rendell Rhoades', 1 September 1973 (*3–5*), text, signed 'Harry of Carmel' (*6–9*), text (other items) (*10–14*), name of publisher and printer (*15*), blank (*16*)

Binding: Pale orange Yellow (73) laid paper, stapled, no spine or endpapers. FC: reproduction of the TP in deep yellowish Green (137). Inside FC: blank. RC: facsimile of text (advertisement) on p *10*, in Green. Inside RC: blank

Copy seen: CA

Fingerprint: ngn- 0.*s*, edy, *Hi*EA 3 1973A

Notes: Published and printed by Rhodopress of Ashland, Ashland, Ohio.

This work, evidently edited by R Rhoades, reprints contributions on croquet — principally an article in *Highland Weekly News* (8 September 1870) by a regular columnist 'Harry of Carmel' — which appeared in various Highland County newspapers during the years 1870–86.

A190   PROCEEDINGS OF THE CHICAGO CROQUET CONVENTION.   1973
MC Reifsnider *et al*

Proceedings | *of the* | **Chicago Croquet Convention** | *held at* | **The Palmer House.** | September 23-24, 1879. | M. C. Reifsnider, Sec'y. | [publisher's device: twin trees in silhouette set at the ends of a long rule] | [in gothic-revival script] Rhodopress of Ashland ◆ Ashland, Ohio. | 1973

[TP verso]

[the lettering set within a diagram of a croquet lawn, each hoop represented by an inverted letter U and each stake by a letter I] *The Croquet Series.* | [do] *One of fifty copies.*

Formula: [1⁶]. 6 leaves, unnumbered [pp 1–16]

Technical notes: 98 × 76 mm (p 6). 24 lines, 20 = 84 mm. Leaf size 132 × 108 mm; thickness 0.18 mm; wove, unwatermarked, rough, white

Contents: Title (*1*), TP verso (*2*), foreword, quoting announcement, signed 'Rendell Rhoades', 20 November 1973 (*3*), text (convention of croquet players) (*4–8*), text (the convention ended) (*9–10*), sources of text (*11*), blank (*12*)

Binding: Very pale Green (148) card, stapled, no spine or endpapers. FC: reproduction of the TP in black. Inside FC: blank. RC: advertisement. Inside RC: blank

Copy Seen: CA

Fingerprint: tone anp- tes- t.h- C 1973A [all groups taken from p *3*]

Notes: Published and printed by Rhodopress of Ashland, Ashland, Ohio. Edited by Rendell Rhoades.

The text reprints articles in the *Chicago Tribune* (31 August 1879, 24 September 1879, 25 September 1879).

1974

A191   THAT CONFOUNDED CROQUET. 'Knickolas Knickerbocker'   1974

That | Confounded Croquet. | [flourish] | *By* | Knickolas Knickerbocker | • • • • | [publisher's device: twin trees in silhouette set at the ends of a long rule] | [in gothic-revival script] Rhodopress of Ashland ◆ Ashland, Ohio. | 1974

[TP verso]

Rhodopress of Ashland | May 20, 1974. | [the lettering set within a diagram of a croquet lawn, each hoop represented by an inverted letter U and each stake by a letter I] *The Croquet Series.* | [*do*] *One of fifty copies.* | From *The New York Times*, 1872 | and 1877, with illustrations from *Punch* (1869 and 1873).

Formula: [1¹²]. 12 leaves, unnumbered [pp 1–24]

Technical notes: 93 × 76 mm (p 6). 22 lines, 20 = 84 mm. Leaf size 132 × 107 mm; thickness 0.17 mm; wove, unwatermarked, rough, white

Contents: Blank (*1*), frontispiece (engraving entitled 'The curate's game') (*2*), title (*3*), TP verso (*4*), text ('The curate's game') (*5–9*), text ('Croquet & conciliation') (*10–17*), text ('Rev. Mr. Israels' fall') (*18–24*)

Binding: Very pale Green (148) smooth card, stapled, no spine or endpapers. FC: printed in black within a triple-ruled frame in dark reddish Orange (38) ([at R] THAT | [the letter *C*, serving as the initial letter for this line and the following line, in artist's shaded script, containing an engraved illustration of a man in clerical dress instructing a young woman player] [C]*onfounded* | [C]*roquet* • | By KNICKOLAS KNICKERBOCKER | • • • • • | [publisher's device: twin trees in silhouette set at the ends of a long rule] | [in gothic-revival script] Rhodopress of Ashland ◆ Ashland, Ohio. | 1974). Inside FC: blank. RC: blank. Inside RC: blank

Copy seen: CA

Fingerprint: etw- a-ed *6.m-* bewa 7 1974A

Notes: Published, on 20 May 1974, and printed by Rhodopress of Ashland, Ashland, Ohio.

This work reprints articles which appeared in *The New York Times* (8 August 1872, 14 December 1877, 3 September 1877). None of these articles contain any reference to the pseudonymous author.

1975

A192   BASIC LAWS OF CROQUET [and BASIESE WETTE VAN   1975
CROQUET]. BG Neal

(a) *First edition (1975)*

BASIC LAWS OF | [in shaded display script] **Association Croquet** | [*do*] AND
GOLF CROQUET | by B. G. NEAL | FIRST EDITION | *Published by* | THE
CROQUET ASSOCIATION | THE HURLINGHAM CLUB, LONDON, S.W.6 | 1975

Formula: [1⁸]. 8 leaves, pp *i–ii* iii *iv* v, 6–16

Technical notes: 128 × 84 mm (p 12). 46 lines, 20 = 56 mm. Leaf size 164 × 104
mm; thickness 0.08 mm; wove, unwatermarked, smooth, white

Contents: Title (*i*), TP verso (*ii*), preface (iii), blank (*iv*), contents (v), text (6–16)

Binding: Dark greenish Yellow (103) stiff card, stapled through the wrapper, no
spine or endpapers. FC: printed in black within a double-ruled frame, the outer
frame in bold ([in shaded display script] **BASIC LAWS** | [*do*] **OF** | [*do*] **CROQUET**).
Inside FC: advertisement. RC: blank. Inside RC: advertisement

Copy seen: PC

Fingerprint: t.he opop).u- arEi 3 1975A [group 2 taken from the caption to the
diagrams on p 11]

Notes: Printed by RH Johns, Newport, Gwent.

(b) *Second edition (1978)*

[in shaded display script] BASIC LAWS OF | [*do*] **Association Croquet** | [*do*] AND
GOLF CROQUET | by B. G. NEAL | SECOND EDITION | *Published by* | THE
CROQUET ASSOCIATION | THE HURLINGHAM CLUB, LONDON, S.W.6 | 1978

Formula: As that of (a)

Technical notes: 128 × 84 mm (p 12). 46 lines, 20 = 56 mm. Leaf size 165 × 104
mm; thickness 0.09 mm; wove, unwatermarked, smooth, white

Contents: As the contents of (a)

Binding: As that of (a)

Copy seen: BOD: 38464 f 19

Fingerprint: t.he opop).u- arEi 3 1978A [group 2 taken from the caption to the
diagrams on p 11]

Notes: Printed by RH Johns, Newport, Gwent.

(c) *Third edition (1981)*

BASIC LAWS OF | **Association Croquet** | AND GOLF CROQUET | by B. G. NEAL
| THIRD EDITION | *Published by* | THE CROQUET ASSOCIATION | THE
HURLINGHAM CLUB, LONDON, S.W.6 3PR | 1981

Formula: [1⁸]. 8 leaves, pp *i–ii* iii *iv* v, 6–16

Technical notes: 128 × 85 mm (p 12). 46 lines, 20 = 56 mm. Leaf size 154 × 99 mm;
thickness 0.11 mm; wove, unwatermarked, smooth, white

Contents: Title (*i*), TP verso (*ii*), preface (iii), blank (*iv*), contents (v), text (6–16)

Binding: Light Olive (106) stiff card, stapled through the folds of the sheets and
wrapper, no spine or endpapers. FC: printed in black within a double-ruled frame,
the outer frame in bold (**BASIC LAWS** | OF | **CROQUET**). Inside FC: advertise-
ment. RC: blank. Inside RC: advertisement

Copy seen: PC

Fingerprint: t.et opop J.nd enEi 3 1981A

Notes: Published by the CA, printed by RH Johns, Newport, Gwent.

(d) *Fourth edition (1984)*

BASIC LAWS OF | **Association Croquet** | AND GOLF CROQUET | by B. G. NEAL | FOURTH EDITION | *Published by* | THE CROQUET ASSOCIATION | THE HURLINGHAM CLUB, LONDON, SW6 3PR | 1984

Formula: [1^8]. 8 leaves, pp i–v, 6–16

Technical notes: 128 × 84 mm (p 12). 46 lines, 20 = 56 mm. Leaf size 149 × 103 mm; thickness 0.09 mm; wove, unwatermarked, smooth, white

Contents: Title (i), advertisement (ii), surrogate TP verso (iii), preface (iv), contents (v), text (6–16)

Binding: Vivid greenish Yellow (97) card, stapled through the folds of the sheets and wrapper, no spine or endpapers. FC: printed in black within a double-ruled frame, the outer frame in bold (**BASIC LAWS** | OF | **CROQUET**). Inside FC: blank. RC: blank. Inside RC: blank

Copy seen: PC

Fingerprint: erd. opop J.ee enEi 3 1984A

Notes: Published by the CA, printed by Stoate & Bishop (Printers), Cheltenham and Gloucester. The text is essentially the same as that of (c), though references to the full laws and regulations of the game (A100) and related publications are updated and the text is reset throughout.

(e) *Afrikaans translation (1987)*

BASIESE WETTE VAN | **Association Croquet** | EN GOLF CROQUET | deur B.G. NEAL | Vertaal deur Sy Ed. Regter G. Marais | Met Vergunning van Professor B.G. Neal | Outeursreg Voorbehou | *Uitgewer* | **SUID-AFRIKAANSE CROQUET** | **VERENIGING** | LATE VINTAGE, RUST & VREDE LAAN, | CONSTANTIA 7800

Formula: [1^{10}]. 10 leaves, pp i–iii, 1–14 *15–17*

Technical notes: 125 × 87 mm (p 6, ragged). 30 lines, 20 = 83 mm. Leaf size 148 × 103 mm; thickness 0.10 mm; wove, unwatermarked, smooth, white

Contents: Title (i), foreword (ii), contents (iii), text (1–14), blank page for notes, incorporating name of printer (*15*), blank (*16–17*)

Binding: Brilliant Yellow (83) leather-effect embossed card, stapled through the folds of the sheets and wrapper, no spine or endpapers. FC: printed in black within a double-ruled frame, the outer frame in bold (**BASIESE WETTE** | van | **CROQUET**). Inside FC: blank. RC: blank. Inside RC: blank

Copy seen: PC

Fingerprint: 1413 ofu, n.te bior C 1987A [groups 1–4 taken from pp iii, 8, 10, 11 respectively]

Notes: Published by Suid-Afrikaanse Croquet Vereniging, August 1987, printed by Prestoprint.

A193   **CROQUET: THE LADIES' GAME.** [Anon]   **1975**

CROQUET: | The Ladies' Game. | Its Implements, Conduct of | the Game, Rules, etc. | • • • • | [three flourishes] | [publisher's device: twin trees in silhouette set at the ends of a long rule] | [in gothic-revival script] Rhodopress of Ashland ◆ Ashland, Ohio. | 1975

[TP verso]

[the lettering set within a diagram of a croquet lawn, each hoop represented by an inverted letter U and each stake by a letter I] *The Croquet Series.* | [*do*] *One of fifty copies.* | Rhodopress of Ashland | February 14, 1975. | From *The New York Weekly News,* | Saturday, June 23, 1866; with illus- | tration from *Punch* (London), 1871.

Formula: [1¹²]. 12 leaves, unnumbered [pp 1–24]

Technical notes: 90 × 75 mm (p 6). 21 lines, 20 = 84 mm. Leaf size 133 × 107 mm; thickness 0.18 mm; wove, unwatermarked, rough, white

Contents: Title (*1*), TP verso (*2*), foreword, signed 'Rendell Rhoades', 14 February 1975 (*3–4*), text (Croquet: the ladies' game) (*5–14*), reprint of contemporary advertisement (*15*), text, concluded (*16–19*), name of printer (*20*), advertisement (*21*), blank (*22–24*)

Binding: Pale Yellow (89) card, stapled, no spine or endpapers. FC: printed in black and dark reddish Orange (38) ([in black] THE | [the letter *L*, partly obscured by the caricature below, in Orange] Ladies' | [at L, caricature of a woman player in Orange] | [set vertically at R in black] Game ● | [publisher's device in black: twin trees in silhouette set at the ends of a long rule] | [in black gothic-revival script] Rhodopress of Ashland ◆ Ashland, Ohio. | [in black] 1975). Inside FC: blank. RC: blank. Inside RC: blank

Copy seen: CA

Fingerprint: n.t- heth tsof twth 3 1975A

Notes: Published, on 14 February 1975, and printed by Rhodopress of Ashland, Ashland, Ohio.

This work reprints an article in *The New York Weekly News* (23 June 1866), including a code of 17 numbered rules, some with numbered sub-clauses.

A194   **THE LITERATURE OF CROQUET. 'The Editor of *The Reader*'**   **1975**

THE LITERATURE OF CROQUET. | *By the Editor of* The Reader, | *with Comments by* | Frederick J. Foot. | [device in dark reddish Orange (38): a scroll and a plume] | [publisher's device: twin trees in silhouette set at the ends of a long rule] | [in gothic-revival script] Rhodopress of Ashland ◆ Ashland, Ohio. | 1975

[TP verso]

[the lettering set within a diagram of a croquet lawn, each hoop represented by an inverted letter U and each stake by a letter I] *The Croquet Series.* | [*do*] *One of fifty copies.* | Reprinted from THE READER | (London) of October 15 and 22, 1864. | [double rule] | Rhodopress of Ashland | March 17, 1975.

Formula: [1¹⁰]. 10 leaves, unnumbered [pp 1–20]

Technical notes: 92 × 76 mm (p 4). 22 lines, 20 = 84 mm. Leaf size 132 × 108 mm; thickness 0.17 mm; wove, unwatermarked, rough, white

Contents: Title (*1*), TP verso (*2*), text (The literature of croquet) (*3–16*), text (letter to the Editor of *The Reader*) (*16–18*), name of printer (*18*), blank (*19–20*)

Binding: Very pale Green (148) card, stapled, no spine or endpapers. FC: reproduction of the TP in black and Orange. Inside FC: blank. RC: blank. Inside RC: blank.

Copy seen: CA

Fingerprint: l-nd p-as leit grha 3 1975A

Notes: Published on 17 March 1975, printed by the publisher. Editorship by Rendell is inferred from the known origins of the Rhodopress of Ashland Croquet Series. See, for example, NL Rhoades, *Croquet: A Bibliography from the Rendell Rhoades Croquet Collection* (A263) and *Notes* to A254.

The text reproduces a humorous leader in *The Reader* (15 October 1864) and a replication by Foot (*op cit*, 29 October 1864, not 22 October as stated on p 2). A footnote on p 8 is thought to be by Rendell.

AA195 NOTES ON THE CONSTRUCTION OF CROQUET LAWNS.   1975
RF Rothwell

(a) **First edition (1975)*

[Title heading, f *1*]

NOTES on the construction of CROQUET LAWNS | by R. F. Rothwell

Formula: [1–8¹]. 8 leaves, ff *1 2–8* [misprinting *8* as '4']

Technical notes: 282 × 180 mm (f 2, ragged). 67 lines, 20 = 84 mm. Leaf size 331 × 205 mm; thickness 0.16 mm; wove, watermarked (RONEO), smooth, white

Contents: Title heading (*1*), text (*1–7*), plan of lawn (*8*)

Binding: Fastened by a staple in the top L corner

Copy seen: PC

Fingerprint: seen d.ed beng noat C 1975Q [group 1 taken from f 2, groups 2–4 taken from f 6]

Notes: Presumably printed by the CA and issued on demand. Year of publication is inferred from dates cited in the text.

(b) *Other edition [1975]*

[Title heading, f *1*]

NOTES on the construction of CROQUET LAWNS | by R. F.Rothwell

Formula: [1–8¹]. 8 leaves, ff *1 2–7 8*

Technical notes: 265 × 177 mm (f 4, ragged). 63 lines, 20 = 84 mm. Leaf size 297 × 210 mm; thickness 0.10 mm; wove, unwatermarked, smooth, white

Contents: As the contents of (a)

Binding: The copy examined consists of loose sheets

Copy seen: PC

Fingerprint: g.is ofes toss uter C 1975Q [group 1 taken from f 2, groups 2–4 taken from f 6]

Notes: Printed anonymously, presumably in small batches by the CA when stocks of (a) had been exhausted. Year of publication is conjectural. The text is apparently identical in substance to that of (a).

1976

A196 CROQUET — A CHALLENGE. [Rendell Rhoades (ed)]   1976

CROQUET – A CHALLENGE. | • • • • | The Ravenna-Newburg Match of 1875 | and the Description of an | Impromptu Game. | • • • | • | [publisher's device: twin trees in silhouette set at the ends of a long rule in bold] | [in gothic-revival script] Rhodopress of Ashland – – – – – – – – Ashland, Ohio. | 1976

[TP verso, the lettering set within a diagram of a croquet lawn, each hoop represented by an inverted letter U and each stake by a letter I]

The Croquet Series. | *One of fifty copies.* | Rhodopress of Ashland | [rule in bold] | February 7, 1976

Formula: [1¹⁰]. 10 leaves, unnumbered [pp 1–20]

Technical notes: 92 × 76 mm (p 7). 22 lines, 20 = 83 mm. Leaf size 133 × 107 mm; thickness 0.18 mm; wove, unwatermarked, rough, white. The advertisement on p *19* includes a device — a schematic illustration of a ball — in dark reddish Orange (38)

Contents: Title (*1*), TP verso (*2*), text ('Croquet – A Challenge') (*3*), text ('Croquet: The Iron-Ward Challenge Accepted by the Ravenna Team') (*4–5*), text ('Croquet: The Ravenna-Newburg Match [*etc*]') (*6–16*), advertisement (The Croquet Series) (*17*), blank (*18*), advertisement (*19*), blank (*20*)

Binding: Light Yellow (86) leather-effect embossed card, stapled, no spine or endpapers. FC: reproduction of the TP, in black. Inside FC: blank. RC: blank. Inside RC: blank

Copy seen: CA

Fingerprint: 5.*nd* heto 6.a- 5.il C 1976A

Notes: Published on 7 February 1976, printed by the publisher. Editorship by Rendell is inferred from the known origins of the Rhodopress of Ashland Croquet Series. See, for example, NL Rhoades, *Croquet: A Bibliography from the Rendell Rhoades Croquet Collection* (A263) and *Notes* to A254.

The text reprints articles in the *Cleveland Leader* (15 July 1875, 17 July 1875) and *Portage County Republican-Democrat* (21 July 1875, 28 July 1875) with some connecting editorial matter.

1977

A197   **CROQUET LOVER AT THE DINNER TABLE.** Jonathan Aldrich   1977

Croquet Lover at the Dinner Table/ Poems by Jonathan Aldrich | [R justified, at the foot] A Breakthrough Book/ University of Missouri Press | [*do*] Columbia & London, 1977

Formula: [1–4⁸]. 32 leaves, pp *1–7* 8–26 *27* 28 *29* 30–34 *35* 36–43 ~~44~~ *44* 46–64

Technical notes: 167 mm × variable width. 34 lines, 20 = 99 mm. Leaf size 215 × 163 mm; thickness 0.14 mm; wove, watermarked ([in a convex arc] WARREN'S | OLDE STYLE), rough, white

Contents: Half-title and dedication (*1*), blank (*2*), title (*3*), TP verso (*4*), contents (*5*), blank (*6*), text, continued (*7–43*), blank (*44*), text, concluded (*45–64*)

Binding: Brilliant greenish Blue (168) sail cloth over heavy boards, sewn, the endpapers embossed and coloured vivid Yellow (82). FC: blank. RC: blank. Spine: silver-blocked downwards ([‡] the Dinner Table / Aldrich [at the foot] Missouri)

Copy seen: BL: X 989/51755

Notes: Printed anonymously, © 1977 by Jonathan Aldrich, ISBN 0–8262–0205–5.

The text consists of a collection of verse. The title poem, 'Croquet Lover at the Dinner Table (at a Writer's Conference)' ('She passes muffins, orders the most remote...'), extends to 14 lines. It is stated on the TP verso that it was first published in *American Weave* magazine and then in a pamphlet by the Academy of American Poets.

A198 CROQUET: THE COMPLETE GUIDE TO HISTORY, 1977
STRATEGY, RULES AND RECORDS.
James Charlton and William Thompson

(a) *First edition (1977)*

[Mostly on p *3*]

Croquet | [p *2*] **The Complete Guide to History,** [p *3*] **Strategy, Rules and Records** | by **James Charlton & William Thompson** | Illustrations by Katherine Freeman | Photographs by Roger Adler | Book and cover design by Andrew Bromberg | [publisher's device] | TURTLE PRESS | • | CHARLES SCRIBNER'S SONS | New York • New York

Formula: [1–11^8]. 88 leaves, pp *1–14* 15–21 *22* 23–29 *30* 31–32 *33–34* 35–38 *39–40* 41–49 *50* 51–55 *56* 57–61 *62* 63–76 *77–78* 79–83 *84* 85–89 *90* 91–94 *95–96* 97–100 *101–102* 103–104 *105–106* 107–113 *114* 115–117 *118* 119–125 *126* 127–161 *162* 163–174 *175–176*

Technical notes: 195 × 134 mm (p 17). 40 lines, 20 = 97 mm. Leaf size 252 × 199 mm; thickness 0.13 mm; wove, unwatermarked, smooth, white

Contents: Half-title (*1*), extension to TP (*2*), title (*3*), TP verso (*4*), acknowledgements (*5*), blank (*6*), contents (*7*), frontispiece (reprint of Tenniel's illustration of Alice and the Duchess from Ch IX of Lewis Carroll, *Alice's Adventures in Wonderland*) (*8*), foreword, signed 'Jack R Osborn' (*9–10*), blank (*11*), illustration (of sheet music cover entitled 'Croquet') (*12*), introduction, signed 'Andrew I Adler, Roger Adler, Editors' (*13*), reprint of an early engraving and quotations from *Living Age* and *The American Past* (*14*), text (*15–126*), the official rules of the USCA American six-wicket game (*127–145*), USCA official rules for the nine-wicket game (*146–154*), text, concluded (*155–175*), blank (*176*)

Binding: Brilliant bluish Green (159) linen grain paper over stiff boards, apparently sewn. FC: printed in white (**Croquet** | **The Complete Guide to History, Strategy, Rules and Records**). RC: blank. Spine: printed in white downwards ([near the head] **Croquet** [centrally] by **James Charlton & William Thompson** | [near the foot] Turtle Press / Scribners).

Dust wrapper: Printed in full colour on glossy white paper laminate. FP: ([in black] **Croquet** | [in vivid reddish Orange (34)] **The Complete Guide to History, Strategy, Rules and Records** | [in black] by **James Charlton & William Thompson** | [colour photograph taken from rear at low level of player preparing to take hoop shot] | [in Orange] **An Illustrated Introduction to the Stings and Subtleties of America's Most Misunderstood Sport** | [in black] **Foreword by Jack Osborn**). FF: price and publisher's blurb. RP: publisher's blurb. RF: illustration of croquet stand and publisher's notes about the authors. Spine: downwards in black ([from near top edge] **Croquet** [above centre] by **James Charlton & William Thompson** [to near the foot] Turtle Press / Scribners)

Copy seen: PC

Fingerprint: n.nd rser ofy, ThCr 7 1977A

Notes: Printed anonymously, price $9.95.

This work contains the first published edition of *The Official Rules of The United States Croquet Association American Six-wicket Game* (including a code of 68 numbered rules) and *United States Croquet Association Official Rules for the Nine-wicket Game*. See also A212.

(b) *Second edition (1988)*

[in display script] CROQUET | ITS HISTORY, STRATEGY, RULES, | AND

RECORDS | JAMES CHARLTON and WILLIAM THOMPSON | with ROGER, KATHERINE, and ANDREW ADLER | THE STEPHEN GREENE PRESS | Lexington, Massachusetts

Formula: [1–88¹]. 88 leaves, pp *i–viii* ix–x *xi–xii*, 1–11 *12* 13–19 *20* 21–27 *28 29 30* 31–34 *35–36* 37–45 *46* 47–51 *52* 53–57 *58* 59–72 *73–74* 75–79 *80* 81–85 *86* 87–90 *91–92* 93–96 *97–98* 99–100 *101–102* 103–109 *110* 111–113 *114* 115–121 *122* 123–138 *139–140* 141–147 *148* 149–160 *161–164*

Technical notes: 191 × 134 mm (p 9). 39 lines, 20 = 99 mm. Leaf size 253 × 203 mm; thickness 0.10 mm; wove, unwatermarked, smooth, white

Contents: Half-title (*i*), blank (*ii*), title (*iii*), TP verso (*iv*), acknowledgements (*v*), blank (*vi*), contents (*vii*), plate (reproduction of an engraving) (*viii*), foreword, signed 'Jack R. Osborn' (*ix–x*), half-title (*xi*), frontispiece (cartoon signed 'Ketcham 8-1') (*xii*), text (1–*161*), blank (*162–164*)

Binding: High-gloss yellowish White (92) paper laminate wrapper glued to the edges of the leaves. FC: printed within a very deep Purple (220) ruled frame, broken at the top R corner by a deep reddish Orange (36) diagonal band ([white out of Orange] NEWLY | UPDATED) ([in Purple] "Fills a huge vacuum in the literature of croquet." | [*do*] —JACK R. OSBORN, President, U.S. Croquet Association | [in black and deep orange Yellow (69) display script] CROQUET | [in dark olive Green (126)] ITS HISTORY, STRATEGY, RULES, | [*do*] AND RECORDS | [close-up colour photograph of a player's legs, mallet, two hoops, two balls, and peg, set on a lush lawn, within an Orange ruled panel] | [in Purple] JAMES CHARLTON and WILLIAM THOMPSON | with ROGER, KATHERINE, and ANDREW ADLER). Inside FC: blank. RC: publisher's blurb *etc* in Purple, Green, and Orange on Yellow. Inside RC: blank. Spine: downwards on Yellow ([in Green] James Charlton and William Thompson | [set below line above, in Green] with Roger, Katherine, and Andrew Adler | [in Purple] CROQUET [in Green] Its History, Strategy, Rules, and Records [in black] ISBN 0-8289-0666-1 [publisher's device, a monogram, crosswise, in black]

Copy seen: PC

Fingerprint: n.va ndon lyhe foTh 3 1988A

Notes: Printed by The Alpine Press, USA, price $19.95 (Australia), $16.95 (Canada), $11.95 (USA).

The text and illustrations depart extensively from (a). The main revisions are the addition of a new introductory chapter ('In the Swing'), changes in the order of other chapters, insertion of new illustrations, omission and variation of others, replacement of a simplified code of 42 'basic rules' with the USCA six-wicket and nine-wicket games, and updating of records, addresses, and bibliography.

A199   **MANLY CROQUET CLUB: SPECIAL COOK BOOK.**   [1977]
[Manly Croquet Club]

[The FC, within a cross-banded frame, in black]

MANLY | [artist's swelled rule] | **CROQUET CLUB** | [sketch of a hoop, two crossed mallets, and a cluster of four balls] | [sketch of a birthday cake with lighted candles and a vase of flowers] | [half-outlined *S*] **SPECIAL** | [half-outlined *C*] **COOK** | [half-outlined *B*] **BOOK** | **To celebrate the Seventy-** | **Fifth Birthday of the above** | **Club.**

Formula: [1³⁰]. 30 leaves, pp *i–iii*, 1–57

Technical notes: 188 × 140 mm (p 4). 52 lines, 20 = 73 mm. Leaf size 202 × 161 mm; thickness 0.10 mm; wove, unwatermarked, smooth, white

Contents: Foreword by Kylie Scotter (*i*), blank (*ii*), contents (*iii*), text (1–57)

Binding: Grey paper, stapled, no spine or endpapers. FC: as above. Inside FC: blank. RC: blank. Inside RC: blank

Copy seen: PC

Fingerprint: 77'. **ceur gged fe1b** C 1977Q [groups 1–4 taken from pp *i*, 6, 10, 11 respectively]

Notes: Published and printed anonymously. Year of publication is inferred from the date appended to the foreword.

AA200 RULES OF THE CROQUET ASSOCIATION.   **1977**
[The Croquet Association]
RULES | of | THE CROQUET ASSOCIATION

Formula: [1⁴]. 4 leaves, unnumbered [pp 1–8]

Technical notes: 181 × 107 mm (p 3, ragged). 52 lines, 20 = 70 mm. Leaf size 206 × 146 mm; thickness 0.11 mm; wove, watermarked ([in a convex arc] **CROXLEY** | [in a concave arc] **SCRIPT**), smooth, white

Contents: Title (*1*), text (2–8), authority, signed 'R.F. Rothwell', Secretary, January 1977 (*8*)

Binding: No wrapper, stapled.

Copy seen: CA

Fingerprint: g.ll beg. ofto d.ng C 1977A [all four groups taken from p *3*]

Notes: Published in January 1977 by the CA, printed anonymously by FH Brown.

1978

AA201 CANBERRA CROQUET CLUB: 50TH ANNIVERSARY   **[1978]**
CELEBRATIONS. [Mrs L Jorgensen (ed)]
[The FC]
[club device] | [in a calligraphic script] **CANBERRA CROQUET CLUB** | [half-tone photograph of clubhouse] | [in a calligraphic script] **50th ANNIVERSARY** | [*do*] **CELEBRATIONS**

Formula: [1⁴]. 4 leaves, unnumbered [pp 1–8]

Technical notes: †190 × †114 mm (p 2). 72 lines, 20 = †53 mm, variable. Leaf size †230 × †138 mm

Contents: Canberra Croquet Club, sundry details (*1*), president's message, signed '*PHYLLIS MANNING*', champions and presidents (*2*), anniversary celebrations (3–8)

Binding: Apparently pale coloured paper or card, stapled through the folds, no spine or endpapers. FC: wanting from the photocopy examined. Inside FC: blank. RC: wanting from the photocopy examined. Inside RC: blank

Copy seen: NLA: NP 796 354060947 C214 (incomplete photocopy of unknown scale)

Fingerprint: s.26 s.od **s.RS** y.** C 1978Q

Notes: Printed anonymously. A curiosity of this work is the unfinished state of p *8*, which merely gives captions for photographs of two prospective celebration events, not the planned photographs themselves. This would suggest either that it was intended as the only edition, in the anticipation that interested readers would paste in the wanting photographs when they became available, or that it was issued for preview purposes with the intention that a definitive edition would be issued later in the year when the photographs could be inserted by the printer.

AA202 IVC CROQUET SUB-CLUB HANDBOOK 1978. [E Solomon]   1978

IVC CROQUET SUB-CLUB | HANDBOOK | 1978

Formula: [1⁶]. 6 leaves, pp *i–ii*, 1–8 *9–10*

Technical notes: 186 × 121 mm (p 1). 43 lines, 20 = 86 mm. Leaf size 210 × 148 mm; thickness 0.09 mm; wove, unwatermarked, smooth, white

Contents: Title (*i*), officers (*ii*), text (*1–10*)

Binding: No wrapper, stapled

Copy seen: PC

Fingerprint: lele 6.st lys. alnd C 1978A [all four groups taken from p 1]

Notes: Printed anonymously. The identity of the author is inferred from the responsibilities of the officers cited on p *ii*. The sub-club was a section of the Inter Varsity Club.

A203   KROCKET REGLER. Göran Fick and Ingmar Tönnby   1978

(a) *First edition (1978)*

Not seen. The year of publication of the first edition is cited on the surrogate TP verso of (b).

(b) *Andra tryckningen (1985)*

[The FC]

KROCKET REGLER | GODKÄNDA AV | SVENSKA CROQUETFÖRBUNDET | [publisher's device] | Göran Fick | Ingmar Tönnby

Formula: [1¹⁴]. 14 leaves, pp 1–28

Technical notes: 116 × 76 mm (p 15, ragged). 46 lines, 20 = 51 mm. Leaf size 143 × 105 mm. Pp 1–12, 17–28: thickness 0.10 mm, wove, unwatermarked, smooth, white. Pp 13–16: thickness 0.10 mm, wove, unwatermarked, smooth, brilliant greenish Yellow (98)

Contents: Frontispiece, engraving and verse reprinted from *The Boy's Own Book* (Crosby Lockwood & Co, 1878) (1), surrogate TP verso (2), contents (3), foreword, signed 'Göran Fick och Ingmar Tönnby', May 1978 (4–5), text (6–27), engraving reprinted from *Pictures for Our Pets* (source unknown) (28)

Binding: Yellow (98) paper, stapled through the folds of the leaves, no spine or endpapers. FC: printed in black as above. Inside FC: blank. RC: blank. Inside RC: blank

Copy seen: PC

Fingerprint: y.y, g.3. g.en kaen 3 1885A [group 1 taken from p 1, group 2 taken from p 9, group 3 taken from the caption and one of the legends to the illustration on p 13, group 4 taken from p 14]

Notes: Printed anonymously. The text evidently describes a version of croquet resembling the game as played in the UK in the early 1860s, employing a nine-hoop setting with two pegs. It includes a schedule of 26 numbered definitions and a code of 42 numbered rules.

1979

AA204 FROM THE BEGINNING TO THE END. John Solomon   1979

(a) *First printing (1979)*

[The FC]

<u>FROM THE BEGINNING TO THE END</u> | A PERSONAL CROQUET HISTORY | BY | JOHN SOLOMON

Collation: Loose-leaf typescript. 40 leaves, pp *1 2, 1 2–78*

Technical notes: 224 × 155 mm (p 3, ragged). 31 lines, 20 = 146 mm. Leaf size 297 × 210 mm; thickness 0.11 mm; wove, unwatermarked, smooth, white

Contents: Apology (*1–2*), text (*1–78*), signed in MS, 'John Solomon', March 1979 (*78*)

Binding: The copy examined is fastened by a deep Blue (179) extruded plastic binder between strong orange Yellow (68) leather-effect card covers. FC: in typescript (as above) on a white stick-on label. Inside FC: blank. RC: blank. Inside RC: blank. Spine: blank

Copy seen: PC

Fingerprint: n.ed t.er e.it info 3 1979A [groups 1–4 taken from pp *1* ('Apology'), 7, 13, 14 respectively]

Notes: Unpublished typescript. In 1979 the author duplicated ten copies of this work, of which some were sent to leading figures in the croquet world and two were deposited with the CA.

(b) *Second printing (ca 1994)*

Not seen. The existence of this issue is attested by the author.

Notes: In or about 1994 the author added two appendices to this work, listing and analysing his results, and produced two copies which he presented to the CA. The text is unaltered, but the title is reset on a new front page, visible through a cut-out in the FC.

1970–79

AA205 RULES OF PLAY: KOURT KING CROQUET SETS. [Anon]   *ca* 1970

[Within a ruled frame]

Rules of Play | [in vivid Green (137) MS-style script] *Kourt King* | CROQUET SETS | [Green illustration of a croquet ball] | *Croquet for Health* | *"Old fashioned Game | that never grows Old"* | **INDIANA HANDLE COMPANY** | **PAOLI, INDIANA**

Formula: [1²]. 2 leaves, unnumbered [pp 1–4]

Technical notes: 184 × 113 mm (p *3*). 52 lines, 20 = 71 mm. Leaf size 215 × 139 mm; thickness 0.14 mm; wove, unwatermarked, smooth, white; printed in black and vivid Green (137)

Contents: Title (*1*), text (*2–4*)

Binding: None

Copy seen: PC

Fingerprint: d.is y.he l.ot htt. C 1970Q [all four groups taken from p *3*]

Notes: This work was evidently issued by the Indiana Handle Company with its croquet sets. Approximate year of publication is inferred from the fact that a copy of the same work described by NL Rhoades (A263) includes, as an insert, a related price list dated 1 October 1970.

The text includes a code of unnumbered rules, thought to be typical of the game as played in most parts of the USA before the foundation of the USCA.

1980

A206   A HISTORY OF CROQUET IN VICTORIA: 1866 TO 1980.   1980
Joyce Ridley

A History | of | Croquet | in | Victoria | 1866 to 1980 | by Joyce Ridley | Approved by Victorian Croquet Association

Formula: [1⁴⁴]. 44 leaves, pp *i–vi*, 1–80 *81–82*

Technical notes: 187 × 113 mm (p 2). 49 lines, 20 = 77 mm. Leaf size 215 × 137 mm

Contents: Title (*i*), TP verso (*ii*), contents (*iii*), blank (*iv*), preface, signed 'Joyce Ridley' (*v*), blank (*vi*), text (1–80), blank (*81–82*)

Binding: White semi-gloss card, stapled, no spine or endpapers. FC: the TP reproduced in black over a faint half-tone photograph in gradations of pale Yellow Green (121) of a woman player in profile, dressed in crinoline and bonnet. Inside FC: blank. RC: blank, in gradations of white and Yellow Green. Inside RC: blank.

Copies seen: PC (and photocopy of another original copy)

Fingerprint: 7976 rs2, asA. arth 3 1980A

Notes: Printed by Allanby Press Printers. Both copies examined bear the following inscription in the author's hand on the TP verso: 'ISBN 0 9594184 0 7'. Both copies also bear identical corrections to the text in the author's hand.

AA207 SPECTATOR[']S GUIDE TO ASSOCIATION CROQUET.   1980
[The Croquet Association]

(a) *First edition (1980)*

[Titled heading, p *1*]

[device of the CA] | Pimm's | Association | Croquet Internationals | SPECTATORS GUIDE TO ASSOCIATION CROQUET

Formula: [1²]. 2 leaves, unnumbered [pp *1–4*]

Technical notes: 259 × 177 mm, divided into two columns (p 2). 74 lines, 20 = 70 mm. Leaf size 297 × 209 mm; thickness 0.12 mm; wove, unwatermarked, smooth, white

Contents: Title heading (*1*), text (*1–4*)

Binding: None

Copy seen: PC

Fingerprint: l.he e,er erwo lyhe C 1980Q [all four groups taken from the L column of p 3]

Notes: Published by the CA on the occasion of the Home International Championships in 1980, sponsored by Pimm's, and issued free of charge to spectators. Printed anonymously, probably by Sevenoaks Advertising Studios. The accounts of the CA show that in June 1980 this company was paid £309 for printing 10000 copies of a 'new Association croquet leaflet'.

This work was evidently intended to serve much the same function as *Croquet — A Simple Synopsis* (A151), but is entirely rewritten, expanded, and updated to incorporate subsequent changes in the laws.

(b) *Debenham Tewson & Chinnocks edition [ca 1984]*

[Title heading, p *1*]

[device featuring croquet goods, at L] | [one of three lines to the R of device above]
DEBENHAM | [*do*] **TEWSON &** | [*do*] **CHINNOCKS** | Chartered Surveyors |
International Real Estate Consultants | SPECTATOR'S GUIDE TO | ASSOCIATION
CROQUET

Formula: [1³]. 3 leaves, unnumbered [pp 1–6], on a single sheet in a C-fold, pp *1–6*
in the order 1, 2, 6, 3, 4, 5 of the external contours of the letter C (from top to
bottom and L to R) [pp 1–6]

Technical notes: 228 × 93 mm (p *2*). 65 lines, 20 = 70 mm. Leaf size 253 × 118 mm;
thickness 0.14 mm; wove, unwatermarked, smooth, white, printed in deep Blue (179)

Contents: Title heading (*1*), text (*1–6*), publishing information (*6*)

Binding: None

Copy seen: PC

Fingerprint: p.an hato keer ngen C 1984Q [all four groups taken from p *3*]

Notes: Produced for the CA by Debenham Tewson & Chinnocks, sponsors, on the
occasion of the CA Open Championships, probably during the period (1984–86) of
their sponsorship. Year of publication is presumed to be within that period. Printed
anonymously.

The text is an abridgment of (a).

(c) *Bombay Dry Gin edition [1987]*

[Within a ruled frame, with rounded corners and an arched extension at the head]
[device of Bombay Dry Gin] | SPECTATOR'S | GUIDE TO | ASSOCIATION |
CROQUET | Association Croquet is one of the | finest of all outdoor games. | It
requires delicate skill | rather than strength and tactical ability | rather than quick
reflexes.

Formula: [1⁴]. 4 leaves, unnumbered [pp 1–8], on a single sheet in a W-fold, pp *1–8*
in the order 1, 2, 3, 8, 7, 4, 5, 6 of the external contours of the letter W (from L to
R) [pp 1–8]

Technical notes: 190 × 80 mm (p *3*, ragged). 55 lines, 20 = 70 mm. Leaf size 210 ×
99 mm; thickness 0.18 mm; wove, unwatermarked, smooth, pale Yellow (89),
printed in strong Green (141)

Contents: Title (*1*), text (*1–8*), advertisement (*8*)

Binding: None

Copy seen: CA

Fingerprint: ldgo les6 nech hyhe C 1987Q [all four groups taken from p *3*]

Notes: Printed anonymously. Year of publication is deduced from the following
indications:

(i) Bombay Dry Gin was a prominent sponsor of the CA during the years 1987–88.

(ii) A copy of this work is contained within a Starter Pack of publicity material
issued by the Publicity Committee of the CA in June 1987.

1981

A208   **THE HISTORY OF CROQUET.** DMC Prichard   1981

The History of | **CROQUET** | [swelled rule] | **D.M.C. PRICHARD** | CASSELL |
LONDON

[TP verso]

CASSELL LTD. | 35 Red Lion Square, London WC1R 4SG | and at Sydney, Auckland, Toronto, Johannesburg, | an affiliate of | Macmillan Publishing Co., Inc., | New York | Copyright © D.M.C. Prichard 1981 | [assertion of copyright] | First published 1981 | ISBN 0 304 30759 9 | Typeset by Inforum Ltd., Portsmouth | Printed in Great Britain by | Fletcher & Son Ltd, Norwich

Formula: [1–8^{16}]. 128 leaves including the front and rear endpapers, pp *i–xii, 1 2 3 4–6 7 8 9–11 12–13 14–18 19–22 23–24 25–27 28–30 31–39 40–42 43–48 49 50 51 52 53 54 55 56–60 61 62–63 64–65 66–67 68–69 70–71 72–75 76–80 81–82 83 84 85–89 90 91–96 97 98–105 106–107 108–116 117–118 119–125 126 127–137 138–140 141–148 149–150 151–152 153 154 155–158 159 160 161 162–164 165 166 167–170 171–172 173 174 175–177 178–181 182–183 184 185–191 192–193 194–196 197 198–207 208 209–231 232–233 234 235 236–239 240–244*

Technical notes: 189 × 113 mm (p 2). 45 lines, 20 = 84 mm. Leaf size 233 × 153 mm; thickness 0.14 mm; wove, unwatermarked, smooth, white

Contents: Glued to the FC (*i*), blank (*ii–iv*), half-title (*v*), frontispiece (black-and-white photograph) (*vi*), title (*vii*), TP verso (*viii*), contents (*ix–x*), author's preface, dated 1981 (*xi–xii*), text (*1–239*), blank (*240–243*), glued to the RC (*244*)

Binding: Moderate Green (145) buckram grain paper over stiff boards, sewn. FC: blank. RC: blank. Spine: gold-blocked downwards ([near the head] *The History of Croquet* [centrally] D.M.C. *PRICHARD* [near the foot] CASSELL).

Dust wrapper: Glossy paper laminate. FP: title *etc* in white out of a colour photograph of a mallet, a set of four first colour balls, and a hoop crowned by a single red clip ([rule] **THE HISTORY OF** [rule] | **CROQUET** | [rule] | **D.M.C.PRICHARD**). FF: publisher's blurb and price. RP: against and out of a black background ([black-and-white photograph] | Tea at Devonshire Park 1902 | ISBN 0 304 307599). RF: about the author. Spine: in white out of a black background, mostly downwards ([near the head] THE HISTORY OF [below] **CROQUET** | [slightly above centre] D.M.C.PRICHARD [crosswise, near the foot] CASSELL)

Copy seen: PC

Fingerprint: 1715 y)me tsus Waha 3 1981A

Notes: Printed by Fletcher & Son, price £8.95 net. A notice of *corrigenda* appeared in *The Croquet Gazette* (December 1981).

A209   THE STOCKYARD AND THE CROQUET LAWN. GA Wilkes   1981

(a) *First edition (1981)*

Not seen. The existence of this edition is inferred from the citation on the TP verso of (b).

(b) *First UK edition (1981)*

[L justified]

Studies in Australian Culture | [rule] | *The Stockyard and the* | *Croquet Lawn* | Literary Evidence for Australian | Cultural Development | **G. A. Wilkes** | Challis Professor of English Literature. | University of Sydney | [publisher's device] | Edward Arnold

[From the TP verso, L justified]

First published 1981 by | Edward Arnold (Australia) Pty Ltd | This edition published 1981 by | Edward Arnold (Publisher) Ltd | 41 Bedford Square, London WC1B 3DQ

Formula: [1–5¹⁶]. 80 leaves, pp *i–vi, 1* 2–8 *9* 10–31 *32* 33–55 *56* 57–77 *78* 79–100 *101* 102–114 *115* 116–140 *141* 142–145 *146* 147–150 *151* 152–153 *154*

Technical notes: 164 × 109 mm (p 2). 39 lines, 20 = 84 mm. Leaf size 216 × 139 mm; thickness 0.11 mm; wove, unwatermarked, smooth, white

Contents: Series introduction by John Colmer, general editor (*i*), blank (*ii*), title (*iii*), TP verso (*iv*), contents (*v*), blank (*vi*), text (*1–153*), blank (*154*)

Binding: Dark greyish Green (151) cloth over heavy boards, sewn. FC: blank. RC: blank. Spine: silver-blocked, downwards ([the extreme L obscured on the copy examined by library labels] G. A. Wilkes   The Stockyard and the Croquet Lawn Arnold)

Copy seen: BL: X529/46190

Fingerprint: 5146 g'in he*th* toWe 3 1981A

Notes: Printed by Brown Prior Anderson Pty, Burwood, Victoria, ISBN 0 7131 8042 0.

In the author's words, 'The antithesis of the genteel and the robust, the refined and the crude, the old world and the new, and the contest between them for mastery, is the most familiar model of Australian cultural development.... Stockyard versus croquet lawn is but one way of formulating a relationship that had a variety of manifestations' (p 3).

1982

A210 **THE AUSTRALIAN CROQUET MANUAL. CR Sloane**   **1982**

(a) *First edition (1982)*

[at the head, R justified] 1 | [in a calligraphic script] **THE** | [*do*] **AUSTRALIAN** | [*do*] **CROQUET** | [*do*] **MANUAL** | [*do*] **C. R. SLOANE** | [*do*] **ABB PRINTING** | [*do*] **121 FLINDERS LANE** | [*do*] **MELBOURNE**

Formula: [1–84¹]. 84 leaves, pp 1–3, *i*, 4–167 [= 168]

Technical notes: 168 × 104 mm (p 22). 58 lines, 20 = 59 mm. Leaf size 209 × 146 mm; thickness 0.12 mm; wove, unwatermarked, smooth, white

Contents: Title (1), TP verso (2), contents, continued (3), blank (*i*), contents, concluded (4), foreword, by Neil Spooner (5), an aboriginal legend (6), acknowledgements (7), list of diagrams (8–9), list of photographs (10), list of appendices (11), text (12–167)

Binding: White linen-textured card glued to the edges of the leaves, no endpapers. FC: printed in black and strong Green (141) ([in MS-style display script, in Green on white, R justified] **The Australian** | [*do*] **Croquet** | [*do*] **Manual** | [in a calligraphic script in black on white, to the R of a sketch in black, signed in MS 'Kerr', featuring a man player seen through a hoop in close-up] **C.R. SLOANE** | [within a ruled panel in bluish Grey (191) on Green] THIS BOOK HAS BEEN | [*do*] AWARDED THE | [*do*] CONFEDERATION OF | [*do*] AUSTRALIAN SPORT | [*do*] STAMP OF APPROVAL.). Inside FC: in black near the foot (Published by C. R. Sloane 1982, ISBN 0 9592760 0 9). RC: sponsors' joint advertisement in Blue on white. Inside RC: advertisement. Spine: blank

Copy seen: CA

Fingerprint: 9090 6362 ".s, inTh C 1982A [groups 1–4 taken from pp 3, 10, 12, 13 respectively]

Notes: Published by the author, printed by ABB Printing, Melbourne.

(b) *Second edition (1983)*

[Mostly in a calligraphic script]

[at the head, R justified, in typescript] 1 | THE | AUSTRALIAN | CROQUET | MANUAL | C.R. SLOANE | ABB PRINTING | 121 FLINDERS LANE | MELBOURNE

Formula: Not ascertainable from the photocopy examined. Apparently 92 leaves, pp 1–3, *i*, 4–183 [= 184]

Technical notes: †234 × †147 mm (p 19). 56 lines, 20 = †84 mm. Leaf size †281 × †195 mm

Contents: Title (1), TP verso (2), contents, continued (3), blank (*i*), contents, concluded (4), foreword, by Neil Spooner (5), an aboriginal legend (6), acknowledgements (7), list of diagrams (8–9), list of photographs (10), list of appendices (11), text, apparently continued (12–20), wanting from the photocopy examined ([21–182]), text, concluded (183)

Binding: FC: ([in MS-style display script, R justified] **The Australian** | [*do*] **Croquet** | [*do*] **Manual** | [in a calligraphic script, to the R of a sketch in black, featuring the front view of a man player seen through a hoop in close-up] **C.R. SLOANE** | [within a ruled panel] THIS BOOK HAS BEEN | [*do*] AWARDED THE | [*do*] CONFEDERATION OF | [*do*] AUSTRALIAN SPORT | [*do*] STAMP OF APPROVAL). Inside FC: in black near the foot (Published by C. R. Sloane [. . .]). RC: wanting from the photocopy examined. Spine: wanting from the photocopy examined

Copy seen: NLA: 796 3540994 S634 (incomplete photocopy of unknown scale)

Fingerprint: 9090 7878 ".s, 3528 C 1983A [group 2 taken from p 12, group 3 taken from p 12, group 4 taken from p 13]

Notes: Published by the author.

This enlarged edition is modelled closely on (a). The enlargement, including the FC, was evidently achieved by photographic magnification of the original copy. Very little of the original text would appear to be altered: the present edition would appear to have an extra appendix (pp [168]–[183]) and the panel and its contents at the lower R of the FC is evidently reset.

(c) *Third edition (1988)*

[at the head, R justified] 1 | [in a calligraphic script] **THE** | [*do*] **AUSTRALIAN** | [*do*] **CROQUET** | [*do*] **MANUAL** | Quick Brown Fox Printers, | 4/19 Hicks Street, | Southport. Qld. 4215

Formula: [1–95¹]. 95 leaves, pp 1–190

Technical notes: 234 × 147 mm (p 19). 56 lines, 20 = 84 mm. Leaf size 281 × 195 mm; thickness 0.10 mm; wove, unwatermarked, smooth, white

Contents: Title (1), TP verso (2), contents (3–4), foreword, by Neil Spooner (5), an aboriginal legend (6), acknowledgements (7), list of diagrams (8–9), list of photographs (10), list of appendices (11), text (12–190)

Binding: White Astrolux board glued to the edges of the leaves, hinged at the front, no endpapers. FC: printed in black and vivid yellowish Green 129) ([in MS-style display script, in Green on white, R justified] **The Australian** | [*do*] **Croquet** | [*do*] **Manual** | [in a calligraphic script in black on white, to the R of a sketch in black, signed in MS 'Kerr', featuring a front view of a man player seen through a hoop in close-up] **C.R. SLOANE** | [within a ruled panel in black on Green] THIS BOOK HAS BEEN | [*do*] AWARDED THE | [*do*] CONFEDERATION OF | [*do*]

AUSTRALIAN SPORT | [*do*] STAMP OF APPROVAL). Inside FC: in black near the foot (Published by C. R. Sloane 1988, ISBN 0 9592760 2 5). RC: blank. Inside RC: advertisement. Spine: the lower portion is printed in Green and divided from the upper portion, in white, by a black rule, the upper and lower portions being continuous with the background colours on the FC

Copy seen: PC

Fingerprint: 9090 f)90 m.m. Si1. 3 1988A

Notes: Published by the author, printed by Quick Brown Fox Printers, Southport, Queensland.

This edition, enlarged and extended, is modelled closely on earlier editions. Most of the pages left incomplete in (a) and (b) are extended with interpolated matter and the present edition has an extra appendix N ('Afterthoughts and Additions', pp 168–190). It has not be collated systematically with (b).

A211   COACHING HANDBOOK. [The Croquet Association]   [1982]

[The FC]

Coaching | Handbook | for the coaching of | beginners and more | advanced players | Published by the Croquet Association

Formula: [1–51¹]. 51 leaves, ff 1–51

Technical notes: 257 × 160 mm (variable) (p 3, ragged). 61 lines, 20 = 84 mm. Leaf size 297 × 210 mm; thickness 0.10 mm; wove, unwatermarked, smooth, white

Contents: Text (1–51), name of publisher (51)

Binding: Astrolux boards front and rear, slotted, fastened by a white plastic comb, no endpapers. FC: printed in black as above. Inside FC: blank. RC: blank. Inside RC: blank. Spine: blank

Copy seen: PC

Fingerprint: n.ne e.ct e.ng).ng 3 1982Q [groups 1–4 taken from pp 1, 5, 13, 13 respectively]

Notes: Printed anonymously. Year of publication is inferred from the review cited below.

Review: *The Croquet Gazette* (Winter 1982, p 9).

**A212   THE OFFICIAL RULES OF THE UNITED STATES CROQUET   1982
ASSOCIATION AMERICAN SIX WICKET GAME AND
AMERICAN NINE WICKET GAME AND GOLF CROQUET.**
[The United States Croquet Association]

(a) *First edition (1982)*

[The FC]

1982 | [device of the USCA] | The Official Rules of The | UNITED STATES | CROQUET ASSOCIATION | American Six Wicket Game | and | American Nine Wicket Game | and | Golf Croquet

Formula: [1¹⁸]. 18 leaves, pp *1* 2–36

Technical notes: 137 × 89 mm (p 6). 43 lines, 20 = 65 mm. Leaf size 152 × 101 mm; thickness 0.09 mm; wove, unwatermarked, smooth, white

Contents: Title (*1*), contents and assertion of copyright (2), foreword by Jack R Osborn (3), official USCA 6-wicket layout (4), USCA American six-wicket game —

the court, setting, equipment, and accessories (5–8), — basic principles of play (9–12), — customs and etiquette (13–14), — rules, numbered 1–68, and advanced rule amendments 1–2 (15–26), official rules for the nine-wicket game (27–33), rules of golf croquet, numbered 1–10 (34), advertisements (35–36)

Binding: Pale Blue (185) card printed in deep Blue (179), stapled, no spine or endpapers. FC: title *etc* as above. Inside FC: blank. RC: about the USCA. Inside RC: blank

Copy seen: PC

Fingerprint: a.ss e.re e.be arun 3 1982A [group 1 taken from p 3]

Notes: Printed anonymously.

The official rules of the USCA American six-wicket and nine-wicket games had first appeared in Charlton and Thompson (A198) in 1977, and had subsequently been reprinted in the *US Croquet Gazette* (1980).

(b) *Official 1986–7 edition (1986)*

Not seen. The FC of this edition is illustrated in an advertisement in (c).

(c) *Official 1987–8 edition (1987)*

[The FC]

1987-8 | [device of the USCA] | The Official Rules of The | UNITED STATES | CROQUET ASSOCIATION | American Six Wicket Game | and | American Nine Wicket Game | and | Golf Croquet

Formula: [1²⁸]. 28 leaves, pp *1–3* 4–26, *i–iv*, 27–52 [= 56]

Technical notes: 139 × 76 mm (p 23). 42 lines, 20 = 67 mm. Leaf size 152 × 97 mm; thickness 0.11 mm; wove, unwatermarked, smooth, white

Contents: Title (*1*), contents (*1–3*), foreword by Jack R Osborn (4), introduction (5), official USCA 6-wicket layout (6), USCA American six-wicket game — the court, setting, equipment, and accessories (7–11), — basic principles of play (12–15), — customs and etiquette (16–19), — rules, numbered 1–69, and optional advanced rule, continued (20–26), advertisement (*i–iv*), — rules, concluded (27–34), official rules for the nine-wicket game (35–43), rules of golf croquet, numbered 1–8 (43–45), glossary (46–49), advertisements (50–52)

Binding: Strong orange Yellow (68) leather-effect embossed card printed in black, stapled, no spine or endpapers. FC: title *etc* as above. Inside FC: blank. RC: about the USCA. Inside RC: blank

Copy seen: PC

Fingerprint: 49y* AYON 2;t; daof 3 1987A

Notes: Printed anonymously.

(d) *Official 1989 edition [1989]*

[The FC]

[device of the USCA] | The Official Rules of The | UNITED STATES | CROQUET ASSOCIATION | American Six Wicket Game | and | American Nine Wicket Game | and | Golf Croquet

Formula: [1³⁴]. 34 leaves, pp *1–3* 4–32, *i–iv*, 33–64 [= 68]

Technical notes: 132 × 76 mm (p 17). 38 lines, 20 = 70 mm. Leaf size 152 × 94 mm; thickness 0.09 mm; wove, unwatermarked, smooth, white

Contents: Title (*1*), contents (*1–3*), foreword by Jack R Osborn (*4*), introduction by Dan Shepherd (*5*), official USCA 6-wicket layout (*6*), USCA American six-wicket game — the court, setting, equipment, and accessories (*7–13*), — basic principles of play (*14–18*), — customs and etiquette (*18–21*), — rules, numbered 1–69, optional advanced rule, and experimental rules 1–4, continued (*22–32*), advertisement (*i–iv*), — rules, concluded (*33–41*), official rules for the nine-wicket game (*42–51*), rules of golf croquet, numbered 1–8 (*52–54*), glossary (*55–58*), advertisements (*59–60*), blank save pagination and heading 'NOTES' (*61–64*)

Binding: Pale Blue (185) leather-effect embossed card printed in deep Blue (179), stapled, no spine or endpapers. FC: title *etc*, as above. Inside FC: blank. RC: about the USCA. Inside RC: blank

Copy seen: PC

Fingerprint: 55y* tsts AYON with 3 1989Q

Notes: Printed anonymously. Year of publication is inferred from the year of copyright.

(e) *Official 1992 edition (1992)*

[The FC, printed in strong Green (141) on very light Green (143)]

[device of the USCA] | The Official Rules of The | UNITED STATES | CROQUET ASSOCIATION | American Six Wicket Game | and | American Nine Wicket Game | and | Golf Croquet

Formula: [1³²]. 32 leaves, pp *1–3 4–59 60–64*

Technical notes: 136 × 77 mm (p 8). 43 lines, 20 = 64 mm. Leaf size 153 × 96 mm; thickness 0.13 mm; wove, unwatermarked, smooth, white

Contents: Title (*1*), contents (*1–3*), foreword by Rudolph E ('Foxy') Carter (*4*), USCA American six-wicket game — the court and setting (*5–6*), — equipment (*7–10*), — the object of the game (*10–13*), — customs and ethics (*13–15*), — rules, numbered 1–73, and experimental rules, numbered 1 and 2 (*16–38*), rules of the standard nine wicket game (*38–47*), rules of golf croquet, numbered 1–8 (*47–49*), glossary (*50–54*), index (*55–58*), advertisements (*59–60*), blank save heading 'NOTES' (*61–64*)

Binding: Very light Green (143) leather-effect embossed card printed in strong Green (141), stapled, no spine or endpapers. FC: title *etc* as above. Inside FC: blank. RC: about the USCA. Inside RC: blank

Copy seen: PC

Fingerprint: 55ex t.or n.en opwh 3 1992A [group 1 taken from p 3]

Notes: Printed anonymously.

(f) *Official 1995–6 edition (1995)*

[The FC, in white out of deep purplish Blue (197)]

[device of the USCA] | **The Official Rules of The | UNITED STATES | CROQUET ASSOCIATION | American Six Wicket Game | and | American Nine Wicket Game | and | Golf Croquet**

Formula: [1⁴⁶]. 46 leaves, pp *1–44, i–iv, 45–88* [= 92]

Technical notes: 135 × 77 mm (p 6). 42 lines, 20 = 64 mm. Leaf size 152 × 98 mm; thickness 0.12 mm; wove, unwatermarked, smooth, white

Contents: Title (*1*), contents (*1–3*), foreword by Bill Berne (*4*), USCA American six-wicket game — the court and setting (*5*), — equipment (*6–9*), — outline of the game (9–11), — customs and etiquette (11–16), — rules, numbered 1–74, continued (17–44), advertisement (*i–iv*), — rules, concluded, and experimental rules, numbered 1–3 (45–52), blank save pagination and heading 'NOTES' (53–55), nine-wicket game — layout (56), — rules (57–62), blank save pagination and heading 'NOTES' (63), rules of golf croquet, numbered 1–8 (64–66), blank save pagination and heading 'NOTES' (67), glossary (68–73), index (74–80), advertisements (81–88)

Binding: Semi-gloss white card, the FC and RC printed in white out of deep purplish Blue (197), stapled, no spine or endpapers. FC: title *etc* as above. Inside FC: advertisement. RC: about the USCA. Inside RC: advertisement

Copy seen: PC

Fingerprint: A.e, n.ny ine. abWh 3 1995 [group 1 taken from p 3]

Notes: Printed anonymously.

1983

A213   WINNING CROQUET: FROM BACKYARD TO   1983
GREENSWARD — THE SKILLS, STRATEGIES AND RULES
OF AMERICA'S MOST SOPHISTICATED OUTDOOR SPORT.
Jack Osborn and Jesse Kornbluth

WINNING | [within the outline of a circle] *From Backyard* | [*do*] *to Greensward* | [*do*] *—the Skills,* | [*do*] *Strategies and Rules* | [*do*] *of America's* | [*do*] *Most Sophisticated* | [*do*] *Outdoor Sport* | *CROQUET* | *Jack Osborn* | *President, United States Croquet Association* | *and* | *Jesse Kornbluth* | *Foreword by Herbert Bayard Swope, Jr.* | *Instructional Photographs by William Powers* | *Illustrations by Alan Scheuch and Willie Espada* | *SIMON AND SCHUSTER / New York*

Formula: [1–112¹]. 112 leaves, pp *1–4* 5 6 *7–9 10* 11–15 *16* 17–65 *66–67* 68–70 *71* 72–80 *81* 82–84 *85* 86–88 *89* 90 *91* 92–98 *99* 100 *101* 102–103 *104* 105 *106–107* 108–113 *114–115* 116 *117* 118 *119* 120–170 *171* 172–207 *208* 209–224

Technical notes: 187 × 109 mm (p 12). 41 lines, 20 = 91 mm. Leaf size 234 × 154 mm; thickness 0.13 mm; wove, unwatermarked, smooth, white

Contents: Publisher's device, line drawing of a walker (*1*), blank (*2*), title (*3*), TP verso (*4*), contents (*5–6*), foreword, signed 'Herbert Bayard Swope, Jr' (*7–8*), acknowledgements (*9*), blank (*10*), authors' introduction (*11–15*), blank (*16*), text, continued (*17–207*), blank (*208*), text, concluded (*209–224*)

Binding: White glossy laminated card glued to the edges of the leaves, no endpapers. FC: printed in brilliant greenish Yellow (98), white, and full colour out of a moderate Green (145) background ([in Yellow] **Winning Croquet** | [in white] **From Backyard to Greensward** | [two posed colour photographs, side by side within a square panel, showing the legs of a player with mallet, hoop, and ball, contrasting the backyard and greensward games] | [in white out of Green] [double rule] **The Skills, Strategies and Rules** | [*do*] **of America's Most** [double rule] | [*do*] **Sophisticated Outdoor Sport** | [in Yellow] Jack Osborn, President, U.S. Croquet Association, | [*do*] [double rule] and Jesse Kornbluth [double rule]). Inside FC: blank. RC: publisher's blurb, incorporating a photograph of Osborn, and price, in black and white. Inside RC: blank. Spine: downwards in white and Yellow out of Green background, continuous with that of the FC ([in white] Osborn and Kornbluth [in Yellow] Winning Croquet [in white] Simon and Schuster)

Copy seen: PC

Fingerprint: 6056 rend e.da iner 7 1983A

Notes: Printed anonymously, paperback price $9.95. ISBN 0-671-45824-8 cloth, 0-671-47276-3 paper. Year of publication is as given in the LC Cataloging in Publication data reproduced on the TP verso.

1984

A214 ASSOCIATION CROQUET. Masaru Ikeda   [1984]

[In strong Green (141)]

[Japanese title *etc* displayed in open script on two lines about a zigzag rule] | **Association** | **Croquet** | [one line of Japanese script]

Formula: [1–79¹]. 79 leaves including the front and rear pastedowns, pp *i–vi, 1–9* 10–14 *15* 16–32 *33* 34–70 *71* 72–96 *97* 98–100 *101* 102–132 *133* 134–145 *146–148, vii–x*

Technical notes: 132 × 90 mm (p 21). 27 lines, 20 = 109 mm. Leaf size 182-127 mm. Pp *i–iv vi–x*: thickness 0.18 mm; wove, unwatermarked, smooth, vivid Yellow Green (115). Pp *v–vi*: thickness 0.11 mm; wove, unwatermarked, smooth, white. Pp *1–148*: thickness 0.13 mm; wove, unwatermarked, smooth, white

Contents: Glued to the FC (*i*), blank (*ii–iv*), title (*v*), blank (*vi*), *1–4* (preliminaries), blank (*5*), contents (*6–7*), blank (*8*), text (*9–145*), blank (*146*), name of printer (*147*), blank (*148–151*), glued to the RC (*152*)

Binding: Light Grey (264) light card glued to the edges of the leaves. FC: blank. RC: blank. Spine: blank

Dust wrapper: High-gloss white paper laminate. FP: (Japanese title displayed in open script on two lines about a zigzag rule, the title in vivid Green (139) outlined in dark yellowish Green (137) and black, and the rule in strong Yellow Green (117) | [colour photograph of a game of croquet in a panel superimposed on a stylised array of four balls in moderate Blue (182), vivid Red (11), black, and strong Yellow (84)] | [one line of Japanese script]). FF: Japanese script in light Grey (264) and black. RP: ([stylised array of four balls in moderate Blue (182), vivid Red (11), black, and strong Yellow (84)] | [in white out of a strong Yellow Green (117) panel superimposed over an array of four balls (as above)] **Association** | [*do*] **Croquet** | [one line of Japanese script] | [R justified, in black] ISBN–583–02434–7 C2075 [Japanese character] 1200E). RF: ([one line of Japanese script in black]). Spine: downwards ([Japanese script in light bluish Green (163) outlined in moderate bluish Green (164) and black]), publisher's device ([in black, a stylised representation of a discus thrower]) crosswise at the foot.

Copy seen: PC

Fingerprint: Not reproducible in an available font

Notes: Apparently published by Baseball Magazine (incorporated within a device on p *147*). Author and year of publication are inferred from the assertion of copyright (p *147*).

AA215 CROQUET: A DEVELOPMENT PLAN FOR THE EASTERN   1984
REGION. [The Eastern Region Croquet Development Committee]

[Folio *1*, interspersed by line drawings of players of several sports]

[Sports Council device at R | <u>CROQUET</u> | A DEVELOPMENT PLAN FOR | THE EASTERN REGION | 1984–87 | [Sports Council device at L] | [one of three lines at R] The Eastern Region Croquet | [*do*] Development Committee | [*do*] January 1984

Formula: [1–14¹]. 14 leaves, unnumbered [ff 1–14]

Technical notes: ca 282 × 187 mm (p 5, ragged). 44 lines, 20 = *ca* 128 mm. Leaf size *ca* 296 × 210 mm.

Contents: Title (*1*), text (*2–13*), blank (*14*)

Binding: Apparently stapled between plain covers, the title visible through a cut-out panel in the FC.

Copy seen: PC (photocopy)

Fingerprint: y.ts on83 81QP rdad C 1984A [groups 3 and 4 taken from the R column of f *13*]

Notes: Printed anonymously, issued in January 1984. The Eastern Region Croquet Development Committee, an *ad hoc* body promoted by the CA to assist in exploiting Sports Council funding in the eastern region, was the forerunner of the East Anglian Croquet Federation.

AA216 [THE] CROQUET ASSOCIATION FORWARD PLAN.   1984
[The Croquet Association]

(a) *First edition, 1985–89 forward plan (1984)*

CROQUET ASSOCIATION FORWARD PLAN | [R justified, at the foot] 9th November, 1984.

Formula: [1–126¹]. 126 leaves, numbered within sections [ff 1–126]

Technical notes: 253 × 170 mm (f 5). 60 lines, 20 = 84 mm. Leaf size 297 × 210 mm; thickness 0.10 mm; wove, unwatermarked, smooth, white

Contents: Title (*1*), contents (*2*), Section 1: introduction (*3*), Section 2: current situation (*4–9*), Section 3: overall aims (*10*), Section 4: summary of individual programmes (*11–22*), Section 5: financial summary and plan targets (*23–24*), Section 6: job description of development officer (*25–27*), Section 7: central programmes (*28–74*), regional programmes (*75–126*)

Binding: Moderate greenish Blue (173) card covers, pierced at two points and bound by a Twingrip metal fastener, no spine or endpapers. FC: blank. Inside FC: blank. RC: blank. Inside RC: blank

Copy seen: CA

Fingerprint: onon s.gh 503) 0)3) C 1984A [groups 3 and 4 taken from the extreme R column of f *13*]

Notes: Issued to officials of the CA and other interested parties, presented to the Sports Council, printed anonymously.

(b) *1988–90 forward plan [1987]*

THE CROQUET ASSOCIATION | FORWARD PLAN: 1988–1990

Formula: [1–37¹]. 126 leaves, numbered within sections [ff 1–37]

Technical notes: 253 × 166 mm (f 4). 60 lines, 20 = 84 mm. Leaf size 297 × 210 mm; thickness 0.10 mm; wove, unwatermarked, smooth, white

Contents: Title (*1*), contents (*2*), Section 1: introduction (*3–6*), Section 2: financial summary (*7*), Section 3: development programmes (*8–35*), Appendix: job description of development officer (*36–37*)

Binding: Strong Red (12) leather-effect card covers, slotted and fastened by a white plastic-coated wire comb, no spine or endpapers. FC: blank. Inside FC: blank. RC: blank. Inside RC: blank

Copy seen: CA

Fingerprint: erns 0.to s.ch etnd C 1987Q [groups 3 and 4 taken from f *13*]

Notes: Issued to officials of the CA and other interested parties, presented to the Sports Council, printed anonymously. Year of publication is well documented in the archives of the CA.

(c) *1991–94 forward plan [1991]*

THE CROQUET ASSOCIATION | FORWARD PLAN: 1991–1994 | [device of the CA]

Formula: [1³⁰]. 30 leaves, numbered within sections and sub-sections only [pp 1–60]

Technical notes: 186 × 118 mm (p *20*). 62 lines, 20 = 60 mm. Leaf size 210 × 146 mm; thickness 0.10 mm; wove, unwatermarked, smooth, white

Contents: Title (*1*), blank (*2*), index (*3*), blank (*4*), Section 1, introduction (*5–13*), blank (*14*), Section 2, financial summary (*15*), blank (*16*), Section 3.1, administration and membership services (*17–22*), blank (*23–24*), Section 3.2, development (*25–27*), blank (*28*), Section 3.3, access (*29–35*), blank (*36*), Section 3.4, publicity (*37–39*), blank (*40*), Section 3.5, coaching (*41–43*), blank (*44*), Section 3.6, international (*45–47*), blank (*48*), Appendix A, regional policies and practices (*49–50*), blank (*51–52*), Appendix B, facility needs (*53*), blank (*54*), Appendix C, statistics (*55–56*), Appendix D, job description of development officer (*57–58*), blank (*59–60*)

Binding: Stapled, no covers, spine or endpapers

Copy seen: PC

Fingerprint: ercs s.CA 4.er arth C 1991Q

Notes: Issued to officials of the CA and other interested parties, presented to the Sports Council, printed anonymously.

(d) *1994 edition, 1995–98 forward plan (1994)*

[device of the CA] | FORWARD PLAN | 1995–1998 | [R justified, at the foot] 5th October, 1994

Formula: [1²⁰]. 20 leaves, pp *i–ii*, 1–36, *37–38*

Technical notes: 178 × 118 mm (p *11*). 60 lines, 20 = 59 mm. Leaf size 210 × 148 mm; thickness 0.11 mm; wove, unwatermarked, smooth, white

Contents: Title (*i*), blank (*ii*), main objective (1), introduction (2–3), summary and recommendations (4–5), recruitment (6–9), facilities provision (10–12), coaching provision (13–15), competition provision (16–19), regional activities (20–21), publicity (22–23), junior and schools (24–25), special projects (26–28), administration (29–30), increasing income (31–32), summary of objectives and targets (33–36), blank (*37–38*)

Binding: The copy examined is stapled and unbound

Copy seen: PC

Fingerprint: 33me s.s. s.ew anPr 3 1994A

Notes: Issued by the CA to officials of the association and other interested parties, presented to the Sports Council, printed anonymously.

A217 WINSLOW HOMER: THE CROQUET GAME. David Park Curry   1984

[in medium Grey (265)] **WINSLOW HOMER** [in light Grey (264)] **THE CROQUET GAME** | By *David Park Curry* | *Yale University Art Gallery* · *New Haven* · *Connecticut*

[TP verso, L justified]

Copyright © 1984 | by Yale University Art Gallery | All rights reserved | Library of Congress catalogue number 84–050421 | ISBN: 0–89467–031–X

Formula: [1⁶ 2⁸ 3⁴]. 18 leaves, unnumbered [pp 1–36], the pages divided into two columns

Technical notes: 232 × 138 mm max (p *10*, ragged). 51 lines, 20 = 92 mm. Leaf size 280 × 194 mm; thickness 0.12 mm; wove, unwatermarked, semi-gloss, white

Contents: Title (*1*), TP verso (*2*), foreword, signed 'Helen A Cooper' (*3*), acknowledgements, signed 'David Park Curry' (*4*), lenders to the exhibition (*5*), text (*6–35*), name of printer (*36*)

Binding: White art paper, with hinge, glued to the gatherings, sewn, no endpapers. FC: blank. RC: blank. Spine: blank

Dust wrapper: Very smooth matt white paper. FP: near the head, a colour reproduction of an oil painting entitled 'A game of croquet' by Homer; near the foot, the title ([in bluish Grey (191)] WINSLOW HOMER [in greyish Yellow (90)] THE CROQUET GAME). FF: the galleries where the exhibition catalogued by this work was held, and the opening and closing dates of the exhibition at each location. RP: blank. RF: blank. Spine: blank

Copy seen: PC

Fingerprint: esus n.er rkm. cobr C 1984A [group 2 taken from the caption to fig 10, group 3 taken from the caption to fig 13]

Notes: Printed by The W[illia]m Mack Co and The Meriden Gravure Co. It is conjectured that this work, produced as the main catalogue for a special exhibition of the croquet works of Homer, was first published when the exhibition opened at the Yale University Art Gallery on 18 April 1984.

1985

A218　EXPERT CROQUET TACTICS. KF Wylie　　　　　　　　　[1985]

(a) *First edition [1985]*

EXPERT CROQUET TACTICS | K. F. Wylie

[TP verso]

[on a stick-on label] I. S. B. N.　0 9511914 0 3 | [*do*] Library of Congress Catalog Number 86-670095 | © Copyright K.F.Wylie 1985 | Printed on acid-free paper by Unitset Limited, Southampton, England

Formula: [1–10⁸]. 80 bound leaves and 1 loose leaf, pp *1–4* 5–150 *151–160, i–ii* [= 162]

Technical notes: 214 × 139 mm (p 15). 40 lines, 20 = 108 mm. Leaf size 270 × 187 mm; thickness 0.15 mm; wove, unwatermarked, smooth, white

Contents: Title (*1*), TP verso (*2*), contents (*3*), dedication (*4*), preface, dated 'All Saints' Day 1985' (*5*), text (6–150), blank (*151–160*), *addenda, corrigenda,* and 'replies to just criticism' (*i*), blank (*ii*)

Binding: Vivid Red (11) cloth over stiff boards, sewn. FC: gold-blocked (**EXPERT** | **CROQUET** | **TACTICS**). RC: blank. Spine: gold-blocked downwards ([from near the top edge] **EXPERT CROQUET TACTICS** [to near the foot] **Wylie**)

Dust wrapper: Plain medium Grey (265) wove paper

Copy seen: PC

Fingerprint: 5049　.)he　t.wn　un(b 3 1985Q

Notes: Published privately in December 1985; printed by Unitset; price £21 (discounted for orders in advance of publication).

The print run comprised some 250 copies, of which this first edition was limited to 200. When stocks had been exhausted, the remaining copies were issued as (b). The combined profits realised by the two issues were donated to the CA.

The loose leaf insert was extended cumulatively as the author and readers noted points which called for revision and further comment.

Review: *Croquet* (1986)

(b) *Surplus to first edition [1986]*

[The TP as that of (a)]

[TP verso]

[over-printed in moderate Blue (182)] SURPLUS | [*do*] TO FIRST | [*do*] EDITION | [on a stick-on label] I. S. B. N. 0 9511914 0 3 | [*do*] Library of Congress Catalog Number 86-670095 | [*do*] Copyright K.F.Wylie 1985 | [*do*] Printed on acid-free paper by Unitset Limited, Southampton, England

Formula: As that of (a)

Technical notes: As at (a)

Contents: As the contents of (a)

Binding: As that of (a)

Dust wrapper: None

Copy seen: PC

Fingerprint: 5049 .)he t.wn un(b 3 1986Q

Notes: Published privately, printed by Unitset. This issue consisted of some few dozen copies, which were sold at a discount by the CA when stocks of (a) had been exhausted.

(c) *Second edition (1991)*

[pagination, R justified] *i* | [rule] | **Expert** | **Croquet** | **Tactics** | by | Keith Wylie | EASTERN ROSE PUBLISHING

[TP verso, L justified]

Second Edition | PUBLISHED BY | Eastern Rose Publishing | No. 17, Wroxham Road | Ipswich | Suffolk IP3 0PH | First Edition Published in 1985 by K F Wylie | Copyright © K F Wylie 1985 – 1991 | ISBN 1 874135 00 2 Expert Croquet Tactics. 2nd Edition.   (pbk) | [...] | Printed by the Benfoy Press | Typeset at Eastern Rose Publishing | [...]

Formula: Not ascertainable from the copy examined. 82 leaves, pp i–ix *x*, 1–153 *154*

Technical notes: 174 × 114 mm (p 5). 40 lines, 20 = 88 mm. Leaf size 214 × 152 mm; thickness 0.11 mm; wove, unwatermarked, very smooth, white

Contents: Title (i), TP verso (ii), contents (iii), dedication (iv), preface to the second edition, signed St Luke's Day 1991 (v–vi), preface, signed All Saints' Day 1985 (vii–viii), notation and technical terms (viii–ix), blank (*x*), text (1–153), blank (*154*)

Binding: White Astrolux laminate board with hinges front and rear, glued over the spine, printed in black, vivid reddish Orange (34), and gold, no endpapers. FC: printed on and out of an Orange background ([in gold] **EXPERT** | [*do*] **CROQUET** | [*do*] **TACTICS** | [perspective drawing of a hoop, in white out of Orange, set at the centre of a three-by-three chequer board, in gold and black] | [in gold] **Keith Wylie** | [publisher's device, in gold within an elliptical white frame]

Copy seen: PC

Fingerprint: 5352 ises lyt2 *lyFi* 3 1991A [group 4 taken from the caption to fig 1.13 on p 14]

Notes: Printed by the Benfoy Press, price £12. Five hundred copies were commissioned by the CA, 200 by the author.

The letterpress in this edition is entirely reset. The last of four 'articles' (on openings) is largely rewritten, the others are reproduced with only minor revisions.

Review: *Croquet* (March/April 1992, p 21).

AA219 SYDNEY CROQUET CLUB: 50TH ANNIVERSARY.   [1985]
T Hooper (ed), Stanley Irwin, *et al*

[The FC]

[sketch of clubhouse] | **SYDNEY CROQUET CLUB** | Clubhouse Log Cabin — Woollahra Park | **50th Anniversary** | Saturday, 27th April, 1985

Formula: [1⁴]. 4 leaves, unnumbered [pp 1–8]

Technical notes: 184 × 122 mm (p *4*). 44 lines, 20 = 84 mm. Leaf size 205 × 145 mm; thickness 0.10 mm; wove, unwatermarked, smooth, white

Contents: Particulars of club and names of officials (*1*), list of club members (*2*), anniversary programme (*3*), club history (*4–8*)

Binding: Moderate orange Yellow (71) textured card printed in black, stapled, no spine or endpapers. FC: as above. Inside FC: blank. RC: blank. Inside RC: blank

Copy seen: PC

Fingerprint: rsys ay00 s.ue Ins) C 1985Q

Notes: Printed anonymously. Year of publication is inferred from the stated anniversary year.

1986

A220 THE BASICS OF CROQUET. Xandra Kayden   [1986]
[The FC]

THE BASICS OF CROQUET | What it is About, How to Play it, and Rules of the | American and British Association Games | Xandra Kayden | The New England Collegiate Croquet Association | 372 Harvard Street, Cambridge, Massachusetts 02138 | (617) 492-6141

Formula: [1¹⁸]. 18 leaves, pp 1–36

Technical notes: 123 × 79 mm (p *12*). 35 lines, 20 = 70 mm. Leaf size 151 × 101 mm; thickness 0.13 mm; wove, unwatermarked, smooth, white

Contents: Preface, signed 'Xandra Kayden', Fall 1986 (*1*), contents (*2*), text (*3–36*)

Binding: Light Grey (264) card, stapled, no spine or endpapers. FC: title *etc*, as above. Inside FC: blank. RC: printer's device at the foot. Inside FC: blank

Copy seen: PC

Fingerprint: 86s. e.nd ..g, plTh 3 1986Q [group 1 taken from p 1, group 2 taken from the text on p 9, group 4 taken from the text on p 14]

Notes: Printed by Allied Printing, Boston. Year of publication is inferred from the date appended to the signature to the preface (p 1).

A221 THE UPS AND DOWNS OF CROQUET PLAYERS.   1986
Dorothy M Edwards

[The FC, over a group of cartoons in the artist's hand]

The Ups and Downs | **of** | **Croquet Players** | [MS in the artist's hand] by | [*do*] Dorothy M. Edwards

Formula: [l¹⁸]. 18 leaves, pp 1 (recto), 1 (verso)–35 [= 36], p 1 duplicated

Technical notes: 196 × 128 mm (p 12, artwork). Leaf size 210 × 148 mm; thickness 0.10 mm; wove, unwatermarked, smooth, white

Contents: Foreword (1), sketches (1–35)

Binding: Very pale Green (148) parchment-effect light card, printed in black, stapled, no spine or endpapers. FC: as above. Inside FC: blank. RC: ([a group of cartoons in the artist's hand, continued on the FC] | [MS in the artist's hand] Prospect Croquet Club 1926-86). Inside RC: blank

Copy seen: PC

Fingerprint: edbe dsn. urwn l.on C 1986Q [all four groups taken from p 1 (recto)]

Notes: Published by the Prospect Croquet Club of Australia and printed anonymously. The identity of the publisher is inferred from an acknowledgement on p 1 (recto). Year of publication is inferred from a reference on p 1 (recto) to the artist having celebrated her 90th birthday in February 1986.

This work consists of a collection of sketches, most with captions in the artist's own hand and some with captions in typescript.

1987

A222 CROQUET HANDBOOK [and THE OBSERVER/LASSALE   [1987]
CROQUET CLASSIC, THE CARLSBERG CROQUET
HANDBOOK]. [The Croquet Association]

(a) *First edition [1987]*

[Page *1*]

[set between upper and lower rules] YOUR CROQUET HANDBOOK | THE OBSERVER/**LASSALE** | CROQUET CLASSIC | [framed half-tone photograph of a man and woman, posing in play] | Organised in Collaboration with The Croquet Association | **LASSALE** | THE MODERN CLASSIC

Formula: [1¹⁰]. 10 leaves, unnumbered [pp 1–20]

Technical notes: 131 × 86 mm (p 7). 27 lines, 20 = 98 mm. Leaf size 146 × 104 mm; thickness 0.15 mm; wove, unwatermarked, smooth, pale Yellow (89), printed in brownish Black (65)

Contents: Title (*1*), advertisements (*2*), text (*3–19*), advertisement for Lassale watches (*20*)

Binding: No wrapper, stapled, no spine or endpapers

Copy seen: CA

Fingerprint: t.ot e.ur).ot st4. C 1987Q

Notes: Printed anonymously. Year of publication is inferred from the following indications:

(i) Lassale was a prominent sponsor of the CA in 1987.

(ii) The copy examined is among the contents of a Starter Pack of publicity material issued by the Publicity Committee of the CA in June 1987.

(b) *Second edition, Carlsberg issue [1988]*

[Page *1*]

The Carlsberg | **Croquet Handbook** | [framed half-tone photograph of a man and woman, posing in play] | [Carlsberg logo]

Formula: [1¹⁰]. 10 leaves, unnumbered [pp 1–20]

Technical notes: 134 × 84 mm (p 8). 27 lines, 20 = 99mm. Leaf size 148 × 105 mm; thickness 0.18 mm; wove, unwatermarked, smooth, white, printed in deep yellowish Green (132)

Contents: Title (*1*), advertisements (*2*), text (*3–19*), advertisement by Carlsberg (*20*)

Binding: No wrapper, stapled, no spine or endpapers

Copy seen: PC

Fingerprint: t.an inhe hely 1.Yo C 1988Q [group 3 taken from the text on p *13*]

Notes: Printed anonymously. Year of publication is inferred from the fact that Carlsberg were prominent sponsors of the CA during the years 1987 and 1988. This issue was produced in connection with a scheme funded by Carlsberg to sell croquet sets to hotels and other institutions.

The text, though reset throughout, is mostly identical to that of (a). The only substantive variations are an expansion of the treatment given to the peg-out and an additional section on wiring lifts. The cover photograph is the same as that of (a).

(c) *Second edition, Royal Bank of Scotland issue [1991]*

[Page *1*]

CROQUET HANDBOOK | [half-tone photograph of man and woman, posing in play, within a double-ruled frame incorporating the device of the CA at the lower R corner] | **Published by** | **The Croquet Association**

Formula: [1¹⁰]. 10 leaves, unnumbered [pp 1–20]

Technical notes: 134 × 84 mm (p 8). 27 lines, 20 = 99mm. Leaf size 148 × 105 mm; thickness 0.18 mm; wove, unwatermarked, smooth, light bluish Grey (190), printed in strong purplish Blue (196)

Contents: Title (*1*), advertisements (*2*), text (*3–19*), advertisement by the Royal Bank of Scotland (*20*)

Binding: No wrapper, stapled, no spine or endpapers

Copy seen: PC

Fingerprint: t.an inhe hely 1.Yo C 1991Q [group 3 taken from the text on p *13*]

Notes: Printed anonymously, (1993) price £0.75 to Associates. Year of publication is inferred from the following indications:

(i) The Royal Bank of Scotland was a prominent sponsor of the CA for several years from 1987.

(ii) The photograph on p *1* is a detail of a photograph in the May 1991 issue of *Croquet* (p 23).

(iii) This issue was offered for sale by the CA in 1993 and subsequent years.

AA223 A PLAN FOR DEVELOPMENT BY THE EAST ANGLIAN   **[1987]**
CROQUET FEDERATION [or CROQUET IN THE EASTERN
REGION]. [East Anglian Croquet Federation and Sports Council
(Eastern Region)]

[The FC, printed in gradations of vivid Yellow Green [115], and black]

[Sports Council device, L justified, in white out of solid Yellow Green] | [device of
East Anglian Croquet Federation, in black on solid Yellow Green, at R] | [in white
out of solid Yellow Green, L justified] **CROQUET** | [*do*] **IN THE** | [*do*] **EASTERN**
REGION | [device of East Anglian Croquet Federation in solid Yellow Green, on
dark gradation, at L] | [one of three lines, in solid Yellow Green, on dark gradation]
A plan for development | [*do*] **by the East Anglian** | [*do*] **Croquet Federation** |
[device of East Anglian Croquet Federation, in solid Yellow Green within white
panel out of medium gradation, at R] | [one of two lines, in solid Yellow Green, on
pale gradation] A Memorandum to the Eastern Council | [*do*] for Sport and
Recreation | [device of East Anglian Croquet Federation in solid Yellow Green,
on pale gradation, R justified] | [one of four lines, in solid Yellow Green on white,
L justified] Produced by the Sports Council | [*do*] (Eastern Region) | [*do*] in co-
operation with the | [*do*] East Anglian Croquet Federation | [other device of the
Sports Council in black on white]

Formula: [l⁴]. 4 leaves, pp 1–8

Technical notes: 265 × 188 mm (p 1), divided into two columns. 69 lines, 20 = 77
mm. Leaf size 296 × 209 mm; thickness 0.10 mm; wove, unwatermarked, smooth,
white

Contents: Text (1–8)

Binding: White semi-gloss light card, stapled, no spine or endpapers. FC: as above.
Inside FC: surrogate TP verso. RC: blank. Inside RC: at the foot (Printed in England
by **Newnorth-Burt**, Kempston, Bedford)

Copy seen: PC

Fingerprint: annt ndor cen, s,he C 1987Q [all four groups taken from p 1]

Notes: Produced by the Sports Council (Eastern Region) in co-operation with the
East Anglian Croquet Federation, printed by Newnorth-Burt, Bedford. Year of
publication is inferred from the text.

A224   PLUS ONE ON TIME. DL Gaunt   **[1987]**

[Mostly within a ruled frame]

PLUS ONE | **ON TIME** | CROQUET TACTICS FOR THE MEDIUM | TO HIGH
HANDICAP PLAYER | [rule] | *D L GAUNT* | [below the frame] *1*

[TP verso]

Published by D L Gaunt | *5 Rosedale Avenue* | *Stonehouse* | *Glos.* | *ISBN No. 0*
9512813 0 5

Formula: [1–80¹]. 80 leaves, pp 1–157 *158–160*

Technical notes: 170 × 109 mm (p 9). 41 lines, 20 = 84 mm. Leaf size 210 × 145
mm; thickness 0.13 mm; wove, unwatermarked, smooth, white

Contents: Title (1), TP verso, including dedication (2), about the author (3), blank
save pagination (4), contents (5), blank save pagination (6), text (7–155), blank save
heading and pagination (156), text, signed 'Don Gaunt', 1987 (157), blank
(158–160)

Binding: White high-gloss laminate card with scored hinge, paperback, no end-papers. FC: the lettering *etc* in white, brilliant greenish Blue (168), vivid greenish Yellow (97), and strong Red (12) over and out of a black background within a white ruled frame ([in Blue] **PLUS ONE** | [*do*] **ON TIME** | [white rule] | [in Yellow] CROQUET TACTICS FOR THE MEDIUM | [*do*] TO HIGH HANDICAP PLAYER | [white rule] | [in Red] *D L GAUNT*). RC: near the foot, in white out of black (ISBN No. 0 9512813 0 5). Spine: downwards, in white out of black ([near the head] PLUS ONE ON TIME [near the foot] D L GAUNT)

Copy seen: PC

Fingerprint: e.e- s.os t.at atPl 7 1987Q

Notes: Published in 1987, printed by the Post Office Research Reprographics Department, price £5.00. The initial printing was of 2000 copies, of which 1024 had been sold by mid-September 1998.

A225   THE WORLD OF CROQUET.   1987
John McCullough and Stephen Mulliner

The World of | Croquet | JOHN McCULLOUGH | and | STEPHEN MULLINER | [publisher's device] | **The Crowood Press**

[TP verso]

First published in 1987 by | The Crowood Press | Ramsbury, Marlborough, | Wiltshire SN8 2HE | © John McCullough and Stephen Mulliner 1987 | [. . .] | ISBN 0 946284 59 8 | [. . .]

Formula: [1–14⁸]. 112 leaves, pp *1–3* 4–224

Technical notes: 198 × 152 mm (p 18), the text divided into two columns. 47 lines, 20 = 84 mm. Leaf size 246 × 189 mm; thickness 0.16 mm; wove, unwatermarked, very smooth, white

Contents: Title (*1*), TP verso (*2*), contents (*3*), acknowledgements (*4*), foreword, signed 'Andrew Hooper' (*5*), text (6–224)

Binding: Deep Yellow Green (118) buckram grain paper over stiff boards, sewn. FC: blank. RC: blank. Spine: gold-blocked, mostly downwards ([near the head] THE WORLD OF | [below] **CROQUET** [slightly L of centre] JOHN McCULLOUGH [below] and [below] STEPHEN MULLINER [publisher's device] [crosswise] CROWOOD)

Dust wrapper: Printed on high-gloss white paper laminate. FP: the lettering set over a colour photograph of G Nigel Aspinall, a noted contemporary player, in play ([in greyish Red (19) and black shaded script] **THE WORLD OF** | [in black and light greenish Blue (172) shaded script] **CROQUET** | [in black] JOHN McCULLOUGH and STEPHEN MULLINER). FF: publisher's blurb and price in black, Red and Blue on a light Grey (264) background. RP: on a Grey background ([colour photograph of a game in play, within a panel framed by a Red border outlined in black] | [summary of contents] | [ISBN bar code]). RF: on a Grey background: black-and-white portrait photographs of, and biographical notes about the authors, notes about the illustrations, ISBN, 'Printed in Great Britain'. Spine: mostly downwards on a Grey background ([in black and Red shaded script] **THE WORLD** | [in Blue and black shaded script below] **CROQUET** [slightly R of centre, in black] JOHN McCULLOUGH [below, in black] and [below, in black] STEPHEN MULLINER [publisher's device, crosswise near the foot] [crosswise near the foot, in black] CROWOOD)

Copy seen: PC

Fingerprint: 2221 n.at s.ld orin 3 1987A [group 2 taken from the caption to fig 4, group 3 taken from the caption to fig 7]

Notes: Printed anonymously.

1988

A226 **BEGINNER'S CROQUET. Barrie Chambers and Stan Hall**   [1988]

[The FC]

[in white out of a vivid Green (139) horizontal band] **BEGINNER'S CROQUET** | [in black on the same Green band] by | [*do*] *BARRIE CHAMBERS* | [*do*] and | [*do*] *STAN HALL* | [half-tone photograph of a woman player and man player on court, apparently printed in black and Green]

Formula: [1¹⁴]. 14 leaves, pp *i–ii*, 1–26

Technical notes: 186 × 137 mm (p 6, ragged). 44 lines, 20 = 84 mm. Leaf size 210 × 163 mm; thickness 0.08 mm; wove, unwatermarked, semi-gloss, white

Contents: Contents (*i*), advertisement and assertion of copyright (*ii*), text (1–26), name of printer (26)

Binding: White laminated light card, stapled, no spine or endpapers. FC: as above. Inside FC: blank. RC: advertisement. Inside RC: blank

Copy seen: PC

Fingerprint: 2626 d.re e.be rees 3 1988Q [group 1 taken from p *i*]

Notes: Printed by Hyland Offset, Artarmon, NSW. Year of publication is conjectural. The list of further reading given on p 26 cites a publication dated 1988, the online system of the NLA cites 'between 1983 and 1990', and the catalogue of the library of the West Australian Croquet Association cites 'c1988'.

AA227 **CROQUET IN NORTHERN CALIFORNIA. Bob Alman (ed)**   1988

[Page *1*]

[double rule] | **CROQUET** | [rule] | IN NORTHERN CALIFORNIA | [double rule] | [half-tone photograph of a man player in play] | [double rule] | Clubs and Membership | [rule] | Facilities | [rule] | Instruction and Coaching | [rule] | Event Planning and Production | [rule] | Publications | [double rule]

Formula: A twice-folded leaflet printed on a single sheet. 4 leaves, unnumbered [pp 1–8]

Technical notes: 190 × 71 mm (p 2, ragged). 55 lines, 20 = 70 mm. Leaf size 216 × 89 mm; thickness 0.15 mm; wove, unwatermarked, smooth, white

Contents: Title (*1*), text (*1–8*), empty panel, perhaps intended for over-printing by any of the participating clubs (*8*), publishing details (*8*)

Binding: None

Copy seen: PC

Fingerprint: y.he ste. heet y.th C 1988A [all four groups taken from p *3*]

Notes: Printed anonymously, published by the five participating croquet clubs of Northern California — *viz* Meadowood, San Francisco Croquet Club, Santa Rosa Croquet Club, Sonoma-Cutrer Croquet Club, and Berkeley Croquet Club.

A228   **CROQUET: THE ART AND ELEGANCE OF PLAYING THE**   [1988]
GAME. Donald Charles Richardson

(a) *First edition [1988]*

[in white out of a deep Green (142) panel within a triple-ruled frame, the outer and inner frames in strong reddish Orange (35) and the central frame in brilliant Yellow (83), within a full colour photograph which extends across the facing verso]

CROQUET | • | The Art and Elegance of Playing the Game | by | DONALD CHARLES RICHARDSON | Photographs by John Falocco | [publisher's device] | HARMONY BOOKS/NEW YORK

[From the TP verso]

10 9 8 7 6 5 4 3 2 1 | First edition

Formula: [1–6⁸]. 48 leaves, pp *1–11* 12–17 *18–19* 20–33 *34–35* 36–41 *42–43* 44–57 *58–59* 60–77 *78–79* 80–93 *94–95* 96

Technical notes: 204 × 147 mm (p 12), divided into two columns, the text set in double-ruled frames. 42 lines, 20 = 103 mm. Leaf size 254 × 188 mm; thickness 0.10 mm; wove, unwatermarked, glossy, white

Contents: Half-title *(1)*, extension of the TP *(2)*, title *(3)*, TP verso *(4)*, dedication *(5)*, two-by-two array of colour photographs *(6)*, contents *(7)*, blank *(8)*, half-title *(9)*, text and illustrations *(10–93)*, blank *(94)*, index *(95–96)*

Binding: Dark Green (146) poplin over heavy boards, sewn. All pages of the endpapers are decorated by a repeated line drawing in black of a hoop, two crossed mallets, and four ringed balls. FC: blank. RC: blocked in white at the foot (ISBN 0-517-56826-8). Spine: blocked downwards in white (• CROQUET •   Donald Charles Richardson   Harmony Books)

Dust wrapper: High-gloss white laminated paper. FP: composed of three adjoining panels, bordered and divided by triple rules, the outer and inner rules in strong reddish Orange (35) and the central rule, in bold, in brilliant Yellow (83). The topmost panel, in deep Green (142), is lettered in white (**CROQUET** | The Art and Elegance of Playing the Game); the central panel consists of a colour photograph, depicting a game of garden croquet; the lowermost panel, in Green, is lettered in white (• DONALD CHARLES RICHARDSON • | PHOTOGRAPHS • BY • JOHN • FALOCCO). FF: publisher's blurb and price in white within a Green triple-framed panel, the outer and inner frames in Orange and the central frame, in bold, in Yellow. RP: within a triple frame, the outer and inner frames in Orange and the central frame, in bold, in Yellow ([a small panel consisting of a colour photograph depicting a standard croquet grip in profile] | [in Orange] CONTENTS | [*do*] • | [*do*] The History | [in brilliant Blue (177)] • | [in Orange] The Equipment | [*do*] • | [*do*] Playing the Game | [in Blue] • | [in Orange] The Social Scene | [*do*] • | [*do*] The Rules | [a small panel consisting of a colour photograph depicting a standard croquet grip in near frontal view, ISBN, and bar code 9 780517 568262 51895]). RF: colour photograph of the author, about the author, production credits, and details of publisher, within a Green triple-framed panel, the outer and inner frames in Orange and the central frame, in bold, in Yellow. Spine: downwards in black ([in Orange] • [in Green] CROQUET [in Orange] • [in Green] Donald Charles Richardson Harmony Books)

Copy seen: PC

Fingerprint: EROR).*et* s.n- Crso 7 1988Q [group 4 taken from p 20]

Notes: Printed anonymously in Japan, ISBN 0–517–56826–8, price $19.95 (higher in Canada). Year of publication is inferred from the Library of Congress cataloging-in-publication data cited on the TP verso.

The text is profusely illustrated with double-page, full-page, and smaller colour photographs, black-and-white half-tone photographs, and diagrams.

(b) *Second impression (ca 1988)*

[The TP as that of (a)]

[From the TP verso]

10 9 8 7 6 5 4 3 2

Formula: As that of (a)

Technical notes: As those of (a)

Contents: As the contents of (a)

Binding: As that of (a)

Dust wrapper: As that of (a) save for a variation in the last five digits of the bar code at the foot of the RF. These read '90000'.

Copy seen: PC

Fingerprint: As that of (a)

Notes: Printed anonymously in Japan. Year of publication is conjectural.

A229   CROQUET: THE COMPLETE GUIDE. AE Gill   1988

[rule] **CROQUET** | [rule] | THE | COMPLETE | GUIDE | A. E. Gill | HEINEMANN [publisher's device] KINGSWOOD

[TP verso]

Heinemann Kingswood | Michelin House, 81 Fulham Road, London sw3 6rb | LONDON   MELBOURNE   AUCKLAND | Copyright © 1988 A. E. Gill | First published 1988 | 0 434 98100 1 | Printed and bound in Great Britain by | Butler & Tanner Ltd., Frome and London

Formula: [1–6¹⁶ 7⁸ 8¹⁶]. 120 leaves including the rear pastedown, pp *i–vii* viii–xi *xii* xiii–xix *xx, 1–2 3–26 27 28–51 52 53–79 80–81 82–86 87–88 89–91 92 93–110 111–112* 113–128 *129–131* 132–145 *146* 147 *148* 149 *150* 151–155 *156* 157 *158* 159–175 *176–178* 179–204 *205–207* 208–215 *216–220*

Technical notes: 182 × 110 mm (p xvi), 40 lines, 20 = 92 mm. Leaf size 233 × 154 mm; thickness 0.13 mm; wove, unwatermarked, very smooth, white

Contents: Half-title *(i)*, blank *(ii)*, title *(iii)*, TP verso *(iv)*, dedication *(v)*, blank *(vi)*, contents *(vii–*viii), list of illustrations (ix–xi), blank *(xii)*, acknowledgements (xiii–xiv), introduction (xv–xix), blank *(xx)*, heading, 'PART ONE' *(1)*, blank *(2)*, text, continued (3–86), heading, 'PART TWO' *(87)*, blank *(88)*, text, continued (89–110), heading, 'PART THREE' *(111)*, blank *(112)*, text, continued (113–175), blank *(176)*, heading, 'APPENDICES' *(177)*, blank *(178)*, text, continued (179–204), heading, 'INDEX' *(205)*, blank *(206)*, text, concluded *(207–215)*, blank *(216–219)*, glued to the RC *(220)*

Binding: Moderate Yellow Green (120) buckram grain paper over stiff boards, sewn. There is no rear endpaper: the last sheet of the end gathering serves also as the rear pastedown. FC: blank. RC: blank. Spine: gold-blocked, mostly downwards ([from near the top] CROQUET [below the word 'CROQUET'] THE COMPLETE GUIDE [near the centre] *A.E. GILL* | [publisher's device crosswise at the foot])

Dust wrapper: White semi-gloss paper, the lettering of the title *etc* on the RP, spine, and FP being printed over and out of an artist's light-hearted illustration in full colour of a croquet game. FP: ([in vivid reddish Orange (34) over illustration] **CROQUET** | [in white out of illustration] THE COMPLETE GUIDE | [in white out of illustration, at the foot] *A.E. GILL*). FF: publisher's blurb and price. RP: ISBN bar code in black over illustration. RF: about the author, and names of illustrator, designer, and publisher. Spine: mostly downwards ([near the head, in Orange over illustration] CROQUET [below the word 'CROQUET', in white] THE COMPLETE GUIDE [in white out of illustration] *A.E. GILL* | [publisher's device crosswise at the foot, in black over illustration]

Copy seen: PC

Fingerprint: psed ofn; cted alMi 7 1988A

Notes: Printed by Butler & Tanner, price £14.95 net.

A230 **CROQUET: THE GENTLE BUT WICKET GAME.** [1988]
Christopher R Reaske

CROQUET | *The Gentle but Wicket Game* | [line drawing of two crossed mallets and two balls] | *Christopher R. Reaske* | E. P. DUTTON [publisher's device] NEW YORK

Formula: [1–80¹]. 80 leaves, pp *1–2*, *i–vii* viii ix x *xi–xii*, 1–122 *123* 124–146 [= 160]

Technical notes: 160 × 143 mm (p 3). 35 lines, 20 = 92 mm. Leaf size 203 × 176 mm; thickness 0.13 mm; wove, unwatermarked, smooth, white

Contents: Half-title (*1*), blank (*2*), title (*i*), TP verso (*ii*), dedication (*iii*), blank (*iv*), significant quotations (*v*), blank (*vi*), contents (*vii*–viii), preface (*ix*–x), acknowledgements (*xi*), blank (*xii*), text (1–146)

Binding: White high-gloss laminated card glued to the edges of the leaves, no endpapers. A design, in vivid reddish Orange (34), strong yellowish Green (131), light greenish Blue (172), and white, with full colour and black-and-white photographs, integrating the FC, RC, and spine. FC: ([in Orange on a white head band] **CROQUET** | [in Green out of a full colour illustration, depicting a stylish croquet scene, within a double-ruled frame in the form of a croquet hoop, flanked by vertical Blue bands] THE GENTLE BUT WICKET GAME | [*do*, but in white] *Christopher R. Reaske* | [*do*] "A splendidly informative treatise | [*do*] on croquet…the next best thing | [*do*] to being out there on the | [*do*] wicket 'sward itself!" | [*do*] —*George Plimpton*). Inside FC: blank. RC: ([over white head band, in black] From backyard to greensward, | [*do*, but in Orange] **CROQUET** | [*do*, but in black] is becoming an American obsession. | [publisher's blurb, incorporating a black-and-white photograph of the author, production credits, price, and ISBN, on a Green background within a double-ruled frame in the form of a croquet hoop, flanked by vertical Blue bands]). Inside RC: blank. Spine: mostly downwards ([in Orange on white] *Reaske* [in Orange out of Blue] **CROQUET** [publisher's device crosswise in black] [in computer-style script] D0385)

Copy seen: PC

Fingerprint: 7)ke s.ng e.an owkn 3 1988Q

Notes: Printed anonymously, ISBN 0–525–48385–3, price $11.95. Year of publication is inferred from the LC cataloging-in-publication data cited on the TP verso.

A231   CROQUET: THE WICKET SPORT. Alan P Baker   [1988]

[The FC]

[The letter *O* in strong Red (12) on white, set as a ball in the jaws of a hoop, the others letters in deep Blue (179) on white] CROQUET | [Red] *THE WICKET SPORT* | [Blue] By | [Blue] ALAN BAKER | [black-and-white photograph of equipment used in Kentucky-style croquet] | [emblem of the Kentucky Croquet Association in Red on L, letterpress in Blue on R] *INCLUDING THE OFFICIAL RULES OF THE KENTUCKY CROQUET ASSOCIATION

[From p 3]

Copyright © 1988 by Alan P. Baker, Springfield, Ky. 40069 | Croquet, The Wicket Sport | Published by | Hayes Printing Co. | 220 East First Street | Campbellsville, Ky. 42718 | *Manufactured in the United States of America* | *TX 326 075* | 3

Formula: [1⁴⁰]. 40 leaves, pp *1* 2–80

Technical notes: 180 × 111 mm (p 8). 48 lines, 20 = 76 mm. Leaf size 214 × 136 mm; thickness 0.13 mm; wove, unwatermarked, smooth, white

Contents: Contents (*1*), blank (*2*), assertion of copyright *etc* (*3*), blank (*4*), text (*5–80*)

Binding: Folded semi-gloss card, stapled, no spine or endpapers. FC: title, as above. Inside FC: blank. RC: blank. Inside RC: publisher's blurb (ABOUT THE AUTHOR | [black-and-white photograph of the author] | [letterpress]).

Copy seen: PC

Fingerprint: 7977 d!ng TEON ViPr 3 1988Q

Notes: This work was apparently printed by the publisher, Hayes Printing Co, Campbellsville, Ky.

AA232 A DEVELOPMENT PLAN FOR CROQUET IN LONDON,   1988
KENT, SURREY, SUSSEX. [South East Croquet Federation]

(a) *First edition (1988)*

[Page *i*, the title set within a ruled panel]

A | DEVELOPMENT PLAN | for | CROQUET | in | LONDON | KENT | SURREY | SUSSEX | A Report prepared by the | SOUTH EAST CROQUET FEDERATION | A memorandum | to Greater London Council | and | to South East Council | for Sport and Recreation | April 1988

Formula: [1–9¹]. 9 leaves, pp *i–ii*, 1–15 *16*

Technical notes: 254 × 169 mm (p 3), pp 1–11 divided into two columns. 61 lines, 10 = 84 mm. Leaf size 297 × 210 mm; thickness 0.10 mm; wove, unwatermarked, smooth, white. The face sheet is coloured pale Yellow (89)

Contents: Title (*i*), foreword (*ii*), contents (*1*), text (*2–15*), blank (*16*)

Binding: Stapled, no spine or endpapers

Copy seen: PC

Fingerprint: cent *dse.* beal s.in C 1988A [group 1 taken from p 1, groups 2–4 taken from p 9]

Notes: Printed anonymously. This work was issued by the South East Croquet Federation (of England) in April 1988, it is thought free of charge, to official bodies, affiliated clubs, and other interested parties.

(b) *Sports Council issue (1988)*

[Page 1, printed in strong greenish Blue (169), the title set within a panel consisting of a repeated stylised figure of a man in play]

A | DEVELOPMENT PLAN | for | CROQUET | in | LONDON | KENT | SURREY | SUSSEX | A Report prepared by the | SOUTH EAST CROQUET FEDERATION | [device of the Sports Council, at L] April 1988

Formula: [1–11^1]. 11 leaves, pp *i–iv*, 1, *v*, 15 *16–17* [= 22]

Technical notes: 254 × 169 mm (p 3), pp 1–11 divided into two columns. 61 lines, 10 = 84 mm. Leaf size 297 × 210 mm; thickness 0.10 mm; wove, unwatermarked, smooth, white

Contents: Title (*i*), blank (*ii*), foreword (*iii*), blank (*iv*), contents (1), blank (*v*), text (2–15), blank (*16–17*)

Binding: The leaves slotted and fastened by a black plastic comb, no endpapers

Slip case: White semi-gloss card, printed in strong Blue (178), vivid greenish Yellow (97), vivid reddish Orange (34), and vivid Yellow Green (115), with a pocket inside the rear flap. FP: ([publisher's device] | [L justified] I N F O R M A T I O N S E R V I C E S | [sketch of sundry sportspeople at L, continued from the RP and spine, in white, Yellow, and Orange out of a Blue panel]). Inside FP: blank. RP: ([publisher's device] | [R justified] 16 UPPER WOBURN PLACE   LONDON WC1H 0QP   TEL: 071 388 127   FAX: 071 383 5740 | [sketch of sundry sportsplayers at R, continued on the spine and FP, in white, Yellow, and Orange out of a Blue panel] FOR REGIONAL SPORTS COUNCIL ADDRESSES SEE ENCLOSURES). Inside RP: blank. Spine: downwards from the head ([in Blue] I N F O R M A T I O N S E R V I C E S [connecting portion of the panel on the FP and RP, as described above])

Copy seen: PC

Fingerprint: n.nt e:of d.s. ThTh C 1988A [group 3 taken from p 14, group 4 taken from the caption to Appendix III on p 15]

Notes: Published by the Sports Council in April 1988, printed anonymously, issued free of charge on demand.

The text is identical to that of (a). The pagination also is identical, except for an irregularity resulting from the insertion of a blank page (p *v*) after p 1. The difference between the fingerprints of the two issues is wholly attributable to this irregularity.

A233   A HISTORY OF THE AUSTRALIAN CROQUET COUNCIL: **1988**
1949 TO 1986. [Winifred Dickinson]

[The FC, within a ruled frame with rounded corners]

[black-and-white photograph of badge] | *A. C. C. President's Badge* | A HISTORY | of | THE AUSTRALIAN | CROQUET COUNCIL | 1949 to 1986

[Page 2]

Published by : Mrs. W. Dickinson O.A.M. | © Copyright 1988 | Printed by | Argus Printing (Kempsey) Pty. Ltd. | Elbow Street, West Kempsey.2440.

Formula: [14^1]. 14 leaves, pp 1–28

Technical notes: 272 × 182 mm (p 7), mostly divided into two columns. 78 lines, 20 = 70 mm. Leaf size 299 × 209 mm; thickness 0.12 mm; wove, unwatermarked, smooth, white

Contents: Preface (1), publishing details (2), contents (3), text (4–28)

Binding: Light yellowish Green (135) leather-effect card front and rear, bound with a moderate yellowish Green (136) cloth strip, stapled, no endpapers. FC: title, as above. Inside FC: blank. RC: blank. Inside RC: blank. Spine: blank

Copy seen: PC

Fingerprint: M.er *iaC.* annt (Iwe 3 1988Q [group 1 taken from p 1, the first two characters of group 4 taken from the caption to the illustration on p 14]

Notes: Printed by Argus Printing (Kempsey), West Kempsey. Year of publication is inferred from the year of copyright cited on p 2.

A234   **PRACTICAL UMPIRING: A HANDBOOK FOR CROQUET**   [1988]
UMPIRES AND PLAYERS. Graeme Roberts

(a) *First edition [1988]*

PRACTICAL UMPIRING | A HANDBOOK FOR CROQUET UMPIRES AND PLAYERS | GRAEME ROBERTS | Member, N.Z.C.C. Laws Committee | Senior Referee | New Zealand Representative 1982 | Published by the New Zealand Croquet Council Inc. | in association with NZI Bank | © Graeme Roberts 1988

Formula: [1²⁴]. 24 leaves, pp *1–4 5–7 8 9 10* 11–48

Technical notes: 179 × 110 mm (p 20). 50 lines, 20 = 72 mm. Leaf size 204 × 143 mm; thickness 0.10 mm; wove, unwatermarked, smooth, white

Contents: Title *(1)*, blank *(2)*, contents *(3–4)*, acknowledgements *(5)*, preface, signed 'Jean Corry' *(6)*, foreword, signed 'A Heenan' *(7)*, blank *(8)*, introduction *(9)*, blank *(10)*, text *(11–45)*, index *(46–48)*

Binding: Very pale Green (148) card, stapled, no spine or endpapers. FC: printed in black (**PRACTICAL UMPIRING** | A HANDBOOK FOR CROQUET UMPIRES AND PLAYERS | GRAEME ROBERTS | Published by the New Zealand Croquet Council Inc. | in association with NZI Bank). Inside FC: blank. RC: in black ([device of NZI Bank] | KEEPING CROQUET IN PLAY). Inside RC: blank

Copy seen: PC

Fingerprint: 3534 .)nt n.at spfu 3 1988A [group 3 taken from the caption to the lowermost diagram on p 13, group 4 taken from the note to the lowermost diagram on p 14]

Notes: Printed anonymously. Year of publication is inferred from the assertion of copyright on the TP.

(b) *Fourth impression (1993)*

[device of the New Zealand Croquet Council, in the form of a medallion] | **PRACTICAL UMPIRING** | A Handbook for Croquet Umpires and Players | **GRAEME ROBERTS** | Member, N.Z.C.C. Laws Committee | Senior Referee | New Zealand Representative 1982 | Published by the New Zealand Croquet Council Inc. | 4th Impression June 1993 | © Graeme Roberts 1988 | *New Zealand Croquet is generously supported by the Hillary* | *Commission and the New Zealand Sports Foundation*

Formula: As that of (a)

Technical notes: 186 × 112 mm (p 20). 50 lines, 20 = 75 mm. Leaf size 210 × 145 mm; thickness 0.10 mm; wove, unwatermarked, smooth, white

Contents: As the contents of (a)

Binding: Very light Green (143) card, stapled, no spine or endpapers. FC: printed in black ([device of the New Zealand Croquet Council, in the form of a medallion] | **PRACTICAL UMPIRING** | **A Handbook for Croquet Umpires and Players** | **GRAEME ROBERTS** | Published by the New Zealand Croquet Council Inc. | 4th Impression June 1993). Inside FC: blank. RC: in white out of a black central panel (*New Zealand Croquet is* | *generously supported by* | *the Hillary Commission* | *and the New Zealand* | *Sports Foundation*). Inside RC: blank

Copy seen: PC

Fingerprint: 3534 .)nt n.at spfu 3 1993A [group 3 taken from the caption to the lowermost diagram on p 13, group 4 taken from the note to the lowermost diagram on p 14]

Notes: Published in June 1993, printed anonymously, price NZ$6.75 in 1996.

A235   SIMPLIFIED CROQUET: THE MINI-BREAK WAY. Peter Danks   1988

THE *Simple* CROQUET SERIES | [rule] | Volume Two | *Simplified* CROQUET | the | MINI-BREAK way | by | PETER DANKS | A Practical Instructional Handbook | for Club and Garden Croquet | Beginners and Improvers | [rule]

[TP verso]

[rule] | [publisher's device, a gate, between upper and lower rules] | The Shillingate Press | Budleigh Salterton | Devon EX9 6SX | © Peter Danks 1988 | First published 1988 | ISBN: 1 871291 01 1 | Printed by *First Impressions*, Budleigh Salterton, Devon. | [rule]

Formula: [1–84¹]. 84 leaves, pp *1–2*, i–iii *iv*, 1–109 *110* 111–157 *158–162* [= 168]

Technical notes: 143 × 101 mm (p 2). 34 lines, 20 = 84 mm. Leaf size 199 × 134 mm; thickness 0.12 mm; wove, unwatermarked, smooth, white

Contents: Title (*1*), TP verso (*2*), index (i–iii), blank (*iv*), text, continued (1–109), blank (*110*), text, concluded (111–157), blank (*158*), conclusion (*159*), blank (*160*), form of application to join the CA (*161*), blank (*162*)

Binding: White Astrolux laminate board printed in strong Red (12), with hinge, glued to the leaves, no endpapers. FC: the letterpress R justified and set within an abstract design incorporating a winning peg, two balls, and a hoop (Simplified | CROQUET | the | MINI-BREAK way | by | PETER DANKS | A Practical Instructional Handbook | for Club and Garden Croquet | Beginners and Improvers). Inside FC: about the author. RC: publisher's blurb, ISBN, and price. Inside RC: blank. Spine: downwards (*Simplified* CROQUET – the MINI-BREAK way by PETER DANKS)

Copy seen: PC

Fingerprint: 6564 t.ot 3.ke b⁵b⁴ 3 1988A

Notes: Published privately, printed by First Impressions, Budleigh Salterton, Devon, price £7.95.

A curiosity of this work is that it is designated 'Volume Two' but was published before the companion work *Simply Teach Yourself Croquet* (A244) by the same author, which is designated 'Volume One'. Volume I is addressed more particularly to beginners, vol II to improvers.

A236   TOWNSEND'S CROQUET ALMANACK. John Walters (ed)   1988
(a) *First (1989) edition (1988)*

[in a convex arc] **TOWNSEND'S CROQUET** | [publisher's device: two crossed mallets, a hoop, and a ball] | **ALMANACK** | [rule] | **1989** | [rule] | **Edited by** | **JOHN WALTERS** | TOWNSEND CROQUET LTD | Kirby Cross | Frinton-on-Sea | Essex | 1

[TP verso, L justified]

First published in 1988 by | Townsend Croquet Ltd | Kirby Cross, Frinton-on-Sea | Essex CO13 0LX | © Townsend Croquet Ltd 1988 | [...]

Formula: [1–12^8 13^4 14^8]. 108 leaves, pp 1–216

Technical notes: 182 × 119 mm (p 9). 57 lines, 20 = 64 mm. Leaf size 209 × 144 mm; thickness 0.10 mm; wove, unwatermarked, smooth, white

Contents: Title (1), TP verso (2), contents (3–5), acknowledgements, signed 'John Walters', November 1988 (6), foreword by Martin Murray (7), review of 1988 (8–11), preface to international review, by David Openshaw (12–13), croquet in Australia, edited by Carolyn Spooner (13–21), croquet in New Zealand, by Graham Beale (21–25), croquet in America, by Tremaine Arkley (26–29), world's top 12 players (30–34), guide to croquet (35–40), croquet records (41–49), player statistics (50–63), 1988 championship results (64–68), results of 1988 invitation events (69–70), 1988 tournament results (71–130), past national championships (131–154), past major tournaments (155–161), British and foreign events (162–170), international matches (171–197), dates in croquet history (198–199), croquet addresses (200–209), national garden croquet players register (210–213), glossary (214–216)

Binding: Dark greyish Blue (187) buckram grain paper over stiff boards, sewn. FC: gold-blocked ([in a convex arc] **TOWNSEND'S CROQUET** | [publisher's device: two crossed mallets, a hoop, and a ball] | **ALMANACK** | [rule] | **1989** | [rule]). RC: blank. Spine: gold-blocked downwards (TOWNSEND'S CROQUET ALMANACK [underlined and overlined] 1989)

Copy seen: PC

Fingerprint: 2924 ?"as m.ms teCa 3 1988A

Notes: Printed by The Lavenham Press.

(b) *1990 edition (1990)*

[in a convex arc] TOWNSEND'S CROQUET | [publisher's device: two crossed mallets, a hoop, and a ball] | ALMANACK | [rule] | **1990** | [rule] | *Edited by* | *JOHN WALTERS* | *Proprietor and Editor-in-Chief* | *Charles Townsend, TOWNSEND CROQUET LTD* | *Kirby Cross, Frinton-on-Sea, Essex* | 1

[TP verso]

First published in 1990 by | *Townsend Croquet Ltd* | *Kirby Cross, Frinton-on-Sea* | *Essex CO13 0LX* | *c Townsend Croquet Ltd 1988, 1989, 1990* | *[...]*

Formula: [1–13^8 14^8 χ1)]. 113 leaves, pp 1–93 *94* 95–167 *168* 169–209, i–xvii

Technical notes: 183 × 120 mm (p 6). 44 lines, 20 = 84 mm. Leaf size 208 × 148 mm; thickness 0.10 mm; wove, unwatermarked, smooth, white

Contents: Title (1), TP verso (2), section title, 'Part One' (3), contents of Part 1 (4), guide to croquet (5–12), 1989 review of Great Britain (13–29), 1989 review of New Zealand, by Graham Beale (30–33), 1989 review of Australia, by Carolyn Spooner, Creina Dawson, and Betty Haupt (34–43), 1989 review of America, by Tremaine Arkley (44–54), 'Olde Dorke's Almanack', by Peter Dorke (55–60), croquet records (61–81), glossary (82–85), National Garden Croquet Players Register (86–93), advertisement (*94*), croquet addresses (95–100), contacts (101–106), croquet hotels, and advertisements (107–109), section title, 'Part Two' (110), contents of Part 2

(111–112), World Championship (113), past British championships (113–132), CA silver medallists (133–137), past British events (138–146), New Zealand past winners (147–151), Australian past winners (152–153), American past winners (154), minor countries' past winners (155–157), 1990 MacRobertson Shield (158–159), Solomon Trophy (160–162), British home internationals (163–167), advertisement (*168*), 1990 fixtures (169–173), dates in croquet history (174–179), 1989 results and statistics (180–209), appendix, MacRobertson Shield 1990 (i–xvii), sources of photographs (xvii)

Binding: Dark Blue (183) buckram grain paper over stiff boards, sewn. FC: gold-blocked ([in a convex arc] TOWNSEND'S CROQUET | [publisher's device: two crossed mallets, a hoop, and a ball] | ALMANACK | [rule] | **1990** | [rule]). RC: blank. Spine: gold-blocked downwards (TOWNSEND'S CROQUET ALMANACK [underlined and overlined] 1990)

Copy seen: PC

Fingerprint: NE90 hesy ays- CoAs 3 1990A [the last two characters of group 1 in white out of black]

Notes: Printed anonymously.

(c) *1991 edition (1991)*

[in a convex arc] TOWNSEND'S CROQUET | [device: two crossed mallets, a hoop, and a ball] | ALMANACK | [rule] | **1991** | [rule] | *Edited by John Walters* | [publisher's device, a rose] | *Eastern Rose Publishing, No. 17 Wroxham Road, Ipswich, Suffolk.* | [hatched rule] | [R justified] *Page 1*

[TP verso, L justified]

[rule] | First published in 1991 by | Eastern Rose Publishing | No. 17, Wroxham Road | Ipswich | Suffolk IP3 0PH | © Eastern Rose Publishing 1990, 1991 | portions © Townsend Croquet Ltd 1988, 1989, 1990

Formula: [1–80^1]. 80 leaves, pp 1–57 (white), *i–ii* (blue), 1–46 (blue), 58–112 (white) [= 160]

Technical notes: 180 × 131 mm (p 10, white). 43 lines, 20 = 85 mm. Leaf size 218 × 154. White leaves: thickness 0.14 mm, wove, unwatermarked, smooth, white. Blue leaves: thickness 0.12 mm, wove, unwatermarked, smooth, light Blue (181)

Contents of white pages: Title (1), TP verso (2), contents of white pages (3–4), guide to croquet and top-class tactics (5–14), glossary (15–18), advertisement (19), correspondence from *Croquet* magazine (20–24), advertisement (25), 1990 review of Great Britain, continued (26–40), advertisement (41), 1990 World Championships, by David Openshaw (42–50), world rankings (51–52), 1990 review of Australia, by Carolyn Spooner (53–62), report of overseas tour, by Debbie Cornelius (63–69), 1990 review of Great Britain, concluded (70–79), British rankings (80–81), photograph (82), World Championship (83), past British championships (83–98), past British events (99–102), New Zealand past winners (103–105), Australia past winners (106–107), USA past winners (108), dates in croquet history (109–112)

Contents of blue pages: Advertisement (*i*), blank (*ii*), contents of blue pages (1), 1991 Townsend Croquet medallists (2–3), croquet records (4–20), 1990 world player statistics (21–30), 1990 championship results (31–42), croquet hotels, and advertisements (43–45), advertisements (46)

Binding: Brilliant greenish Blue (168) Astrolux laminate board glued to the edges of the leaves, no endpapers. FC: printed in black and moderate Red (15) ([at L:

perspective transformation of Townsend Croquet's device, two crossed, mallets, a hoop, and a ball, in black] [at R, perspective rendering of title in Blue shaded script out of a Red disc, 'Townsend's Croquet' in a convex arc surmounting 'Almanack'] | [in perspective, in Red, partly on Blue and partly over a panel below] **1991** | [in Blue out of a black panel with a Blue ruled frame] **TOWNSEND'S CROQUET** | [*do*] **ALMANACK 1991** | [*do*] **Edited by John Walters** | [*do*, to the R of the publisher's device, a rose] Eastern | [*do*] Rose | [*do*] Publishing). Inside FC: blank. RC: publisher's blurb and price, within a double-ruled Red frame. Inside RC: blank. Spine: downwards in black (TOWNSEND'S CROQUET ALMANACK [overlined and underlined] 1991 [publisher's device: a rose]

Copy seen: PC

Fingerprint: 0201 k.da iss! suni 3 1991A

Notes: Printed by Ivor Walden, Woodbridge, Suffolk, UK price £6.95 net.

Review: *Croquet* (May 1991, p 22)

(d) *1992 edition (1992)*

[in a convex arc] TOWNSEND'S CROQUET | [Townsend Croquet's device: two crossed mallets, a hoop, and a ball] | ALMANACK | [rule] | **1992** | [rule] | *Edited by* | ***John Walters*** | [publisher's device, a rose] | *Eastern Rose Publishing, No. 17 Wroxham Road, Ipswich, Suffolk IP3 0PH*

[TP verso, L justified]

First published in 1992 by | Eastern Rose Publishing | No. 17, Wroxham Road | Ipswich | Suffolk IP3 0PH | © Eastern Rose Publishing 1990, 1991, 1992 | portions © Townsend Croquet Ltd 1988, 1989, 1990 | [...]

Formula: [1⁴⁰]. 40 leaves, pp i–ii, 1–78, mostly divided into two columns

Technical notes: 191 × 132 mm (p 3). 46 lines, 20 = 84 mm. Leaf size 209 × 151 mm; thickness 0.13 mm; wove, unwatermarked, smooth, white

Contents: Title (i), TP verso (ii), contents (1), 1991 review (2–15), croquet records (16–31), 1991 player statistics (32–42), WCF world rankings and tables (43), 1991 championships (44), World Championship (45), past British championships (45–70), past English events (71–72), USA past winners (73), Australia past winners (74–75), New Zealand past winners (76–78)

Binding: Yellow Astrolux laminate board printed in Blue, stapled, no spine or endpapers. FC: ([in a convex arc] TOWNSEND'S CROQUET | [Townsend Croquet's device: two crossed, mallets, a hoop, and a ball] | ALMANACK | [monochrome photographs of three champions holding trophies] | [overlined and underlined] **1992**). Inside FC: blank. RC: publisher's blurb, price, *etc.* Inside RC: blank

Copy seen: PC

Fingerprint: 7272 Heow stIP opDE 3 1992A

Notes: Printed by Econoprint, Ipswich, UK price £4.95 net.

Review: *Croquet* (March/April 1992, p 21).

1989

A237　CROQUET. Stephen Mulliner　　　　1989

[L justified, within a grey panel] *PLAY · THE · GAME* | **CROQUET** | [rule in grey] | [downwards at R, within a grey vertical panel] Stephen Mulliner | [L justified] Ward Lock Limited · London

[From the TP verso, L justified]

© Ward Lock Limited 1989 | © Illustrations Ward Lock Limited 1989 | First published in Great Britain in 1989 | by Ward Lock Limited, 8 Clifford Street | London W1X 1RB, an Egmont Company | [...] | ISBN 0–7063–6776–6 | [...]

Formula: Not ascertainable from the copy examined. 40 leaves, pp *1–5* 6–38 *39* 40–50 *51* 52–77 *78* 79–80

Technical notes: 184 × 141 mm (p 8, ragged), the text divided into two columns by a vertical rule. 48 lines, 20 = 77 mm. Leaf size 203 × 169 mm; thickness 0.11 mm; wove, unwatermarked, very smooth, white

Contents: Half-title (*1*), frontispiece, black-and-white photograph of noted contemporary player (*2*), title (*3*), TP verso (*4*), contents (*5*), foreword, signed 'Martin Murray' (*6*), text (7–80)

Binding: White high-gloss laminate glued to the leaves or gatherings, no endpapers. FC: the lettering set on and out of a drawing in full colour of a mallet, black and blue balls, a hoop and a winning peg, on a vivid yellowish Green (129) background ([L justified, in vivid reddish Orange (34), on a vivid Yellow (82) panel] *PLAY · THE · GAME* | [in white out of Green] **CROQUET** | [rule in Orange] | [L justified, in black on Green] Endorsed by the Croquet Association | [downwards in Yellow and Orange on a strong Blue (178) vertical panel] Stephen Mulliner ·). Inside FC: blank. RC: publisher's advertisement for 'Play the Game' series including a list of 19 titles, name of cover illustrator, ISBN bar code, and price. Inside RC: blank. Spine: downwards ([Orange disc on a Yellow band, near the head] [black on white] *PLAY · THE · GAME* [Blue on white] **CROQUET** [black on white, near the foot] WARD LOCK)

Copy seen: PC

Fingerprint: 8079 inin n.to C:B: C 1989A [groups 1–4 taken from pp 5, 13, 19, 20 respectively, group 4 from the legend to fig 5]

Notes: Printed anonymously in Great Britain, price £3.99 'NET UK ONLY'.

A238   CROQUET: HOW TO PLAY THE PERFECT GAME. Robert Kroeger 1989

Croquet: | **How to Play the Perfect Game** | *Robert Kroeger* | *Illustrations by Robert Kroeger* | *Cover art by Barbara Levitt* | *Croquet Foundation of America* | *Palm Beach Gardens, Florida* | [rule]

Formula: [1–42¹]. 42 leaves, pp *iii* iv–vi, 1–79 *80* [= 84], plus 1 loose leaf insert (*corrigenda*)

Technical notes: 204 × 168 mm (plus marginalia, variable) divided into two columns (p 2, ragged). 48 lines, 20 = 85 mm. Leaf size 281 × 218 mm; thickness 0.13 mm; wove, unwatermarked, smooth, white. Several illustrations in the text are printed in black, brilliant greenish Blue (168), strong Red (12), and light Yellow (86)

Contents: Title (*iii*), TP verso (iv), contents (v), text (1–79), blank (*80*)

Binding: White card, white coated wire comb, slotted, no spine or endpapers. FC: printed in black, the letterpress L justified (**Croquet:** | **How to Play the Perfect Game** | *Robert Kroeger* | [artist's sketch in pen and ink of a man in play against a background of an abstract landscape] | *Croquet Foundation of America*). Inside FC: blank. RC: blank. Inside RC: about the author

Copy seen: PC

Fingerprint: 7979 2.6, y.it thBl C 1989A [groups 1–4 taken from pp v, 37, 55, 56 respectively]

Notes: Printed by Alden Hauk, USA, sold together with a companion Compact audio tape.

The 'Audio Tape Cassette Corrections' given in the loose insert refer to strokes shown in diagrams which are not shown in the copy seen of the printed book. This might suggest the existence of another (companion) set of diagrams which has not been seen.

A239   CROQUET: THE SPORT. Jack R Osborn *et al*   [1989]

CROQUET | THE SPORT | by | **Jack R. Osborn** | Founder, President Emeritus | United States Croquet Association | Incorporating | **"Winning Croquet—From Backyard to Greensward"** | with | **Jesse Kornbluth** | and | **John C. Osborn** | and | **Dr. Carlton H. Mabee** | Forward by | **Herbert Bayard Swope, Jr.** | Instructional Photographs by William Powers and Lucien Capehart | Illustrations by Allen Scheuch and Diane Ristuccia | **FARSIGHT COMMUNICATIONS, INC. / Palm Beach Gardens, Florida**

Formula: [1–2^{16} 3^8 4–9^{16}]. 136 leaves, pp *1–4* 5–272

Technical notes: 187 × 112 mm (p 12). 41 lines, 20 = 91 mm. Leaf size 229 × 152 mm; thickness 0.10 mm; wove, unwatermarked, smooth, white

Contents: Blank (*1–2*), title (*3*), TP verso (*4*), contents (*5–6*), foreword, signed 'Herbert Bayard Swope, Jr.' (*7–8*), acknowledgements (*9–10*), text (*11–271*), advertisement (*272*)

Binding: Vivid purplish Blue (194) linen grain embossed paper over stiff boards, sewn. FC: blank. RC: blank. Spine: gold-blocked downwards (**CROQUET   The Sport   OSBORN   Farsight** [publisher's device])

Dust wrapper: White high-gloss plastic laminated paper. FP: printed in white and moderate Yellow (87) out of, and at the head of, a full-colour photograph of the USCA International Challenge Cup and sundry croquet equipment ([in Yellow outlined in white] **CROQUET** | [in white] **The Sport** | [in Yellow] **JACK R. OSBORN** | [in white] **Founder, U. S. Croquet Association** | [*do*] **with John C. Osborn**), and out of a dark Blue (183) band at the foot ([in Yellow] **Incorporating** [in white] '**WINNING CROQUET**' [in Yellow] **with Jesse Kornbluth**); the colour photograph and the horizontal band at the foot are both extended across the spine. FF: ISBN, price, and publisher's blurb, continued on the RF. RP: publisher's blurb, full colour photograph of two of the authors, name and address of the publisher in brilliant Blue (177), and ISBN bar code. RF: publisher's blurb concluded from the FF, production credits, and place of printing. Spine: mostly out of an extension to the background photograph of the FP ([in Yellow] **CROQUET** [in white] **The Sport** [in Yellow] **OSBORN** [in white] **Farsight** [publisher's device in Blue, out of an extension to the tail band of the FP])

Copy seen: PC

Fingerprint: 6541 y.be enis clco 7 1989Q

Notes: Printed anonymously in the USA, ISBN 0–9624568–0–2, price $24.95 ('Higher in Canada'). Year of publication is inferred from the year of copyright cited on the TP verso.

The TP verso refers also to a paperback version of the same work, ISBN 0–9624568–1–0.

A240   HI AND LOIS IN CROQUET FOR A DAY.   **1989**
Mort Walker and Dick Browne

® | [in open artist's script] **Hi** [in artist's MS] and [in artist's open script, the letters overlapping one another] **Lois** [in artist's MS] in | **CROQUET** | **FOR A DAY** | [apparently in artist's script] by MORT WALKER and DIK BROWNE | [publisher's device] | A TOM DOCHERTY ASSOCIATES BOOK | NEW YORK

Formula: Apparently [1–4^{16}]. 64 leaves, unnumbered [pp 1–128]

Technical notes: 153 × 85 mm (p 3). The text consists entirely of comic strip. Leaf size 171 × 106 mm; thickness 0.12 mm; wove, unwatermarked, smooth, white, all edges vivid Yellow (82)

Contents: Title (*1*), TP verso (*2*), text (*3–127*), advertisement (*128*)

Binding: White semi-gloss card apparently glued to the folds of the gatherings, no endpapers. FC: design consisting of two areas, a small upper area and a large lower area, divided by a full-width rule in black. Upper area: out of a plain moderate reddish Purple (241) background, the lettering apparently reproduced from that on the TP — or *vice versa* — by a facsimile process ([in black] ® | [in open artist's script, in brilliant Yellow (83) outlined in black] **Hi** [in artist's MS, in black] and [in artist's open script, the letters overlapping one another, in Yellow outlined in black] **Lois** [in artist's MS, in black] in | [in yellow out of Purple] **CROQUET** | [*do*] **FOR A DAY** | [apparently in artist's script, in black] by MORT WALKER and DIK BROWNE). Lower area: cartoon in line and several plain colours with lettering upwards (© 1988 King Features Syndicate | **US/50311-2 ★ $2.95** | CAN/50312-0 ★ $3.95) and crosswise ([publisher's device] | **TOR**). Inside FC: barcodes and numeric decodes. RC: against a Purple background: comic strip in two panels, the upper panel inscribed downwards at the R (© 1988 King Features Syndicate, Inc. World rights reserved), and in black on white in a third panel at the foot ([barcode with numeric decodes] | ISBN 0–812–50311–2) with lettering in black on Purple to the R (A Tom Doherty | Associates, Inc. Book). Inside RC: blank. Spine: lettered against a Purple background crosswise at the top ([publisher's device] | ® | **TOR** | *humor*), downwards centrally ([in open artist's script, in Yellow outlined in black] **Hi** [in artist's MS, in black] and [in artist's open script, the letters overlapping one another, in Yellow outlined in black] **Lois** [in artist's MS, in black] in | [in yellow out of Purple] **CROQUET FOR A DAY** | [apparently in artist's script, in black,] by [*do*, as one of two lines] MORT WALKER [*do*] and DIK BROWNE), and crosswise at the foot (**US/812-** | **50311-2** | **295** | CAN/812- | 50312-0 | 395)

Copy seen: PC

Fingerprint: Indeterminate

Notes: Published in October 1989, printed in the USA, price $2.95 in the US, $3.95 in Canada.

The text, all in black-and-white comic strip, is thought to have been reprinted from contributions syndicated to the American press. Several of the cartoon strips in the text and on the outer wrapper bear copyright claims through the period 1969–88.

A241   HOW TO PLAY CROQUET. [Nigel Aspinall, consultant author]   **1989**

[Most of the letterpress L justified, to the L of a line drawing of a woman player in play]

[on a grey panel underlined and overlined by rules in bold, centred] **How to play** | [in Red, centred, the letters *U*, *E* truncated by the top of the illustration below] **CROQUET** | **a step-by-step** | **guide** | Series editor: | Mike Shaw | Technical consultant: | Nigel Aspinall | 8 times Singles Champion, | British Open Championships | **JARROLD** | [double rule in bold truncated by the illustration above, the upper rule in Grey, the lower rule in Red]

[From the TP verso, L justified]

First published in Great Britain, 1989 | Copyright © Mike Shaw, 1989 | Designed and produced by | Park Sutton Limited, 8 Thorpe Road, | Norwich NR3 1RY | for Jarrold Colour Publications, Barrack Street, | Norwich NR3 1TR | Illustrations by Malcolm Ryan

Formula: Not ascertainable from the copy examined. 24 leaves, pp *1–4* 5 6 7 8 9 *10* 11 *12* 13 *14* 15 *16* 17 *18* 19 *20* 21 *22* 23 *24* 25 *26* 27 *28* 29 *30* 31 *32* 33 *34* 35 *36* 37 *38 39 40* 41 *42* 43 *44 45 46 47 48*

Technical notes: 141 × 140 mm max (p *8*, ragged), the text and illustrations on most pages divided into two or three columns of variable width and printed in several colours. 43 lines, 20 = 66 mm. Leaf size 170 × 162 mm; thickness 0.11 mm; wove, unwatermarked, very smooth, white

Contents: Title (*1*), TP verso (*2*), contents (*3*), text (*4–48*)

Binding: White high-gloss laminate, hinged front and rear, printed in vivid reddish Orange (34), brilliant Yellow (83), dark greyish Yellow (91), and yellowish Grey (93) on a vivid Green (139) background, glued to the edges of the leaves or folds of the gatherings, no spine or endpapers. FC: ([Yellow (83) rule] | [in white out of Green] How to play | [Yellow (83) rule] | **CROQUET** | [full-tone sketch of a hoop with a red clip on an upright and a red ball, at R] | [in white out of Green, L justified, opposite sketch] a step-by-step | [*do*] guide | [*do*] **JARROLD** | [double rule, truncated by the sketch above, the upper rule in white out of Green, the lower rule in Yellow (83)]). Inside FC: blank. RC: publisher's blurb, sketch of a man player in play, name of publisher, ISBN bar code (ISBN 0–7114–0423–6), and publisher's price sticker. Inside RC: blank. Spine: downwards ([Yellow (83) on a Green background, near the head] HOW TO PLAY [in white out of Green] CROQUET [in white out of Green, near the foot] **JARROLD**)

Copy seen: PC

Fingerprint: 2222).k, s.in Reya 3 1989A [group 4 taken from legends to the lower L illustration on p *14*]

Notes: Printed anonymously in Portugal, price £3.50. The identity of the author of the original script is unknown.

AA242 PUBLICITY FOR CROQUET IN WESTERN AUSTRALIA.   [1989]
Margaret McPhee and Judith Faulkner

<u>PUBLICITY FOR CROQUET IN WESTERN AUSTRALIA</u> | A report prepared by Margaret McPhee and Judith Faulkner | July 1898 [*sic*]

Formula: [1–11¹]. 11 folios, ff *i–iii*, *1–2* 3 *4–5* 6 7 8

Technical notes: 259 × 165 mm (f *5*, ragged). 42 lines, 20 = 125 mm. Leaf size 297 × 210 mm; thickness 0.11 mm; wove, unwatermarked, smooth, white

Contents: Title (*i*), verse quoted by Charlton and Thompson (A198) (*ii*), contents (*iii*), text (*1–8*)

Binding: Fastened by a single staple in the top L corner

Copy seen: PC

Fingerprint: 7.on etnt e?is hee. C 1989Q [group 1 taken from f *ii*, groups 2–4 taken from f *3*]

Notes: Issued to interested parties. Year of issue is inferred from dates cited in the text.

A243 SCOTTISH CROQUET ASSOCIATION HANDBOOK. 1989
[Scottish Croquet Association]

(a) *First edition, 1989 (1989)*

SCOTTISH CROQUET ASSOCIATION | HANDBOOK 1989 | [device of the SCA] | [at the foot, R justified] Corla van Griethuysen | Editor

Formula: [1²⁴]. 24 leaves, pp 1–43 *44 45 46 47 48*

Technical notes: 160 × 115 mm (p 17). 54 lines, 20 = 59 mm. Leaf size 209 × 146 mm; thickness 0.10 mm; wove, unwatermarked, smooth, white

Contents: Title (1), contents and office holders (2), introduction (3), 1989 fixtures (4), croquet in Scotland (5–6), advertisement (6), SCA events (7–22), inter-club competition (23–24), club events (25–27), CA events (28–29), coaching (30), affiliated clubs (31–38), membership list (39–42), tournament entry forms (43–48)

Binding: Pale orange Yellow (73) Astrolux board, stapled, no spine or endpapers. FC: printed in black (Scottish Croquet Association | [device of the SCA] | HANDBOOK 1989). Inside FC: blank. RC: printed in black ([device of The Royal Bank of Scotland] | The Royal Bank | of Scotland). Inside RC: blank

Copy seen: PC

Fingerprint: htms .5.5 tten C.M. 3 1989A

Notes: Published by the SCA, printed anonymously.

(b) *1990 edition (1990)*

SCOTTISH CROQUET ASSOCIATION | HANDBOOK 1990 | [device of the SCA] | [at the foot, R justified] Corla van Griethuysen | Editor

Formula: [1³⁸]. 38 leaves, pp 1–69 *70 71 72 73 74–76*

Technical notes: 172 × 119 mm (p 4). 61 lines, 20 = 57 mm. Leaf size 210 × 147 mm; thickness 0.11 mm; wove, unwatermarked, smooth, white

Contents: Title (1), contents, subscription rates, editorial note, and acknowledgements (2), fixtures (3), croquet in Scotland, signed 'Ian H. Wright' (4–5), top players (6–12), SCA events and representative matches (13–36), inter-club competition (37–39), club events (40–48), CA events (49–52), coaching (53), players' statistics (54–56), affiliated clubs (57–63), membership list (64–68), tournament entry forms (69–74), blank (75–76)

Binding: Brilliant greenish Blue (168) Astrolux board, stapled, no spine or endpapers. FC: printed in black (SCOTTISH CROQUET | ASSOCIATION | [device of the SCA] | **HANDBOOK 1990**). Inside FC: blank. RC: printed in black (HOME INTERNATIONALS | JUNE 16/17 | GLASGOW | [device of Glasgow 1990] | [device of Glasgow Sports Promotion Council] | [device of University of Strathclyde] | [device of Glasgow District Council] | Partly funded from Glasgow District Council's Festival Budget | Glasgow Sports Promotion Council and University of Strathclyde). Inside RC: advertisement

Copy seen: PC

Fingerprint: d.35 n.n, !!ny GeCo 3 1990A

Notes: Published by the SCA, printed anonymously.

(c) *1991 edition (1991)*

SCOTTISH CROQUET ASSOCIATION | HANDBOOK 1991 | [device of the SCA] | [at the foot, R justified] Corla van Griethuysen | Editor

Formula: [1⁴²]. 42 leaves, pp 1–81 *82–84*

Technical notes: 168 × 116 mm (p 5). 62 lines, 20 = 54 mm. Leaf size 210 × 144 mm; thickness 0.10 mm; wove, unwatermarked, smooth, white

Contents: Title (1), contents, subscription rates, editorial note, and acknowledgement (2), fixtures (3), guide to Association Croquet, by Rod Williams (4–8), croquet in Scotland, by Ian H Wright (9–10), top players (11–20), SCA events and representative matches (21–45), inter-club competition (46–47), club events (48–57), CA events (58–60), coaching (61), players' statistics (62–64), affiliated clubs (65–71), membership list (72–76), tournament entry forms (77–82), blank (*83–84*)

Binding: Light Orange (52) Astrolux board, stapled, no spine or endpapers. FC: printed in black (SCOTTISH CROQUET | ASSOCIATION | [device of the SCA] | **HANDBOOK 1991**). Inside FC: blank. RC: printed in black (HOME INTERNATIONALS | JUNE 15/16 | GLASGOW | **Sponsored by:** | [device of Glasgow Sports Promotion Council]). Inside RC: blank

Copy seen: PC

Fingerprint: d.44 s.ng p.he 3 1991A

Notes: Published by the SCA, printed anonymously.

(d) *1992 edition (1992)*

SCOTTISH CROQUET ASSOCIATION | HANDBOOK 1992 | [device of the SCA] | [at the foot, R justified] Corla van Griethuysen | Editor

Formula: [1³²]. 32 leaves, pp 1–63 *64*

Technical notes: 171 × 117 mm (p 5). 61 lines, 20 = 56 mm. Leaf size 206 × 145 mm; thickness 0.10 mm; wove, unwatermarked, smooth, white

Contents: Title (1), contents, subscription rates, editorial note, and acknowledgement (2), fixtures (3), guide to Association Croquet, by Rod Williams (4–8), croquet in Scotland, by Ian H Wright (9–10), who's who (11–14), SCA events and representative matches (15–30), inter-club competition (31–32), club events (33–38), CA events (39–41), coaching (42), players' statistics (43–45), affiliated clubs (46–52), membership list (53–57), blank save pagination (58), application form for invitation events (59–60), tournament entry forms (61–64)

Binding: Light bluish Grey (190) Astrolux board, stapled, no spine or endpapers. FC: printed in black (SCOTTISH CROQUET | ASSOCIATION | [device of the SCA] | **HANDBOOK 1992**). Inside FC: blank. RC: printed in black (HOME INTERNATIONALS | JUNE 13/14 | GLASGOW | **Sponsored by:** | [device of University of Strathclyde] | [device of Glasgow Sports Promotion Council]). Inside RC: blank

Copy seen: PC

Fingerprint: d.29 n.91 e.He wocr 3 1992A

Notes: Published by the SCA, printed anonymously.

(e) *1993 edition (1993)*

SCOTTISH CROQUET ASSOCIATION | HANDBOOK 1993 | [device of the SCA] | [at the foot, R justified] Corla van Griethuysen | [*do*] Editor

Formula: [1³⁶]. 36 leaves, pp 1–69 *70–72*

Technical notes: 174 × 111 mm (p 5). 66 lines, 20 = 53 mm. Leaf size 210 × 144 mm; thickness 0.10 mm; wove, unwatermarked, smooth, white

Contents: Title (1), contents, subscription rates, and acknowledgement (2), fixtures (3), guide to Association Croquet, by Rod Williams (4–8), croquet in Scotland, by Ian H Wright (9–10), SCA events and representative matches (11–32), inter-club competition (33–34), club events (35–42), short croquet events (43), golf croquet events (44), CA events (45–47), coaching (48), players' statistics (49–51), affiliated clubs (52–58), membership list (59–63), blank save pagination (64), application form for invitation events (65–66), tournament entry forms (67–70), blank (70–72)

Binding: Pale Yellow (89) Astrolux board, stapled, no spine or endpapers. FC: printed in black (SCOTTISH CROQUET | ASSOCIATION | [device of the SCA] | **HANDBOOK 1993**). Inside FC: blank. RC: blank. Inside RC: blank

Copy seen: PC

Fingerprint: d.31 !!s: h.ne 1919 3 1993A

Notes: Published by the SCA, printed anonymously.

(f) *1994 edition (1994)*

[The FC]

SCOTTISH CROQUET | ASSOCIATION | [device of the SCA] | **HANDBOOK 1994** | Editor : Corla van Griethuysen

Formula: [1³²]. 32 leaves, pp 1–64

Technical notes: 180 × 124 mm (p 5). 61 lines, 20 = 59 mm. Leaf size 210 × 144 mm; thickness 0.10 mm; wove, unwatermarked, smooth, white

Contents: Contents, subscription rates, and acknowledgement (1), fixtures (2–3), guide to Association Croquet, by Rod Williams (4–8), croquet in Scotland, by Ian H Wright (8–11), SCA events and representative matches (12–32), inter-club competition (33–34), club events (35–41), short croquet events (42–43), golf croquet events (44), CA events (45–47), coaching (48), automatic handicapping system (49–51), players' statistics (52–54), affiliated clubs (55–60), membership list (60–64)

Binding: Brilliant Blue (177) Astrolux board, stapled, no spine or endpapers. FC: printed in black, as above. Inside FC: blank. RC: blank. Inside RC: blank

Copy seen: PC

Fingerprint: n.to d.ng onaw gaSi 3 1994A [group 1 taken from p 1]

Notes: Published by the SCA, printed anonymously.

(g) *1995 edition (1995)*

[The FC]

SCOTTISH CROQUET ASSOCIATION | HANDBOOK 1989 | [device of the SCA] | [at the foot, R justified] Corla van Griethuysen | [*do*] Editor

Formula: [1³⁸]. 38 leaves, pp 1–73 74–76

Technical notes: 164 × 113 mm (p 5). 61 lines, 20 = 54 mm. Leaf size 210 × 145 mm; thickness 0.10 mm; wove, unwatermarked, smooth, white

Contents: Contents, subscription rates, and acknowledgement (1), fixtures (2–3), guide to Association Croquet, by Rod Williams (4–8), croquet in Scotland, by Ian H Wright (8–11), SCA events and representative matches (12–35), inter-club competition (36–37), club events (38–46), short croquet events (47), golf croquet events (48), CA events (49–51), coaching (52–53), automatic handicapping system (54–56), players' statistics (57–59), affiliated clubs (60–66), membership list (67–73), useful addresses (73)

Binding: White Astrolux board, printed in strong Blue (178), stapled, no spine or endpapers. FC: as above. Inside FC: blank. RC: blank. Inside RC: blank

Copy seen: PC

Fingerprint: n.to ngya erll D.G. 3 1995A [group 1 taken from p 1]

Notes: Published by the SCA, printed anonymously.

(h) *1996 edition (1996)*

[The FC]

SCOTTISH CROQUET | ASSOCIATION | [device of the SCA] | **HANDBOOK 1996** | EDITOR: CORLA VAN GRIETHUYSEN

Formula: [1⁴⁰]. 40 leaves, pp 1–79 *80*

Technical notes: 173 × 118 mm (p 5). 61 lines, 20 = 57 mm. Leaf size 211 × 144 mm; thickness 0.10 mm; wove, unwatermarked, smooth, white

Contents: Contents, subscription rates, and acknowledgement (1), fixtures (2–3), guide to Association Croquet, by Rod Williams (4–8), constitution (8–10), croquet in Scotland, by Ian H Wright (10–13), SCA events and representative matches (14–37), inter-club competition (38–39), club events (40–49), short croquet events (50), golf croquet events (51), CA events (52–54), coaching (55–56), automatic handicapping system (57–59), players' statistics (60–62), affiliated clubs (63–68), SCA officers (69), club officials (69–70), membership list (71–77), useful addresses (77–78), the 'Egyptian' system

Binding: Very light Purple (221) Astrolux board, printed in black, stapled, no spine or endpapers. FC: as above. Inside FC: blank. RC: blank. Inside RC: blank

Copy seen: PC

Fingerprint: n.to a.ng d.to <u>Pl</u>In 3 1996A [group 1 taken from p 1]

Notes: Published by the SCA, printed anonymously.

(j) *1997 edition (1997)*

[The FC, the letterpress in MS-style script]

SCOTTISH CROQUET | ASSOCIATION | [device of the SCA] | HANDBOOK 1997 | Editor: Fergus McInnes

Formula: [1⁴⁶]. 46 leaves, pp 1–89 *90–92*

Technical notes: 169 × 110 mm (p 45, ragged). 43 lines, 20 = 80 mm. Leaf size 210 × 144 mm; thickness 0.11 mm; wove, unwatermarked, smooth, white

Contents: Contents (1), subscription rates (2), chairman's preface, signed '*David Appleton*' (3) editor's introduction, signed '*Fergus McInnes*' (4) events and competitions (5–43) croquet in Scotland (44–58), miscellaneous (59–71), players' statistics (72–73), directory (74–89), blank (*90–92*)

Binding: Very pale Blue (184) Astrolux board, printed in black, stapled, no spine or endpapers. FC: as above. Inside FC: blank. RC: blank. Inside RC: blank

Copy seen: PC

Fingerprint: 8979 hton ery9 1919 3 1997A [group 1 taken from p 1, groups 2 and 3 taken from the line ends of pp 9 and 13, group 4 taken from the L column of p 14]

Notes: Published by the SCA, printed anonymously.

(k) *1998 edition (1998)*

[The FC, the letterpress in MS-style script]

SCOTTISH CROQUET | ASSOCIATION | [device of the SCA] | HANDBOOK 1998 | Editor: Fergus McInnes

Formula: [1–46¹]. 46 leaves, pp 1–92

Technical notes: 171 × 112 mm (p 45, ragged). 42 lines, 20 = 82 mm. Leaf size 205 × 144 mm; thickness 0.10 mm; wove, unwatermarked, smooth, white

Contents: Contents (1), subscription rates (2), chairman's preface, signed '*George Anderson*' (3) editor's introduction, signed 'Fergus McInnes' (4) events and competitions (5–43) croquet in Scotland (44–60), miscellaneous (61–74), players' statistics (75–76), directory (77–92)

Binding: Brilliant greenish Blue (168) Astrolux board, printed in black, glued to the edges of the leaves, scored for hinges front and rear, no endpapers. FC: as above. Inside FC: blank. RC: blank. Inside RC: blank. Spine: blank

Copy seen: PC

Fingerprint: 9282 onon).ap 1919 3 1998A [group 1 taken from p 1]

Notes: Published by the SCA, printed anonymously.

A244   SIMPLY TEACH YOURSELF CROQUET. Peter Danks   1989

THE Simple CROQUET SERIES | [rule] | Volume One | Simply TEACH YOUR-SELF | C R O Q U E T | by | PETER DANKS | A Practical Instructional Handbook | for Club and Garden Croquet | Beginners and Improvers. | [rule]

[TP verso]

[rule] | [publisher's device, a gate, between upper and lower rules] | The Shillingate Press | Budleigh Salterton | Devon EX9 6SX | © Peter Danks 1989 | First published 1989 | ISBN: 1 871291 00 3 | Printed by First Impressions, Budleigh Salterton, Devon. | [rule]

Formula: [1–86¹]. 85 leaves, and 1 half-leaf glued to the RC, pp 1–2, i–viii, 1–58 57–141 142 143–155 156–158, i–ii [= 172], pp 57–58 repeated in error in the copy examined

Technical notes: 141 × 104 mm (p 11). 34 lines, 20 = 84 mm. Leaf size 200 × 146 mm. All leaves except the last: thickness 0.12 mm; wove, unwatermarked, smooth, white. End half-leaf (pp i–ii): white card

Contents: Title (1), TP verso (2), index (i–viii), text, continued (1–141), blank save for header and footers (142), text, concluded (143–155), blank (156), form of application to join the CA (157), blank (158), blank (i), glued to the RC (ii)

Binding: White Astrolux board, printed in vivid purplish Blue (194), attached to the end (card) half-leaf, all leaves slotted and fastened by a white wire comb, no endpapers. FC: the letterpress mostly R justified and set within an abstract design incorporating a winning peg, two balls, and a hoop (Simply | TEACH YOURSELF | C R O Q U E T | by | PETER DANKS | [centred] A Practical Instructional Handbook | [*do*] for | [*do*] Club and Garden Croquet Beginners). Inside FC: about the author. RC: publisher's blurb, ISBN, and price. Inside RC: blank. Spine: downwards (Simply TEACH YOURSELF CROQUET by PETER DANKS)

Copy seen: PC

Fingerprint: 3130 t?or r.es ScIS 3 1989A [group 4 taken from legends to Diagram 3 on p 14]

Notes: Published privately, printed by First Impressions, Budleigh Salterton, Devon, price £7.95.

A curiosity of this work is that it is designated 'Volume One' but was published after the companion work *Simplified Croquet: The Mini-break Way* (A235) by the same author, which is designated 'Volume Two'. Volume I is addressed more particularly to beginners, vol II to improvers.

1980–89

AA245 ASSOCIATION CROQUET: A GUIDE TO ASSOCIATION   *ca* 1985
CROQUET FOR LOCAL AUTHORITIES.
[The Croquet Association]

[Page *1*, heading]

[in outlined display script] *ASSOCIATION CROQUET* | A guide to Association Croquet for Local Authorities

Formula: [1²]. 2 leaves, unnumbered [pp 1–4]

Technical notes: 188 × 127 mm (p 2). 60 lines, 20 = 63 mm. Leaf size 210 × 148 mm; thickness 0.11 mm; wove, unwatermarked, semi-gloss textured, white; printed in moderate Brown (58)

Contents: Title heading (*1*), text (*1–4*)

Binding: None

Copy seen: PC

Fingerprint: d.to ndhe ofTY y.s, C 1985Q [all four groups taken from p *3*]

Notes: Issued by the CA, printed anonymously. The identity of the publisher and approximate year of publication are inferred from the text.

A246   **CROQUET BEGINNERS' COACHING COURSE.** Kevin Fellows   *ca* 1989

(a) *First edition* (ca *1989*)

Not seen. The existence of this edition is implied by the description of (b) as the second edition. Year of publication is conjectural.

(b) *Second edition* (*1995*)

[The FC]

Croquet Beginners' Coaching Course | A course of six lessons offering a | structured introduction to the game | **by Kevin Fellows** | 2nd edition, © 1995

Formula: [1–14¹]. 14 leaves including the FC, unnumbered [ff 1–14]

Technical notes: 230 × 170 mm (f *11*). 47 lines, 20 = 98 mm. Leaf size 297 × 210 mm; thickness 0.10 mm; wove, unwatermarked, smooth, white

Contents: Title (*1*), contents (*2*), text (*3–14*)

Binding: White plastic comb with a clear acetate sheet over the FC and an RC of vivid Orange (48) paper, slotted. FC: as above. RC: blank. Inside RC: blank

Copy seen: PC

Fingerprint: e!on t,be k!ep memo C 1995A [group 1 taken from f *2*, group 2 taken from the L column of f *6*, groups 3 and 4 taken from f *13*]

Notes: Published and printed anonymously, offered by the NZCC in 1996 at NZ$7.00 including GST.

A247   CROQUET COACHING HANDBOOK. Kevin Brereton   *ca* 1989

(a) *First edition (ca 1989)*

Not seen. The existence of this edition is implied by the description of (b) as the second edition. Year of publication is conjectural.

(b) *Second edition (1992)*

CROQUET | COACHING | HANDBOOK | by KEVIN BRERETON | T.S.T.C., B.A., B.Arch. | [computer-generated profile of a croquet mallet, each face of the head flanked by two balls] | [within a rectangular ruled frame] **AN ILLUSTRATED GUIDE AND COACHING** | [*do*] **PROGRAM FOR THE SPORT OF CROQUET**

Formula: [1³⁴]. 34 leaves, pp *i–iv*, i| |1–6, *v–vi*, I|i|1–12, I|1|1–2, I|2|1, I|3|1, *vii–viii*, II|i|1, II|1|1, II|2|1, II|3|1, *ix–x*, III|i|1, III|1|1, III|2|1, III|2|1, III|3|1, *xi–xii*, IV|i|1–6, IV|1|1–2, IV|2|1, IV|3|1, *xiii–xiv*, V|i|1–2, V|1|1, V|2|1–2, V|3|1, *xv–xxii* [= 68, the pagination running systematically by 'levels' (i, 1, 2, 3) within 'topics']

Technical notes: 220 × 156 mm (p i| |1, variable, some pages divided into two columns). 39 lines (variable), 20 = 113 mm (variable). Leaf size 295 × 206 mm; thickness 0.12 mm; wove, unwatermarked, smooth, white

Contents: Title (*i*), TP verso (*ii*), contents (*iii*), blank (*iv*), introduction (topic i) (i| |1–6), heading (topic I) (*v*), blank (*vi*), text (topic I) (I|i|1–I|3|1), heading (topic II) (*vii*), blank (*viii*), text (topic II) (II|i|1–II|3|1), heading (topic III) (*ix*), blank (*x*), text (topic III) (III|i|1–III|3|1), heading (topic IV) (*xi*), blank (*xii*), text (topic IV) (IV|i|1–IV|3|1), heading (topic V) (*xiii*), blank (*xiv*), text (topic V) (V|i|1–V|3|1), heading (appendices) (*xv*), blank (*xvi*), appendix 1 (*xvii*), blank, save heading 'NOTES' (*xviii*), appendix 2 (*xix*), blank, save heading 'NOTES' (*xx*), appendix 3 (*xxi*), blank (*xxii*)

Binding: Vivid Yellow Green (115) Astrolux board, stapled, no spine or endpapers. FC: L justified to the R of a full-length artist's sketch of a croquet mallet (**CROQUET | COACHING | HANDBOOK | by | Kevin Brereton** | *Second Edition*). Inside FC: blank. RC: blank. Inside RC: blank.

Copy seen: PC

Fingerprint: 1)1) **NGCI** k.er avat C 1992A

Notes: Published by EX-ACT CRAFTS, Canberra, printed anonymously, ISBN 0 646 02134 6.

To quote from a note on p *ii*, 'Whilst the original text [of the first edition] and hand-book concept is retained some minor alterations regarding the practical use of the book have been made to suit the new format. Instructional coaching tapes in PAL and NTSC video formats are now available from the publisher to supplement the Croquet Coaching Handbook.'

AA248   THE CROQUET SPONSOR'S HANDBOOK.   *ca* 1986
[The Croquet Association]

(a) *First edition (ca 1986)*

Not seen. This work was compiled by Simon Garrett. Approximate year of publication is conjectural.

(b) *1993 edition (1993)*
[The FC, p *1*]
THE | CROQUET | SPONSOR'S | HANDBOOK

Formula: [1⁶]. 6 leaves, unnumbered [pp 1–12]

Technical notes: 94 × 194 mm (p *3*, ragged). 20 lines, 20 = 97mm. Leaf size 100 × 203 mm; thickness 0.11 mm; wove, unwatermarked, smooth, white; printed in black and vivid purplish Blue (194). Some pages of the text are superimposed on faint half-tone illustrations

Contents: Title (*1*), half-tone photograph of croquet match (*2*), introduction by Christopher Hudson (*3*), text (*4–12*), name of publisher (*12*)

Binding: White card, stapled, no spine or endpapers. FC: as above. Inside FC: as above. RC: as above. Inside RC: as above

Copy seen: PC

Fingerprint: n.r. n.e. ous. ndch C 1993Q [all four groups taken from p *3*]

Notes: Published by the CA, printed anonymously. The text was compiled by David Hudson under the direction of Christopher Hudson, CA Development Officer.

AA249 GOLF CROQUET. [The Croquet Association]   *ca 1985*

(a) *First edition (ca 1985)*

Not seen. It is thought that the first edition of this work, which was intended to promote the game of golf croquet, was one of the first leaflets funded by commercial sponsorship during the 1980s.

(b) *First Atco edition (ca 1990)*

[Page *1*, heading]

[in shaded display script] **GOLF CROQUET**

Formula: [1²]. 2 leaves, unnumbered [pp 1–4]

Technical notes: 193 × 135 mm (p *2*), pp *2, 3* divided into two columns, printed in black and deep yellowish Green (132). 62 lines, 20 = 63 mm. Leaf size 211x 149 mm; thickness 0.10 mm; wove, unwatermarked, semi-gloss, white

Contents: Title heading and advertisement by Atco (*1*), text (*1–4*), advertisement by Atco and name of printer (*4*)

Binding: None

Copy seen: PC

Fingerprint: e.n: seut here s.y. C 1990Q [all four groups taken from the L column of p *3*, the first two characters of group 1 taken from the caption to a half-tone illustration]

Notes: Published by the CA, sponsored by Atco Ltd, printed by Print Seventy, Crewe, Cheshire. Approximate year of publication is inferred from the style of the Atco logo — the coloured lettering outlined in black — used in their advertisements and from the fact that Atco sponsored the CA Open Championships during the years 1990–93.

(c) *Atco edition, 1992 issue (ca 1992)*

[Title heading as that of (a)]

Formula: As that of (a)

Technical notes: As at (a)

Contents: As the contents of (a)

Binding: None

Copy seen: PC

Fingerprint: **e.n**: seut here **s.y.** C 1992Q [all four groups taken from the L column of p 3, the first two characters of group 1 taken from the caption to a half-tone illustration]

Notes: Published by the CA, sponsored by Atco Ltd, printed by Print Seventy, Crewe, Cheshire. Approximate year of publication is inferred from the new style of the Atco logo — no longer outlined — used in their advertisements and from the fact that Atco sponsored the CA Open Championships during the years 1990–93. During this period Atco advertised regularly in *Croquet*. Their first advertisement with the new style logo appeared in Issue 221 (May/June 1992, p 5).

The text of this issue is identical to that of (a).

(d) *Selsdon Park edition (ca 1994)*

[Printed mostly in vivid reddish Orange (34) against a light Yellow Green (119) background]

[Selsdon Park device] | [artist's sketch of croquet goods in full colour within a triple-ruled panel] | GOLF CROQUET | [rule] | FORTY MINUTES OF FUN-FILLED ACTION

Formula: As that of (a)

Technical notes: 174 × 125 mm (p 2, ragged), divided into two columns, mostly printed over coloured panels. 50 lines, 20 = 70 mm. Leaf size 210x 149 mm; thickness 0.13 mm; wove, unwatermarked, semi-gloss, white

Contents: Title (*1*), text (*2–4*), notice by the CA and advertisement by Selsdon Park

Binding: None

Copy seen: PC

Fingerprint: y.he rant ngs. rnie C 1994Q [all four groups taken from the L column of p 3, group 1 taken from the text of that column]

Notes: Published by the CA, sponsored by Selsdon Park, printed anonymously. Approximate year of publication is as stated by the CA.

The text of this edition is identical, or virtually identical, to those of (a) and (b) but is entirely reset and rearranged.

AA250 AN INTRODUCTION TO THE LAWS OF SHORT CROQUET.   *ca* 1987
[The Croquet Association]

(a) **First edition (ca 1987)*

[Page *1*, heading, printed in Blue]

AN INTRODUCTION TO | THE LAWS OF | SHORT CROQUET

Formula: [1³]. 3 leaves, unnumbered [pp 1–6], on a single sheet in a C-fold, pp *1–6* in the order 1, 2, 6, 3, 4, 5 of the external contours of the letter C (from top to bottom and L to R)

Technical notes: 201 × 80 mm (p 2). 52 lines, 20 = 78 mm. Leaf size 210 × 99 mm; thickness 0.10 mm; wove, unwatermarked, semi-gloss, white; printed in black, deep reddish Orange (36), brilliant Blue (177), brilliant Yellow (83), and light yellowish Green (135)

Contents: Title heading and advertisement by John Jaques (*1*), text (*1–6*), announcement by the CA (*6*)

Binding: None

Copy seen: PC

Fingerprint: nes. urve ofe. d.ng C 1989Q [all four groups taken from p *3*]

Notes: Printed anonymously. Probably published by the CA early in 1987. A copy of this work is contained within a Starter Pack of publicity material issued by the Publicity Committee of the CA in June 1987.

(b) *Townsend Croquet edition (ca 1992)*

[Page *1*, heading, in black on a vivid reddish Orange (34) band, overlined and underlined in black]

[in MS-style script, slanting upwards] **An introduction to** [in display script] **SHORT CROQUET**

Formula: [1²]. 2 leaves, unnumbered [pp 1–4]

Technical notes: 193 × 130 mm (p *3*), mostly divided into two columns. 55 lines, 20 = 70 mm. Leaf size 211 × 149 mm; thickness 0.11 mm; wove, unwatermarked, semi-gloss, white, printed in black and Orange

Contents: Title heading and advertisement by Townsend Croquet (*1*), text (*1–4*), advertisement by Townsend Croquet and name of printer (*4*)

Binding: None

Copy seen: PC

Fingerprint: bell urTO ixIL utix C 1992Q [all four groups taken from the L column of p *3*]

Notes: Published by the CA, printed by Print Seventy, Crewe, Cheshire. The text is modelled closely on (a); revisions include both omissions and additions.

1990

A251 ATTAIN BETTER CROQUET. Cliff Anderson   [1990]

[The FC, over a sketch printed in black of a mallet and ball against a patterned background of regular vertical and horizontal rules in medium Grey (265)]

ATTAIN | BETTER CROQUET | By Cliff Anderson

Formula: [1¹⁴]. 14 leaves, pp *i–iv*, 1–21 *22–24*

Technical notes: 127 × 88 mm (p *2*). 43 lines, 20 = 60 mm. Leaf size 150 × 105 mm; thickness 0.12 mm; wove, unwatermarked, smooth, white

Contents: About the author, and publishing details (*i*), blank (*ii*), contents (*iii*), blank (*iv*), text (*1–21*), advertisement (*21*), blank (*22–24*)

Binding: Very light greenish Blue (171) card, stapled, no spine or endpapers. FC: as above. Inside FC: blank. RC: blank. Inside RC: blank

Copy seen: PC

Fingerprint: r.ed rder *e.es* 3 1990Q [group 3 taken from the caption to illustration 1 on p 13]

Notes: Published and printed anonymously. Year of publication is inferred from a notice in *New Zealand Croquet Gazette* (December 1990, p 15).

A252 LE CROQUET. [Anon]   1990

[The FC, between strong Yellow Green (117) broad head- and narrow tail-bands outlined by rules, and at L of a line drawing of a man player preparing to execute a stroke, in MS-style script]

Le Croquet | • règle du jeu | • comment jouer | • le golf croquet

Formula: [1¹⁶]. 16 leaves, pp *i–ii*, 1–27 28–30

Technical notes: 116 × 192 mm (p 20, ragged), some pages divided into two columns. Variable line spacing. Leaf size 148 × 210 mm; thickness 0.09 mm; wove, unwatermarked, semi-gloss, pale Yellow Green (121). Illustrations in the text are printed in black and light Yellow Green (119)

Contents: Title (*i*), TP verso (*ii*), contents (1), text (2–28), publishing details and production credits (29), name and details of publisher (30)

Binding: Stapled through the folds, no wrapper, spine, or endpapers.

Copy seen: PC

Fingerprint: 1413 s.up à.re r... 3 1990A [groups 1–4 taken respectively from the L column of p 1, the L column of p 11, the legend to the lowermost illustration in the L column of p 13, the legend to the lowermost illustration in the L column of p 14]

Notes: Published by Tectona, Paris, printed by Néographê.

The text includes a code of seven rules of golf croquet, none of (Association) Croquet.

A253   CROQUET: SKILLS OF THE GAME. Bill Lamb   **1990**

(a) *First edition (1990)*

[R justified]

CROQUET | Skills of the Game | BILL LAMB | THE CROWOOD PRESS [publisher's device]

[TP verso, L justified]

First published in 1990 by | The Crowood Press | Gipsy Lane, Swindon | Wiltshire SN2 6DQ | © W. E. Lamb 1990 | [...] | ISBN 1 85223 359 1 | [...]

Formula: [1–4¹⁶]. 64 leaves, pp *i–vi*, 1–122

Technical notes: 183 × 139 mm (p 17). 44 lines, 20 = 84 mm, divided into two columns. Leaf size 234 × 164 mm; thickness 0.13 mm; wove, unwatermarked, very smooth, white

Contents: Half-title (*i*), frontispiece (black-and-white photograph) (*ii*), title (*iii*), TP verso (*iv*), contents (*v*), forewords, signed 'Chris Hudson', 'John McCullough', and 'Joseph Hogan' (*vi*), text (1–122)

Binding: Glossy white paper, printed in full colour, over stiff boards, sewn. FC: the title *etc* printed within a colour photograph of Colin Irwin in play at Hurlingham ([within an extended vivid Green (139) panel outlined in white] **CROQUET** | [in vivid greenish Yellow (97), otherwise as the line above] The Skills of the Game | [in white out of photograph] Bill Lamb). RC: on and out of a vivid Red (11) background ([publisher's blurb, testimonials, and colour photograph, within an extended vivid Green (139) panel outlined in white] | [in white out of Red, L justified, to near the bottom edge] Endorsed by The Croquet Association | [*do*] Front cover photograph Allsport/Simon Bruty | [*do*] Back cover photograph Allsport/Dan Smith | [*do*] ISBN 1 85223 359 1 | [*do*] Printed in Great Britain | [ISBN bar code in white panel out of Red, at R to near the foot]). Spine: downwards out of a Red background ([a white bar linking the extensions of the upper panels on the FC and RC] [in white] CROQUET [in Yellow] Bill Lamb [publisher's device in Green, crosswise])

Copy seen: PC

Fingerprint: 2117 s.d- n-e- *seFi* 3 1990A [group 4 taken from the caption to fig 10(a) on p 14]

Notes: Published in the autumn of 1990, printed by BPCC Hazell Books, price £10.99. In anticipation of the publication of the paperback issue (b), 800 copies were remaindered to the CA at £1.00 per copy.

(b) *Paperback (1994)*

[The TP as that of (a)]

[From the TP verso, L justified]

First published in 1990 by | The Crowood Press Ltd | Ramsbury, Marlborough | Wiltshire SN8 2HR | Paperback edition 1994 | © W. E. Lamb 1990 | [...] | ISBN 1 85223 828 3 | [...]

Formula: As that of (a)

Technical notes: 183 × 139 mm (p 17). 44 lines, 20 = 84 mm, divided into two columns. Leaf size 234 × 164 mm; thickness 0.13 mm; wove, unwatermarked, smooth, white

Contents: As the contents of (a)

Binding: High-gloss white card laminate, printed in full colour, glued to the folds of the gatherings, scored for hinges front and rear, no endpapers. FC: the title *etc* printed within a colour photograph of Colin Irwin in play at Hurlingham ([within an extended vivid yellowish Green (129) panel outlined in white] **CROQUET** | [*do*, in vivid greenish Yellow (97)] The Skills of the Game | [in white out of photograph, at the foot] Bill Lamb). RC: on and out of a vivid reddish Orange (34) background ([publisher's blurb, testimonials, and colour photograph, within an extended vivid Green (139) panel outlined in white] | [in white out of Orange, L justified, near the foot] ISBN 1 85223 816 X | [*do*] Cover photographs by Allsport [*do*] Printed in Great Britain | [*do*] Endorsed by the Croquet Association | [ISBN bar code in white panel out of Orange, at R to near the foot]). Spine: downwards out of an Orange background ([a white bar linking the extensions of the upper panels on the FC and RC] [in white] CROQUET [in Yellow] Bill Lamb [publisher's device in Green, cross-wise])

Copy seen: PC

Fingerprint: 2117 s.d- n-e- *seFi* 3 1994A [group 4 taken from the caption to fig 10(a) on p 14]

Notes: Published in the spring of 1994, price £7.99. Save for the correction of a few minor errors, the text is identical to that of (a). The only variations in substance are to be found on the FC and in the publisher's blurb and testimonials on the RC.

A254   **STROKES FROM HERE AND THERE.** [Rendell Rhoades (ed)]   **1990**

STROKES FROM HERE AND THERE. | Columbus & Cincinnati | • • | [publisher's device: twin trees in silhouette set at the ends of a long rule in bold] | [in gothic-revival script] Rhodopress of Ashland – – – – – – – Ashland, Ohio. | 1976

[TP verso, the lettering set within a diagram of a croquet lawn, each hoop represented by an inverted letter U and each stake by a letter I]

The Croquet Series. | One of fifty copies. | Rhodopress of Ashland | [rule in bold] | February 22, 1976

Formula: [1⁴]. 4 leaves, unnumbered [pp 1–8]

Technical notes: 90 × 86 mm (p *4*). 22 lines, 20 = 83 mm. Leaf size 134 × 108 mm; thickness 0.16 mm; laid, watermarked (Hamilton |[?] Library), rough, white

Contents: Title (*1*), TP verso (*2*), text (*3–8*), name of printer (*8*)

Binding: Light Yellow (86) leather-effect embossed card, stapled, no spine or end-papers. FC: as the TP, printed in black. Inside FC: blank. RC: blank. Inside RC: publisher's blurb [see *Notes* below]

Copy seen: CA

Fingerprint: n,e: ine. reed s;n. C 1990A [all four groups taken from p *3*]

Notes: Published posthumously, apparently in June 1990, and printed by Mr Myron Sattler of Art Printing Co, Ashland, Ohio. To quote from the publisher's blurb:

'Rhodopress Publications, listed as a private press since 1958, and as Rhodopress of Ashland, 1962–1976, was owned and operated by Rendell Rhoades as a hobby.

'The Croquet Series, nos. 1–8, was published 1973–1976. No. 9, "Strokes from Here and There" had been composed, type set, and proof pulled, but corrections and printing had not been completed at the time of his death, Sept. 26, 1976.

'Mr. Myron Sattler of the Art Printing Co., Ashland, Ohio, has graciously made the necessary changes and run the 50 copies on his professional presses. It is with gratitude we can include this last bit of croquet ephemera in the bibliography as Rendell Rhoades would have wanted it.'

A *catalogue raisonnée* of Rhoades's croquet collection was later completed by Nancy L Rhoades, his widow, in 1992 (A263). It would be fruitless to speculate how Rhoades's own bibliography might have compared with that work if he had lived to complete it.

The text reprints articles which appeared in the *Ohio State Journal* (23 June 1930) and *Cincinnati Enquirer* (15 December 1935). A footnote on p 6 is apparently by Rhoades.

1991

A255   CROQUET COACHING MANUAL. [The Croquet Association]   **[1991]**

[The FC, printed in strong purplish Blue (196), L justified]

Croquet | **Coaching** | **Manual** | [in white out of a rectangular Blue panel] *Published by the* **Croquet Association** | [publisher's device at the bottom R]

Formula: [1³²]. 32 leaves, pp 1–32

Technical notes: 233 × 155 mm (p *4*). 47 lines, 20 = 100 mm. Leaf size 298 × 207 mm; thickness 0.10 mm; wove, unwatermarked, smooth, white

Contents: Introduction, signed 'Bill Lamb', May 1991 (*1*), publishing details (*1*), contents (*2*), text (*3–64*)

Binding: White semi-gloss light card, stapled, no spine or endpapers. FC: as above. Inside FC: blank. RC: blank. Inside RC: blank

Copy seen: PC

Fingerprint: 91*on* n.ns s.ny anro 3 1991Q [group 1 taken from p *1*]

Notes: Published by the CA in the autumn of 1991, printed anonymously, originally priced £10.00 and discounted to registered CA coaches at £7.50. The initial print run was of about 500 copies. This work was intended as a replacement for the CA's *Coaching Handbook* (A211).

Authorship was shared by Bill Lamb, D Purdon, and K Aiton. Bill Lamb acted as editor.

A256 CROQUET HISTORY: MAINLY AUSTRALIA, ESPECIALLY   [1991]
NEW SOUTH WALES. Max Hooper

CROQUET | HISTORY | Mainly Australia, | especially New South Wales | [reproduction of a well known image of a woman dressed in crinoline and bonnet, preparing to take tight croquet] | **MAX HOOPER**

Formula: [1–2¹² 3¹²(3₂+χ1) 4¹²]. 49 leaves, pp *1–5 6 7 8–20 21 22–25 26–27 28–33 34–35 36–47 48–49 50–51 52–53 54–64 65 66–71 72–73 74 75 76 77–79 80–88 89–90 91–97 98* [pp *53–54* wanting from one of the copies examined]

Technical notes: 158 × 91 mm (p 8). 33 lines, 20 = 96 mm. Leaf size 193 × 112 mm; thickness 0.11 mm; wove, unwatermarked, smooth, white

Contents: Title (*1*), TP verso (*2*), contents (*3*), dedication (*4*), introduction, signed 'Max Hooper' (*5–6*), text, continued (*7–25*), blank (*26*), text, continued (*27–33*), blank (*34*), text, continued (*35–47*), blank (*48*), text, continued (*49–51*), blank (*52*), text, continued (*53–71*), blank (*72*), text, continued (*73–77*), blank (*78*), text, concluded (*79–97*), blank (*98*)

Binding: Gold Astrolux board glued to the folds of the gatherings, printed in black, apparently sewn, no endpapers. FC: as the TP. Inside FC: blank. RC: publisher's blurb and ISBN (0 646 03515 0). Inside RC: blank. Spine: downwards (**CROQUET HISTORY   MAX HOOPER**)

Copies seen: PC

Fingerprint: 7977 3,re edry rure 3 1991Q [group 2 taken from the text on p 11]

Notes: Printed by Posh Printing, Surry Hills, NSW. Year of publication is inferred from the assertion of copyright (p *2*).

A257 THE FIRST TWENTY YEARS: A BRIEF HISTORY OF THE   1991
CHELTENHAM CROQUET CLUB. H Barr

[The FC]

THE FIRST TWENTY YEARS | A BRIEF HISTORY OF THE CHELTENHAM | CROQUET CLUB | H. BARR | DARAM PRINTING PTY LIMITED

Formula: [1⁸]. 16 leaves, pp [i–ii], *1* 2–5 [6–11] 12–13 [14]

Technical notes: †169 x †115 mm (p 3). 52 lines 20 = †65 mm. Leaf size †210 × †147 mm

Contents: Wanting from the photocopy examined ([i]), TP verso ([ii]), wanting from the photocopy examined ([*1*]) text, continued (2–5), wanting from the photocopy examined ([6–11]), text, continued (12–13), wanting from the photocopy examined ([14])

Binding: Apparently printed on light coloured paper or card, stapled, no spine or endpapers. FC: printed as above. Inside FC: wanting from the photocopy examined. RC: printed, at the foot ([rule] | **Daram Printing Pty. Limited** | Telephone: (02) 674 2777 Fax: (02) 624 7264 | [rule]). Inside RC: wanting from the photocopy examined

Copy seen: NLA: NP 796 354099441 B268 (photocopy of unknown scale, wanting the inside pages of the wrapper and pp [i–ii, 6–11, 14])

Fingerprint: Not ascertainable from the photocopy examined

Notes: Printed by Daram Printing Pty.

AA258 FIXTURES LIST [ABRIDGED EDITION].   1991
[The Croquet Association]

(a) *First edition (1991)*

Not seen. The publication of the first edition of this work early in 1991 is well documented in the archives of the CA. It was conceived as an economical medium for informing overseas Associates of the principal events sponsored by the association.

(b) *1992 edition (1992)*

[Page *1*]

The Croquet Association | [device of the CA] | Fixtures List 1992 | (Abridged) | Published by: The Croquet Association | The Hurlingham Club | Ranelagh Gardens | London SW6 3PR | Tel: 071 736 3148

Formula: [1⁶]. 6 leaves, unnumbered [pp 1–12]

Technical notes: 170 × 115 mm (p 9, ragged). 57 lines, 20 = 60 mm, variable. Leaf size 210 × 148 mm; thickness 0.10 mm; wove, unwatermarked, smooth, white

Contents: Title (*1*), calendar of fixtures with page references to the complete *The Croquet Association Fixtures List* (A183y) (*2–5*), announcement (*6*), subscriptions and levy (*7–8*), general conditions and information (*8–10*), tournament entry form (*11–12*)

Binding: Stapled through the folds of the leaves, no wrapper, spine, or endpapers.

Copy seen: CA

Fingerprint: 6848 s)ME TEy. edte C 1992A [group 1 taken from p *3*, groups 2–4 taken from p *11*]

Notes: Issued early in April 1992 free of charge to overseas Associates, printed anonymously. It is believed that the print run numbered about 200.

(c) *1998 edition (1998)*

[Within a panel framed by an ornamental border] **FIXTURES LIST 1998** | [device of the CA] | Published by: The Croquet Association | The Hurlingham Club | Ranelagh Gardens | London SW6 3PR | Tel: 0171-736-3148 | Email: caoffice@ croquet.org.uk | [R justified] Typed and edited by D.L. Gaunt

Formula: [1⁸]. 8 leaves, unnumbered [pp 1–16]

Technical notes: 165 × 114 mm (p *4*). 55 lines, 20 = 60 mm, variable. Leaf size 211 × 148 mm; thickness 0.10 mm; wove, unwatermarked, smooth, pale Yellow (89)

Contents: Title (*1*), preface, signed 'Paul Campion' (*2*), calendar of fixtures with page references (*3–8*), subscriptions and levy (*9*), general conditions and informa-tion (*10–11*), introduction by the chairman of the tournament committee, signed 'Bill Arliss', and notice by the chairman of the trophies committee, signed 'A Oldham' (*12*), tournament entry forms (*13–16*)

Binding: None, the leaves loosely quired

Copy seen: PC

Fingerprint: 7874 e.t. net. ofce C 1998A [group 1 taken from p *3*, groups 2–4 taken from p *11*]

Notes: Printed anonymously, issued free of charge to overseas Associates *etc* plan-ning to visit the UK and enter tournaments. The text, as abridged, is reproduced without alteration from the full edition of *Croquet Association Fixtures 1998* (A183ee).

A259 A GUIDE TO CROQUET COURT PLANNING, BUILDING,   1991
& MAINTENANCE. Dr Carleton H Mabee

A Guide | *to* | *CROQUET COURT* | *Planning, Building,* | *& Maintenance* | by | **Dr. Carleton H. Mabee** | Chairman, Courts and Greens Committee | United States Croquet Association | Illustrations by Pat Hardy | Introduction by Jack R. Osborn | [at the foot, L justified] BASS COVE BOOKS • KENNEBUNKPORT, MAINE • 1991

Formula: [1–7⁸ 8⁴]. 60 leaves, pp *1–7* 8–13 *14* 15–16 *17* 18–19 *20* 21–102 *103* 104–119 *120*

Technical notes: 157 × 167 mm divided into two columns (p 21, ragged). 32 lines, 20 = 99 mm. Leaf size 213 × 275 mm; thickness 0.16 mm; wove, unwatermarked, smooth, white

Contents: Half-title (*1*), blank (*2*), title (*3*), TP verso (*4*), dedication (*5*), quotation from Bert Myer, 1989 (*6*), contents (*7*), list of illustrations (*8*), list of tables (*9*), acknowledgements (*10*), author's preface (*11*), introduction, signed 'Jack R. Osborn', November 1990 (*12–13*), text (*14–119*), blank save heading 'Notes' (*120*)

Binding: White high-gloss laminated card, glued to the folds of the gatherings, no endpapers. FC: printed in strong yellowish Green (131) and black ([at the top R of artist's sketch, mostly in black] ***A Guide to*** | [*do*, in Green, under- and over-lined in black] **CROQUET COURT** | [at the top R of artist's sketch, in black] Planning, Building | [*do*] ***& Maintenance*** | [artist's line drawing of game in play, with Green infill] | [at the foot, in black, on Green infill to the sketch above] **Dr. Carleton H. Mabee** | [*do*] ***With an Introduction by Jack Osborn*** | [*do*] ***and Drawings by Pat Hardy***). RC: in black ([artist's line drawing, presumably of the author, and publisher's blurb] | [one of three lines to the L] **Bass Cove Books** | [*do*] Kennebunkport, Maine 04046 | [*do*] $45.00 | [at R, in computer-style script] ISBN 0-9630074-0-8 | [*do*, bar code]). Spine: in black, downwards (***Mabee* • A Guide to Croquet Court Planning, Building & Maintenance**) and crosswise at the foot (BASS | COVE)

Copy seen: PC

Fingerprint: 4343 ceof tos, reNE 7 1991A [groups 1–4 taken from pp 7, 15, 19, 20 respectively]

Notes: Printed anonymously in the USA, price $45.00

A262 HOOP & ROQUET: A HISTORY OF THE NORTHERN   1991
  • DISTRICT CROQUET ASSOCIATION. Dorothy Dettman

HOOP & | **ROQUET** | *A History of the* | *Northern District Croquet* | *Association* | *by* | Dorothy Dettmann

Formula: [1²⁸]. 28 leaves, pp *i–v vi*, 1 2 3–49 *50*

Technical notes: 168 × 110 mm (p 4). 40 lines, 20 = 84 mm. Leaf size 206 × 136 mm; thickness 0.12 mm; wove, unwatermarked, semi-gloss, white

Contents: Title (*i*), TP verso (*ii*), major events won by Mrs MM Harrison (*iii*), blank (*iv*), contents (*v*), foreword, signed in MS 'Gladys E Thompson' (*vi*), about the author (*1–2*), text (*3–49*), blank (*50*)

Binding: Semi-gloss white card printed in vivid yellowish Green (129), stapled, no spine or endpapers. FC: against a predominantly Green background, a vertical band close to the inner edge continuing the design on the RC ([in white out of Green] **HOOP &** | [*do*] **ROQUET** | [device of the NDCA in Green on white out of Green background] | [in white panel out of Green] *A History of the* | [*do*] **NORTHERN DISTRICT CROQUET** | [*do*] **ASSOCIATION** | [*do*, R justified] by | [*do*] ***Dorothy***

Dettman). Inside FC: 'Instructions for playing the Game of Croquet' in MS, printed in Green, concluded inside RC. RC: names of associated clubs, occupying six lines, repeated continuously as on wallpaper, printed in Green, extended laterally to form a narrow vertical strip at the L of the FC. Inside RC: 'Instructions for playing the Game of Croquet', concluded from inside the RC

Copy seen: PC

Fingerprint: amhe o)e: s.H. Bgin 3 1991A [group 4 taken from the caption to the illustration on p 14]

Notes: Printed by Eastside Printing, Hawthorn East, Victoria.

A261   **IT'S A WICKET KITCHEN.** Anne D Bessette   [1991]

IT'S A WICKET KITCHEN | **181 WAYS TO WINE, DINE** | **AND AMUSE YOUR FRIENDS** | [cartoon, a line drawing] | A selection of recipes contributed by | croquet enthusiasts from throughout the United States, | Canada, Mexico, France and Bermuda. | Compiled, edited and illustrated by Anne D. Bessette | **A PORTION OF THE PROFITS FROM THIS BOOK WILL BE** | **DONATED TO** | **THE CROQUET FOUNDATION OF AMERICA**

Formula: 95 loose leaves, pp *i* ii–xii, 13–190

Technical notes: 172 × 99 mm (p 34, ragged). 38 lines, 20 = 91 mm. Leaf size 213 × 139 mm; thickness 0.10 mm; wove, unwatermarked, semi-gloss, white. Page dividers of white card, printed on the recto only in black, strong Blue (178), strong Red (12), and vivid greenish Yellow (97), precede pp 13 (drinks), 19 (firsts), 55 (breads), 63 (breakfast and lunch), 71 (fish and fowl), 95 (meats), 109 (sauces), 121 (vegetables), 135 (salads), 149 (desserts), 159 (cakes *etc*)

Contents: Title (*i*), TP verso (ii), foreword, signed 'A.D.B.' (iii), dedication and acknowledgements (iv), contents (v), weights, measures, and notes (vi–vii), list of croquet clubs (viii–ix), list of contributors (x–xi), advertisement (xii), text (13–189), space for notes (189), conclusion (190)

Binding: Semi-gloss white card front and rear, vivid Red (11) plastic comb, slotted, no endpapers. FC: the title (**IT'S A** | **WICKET** | **KITCHEN**) set within a hoop which features in a cartoon printed in black, strong Blue (178), strong Red (12), and vivid greenish Yellow (97). Inside FC: blank. RC: ([a cartoon in black, Blue, Red, and Yellow] | **Compiled,** | **illustrated and edited by** | **Anne D. Bessette** | A portion of the profit from this book is being donated to | The Croquet Foundation of America)

Copy seen: PC

Fingerprint: B.!! chfo **sene PoFr** 3 1991Q

Notes: Published anonymously, printed in December 1991 by Pine Prints of the Sandhills, Southern Pines, NC, price $16.00. Year of publication is inferred from the stated year of printing.

A262   **QUEEN OF GAMES: A HISTORY OF CROQUET.** Nicky Smith   1991

[a vignette: two crossed mallets in front of two arched hoops and a ball] | [in artist's display script, swash *Q*] **QUEEN** *of* | [*do*, displaced to the R by the letter *Q*] **GAMES** | A HISTORY OF CROQUET | Nicky Smith | Weidenfeld and Nicolson | London

[TP verso]

First published in Great Britain in 1991 | by George Weidenfeld & Nicolson Ltd | 91 Clapham High Street, London SW4 7TA | Copyright © Nicky Smith 1991 |

[assertion of copyright] | [BL Cataloguing in Publication Data] | ISBN 0 297 81176 2 | Typeset at The Spartan Press Ltd, Lymington, Hants | Printed and bound in Great Britain by | Butler and Tanner Ltd, Frome and London

Formula: [1–6¹⁶]. 96 leaves, pp *i–vi* vii–xiii *xiv*, 1–171 *172* 173–177 *178*

Technical notes: 177 × 114 mm (p 3). 39 lines, 20 = 91 mm. Leaf size 233 × 152 mm; thickness 0.17 mm; wove, unwatermarked, rough, white. Six leaves of plates on semi-gloss paper (12 unnumbered pages of black-and-white photographs) follow p 82

Contents: Half-title (*i*), by the same author (*ii*), title (*iii*), TP verso (*iv*), dedication (*v*), blank (*vi*), contents (vii), list of illustrations (viii), acknowledgements (ix–x), introduction (xi–xiii), blank (*xiv*), text (1–177), blank (*178*)

Binding: Moderate Green (145) linen grain paper over stiff boards, sewn. FC: blank. RC: blank. Spine: Gold-blocked ([title in the same style as on the FP of the dust wrapper, in two lines downwards] [subtitle in the same script as on the FP, cross-wise over a small disc] [author's name in the same script as on the FP, downwards] [crosswise] Weidenfeld | [*do*] & Nicolson)

Dust wrapper: Printed in full colour on glossy white paper laminate. FP: against a background of alternate broad stipes of brilliant Yellow Green (116) and strong yellowish Green (131) ([in the same style as the title lettering on the TP, in strong Red (12)] **QUEEN** *of* | [*do*] **GAMES** | [in black shaded script] **THE HISTORY OF CROQUET** | [drawing in full colour after Lucien Davis of a scene from a croquet match, in a panel outlined by a double-ruled frame flanked by stylised mallets and balls] | [in Red shaded script] **NICKY SMITH**). FF: publisher's blurb and price. RP: monochrome cartoon from Crowther Smith's *A Croquet Nonsense Book* (A144) and ISBN bar code. RF: in black on white ([portrait of the author] | [about the author] | [attribution of illustrations] | [name and address of publisher]). Spine: against a background of alternate broad stipes of brilliant Yellow Green (116) and strong yellowish Green (131), continuous with that on the FP ([title in the same style and colours as on the FP, in two lines downwards from near the head] [subtitle in the same script and colours as on the FP, crosswise over two stylised crossed mallets and a Red ball] [author's name in the same script and colours as on the FP, downwards] [crosswise near the foot, in black] Weidenfeld | [*do*] & Nicolson)

Copy seen: PC

Fingerprint: onll s.nd inat onme 3 1991A

Notes: Printed by Butler & Tanner, Frome and London, price £16.95 in UK only.

Reviews: *Croquet* (May 1991, p 22; March/April 1992, p 21)

1992

A263   **CROQUET: AN ANNOTATED BIBLIOGRAPHY FROM THE**   1992
        RENDELL RHOADES CROQUET COLLECTION.
        Nancy L Rhoades

[set between two stylised hoops] CROQUET | An Annotated Bibliography | from the Rendell Rhoades | Croquet Collection | by | NANCY L. RHOADES | [publisher's device] | The Scarecrow Press, Inc. | Metuchen, N.J., & London | 1992

Formula: [1–2¹⁶ 3⁸ 4–8¹⁶]. 120 leaves, pp *1–2, i–ii* iii *iv* v *vi* vii *viii* ix–xx, 1–197 *198* 199–214 *215–218*

Technical notes: 181 × 109 mm (p xii). 55 lines, 20 = 66mm. Leaf size 216 × 134 mm; thickness 0.11 mm; wove, unwatermarked, smooth, white. Eight pages of half-tone black-and-white plates, unnumbered, on semi-gloss paper are inset following p 90

Contents: Blank (*1*), frontispiece, a black-and-white half-tone photograph (*2*), title (*i*), TP verso (*ii*), contents (iii), blank (*iv*), acknowledgements (v), blank (*vi*), notes and apologia (vii), blank (*viii*), biography of Rendell Rhoades (ix–xx), text (1–197), blank (198), checklist of croquet publications published up to 1904 (199–202), index (203–214), blank (215–218)

Binding: Dark Green (146) cloth over stiff boards, sewn. FC: printed mostly in white ([set between two stylised hoops in gold] CROQUET | An Annotated Bibliography | from the Rendell Rhoades | Croquet Collection | NANCY L. RHOADES). RC: blank. Spine: the lettering downwards, in white (RHOADES   CROQUET [publisher's device, crosswise])

Copy seen: PC

Fingerprint: 0399 s.th nyhe inim 3 1992A

Notes: Printed anonymously, price £22.15 from the CA.

A264   CROQUET ASSOCIATION OF IRELAND HANDBOOK.   **1992**
[Croquet Association of Ireland]

(a) ****First edition (1992)*

[The FC]

[open outlined initial capital] Croquet | [*do*] Association | of | [open outlined initial capital] Ireland | [artist's perspective sketch of Irish land mass in the form of a modern court setting] | HANDBOOK 1992 [sketch of a mallet standing upright]

Formula: [1⁶]. 6 leaves, unnumbered [pp 1–12], and 5 loose leaves stapled inside the RC [ff 1–5]

Technical notes: 184 × 137 mm (p 9, ragged). 37 lines, 20 = 100 mm, variable. Leaf size 210 × 149 mm; thickness 0.10 mm; wove, unwatermarked, smooth, white

Contents: Subscriptions and officers (*1*), international matches (*1–3*), fixtures (*4*), general conditions for tournaments (*5*), selection regulations (*6–7*), directory of associates (*8–10*), clubs, affiliated bodies, and other addresses (*11*), equipment prices (*12*), entry forms for specific tournaments (ff *i–v*)

Binding: Very pale Green (148) light card, stapled through the folds of the leaves, no spine or endpapers. FC: printed in black (as above). Inside FC: blank. RC: monogram at the foot, perhaps the printer's device. Inside RC: blank

Copy seen: PC

Fingerprint: odin ck10 1212 1212 C 1992A [group 1 taken from p *1*, groups 2–4 from p 9]

Notes: Edited by Leslie Bryan, printed anonymously, issued free of charge to members of the CAI.

(b) 1993 *edition (1993)*

[The FC]

[open outlined initial capital] Croquet | [*do*] Association | of | [open outlined initial capital] Ireland | [artist's perspective sketch of Irish land mass in the form of a modern court setting] | HANDBOOK 1993

Formula: [1¹⁰]. 10 leaves, pp 3–11 *12* 13–21 *22*, and 7 loose leaves stapled inside the RC

Technical notes: 185 × 126 mm (p 6), mostly divided into two columns. 53 lines, 20 = 70 mm, variable. Leaf size 210 × 149 mm; thickness 0.10 mm; wove, unwatermarked, smooth, white

Contents: Subscriptions and officers (3), fixtures (4), general conditions for tournaments (5–7), proposed changes of the 1987 constitution (7), draft constitution (1993) (8–11), laws of croquet (*12–15*), advertisement (15), international matches (16–17), directory of associates (18–20), clubs, affiliated bodies, and other addresses (20–21), equipment prices (*22*), entry forms for specific tournaments (ff *i–vii*)

Binding: Light greenish Yellow (101) card, stapled through the folds of the leaves, no spine or endpapers. FC: printed in black (as above). Inside FC: blank. RC: monogram at the foot, perhaps the printer's device. Inside RC: blank

Copy seen: PC

Fingerprint: S)L) esrs ndnt th'w 3 1993A [group 1 taken from p 3]

Notes: Edited by Simon Williams, printed anonymously.

(c) 1994 *edition (1994)*

[Front cover]

[open outlined initial capital] Croquet | [*do*] Association | of | [open outlined initial capital] Ireland | [artist's perspective sketch of Irish land mass in the form of a modern court setting] | HANDBOOK 1994

Formula: [1¹⁴]. 14 leaves, pp 3–30, 31 (inside the RC), and loose insert

Technical notes: 186 × 115 mm (p 9), mostly divided into two columns. 52 lines, 20 = 72 mm, variable. Leaf size 214 × 148 mm; thickness 0.10 mm; wove, unwatermarked, smooth, white

Contents: Contents, assertion of copyright, and name of editor (3), subscriptions and officers (4), fixtures (5), general conditions for tournaments (6–7), constitution (8–11), laws of croquet (12–15), advertisement (15), international matches (16–17), directory of associates (18–20), clubs, affiliated bodies, and other addresses (21), equipment prices (22), alternative games (23–31), selection availability form (loose insert)

Binding: Light greenish Blue (172) light card, stapled, no spine or endpapers. FC: printed in black (as above). Inside FC: blank. RC: monogram at foot, perhaps printer's device. Inside RC: conclusion of text (p 31)

Copy seen: PC (wanting loose insert)

Fingerprint: msed esrs ndnt th'w 3 1994A [group 1 taken from p 3]

Notes: Edited by Simon Williams, printed anonymously.

(d) 1998 *edition (1998)*

[The FC]

[open outlined script, the initial letter shaded] Croquet | [*do*] Association of | [*do*] Ireland | [artist's perspective sketch of Irish land mass in the form of a modern court setting] | [in open outlined script] 1998 HANDBOOK

Formula: [1¹⁴]. 14 leaves, pp *1* 2–28, and two loose inserts

Technical notes: 180 × 118 mm (p 8), mostly divided into two columns. 62 lines, 20 = 60 mm, variable. Leaf size 210 × 148 mm; thickness 0.10 mm; wove, unwatermarked, smooth, white

Contents: Contents, assertion of copyright, and name of editor (*1*), subscriptions and officers (2), fixtures (3), general conditions for tournaments (4–5), constitution (6–8), laws of croquet for beginners (9–12), directory of associates (13–16), clubs, other addresses, and equipment prices (17), winners of principal events (18–19), alternative games (20–22), the Egyptian draw and modified games (23–24), notes for novices (25–28), selection availability form and coaching application form (loose inserts)

Binding: Very pale Green (148) light card, stapled, no spine or endpapers. FC: printed in black (as above). Inside FC: blank. RC: monogram at the foot, perhaps the editor's personal device. Inside RC: blank

Copy seen: PC (wanting loose inserts)

Fingerprint: 98ed r.em rkes PaJo 3 1998A [group 1 taken from p 3]

Notes: Edited by L Dungan, printed anonymously. Publication of this handbook was resumed in 1998 after a lapse of some years.

A265 CROQUET COACHING: ERROR CORRECTION. John Riches   [1992]

(a) *First edition [1992]*

[The FC, within a ruled frame]

CROQUET | COACHING: | ERROR | CORRECTION | [abstract sketch of player about to make a stroke] | by John Riches

Formula: [1–15^1]. 15 leaves, unnumbered, [pp 1–30]

Technical notes: 226 × 153 mm (p 5). 41 lines, 20 = 112 mm. Leaf size 297 × 210 mm; thickness 0.10 mm; wove, unwatermarked, smooth, white

Contents: Text (*1–29*), advertisement (*30*)

Binding: Vivid reddish Orange (34) light card front and rear, stapled, the spine wrapped with deep reddish Orange (36) stippled plastic tape, no endpapers. FC: printed in black, as above. Inside FC: blank. RC: blank. Inside RC: blank. Spine: blank

Copy seen: PC

Fingerprint: t.of n.n- orhe qudi C 1992Q [group 1 taken from p 1]

Notes: Printed and published privately in Enfield SA, price Aus$6.00 including postage within Australia. Year of publication is inferred from a note in a supplementary advertisement to a companion work (A267). The author, however, has subsequently stated that this work was first published in 1990.

Several variants of this edition may have appeared (see *Notes* to a companion work, A294). It was, and continues to be, produced in small batches to meet current orders, both privately in Australia and by the NZCC. Excluding sales by the NZCC, about 400 copies had been sold up to June 1999.

(b) *First English edition (1995)*

[The TP as that of (a)]

Formula: [1–33^1]. 33 leaves, unnumbered, [ff 1–33]

Technical notes: 226 × 152 mm (f 5). 41 lines, 20 = 112 mm. Leaf size 297 × 210 mm; thickness 0.10 mm; wove, unwatermarked, smooth, white

Contents: Text, continued (*1–29*), advertisement, revision of that in (a) (*30*), text, concluded (*31–32*), advertisement (*33*)

Binding: Pale Yellow (89) paper FC protected by clear acetate sheet and RC of white light Astrolux board, slotted and fastened with a white plastic comb, no endpapers. FC: printed in black, as above. Inside FC: blank. RC: blank. Inside RC: blank. Spine: blank

Copy seen: PC

Fingerprint: t.of upin orhe e.ea C 1995A [group 1 taken from f *1*, group 2 taken from f *5*, groups 3 and 4 taken from f *13*]

Notes: Published in October 1995 by D Drazin, Croxley Green, Herts, for distribution in the UK and Ireland, printed anonymously, price £6.00. The text is identical, or virtually identical, to that of (a). Apparently the only variations are revisions to the earlier advertisement (incorporating Australian prices as at November 1992), the addition of an *addendum* to the text (ff *31–32*), and the addition of an advertisement addressed to the UK market (f *33*).

Fifty copies were produced in small batches in 1995 and 1996, of which 24 remained unsold in October 1998.

A266   CROQUET TECHNIQUE. John Riches   [1992]

(a) *First edition [1992]*

[The FC, within a ruled frame]

CROQUET | **TECHNIQUE** | [abstract sketch of a player about to make a stroke] | by John Riches

Formula: [1–12¹]. 12 leaves, pp 1–9 *10* 11–23 *24*

Technical notes: 242 × 162 mm (p 3). 47 lines, 20 = 99 mm. Leaf size 297 × 210 mm; thickness 0.10 mm; wove, unwatermarked, smooth, white

Contents: Contents (1), text (2–22), advertisement (23), blank (*24*)

Binding: Moderate yellowish Green (136) light card front and rear, stapled, the spine wrapped with dark yellowish Green (137) plastic-laminated cloth tape, no endpapers. FC: printed in black, as above. Inside FC: blank. RC: blank. Inside RC: blank. Spine: blank

Copy seen: PC

Fingerprint: 2220 n.he r-ny thin 3 1992Q [group 1 taken from p 1]

Notes: Printed and published privately in Enfield SA, price Aus$6.00 including postage within Australia. Year of publication is inferred from a note in a supplementary advertisement to a companion work (A267). The author, however, has subsequently stated that this work was first published in 1989.

Several variants of this edition may have appeared (see *Notes* to a companion work, A294). It was, and continues to be, produced in small batches to meet current orders, both privately in Australia and by the NZCC. Excluding sales by the NZCC, about 800 copies had been sold up to June 1999.

(b) *First English edition (1995)*

[The TP as that of (a)]

Formula: [1–13¹]. 13 leaves, pp *i*, 1–9 *10* 11–21, *ii–iii*, 22–23 [= 26]

Technical notes: 241 × 162 mm (p 3). 47 lines, 20 = 98 mm. Leaf size 297 × 210 mm; thickness 0.10 mm; wove, unwatermarked, smooth, white

Contents: Blank (*i*), contents (1), text, continued (2–21), author's supplementary note (21, *ii–iii*), text, concluded (22), other booklets by the same author (23)

Binding: Very light Green (143) paper FC protected by clear acetate sheet and RC of white light Astrolux board, slotted and fastened with a white plastic comb, no endpapers. FC: printed in black, as above. Inside FC: blank. RC: blank. Inside RC: blank. Spine: blank

Copy seen: PC

Fingerprint: n.is nth. d.er masu C 1995A [groups 1–4 taken from pp 2, *10*, 12, 13 respectively]

Notes: Published in October 1995 by D Drazin, Croxley Green, Herts, for distribution in the UK and Ireland, printed anonymously, price £6.00. The text is for the most part identical, or virtually identical, to that of (a). Apparently the only variations are a few minor revisions in MS, the interpolation of a supplementary note (pp 21, *ii–iii*), and substitution (at p 23) of the original advertisement (incorporating Australian prices as at November 1992) by an advertisement addressed to the UK market.

Sixty-five copies were produced in small batches in 1995 and 1996, of which 13 remained unsold in October 1998.

A267   CROQUET: THE MENTAL APPROACH. John Riches   [1992]

(a) *First edition [1992]*

[The FC, within a ruled frame]

[swash Q] **CROQUET:** | **THE** | **MENTAL** | **APPROACH** | [abstract sketch of a player about to make a stroke] | by John Riches

Formula: [1–23¹]. 23 leaves, pp 1–46

Technical notes: 248 × 148 mm (p 4). 51 lines, 20 = 98 mm. Leaf size 297 × 210 mm; thickness 0.10 mm; wove, unwatermarked, smooth, white

Contents: Contents, author's note, and acknowledgements (1), text (2–46), advertisement (46)

Binding: Brilliant greenish Yellow (98) light card front and rear, stapled, the spine wrapped with stippled black plastic tape, no endpapers. FC: printed in black, as above. Inside FC: blank. RC: blank. Inside RC: blank. Spine: blank

Copy seen: PC

Fingerprint: d.ve n.er ng,- plne 3 1992Q [group 1 taken from p 1]

Notes: Printed and published privately in Enfield SA, price Aus$11.00 within Australia. Year of publication is inferred from a note in the supplementary advertisement (p 46) and confirmed by the author.

Several variants of this edition may have appeared (see *Notes* to a companion work, A294). It was, and continues to be, produced in small batches to meet current orders, both privately in Australia and by the NZCC. Excluding sales by the NZCC, about 400 copies had been sold up to June 1999.

(b) *First English edition (1995)*

[The TP as that of (a)]

Formula: [1–47¹]. 47 leaves, ff 1–46 47

Technical notes: 250 × 148 mm (f 4). 51 lines, 20 = 99 mm. Leaf size 297 × 210 mm; thickness 0.10 mm; wove, unwatermarked, smooth, white

Contents: Contents, author's note, and acknowledgements (1), text (2–46), advertisement (47)

Binding: Pale greenish Yellow (104) paper FC protected by clear acetate sheet and RC of white light Astrolux board, slotted and fastened with a white plastic comb, no endpapers. FC: printed in black, as above. Inside FC: blank. RC: blank. Inside RC: blank. Spine: blank

Copy seen: PC

Fingerprint: d.ve n.ms vent toff C 1995A [group 1 taken from f 1, group 2 taken from f 5, groups 3 and 4 taken from f 13]

Notes: Published in October 1995 by D Drazin, Croxley Green, Herts, for distribution in the UK and Ireland, printed anonymously, price £7.50. The text is identical, or virtually identical, to that of (a). Apparently the only variation is substitution (at f 47) of the original advertisement (incorporating Australian prices as at November 1992) by an advertisement addressed to the UK market.

Fifty copies were produced in small batches in 1995 and 1996, of which eight remained unsold in October 1998.

A268   KYABRAM CROQUET THEN & NOW: 1922–1992.   [1992]
Dorothy Austin

KYABRAM CROQUET | THEN & NOW | 1922 - 1992 | Researched & Written By; | Mrs. Dorothy Austin | 1992 | Typed By; | Mrs. Noelene Cook | Printed & Prepared By; | Fred de Rooze | Orm Cook | Noelene Cook

Formula: [1²⁰]. 20 leaves, pp *i–iv*, 1–33 *34–36*

Technical notes: 176 × 104 mm (p 2). 42 lines, 20 = 84 mm. Leaf size 210 × 144 mm; 0.10 mm; wove, unwatermarked, smooth, white

Contents: Significant quotation (*i*), blank (*ii*), title (*iii*), list of life members (*iv*), text, continued (1–35), advertisement (36), text, concluded (inside RC)

Binding: Very light Blue (180) leather-effect embossed paper, printed in black, stapled, no spine or endpapers. FC: in display script (*KYABRAM* | *CROQUET* | *CLUB* | **Then & Now** | **1922** [a two-headed arrow] **1992**). Inside FC: blank. RC: blank; the copy examined is marked '1067'

Copy seen: PC

Fingerprint: eeet soar s.ur be"A 3 1992Q

Notes: Printed and prepared by Fred de Rooze, Orm Cook, and Noelene Cook. Year of publication is inferred from the citation on the TP.

A269   RECOMMENDATIONS FOR A CHAMPIONSHIP CROQUET   1992
COURT. Dr Carleton H Mabee

RECOMMENDATIONS FOR A | CHAMPIONSHIP CROQUET COURT | by | Dr. Carleton H. Mabee | Chairman, | Courts and Greens Committee | Produced in cooperation with the | United States Croquet Association | and the | Croquet Foundation of America | Published by | Bass Cove Books | RR1, Box 933, North Street | Kennebunkport, Maine 04046 | 1992

Formula: [1¹⁰]. 10 leaves, pp *i–iii*, 1–17

Technical notes: 186 × 112 mm (p 1, ragged). 46 lines, 20 = 81 mm. Leaf size 213 × 136 mm; thickness 0.10 mm; wove, unwatermarked, smooth, white

Contents: Title (*i*), open letter to 'court builder', signed 'Courts and Greens Committee' (*iii*), text (1–17)

Binding: Yellowish White (92) light card, stapled, no spine or endpapers. FC: printed in black (**RECOMMENDATIONS** | **FOR A CHAMPIONSHIP** | **CROQUET COURT** | [frameless reprint of engraved illustration entitled 'Preparing for croquet' first published in *Illustrated London News* (24 June 1871)]). Inside FC: blank. RC: blank. Inside RC: advertisement

Copy seen: PC

Fingerprint: 1716 r.nd llon 2.1. C 1992A [groups 1–4 taken from pp *iii*, 8, 10, 11 respectively]

Notes: Printed anonymously.

A270   REFEREES HANDBOOK: AN INTERPRETATIVE GUIDE TO   1992 THE REGULATIONS AND LAWS OF ASSOCIATION CROQUET. Graeme Roberts

[device of the NZCC, the initials *N, Z, C, C,* the letter *N* set over a ball] | **REFEREES | HANDBOOK | An Interpretative Guide to the Regulations | and Laws of Association Croquet** | **Graeme Roberts** | Chairman, N.Z.C.C. Laws Committee | Senior Referee | New Zealand Representative 1982, 1990 | Author: Practical Umpiring

Formula: 118 loose leaves, unnumbered [ff 1–118]

Technical Notes: 166 × 113 mm (f 12). 40 lines, 20 = 84 mm. Leaf size 209 × 149 mm; thickness 0.10 mm; wove, unwatermarked, smooth, white, punched to fit a ring binder

Contents: Title (*1*), TP verso (*2*), contents (*3–6*), acknowledgements (*7*), foreword, signed 'Ashley Heenan' (*8–9*), introduction (*10*), Part I, the regulations (*11–42*), Part II, the laws (*43–101*), index (*102–118*)

Binding: A trade ring binder with three equally spaced spring-loaded clasps, covered in white leather-effect PVC printed in black, with a clear PVC pocket inside the FC. FC: ([device of NZCC, the initials *N, Z, C, C,* the letter *N* set over a ball] | **REFEREES | HANDBOOK | An Interpretative Guide to the | Regulations and Laws of | Association Croquet** | [rule, in bold] | **Graeme Roberts**). Inside FC: blank. RC: blank. Inside RC: blank. Spine: across the top ([device of the NZCC]); downwards, centred (**REFEREES HANDBOOK | An Interpretative Guide to the | Regulations and Laws of Association Croquet**); across the foot ([rule, in bold] | **Graeme Roberts**)

Copy seen: PC

Fingerprint: c.92 k.s. t.ng onat 3 1992A [group 4 taken from f 13]

Notes: Printed anonymously, offered by the NZCC in 1996 to affiliated players at NZ$25.00.

AA271 REFLECTIONS ON THE SUSSEX COUNTY CROQUET   1992 CLUB AT SOUTHWICK. John Eardley-Simpson

[In MS]

Reflections | on | The Sussex County Croquet Club | at Southwick | [line drawing of club grounds] | written and illustrated | by | John Eardley-Simpson

Formula: [1¹⁰]. 10 leaves, unnumbered [pp 1–20]

Technical notes: ca 180 × 103 mm (p *11*, ragged). 61 lines, 20 = *ca* 59 mm. Leaf size *ca* 210 × 148 mm

Contents: Title (*1*), blank (*2*), acknowledgements and assertion of copyright, March 1992 (*3*), text (*4–20*)

Binding: Apparently stapled, no wrapper, spine, or endpapers

Copy seen: PC (photocopy)

Fingerprint: 92on n.of s.l, ofpr C 1992A

Notes: Printed and published privately.

A272   TAKE A BISQUE. Nell Hass   1992

TAKE | A | BISQUE | LESSONS IN WAYS TO TAKE BISQUES AND USE THEM | TO GOOD ADVANTAGE | NELL HASS | 19 DOON DOON STREET | CURRIMUNDI QLD 4551

Formula: [1–21¹]. 21 leaves, pp *1* 2–42

Technical notes: 223 × 156 mm (variable) (p 3, ragged). 30 lines, 20 = 147 mm. Leaf size 297 × 209 mm; thickness 0.10 mm; wove, unwatermarked, smooth, white

Contents: Title (*1*), TP verso (*2*), text (3–42)

Binding: Very light greenish Blue (171) light card, black plastic comb, slotted, no spine or endpapers. FC: printed in black, the title within a double frame, the inner frame ruled, the outer frame defined by a repeated figure composed of a croquet mallet, ball, and hoop (*TAKE* | *A* | *BISQUE* | *NELL HASS* | [swelled rule composed of the same repeated figure used to define the outer frame above]). Inside FC: blank. RC: blank. Inside RC: blank

Copy seen: PC

Fingerprint: s.or k.ay k.ay 20BI 3 1992A [group 4 taken from p 16]

Notes: Published by Nell Hass, printed anonymously, ISBN 0 646 11446 8.

A273   TEACH YOURSELF CROQUET. Don L Gaunt   1992

[publisher's device] **TEACH YOURSELF** | [rule in bold] | **CROQUET** | [in white out of a black panel] INCLUDING GAMES FOR THE GARDEN AND | [*do*] THE CROQUET ASSOCIATION RULES | **Don Gaunt** | Hodder & Stoughton | LONDON SYDNEY AUCKLAND

[From the TP verso, L justified]

ISBN 0–340–56528–4 | First published 1992 | © 1992 Don Gaunt | [assertion of copyright] | Typeset by Rowland Phototypesetting Ltd, Bury St Edmunds, Suffolk | Printed in Great Britain for the educational publishing division of Hodder & Stoughton | Ltd, Mill Road, Dunton Green, Sevenoaks, Kent by Clays Ltd, St Ives plc, Bungay, | Suffolk

Formula: Apparently [1–9⁸]. 72 leaves, pp *i–iii* iv–vi, 1– 46 *47* 48–136 *137–138*

Technical notes: 169 × 103 mm (p 2). 42 lines, 20 = 81 mm. Leaf size 197 × 128 mm; thickness 0.12 mm; wove, unwatermarked, smooth, white. Four inset leaves of plates on semi-gloss paper, each page containing two colour photographs (numbered 1–16), follow p 58

Contents: Title (*i*), TP verso (*ii*), contents (*iii*), about the author (iv), 'How to use this book' (v–vi), acknowledgements (vi), text (1–136), advertisement (*137*), blank (*138*)

Binding: White glossy laminate glued to the folds of the gatherings, no endpapers. FC: ([publisher's device in white and brilliant Yellow (83) out of a black horizontal band] [in Yellow out of black] **TEACH YOURSELF** | [colour photograph of man and woman players in play] | [vivid purplish Red (254) rule, in bold, out of colour photograph] | [in very light Blue (180) out of colour photograph] **CROQUET** | [in white out of a medium Grey (265) panel] INCLUDING GAMES FOR THE GARDEN AND | [*do*] THE CROQUET ASSOCIATION RULES). Inside FC: the FCs of six titles in the Teach Yourself series reproduced in colour. RC: ([publisher's device in white and Yellow out of a black horizontal band] [in Yellow out of black] **TEACH YOURSELF** | [Red rule, in bold, out of a Blue background] | [publisher's blurb, with colour illustration, on Blue background] | [publisher's device and name,

ISBN bar code, and price, in black on a white panel out of Blue background]). Inside RC: blank. Spine: ([publisher's device in Yellow and white crosswise out of a black background] [downwards in Yellow out of black] **TEACH YOURSELF** [downwards in white out of black] **CROQUET** [detail from colour photograph of croquet lawn, crosswise, out of black])

Copy seen: PC

Fingerprint: 3231 tod. ntnt (a'I 3 1992A [group 2 taken from p 7, the first two characters of group 3 taken from the caption to fig 4 on p 13, the last two characters of group 3 taken from the caption to fig 4(f) on p 13]

Notes: Printed by Clays, Bungay, Suffolk, price £5.99 net in the UK, NZ$19.95 in New Zealand. The initial printing was of 8000 copies. A separate edition was published in America.

Reviews: *Croquet* (July/August 1992, p 17), *Croquet Update* (December 1992).

1993

A274   **APPROACHING CROQUET: PART 1. Peter Hirst and Ashley**   1993
        Heenan (ed)

[The letterpress, mostly L justified, to the R of devices of the Hillary Commission and Coaching New Zealand, and flanked on the R by a thumb-nail cartoon]

[R justified, the figure *1* in white out of a right-facing tailless arrow] **PART 1** | **APPROACHING** | [rule] | **C R O Q U E T** | *Devised by* | *Peter Hirst CNZ* | *Ashley Heenan NZCC* | ***From Material Supplied by*** | *Dennis Bulloch* | *Madeline Hadwin* | *NZCC Coaching Panel* | ***Designer*** | *Aleck Yee* | ***Illustrations*** | *John Prince* | ***This Publication made possible with the*** | *generous financial support of* | *The Hillary Commission* | ***and the advice and assistance of*** | *Coaching New Zealand* | ***Published by*** | *New Zealand Croquet Council* | *Incorporated* | ***Produced by*** | *Alltex Electronic Publishing and Design* | © *New Zealand Croquet Council Inc.* | [indented] *August 1993* | *ISBN 0-473-02166-8*

Formula: [1⁸]. 8 leaves, pp *1* 2–17 including the inside of the RC

Technical notes: 236 × 162 mm, variable (p 4, ragged). 52 lines, 20 = 94 mm. Leaf size 297 × 210 mm; thickness 0.09 mm; wove, unwatermarked, semi-gloss, white

Contents: Title (*1*), foreword, signed 'Roger Murfitt' (2), preface, signed 'Peter A Hirst' and introduction (3), text (4–17)

Binding: White semi-gloss card, stapled, no spine or endpapers. FC: printed mostly in black over and out of a background design divided diagonally, the top-L coloured black and the bottom-R brilliant Blue (177), the whole overlaid by a regular matrix of medium Grey (265) dots ([in white out of black background] **APPROACHING** | [*do*, rule] | [*do*] **C R O Q U E T** | [artist's sketch of hands gripping a mallet shaft, centrally on a white panel out of both black and Blue portions of the background design] | [the figure *1* in white out of a right-facing tailless arrow in black, over the Blue portion of the Background design] **PART 1** | [publisher's device, incorporating schematic illustration of a ball in Grey]). Inside FC: blank. RC: printed in black near the foot over a very light Blue (180) background (*New Zealand Croquet is generously supported by the Hillary Commission* | *and the New Zealand Sports Foundation* | [device of the Hillary Commission]).

Copy seen: PC

Fingerprint: t.nd g.ha l.es taco 3 1993A [group 4 taken from the text on p 14]

Notes: Produced by Alltex Electronic Publishing and Design, offered by the NZCC together with Parts 2 and 3 in 1996 at NZ$15.00.

A275 APPROACHING CROQUET: PART 2. Peter Hirst and Ashley   **1993**
Heenan (ed)

[The letterpress, mostly L justified, to the R of devices of the Hillary Commission and Coaching New Zealand, and flanked on the R by a thumb-nail cartoon]

[R justified, the figure *2* in white out of a right-facing tailless arrow] **PART 2** | **APPROACHING** | [rule] | **C R O Q U E T** | *Devised by* | *Peter Hirst CNZ* | *Ashley Heenan NZCC* | ***From Material Supplied by*** | *Dennis Bulloch* | *Madeline Hadwin* | *NZCC Coaching Panel* | ***Designer*** | *Aleck Yee* | ***Illustrations*** | *John Prince* | ***This Publication made possible with the*** | ***generous financial support of*** | *The Hillary Commission* | ***and the advice and assistance of*** | *Coaching New Zealand* | ***Published by*** | *New Zealand Croquet Council* | *Incorporated* | ***Produced by*** | *Alltex Electronic Publishing and Design* | © *New Zealand Croquet Council Inc.* | [indented] *August 1993* | *ISBN 0-473-01267-6*

Formula: [1⁸]. 8 leaves, pp *1* 2–17 including the inside of the RC

Technical notes: 236 × 157 mm, variable (p 6, ragged). 52 lines, 20 = 94 mm. Leaf size 296 × 208 mm; thickness 0.09 mm; wove, unwatermarked, semi-gloss, white

Contents: Title and publishing details (*1*), text (2–17)

Binding: White semi-gloss card, stapled, no spine or endpapers. FC: printed mostly in black over and out of a background design divided diagonally, the top-L coloured black and the bottom-R vivid reddish Orange (34), the whole overlaid by a regular matrix of medium Grey (265) dots ([in white out of black background] **APPROACHING** | [*do*, rule] | [*do*] **C R O Q U E T** | [artist's sketch of a man playing a croquet stroke, centrally on a white panel out of both black and Orange portions of the background design] | [the figure *2* in white out of a right-facing tailless arrow in black, over the Orange portion of the background design] **PART 2** | [publisher's device, incorporating a schematic illustration of a ball]). Inside FC: blank. RC: printed in black near the foot over a strong Pink (2) background (*New Zealand Croquet is generously supported by the Hillary Commission* | *and the New Zealand Sports Foundation* | [device of the Hillary Commission]).

Copy seen: PC

Fingerprint: n.ll g.ry y.is pema 3 1993A [group 1 taken from the text on p 3]

Notes: Produced by Alltex Electronic Publishing and Design, offered by the NZCC together with Parts 1 and 3 in 1996 at NZ$15.00.

A276 APPROACHING CROQUET: PART 3. Peter Hirst and Ashley   **1993**
Heenan (ed)

[The letterpress, mostly L justified, to the R of devices of the Hillary Commission and Coaching New Zealand, and flanked on the R by a thumb-nail cartoon]

[R justified, the figure *3* in white out of a right-facing tailless arrow] **PART 3** | **APPROACHING** | [rule] | **C R O Q U E T** | *Devised by* | *Peter Hirst CNZ* | *Ashley Heenan NZCC* | ***From Material Supplied by*** | *Dennis Bulloch* | *Madeline Hadwin* | *NZCC Coaching Panel* | ***Designer*** | *Aleck Yee* | ***Illustrations*** | *John Prince* | ***This Publication made possible with the*** | ***generous financial support of*** | *The Hillary Commission* | ***and the advice and assistance of*** | *Coaching New Zealand* | ***Published by*** | *New Zealand Croquet Council* | *Incorporated* | ***Produced by*** | *Alltex Electronic Publishing and Design* | © *New Zealand Croquet Council Inc. August 1993* | *ISBN 0-473-01268-4*

Formula: [1⁸]. 8 leaves, pp *1* 2–17 including the inside of the RC

Technical notes: 245 × 125 mm, variable (p 3, ragged). 54 lines, 20 = 94 mm. Leaf size 298 × 209 mm; thickness 0.09 mm; wove, unwatermarked, semi-gloss, white

Contents: Title and publishing details (*1*), text (2–17)

Binding: White semi-gloss card, stapled, no spine or endpapers. FC: printed mostly in black over and out of a background design divided diagonally, the top-L coloured black and the bottom-R brilliant Green (140), the whole overlaid by a regular matrix of medium Grey (265) dots ([in white out of black background] **APPROACHING** | [*do*, rule] | [*do*] C R O Q U E T | [cartoon centrally on a white panel out of both black and Green portions of the background design] | [the figure 3 in white out of a right-facing tailless arrow in black, over the Green portion of the background design] **PART 3** | [publisher's device, incorporating a schematic illustration of a ball]). Inside FC: blank. RC: printed in black near the foot over a very light Green (143) background (*New Zealand Croquet is generously supported by the Hillary Commission* | *and the New Zealand Sports Foundation* | [device of the Hillary Commission])

Copy seen: PC

Fingerprint: e.ny g.ng d!en of-m 3 1993A [group 3 taken from the text on p 13]

Notes: Produced by Alltex Electronic Publishing and Design, offered by the NZCC together with Parts 1 and 2 in 1996 at NZ$15.00.

AA277 CLUB MEMBERSHIP BOOKLET [and 'UPDATES'].   1993
[Victorian Croquet Association]

(a) *First edition (1993)*

[The FC]

[device of Sport and Recreation Victoria] | [device of the VCA] | **CLUB MEMBER-SHIP** | **BOOKLET** | [between devices of Arthritis Foundation of Victoria and VicHealth Foundation, one of three lines] *"Move It or Lose It"* | [*do*] Another project funded by VicHealth | [*do*] with the Arthritis Foundation of Victoria

Formula: [1²⁸]. 28 leaves, pp *i–iv*, 1–50 *51–52*

Technical notes: 172 × 124 mm (p 9, ragged). 58 lines, 20 = 60 mm. Leaf size 210 × 146 mm; thickness 0.10 mm; wove, unwatermarked, smooth, white

Contents: The VCA (*i*), blank (*ii*), contents (*iii*), blank (*iv*), metropolitan referees (1–3), membership of metropolitan clubs (4–15), country clubs listed by associations (16–17), country referees (18–22), membership of country clubs (23–50), blank (*51–52*)

Binding: Very light Green (143) card, stapled, no spine or endpapers. FC: printed in black as above. Inside FC: blank. RC: blank. Inside RC: blank

Copy seen: PC

Fingerprint: 72RY 6328 7171 BaAu 3 1993A [group 1 taken from p *i*]

Notes: Printed anonymously.

(b) *Update December 1993 (1993)*

[Page *i*]

[device of Sport and Recreation Victoria] | [device of the VCA] | **CLUB MEMBER-SHIP** | **BOOKLET** | UPDATE DEC 1993 | [between devices of Arthritis Foundation of Victoria and VicHealth Foundation, one of three lines] *"Move It or Lose It"* | [*do*] Another project funded by VicHealth | [*do*] with the Arthritis Foundation of Victoria

Formula: [1^{18}]. 18 leaves, pp *i*, 1–35

Technical notes: 174 × 128 mm (p 4). 57 lines, 20 = 61 mm. Leaf size 210 × 146 mm; thickness 0.11 mm; wove, unwatermarked, smooth, moderate Pink (4)

Contents: Title (*i*), metropolitan referees (1–3), amendments to membership of metropolitan clubs to 15 December 1993 (4–11), country referees (12–16), amendments to membership of country clubs to 15 December 1993 (17–35)

Binding: Stapled, no wrapper

Copy seen: PC

Fingerprint: 9059 8561 0702 Co** C 1993A [group 1 taken from p 2, group 2 taken from p 10, group 3 taken from p 12, group 4 taken from p 13]

Notes: Printed anonymously.

(c) ***Update December 1994 (1994)***

[Page *i*]

[device of Sport and Recreation Victoria] | [device of the VCA] | **CLUB MEMBER-SHIP** | **BOOKLET** | UPDATED TO DECEMBER 1994 | [devices of VicHealth Foundation and Arthritis Foundation of Victoria] | Another project funded by VicHealth | with the Arthritis Foundation of Victoria

Formula: [1^{12}]. 12 leaves, pp *i*, 1–23

Technical notes: 168 × 97 mm (p 2). 56 lines, 20 = 60 mm. Leaf size 210 × 146 mm; thickness 0.10 mm; wove, unwatermarked, smooth, pale Yellow (89)

Contents: Title (*i*), amendments to membership of metropolitan clubs to 19 December 1994 (1–7), amendments to membership of country clubs to 19 December 1994 (8–23)

Binding: Stapled, no wrapper

Copy seen: PC

Fingerprint: 4084 5050 bs50 Va*A C 1994A [groups 1–4 taken from pp 2, 10, 12, 13 respectively]

Notes: Printed anonymously.

A278   CROQUET: LESSONS IN TACTICS. John Riches   [1993]

(a) *First edition [1993]*

[The FC, within a ruled frame]

CROQUET: | **LESSONS IN** | **TACTICS** | [abstract sketch of a player about to make a stroke] | by John Riches

Formula: [1–30^1]. 30 leaves, pp 1–59 *60*

Technical notes: 215 × 145 mm (p 5). 44 lines, 20 = 99 mm. Leaf size 297 × 210 mm; thickness 0.10 mm; wove, unwatermarked, smooth, white

Contents: Contents (1), introduction, signed 'John Riches' (2), text (3–58), advertisement (59), blank (*60*)

Binding: Light bluish Grey (190) light card front and rear, stapled, the spine wrapped with bluish Black (193) stippled plastic tape, no endpapers. FC: printed in black, as above. Inside FC: blank. RC: blank. Inside RC: blank. Spine: blank

Copy seen: PC

Fingerprint: 5750 e.me y.to doyo 3 1993Q [group 1 taken from p 1]

Notes: Printed and published privately in Enfield SA, price Aus$11.00 including postage within Australia. Year of publication is inferred from a note in a supplementary advertisement to a companion work (A267) and confirmed by the author. Several variants of this edition may have appeared (see *Notes* to a companion work, A294). It was, and continues to be, produced in small batches to meet current orders, both privately in Australia and by the NZCC. Excluding sales by the NZCC, about 500 copies had been sold up to June 1999.

(b) *First English edition (1995)*

[The FC as that of (a)]

Formula: [1–30¹]. 30 leaves, pp 1–58, *59–60*

Technical notes: As at (a)

Contents: Contents (1), introduction, signed 'John Riches' (2), text (3–58), advertisement (59), blank (60)

Binding: Light Grey (264) paper FC protected by clear acetate sheet and RC of white light Astrolux board, slotted and fastened with a white plastic comb, no endpapers. FC: printed in black, as above. Inside FC: blank. RC: blank. Inside RC: blank. Spine: blank

Copy seen: PC

Fingerprint: 5750 e.me y.to doyo 3 1995A [group 1 taken from p 1]

Notes: Published in October 1995 by D Drazin, Croxley Green, Herts, for distribution in the UK and Ireland, printed anonymously, price £7.50. The text is identical, or virtually identical, to that of (a). Apparently the only variation is substitution (at p 59) of the original advertisement (incorporating Australian prices as at November 1992) by an advertisement addressed to the UK market.

Sixty-five copies were produced in small batches in 1995 and 1996, of which twelve remained unsold in October 1998.

A279   CROQUET: NEXT BREAK STRATEGY. John Riches   [1993]

(a) *First edition (1993)*

[The FC, within a ruled frame]

CROQUET: | NEXT BREAK | STRATEGY | [abstract sketch of a player about to make a stroke] | by John Riches

Formula: [1–26¹]. 26 leaves, pp 1–52

Technical notes: 232 × 144 mm (p 4). 47 lines, 20 = 99 mm. Leaf size 297 × 210 mm; thickness 0.10 mm; wove, unwatermarked, smooth, white

Contents: Contents and publishing details (1), text (2–49), advertisement (50), Appendix A (51), Appendix B (52)

Binding: Very light greenish Blue (171) light card front and rear, stapled, the spine wrapped with deep Blue (179) stippled plastic tape, no endpapers. FC: printed in black, as above. Inside FC: blank. RC: blank. Inside RC: blank. Spine: blank

Copy seen: PC

Fingerprint: 57.A e.ld k.ed ouot 3 1993Q [group 1 taken from p 1]

Notes: Printed and published privately in Enfield SA, price Aus$11.00 including postage within Australia. Year of publication is conjectural. According to a note on p 1, this work was first published as *Croquet Tactics* in 1991, a claim subsequently confirmed by the author.

Several variants of this edition may have appeared (see *Notes* to a companion work, A294). It was, and continues to be, produced in small batches to meet current orders, both privately in Australia and by the NZCC. Excluding sales by the NZCC, about 500 copies had been sold up to June 1999.

(b) *First English edition (1995)*

[The FC as that of (a)]

Formula: [1–26¹]. 26 leaves, pp 1–49 *50* 51–52

Technical notes: As at (a)

Contents: Contents and publishing details (1), text (2–49), advertisement (*50*), Appendix A (51), Appendix B (52)

Binding: Very light greenish Blue (171) paper FC protected by clear acetate sheet and RC of white light Astrolux board, slotted and fastened with a white plastic comb, no endpapers. FC: printed in black, as above. Inside FC: blank. RC: blank. Inside RC: blank. Spine: blank

Copy seen: PC

Fingerprint: 57.A e.ld k.ed ouot 3 1995A [group 1 taken from p 1]

Notes: Published in October 1995 by D Drazin, Croxley Green, Herts, for distribution in the UK and Ireland, printed anonymously, price £7.50. The text is identical, or virtually identical, to that of (a). Apparently the only variation is substitution (at p *50*) of the original advertisement (incorporating Australian prices as at November 1992) by an advertisement addressed to the UK market.

Sixty-five copies were produced in small batches in 1995 and 1996, of which ten remained unsold in October 1998.

A280 **HELP: A HUMEROUS GUIDE TO ENLIGHTEN LOST**   [1993]
      CROQUET PLAYERS IN THE NORTHERN LEAGUE.
      Mike Evans (ed)

(a) *First edition [1993]*

[The FC]

[device, a mallet head and a ball] | Confederation of Northern Croquet Clubs. | H E L P | [a cartoon] | A <u>H</u>umerous guide to <u>E</u>nlighten <u>L</u>ost | Croquet <u>P</u>layers in the Northern League. | Published by **BEVERLEY CROQUET CLUB** | Editor Mike Evans

Formula: [1¹⁰]. 10 leaves, pp *i, 1* 2–4, *ii,* 5–18 [= 20]

Technical notes: 157 × 111 mm (p 14). 37 lines, 20 = 86 mm. Leaf size 211 × 148 mm; thickness 0.10 mm; wove, unwatermarked, smooth, white

Contents: Index (*i*), blank (*1*), disclaimers and copyright (2), introduction (3), apologia, historical note, and dedication (4), blank (*ii*), text (5–18)

Binding: Strong yellowish Green (131) light card, stapled, no spine or endpapers. FC: as above, printed in black. Inside FC: at the foot (C Copyright Beverley Croquet Club 1993). RC: blank. Inside RC: blank

Copy seen: PC

Fingerprint: 8.7. n.or !.om coMo 3 1993Q [group 1 is taken from p *i*]

Notes: Printed anonymously, published privately, price £2.50. Year of publication is as given in the historical note in (b) (p 3).

(b) *Second edition [1995]*

[The FC]

HELP II | The <u>H</u>umorous Guide | To <u>E</u>nlighten <u>L</u>ost | Croquet <u>P</u>layers | *Sponsored* *by* | [device of sponsor, Manor House] | ***All funds raised by this book go to the*** | ***Beverley & Tyneside Croquet Clubs***

Formula: [1³⁸]. 38 leaves, pp 1–76

Technical notes: 184 × 121 mm (p 13). 49 lines, 20 = 76 mm. Leaf size 211 × 144 mm; thickness 0.10 mm; wove, unwatermarked, smooth, white

Contents: Acknowledgements (1), disclaimers and copyright (2), historical note and dedication (3), introduction (4), contents (5–7), text (8–75), space for notes (76)

Binding: Very pale Green (148) card printed in black, stapled, no spine or end-papers. FC: as above. Inside FC: blank. RC: advertisement. Inside RC: advertisement

Copy seen: PC

Fingerprint: h.ke m.t. !)t. SnDe 3 1995Q [group 1 taken from p 1]

Notes: Edited by JMC Evans and G Curry, published privately, printed anony-mously, price £4.50. The year of publication given is that in which this edition first became available from the publishers.

A281   **MONOGRAPH SERIES ON CLUB-BUILDING,**   [1993]
         ORGANIZATION AND MANAGEMENT. VOLUME ONE:
         GETTING STARTED. Bob Alman *et al*

[L justified] • [R justified] *Monograph — Volume 1 • 1* | [rule] | [superimposed on a grey-effect horizontal band] **VOLUME ONE: GETTING STARTED** | [rule in bold, heading a ruled frame which contains most of all the following letterpress] | The | Croquet Foundation of America | *presents the* | **Monograph Series on Club-Building,** | **Organization and Management** | Bob Alman, Editor and Chief Writer | Anne C. Frost, Executive Editor | Gail Arkley and Tremaine Arkley, Copy Editors | Sandra A. Larson, Design and Layout | published by | The Croquet Foundation of America | 500 Avenue of Champions | Palm Beach Gardens, Florida 33418 | (407) 627-4188 | Copyright © 1993 The Croquet Foundation of America | [rule, in bold below the frame]

Formula: [1–22¹]. 22 leaves, pp 1–5 *6* 7–9 *10* 11 *12* 13–23 *24* 25–44

Technical notes: 243 × 179 mm, variable (p 7, ragged), mostly divided into three columns. 53 lines, 20 = 84 mm. Leaf size 276 × 212 mm; thickness 0.12 mm; wove, unwatermarked, smooth, speckled yellowish White (92)

Contents: Title (1), publisher's foreword, signed 'W. *Ellery McClatchy*' (2), contents (3), acknowledgements (4), preface, signed '*Bob Alman*', 1993 (5), founder clubs of the USCA (6), text (7–9), foundation of the USCA (10), text, continued (11), extra-neous illustration (*12*), text, continued (13–23), extraneous illustration (*24*), text, concluded (25–41), advertisements (42–44)

Binding: Speckled yellowish White (2) light card glued to the edges of the leaves, no endpapers. FC: printed in black and medium Grey (265), all the letterpress L justi-fied and partly over a broad vertical grey-effect band, extending from near the head to near the foot at the L, with a framed black-and-white photograph of two players shaking hands on court at the foot ([in Grey] **THE CROQUET** | [in black] **FOUNDATION** | [in Grey] **OF AMERICA** | [in Grey] **INC.** | [in black] *Monograph Series on Club-Building,* | [in black] *Organization and Management* | [rule, in bold] | [indented, in black] *Volume 1* | [do] *Getting* | [do] *Started*). Inside FC: blank. RC: printed in black (Cover Photo by Dave Dondero | **Croquet Foundation of America** | **(407) 627-4188** | 500 Avenue of Champions, Palm Beach Gardens, FL 33418). Inside RC: blank. Spine: blank

Copy seen: PC

Fingerprint: **3923** s,om Weew inpl 3 1993Q

Notes: Printed anonymously, price US$9.95. Year of publication is inferred from the assertion of copyright (p 1). This work and two companion monographs — *viz* A289 and A290 — were sponsored by Ellery McClatchy.

The text includes chapters by Anne Frost, William Sullivan, Jed Rotella, Dr Carl Mabee, Ed Merill, and Ross Robinson.

<h2 style="text-align:center">1994</h2>

**A282 70 YEARS THROUGH THE HOOPS: THE HISTORY OF THE   1994
SHEPPARTON CROQUET CLUB INC 1924–1994. Elsie Brady**

70 YEARS THROUGH THE HOOPS | THE HISTORY OF THE | SHEPPARTON CROQUET CLUB INC. | 1924 — 1994 | [black-and-white photograph of club-house] | [as caption to photograph above] SHEPPARTON CROQUET CLUB CLUBHOUSE | [R justified at the foot] by ELSIE BRADY

[From p 2]

Published by | The Shepparton Croquet Club Inc. | Printed by | Shepparton Printing Service Pty. Ltd.

Formula: [1^{16}]. 16 leaves, pp *1* 2–32

Technical notes: 269 × 189 mm (p 9), mostly divided into two columns. 63 lines, 20 = 86 mm. Leaf size 301 × 214 mm; wove, unwatermarked, very smooth, white

Contents: Title (*1*), works by the same author and 'Croquet Players' "If"' (verse with apologies to Kipling) (2), publishing details (2), foreword, signed 'Kevin F. Riordan' (3), a message from the President, signed 'Dawn Judd' (3), author's preface (4), text (5–32)

Binding: White linen grain card, stapled, no spine or endpapers. Printed in deep yellowish Green (132) and gold ([club emblem in the form of a medallion, in gold and Green] | **70 YEARS THROUGH THE HOOPS** | [displaced to the L of centre by the illustration described below, in Green] THE HISTORY OF THE | [*do*] SHEPPARTON CROQUET CLUB | [*do*] INC. | [*do*] 1924 — 1994 | [drawing of a mallet standing upright, a hoop, and a ball, in gradations of Green and gold] | [at the foot, in Green] by ELSIE BRADY). Inside FC: blank. RC: blank. Inside RC: blank

Copy seen: PC

Fingerprint: ddr. t.4. onge n.ed 3 1994A [group 2 taken from the caption to the photograph at the foot of the L column of p 11, group 3 taken from the caption to the photograph at the foot of p 13]

Notes: Printed by Shepparton Printing Service.

**AA283 CLUB REGISTRATION PACK [and REGISTERED CLUB   1994
HANDBOOK]. [The Croquet Association]**

(a) *First edition (1994)*

[Folio 1]

The Croquet Association | Development Committee | [device of the CA] | **CLUB** | **REGISTRATION** | **PACK** | WELCOME TO THE CROQUET ASSOCIATION | We are pleased that you have decided to join us and we hope that this Registration Pack will help | inform your Club and its members of some of the opportunities made possible by your registration. | We hope that this pack can remain in your clubhouse so that it is available for all your members | to read. Some pages will be updated at the beginning of each season, as necessary, but please do | let us know of any errors in the text or items that you think should be included. | We hope that you enjoy this pack and good luck with anything you gain by having used it. | Syd Jones, | Chairman of the Development Committee, | The Croquet Association, | c/o The Hurlingham Club, | Ranelagh Gardens, London SW6 3PR | Issued Feb 1994 (ref: cacrp4b1.doc) | [rule] | The Croquet Association - Club Registration Pack   Feb 1994   Page 1 of 1

Formula: [1–30¹]. 30 leaves, ff 1–19, pp 20/1–2, ff 21–30, numbered within sections

Technical notes: 230 × 160 mm (f 3, ragged), variable, some pages divided into columns. Variable number of lines and line spacing. Leaf size 297 × 210 mm; thickness 0.10 mm; wove, unwatermarked, smooth, white

Contents: Title (*1*), contents (*2*), I. federation information (*3*), II. local federation information (*4*), III. CA Council members (*5*), IV. CA Council committees (*6*), V. handicap system (*7–8*), VI. etiquette and customs (*9–10*), VII. commercial break (*11–12*), VIII. membership application form (*13*), IX. tournaments (*14*), X. equipment and suppliers (*15–18*), XI. club competitions (*19*), XII and XIII. club awards (*20/1–2, 21–22*), XIV. world croquet (*23*), XV. development grants (*24*), XVI. insurance (*25*), XVII. indoor carpet croquet (*26*), XVIII. sponsorship (*27–28*), XIX. schools (*29*), XX. leaflets available (*30*). Sections VIII, IX, and XX are accompanied by sundry forms and leaflets

Binding: Trade binder, the FC made of clear polypropylene, the RC of strong Green (141) PVC, and the spine of moderate Green (145) PVC. The FC encloses a paper titling strip. The RC encloses a clasp constructed of sheet metal which fastens 14 clear polypropylene wallets within which the contents are arranged in order.

Copy seen: CA

Fingerprint: Indeterminate

Notes: Issued by the CA to registered clubs in February 1994 with the intention that amendments would be issued from time to time, updating the original contents. Amended sheets were issued in 1995, 1996, and 1997. Most of the original sheets are dated February 1994.

(b) *Registered Club Handbook, 1998 (1998)*

THE CROQUET ASSOCIATION | [device of the CA at L, ruled across the page] | [device of the CA] | **REGISTERED** | **CLUB** | **HANDBOOK** | WELCOME TO THE CROQUET ASSOCIATION | We are pleased that you have decided to join us and hope that this Handbook will help inform your Club and | its members of some of the opportunities made possible by your registration. | We ask all club committees to **make this handbook permanently available in your** | clubhouse so that it is available for **all your members** to read. Some pages will be updated at | the beginning of each season, as necessary. Please do let us know of any errors in the text or items that you | think should be included. | We hope that you enjoy the Handbook and good luck with anything that you gain by using it. | Additional or replacement copies of the complete Handbook may be obtained from Paul Campion at the CA | Office at £3.00 per copy. | **Issued by the Croquet Association** | **c/o The Hurlingham Club, Ranelagh Gardens** | **London SW6 3PR**

Formula: [1–41¹]. 41 leaves, unnumbered [ff 1–41]

Technical notes: ca 220 × *ca* 170 mm, variable. Variable line spacing. Leaf size 297 × 210 mm; thickness 0.11 mm; wove, unwatermarked, smooth, white

Contents: Title (*1*), contents (*2*), section 1, Council and its committees (*3–5*), section 2, the federations (*6–7*), section 3, in play (*8–18*), section 4, world croquet (*19*), section 5, CA facilities (*20–36*), section 6, the CA shop (*37–41*)

Binding: Pale yellowish Pink (31) card covers front and rear, punched and bound by a two-part pressed-metal fastener, no spine or endpapers. FC: reprint of the TP. Inside FC: blank. RC: blank. Inside RC: blank

Copy seen: PC

Fingerprint: 98op nsn. 0182 7364 C 1998A [group 1 taken from f 2, group 2 taken from the L column of f 6, groups 3 and 4 taken from the second and third columns of the lowermost table on f *13*]

Notes: Printed anonymously, issued to secretaries of affiliated clubs and friends of the association. This loose-leaf edition, published after a lapse of some years, was intended to serve as a permanent basis for periodic revision by occasional subsequent issue of replacement sheets.

AA284 CROQUET: BASIC PRINCIPALS OF PLAY.   [1994]
[United States Croquet Association]

[Title heading, p *1*, divided into two columns by a vertical rule in bold]

[at L] **Croquet** | *Basic Principals of Play* | [at R] AN INTRODUCTION TO | [*do*] THE SPORT OF USCA CROQUET | [*do*] the basic principals of play for the | [*do*] UNITED STATES | [*do*] CROQUET ASSOCIATION'S | [*do*] American Six-Wicket croquet game.

Formula: [1²]. 2 leaves, unnumbered [pp 1–4]

Technical notes: 196 × 114 mm (p *2*). 42 lines, 20 = 93 mm. Leaf size 216 × 139 mm; thickness 0.10 mm; wove, unwatermarked, smooth, white, printed in brilliant Blue (177)

Contents: Title heading (*1*), text (*1–4*), publisher's notice (*4*)

Binding: None

Copy seen: PC

Fingerprint: tsts r:xt dsis **TSOF** C 1994Q [all four groups taken from captions of the diagrams in the L column of p *3*]

Notes: Published by the USCA, printed anonymously. Year of publication is inferred from the circumstances in which a copy of this leaflet was received from the publisher in 1994.

A285   CROQUET REFEREES GUIDE. John Riches   1994

(a) *First edition (1994)*

[The FC, within a ruled frame with rounded corners]

CROQUET | REFEREES | GUIDE | by John Riches

Formula: [1–18¹]. 18 leaves, ff 1–18

Technical notes: 249 × 167 mm (p *3*). 51 lines, 20 = 98 mm. Leaf size 297 × 210 mm; thickness 0.10 mm; wove, unwatermarked, smooth, white

Contents: Contents and publishing details (*1*), text (*2–18*)

Binding: Very light yellowish Green (134) paper front and rear, stapled, no spine or endpapers. FC: printed in black, as above. Inside FC: blank. RC: blank. Inside RC: blank. Spine: blank

Copy seen: PC

Fingerprint: 575. ishe own. ine. 3 1994A [group 1 taken from p 1, group 2 taken from the text on p 5, groups 3 and 4 taken from the text on p 13]

Notes: Printed and published privately in Enfield SA in October 1994, price Aus\$6.00 including postage within Australia.

Several variants of this edition may have appeared (see *Notes* to a companion work, A294). It was, and continues to be, produced in small batches to meet current orders, both privately in Australia and by the NZCC. Excluding sales by the NZCC, about 500 copies had been sold up to June 1999.

(b) ***First English edition (1995)***

[The FC as that of (a)]

Formula: [1–19¹]. 18 leaves, ff 1–18 *19*

Technical notes: As at (a)

Contents: Contents and publishing details (1), text (2–18), advertisement (*19*)

Binding: Very light yellowish Green (134) paper FC protected by clear acetate sheet and RC of white light Astrolux board, slotted and fastened with a white plastic comb, no endpapers. FC: printed in black, as above. Inside FC: blank. RC: blank. Inside RC: blank. Spine: blank

Copy seen: PC

Fingerprint: 575. ishe own. ine. 3 1995A [group 1 taken from p 1, group 2 taken from the text on p 5, groups 3 and 4 taken from the text on p 13]

Notes: Published in October 1995 by D Drazin, Croxley Green, Herts, for distribution in the UK and Ireland, printed anonymously, price £6.00. The text is identical, or virtually identical, to that of (a). Apparently the only variation is the addition of an advertisement addressed to the UK market.

Thirty-five copies were produced in small batches in 1995 and 1996, of which the last was sold in June 1998 .

A286 CROQUET SHOT-MAKING MANUAL. Bob Kroeger   [1994]

[Black reproduction of the FC, the letterpress superimposed over a sketch of a jump stroke against a diagonally striped background within a rectangular panel which extends from near the head to the near the foot at the L]

[broad rule] | [L justified] **United States** | [*do*] **Croquet Association** | [device of USCA, to the R of the two foregoing lines] | **Croquet** | **Shot-Making** | **Instruction Manual** | **By Bob Kroeger** | **USCA Instructional School Director** | *Produced in part through a grant from the* | **Croquet Foundation of America** | [rule]

Formula: [1–18¹]. 18 leaves, pp *1* 2–34 *35–36*

Technical notes: 231 × 155 mm, variable (p 11, ragged), several pages divided into columns. 50 lines, 20 = 93 mm. Leaf size 280 × 216 mm; thickness 0.18 mm; wove, uwatermarked, rough, white

Contents: Title (*1*), blank save footer including pagination (2), contents (3), blank save footer including pagination (4), introduction, signed '*Bob Kroeger*' (5), blank save footer including pagination (6), text (7–31), blank save footer including pagination (32), text, concluded (33), acknowledgements and name of printer (34), about the author, and advertisement (*35*), blank (*36*)

Binding: White semi-gloss card at the front and matt white card at the rear, slotted, fastened by a vivid Red (11) plastic comb, no spine or endpapers. FC: printed mostly in vivid purplish Blue (194) with selective use of Red (for stripes within the publisher's device, one of the balls in the illustration, and the lines '*By Bob Kroeger*' and '*Croquet Foundation of America*'), otherwise as the TP. Inside FC: blank. RC: blank. Inside RC: blank

Copy seen: PC

Fingerprint: **ONts** *h.he n.ed* deca 3 1994Q

Notes: Printed anonymously. Year of publication is inferred from the assertion of copyright on p 34.

A287 **FIXTURES AND TOURNAMENTS: SEASON 1994–1995**   1994
[The Victorian Croquet Association]

[Page *1*]

THE VICTORIAN CROQUET ASSOCIATION INC. | (Affiliated with the Croquet Association of England | and the Australian Croquet Association) | **FIXTURES AND TOURNAMENTS** | **Season 1994-1995** | [device of Sport and Recreation Victoria] | [devices of Arthritis Foundation of Victoria and VicHealth] | ENQUIRIES: Mrs Lyn Bowey (03) 544-8608 | Mrs Inga Quaine (03) 598-3285 | PRESIDENT | Mrs Lyell Squire | (03) 598-9366

Formula: [1⁴]. 4 leaves, pp *1* 2–8

Technical notes: 126 × 87mm (p 2). 45 lines, 20 = 56 mm. Leaf size 147 × 105 mm; thickness 0.14 mm; wove, unwatermarked, smooth, white, printed in strong purplish Blue (196)

Contents: Title (*1*), conditions for 1994–95 Association fixtures (2), Association fixtures (3–4), metropolitan tournaments (4), country tournaments (5–6), VCA Sunday League tournaments (6), metropolitan Pennant fixtures (7–8)

Binding: Stapled, no wrapper or spine

Copy seen: PC

Fingerprint: ls5) ths. 1)2) ls1) C 1994A [all four groups taken from p 3]

Notes: Printed anonymously. Subsequent editions of this work are believed to have been issued annually.

A288 **THE LAWS OF ASSOCIATION CROQUET AND THE**   1994
      OFFICIAL RULINGS. [The Victorian Croquet Association]

(a) *First edition (1994)*

Not seen. The existence of this work and its year of publication are inferred from a citation on the TP of (b).

(b) *August 1995 issue, Change 4 (1995)*

THE LAWS | OF | ASSOCIATION CROQUET | AND | THE OFFICIAL RULINGS | Issued by: The Victorian Croquet Association Inc. | P.O. Box 2091, North Brighton, Vic. 3186 | November, 1994 | Revised August 1995, Change 4

Formula: [1⁴¹], excluding the front cover sheet. 41 leaves, pp *i*–vi, 1–75 76

Technical notes: 188 × 97 mm (p 42). 44 lines, 20 = 85 mm. Leaf size 210 × 149 mm; thickness 0.11 mm; wove, unwatermarked, smooth, white

Contents: Front cover sheet (see *Binding*), title (*i*), preface (ii), contents (iii–vi), text, continued (*1–66*), blank save pagination (*67–68*), text, concluded (*69–75*), blank (*76*)

Binding: Loose leaves, punched at two points, secured by a folding fastener of strip metal within a plain trade binder, the FC in clear polypropylene attached by two vertical welds to the spine in deep Blue (179) PVC sheet and the RC, also in Blue PVC, attached to the spine by two vertical welds. The pocket between the two welds of the FC, which lies at the front close to the spine, contains a white paper strip. The transparent FC reveals a brilliant greenish Blue (168) paper front cover sheet, printed in black ([devices of the Victorian Croquet Association and Sport and Recreation Victoria in the top L and R corners] | **The Victorian Croquet Association Inc.** | [in MS-style script] **Official Handbook** | incorporating | **THE LAWS OF ASSOCIATION CROQUET** | **AND THE OFFICIAL RULINGS** | **THE VICTORIAN REGULATIONS** | **FOR TOURNAMENTS** | [devices of VicHealth and the Arthritis Foundation of Victoria at the foot in the L and R corners).

Copy seen: PC

Fingerprint: 1313).nd 3)h. 38po 3 1995A.

Notes: Printed anonymously. In the preface it is stated that 'amendments and additions to this handbook will be issued from time to time'. The existence of new matter in this issue is suggested by vertical rules in the L margins of pp 48, 54, 58, and 74, and by the signature 'Change 4 August 1995' which appears at the foot of pp 49–51, 53, 54, 57, 58, 61, 69, 74, and 75.

Parts of the text relating to official rulings and interpretations are signed 'Ian S. Reid', 'Dr Ian Reid', and 'Shirley Muir'.

A289   **MONOGRAPH SERIES ON CLUB-BUILDING,**   [1994]
      ORGANIZATION AND MANAGEMENT. VOLUME TWO:
      ORGANIZING FOR SUCCESS. Bob Alman *et al*

[L justified] • [R justified] *Monograph — Volume 2 • 1* | [rule] | [superimposed on a grey-effect horizontal band] **VOLUME TWO: ORGANIZING FOR SUCCESS** | [rule in bold, heading a ruled frame which contains most of all the following letterpress] | The | Croquet Foundation of America | *presents the* | **Monograph Series on Club-Building,** | **Organization and Management** | Bob Alman, Editor and Chief Writer | Anne Frost, Executive Editor | Sandra A. Larson, Design and Layout | Gail Arkley and Tremaine Arkley, Copy Editors | published by | The Croquet Foundation of America | 500 Avenue of Champions | Palm Beach Gardens, Florida 33418 | (407) 627-4188 | Copyright © 1994 The Croquet Foundation of America | [rule, in bold below the frame]

Formula: [1–26¹]. 26 leaves, pp 1–5 6 7–25 26 27–31 32 33–41 42 43–52

Technical notes: 224 × 176 mm, variable (p 7, ragged), divided into two and three columns. 56 lines, 20 = 84 mm. Leaf size 275 × 211 mm; thickness 0.14 mm; wove, unwatermarked, smooth, speckled bluish White (189)

Contents: Title (1), publisher's foreword, signed '*W. Ellery McClatchy*' (2), contents (3), preface, signed '*Bob Alman*', 1994 (4), publisher's announcement (5), blank (6), text, continued (7–25), blank (*26*), text, continued (27–31), blank (*32*), text, continued (33–41), blank (*42*), text, concluded (43–38), advertisements (49–52)

Binding: Speckled bluish White (189) light card glued to the edges of the leaves, no endpapers. FC: printed in black and medium Grey (265), all the letterpress L justified and partly over a broad vertical grey-effect band, extending from near the head to near the foot at the L, with a framed black-and-white photograph of a group of players at the foot ([in Grey] **THE CROQUET** | [in black] **FOUNDATION** | [in Grey] **OF AMERICA** | [in Grey] **INC.** | [in black] *Monograph Series on Club-Building,* | [in black] *Organization and Management* | [rule, in bold] | [indented, in black] *Volume 2* | [*do*] *Organizing* | [*do*] *for Success*). Inside RC: blank. RC: printed in black (Cover Photo by Jon Werolin | **Croquet Foundation of America** | (407) 627-4188 | 500 Avenue of Champions, Palm Beach Gardens, FL 33418). Inside RC: blank. Spine: blank

Copy seen: PC

Fingerprint: **45***HE* hein hewe anpa 3 1994Q

Notes: Printed anonymously, price US$9.95. Year of publication is inferred from the assertion of copyright (p 1).

The text includes a chapter by Warren Hernand.

A290   MONOGRAPH SERIES ON CLUB-BUILDING,   [1994]
        ORGANIZATION AND MANAGEMENT. VOLUME THREE:
        PRODUCING PROGRAMS & EVENTS THAT WORK.
        Bob Alman *et al*

[L justified] • [R justified] *Monograph — Volume 3* • *1* | [rule] | [superimposed on a grey-effect horizontal band] **VOLUME THREE: PRODUCING** | [*do*] **PROGRAMS & EVENTS THAT WORK** | [rule in bold, heading a ruled frame which contains most of the following letterpress] | The | Croquet Foundation of America | *presents the* | **Monograph Series on Club-Building,** | **Organization and Management** | Bob Alman, Editor and Chief Writer | Anne C. Frost, Executive Editor | Sandra A. Larson, Design and Layout | Gail Arkley and Tremaine Arkley, Copy Editors | published by | The Croquet Foundation of America | 500 Avenue of Champions | Palm Beach Gardens, Florida 33418 | (407) 627-4188 | Copyright © 1994 The Croquet Foundation of America | [rule, in bold below the frame]

Formula: [1–36¹]. 36 leaves, pp 1–72

Technical notes: 235 × 178 mm, variable (p 8, ragged), mostly divided into three columns. 56 lines, 20 = 84 mm. Leaf size 276 × 211 mm; thickness 0.14 mm; wove, unwatermarked, smooth, speckled yellowish White (92)

Contents: Title (1), publisher's foreword, signed 'W. *Ellery McClatchy*' (2), contents (3–4), black-and-white photograph (4), preface, signed '*Bob Alman*', 1994 (5), text (6–67), advertisements (68–71), blank save for running header, heading ('NOTES'), and ruled frame (72)

Binding: Speckled yellowish White (2) light card glued to the edges of the leaves, no endpapers. FC: printed in black and medium Grey (265), all the letterpress L justified and partly over a broad vertical grey-effect band, extending from near the head to near the foot at the L, with a framed black-and-white photograph of a group of players (celebrating) at the foot ([in Grey] **THE CROQUET** | [in black] **FOUNDATION** | [in Grey] **OF AMERICA** | [in Grey] **INC.** | [in black] *Monograph Series on Club-Building,* | [in black] *Organization and Management* | [rule, in bold] | [indented, in black] *Volume 3* | [*do*] *Producing* | [*do*] *Programs* | [*do*] *And Events* | [*do*] *That Work*). Inside FC: blank. RC: printed in black (Cover Photo by Mike Orgill | **Croquet Foundation of America** | (407) 627-4188 | 500 Avenue of Champions, Palm Beach Gardens, FL 33418). Inside RC: blank. Spine: blank

Copy seen: PC

*Fingerprint: ed*n. ndn- hel. enTh 3 1994Q

Notes: Printed anonymously, price US$9.95. Year of publication is inferred from the assertion of copyright (p 1).

The text includes chapters by Doug Merrill, Stanley Palmer, and Anne C Frost.

1995

A291   CROQUET. Steven Boga   [1995]

[in display script] **CROQUET** | [in display script] **Steven Boga** | STACKPOLE | BOOKS

Formula: [1–48^1]. 48 leaves, pp *i–iii* iv–vi, 1–7 *8 9 10* 11–38 *39* 40–41 *42* 43–44 *45* 46–90

Technical notes: 164 × 102 mm (p v). 39 lines, 20 = 85 mm. Leaf size 209 × 138 mm; thickness 0.14 mm; wove, unwatermarked, smooth, white

Contents: Title (*1*), TP verso (*2*), contents (*iii*), introduction (iv–vi), text (1–90)

Binding: White laminated Astrolux board, glued to the edges of the leaves, printed in black, deep reddish Orange (36), and dark Grey (266), no endpapers. FC: the title ([in Orange and Grey shaded script, slanted from bottom L to top R out of a black diagonal area at the top L] **Croquet**) above a sketch composed of a mallet, ball, peg, and two hoops, and other lettering in MS style (A handbook | of all the rules, | strategies, | techniques, and | tips you need | to be a | better player | [slanted from bottom L to top R (**Steven** | [*do*] **Boga**). Inside FC: blank. RC: publisher's blurb embellished by two sketches in Orange and Grey composed of a peg, hoop, balls, and a mallet head, price ($10.00 U.S.), ISBN (0–8117–2489–1), and bar code. Inside RC: blank. Spine: downwards, mostly in white out black, the author's name and the title in MS-style script (Boga [a ball in Orange and Grey] Croquet [near the foot] STACKPOLE BOOKS)

Copy seen: PC

Fingerprint: 8278 u-d. rek- care 3 1995Q

Notes: Printed anonymously, ISBN 0–8117–2489–1, price $10.00 in USA. Year of publication is inferred from the stated year of copyright and from the given LC cataloguing-in-publication data.

A292   CROQUET AND OTHER BALL SPORTS. Peter Rudge   1995

CROQUET | AND OTHER BALL SPORTS | by | Peter Rudge | Illustrated by | Frank Atack | CORAT | 1995

Formula: [1^{16}]. 16 leaves, unnumbered [pp 1–32]

Technical notes: 182 × 126 mm (p *4*). 38 lines, 20 = 97. Leaf size 208 × 148 mm; thickness 0.11 mm; wove, unwatermarked, very light yellowish Green (134)

Contents: Title (*1*), TP verso (*2*), contents (*3*), introduction (*4–5*), text (*6–32*)

Binding: Very pale Green (148) Astrolux board, printed in black, stapled, no spine or endpapers. FC: ([in shaded script] **CROQUET** | [ditto] **AND OTHER BALL SPORTS** | **by** | **Peter Rudge** | **Illustrated by Frank Atack**). Inside FC: blank. RC: about the author and illustrator. Inside RC: blank

Copy seen: PC

Fingerprint: **tson** y.re e.xt omwi C 1995A

Notes: Published by CORAT, Coolangatta, Queensland, printed anonymously, price Aus$10.00 (mail order), £5.00 (UK).

Review: *Croquet Newsletter* [Queensland] (February 1996).

AA293 THE CROQUET ASSOCIATION HANDBOOK.   1995
[The Croquet Association]

Foreword: From 1995 a small booklet, variously entitled, has been issued by the CA free of charge to Associates, *ie* members, together with their membership cards and other literature, at the start of each season. The contents of the early editions have also varied widely from year to year. This work is distinguished by its brevity from the association's year book (A110), variously entitled, which was also issued free of charge to Associates for many years.

(a) **First edition, 1995 (1995)*

[The FC, printed in black, divided into three columns by vertical rules. L column:] [in open shaded script] **THANK** | [*do*] **YOU** | [within a ruled frame, which also encloses the final line] THE CROQUET | [*do*] ASSOCIATION

[Central column:]

[device of the CA]

[R column:]

for renewing your subscription to | the Croquet Association. | We are most grateful for your | support, and wish you every | success in the coming season. | [within a ruled frame, which also encloses the final line] 1995 MEMBER'S | [ditto] HAND-BOOK

Formula: [1⁶]. 6 leaves, unnumbered [pp 1–12]

Technical notes: 47 × 183 mm (p *8*, ragged), divided by vertical rules into 2–5 columns. Variable number of lines and line spacing. Leaf size 83 × 209 mm; thickness 0.12 mm; wove, unwatermarked, smooth, brilliant yellowish Green (130)

Contents: Committee chairmen and sponsor (inside FC), introduction (*1*), prospects for 1995 season (*2–5*), CA shop and services (*6–7*), future prospects (*8*), milestones and achievements (*9*), recruitment programme (*10–12*, inside RC), 1994 honours (RC)

Binding: Brilliant yellowish Green (130) light card, stapled, no spine or endpapers. FC: as above. Inside FC: text, continued. RC: text, concluded. Inside RC: text, continued

Copy seen: PC

Fingerprint: s.rs m.at s.t. d.ts C 1995A [group 1 taken from the L column of p *1*, groups 2–4 taken from the L columns of p *9*]

Notes: Printed anonymously.

(b) *1996 edition (1996)*

[The FC]

[device of the CA] | **HANDBOOK** | **1996**

Formula: [1²]. 2 leaves, unnumbered [pp 1–4]

Technical notes: 114 × 67 mm (p *1*), mostly divided into two or three columns. 34 lines, 20 = 68 mm. Leaf size 138 × 89 mm; thickness 0.10 mm; wove, unwatermarked, smooth, white

Contents: The CA (inside FC and *1*), dates of events (*2*), CA shop (*3*), membership statistics, recruitment, and subscriptions (*4*), automatic handicapping system (inside RC), courses, merit awards, and advertisement by sponsor (RC)

Binding: Very light greenish Blue (89) Astrolux board, stapled, no spine or endpapers. FC: printed in black, as above. Inside RC: as above. RC: as above. Inside RC: as above

Copy seen: PC

Fingerprint: t123 r926 r5h2 25s: C 1996A [all four groups taken from p *1*, the first two characters of group 1 from the lowermost line, the first two characters of group 4 from the L column, and all other characters from the central column of the text]

Notes: Sponsored, and apparently also printed by Kall-Kwik Printing, Putney, London.

(c) *1997 edition (1997)*

[The FC]

[1997 centenary device of the CA] | **HANDBOOK** | 1997

Formula: [1²]. 2 leaves, unnumbered [pp 1–4]

Technical notes: 114 × 67 mm (p *1*), mostly divided into two or three columns. 32 lines, 20 = 66 mm. Leaf size 135 × 89 mm; thickness 0.12 mm; wove, unwatermarked, smooth, white

Contents: The CA (inside FC and *1*), dates of events (*2*), CA shop (*3*), membership statistics, recruitment, and subscriptions (*4*), automatic handicapping system (inside RC), courses, merit awards, and advertisement by sponsor (RC)

Binding: Gold Astrolux board, stapled, no spine or endpapers. FC: printed in black, as above. Inside FC: as above. RC: as above. Inside RC: as above

Copy seen: PC

Fingerprint: 22r8 r125 r4h8 h115 C 1997A [all four groups taken from the central column of p *1*]

Notes: Sponsored, and apparently also printed by Kall-Kwik Printing, Putney, London.

A294 **CROQUET: FINER POINTS. John Riches** 1995

(a) *First edition (1995)*

[The FC, within a ruled frame]

CROQUET: | **FINER** | **POINTS** | [abstract sketch of player about to make a stroke] | by John Riches

Formula: [1–49¹]. 49 leaves, pp *i*, 1–97

Technical notes: 259 × 175 mm (p *40*). 52 lines, 20 = 100 mm. Leaf size 297 × 210 mm; thickness 0.10 mm; wove, unwatermarked, smooth, white

Contents: Author's notes and publishing details (*i*), contents (*1*), introduction, signed 'John Riches', and about the author (*2*), text (*3–96*), advertisement (*97*)

Binding: Very pale Purple (226) light card front and rear, stapled, the spine wrapped with bluish Grey (191) stippled plastic tape, no endpapers. FC: printed in black, as above. Inside FC: blank. RC: blank. Inside RC: blank. Spine: blank

Copy seen: PC

Fingerprint: 5785 o.ay e.rd siTh C 1995A [group 1 taken from p *i*, group 2 taken from p 8, group 3 taken from p 12, group 4 taken from the text on p 13]

Notes: Printed and published privately in Enfield SA, price Aus$11.00 including postage within Australia. According to the publishing details given on p *i*, this work was published in January 1995. The author has subsequently stated that it was first published in June of that year. It was, and continues to be, produced in small batches to meet current orders, both privately in Australia and by the NZCC. Excluding sales by the NZCC, about 400 copies had been sold up to June 1999.

Several variants of this edition may have appeared. To quote from the author's notes (p *i*): 'This booklet, like the author's previous booklets, has been written, typed, illustrated, photocopied, assembled, stapled, bound and published by him alone. For this reason print-runs are necessarily small, usually of about 20–30 copies. It is quite likely that errors found after one print-run will be corrected in the next, with the result that copies of the booklet may not be identical to each other.'

(b) *First English edition (1995)*

[The FC as that of (a)]

Formula: [1–49¹]. 49 leaves, pp *i*, 1–96 97

Technical notes: As at (a)

Contents: Author's notes and publishing details (*i*), contents (1), introduction, signed 'John Riches', and about the author (2), text (3–96), advertisement (97)

Binding: Very pale Purple (226) paper FC protected by clear acetate sheet and RC of white light Astrolux board, slotted and fastened with a white plastic comb, no endpapers. FC: printed in black, as above. Inside FC: blank. RC: blank. Inside RC: blank. Spine: blank

Copy seen: PC

Fingerprint: As at (a)

Notes: Published by D Drazin, Croxley Green, Herts, for distribution in the UK and Ireland, printed anonymously, price £10.00. The text is identical to that of (a). The only variation is the advertisement on p 97.

Fifty-five copies were produced in small batches in 1995 and 1996, of which nine remained unsold in October 1998.

A295   CROQUET MANAGEMENT. Don Gaunt and Roger Wheeler   1995

[The FC, printed in black within a ruled frame with head extension representing a clipboard, with the stylised image of a pen or pencil retained by two clips at the R, the text and frame *etc* here rendered being repeated at progressive scale reductions of 60% so as to give the impression of infinite recession, the ninth repeat being the last clearly recognisable]

CROQUET | MANAGEMENT | [successive repeats of the frame and titling *etc*] | **Don Gaunt & | Roger Wheeler**

Formula: [1–62¹]. 62 leaves, pp *i–ii*, 1 2 3 4 5–23 *24* 25–51 *52* 53–59 *60* 61–65 *66* 67–69 *70* 71–83 *84* 85–93 *94* 95–107 *108* 109–113 *114* 115–121 *122*

Technical notes: 224 × 158 mm (p 13). 49 lines, 20 = 92 mm. Leaf size 297 × 210 mm; thickness 0.10 mm; wove, unwatermarked, smooth, white

Contents: Contents (*i*), blank (*ii*), introduction, signed 'DLG & RFW', March 1995 (1), blank (2), dedication (3), blank (4), foreword by Edgar Jackson, signed 'EJ 19/9/91' (5–6), text (7–23), blank (*24*), text, continued (25–51), blank (*52*), text, continued (53–59), blank (*60*), text, continued (61–65), blank (*66*), text, continued (67–69), blank (*70*), text, continued (71–83), blank (*84*), text, continued (85–93), blank (*94*), text, continued (95–107), blank (*108*), text, continued (109–113), blank (*114*), text, concluded (115–121), blank (*122*)

Binding: Light Yellow Green (119) card front and rear, fastened by a white plastic comb, slotted, no endpapers. FC: printed in black, as above. Inside FC: blank. RC: blank. Inside RC: blank.

Copy seen: PC

Fingerprint: 1509 e.ne meho k-to C 1995A [groups 3 and 4 taken from p 13]

Notes: Published in 1995, printed anonymously, price £10. The initial printing was of 600 copies, of which about 180 had been sold by September 1998.

AA296 CROQUET MECHANICS: A NUMERICAL ANALYSIS.   1995
Doug Sutherland

CROQUET MECHANICS | [displaced to R of centre] - a Numerical Analysis | [*do*] by Doug Sutherland | [*do*] Warrawee Croquet Club | [*do*] June 1995

Formula: [1–20^1]. 20 leaves, ff *i*, 1–17, *i–ii* [= 20]

Technical Notes: *ca* 241 × 145 mm (f 2, ragged). 38 lines, 20 = *ca* 127 mm. Leaf size *ca* 297 × 210 mm

Contents: Title (*i*), text (1, 2 and verso, 3, 4 and verso, 5–17), letter dated 11 September 1995, signed 'Keith Wylie' (*i–ii*)

Binding: The photocopy examined is fastened by a single staple in the top L corner and is bound in a white extruded plastic binder

Copy seen: PC (photocopy of unknown provenance)

Fingerprint: heas atl, d.ta hehe 3 1995A [groups 3 and 4 taken from f 13]

Notes: This work, produced in typescript, is thought to be unpublished, though several copies are believed to have been produced.

AA297 CROQUET PASSION: IMAGES FROM THE COLLECTION   [1995]
OF ALLEN SCHEUCH. [Allen Scheuch]

[Page *1*, within a ruled frame]

CROQUET PASSION | Images from the Collection of Allen Scheuch | [engraved illustration, reproduced from an advertisement in *Our Young Folks*, May 1869] | The National Croquet Gallery | Hall of Fame & Archives | at the Newport Art Museum | 1995-96

Formula: [1^4]. 4 leaves, unnumbered [pp 1–8]

Technical notes: 196 × 121 mm (p *4*). Pp *1–3*: 43 lines, 20 = 91 mm. Pp *4–7*: 51 lines, 20 = 77 mm. Leaf size 216 × 139 mm; thickness 0.14 mm; wove, unwatermarked, smooth, light Grey (264), flecked

Contents: Title (p *1*), foreword, signed 'Theo Holcomb', note from the collector, signed 'Allen Scheuch', and attribution of illustration on the TP (2), introduction, signed 'A.S.' (3), notes to the exhibit (4–7), blank (8)

Binding: Stapled, no wrapper

Copy seen: PC

Fingerprint: S.se edhe gere nash C 1995Q [all four groups taken from p *3*]

Notes: Printed anonymously. This work was evidently issued to visitors to a special exhibition held by the National Croquet Gallery, Newport Art Museum, Newport RI, during the years 1995–96.

A298 SEEING THE SCIENCE IN CROQUET. Peter Rudge   1995

SEEING THE SCIENCE IN | CROQUET | by | Peter Rudge | Illustrated by | Frank Atack | CORAT | 1995 | [rule, in bold]

Formula: [1^{16}]. 16 leaves, unnumbered [pp 1–32]

Technical notes: 177 × 125 mm (p 5). 38 lines, 20 = 93 mm. Leaf size 207 × 146 mm; thickness 0.11 mm; wove, unwatermarked, smooth, light Yellow (86)

Contents: Title (*1*), TP verso (*2*), contents (*3*), text (*4–32*)

Binding: Vivid greenish Yellow (97) Astrolux board, printed in black, sewn, no spine or endpapers. FC: ([in shaded script] **SEEING THE SCIENCE IN** | [*do*] **CROQUET | by | Peter Rudge | Illustrated by Frank Atack**). Inside FC: blank. RC: about the author and illustrator. Inside RC: blank

Copy seen: PC

Fingerprint: **eson** e.ly l.he ·eba C 1995A

Notes: Published by CORAT, Coolangatta, Queensland, printed anonymously, price Aus$10.00 (mail order), £5.00 (UK).

Review: *Croquet Newsletter* [Queensland] (February 1996).

1996

A299 [CH°UI CH°IU CHIAO SHIH].   1996

[One line of Chinese script] | [colour photograph of a mallet, hoop, and two balls] | [twelve lines of Chinese script]

Formula: [1^2 2–7^{16} 8^2]. 100 leaves, pp *i–iv*, *1–2* 3–192, *v–viii*. The pagination runs 'backwards'

Technical notes: 161 × 105 mm (p 39). 19 columns, 20 = 113 mm. Leaf size 209 × 148 mm. Pages *i–iv*, *v–viii*: thickness 0.12 mm, wove, unwatermarked, smooth, very light bluish Green (162), printed in brilliant bluish Green (159). Pages *1–32*: thickness 0.10 mm, wove, unwatermarked, smooth, white. Pages 33–192: wove, unwatermarked, smooth, white

Contents: Blank (*i*), artist's sketch in Blue (*ii–iii*), blank (*iv*), title (*1*), TP verso (*2*), contents, printed in black and light purplish Pink (249) (*3–5*), several unnumbered colour photographs with captions (*6–20*), several unnumbered black-and-white photographs with captions (*21–32*), text (*33–192*)

Binding: High-gloss paper laminate glued to the folds of the gatherings, the FC and RC folded inwards to create flaps, the whole having a common background consisting of a stylised photographic representation of textured cloth in gradations of vivid greenish Yellow (97) flecked with red, surmounted by a broad horizontal band in deep yellowish Green (132), sewn. FC (at the 'rear'): ([one line of Chinese script, R justified, in Yellow out of a Green band)] | [one line of Chinese script, R justified, in white out of Green band] | [one line of Chinese script in black, centred, over Yellow background] | [two colour photographs in rectangular panels side by side, that on the L (in solid colours) being of an artist's sketch of a man player driving a ball through a hoop and that on the R being the same as the illustration on the TP]). FP (at the 'rear'): Chinese script in two lines and six columns, respectively in black and moderate bluish Green (164), over Yellow background. Inside FC: blank. RC (at the 'front'): ([publisher's device in strong Blue (178) on Yellow background] | [group of six characters in Chinese script, in black] | K126 NT$180 | ISBN 957-617-153-9 | [bar code] | 9 789576 171536). RF: Chinese script in Blue and black. Inside RC: blank. Spine: downwards ([Chinese script and the characters *26*, in Yellow out of Green] [Chinese script and device in Green on Yellow] [Chinese script in very dark Purple (225) on Yellow)

Copy seen: PC

Fingerprint: Not reproducible in an available font

Notes: Published in Chinese by Megas Publishing Co, Taipei, it is believed in 1996, price NT$180. Year of publication is inferred from the characters '9' and '6' which appear in close proximity on the TP and from the fact that a search of the online systems of the principal libraries in Hong Kong conducted in 1995 failed to reveal any publication about croquet in the Chinese language.

The transliteration of the title given above follows a citation generated by the CNIDR http–>Z39.50 gateway, with LOC modifications. The same citation quotes 'Lien kuang t°u shu kung ssu. Pien chi pu' as 'other authors'.

**A300   CROQUET: PROBLEMS OF LAWS INTERPRETATION.   1996
John Riches and John Hanscomb**

(a) *First edition (1996)*

[The FC, within a ruled frame]

CROQUET: | PROBLEMS | OF | LAWS | INTERPRETATION | [abstract sketch of player about to make a stroke] | by John Riches | and John Hanscomb

Formula: [1–74¹]. 74 leaves, pp 1–147 *148*

Technical notes: 245 × 159 mm (p 4). 50 lines, 20 = 98 mm. Leaf size 297 × 210 mm; thickness 0.10 mm; wove, unwatermarked, smooth, white

Contents: Contents (1), about the author, and dedication (2), introduction, signed 'John Riches' (3–5), text (6–146), advertisement (147), blank (*148*)

Binding: Vivid reddish Orange (34) light card front and rear, stapled, the spine wrapped with deep reddish Orange (36) stippled plastic tape, no endpapers. FC: printed in black, as above. Inside FC: blank. RC: blank. Inside RC: blank. Spine: blank

Copy seen: PC

Fingerprint: 2.1. w.**ME** .)n. "CTh 3 1996A

Notes: Printed and published privately in Enfield SA, in November 1996, price Aus$11.00 including postage within Australia. This work was, and continues to be, produced in small batches to meet current orders, both privately in Australia and by the NZCC. Excluding sales by the NZCC, about 80 copies had been sold up to June 1999.

(b) *First English edition (1997)*

[The FC as that of (a)]

Formula: [1–74¹]. 74 leaves, pp 1–146 *147–148*

Technical notes: As at (a)

Contents: Contents (1), about the author, and dedication (2), introduction, signed 'John Riches' (3–5), text (6–146), advertisement (*147*), blank (*148*)

Binding: Strong yellowish Pink (26) paper FC protected by clear acetate sheet and RC of white light Astrolux board, slotted and fastened with a white plastic comb, no endpapers. FC: printed in black, as above. Inside FC: blank. RC: blank. Inside RC: blank. Spine: blank

Copy seen: PC

Fingerprint: 2.1. w.**ME** .)n. "CTh 3 1997A

Notes: Published in 1997 by D Drazin, Croxley Green, Herts, for distribution in the UK and Ireland, printed anonymously, price £15.00. The text is identical, or virtually identical, to that of (a). Apparently the only variation is substitution (at p *50*) of the original advertisement (incorporating Australian prices as at January 1997) by an advertisement addressed to the UK market.

Thirty-five copies were printed in 1997, of which 24 remained unsold in October 1998.

A301 **THE LIGHTER SIDE OF SERIOUS CROQUET. David Appleton** 1996

The Lighter Side | of | Serious Croquet | David Appleton

[From the TP verso, L justified]

Published in Great Britain by David Appleton, | Newcastle upon Tyne, 1996. | [...] | ISBN 0 9520246 1 6

Formula: [1–50¹]. 50 leaves, pp *1–2*, i–iv, *1 2–93 94*

Technical notes: 196 × 140 mm (p *4*), mostly in two columns. 40 lines, 20 = 99 mm. Leaf size 241 × 176 mm; thickness 0.13 mm; wove, unwatermarked, very smooth, white

Contents: Title (*1*), TP verso (*2*), preface, signed 'Rod Williams' (i), author's foreword (ii–iii), contents (iv), text (*1–93*), blank (*94*)

Binding: High-gloss white laminate with hinge, printed in black, glued to the edges of the leaves, no endpapers. FC: ([at L] *David Appleton* | [do] *looks at* | [cartoon line drawing at R, opposite the two lines above] | [centred within a photograph of a trophy modelled on a mallet head] *The Lighter Side* | [do] *of* | [do] *Serious Croquet* | [at R] *with a little help from his friends* | [do] *including more than 70 cartoons by* | [do] *Jack Shotton* | [cartoon line drawing at L, opposite the three lines above]). Inside FC: blank. RC: ISBN and bar code. Spine: blank

Copy seen: PC

Fingerprint: msy. w.e. t?th Idwi 3 1996A [group 4 taken from the L column of p 14]

Notes: Printed anonymously, price £10.00.

A302 **PRINCIPLES OF HANDICAPPING. Bill Lamb** 1996

[The FC]

[publisher's device] | **PRINCIPLES OF HANDICAPPING** | By | Bill Lamb

Formula: [1⁸]. 8 leaves, pp 1–16

Technical notes: 176 × 123 mm (p *2*). 42 lines, 20 = 84 mm. Leaf size 211 × 144 mm; thickness 0.11 mm; wove, unwatermarked, smooth, white

Contents: TP verso and contents (inside FC), text (1–16)

Binding: Pale Blue (185) light card, printed in black, stapled, no spine or endpapers. FC: as above. Inside FC: TP verso and contents. RC: blank. Inside RC: blank

Copy seen: PC

Fingerprint: e.in iter othe anws 3 1996A [group 1 taken from p 1]

Notes: Published by the CA, printed and bound by Kall-Kwik Printing, initially priced £3.00 but issued free of charge to registered clubs. The CA subsequently issued this work free of charge more generally, bundled with other publications.

The initial print run ordered was of 500 copies, but an extra 1000 copies were printed in error and purchased by the CA at a nominal price.

1997

A303 THE CROQUET ASSOCIATION CENTENARY YEAR BOOK: 1997
1897–1997. [The Croquet Association] and Colin Prichard

THE CROQUET ASSOCIATION | CENTENARY YEAR BOOK | 1897–1997 | *TOGETHER WITH* | **A CONCISE HISTORY OF** | THE CROQUET ASSOCIA-TION | *BY* | **COLIN PRICHARD** | [centenary device of the CA] | LONDON: | THE CROQUET ASSOCIATION | 1997 | [rule] | *SPONSORED BY* | JOHN JAQUES AND SON

Formula: [1–76¹]. 76 leaves, pp *i–iv*, 1–2 3–146 *147–148*

Technical notes: 173 × 116 mm (p 13). 42 lines, 20 = 82 mm. Leaf size 210 × 147 mm; thickness 0.12 mm; wove, unwatermarked, smooth white. There are six leaves of inset half-tone black-and-white photographs, comprising 20 plates: plate 1 faces p *1*, plate 2 faces p 7, plate 3 faces p 10, plate 4 faces p 11, plates *5–20* are set between pp 28 and 29

Contents: Blank (*i*), advertisement (*ii–iii*), blank (*iv*), title (*1*), TP verso (*2*), message from HM the Queen (3), preface, signed 'Stephen Badger', April 1997 (4), contents (5), list of plates (6), presidents, vice-presidents, and officials (7–8), Council (9–10), rules of the association (11–18), benefactors (19), membership, 1897–1997 (20), annual subscription rates, 1897–1997 (21), subscription rates, 1997 (22), challenge trophies and other prizes (23–28), winners of principal association events (29–69), winners of principal international events (70–73), registered clubs (74–83), federa-tions of clubs (84--85), other national associations (86), a concise history of the association by Colin Prichard (87–145), books available from the association (146), blank (*147–148*)

Binding: Light Grey (264) laminated Astrolux board printed in black, hinged front and rear, glued to the edges of the leaves, no endpapers. FC: (**THE CROQUET ASSOCIATION** | **CENTENARY YEAR BOOK** | **1897–1997** | *TOGETHER WITH* | **A CONCISE HISTORY OF** | **THE CROQUET ASSOCIATION** | *BY* | **COLIN PRICHARD** | [centenary device of the CA]). Inside FC: blank. RC: blank. Inside RC: blank. Spine: downwards (**The Croquet Association Centenary Year Book 1897–1997**)

Copy seen: PC

Fingerprint: 6.R. 94er alee th(f 3 1997A

Notes: Printed by Imediaprint (City), London, and published by the Croquet Association on 1 May 1997, ISBN 0 902758 05 5, price £12.00 to Associates (*ie* members of the Association).

Thee hunded copies were produced, of which 294 were bound as here described.

A304 **CROQUET: FUN AND GAMES.** Peter Rudge 1997

CROQUET: | **FUN AND GAMES** | by | Peter Rudge | Illustrated by | Frank Atack | CORAT | 1997 | [rule]

Formula: [1¹⁶]. 16 leaves, some numbered irregularly [pp 1–32]

Technical notes: 180 × 123 mm (p 4). 37 lines, 20 = 97 mm, variable. Leaf size 209 × 147 mm; thickness 0.10 mm; wove, unwatermarked, smooth, light purplish Pink (249)

Contents: Title (*1*), publishing details (*2*), contents (*3*), text (*4–31*), other books by the author (*32*)

Binding: Moderate purplish Pink (250) card, printed in black, stapled, no spine or endpapers. FC: ([in shaded display script] **CROQUET:** | [*do*] **FUN AND GAMES** | **by** | **Peter Rudge** | Illustrated by Frank Atack). Inside FC: blank. RC: about the author (23 lines) and about the illustrator (5 lines). Inside RC: blank

Copy seen: PC

Fingerprint: **oron** t.ds e.op 12on C 1997A

Notes: ISBN 1 875383 04 2; published by CORAT, Queensland; printed by Panther Publishing and Printing, Fyshwick, ACT.

A305   CROQUET: VARIATIONS ON A THEME. Peter Rudge   1997

CROQUET: | **VARIATIONS ON A THEME** | by | Peter Rudge | Illustrated by | Frank Atack | CORAT | 1997 | [rule]

Formula: [1¹⁶]. 16 leaves, some numbered irregularly

Technical notes: 182 × 123 mm (p 7). 37 lines, 20 = 99 mm. Leaf size 209 × 145 mm; thickness 0.10 mm; wove, unwatermarked, smooth, very pale Purple (226)

Contents: Title (*1*), publishing details (*2*), contents (*3*), text (*4–31*), other books by the author (*32*)

Binding: Moderate Purple (223) card, printed in black, stapled, no spine or endpapers. FC: ([in shaded display script] **CROQUET:** | [*do*] **VARIATIONS ON A** | **THEME** | **by** | **Peter Rudge** | Illustrated by Frank Atack). Inside FC: blank. RC: about the author (20 lines) and about the illustrator (6 lines). Inside RC: blank

Copy seen: PC

Fingerprint: **oron** t.al t.om Atth C 1997A

Notes: Published by CORAT, Queensland; printed by Panther Publishing and Printing, Fyshwick, ACT, ISBN 1 875383 03 4.

A306   GUIDELINES FOR TOURNAMENT MANAGERS.   [1997]
David Curtis *et al*

[The FC]

GUIDELINES FOR | **TOURNAMENT** | **MANAGERS** | *A manual of guidelines to assist tournament managers with the* | *organisation and administration of national,* *regional and local* | *tournaments for croquet players* | *Produced by the New Zealand Croquet Council Inc.*

Formula: [1–32¹]. 32 leaves, ff 1–32

Technical notes: 260 × 170 mm (p 4, ragged). 43 lines, 20 = 121 mm. Leaf size 297 × 210 mm; thickness 0.10 mm; wove, unwatermarked, smooth, white

Contents: Contents (1), introduction, signed 'Edwina Thompson' (2), manager's manual, each page signed '© *David Curtis 1 June 1996*' (3–9), text, concluded (10–32)

Binding: Brilliant Violet (206) card, the FC protected by a clear acetate sheet, bound by a white plastic comb, slotted, no endpapers. FC: printed in black, as above. Inside FC: blank. RC: blank. Inside RC: blank. Spine: blank

Copy seen: PC

Fingerprint: idws t.he e.e. **GEer** 3 1997Q [groups 3 and 4 taken from p 13]

Notes: Published by the New Zealand Croquet Council in April 1997, printed anonymously. Date of publication is inferred from the date appended to the introduction (p 2).

The text of this work includes contributions attributed to Edwina Thompson, John Prince, and Graeme Roberts.

A307   HISTORY OF CROQUET CLUBS IN QUEENSLAND.   1997
Mrs M Woff (ed)

[The FC]

HISTORY | *OF* | *CROQUET CLUBS* | *IN* | *QUEENSLAND* | [device of Bank of Queensland] | **"PROUDLY SUPPORTS QUEENSLAND CROQUET"** | *Published by: Southport Croquet Club Inc.* | *P.O. Box 2034* | *SOUTHPORT QLD 4215* | *Editor: Mrs M Woff* | *Phone: (07) 5532 2686*

Formula: [1^{16}]. 16 leaves excluding pages of the wrapper, pp *i*, *1* 2–31

Technical notes: 185 × 121 mm (p 7). 46 lines, 20 = 80 mm. Leaf size 211 × 148 mm; thickness 0.10 mm; wove, unwatermarked, smooth, white

Contents: Title (FC), notice to readers (inside FC), contents (*i*), text, continued (1–31), text, concluded (32, inside RC)

Binding: Pale greenish Yellow (104) paper, stapled through the folds, no spine or endpapers. FC: printed in black as above. Inside FC: notice to readers. RC: advertisement. Inside RC: conclusion of text

Copy seen: PC

Fingerprint: 3231 s.oy enp. reTh C 1997A [groups 1–4 taken from pp *i*, 8, 12, 13 respectively]

Notes: Published by Southport Croquet Club, QLD, in association with Queensland Croquet Association, printed anonymously, issued free of charge to subscribers to the club.

The text consists mostly of brief histories of associated clubs signed by or attributed to named contributors. The copy examined contains two loose inserts, each consisting of a brief history of a club omitted from the text, one photocopied from *The Australian Croquet Gazette* (October 1967). Either or both of these inserts may have been intended for issue with this work.

A308   HUMAN CROQUET. Kate Atkinson   1997

(a) *First edition (1997)*

HUMAN CROQUET | [rule] | Kate Atkinson | [publisher's device, a dolphin entwined about an anchor] | Doubleday | LONDON · NEW YORK · TORONTO · SYDNEY · AUCKLAND

Formula: [1–176¹]. 176 leaves, pp *1–10* 11–20 *21–22* 23–78 *79–80* 81–120 *121–122* 123–148 *149–150* 151–187 *188–190* 191–214 *215–216* 217–225 *226–228* 229–265 *266–270* 271–282 *283–284* 285–310 *311–312* 313–323 *324–326* 327–334 *335–336* 337–343 *344* 345 *346* 347–349 *350–352*

Technical notes: 167 × 113 mm (p 14). 35 lines, 20 = 96 mm. Leaf size 233 × 153 mm; thickness 0.14 mm; wove, unwatermarked, smooth, white

Contents: Half-title (*1*), by the same author (*2*), title (*3*), TP verso (*4*), dedication (*5*), blank (*6*), verse quotation (*7*), blank (*8*), part title (*9*), blank (*10*), text, continued (11–20), part title (*21*), blank (*22*), text, continued (23–78), part title (*79*), blank (*80*), text, continued (*81–120*), part title (*121*), blank (*122*), text, continued (*123–148*), part title (*149*), blank (*150*), text, continued (*151–187*), blank (*188*), part title (*189*), blank (*190*), text, continued (*191–214*), part title (*215*), blank (*216*), text, continued (*217–225*), blank (*226*), part title (*227*), blank (*228*), text, continued (*229–265*), blank (*266*), part title (*267*), blank (*268*), part title (*269*), blank (*270*), text, continued (*271–282*), part title (*283*), blank (*284*), text, continued (*285–310*), part title (*311*), blank (*312*), text, continued (*313–323*), blank (*324*), part title (*325*), blank (*326*), text, continued (*327–334*), part title (*335*), blank (*336*), text, concluded (*337–343*), blank (*344*), verse quotation (*345*), blank (*346*), epilogue (*347–349*), blank (*350*), conclusion (*351*), blank (*352*)

Binding: Deep Orange (51) buckram grain paper over stiff boards, the leaves glued together, dark Green (146) endpapers. FC: blank. RC: blank. Spine: gold-blocked, mostly downwards (HUMAN CROQUET Kate Atkinson) and crosswise at the foot ([publisher's device] | Doubleday)

Dust wrapper: White high-gloss laminated paper, in white and black out of an imaginative full colour collage of artwork and photographic images, extending across the RP, spine, and FP. FP: in white out of a full colour collage (KATE ATKINSON | Author of Behind the Scenes at the Museum | [R justified] HUMAN | [*do*] CROQUET). FF: publisher's blurb, ISBN, and price. RP: publisher's blurb in relation to *Behind the Scenes at the Museum*, by the same author, in white out of full colour collage, and ISBN and bar code in black in a white panel out of full colour collage. RF: portrait of the author, brief biographical note, and production credits. Spine: downwards in white out of full colour collage (KATE ATKINSON | HUMAN CROQUET), and crosswise near the foot ([publisher's device in black and Red] | [in black] Doubleday

Copy seen: PC

Fingerprint: chr, s.rs llhe onbe 7 1997A

Notes: Printed by Mackays of Chatham, Chatham, Kent, price £15.99.

The epilogue (pp 347–349), entitled 'A GOOD GAME FOR A PARTY', is an excerpt from S Hedges, *The Home Entertainer* (London: Odhams Press, 1939). It describes a version of croquet in which the participants also take the roles of the balls and hoops.

(b) *Picador American paperback (1998)*

[in shaded script] **Human Croquet** | [rule] | Kate Atkinson | Picador USA | New York | [publisher's device]

Formula: As that of (a)

Technical notes: 158 × 106 mm (p 14). 35 lines, 20 = 90 mm. Leaf size 208 × 136 mm; thickness 0.13 mm; wove, unwatermarked, smooth, white

Contents: As the contents of (a)

Binding: White laminated high-gloss card glued to the edges of the leaves. FC: against an artist's sketch printed in several colours on a vivid Yellow Green (115) background ([in vivid Yellow (82) out of a strong purplish Red (255) band at the head] A *NEW YORK TIMES* NOTABLE BOOK OF THE YEAR] | [within a clockface which forms part of the artist's sketch, in black on deep reddish Orange (36)] a | [*do*] *novel* | [in artist's script, in an irregular curve, in black] **Human Croquet** | [in moderate Purple (223)] *Kate Atkinson* | [in black] **AUTHOR OF** ***BEHIND THE SCENES AT THE MUSEUM*** | [downwards in white out of Orange on the vertical of an L-shaped band at the foot] Picador USA | [at R of publisher's name] *"Intelligent, sympathetic, and terribly funny, this is a simply* | *[do] wonder-ful book." — Kate Tuttle, <u>Boston Book Review</u>*). Inside FC: blank, coloured Yellow. RC: set in two columns over a faint artist's sketch. L column: publisher's blurb, incorporating quotations from reviews, printed in Red and black, partly over a Yellow panel and partly over a Yellow Green reverse L-shaped area. R column: printed in Red and black ([black-and-white photograph of the author] | [about the author] | \$14.00 | [in a white panel over bar code] ISBN 0-312-18688-6). The RC has a narrow Orange foot band which extends across its full width, the spine, and the FC. Inside RC: blank, coloured Yellow. Spine: downwards, mostly in black ([head band] *Kate Atkinson   HUMAN CROQUET*   [crosswise near the foot on three lines] **PICADOR** [rule] USA [Orange tailband continued on both the FC and RC])

Copy seen: PC

Fingerprint: chr, s.rs llhe onbe 7 1998A

Notes: Printed anonymously in the USA, price \$14.00. The text is evidently a photo-reduced facsimile of (a).

Reviews: Boston Book Review, Commonweal, The Independent, The New York Times Book Review, The San Francisco Examiner and Chronicle.

AA309 HUMAN RESOURCE PLAN. [New Zealand Croquet Council]   [1997]

[The FC]

NEW ZEALAND CROQUET COUNCIL INC. | **HUMAN** | **RESOURCE** | **PLAN** | *This manual has been developed to assist people* | *involved in the delivery of sport, namely croquet.*

Formula: [1–11¹]. 11 leaves, ff 1–11

Technical notes: 264 × 167 mm (p 8, ragged). 42 lines, 20 = 127 mm. Leaf size 297 × 210 mm; thickness 0.10 mm; wove, unwatermarked, smooth, white

Contents: Text (1–11)

Binding: The FC is of pale orange Yellow (73) paper protected by a clear acetate sheet, the RC of light Grey (264) paper, bound by a white plastic comb, slotted, no endpapers. FC: printed in black, as above. Inside FC: blank. RC: blank. Inside RC: blank. Spine: blank

Copy seen: PC

Fingerprint: veve es*n:* s.ld cyty C 1997Q [groups 2–4 taken from f 5]

Notes: Published by NZCC, printed anonymously. Year of publication is inferred from the circumstances in which a copy of this work came into the hands of the compiler and from the close similarity of its format to that of A306.

AA310 LAWS RECOMMENDATIONS IN RESPONSE TO   1997
PROPOSALS BY THE CA LAWS COMMITTEE.
[Australian Croquet Association Laws Committee]

[The FC]

CROQUET AUSTRALIA | **LAWS COMMITTEE** | **LAWS RECOMMENDA-TIONS** | *IN RESPONSE TO PROPOSALS BY THE* | *C.A. LAWS COMMITTEE* | July 1997

Formula: [1–13¹]. 13 leaves, unnumbered [ff 1–13]

Technical notes: 246 × 162 mm (p 7, ragged). 50 lines, 20 = 99 mm. Leaf size 297 × 210 mm; thickness 0.11 mm; wove, unwatermarked, smooth, white

Contents: Open letter to 'laws person', signed 'John Riches' (*1*), text (*2–13*)

Binding: Light yellowish Green (135) paper front and rear, stapled, no spine or end-papers. FC: printed in black as above. Inside FC: blank. RC: blank. Inside RC: blank

Copy seen: PC

Fingerprint: et7. nd*s: et57 85e*) C 1997A [group 1 taken from f *1*, group 2 taken from f *5*, groups 3 and 4 taken from f *13*]

Notes: Issued to interested parties in July 1997 in preparation for the International Laws Meeting due to be held at Bunbury the following November, printed anonymously.

A311   **PEEL APPEAL. Steve Jones**   1997

Peel Appeal | by | Steve Jones | PUBLISHED BY [in a calligraphic script] *WriteRight* | **LOWER HUTT 1997**

Formula: [1–82¹]. 82 leaves, pp *1–8, i* ii–iii *iv* v–vi, *1* 2–10 *11* 12–17 *18* 19–35 *36* 37–42 *43* 44–61 *62* 63–71 *72* 73–79 *80* 81–103 *104* 105–112 *113* 114–121 *122* 123–137 *138–139* 140–148 *149–150* [= 164]

Technical notes: 173 × 107 mm (p ii). 41 lines, 20 = 85 mm. Leaf size 210 × 145 mm; thickness 0.14 mm; wove, unwatermarked, smooth, white

Contents: Blank (*1–2*), title (*3*), TP verso (*4*), dedication (*5*), sponsor's advertisement (*6*), contents (*7*), blank (*8*), foreword, signed 'Charles Jones, JP', February 1997 (*i–iii*), introduction (*iv*–vi), text (*1–137*), blank (*138*), index (*139–148*), blank (*149–150*)

Binding: White laminated Astrolux board, hinged front and rear, printed in full colour on a strong Blue (178) background, glued to the leaves, no endpapers. FC: ([in white out of Blue] **Peel Appeal** | [colour photograph of three croquet balls stacked vertically in the jaws of a hoop bearing correspondingly coloured clips on the uprights, within a rectangular panel] | [in white out of Blue] **by** | [*do*] **Steve Jones** | [rule, in black] | [in black] **with contributions from Ashley Heenan O.B.E., Bob Jackson, John Prince, | Paul Skinley, Aaron Westerby and many other leading New Zealand** | [*do*] **players, and a Foreword by Charles Jones, JP** | [in black, in a calligraphic script] *WriteRight*. Inside FC: blank. RC: publisher's blurb, incorporating a colour photograph of the author and ISBN number. Inside RC: blank. Spine: downwards in black (**PEEL APPEAL   STEVE JONES**   [in a calligraphic script] *WriteRight*)

Copy seen: PC

Fingerprint: vea, ndr, e,ry Huve 3 1997A [group 4 taken from p 16]

Notes: Published in March 1997, printed by Wright and Carman (NZ), Upper Hutt, NZ, price NZ$9.95.

1990–97

A312   **A CROQUET PLAYER'S GUIDE TO THE SWING.**   *ca* 1990
Kevin Brereton

[The FC]

A Croquet Player's Guide | to | **THE SWING** | BY KEVIN BRERETON | [schematic line drawing of a man player, illustrating several stages of a swing] | Published by **EX-ACT CRAFTS** (Custom made mallets)

Formula: [1⁸]. 8 leaves, pp 1–16

Technical notes: 161 × 110 mm (p 5, ragged). 38 lines, 20 = 86 mm. Leaf size 210 × 148 mm; thickness 0.11 mm; wove, watermarked ([device] | [in open script] **Abermill**), smooth, white

Contents: Text (1–16)

Binding: Moderate Yellow (87) leather-effect embossed light card, stapled, no spine or endpapers. FC: printed in black, as above. Inside FC: blank. RC: blank. Inside RC: blank

Copy seen: PC

Fingerprint: s.ly y.ap t.ch atst 3 1990Q [groups 1–4 taken respectively from p 1, the caption to fig 11 on p 9, the text on p 13, the text on p 14]

Notes: Printed anonymously. Year of publication is uncertain.

A313   **FUN GAMES FOR CROQUET. John Prince**   *ca* **1996**

[The FC]

[device of the NZCC] | FUN GAMES | FOR CROQUET | SKILLS | DEVELOP-MENT | *Produced by the New Zealand Croquet Council with the | assistance of John Prince.*

Formula: [1–9¹], excluding the FC. 9 leaves, ff 1–9

Technical notes: 239 × 154 mm (p 7, ragged). 45 lines, 20 = 106 mm. Leaf size 297 × 210 mm; thickness 0.11 mm; wove, unwatermarked, smooth, white

Contents: Text (1–9)

Binding: Front and rear cover sheets of vivid Orange (48) paper, the front sheet protected by a clear acetate sheet, slotted and bound by a white plastic comb, no endpapers. FC: as above. Inside FC: blank. RC: blank. Inside RC: blank

Copy seen: PC

Fingerprint: s.p. k.n. p.e. p.ON C 1996Q [groups 2–4 taken from f 5, group 4 taken from the heading of f 5]

Notes: Printed anonymously, price NZ$5.00 including GST. The citation on the TP is taken to signify that this work was published by the NZCC.

A314   **PRACTICE WITH A PURPOSE: A SELF HELP GUIDE TO**   *ca* **1996**
            BETTER CROQUET. John Prince

PRACTICE WITH A | PURPOSE | A SELF HELP GUIDE | TO BETTER CROQUET | COMPILED BY JOHN PRINCE | FOR THE | NEW ZEALAND CROQUET COUNCIL INC.

Formula: [1–31¹], excluding the FC. 31 leaves, ff 1–31

Technical notes: 266 x 194 mm, variable (f 6, ragged). Variable number of lines and line spacing. Leaf size 297 × 210 mm; thickness 0.10 mm; wove, unwatermarked, smooth, white

Contents: Contents (1), introduction (2), quotations from leading players (3), text (4–31)

Binding: Front and rear cover sheets respectively of strong greenish Blue 169) and light Grey (264) paper, the front sheet protected by a clear acetate sheet, slotted and bound by a white plastic comb, no endpapers. FC: as above. Inside FC: blank. RC: blank. Inside RC: blank

Copy seen: PC

Fingerprint: NGTS K... H.OR ORER C 1996Q [groups 3 and 4 taken from f 13]

Notes: Printed anonymously, price NZ$10.00 plus postage including GST. The citation on the TP is taken to signify that this work was published by the NZCC.

All the leaves, save the FC and RC, bear the signature '© *John Prince*'.

Part B:
Patents of Inventions
Related to the Game of Croquet

B1 **CROQUÊT MARKER AND MALLET. John Jaques. GB 999/1862**   1862

IMPROVEMENTS IN THE INSTRUMENTS USED IN THE GAME OF CROQUÊT

Material dates: Petition filed 8 April 1862, sealed 3 October 1862, specification filed 6 October 1862

Contents: Title (*1*), provisional specification (*1–2*), complete specification (*2–5*), name of printer (*5*), figs 1–4 (1 sheet of diagrams)

Copy seen: BLSRL (photocopy)

Notes: Published for the Queen's most Excellent Majesty, printed by George Edward Eyre and William Spottiswoode, London.

B2 **MARKING PROGRESS IN THE GAME OF CROQUÊT.**   1864
Henry McEvoy. GB 1894/1864

IMPROVEMENTS IN THE APPARATUS OR ARTICLES USED IN THE GAME OF CROQUÊT

Material dates: Petition filed 30 July 1864, sealed 24 January 1865, specification filed 30 January 1865

Contents: Title (*1*), provisional specification (*1–2*), complete specification (*3–7*), name of printer (*7*), figs 1–9 (1 sheet of diagrams)

Copy seen: BLSRL (photocopy)

Notes: Published for the Queen's most Excellent Majesty, printed by George Edward Eyre and William Spottiswoode, London.

B3 **CROQUET MALLETS. Joseph Frederick Feltham. GB 1181/1865**   1865

AN IMPROVEMENT IN MALLETS USED IN THE GAME OF CROQUET AND OTHER SIMILAR GAMES

Material dates: Petition filed 27 April 1865, sealed 24 October 1865, specification filed 27 October 1865

Contents: Title (*1*), provisional specification (*1–2*), complete specification (*2–3*), name of printer (*3*), figs 1–2 (1 sheet of diagrams)

Copy seen: BLSRL (photocopy)

Notes: Published for the Queen's most Excellent Majesty, printed by George Edward Eyre and William Spottiswoode, London.

B4 **CROQUET STAND. Walter Thomas Whitmore Jones. GB 1214/1865**   1865

AN IMPROVED CROQUET STAND

Material date: Petition filed 1 May 1865

Contents: Title (*1*), provisional specification (*1–2*), name of printer (2)

Copy seen: BLSRL (photocopy)

Notes: Published for the Queen's most Excellent Majesty, printed by George Edward Eyre and William Spottiswoode, London. This invention received provisional protection only.

B5　　**CROQUET MALLETS. Samuel Stephen Bateson. GB 1704/1865**　　　**1865**

IMPROVEMENTS IN CROQUET MALLETS

Material date: Petition filed 26 June 1865

Contents: Title, provisional specification, name of printer (*1*)

Copy seen: BLSRL (photocopy)

Notes: Published for the Queen's most Excellent Majesty, printed by George Edward Eyre and William Spottiswoode, London. This invention received provisional protection only.

B6　　**MARKING THE GAME OF CROQUET, &C. James Soutter Sr.**　　**1865**
　　　　GB 1829/1865

IMPROVED MEANS FOR MARKING PROGRESS IN THE GAME OF CROQUET AND OTHER GAMES

Material dates: Petition filed 11 July 1865, sealed 9 January 1866, specification filed 10 January 1866

Contents: Title (*1*), provisional specification (*1–2*), complete specification (2–5), name of printer (5), figs 1–6 (1 sheet of diagrams)

Copy seen: BLSRL (photocopy)

Notes: Published for the Queen's most Excellent Majesty, printed by George Edward Eyre and William Spottiswoode, London.

B7　　**INDOOR CROQUET. Henry Jones. GB 2821/1865**　　　**1865**

IMPROVEMENTS IN THE IMPLEMENTS OR ARTICLES EMPLOYED IN THE GAME OF INDOOR CROQUET

Material dates: Petition filed 2 November 1865, specification filed 1 May 1866

Contents: Title (*1*), provisional specification (*1–2*), complete specification (2–5), name of printer (5), figs 1–7 (1 sheet of diagrams)

Copy seen: BLSRL (photocopy)

Notes: Published for the Queen's most Excellent Majesty, printed by George Edward Eyre and William Spottiswoode, London.

B8　　**CRICKET BALLS. Charles Huntley. GB 2328/1865**　　　**1865**

IMPROVEMENTS IN CRICKET, RACKET, TENNIS, AND FOOT BALLS

Material date: Petition filed 11 September 1865

Contents: Title (*1*), provisional specification (*1–2*), name of printer (2)

Copy seen: BLSRL (photocopy)

Notes: Published for the Queen's most Excellent Majesty, printed by George Edward Eyre and William Spottiswoode, London. This invention received provisional protection only.

B9   **IMPROVEMENT IN CROQUET MALLETS. Lawrence Byrnes.**   **1865**
US 51016

Material date: Letters Patent dated 21 November 1865

Contents: Title, specification (1), figs A, B (1 sheet of diagrams)

Copy seen: BL (photocopy)

Notes: Published by United States Patent Office.

B10   **CRICKET AND OTHER BALLS. Charles Huntley. GB 739/1866**   **1866**

Improvements in Cricket Balls, Racket, Tennis, and Foot Balls

Material date: Petition filed 10 March 1866

Contents: Title (1), provisional specification (1–2), name of printer (2)

Copy seen: BLSRL (photocopy)

Notes: Published for the Queen's most Excellent Majesty, printed by George Edward Eyre and William Spottiswoode, London. This invention received provisional protection only.

B11   **CROQUÊT BALLS. Walker Moseley. GB 884/1866**   **1866**

Improvements in Croquêt Balls

Material date: Petition filed 24 March 1866

Contents: Title (1), provisional specification (1–2), name of printer (2)

Copy seen: BLSRL (photocopy)

Notes: Published for the Queen's most Excellent Majesty, printed by George Edward Eyre and William Spottiswoode, London. This invention received provisional protection only.

B12   **IMPROVEMENT IN CROQUETERIE. Lewis Bradley and**   **1866**
Milton Bradley. US 54848

Material dates: Letters Patent dated 22 May 1866, antedated 17 April 1866

Contents: Title (1), specification (1–4), figs 1–8 (1 sheet of diagrams)

Copy seen: BL (photocopy)

Notes: Published by United States Patent Office.

B13   **IMPROVEMENT IN CROQUETERIES. G Livingston Morse.**   **1867**
US 62495

Material dates: Application signed 5 December 1866, Letters Patent dated 26 February 1867

Contents: Title (1), specification (1–2), apparently figs 1–6 (apparently 1 sheet of diagrams)

Copy seen: BL (incomplete photocopy, wanting diagrams)

Notes: Published by United States Patent Office.

B14   **STANDS FOR CROQUET BALLS, &C. John Bolton. GB 1960/1867**   **1867**

IMPROVEMENTS IN STANDS OR HOLDERS FOR CROQUET BALLS AND IMPLEMENTS

Material dates: Petition filed 4 July 1867, sealed 31 December 1867, specification filed 3 January 1868

Contents: Title (*1*), provisional specification (*1–2*), complete specification (*2–4*), name of printer (4), figs 1–7 (1 sheet of diagrams)

Copy seen: BLSRL (photocopy)

Notes: Published for the Queen's most Excellent Majesty, printed by George Edward Eyre and William Spottiswoode, London.

B15   **CROQUET MALLETS. James Asser. GB 3024/1867**   **1867**

IMPROVEMENTS IN CROQUET MALLETS

Material dates: Petition filed 26 October 1867

Contents: Title (*1*), provisional specification (*1–2*), name of printer (2)

Copy seen: BLSRL (photocopy)

Notes: Published for the Queen's most Excellent Majesty, printed by George Edward Eyre and William Spottiswoode. This invention received provisional protection only.

B16   **CROQUET MALLETS. Edwin Gillard Camp. GB 1437/1868**   **1868**

IMPROVEMENTS IN MALLETS USED IN PLAYING THE GAME OF CROQUET AND IN SIMILAR GAMES

Material dates: Petition filed 2 May 1868

Contents: Title (*1*), provisional specification (*1–2*), name of printer (2)

Copy seen: BLSRL (photocopy)

Notes: Published for the Queen's most Excellent Majesty, printed by George Edward Eyre and William Spottiswoode, London. This invention received provisional protection only.

B17   **IMPROVEMENT IN CROQUET-WICKETS. Friend W Smith.**   **1869**
          US 88335

Material date: Letters Patent dated 30 March 1869

Contents: Title, specification (*1*), figs 1–2 (1 sheet of diagrams)

Copy seen: BL (photocopy)

Notes: Published by United States Patent Office.

B18   **MARKERS FOR CROQUET. Langrishe Fyers Banks. GB 1987/1869**   **1869**

IMPROVEMENTS IN MARKERS FOR THE GAME OF CROQUET

Material dates: Petition filed 1 July 1869, sealed 22 December 1869, specification filed 1 January 1870

Contents: Title (1), provisional specification (1–2), complete specification (2–5), name of printer (5), figs 1–6 (1 sheet of diagrams)

Copy seen: BLSRL (photocopy)

Notes: Published for the Queen's most Excellent Majesty, printed by George Edward Eyre and William Spottiswoode.

B19   STAINING CROQUET BALLS, MALLETS, &C. Walter Rogers   1869 and George Tidcombe. GB 3026/1869

Improvements in the Manufacture of Balls and Mallets used in the Game of Croquet and other Games, and in Apparatus employed therein

Material date: Petition filed 18 October 1869

Contents: Title (1), provisional specification (1–2), name of printer (2)

Copy seen: BLSRL (photocopy)

Notes: Published for the Queen's most Excellent Majesty, printed by George Edward Eyre and William Spottiswoode, London. This invention received provisional protection only.

B20   CROQUET MALLETS. Ernest De la Rue. GB 1107/1870   1870

Improvements in Markers for the Game of Croquet

Material dates: Petition filed 14 April 1870, specification filed 13 October 1870

Contents: Title (1), provisional specification (1–2), complete specification (2–4), name of printer (4), figs 1–4 (1 sheet of diagrams)

Copy seen: BLSRL (photocopy)

Notes: Published for the Queen's most Excellent Majesty, printed by George Edward Eyre and William Spottiswoode, London.

B21   COLOURING INDIA-RUBBER, &C. Alfred Ford. GB 2761/1870   1870

An Improved Mode of Colouring India-rubber and other like Waterproof Fabrics or Materials

Material dates: Petition filed 20 October 1870, sealed 18 April 1871, specification filed 20 April 1871

Contents: Title (1), provisional specification (1–2), complete specification (2–5), name of printer (5)

Copy seen: BLSRL (photocopy)

Notes: Published for the Queen's most Excellent Majesty, printed by George Edward Eyre and William Spottiswoode, London.

B22   IMPROVEMENT IN APPARATUS FOR PARLOR-CROQUET.   1870 Albert P Eastman. US 109120

Material date: Specification dated 8 November 1870

Contents: Title, specification (1), figs 1–4 (1 sheet of diagrams)

Copy seen: BL (photocopy)

Notes: Published by United States Patent Office, printed anonymously.

B23   **REGISTERING CROQUET. Mayne Reid. GB 875/1871**   **1871**

AN IMPROVED MODE OF REGISTERING THE GAME OF CROQUET

Material dates: Petition filed 1 April 1871, sealed 26 September 1871, specification filed 26 September 1871

Contents: Title (*1*), provisional specification (*1–2*), complete specification (*2–4*), name of printer (4)

Copy seen: BLSRL (photocopy)

Notes: Published for the Queen's most Excellent Majesty, printed by George Edward Eyre and William Spottiswoode.

B24   **IMPROVEMENT IN CROQUET-ARCHES. Frederick M Clarke.**   **1871**
       US 117865

Material date: Specification dated 8 August 1871

Contents: Title, specification (*1*), 1 unnumbered diagram on a single sheet

Copy seen: BL (photocopy)

Notes: Published by United States Patent Office, printed anonymously.

B25   **CROQUET STANDS, &C. Alfred Barrett. GB 3378/1871**   **1871**

IMPROVEMENTS IN CROQUET STANDS, APPLICABLE ALSO TO RECEPTACLES FOR IMPLEMENTS USED IN OTHER GAMES

Material dates: Petition filed 13 December 1871, sealed 30 April 1872, specification filed 7 June 1872

Contents: Title (*1*), provisional specification (*1–2*), complete specification (*2–5*), name of printer (5), figs 1–3 (1 sheet of diagrams)

Copy seen: BLSRL (photocopy)

Notes: Published for the Queen's most Excellent Majesty, printed by George Edward Eyre and William Spottiswoode, London.

B26   **IMPROVEMENT IN CROQUET-MALLETS. Edward A Ross.**   **1873**
       US 136388

Material date: Specification dated 4 March 1873

Contents: Title, specification (*1*), figs 1–2 (1 sheet of diagrams)

Copy seen: BL (photocopy)

Notes: Published by United States Patent Office, printed anonymously.

B27   **IMPROVEMENT IN CROQUET WICKET-DRIVERS.**   **1873**
       Edwin A Barker. US 142072

Material dates: Application filed 14 May 1873, specification dated 26 August 1873

Contents: Title, specification (*1*), figs 1–2 (1 sheet of diagrams)

Copy seen: BL (photocopy)

Notes: Published by United States Patent Office, printed anonymously.

B28   CROQUET BALLS. William Webster. GB 1548/1874   1874

Improvements in the Manufacture of Balls to be used in the Game of Croquet or other Games

Material date: Petition filed 2 May 1874

Contents: Title (*1*), provisional specification (*1–2*), name of printer (*2*)

Copy seen: BLSRL (photocopy)

Notes: Published for the Queen's most Excellent Majesty, printed by George Edward Eyre and William Spottiswoode, London. This invention received provisional protection only.

**B29   IMPROVEMENT IN CROQUET-MALLETS. Thomas H Logan.   1875
US 159193**

Material dates: Application filed 10 September 1874, specification dated 26 January 1875

Contents: Title, specification (*1*), figs 1–2 (1 sheet of diagrams)

Copy seen: BL (photocopy)

Notes: Published by United States Patent Office, printed anonymously.

**B30   IMPROVEMENT IN CROQUET APPARATUS. Presbury West.   1875
US 161080**

Material dates: Application filed 5 January 1875, specification dated 23 March 1875

Contents: Title (*1*), specification (*1–2*), figs 1–7 (2 sheets of diagrams)

Copy seen: BL (photocopy)

Notes: Published by United States Patent Office, printed anonymously.

**B31   IMPROVEMENT IN GAME APPARATUS. Melbourne C Burr.   1875
US 170707**

Material dates: Application filed 1 November 1875, specification dated 7 December 1875

Contents: Title, specification (*1*), figs 1–2 (1 sheet of diagrams)

Copy seen: BL (photocopy)

Notes: Published by United States Patent Office, printed anonymously.

**B32   IMPROVEMENT IN CROQUET APPARATUS. Albert Angell.   1876
US 172685**

Material dates: Application filed 28 August 1875, specification dated 25 January 1876

Contents: Title (*1*), specification (*1–2*), figs 1–4 (1 sheet of diagrams)

Copy seen: BL (photocopy)

Notes: Published by United States Patent Office, printed anonymously.

B33   **IMPROVEMENT IN CROQUET-MALLETS. Silas E Bauder.**   1876
US 173578

Material dates: Application filed 11 September 1875, specification dated 15 February 1876

Contents: Title, specification (*1*), fig 1 (1 sheet of diagrams)

Copy seen: BL (photocopy)

Notes: Published by United States Patent Office, printed anonymously.

B34   **IMPROVEMENT IN CROQUET-MALLETS. Harry Malin.**   1876
US 183582

Material dates: Application filed 14 August 1875, specification dated 24 October 1876

Contents: Title, specification (*1*), 1 unnumbered diagram on a single sheet

Copy seen: BL (photocopy)

Notes: Published by United States Patent Office, printed anonymously.

B35   **IMPROVEMENT IN CROQUET-STANDS. Adolph Erlebach.**   1877
US 187259

Material dates: Application filed 25 January 1877, specification dated 13 February 1877

Contents: Title, specification (*1*), figs 1–3 (1 sheet of diagrams)

Copy seen: BL (photocopy)

Notes: Published by United States Patent Office, printed anonymously.

B36   **IMPROVEMENT IN GAME-INDICATORS. Abner H Jones and**   1879
Isaac Osgood. US 213113

Material dates: Application filed 17 August 1878, specification dated 11 March 1879

Contents: Title, specification (*1*), 1 unnumbered diagram on a single sheet

Copy seen: BL (photocopy)

Notes: Published by United States Patent Office, printed anonymously.

B37   **CROQUET-STAND. Hubbard C Chester. US 255596**   1882

Material dates: Application filed 3 January 1882, specification dated 28 March 1882

Contents: Title (*1*), specification (*1–2*), figs 1–4 (2 sheets of diagrams)

Copy seen: BL (photocopy)

Notes: Published by United States Patent Office, printed anonymously.

B38   **COUNTING OR CHECKING APPARATUS, &C.**   1882
Frederi[c]k Petersen and John Henry Richardson Dinsmore.
GB 2887/1882

IMPROVEMENTS IN AND RELATING TO COUNTING OR CHECKING APPARATUS PART OF WHICH INVENTION IS APPLICABLE TO BELLS OR GONGS USED FOR OTHER PURPOSES

Material dates: Petition filed 19 June 1882, specification filed 19 December 1882

Contents: Title, price (*1*), provisional specification (*1–3*), complete specification (*4–9*), name of printer (*5*), figs 1–18 (3 sheets of diagrams)

Copy seen: BLSRL (photocopy)

Notes: Published by HMSO, printed by George EB Eyre and William Spottiswoode, London, price 10d.

B39   CROQUET-WICKET. Henry J England. US 266355   1882

Material dates: Application filed 30 September 1882, specification dated 24 October 1882

Contents: Title, specification (*1*), figs 1–4 (1 sheet of diagrams)

Copy seen: BL (photocopy)

Notes: Published by United States Patent Office, printed anonymously.

B40   CROQUET-SET. Alfred DF Farley. US 280807   1883

Material dates: Application filed 26 February 1883, specification dated 10 July 1883

Contents: Title, specification (*1*), figs 1–4 (1 sheet of diagrams)

Copy seen: BL (photocopy)

Notes: Published by United States Patent Office, printed anonymously.

**B41   A NOVEL APPLICATION OF PULPED PAPER STOCK.   1889
Walter Herbert Cook. GB 363/1889**

Material dates: Application filed 8 January 1889, accepted 23 March 1889

Contents: Title, price (*1*), complete specification (*1–2*), name of printer (*2*)

Copy seen: BLSRL (photocopy)

Notes: Published by HMSO, printed by Darling and Son, London, price 4d.

**B42   IMPROVEMENTS IN THE MANUFACTURE OF HANDLES   1889
APPLICABLE FOR TOOLS, IMPLEMENTS, FIREARMS, OR
THE LIKE. Charles A Davis and William W Herron. GB 16216/1889**

Material dates: Application filed 15 October 1889, specification filed 15 July 1890, accepted 16 August 1890

Contents: Title, price (*1*), provisional specification (*1–3*), complete specification (*3–6*), name of printer (*6*), figs 1–5 (1 sheet of diagrams)

Copy seen: BLSRL (photocopy)

Notes: Published by HMSO, printed by Darling and Son, London, price 8d.

**B43   RAISER AND COLLECTOR FOR LAWN TENNIS BALLS OR   1890
OTHER BALLS OR ARTICLES. Ernest Latham. GB 9595/1890**

Material dates: Application filed 20 June 1890, specification filed 4 April 1891, accepted 9 May 1891

Contents: Title, price (*1*), provisional specification (*1*), complete specification (*1–4*), name of printer (*4*), figs 1–8 (3 sheets of diagrams)

Copy seen: BLSRL (photocopy)

Notes: Published by HMSO, printed by Darling and Son, London, price 8d.

B44 ADJUSTABLE CROQUET-WICKET. Frank K Ward. US 438392 1890

Material dates: Application filed 11 August 1890, specification dated 14 October 1890

Contents: Title (*1*), specification (*1–2*), figs 1–2 (1 sheet of diagrams)

Copy seen: BL (photocopy)

Notes: Published by United States Patent Office, printed anonymously.

B45 IMPROVEMENTS IN THE MANUFACTURE OF CROQUET 1891
MALLETS. Albert Joseph Altman. GB 9544/1891

Material dates: Application filed 5 June 1891, specification filed 24 December 1891, accepted 6 February 1892

Contents: Title, provisional specification, complete specification, name of printer, price (*1*), one unnumbered figure (1 sheet of diagrams)

Copy seen: BLSRL (photocopy)

Notes: Published by HMSO, printed by Darling and Son, London, price 8d.

B46 CROQUET TALLY-BOARD. Henry Mortensen and Peter C Larsen. 1893
US 507444

Material dates: Application filed 14 November 1892, specification dated 24 October 1893

Contents: Title (*1*), specification (*1–2*), figs 1–3 (1 sheet of diagrams)

Copy seen: BL (photocopy)

Notes: Published by United States Patent Office, printed anonymously.

B47 AN IMPROVEMENT IN THE MANUFACTURE OF CROQUET 1894
HOOPS. Albert Joseph Altman. GB 351/1894

Material dates: Application filed 6 January 1894, specification filed 20 April 1894, accepted 25 May 1894

Contents: Title, provisional specification, price (*1*), complete specification (*1–2*), name of printer (2), figs 1–4, 2 supernumerary diagrams (2 sheets of diagrams)

Copy seen: BLSRL (photocopy)

Notes: Published by HMSO, printed by Darling and Son, London, price 8d.

B48 IMPROVEMENTS IN CROQUET HOOPS. Frederick Henry Ayres. 1894
GB 6739/1894

Material dates: Application filed 4 April 1894, specification filed 22 December 1894, accepted 26 January 1895

Contents: Title, provisional specification, price (*1*), complete specification (*1–2*), name of printer (2), figs 1–3 (1 sheet of diagrams)

Copy seen: BLSRL (photocopy)

Notes: Published by HMSO, printed by Darling and Son, London, price 8d.

B49 **IMPROVEMENTS IN MALLETS OR LIKE STRIKERS FOR USE**   **1894**
IN PLAYING GAMES WITH BALLS. Frederick Henry Ayres.
GB 8187/1894

Material dates: Application filed 25 April 1894, specification filed 18 January 1895, accepted 23 February 1895

Contents: Title, provisional specification, price (*1*), complete specification (*1–2*), name of printer (*2*), figs 1–3 (1 sheet of diagrams)

Copy seen: BLSRL (photocopy)

Notes: Published by HMSO, printed by Darling and Son, price 8d.

B50 **IMPROVEMENTS IN STANDS OR HOLDERS FOR ARROWS**   **1895**
AND OTHER ARTICLES. Hubert Haes and Robert George Ivey.
GB 14448/1895

Material dates: Application filed 30 July 1895, specification filed 30 April 1896, accepted 13 June 1896

Contents: Title, price (*1*), provisional specification (*1–2*), complete specification (*2–4*), name of printer (*4*), figs 1–3 (1 sheet of diagrams)

Copy seen: BLSRL (photocopy)

Notes: Published by HMSO, printed by Darling and Son, London, price 8d.

B51 **IMPROVEMENTS IN THE MANUFACTURE OF CROQUET**   **1896**
BALLS. George Williams. GB 19820/1896

Material dates: Application filed 8 September 1896, specification filed 17 December 1896, accepted 13 February 1897

Contents: Title, provisional specification, price (*1*), complete specification (*1–2*), name of printer (*2*), figs 1–3 (1 sheet of diagrams)

Copy seen: BLSRL (photocopy)

Notes: Published by HMSO, printed by Darling and Son, London, price 8d.

B52 **HANDLE GRIP FOR RACKETS FOR TENNIS, LAWN TENNIS,**   **1897**
RACKETS, FIVES, BADMINTON, GOLF CLUBS, CRICKET
BATS, LACROSSE BATS, HOCKEY STICKS, INDIAN CLUBS,
BASE BALL, CROQUET MALLETS, AND OTHER GAMES
WHERE BATS OR CLUBS ARE USED. Thomas H Oyler.
GB 20813/1897

Material dates: Application filed 10 September 1897, specification filed 30 April 1898, accepted 23 July 1898

Contents: Title, provisional specification, complete specification, name of printer, price (*1*)

Copy seen: BLSRL (photocopy)

Notes: Published by HMSO, printed by Malcomson & Co, Redhill, price 8d.

B53 **IMPROVEMENTS IN AND RELATING TO HOOPS USED IN**   1898
PLAYING CROQUET AND LIKE GAMES. John Jaques Jr and
Percy Nathaniel Jaques. GB 4314/1898

Material dates: Application filed 21 February 1898, accepted 30 April 1898

Contents: Title, price (*1*), complete specification (*1–2*), name of printer (2), figs 1–4
(1 sheet of diagrams)

Copy seen: BLSRL (photocopy)

Notes: Published by HMSO, printed by Malcomson & Co, Redhill, price 8d.

B54 **IMPROVEMENTS RELATING TO CROQUET HOOPS.**   1898
Joseph George Longhurst. GB 12846/1898

Material dates: Application filed 21 February 1898, specification filed 8 March 1899,
accepted 6 May 1899

Contents: Title, provisional specification, price (*1*), complete specification (*1–2*),
name of printer (2), figs 1–3 (1 sheet of diagrams)

Copy seen: BLSRL (photocopy)

Notes: Published by HMSO, printed by Malcomson & Co, Redhill, price 8d.

B55 **A HAND TOOL FOR SCORING CONCENTRIC GROOVES**   1898
IN THE STRIKING FACES OF CROQUET MALLETS AND
THE LIKE. Albert Egerton Legh Slazenger. GB 15488/1898

Material dates: Application filed 14 July 1898, accepted 1 April 1899

Contents: Title, complete specification, name of printer, price (*1*), one unnumbered
figure (1 sheet of diagrams)

Copy seen: BLSRL (photocopy)

Notes: Published by HMSO, printed by Malcomson & Co, Redhill, price 8d.

B56 **A SELF-ACTING SCORE INDICATING APPARATUS FOR**   1898
USE IN PLAYING GAMES OF SKILL WITH PROJECTILES.
John Edward Austin. GB 20733/1898

Material dates: Application filed 1 October 1898, accepted 19 November 1898

Contents: Title, price (*1*), complete specification (*1–2*), name of printer (2), figs 1–4
(1 sheet of diagrams)

Copy seen: BLSRL (photocopy)

Notes: Published by HMSO, printed by Malcomson & Co, Redhill, price 8d.

B57 **IMPROVEMENTS IN OR CONNECTED WITH HANDLES**   1898
OF BATS, HAMMERS, STICKS, OR CLUBS FOR CRICKET,
TENNIS, HOCKEY, GOLF, AND OTHER IMPLEMENTS USED
IN GAMES OR MANUFACTURES. James Darling. GB 22682/1898

Material dates: Application filed 20 October 1898, specification filed 28 July 1899,
accepted 30 September 1899

Contents: Title, price (*1*), provisional specification (*1–2*), complete specification
(*2–4*), name of printer (4), figs 1–5 (1 sheet of diagrams)

Copy seen: BLSRL (photocopy)

Notes: Published by HMSO, printed by Malcomson & Co, Redhill, price 8d.

B58   GAME DEVICE. Henry Clarance Gallup. US 612965   1898

Material dates: Application filed 4 November 1897, specification dated 25 October 1898

Contents: Title, specification (*1*), figs 1–4 (1 sheet of diagrams)

Copy seen: BL (photocopy)

Notes: Published by United States Patent Office, printed anonymously.

**B59   IMPROVEMENTS IN CROQUET HOOPS. Walter Davidson   1898
and John Edward Austin. GB 26994/1898**

Material dates: Application filed 21 December 1898, accepted 28 January 1899

Contents: Title, price (*1*), complete specification (*1–2*), name of printer (*2*), figs 1–5 (1 sheet of diagrams)

Copy seen: BLSRL (photocopy)

Notes: Published by HMSO, printed by Malcomson & Co, Redhill, price 8d.

B60   CROQUET GAME. Warner G Lake. US 620460   1899

Material dates: Application filed 20 January 1898, specification dated 28 February 1899

Contents: Title, specification (*1*), figs 1–3 (1 sheet of diagrams)

Copy seen: BL (photocopy)

Notes: Published by United States Patent Office, printed anonymously.

**B61   IMPROVEMENTS IN AND RELATING TO APPLIANCES   1899
USED IN PLAYING THE GAME OF CROQUET.
Herbert Giles Braband Smith. GB 10224/1899**

Material dates: Application filed 15 May 1899, complete specification filed 15 February 1900, accepted 17 March 1900

Contents: Title, provisional specification, price (*1*), complete specification (*2–3*), name of printer (*3*), figs 1–8 (1 sheet of diagrams)

Copy seen: BLSRL (photocopy)

Notes: Published by HMSO, printed by Malcomson & Co, Redhill, price 8d.

**B62   IMPROVEMENTS IN APPARATUS FOR PLAYING TABLE   1899
CROQUET. Frederick James Strong. GB 14440/1899**

Material dates: Application filed 13 July 1899, specification filed 19 August 1899, specification accepted 23 September 1899

Contents: Title, provisional specification, complete specification, name of printer, price (*1*), figs 1–2 (1 sheet of diagrams)

Copy seen: BLSRL (photocopy)

Notes: Published by HMSO, printed by Malcomson & Co, Redhill, price 8d.

B63   **MEANS EMPLOYED IN PLAYING GAME OF TABLE-CROQUET. Frederick James Strong. US 650996**   1900

Material dates: Application filed 7 November 1899, specification dated 5 June 1900

Contents: Title, specification (*1*), figs 1–7 (1 sheet of diagrams)

Copy seen: BL (photocopy)

Notes: Published by United States Patent Office, printed anonymously.

B64   **CROQUET-GOLF MALLET. Henry McRae. US 653483**   1900

Material dates: Application filed 1 May 1900, specification dated 10 July 1900

Contents: Title (*1*), specification (*1–2*), figs 1–2 (1 sheet of diagrams)

Copy seen: BL (photocopy)

Notes: Published by United States Patent Office, printed anonymously.

B65   **IMPROVEMENTS IN MALLETS FOR THE GAME OF CROQUET GOLF. Henry McCrea and John Corry Fell (Patent Agent). GB 12428/1900**   1900

Material dates: Application filed 10 July 1900, accepted 29 September 1900

Contents: Title, price (*1*), complete specification (*1–2*), name of printer (*2*), figs 1–2 (1 sheet of diagrams)

Copy seen: BLSRL (photocopy)

Notes: Published by HMSO, printed by Malcomson & Co, Redhill, price 8d.

B66   **IMPROVEMENTS IN OR RELATING TO CROQUET HOOPS. Albert Egerton Legh Slazenger. GB 17538/1900**   1900

Material dates: Application filed 3 October 1900, complete specification filed 3 July 1901, accepted 17 August 1901

Contents: Title, provisional specification, price (*1*), complete specification (*1–2*), name of printer (*2*), figs 1–5 (1 sheet of diagrams)

Copy seen: BLSRL (photocopy)

Notes: Published by HMSO, printed by Malcomson & Co, Redhill, price 8d.

B67   **IMPROVEMENTS ON CROQUET MALLETS. Charles Alexander Stevenson. GB 22639/1900**   1900

Material dates: Application filed 12 December 1900, accepted 9 February 1901

Contents: Title, complete specification, name of printer, price (*1*), figs 1–3 (1 sheet of diagrams)

Copy seen: BLSRL (photocopy)

Notes: Published by HMSO, printed by Malcomson & Co, Redhill, price 8d.

B68 **AN IMPROVED CROQUET STAND. Thomas Starling Usborne.**   1901
GB 16804/1901

Material dates: Application filed 21 August 1901, accepted 21 September 1901

Contents: Title, price (*1*), complete specification (*1–2*), name of printer (2), one unnumbered diagram on a single sheet

Copy seen: BLSRL (photocopy)

Notes: Published by HMSO, printed by Malcomson & Co, Redhill, price 8d.

B69 **IMPROVEMENTS RELATING TO GOLF AND SIMILAR**   1901
BALLS. Addison Tresize Saunders. GB 8069/1901

Material dates: Application filed 21 August 1901, accepted 21 September 1901

Contents: Title, price (*1*), complete specification (*1–4*), name of printer (4), figs 1–3 (1 sheet of diagrams)

Copy seen: BLSRL (photocopy)

Notes: Published by HMSO, printed by Malcomson & Co, Redhill, price 8d.

B70 **IMPROVEMENTS IN OR APPLICABLE TO CROQUET**   1902
HOOPS. Charles Crankshaw. GB 11124/1902

Material dates: Application filed 15 May 1902, complete specification filed 6 September 1902, accepted 6 November 1902

Contents: Title, price (*1*), complete specification (*1–2*), name of printer (2), figs 1–6 (1 sheet of diagrams)

Copy seen: BLSRL (photocopy)

Notes: Published by HMSO, printed by Love & Malcomson, Redhill, price 8d.

B71 **IMPROVEMENTS IN OR CONNECTED WITH LAWN**   1902
TENNIS OR OTHER BATS, CROQUET MALLETS AND
THE LIKE. Howard Speare Cole. GB 11893/1902

Material dates: Application filed 24 May 1902, complete specification filed 24 February 1903, accepted 16 April 1903

Contents: Title, provisional specification, price (*1*), complete specification (*1–3*), name of printer (3), figs 1–7 (1 sheet of diagrams)

Copy seen: BLSRL (photocopy)

Notes: Published by HMSO, printed by Love & Malcomson, Redhill, price 8d.

B72 **IMPROVEMENTS IN GOLF CLUBS, CROQUET MALLETS**   1902
AND THE LIKE. Arthur Howard Procter. GB 26975/1902

Material dates: Application filed 6 December 1902, complete specification filed 5 September 1903, accepted 15 October 1903

Contents: Title, price (*1*), provisional specification (*1–2*), complete specification (2–4), name of printer (4), figs 1–7 (1 sheet of diagrams)

Copy seen: BLSRL (photocopy)

Notes: Published by HMSO, printed by Love & Malcomson, Redhill, price 8d.

B73   MANUFACTURE OF BALLS FOR GAMES AND PASTIMES.   1903
The British Xylonite Company Limited and Samuel Edward Bain.
GB 3557/1903

Material dates: Application filed 14 February 1903, complete specification filed 22 October 1903, accepted 26 November 1903

Contents: Title, provisional specification, price (*1*), complete specification (*1–2*), name of printer (*2*)

Copy seen: BLSRL (photocopy)

Notes: Published by HMSO, printed by Love & Malcomson, Redhill, price 8d.

B74   IMPROVEMENTS IN SEATS. Joseph Greenough. GB 6092/1904   1904

Material dates: Application filed 12 March 1904, complete specification filed 12 December 1904, accepted 2 February 1905

Contents: Title, price (*1*), provisional specification (*1–2*), complete specification (*2–4*), name of printer (*4*), figs 1–9 (1 sheet of diagrams)

Copy seen: BLSRL (photocopy)

Notes: Published by HMSO, printed by Love & Malcomson, Redhill, price 8d. The stated year of printing, 1904, is ostensibly inconsistent with the stated date of acceptance.

B75   IMPROVEMENTS IN CROQUET BALLS. Arthur Griffith.   1904
GB 7874/1904

Material dates: Application filed 5 April 1904, accepted 5 May 1904

Contents: Title, price (*1*), complete specification (*1–2*), name of printer (*2*)

Copy seen: BLSRL (photocopy)

Notes: Published by HMSO, printed by Love & Malcomson, Redhill, price 8d.

B76   IMPROVEMENTS IN OR RELATING TO HANDLES FOR   1904
RACQUETS, BATS AND OTHER ARTICLES.
Henry Osmer Clarke and James William Weeks. GB 22147/1904

Material dates: Application filed 14 October 1904, complete specification filed 24 May 1905, accepted 29 June 1905

Contents: Title, provisional specification, price (*1*), complete specification (*2–3*), name of printer (*3*), figs 1–4 (1 sheet of diagrams)

Copy seen: BLSRL (photocopy)

Notes: Published by HMSO, printed by Love & Malcomson, Redhill, price 8d.

B77   IMPROVED SOCKETS FOR CROQUET HOOPS.   1905
William Edward Martin. GB 18919/1905

Material dates: Application filed 19 September 1905, accepted 2 November 1905

Contents: Title, price (*1*), complete specification (*1–2*), name of printer (*2*), figs 1–7 (1 sheet of diagrams)

Copy seen: BLSRL (photocopy)

Notes: Published by HMSO, printed by Love & Malcomson, Redhill, price 8d.

B78 **IMPROVEMENT IN CROQUET CLIPS OR INDICATORS.**   1905
Travers James Briant. GB 22315/1905

Material dates: Application filed 1 November 1905, accepted 14 December 1905

Contents: Title, complete specification, name of printer, price (*1*), figs 1–6 (1 sheet of diagrams)

Copy seen: BLSRL (photocopy)

Notes: Published by HMSO, printed by Love & Malcomson, Redhill, price 8d.

B79 **CROQUET APPARATUS. George Wm Griswold. US 810853**   1906

Material dates: Application filed 10 January 1905, patented 23 January 1906

Contents: Title (*1*), specification (*1–2*), figs 1–7 (1 sheet of diagrams)

Copy seen: BL (photocopy)

Notes: Published by United States Patent Office, printed anonymously.

B80 **IMPROVEMENT IN THE POINTS OR FANGS OF CROQUET**   1907
HOOPS AND POSTS AND THE LIKE, WHICH ENTER THE
GROUND FOR THE PURPOSE OF FASTENING THEM.
William Wardley. GB 9688/1907

Material dates: Application filed 26 April 1907, complete specification filed 25 November 1907, accepted 20 February 1908

Contents: Title, provisional specification, price (*1*), complete specification (*1–2*), name of printer (*2*), figs 1–2 (1 sheet of diagrams)

Copy seen: BLSRL (photocopy)

Notes: Published by HMSO, printed by Love & Malcomson, Redhill, price 8d.

B81 **A NEW OR IMPROVED 'BISQUE' REGISTER FOR THE**   1908
GAME OF CROQUET. William Senhouse Clarke. GB 244/1908

Material dates: Application filed 4 January 1908, complete specification filed 29 June 1908, accepted 27 August 1908

Contents: Title, provisional specification, price (*1*), complete specification (*2–3*), name of printer (*3*), figs 1–3 (1 sheet of diagrams)

Copy seen: BLSRL (photocopy)

Notes: Published by HMSO, printed by Love & Malcomson, Redhill, price 8d.

B82 **IMPROVEMENTS IN CROQUET HOOPS. John William Wardley.**   1909
GB 3376/1909

Material dates: Application filed 11 February 1909, complete specification filed 6 July 1909, accepted 9 December 1909

Contents: Title, provisional specification, price (*1*), complete specification (*1–3*), name of printer (*3*), figs 1–3 (1 sheet of diagrams)

Copy seen: BLSRL (photocopy)

Notes: Published by HMSO, printed by Love & Malcomson, Redhill, price 8d.

B83 DISPOSITIF POUR LE TRANSPORT DES ACCESSOIRES DU   1909
JEU DE CROQUET. Société H Gavelle et Cie. FR 402129

Material dates: Application filed 16 April 1909, granted 21 August 1909, published 29 September 1909, the original of the photocopy examined is evidently over-printed '2 October 1909'

Contents: Title, price (*1*), specification (*1–2*), name of printer (2), figs 1–3 (1 sheet of diagrams)

Copy seen: BLSRL (photocopy)

Notes: Printed by l'Imprimerie Nationale, Paris, price 1 franc.

B84 IMPROVEMENTS IN SOCKET POSTS FOR SUPPORTING   1909
CROQUET ARCHES. Henry Burgess Collier. GB 25234/1909

Material dates: Application filed 20 May 1909, accepted 2 September 1909

Contents: Title, price (*1*), complete specification (*1–2*), name of printer (2), figs 1–4 (1 sheet of diagrams)

Copy seen: BLSRL (photocopy)

Notes: Published by HMSO, printed by Love & Malcomson, Redhill, price 8d.

B85 IMPROVED CONSTRUCTION OF PEG FOR USE IN   1909
PLAYING CROQUET AND OTHER OUTDOOR GAMES
OR MARKING OR INDICATING EXTENT OF GROUND.
Harold Montague Bryans. GB 11936/1909

Material dates: Claimed as date of first foreign application (in the US) 6 November 1908, application filed 2 November 1909, accepted 31 December 1909

Contents: Title (under International Convention), price (*1*), complete specification (*1–2*), name of printer (2), figs 1–2 (1 sheet of diagrams)

Copy seen: BLSRL (photocopy)

Notes: Published by HMSO, printed by Love & Malcomson, Redhill, price 8d.

B86 IMPROVEMENTS RELATING TO GOLF CLUBS, CRICKET   1910
AND BASE BALL BATS, RACQUETS, HOCKEY STICKS,
CROQUET MALLETS, BILLIARD CUES, AND SIMILAR
SPORTING REQUISITES. Clement George Fletcher. GB 3489/1910

Material dates: Application filed 12 February 1910, complete specification filed 30 July 1910, accepted 3 November 1910

Contents: Title, price (*1*), provisional specification (*1–2*), complete specification (3–6), name of printer (6), figs 1–27 (2 sheets of diagrams)

Copy seen: BLSRL (photocopy)

Notes: Published by HMSO, printed by Love & Malcomson, Redhill, price 8d.

B87 IMPROVEMENTS IN GOLF CLUBS AND THE LIKE.   1912
Percy Gordon Eckersley. GB 17579/1912

Material dates: Application filed 5 December 1912, accepted 3 April 1913

Contents: Title, price (*1*), complete specification (*1–3*), name of printer (*3*), figs 1–5 (1 sheet of diagrams)

Copy seen: BLSRL (photocopy)

Notes: Published by HMSO, printed by Love & Malcomson, Redhill, price 8d.

B88   **IMPROVEMENTS IN MEANS FOR SECURING HANDLES**   **1913**
TO THE HEADS OF BROOMS, BRUSHES AND OTHER
IMPLEMENTS. William Acraman Greenslade and
Frederick Bernard Miles. GB 15743/1913

Material dates: Application filed 8 July 1913, complete specification filed 18 September 1913, accepted 15 January 1914

Contents: Title, provisional specification, price (*1*), complete specification (*1–3*), name of printer (*3*), figs 1–6 (1 sheet of diagrams)

Copy seen: BLSRL (photocopy)

Notes: Published by HMSO, printed by Love & Malcomson, Redhill, price 8d.

B89   **IMPROVEMENTS IN AND RELATING TO CROQUET**   **1914**
HOOPS. Bentley Lyonel John Tollemache. GB 207/1914

Material dates: Application filed 3 January 1914, complete specification filed 3 July 1914, accepted 26 November 1914

Contents: Title, price (*1*), provisional specification (*1–2*), complete specification (*2–3*), name of printer (*3*), figs 1–2 (1 sheet of diagrams)

Copy seen: BLSRL (photocopy)

Notes: Published by HMSO, printed by Love & Malcomson, Redhill, price 8d.

B90   **IMPROVEMENTS IN GOLF CLUBS, TENNIS AND OTHER**   **1915**
RACQUETS, CRICKET AND OTHER BATS, AND SIMILAR
SPORTING REQUISITES. David Wightman. GB 1819/1915

Material dates: Application filed 4 February 1915, complete specification filed 13 March 1915, accepted 4 February 1916

Contents: Title, price (*1*), provisional specification (*1–2*), complete specification (*2–4*), name of printer (*4*), figs 1–7 (1 sheet of diagrams)

Copy seen: BLSRL (photocopy)

Notes: Published by HMSO, printed by Love & Malcomson, Redhill, price 6d.

B91   **CROQUET-MALLET AND THE LIKE. Thomas Taylor Jr.**   **1916**
US 1166946

Material dates: Application filed 20 December 1913, patented 4 January 1916

Contents: Title (*1*), specification (*1–2*), price (*2*), figs 1–4 (1 sheet of diagrams)

Copy seen: BL (photocopy)

Notes: Published by United States Patent Office, printed anonymously, price 5 cents.

B92   **WICKET OR ARCH FOR PLAYING CROQUET AND THE**   1919
          LIKE. Sylvester N Stewart. US 1299055

Material dates: Application filed 3 October 1918, patented 1 April 1919

Contents: Title (*1*), specification (*1–2*), price (*2*)

Copy seen: BL (photocopy)

Notes: Published by United States Patent Office, printed anonymously, price 5 cents.

B93   **IMPROVEMENTS IN HOOPS OR ARCHES FOR PLAYING**   1919
          CROQUET AND LIKE GAMES. Sylvester Noble Stewart.
          GB 133675 (23621/19)

Material dates: Convention Date (US): 3 October 1918. Application (in the UK)
filed 25 September 1919, complete specification accepted 5 February 1920

Contents: Title, price (*1*), complete specification (*1–2*), name of printer (*2*), one
diagram on a single sheet

Copy seen: BLSRL (photocopy)

Notes: Published by HMSO, printed by Love & Malcomson, Redhill, price 6d.

B94   **IMPROVEMENTS IN CROQUET HOOPS. Francis Colchester-**   1922
          Wemyss. GB 192928 (4608/22)

Material dates: Application filed 16 February 1922, complete specification filed
24 May 1922, accepted 15 February 1923

Contents: Title, provisional specification, price (*1*), complete specification (*1–2*),
name of printer (*2*), figs 1–8 (1 sheet of diagrams)

Copy seen: BLSRL (photocopy)

Notes: Published by HMSO, printed by Love & Malcomson, Redhill, price 1/–.

B95   **WICKET AND STAKE FOR INDOOR CROQUET.**   1925
          Edward S Foster. US 1540771

Material dates: Application filed 15 March 1924, patented 9 June 1925

Contents: Title (*1*), specification (*1–2*), figs 1–3 (1 sheet of diagrams)

Copy seen: BL (photocopy)

Notes: Published by United States Patent Office, printed anonymously.

B96   **IMPROVEMENTS IN OR RELATING TO GOLF CLUBS AND**   1928
          OTHER STRIKING IMPLEMENTS FOR GAMES. [Dunlop
          Rubber Company Limited], Charles Frederick Griffin, James Dodds
          McDonald, John Thomas Turney Randles. GB 323897 (37336/28)

Material dates: Application filed 18 December 1928, complete specification filed
17 September 1929, accepted 16 January 1930

Contents: Title, price (*1*), provisional specification (*1–2*), complete specification
(*2–3*), name of printer (*3*), figs 1–4 (2 sheets of diagrams)

Copy seen: BLSRL (photocopy)

Notes: Published by HMSO, printed by Love & Malcomson, Redhill, price 1/–.

B97   **GAME. Lewis C Bump. US 1784818**   **1930**

Material dates: Application filed 27 December 1928, patented 16 December 1930

Contents: Title (*1*), specification (*1–2*), figs 1–4 (1 sheet of diagrams)

Copy seen: BL (photocopy)

Notes: Published by United States Patent Office, printed anonymously.

B98   **IMPROVEMENTS IN OR RELATING TO CROQUET**   **1931**
MALLETS. Richard Wedderspoon and Isabella Wedderspoon.
NZ 66526

Material dates: Complete specification filed 24 February 1931, Journal entry dated
30 July 1931

Contents: Title, patent office's documentation, agent's documentation (1), complete
specification (1–6), agent's certification as a true copy, figs 1–2 (1 sheet of diagrams)

Copy seen: BL (photocopy of certified true copy made by Robert Wales, Wellington
NZ, Certified Patent Agent)

Notes: The original patent document is taken to have been published by New
Zealand Patent Office, printed anonymously.

B99   **IMPROVEMENTS IN OR RELATING TO MALLETS.**   **1933**
Richard Wedderspoon. NZ 71655

Material dates: Provisional specification filed 7 November 1933, complete specification dated 26 September 1934, received 28 October 1934, Journal entry dated
13 December 1934

Contents: Title, patent office's documentation, attorney's documentation (1), complete specification (1–5), attorney's certification as a true copy, figs 1–4 (1 sheet of
diagrams)

Copy seen: BL (photocopy of certified true copy made by Baldwin Son & Carey,
Wellington NZ, Patent Attorneys)

Notes: The original patent document is taken to have been published by New
Zealand Patent Office, printed anonymously.

B100   **GAME. John E Ziebarth. US 1936220**   **1933**

Material dates: Application filed 12 September 1931, patented 21 November 1933

Contents: Title, specification (*1*), figs 1–7 (1 sheet of diagrams)

Copy seen: BL (photocopy)

Notes: Published by United States Patent Office, printed anonymously.

B101   **DISPLAY AND STORAGE RACK. John E Ziebarth. US 1951894**   **1934**

Material dates: Application filed 5 June 1933, patented 20 March 1934

Contents: Title (*1*), specification (*1–2*), figs 1–4 (1 sheet of diagrams)

Copy seen: BL (photocopy)

Notes: Published by United States Patent Office, printed anonymously.

B102   **IMPROVEMENTS IN CROQUET MALLET HANDLES.**   1936
Aubrey George Fortescue Hoare. NZ 76168

Material dates: Patent dated 8 June 1936, complete specification dated 1 March 1937, received 1 March 1937, Journal entry dated 15 July 1937

Contents: Title, patent office documentation (*1*), complete specification (*1–5*), agent's signature (*5*), figs 1–6 (1 sheet of diagrams)

Copy seen: BL (photocopy)

Notes: Apparently published by New Zealand Patent Office, printed anonymously.

B103   **IMPROVEMENTS IN CROQUET MALLET HANDLES.**   1936
Aubrey George Fortescue Hoare. AU 100709 (2183/36)

Material dates: Application and provisional specification accepted 19 June 1936, complete specification lodged 22 February 1937, accepted 2 April 1937

Contents: Title, price (*1*), complete specification (*1–3*), names of publisher and printer (*3*), figs 1–6 (1 sheet of diagrams)

Copy seen: BL (photocopy)

Notes: Printed and published for the Department of Patents, Commonwealth of Australia, by LF Johnston, Commonwealth Government Printer, Canberra, price 1/6 post free.

B104   **IMPROVEMENTS IN AND RELATING TO SPORTS GOODS**   1936
**SUCH AS HOCKEY STICKS, CRICKET BATS AND OTHER
STRIKING SPORTING IMPLEMENTS. William Wright.
GB 481625 (30793/36)**

Material dates: Application filed 11 November 1936, complete specification filed 3 November 1937, accepted 15 March 1938

Contents: Title, provisional specification, price (*1*), complete specification (*1–2*), name of printer (*2*), figs 1–5 (1 sheet of diagrams)

Copy seen: BLSRL (photocopy)

Notes: Published by HMSO, printed by The Courier Press, Leamington Spa, price 1/–.

B105   **IMPROVEMENTS RELATING TO MALLETS. Elmer Elsworth**   1937
Hosier. GB 487113 (22897/37)

Material dates: Application filed 20 August 1937, complete specification accepted 15 June 1938

Contents: Title, price (*1*), complete specification (*1–2*), name of printer (*2*), figs 1–5 (1 sheet of diagrams)

Copy seen: BLSRL (photocopy)

Notes: Published by HMSO, printed by The Courier Press, Leamington Spa, price 1/–.

B106   **RUG CROQUET WICKET. L Julian Smith. US 2162867**   1939

Material dates: Application filed 5 February 1937, patented 20 June 1939

Contents: Title, specification (*1*), figs 1–3 (1 sheet of diagrams)

Copy seen: BL (photocopy)

Notes: Published by United States Patent Office, printed anonymously.

**B107   AN IMPROVED DEVICE FOR SECURING RODS IN SOCKETS   1943
PARTICULARLY BROOMSTICKS AND CHAIR LEGS.**
Walter Clay Peters. GB 568151 (11111/43)

Material dates: Application filed 8 July 1943, complete specification filed 16 August 1943, accepted 21 March 1945

Contents: Title, provisional specification, price (*1*), complete specification (*1–2*), name of printer (*2*), figs 1–2 (1 sheet of diagrams)

Copy seen: BLSRL (photocopy)

Notes: Published by HMSO, printed by The Courier Press, Leamington Spa, price 1/–.

B108   HOOPS FOR GAMES. Ernest Lawrence Hillman. GB 658096   1949
(28237/49)

Material dates: Application and complete specification filed 4 November 1949, published 3 October 1951

Contents: Title, price (*1*), complete specification (*1–2*), name of printer (*2*), figs 1–5 (1 sheet of diagrams)

Copy seen: BLSRL (photocopy)

Notes: Published by HMSO, printed by The Courier Press, Leamington Spa, price 2/–. Index at acceptance: Class 132(ii), I(1b: 2a).

B109   BALL CONFINING CLUB FOR CROQUET. Johannes Sorteberg.   1953
US 2657056

Material dates: Application filed 31 January 1952, patented 27 October 1953

Contents: Title (*1*), specification (*1–2*), figs 1–7 (1 sheet of diagrams)

Copy seen: BL (photocopy)

Notes: Published by United States Patent Office, printed anonymously.

**B110   TAPE CONSTRUCTIONS FOR USE IN LAYING OUT   1962
CROQUET COURTS.** Tilden G Abbott. US 3039197

Material dates: Application filed 27 March 1958, patented 19 June 1962

Contents: Title (*1*), specification (*1–3*), figs 1–7 (1 sheet of diagrams)

Copy seen: BL (photocopy)

Notes: Published by United States Patent Office, printed anonymously.

B111   BALL STRIKING HEAD. John E Borah. US 3226120   1965

Material dates: Application filed 3 May 1963, patented 28 December 1965

Contents: Title (*1*), specification (*1–2*), figs 1–13 (2 sheets of diagrams)

Copy seen: BL (photocopy)

Notes: Published by United States Patent Office, printed anonymously.

B112   MALLET ASSEMBLY. Daniel E Berry. US 3472512   1969

Material dates: Application filed 20 February 1967, patented 14 October 1969

Contents: Title (*1*), specification (*1–4*), figs 1–6 (2 sheets of diagrams)

Copy seen: BL (photocopy)

Notes: Published by United States Patent Office, printed anonymously.

B113   CROQUET WICKET ASSEMBLY. Arnold M Thompson.   1972
US 3695610

Material dates: Application filed 21 September 1970, patented 3 October 1972

Contents: Title, details in standard form with INID codes, one unnumbered diagram (*i*), specification (*1–3*), figs 1–4 (1 sheet of diagrams)

Copy seen: BL (photocopy)

Notes: Published by United States Patent Office, printed anonymously.

B114   GAME BALL RAMMER. John M Molinaro. US 3908996   1975

Material dates: Application filed 2 August 1974, patented 30 September 1975

Contents: Title, details in standard form with INID codes, one unnumbered diagram (*i*), specification (*1–2*), figs 1–4 (1 sheet of diagrams)

Copy seen: BL (photocopy)

Notes: Published by United States Patent Office, printed anonymously.

B115   ACTION CROQUET POST. John T Sahler. US 4531736   1985

Material dates: Application filed 9 February 1984, patented 30 July 1985

Contents: Title, details in standard form with INID codes, one unnumbered diagram (*i*), specification (*1–2*), figs 1–2 (1 sheet of diagrams)

Copy seen: BL (photocopy)

Notes: Published by United States Patent Office, printed anonymously.

B116   IMPROVEMENTS RELATING TO CROQUET BALLS.   1988
Bryan James Dawson and Leonard Julian Hill. GB 2204245

Material dates: Application filed 25 March 1988, published 9 November 1988

Contents: Title, details in standard form with INID codes (*i*), description (*1–8*), publishing details (8)

Copy seen: BL (photocopy)

Notes: Published by The Patent Office, printed anonymously.

B117   CASE FOR CROQUET EQUIPMENT. Mao-Jung Chang.   1989
CA 1318292

Material dates: Application filed 17 March 1989, issued 25 May 1993

Contents: Cover page in standard form with INID codes (*1*), abstract (*2*), claim (*3*), fig 1 (1 sheet of diagrams)

Copy seen: CIPO (downloaded from the CIPO Canadian Patent Office internet website)

Notes: Published by CIPO, printed anonymously. A French language version is also available.

B118   A GAME. Antony John Minton Courtauld. GB 2237211   1990

Material dates: Application filed 16 March 1990, published 29 September 1993

Contents: Title, details in standard form with INID codes (*i*), description (*1–9*), fig 1 (1 sheet of diagrams)

Copy seen: BL (photocopy)

Notes: Published by The Patent Office, printed anonymously.

B119   CROQUET GAME MODIFIED. John J Major and George Spector.   1990
US 4957290

Material dates: Application filed 13 November 1989, patented 18 September 1990

Contents: Title, details in standard form with INID codes, two unnumbered diagrams (*i*), specification (*1*), figs 1–5 (1 sheet of diagrams)

Copy seen: BL (photocopy)

Notes: Published by United States Patent Office, printed anonymously.

B120   CROQUET SET. Charles Peter Townsend. GB 2252051   1991

Material dates: Application filed 25 January 1991, application published 29 July 1992, patent published 6 April 1994

Contents: Title, details in standard form with INID codes (*i*), description (*1–3*), claims (*4*)

Copy seen: BL (photocopy)

Notes: Published by The Patent Office, printed anonymously.

B121   PORTABLE CROQUET PRACTICE WICKET ASSEMBLY.   1992
Wayne Herkness 2nd. US 5158283

Material dates: Application filed 10 February 1992, patented 27 October 1992

Contents: Title, details in standard form with INID codes, one unnumbered diagram (*i*), specification (*1–2*), figs 1–3 (1 sheet of diagrams)

Copy seen: BL (photocopy)

Notes: Published by United States Patent Office, printed anonymously.

B122   DIRECTIONAL MEANS FOR DETERMINING THE LINE   1993
A BALL SHOULD TAKE WHEN STRUCK BY A CLUB.
In Ju Kim. CA 2105022

Material dates: Application filed 27 August 1993, laid open 28 February 1995

Contents: Cover page in standard form with INID codes (*1*), abstract (*2*), specification (*3–4*), figs 1–2 (1 sheet of diagrams)

Copy seen: CIPO (downloaded from the CIPO Canadian Patent Office internet website)

Notes: Published by CIPO, printed anonymously. A French language version is also available.

B123   CROQUET STICK. Lin C Jen. US 5308064   **1994**

Material dates: Application filed 24 June 1993, patented 3 May 1994

Contents: Title, details in standard form with INID codes, one unnumbered diagram (*i*), specification (*1*), figs 1–5 (5 sheets of diagrams)

Copy seen: BL (photocopy)

Notes: Published by United States Patent Office, printed anonymously.

B124   CROQUET MALLET WITH FOAM OR CUSHION OUTER   **1994**
LAYER. Chiu-Yuan Chen. US 5326100

Material dates: Application filed 20 August 1993, patented 4 July 1994

Contents: Title, details in standard form with INID codes, one unnumbered diagram (*i*), specification (*1–2*), figs 1–3 (3 sheets of diagrams)

Copy seen: BL (photocopy)

Notes: Published by United States Patent Office, printed anonymously.

B125   ILLUMINATED CROQUET SET. Wayne L Swanson. US 5370390   **1994**

Material dates: Application filed 26 October 1993, patent dated 6 December 1994

Contents: Title, details in standard form, and abstract, with INID codes, one unnumbered diagram (*i*), specification (*1–3*), figs 1–11 (3 sheets of diagrams)

Copy seen: BL (photocopy)

Notes: Published by United States Patent Office, printed anonymously.

Part C:
Checklist of Other Specialist Books and Pamphlets Thought To Exist

(including some, indicated thus ¶, seen after completion of Part A)

C1   Adams, J: *History of Mandurah Croquet and Recreation Club* (1991)

C2   ¶[All England Croquet Club]: *The All England Croquet Club* [prospectus] (Chastleton House, Moreton-in Marsh: AECC, [1868])

C3   ¶[All England Croquet Club]: *All England Croquet Club* [prospectus for 1870 Annual Prize Meeting] (np: AECC, [1870])

C4   ¶[All England Croquet Club]: *All England Croquet Club: The First Annual Grand Prize Meeting* [prospectus] (np: AECC, [1869])

C5   ¶[All England Croquet Club]: *Constitution of The All England Croquet Club* (Chastleton House, Moreton-in-Marsh: AECC, 1868)

C6   [Associazione Italiana Croquet]: *Guido per lo spettatore* (AIC, *ca* 1992)

C7   [Australian Croquet Association]: *Australian Croquet Association Development Plan* (ACA, 1994)

C8   [Australian Croquet Council]: [*Constitution of the Australian Croquet Council*] (ACC, *ca* 1988)

C9   [Balmacewen Bowling Tennis and Croquet Club]: *Balmacewen Bowling Tennis and Croquet Club: Souvenir of Opening Season 1906–7* (Dunedin, New Zealand: Balmacewen Bowling Tennis and Croquet Club, *ca* 1906)

C10   Brigstocke, A: *Either Ball* (published privately, 1913)

C11   Bucknall, WR: *The Budleigh Salterton Lawn Tennis & Croquet Club: The First Hundred Years* (1974)

C12   Caigou, AC: *"75 Bisques": Wellington Municipal Croquet Club Diary 1919–1994* (Wellington, New Zealand: Wellington Municipal Croquet Club, 1994)

C13   [Canterbury Croquet Association]: *Rules of the Canterbury Croquet Association* (Canterbury, New Zealand: Canterbury Croquet Association, *ca* 1911)

C14   Cavendish: *Improved Table Croquet: Directions and Rules* (Parkins and Gotto, 1866)

C15   Cavendish: *On the Laws of Croquet* (London: published privately, 1868)

C16   [Ceylon Croquet Association]: [*Membership List*] (Ceylon Croquet Association, *ca* 1903)

C17   Charles, TW: *Croquet: Ladies' Version* [sheet music]

C18   Charrier, ME: *Yale Croquet Team Manual* (Newhaven, CT: *ca* 1991)

C19   Claye, T: *Claye on Croquet* (*ca* 1931)

C20   Creed, JEH: *Croquetisms* [sheet music] (*ca* 1959)

C21   ¶[The Croquet Association]: *Association Croquet* [leaflet] (London: The CA)

C22   ¶[The Croquet Association]: *Croquet Has Won a Brand New Image Since She was Champion* [promotional leaflet addressed to the advertising industry] (London: The CA, [1987])

C23   ¶[The Croquet Association]: *Join the Garden Set: Enter the Observer/Lassale Croquet Classic* (London: The CA, [1987])

C24   [The Croquet Association]: [*Recruiting Handbook*] (London: The CA)

C25   ¶[The Croquet Association]: *The Royal Bank National Schools Croquet Championship* (London: The CA, [1987])

C26   ¶[The Croquet Association]: *Snooker, Darts, Chess, Bowls: What's Next in Line for Sponsorship* [promotional leaflet addressed to the public relations industry] (London: The CA, *ca* 1987)

C27   [Croquet Association of Kentucky]: [*Rules of Kentucky Style Croquet*] (Louisville, KY: Croquet Association of Kentucky, 1937)

C28   Donavan, A: *Kelburn Municipal Croquet Club (Inc): Diamond Jubilee 1913–1973*, (Wellington, New Zealand: Kelburn Municipal Croquet Club, *ca* 1973)

C29   Elvey, GFH: *Will You Help?* (London: The CA, *ca* 1961)

C30   Gordon, WR: *Croquet, or Social Prayer Illustrated* (New York: Board of Publication of Reformed Church in America, 1871)

C31   ¶[Grand National Croquet Club]: *Rules of the Grand National Croquet Club* (np: GNCC, [1872])

C32   Grant, WA: *Bleatings from Bognor* (Bognor: published privately, 1934)

C33   Grove, J: *The History of the North Perth Croquet Club* (1992)

C34   Hass, N: *Sequences and Challenges* (*ca* 1994)

C35   Howard, Milly: *Croquet* [sheet music] (London: Duff and Stewart, *ca* 1870)

C36   Hughes, R: *Croquet for Everybody* [sheet music] (Charles Sheard, *ca* 1870)

C37   ¶[Hydro Hotel]: *Croquet* (Hydro Hotel)

C38   Laun, M: *Croquet et tennis* (1904)

C39   Laun, M: *Règle des jeux de croquet et de lawn tennis* (Paris: Delarue, *ca* 1878)

C40   Laurent, C-M: *Le croquet* (Paris: Éditions Bornemann, 1970)

C41   Lawreen, JB: *Playing at Croquet* [sheet music] (London: Duff and Stewart, *ca* 1870)

C42   Locock, CD: *An Unofficial Calendar* (published privately, 1908 and 1913)

C43 McDonald, N: *Kelburn Municipal Croquet Club (Inc), 1973–88* (Wellington, New Zealand: Kelburn Municipal Croquet Club, *ca* 1988)

C44 'Manu Forti': *Rules of Golf Croquet with Hints How to Play It* (Hereford: Jakeman & Carver, *ca* 1915)

C45 Melnyk, D: *Naked Croquet* (Winnipeg: Turnstone Press, 1987)

C46 Mohawk: *Croquet: The Toronto Laws* (Toronto: WC Chewett, 1866)

C47 Moran, RM: *Standard Croquet Rules* (USA)

C48 ¶[National Croquet Club]: *National Croquet Club: Contest for the Championship Badge* [tournament prospectus] (np: NCC, [1870])

C49 ¶[National Croquet Club]: *National Croquet Club: Oxford Croquet Tournament* [tournament prospectus] (np: NCC, [1870])

C50 ¶[National Croquet Club]: *Rules of the National Croquet Club* (np: NCC, [1870])

C51 Pemberton, JH: *Notes for the Guidance of Hon Secretaries of Calendar Fixtures* (London: The CA, *ca* 1908)

C52 Poulain, L: *Le croquet* (*ca* 1947)

C53 ¶Prince, J: *The Delayed and Straight Triple Peel* (NZCC, *ca* 1997)

C54 ¶Prince, J: *Playing the Four Ball Break* (NZCC, *ca* 1997)

C55 ¶Prince, J: *Standard Leaves* (NZCC, *ca* 1997)

C56 ¶Prince, J: *The Standard Opening and Variations for Championship Play* (NZCC, *ca* 1997)

C57 Ross, AGF: *The Powers and Duties of an Umpire* (NZCC, 1946)

C58 Sherman, WRH: [*Rules of Kentucky Style Croquet*] (Louisville, KY: 1935)

C59 [Slazenger & Sons]: *Croquet* [trade catalogue] (London: Slazenger & Sons, 1903)

C60 [La Société Française du Jeu de Croquet]: *Traité du jeu de croquet* (La Société Française du Jeu de Croquet, *ca* 1923)

C61 Sparrow: *A Croquet Record Book* (1911)

C62 Spicer, RA: *Rules of the Union Croquet Club* (New York: Union Croquet Club, 1884)

C63 [Tactical Games]: *Crokey* (Ely, Cambridgeshire: Tactical Games, *ca* 1976)

C64 [Tactical Games]: *Rules of Error Crokey* (Ely, Cambridgeshire: Tactical Games, *ca* 1976)

C65 Turner, G: [TBA] (*ca* 1926)

C66 Veazie, GA: *Croquet, or the Village Doctor* [sheet music] (*ca* 1875)

C67 [Victorian Croquet Association]: [*Constitution of the Victorian Croquet Association*] (Victoria, Australia: VCA, 1979)

C68 [Victorian Croquet Association]: *Regulations for Tournaments* (Victoria, Australia: VCA, 1991)

C69 [Victorian Croquet Association]: *Victorian Croquet Regulations for Official Tournaments* (Victoria, Australia: VCA, 1930)

C70 Watson, RS: *Cricket and Croquet* (Newcastle: A Reid, 1866)

C71 [West Australian Croquet Association]: *Constitution, Rules and Regulations* (WACA, 1957)

C72 Whitaker, E: *Standard Croquet* (New Zealand: 1920)

C73 Whitmore, WJ: *Bye-Laws and Regulations for the Management of Prize Meetings* (Judd & Glass, 1870)

C74 Windsor Richards, W: *A Tale of Enthusiasm* (*ca* 1930)

C75 [World Croquet Federation]: *Report of International Referees Working Party* (WCF, *ca* 1993)

C76 [TBA]: *The Commandments of Croquet*

C77 [TBA]: *Croquet Coaching Manual: Level One Coaching Course* (WACA, 1980)

C78 [TBA]: *Croquet Manual* (VCA, 1967)

C79 [TBA]: *Croquet Records* (London: JC Vickery, 1904)

C80 [TBA]: *Golden Jubilee* [of the] *Maritzburg Croquet Club: 1921 to 1971* (South Africa: *ca* 1972)

C81 [TBA]: *Handbook of Croquet* (Waterfront, South Africa: *ca* 1996)

C82 [TBA]: *The Laws of Croquet* (The Cricket Press, *ca* 1897)

C83 [TBA]: *More Hints on the Game* (Shepparton Croquet Club, 1977)

C84 [TBA]: *The New Way to Play Croquet: Rule Book & Glossary* (Forster Croquet)

C85 [TBA]: *Proposed 3-Year Plan* (WACA, 1981)

C86 [TBA]: *Roquet* [rules for playing a new parlour game] (London: FH Ayres, *ca* 1890)

C87 [TBA]: [*Rules of the Game of*] *Croquet Putting* (Cirencester: WH Smith & Son, 1906)

C88 [TBA]: *Rules of the North Adelaide Croquet Club* (1868)

C89 [TBA]: *A Taste of Croquet* (Wellington: NZCC, 1993)

Part D:
Checklist of Other Putative Patents of Inventions Related to the Game of Croquet

Australia

D1   *Improvements Relating to Croquet Balls.* AU 602966

D2   *Improvements Relating to Croquet Balls.* AU 1372088

D3   AU 1838892

Canada

D4   *Croquet Wickets.* CA 17751

China

D5   *Bat.* CN 1135925

D6   *Croquet Mallet.* CN 2054705U

D7   *Croquet Mallet.* CN 2107294U

D8   *Table Croquet.* CN 2112429U

D9   *Automatic Time Signal Clock for Croquet.* CN 2116247U

D10   *Croquet on Table.* CN 2179180U

D11   *Croquet Terminal Point Pole Fixing Base.* CN 2193186U

D12   *Right Angle Turning Type Croquet Ground Sports Sideline.* CN 2219733U

D13   *Massage Type Cam Locking Adjustable Croquet Mallet.* CN 2221988U

D14   *Insertion Type Numerical Card for Croquet Player.* CN 2230049U

D15   *Multiple Keys Taper Sleeve Locking Adjustable Bat for Croquet.* CN 2238064U

D16   *Bat for Croquet.* CN 2259926U

France

D17   *Croquet Game Played with Balls of Different Colours.* FR 2735700

Germany

D18   DE 9013261U

D19   DE 9013470U

JAPAN

D20   *Device for Croquet.* JP 10118231

NEW ZEALAND

D21   *Crocquet [sic], Table, Apparatus for.* NZ 14974

UNITED KINGDOM

D22   *Miniature Croquet Set.* GB 2222529

D23   *Case for Croquet Equipment.* GB 2229162

D24   *A Game.* GB 2237211

D25   *Miniature Croquet Game.* GB 2265092

USA

D26   *Pool Table Croquet Game Equipment.* US 4147347

D27   *Game Apparatus.* US 4619455

D28   *Case for Croquet Equipment.* US 4842134

D29   *Remote Controlled Deadness Board for Croquet.* US 4868564

D30   *Croquet Ball.* US 4872677

D31   *Croquet Game Apparatus.* US 5029863

D32   *Croquet Set, Particularly, for Miniature Croquet Game.* US 5201519

D33   *Ball and Mallet Game Device.* US 5366220

Index of Titles

Multiple Keys Taper Sleeve Locking Adjustable Bat for Croquet. [TBA]   D15

Naked Croquet. Doug Melnyk   C45

National Croquet Club: Contest for the Championship Badge. [National Croquet Club]   C48

National Croquet Club: Oxford Tournament   C49

New Combination of Parlour Games, The. [Anon]   A113

New Game of Golf-Croquet: A Game for Garden Parties, The. [Anon]   A97

New Handbook of Croquet, The. Edmund Routledge   A39

New or Improved 'Bisque' Register for the Game of Croquet, A. William Senhouse Clarke   B81

New Way to Play Croquet: Rule Book and Glossary, The. [TBA]   C84

New Zealand Croquet Annual, The [and *The New Zealand Croquet Council Year Book*]. [New Zealand Croquet Council]   A140

Notes for the Guidance of Hon Secretaries of Calendar Fixtures. JH Pemberton   C51

Notes on Croquet: And Some Ancient Bat and Ball Games Related to It. RCA Prior   A56

Notes on the Construction of Croquet Lawns. RF Rothwell   AA195

Nouvelle académie des jeux. Jean Quinola   A88

Novel Application of Pulped Paper Stock, A. Walter Herbert Cook   B41

Nude Croquet. Leslie A Fiedler   A172

[Numerical Croquet]. Lewis Carroll   AA57

Observer/Lassale Croquet Classic, The. [The Croquet Association]   A222

Odds and Ends. E Trevor Hartman   A143

Official Croquet: Rules of Play. [Anon]   A152

Official Rules of the United States Croquet Association American Six Wicket Game and American Nine Wicket Game and Golf Croquet, The. [The United States Croquet Association]   A212

Old-Time Croquet in Highland County, Ohio. 'Harry of Carmel'   A189

On the Laws of Croquet. Cavendish   C15

Outdoor Sports and Pastimes. [Anon]   A90

Peel Appeal. Steve Jones   A311

Plan for Development by the East Anglian Croquet Federation, A [or *Croquet in the Eastern Region*]. [East Anglian Croquet Federation and Sports Council (Eastern Region)]   AA223

Playing at Croquet. JB Lawreen   C41

Playing the Four Ball Break. John Prince   C54

Plus One on Time. DL Gaunt   A224

Pocket Guide to Croquet, A. GH Powell   A105

Pocket Guide to Croquet, The. Cavendish   A42

Pool Table Croquet Game Equipment. [TBA]   D26

Portable Croquet Practice Wicket Assembly. Wayne Herkness 2nd   B121

Powers and Duties of an Umpire, The. AGF Ross   C57

Practical Umpiring: A Handbook for Croquet Umpires and Players. Graeme Roberts   A234

Practice with a Purpose: A Self Help Guide to Better Croquet. John Prince   A314

Price List of Croquet, Badminton, and Cricket Goods. FH Ayres   AA81

Principles of Handicapping. Bill Lamb   A302

Proceedings of the Chicago Croquet Convention. MC Reifsnider *et al*   A190

Proposed 3-Year Plan. [TBA]   C85

Publicity for Croquet in Western Australia. Margaret McPhee and Judith Faulkner   AA242

Queen of Games: A History of Croquet. Nicky Smith   A262

Queen's Croquet Ground, The. Lewis Carroll   A160

Raiser and Collector for Lawn Tennis Balls or Other Balls or Articles. Ernest Latham   B43

Recommendations for a Championship Croquet Court. Dr Carleton H Mabee   A269

[Recruiting Handbook]. [The Croquet Association]   C24

Referees Handbook: An Interpretative Guide to the Regulations and Laws of Association Croquet. Graeme Roberts   A270

Reflections on the Sussex County Croquet Club at Southwick. John Eardley-Simpson   AA271

Registered Club Handbook. [See *Club Registration Pack*]

Registering Croquet. Mayne Reid   B23

Règle des jeux de croquet et de lawn tennis. M Laun   C39

Règle du jeu de croquet. [La Société Française du Jeu de Croquet and L'Union des Sociétés françaises de Sports athlétiques]   A134

Regulations for the Management of Prize Meetings. [See *Bye Laws and Regulations for the Management of Prize Meetings*]

Regulations for Tournaments. [Victorian Croquet Association]   C68

Remote Controlled Deadness Board for Croquet. [TBA]   D29

Report of International Referees Working Party. [World Croquet Federation]   C75

Right Angle Turning Type Croquet Ground Sports Sideline. [TBA]   D12

Roquet. [TBA]   C86

Routledge's Handbook of Croquet. Edmund Routledge   A15

Royal Bank National Schools Croquet Championship, The. [The Croquet Association]   C25

Rug Croquet Wicket. L Julian Smith   B106

Rules and Directions for Playing Croquêt — A New Outdoor Game. John Jaques   A3

Rules and Regulations for Playing Field Croquet. [Anon]   A82

Index of Authors and Other Contributors

Jaques, John, Jr
— *Croquêt Marker and Mallet*   B1
— *Croquêt: The Laws and Regulations of the Game*   A12
— *Improvements in and Relating to Hoops Used in Playing Croquet and Like Games*   B53
— *Rules and Directions for Playing Croquêt – A New Outdoor Game*   A3
Jeffery, J. [See 'Straw Hat']
Jellicorse, Maj H
— *History of the Sussex County Croquet and Lawn Tennis Club, Southwick*   A167
Jen, Lin C
— *Croquet Stick*   B123
Jones, Abner H
— *Improvement in Game-Indicators*   B36
Jones, Charles, JP
— *Peel Appeal*   A311
Jones, Harold
— *Croquet Player, The*   A154a
Jones, Henry. [See also 'Cavendish']
— *Indoor Croquet*   B7
— *Laws of Croquet, The*   A52b
Jones, Robert Leetham
— *Croquet: Twelve Hints to Beginners*   A147d
— *Handbook on Modern Croquet, A*   A149
— *Twelve Hints to Long-Bisquers*   A147
Jones, Steve
— *Peel Appeal*   A311
Jones, Syd
— *Club Registration Pack*   AA283a
Jones, Walter Thomas Whitmore. [See Walter Jones Whitmore]
Jorgensen, Mrs L
— *Canberra Croquet Club: 50th Anniversary Celebrations*   AA201
Judd, Dawn
— *70 Years Through the Hoops: The History of the Shepparton Croquet Club Inc 1924–1994*   A282
Kayden, Xandra
— *Basics of Croquet, The*   A220
Keen, Barry
— *Croquet Association Fixtures*   A183r–t
Keene, Charles
— *Mr Punch's Book of Sports*   A133
Kenrick, Jarvis
— *Modern Croquet Tactics*   A115a–c
Kim, In Ju
— *Directional Means for Determining the Line a Ball Should Take when Struck by a Club*   B122
King, Gunning
— *Mr Punch's Book of Sports*   A133
'Knickolas Knickerbocker'
— *That Confounded Croquet*   A191
Kornbluth, Jesse
— *Croquet: The Sport*   A239
— *Winning Croquet: From Backyard to Greensward — The Skills, Strategies and Rules of America's Most Sophisticated Outdoor Sport*   A213
Kramer, S
— *How to Play Croquet: A Pocket Manual*   A73
Kroeger, Robert
— *Croquet: How to Play the Perfect Game*   A238
— *Croquet Shot-Making Instruction Manual*   A286
Lake, Warner G
— *Croquet Game*   B60
Lamb, William E
— *Commentary on the Laws of Croquet*   A186e
— *Croquet*   A176m–o
— *Croquet Coaching Manual*   A255
— *Croquet: Skills of the Game*   A253
— *Principles of Handicapping*   A302
Lane, Maj CS
— *Laws of Croquet, The*   A52b
Larsen, Peter C
— *Croquet Tally-Board*   B46
Latham, Ernest
— *Raiser and Collector for Lawn Tennis Balls or Other Balls or Articles*   B43
Laun, M
— *Croquet et tennis*   C38
— *Règle des jeux de croquet et de lawn tennis*   C39
Laurent, Claude-Marcel
— *Croquet, Le*   C40
Law, Arthur
— *How to Play Croquet*   A102a
Lawreen, JB
— *Croquet*   A51
— *Playing at Croquet*   C41
Lawson, Peter
— *Croquet*   A187
Legaré, Et
— *Manuel et règlement du jeu du croquet*   A87
Levitt, Barbara
— *Take a Bisque*   A272
Lien kuang t°u shu kung ssu. Pien chi pu
— *Ch°ui Ch°iu Chiao Shih*   A299
Lillie, Arthur
— *Book of Croquet: Its Tactics, Laws, & Mode of Play, The*   A54
— *Croquet, Its History, Rules and Secrets*   A98
— *Croquet: The Laws and Regulations of the Game*   A12q, r
— *Croquet Up to Date*   A107
— *Kingball: A Game for Garden Parties*   A99
— *Laws of Croquet, The*   A80
Lilly, Jane
— *Croquet and How to Play It*   A180
Line, Clifton
— *Croquet Player, The*   A154b
Llyn, Fanwy [pseud]
— *Shots and Strokes in Croquet*   A164
Locock, Charles Dealtry

Riley, EJ, Ltd
— *Summer Sports 1937*   AA157
Riordan, Kevin F
— *70 Years Through the Hoops: The History of the Shepparton Croquet Club Inc 1924–1994*   A282
Ristuccia, Diane
— *Croquet: The Sport*   A239
Roberts, Graeme
— *Guidelines for Tournament Managers*   A306
— *Practical Umpiring: A Handbook for Croquet Umpires and Players*   A234
— *Referees Handbook: An Interpretative Guide to the Regulations and Laws of Association Croquet*   A270
Robinson, Ross
— *Monograph Series on Club-Building, Organization and Management. Volume One: Getting Started*   A281
Rogers, Jane
— *Croquet Association Fixtures*   A183v
Rogers, Walter
— *Staining Croquet Balls, Mallets, &c*   B19
Roper, E Antony
— *Laws of Croquet Simplified, The*   A178
Ross, Arthur George Francis
— *Croquet and How to Play It*   A148
— *Croquet Handbook*   A170
— *Powers and Duties of an Umpire, The*   C57
Ross, Edward A
— *Improvement in Croquet-Mallets*   B26
Rotella, Jed
— *Monograph Series on Club-Building, Organization and Management. Volume One: Getting Started*   A281
Rothwell, Richard Francis
— *Notes on the Construction of Croquet Lawns*   AA195
— *Rules of The Croquet Association*   AA200
Routledge, Edmund
— *Game of Croquêt: Its Laws and Regulations, The*   A21
— *Routledge's Handbook of Croquet*   A15
— *Routledge's New Handbook of Croquet*   A39
— *Rules of the Eglinton Castle and Cassiobury Croquet*   A25
Rover, Prof A [pseud]
— *Croquet: Its Principles and Rules*   A31
— *Croquet Manual of Complete Instructions for All Players*   A61
Roy Brothers
— *Croquet*   AA158
Rudge, Peter
— *Croquet and Other Ball Sports*   A292
— *Croquet: Fun and Games*   A304
— *Croquet: Variations on a Theme*   A305
— *Seeing the Science in Croquet*   A298
Ryan, Malcolm
— *How to Play Croquet*   A241
Saffery, MA [?HA]
— *Complete Croquet-Player, The*   A60d, e

Sahler, John T
— *Action Croquet Post*   B115
Sambourne, Linley
— *Mr Punch's Book of Sports*   A133
Sanders, TW
— *Lawns and Greens: Their Formation and Management*   A120
Saunders, Addison Tresize
— *Improvements Relating to Golf and Similar Balls*   B69
Scheuch, Allen
— *Croquet Passion: Images from the Collection of Allen Scheuch*   AA297
— *Croquet: The Sport*   A239
— *Winning Croquet: From Backyard to Greensward — The Skills, Strategies and Rules of America's Most Sophisticated Outdoor Sport*   A213
Scott, Clement
— *Croquet Tactics*   A38
Scotter, Kylie
— *Manly Croquet Club: Special Cook Book*   A199
Scudder, Horace Elisha. [See R Fellow]
Seabury, Paul
— *Game of Croquet: Its Appointment and Laws, The*   A20f
Shaw, DW
— *Croquet Association Fixtures*   A183bb, cc
Shaw, Mike
— *How to Play Croquet*   A241
Shepherd, Dan
— *Official Rules of The United States Croquet Association American Six Wicket Game and American Nine Wicket Game and Golf Croquet, The*   A212d
Shepherd, JA
— *Mr Punch's Book of Sports*   A133
Shepparton Croquet Club
— *Shepparton Croquet Club: Hints on the Game*   AA159
Sherman, Walter RH
— *[Rules of Kentucky Style Croquet]*   C58
Shotton, Jack
— *Lighter Side of Serious Croquet, The*   A301
Simon and Schuster
— *Winning Croquet: From Backyard to Greensward — The Skills, Strategies and Rules of America's Most Sophisticated Outdoor Sport*   A213
Slazenger, Albert Egerton Legh
— *Hand Tool for Scoring Concentric Circular Grooves in the Striking Faces of Croquet Mallets and the Like*   B55
— *Improvements in or Relating to Croquet Hoops*   B66
Slazenger & Sons
— *Croquet*   C59
Sloane, Charles Ronald
— *Australian Croquet Manual, The*   A210
Smith, Friend W

Index of Publishers and Printers

Smith and McDougal
— *Croquet: As Played by the Newport Croquet Club*   A19
Société Française du Jeu de Croquet, La
— *Traité du jeu de croquet*   C60
South Bend Toy Manufacturing Company
— *How to Play Croquet*   A161
— *Lawnplay: Croquet*   AA185
South Eastern Croquet Federation
— *Development Plan for Croquet in London, Kent, Surrey, Sussex, A*   AA232a
Southport Croquet Club, Queensland
— *History of Croquet Clubs in Queensland*   A307
Soutter, James, & Son
— *Laws and Regulations of the Game of Croquet*   A24
Spalding, AG, & Bros
— *Croquet, the Rules Governing the Game, as Adopted by the National American Croquet Association*   A85c
— *Spalding's Official Croquet Manual*   A84
Sparrow
— *Croquet Record Book, A*   C61
Spooner, Chas E, & Co
— *New Zealand Croquet Annual, The*   A140 (1923–24)
Sports Council, The
— *Development Plan for Croquet in London, Kent, Surrey, Sussex, A*   AA232b
Sports Council (Eastern Region)
— *Plan for Development by the East Anglian Croquet Federation, A*   AA223
Sports Press, The
— *Laws of Croquet, The*   A100 (1959)
Spottiswoode & Co
— *Garden Lawns, Tennis Lawns, Croquet Grounds, Bowling Greens, Putting Greens, Cricket Grounds*   A111
Spratt, Isaac
— *Rules of the New Game of Croquet*   A1
Stackpole Books
— *Croquet*   A176n
— *Croquet*   A291
Stacy and Richardson
— *Croquet: The Laws and Regulations of the Game*   A12d, e
Stanley Press, The
— *Croquet*   A176j
Stannard and Co
— *Croquet Galop*   A29c
Steinbach, A
— *Croquet, le badminton, le billard de pelouse, Le*   A162
Stenhouse, A
— *Croquet*   A28
Stevens, R White
— *JN Hearder's Guide to Sea Fishing and the Rivers of South Devon*   A47d
Stevens, William
— *Croquet and Archery*   A18

Stiles, Frank J
— *Croquet: As Played by the Melrose Croquet Club*   A65
Stoate & Bishop (Printers)
— *Basic Laws of Association Croquet and Golf Croquet* [and *Basiese Wette van Croquet*]   A192d
— *Laws of Croquet, The*   A100 (1984, 1986)
Stone, Henry, and Son
— *Croquet Alphabet, A*   A125
Stoothoff, HG
— *Croquet: Rules of the Brooklyn Croquet Association*   A71
Straker Brothers
— *Croquet Handbook*   A170b
Strange The Printer
— *Modern Croquet: Tips and Practice*   A163
Suid-Afrikaanse Croquet Vereniging
— *Basic Laws of Association Croquet and Golf Croquet* [and *Basiese Wette van Croquet*]   A192e
Sunstreet Printing Works (Keighley)
— *Croquet*   A176h
Svenska Croquetförbundet
— *Krocket Regler*   A203
Sydney Croquet Club
— *Sydney Croquet Club: 50th Anniversary*   AA219
Tactical Games
— *Crokey*   C63
— *Rules of Error Crokey*   C64
Tattersall, WB
— *Laws of Croquet, The*   A100 (1949, 1959)
Taylor, Samuel
— *Croquêt: The Laws and Regulations of the Game*   A12k–o
Taylor and Greening
— *Croquêt: The Laws and Regulations of the Game*   A12a–c, f–l
— *Jaques's Croquet*   A34
Tectona
— *Croquet, Le*   A252
Teel & Badet
— *Hand Book of Croquet*   A67
Townsend Croquet
— *Townsend's Croquet Almanack*   A236a, b
Training Associates
— *Croquet*   A187
Trend, Latimer, and Co
— *Croquet and How to Play It*   A180
Tribune Company, Steam Printers
— *Hand Book of Croquet*   A67
Turner, Thomas. [See also Thomas Turner and Co]
— *Rules of the Eglinton Castle and Cassiobury Croquet*   A25
Turner, Thomas, and Co. [See also Thomas Turner]
— *Game of Croquêt: Its Laws and Regulations, The*   A21h